Glencoe Keyboarding with Computer Applications

Your 21st Century Technolo

Solution t

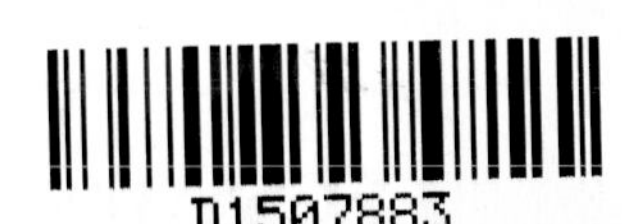

Overview

Comprehensive and Engaging Keyboarding Instruction

- Learn proper technique
- Build speed and accuracy proficiency with skillbuilding in every lesson
- Apply keyboarding skills using word processing, spreadsheet, desktop publishing, and database applications

Technology Resources

- Robust and sophisticated correlated software scores and records every exercise
- Application-specific Student Manuals provide step-by-step instructions to master computer application skills
- Software also includes language arts tutorials and activities

Academic Integration

- Language arts, math, science, social studies, ethics, and portfolio activities reinforce core academic areas
- Language Links emphasize language arts rules and composition skills

Online Learning Center

KeyComps.glencoe.com

- Enrichment activities for core academic areas and careers
- Academic report format guide
- Ergonomic guidelines

Jack E. Johnson, Ph.D.
Dean Emeritus
University of West Georgia
Carrollton, Georgia

Judith Chiri-Mulkey, M.Ed.
Keyboarding and Technology Educator
Aurora, Colorado

Delores Sykes Cotton, M.Ed.
Education Specialist
Business Educator
Detroit, Michigan

Carole Glosup Stanley, M.Ed.
Keyboarding and Technology Educator
Omaha, Texas

New York, New York Columbus, Ohio Chicago, Illinois Peoria, Illinois Woodland Hills, California

Photo Credits

Cover: Images © Photodisc

1, Roger Tully/Tony Stone Images; **29,** Uniphoto; **66,** SW Productions/Brand X Pictures/PictureQuest; **67,** Yomafa Toyohiro/FPG; **71,** Aaron Haupt; **88,** Robert S Semeniuk/The Stock Market; **101,** Aaron Haupt; **116,** Aaron Haupt; **113,** Richard Harrington/FPG; **122,** Telegraph Colour Library/FPG; **127,** Library of Congress; **128,** Aaron Haupt; **131,** Aaron Haupt; **136,** Tom Stewart/CORBIS; **137,** Michael Krasowitz/FPG; **148,** Michele Burgess/The Stock Market; **149,** SuperStock; **164,** Doug Martin; **172,** Syme Thayer/FPG; **179,** Gabe Palmer/The Stock Market; **180,** Michael Keller/The Stock Market; **216,** Royalty-free/CORBIS A; **217,** David Tejada/Tony Stone Images; **223,** KS Studios; **275,** Jose L. Pelaez/The Stock Market; **277,** Robert S. Semeniuk/The Stock Market; **292,** Ed Bock/CORBIS; **293,** Ron Chapple/FPG; **314,** Telegraph Colour Library/FPG; **302,** Aaron Haupt; **314,** Telegraph Colour Library/FPG; **339,** E Nagel/FPG; **342,** Roger Tully/Tony Stone Images; **367,** Palmer Kane/The Stock Market; **434,** David Young-Wolff/PhotoEdit; **435,** Borland; **537,** Ian Murphy/Tony Stone Images; **515,** PhotoDisc/Nick Koudis; **521,** Reuters/Mike Blake/Archive Photos; **548,** SuperStock; **TH1,** Vincent Besnault/Getty Images; **TH1,** Dex Images/CORBIS; **TH1,** Courtesy of International Business Machines Corporation. Unauthorized use not permitted; **TH1,** Mug Shots/Corbis; **TH1,** Michael Newman/PhotoEdit; **TH2,** Royalty-free/Masterfile; **TH2,** Phillip and Karen Smith/SuperStock; **TH2,** Hunter Freeman Photography 2002/Courtesy Apple Computer, Inc.; **TH2,** Aaron Haupt; **TH2,** Lawrence Manning/Royalty Free/CORBIS; **TH2,** Royalty Free/CORBIS; **TH2,** Stephen Swintek/Getty Images; **TH3,** Courtesy of Adesso Inc.; **TH3,** Courtesy of International Business Machines Corporation. Unauthorized use not permitted.; **TH3,** Nikon USA; **TH3,** Royalty Free/CORBIS; **TH3,** Courtesy of Sony; **TH3,** William Whitehurst/CORBIS; **TH3,** Vaughn Youtz/Zuma/CORBIS; **TH4,** Courtesy of International Business Machines Corporation. Unauthorized use not permitted.; **TH4,** Lars Klove/Getty Images; **TH4,** Royalty Free/CORBIS; **TH4,** Courtesy of Sony; **TH5,** Intel Corporation ©2002; **TH6,** Mark Burnett; **TH6,** Cooperphoto/CORBIS; **TH6,** Courtesy of Iomega Corporation; **TH6,** Seagate; **TH7,** Mark Burnett; **TH7,** Hewlitt Packard; **TH7,** Lawrence Manning/Royalty Free/CORBIS; **TH7,** Courtesy of Sony; **TH8,** Tony Freeman/PhotoEdit; **TH8,** Glencoe/McGraw-Hill; **TH8,** Michael Newman/PhotoEdit; **TH8,** Royalty-free/Photodisc/Getty Images.

Image Credits

Abbreviation Key:
MS: © Microsoft Corporation, All rights reserved.

© 1983–2005 MS Office Word 2003, **R18, 182, 366, 370, 387**; © 1991–2003 MS Office Publisher 2003, **382, 404, 405, 407, 409, 413, 416, 421, 425, 429, 432**; © 1981–2003 MS ClipArt, **391**; © 1983–2003 MS Office Excel, **438, 444, 447, 451, 452, 455, 460, 462, 467, 471 475, 479, 493, 495, 500, 504, 507, 508, 511, 512**.

The McGraw-Hill Companies

Printed in the United States of America

Send all inquiries to:
Glencoe/McGraw-Hill
21600 Oxnard Street, Suite 500
Woodland Hills, CA 91367

ISBN-13: 978-0-07-869316-8 (Student Edition; Lessons 1–150)
ISBN 10: 0-07-869316-0 (Student Edition; Lessons 1–150)

ISBN-13: 978-0-07-869315-1 (Student Edition; Lessons 1–80)
ISBN-10: 0-07-869315-2 (Student Edition; Lessons 1–80)

ISBN-13: 978-0-07-873363-5 (Teacher Wraparound Edition)
ISBN-10: 0-07-873363-4 (Teacher Wraparound Edition)

4 5 6 7 027 11 10 09 08 07

OPERATING YOUR COMPUTER

The following tips should be used to operate your computer correctly. Your teacher may provide you with additional instructions.

Turning the computer on

- Make sure there are no diskettes or CD-ROMs in the computer's drives.
- Power on the computer and monitor.
- Wait for the start-up process (*booting*) to finish before starting any programs; you may be required to enter a network user ID and password at this time.
- Insert diskettes and/or CD-ROMs if necessary.

Turning the computer off

- Save data and files if necessary and close all windows.
- Remove any diskettes and CD-ROMs from the drives.
- Use the desktop shut-down procedure; in Windows-based systems, click Start on the taskbar, click Shut Down, choose the Shut down option, and then click OK.
- Power off the computer (if necessary) and monitor.

Diskettes and CD-ROMs

- Handle diskettes and CD-ROMs carefully, holding them by the edges.
- Protect diskettes and CD-ROMs from dirt, scratches, moisture, extremes in temperature, and magnetic fields.
- Insert and remove diskettes and CD-ROMs gently.
- Do not attempt to remove a diskette or CD-ROM when the drive indicator light is on.

Work area

- Keep the area around your computer neat and free from dust and dirt.
- Do not eat or drink near your computer, as spilled food and drinks can cause damage to the computer.

REVIEWERS

Judy Senden
West High School
Anchorage, AK

Betty Gross Malone
Jackson-Olin High School
Birmingham, AL

Debra Scott
Arkansas High School
Texarkana, AR

Donna Green
Mingus Union High School
Cottonwood, AZ

Sue Julian
El Molino High School
Forestville, CA

Rebecca Seher
Education Consultant
California State University
Bakersfield
Bakersfield, CA

Dr. Rita Schnittgrund
Denver West High School
Denver, CO

Janyce Wininger
Stafford High School
Stafford Spring, CT

Marjorie Stewart
Caesar Rodney High School
Camden Wyoming, DE

Patricia McCollough
Fort Walton Beach High School
Fort Walton Beach, FL

Stephanie Rerucha
Winter Haven High School
Winter Haven, FL

Barbara Williams-Mims
Columbus High School
Columbus, GA

Patricia Pierce
Linn-Marr High School
Marion, IA

Dan Petersen
State Division of Vocational Education
Business and Office Technology Education
Boise, ID

Gerrie L. Trossman
Good Counsel High School
Chicago, IL

Ann Rosborough
Decatur Middle School
Indianapolis, IN

Barbara Coleman
Salina High School South
Salina, KS

N. Jean Andrada
Pleasure Ridge High School
Louisville, KY

Terry Smith
Alcee Fortier High School
New Orleans, LA

Elizabeth Nilsen
Cape Elizabeth High School
Cape Elizabeth, ME

Kathy Jensen
Mankato West High School
Mankato, MN

Betty Sue Gregg
South Pariola High School
Batesville, MS

Judy Cox
J. H. Rose High School
Greenville, NC

Nancy Stevens
Manteo High School
Manteo, NC

Mike Opdahl
Larimore High School
Larimore, ND

Betty Sup
Creighton Preparatory School
Omaha, NE

Maria Alvarez
Farmington High School
Farmington, NH

Sandra M. Richardson
Life Center Academy
Burlington, NJ

Bernadine Elmore
New Mexico Military Institution
Roswell, NM

Leesa Lyman
Roy Martin School
Las Vegas, NV

Lorraine Harrison
HS for Arts and Business
Corona, NY

Angela Marquart
Clear Fork High School
Bellville, OH

Michael Prandy
John Marshall High School
Oklahoma City, OK

Sherri Sollars
Westview High School
Portland, OR

Susan Howe
Chariho Regional High School
Wood River Junction, RI

Leah Goldman
White Knoll Middle School
W. Columbia, SC

Patricia B. Hook
Airport High School
West Columbia, SC

Jane Bradfield
O'Gorman High School
Sioux Falls, SD

Edna Earle Bond
Central High School
Memphis, TN

Susan Shirey
Grand Prairie High School
Grand Prairie, TX

Patricia Kay Fordham
Central High School
Salt Lake City, UT

Patricia Smith
Kennewick High School
Kennewick, WA

Gail Springsteen
Waupaca High School
Waupaca, WI

Nancy Byrd
Morgantown High School
Morgantown, WV

1-Minute Timed Writings

Page	Words
52	25
58	25
65	25

2-Minute Timed Writings

Page	Words
71	27
75	27
78	27
81	27
84	27
88	27
93	27
97	30
101	30
104	30
109	30
113	30
116	30

3-Minute Timed Writings

Page	Words
119	31
122	31
127	31
135	32
155	33
163	33
214	33
223	35
238	35
245	35
258	35
269	36
285	36

5-Minute Timed Writings

Page	Words
300	36
315	36
330	37
337	37
354	36
373	38
389	38
400	38
415	38
424	38
437	39
473	39
489	39
498	40
518	40
527	40
536	40
545	40
551	40

CONTRIBUTORS

Erik Amerikaner
Westlake High School
Westlake Village, CA

Sara Armstrong, Ph.D.
Consultant in Professional
Development for Educators
(Former Classroom Educator)
Berkeley, CA

Jo Clark
Georgetown Middle School
Georgetown, SC

Pam Cook
Edwardsville High School
Edwardsville, IL

Jay Edwards
Resource Coordinator
Hemet Unified School District
Hemet, CA

Margaret Erthal, Ph.D.
Assistant Professor
Business Teacher Education
College of Business
Illinois State University
Normal, IL

Patricia Kay Fordham
Central High School
Salt Lake City, UT

Leah Goldman
White Knoll Middle School
W. Columbia, SC

Betty Sue Gregg
South Panola High School
Batesville, MS

Angela Marquart
Clear Fork High School
Bellville, OH

Ann Martin
Georgetown Middle School
Georgetown, SC

Elizabeth Nilsen
Cape Elizabeth High School
Cape Elizabeth, ME

Stephanie Rerucha
Winter Haven High School
Winter Haven, FL

Ann Rosborough
Decatur Middle School
Indianapolis, IN

Rebecca Seher
Education Consultant
California State University,
Bakersfield
Bakersfield, CA

Betty Sup
Creighton Preparatory School
Omaha, NE

Janyce Wininger
Stafford High School
Stafford Springs, CT

Mary L. Young, Ph.D.
Assistant Professor
College of Education
Department of Business and
Technology Education
Florida A&M University
Tallahassee, FL

INDEX *(continued)*

TABLE OF CONTENTS

TABLE OF CONTENTS *(continued)*

UNIT 3 WORD PROCESSING

UNIT 4 WORD PROCESSING

INDEX *(continued)*

TABLE OF CONTENTS *(continued)*

UNIT 5 WORD PROCESSING

INDEX *(continued)*

TABLE OF CONTENTS *(continued)*

UNIT 6 DESKTOP PUBLISHING

INDEX *(continued)*

TABLE OF CONTENTS *(continued)*

UNIT 7 SPREADSHEETS

INDEX

Individual Keys

A

B

C

TABLE OF CONTENTS *(continued)*

UNIT 8 DATABASES

GLOSSARY *(continued)*

U

Undo A software command that reverses the last action taken.

V

Value Numbers, dates, or times entered into a spreadsheet.

Vertical Text Text that is arranged vertically on a page.

W

Widow The last line of a paragraph that is carried forward to the top of the next page.

Wingdings® A font containing special characters or symbols, rather than letters.

WordArt A word processing feature used to create special effects with text.

Word Count The total number of words keyed within a given time limit.

Word Scale The number grid below the last line of text in an exercise.

Word Wrap The automatic wrapping of text from the end of one line to the beginning of the next line.

Workbook A new file in Excel that contains worksheets (spreadsheets).

Wrap Text The automatic wrapping of text from the end of one line to the beginning of the next line.

Z

Zoom A feature used to enlarge or reduce an image on the screen.

ABOUT YOUR BOOK

STRUCTURE

Your book is divided into 8 units. (**Note:** If you are using the book with Lessons 1–80, your book will have just 4 units.) Each unit except the last one is further divided into 20 lessons. Unit 8, because of its complexity, contains only 10 lessons. Each unit opens with two pages which provide a list of the unit objectives (what you will learn in the unit), *Words to Learn* (words that are introduced or used within the unit), and a *Career Byte* (a brief description of a career in which keyboarding skills are helpful).

UNIT 1 KEYBOARDING
LESSONS 1–20

OBJECTIVES

- Demonstrate which fingers control each key on the keyboard.
- Use home key anchors to assist in developing location security.
- Develop and practice correct keyboarding techniques.
- Key at a speed of 25 words per minute for 1 minute with 2 or fewer errors.
- Use proper spacing after common marks of punctuation.
- Compose single word or short phrase responses at the keyboard.

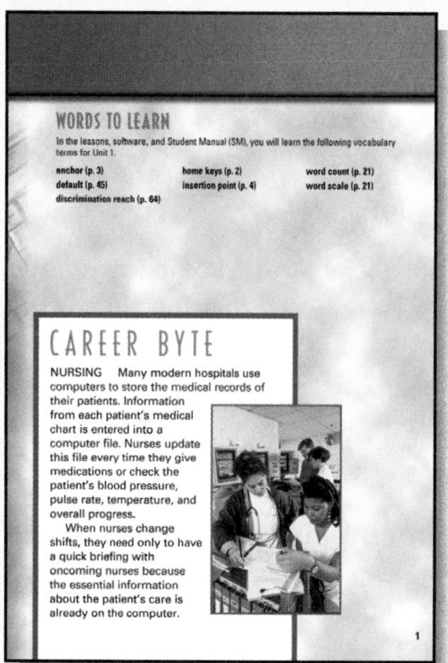

WORDS TO LEARN

In the lessons, software, and Student Manual (SM), you will learn the following vocabulary terms for Unit 1.

anchor (p. 3) home keys (p. 2) word count (p. 21)
default (p. 45) insertion point (p. 4) word scale (p. 21)
discrimination reach (p. 64)

CAREER BYTE

NURSING Many modern hospitals use computers to store the medical records of their patients. Information from each patient's medical chart is entered into a computer file. Nurses update this file every time they give medications or check the patient's blood pressure, pulse rate, temperature, and overall progress.

When nurses change shifts, they need only to have a quick briefing with oncoming nurses because the essential information about the patient's care is already on the computer.

1

UNITS

In Units 1 and 2 you will learn to operate the keyboard by touch with speed and accuracy—a skill you will be able to use throughout your education and career. In Unit 3, you will be introduced to the ten-key numeric keypad and some basic word processing features.

In Units 4 and 5 you will use your keyboarding skills to create documents and to format them correctly. In addition, you will continue to learn about more advanced word processing features as you progress.

Unit 6 includes desktop publishing lessons where you will continue to learn word processing features, such as the Drawing toolbar and WordArt, and use them to create a variety of documents, including some original designs. You will also learn about inserting, sizing, and positioning graphics.

In Unit 7, you will learn about spreadsheets: what they are, how to create them, how to use them for "what if" queries, and how to create pie and bar charts.

Finally, in Unit 8, you will learn about databases: what they are, how they can be used, how to create database tables, how to sort, and how to query databases.

Q

Query A database feature that enables you to locate records that meet certain criteria.

R

Range A group of spreadsheet cells.

Record A group of fields that contain the data that makes up a file.

Reference Initials The initials of the person keying the letter.

Report A database object used for organizing and presenting the information in a database table.

Reveal Codes A software feature available in some programs that enables you to display formatting codes on screen.

Reverse Printing A method of printing type in white or another light color on a black or dark background.

Right Tab A tab stop that aligns text at the right.

Ruler A graphic display that can show margin settings and tab stops.

S

Shading A software feature used to add fill to cells or boxes to add visual interest.

Side Heading Subheadings that break a report into specific sections.

Soft Page Break A page break that is automatically created by the software when text is too long to fit on a page.

Sort A software feature that enables you to rearrange data in a particular order.

Spell Check A software feature that checks the spelling of words in a document.

Spreadsheet A software program that enables you to perform various calculations on the data.

Status Line A line displayed at the bottom of the screen that provides the page number, section number, vertical position in inches, and line number of a document, as well as the horizontal position of the insertion point.

Subscript A character that is positioned a half line below the writing line.

SUM A built-in spreadsheet formula that adds a range of cells.

Superscript A character that is positioned a half line above the writing line.

Symbols Special characters used for special functions. Some are adapted from keyboard keys; others are not available on the regular keyboard.

T

Tab Stop A set position that enables you to quickly move the insertion point to that position.

Table A grid of rows and columns that intersect to form cells into which information can be typed.

Template A predefined document format.

Text Box A created box that can contain text or art and can be placed anywhere in the document.

Thesaurus A software feature that you can use to find words that are similar to words you want to replace.

ABOUT YOUR BOOK *(continued)*

LESSONS

Each lesson is divided into several sections. Every lesson (except the first) begins with a Warmup that you should begin keying as soon as you are settled at your keyboard. In the early lessons, *New Key* sections introduce the new keys for that lesson and provide you with practice lines on these keys.

Every lesson contains a *Skillbuilding* section that is easy to identify because of its blue background. The skillbuilding sections contain a variety of different activities including Technique Timed Writings; Diagnostic Practice; Paced Practice; and 1-, 3-, and 5-Minute Timed Writings.

Many skillbuilding sections include a *Pretest, Practice, Posttest* routine. This routine is designed to help you improve either speed or accuracy through step-by-step procedures. The Pretest helps you identify your speed or accuracy needs. The Practice activities contain a variety of intensive improvement drills. Finally, the Posttest measures your improvement.

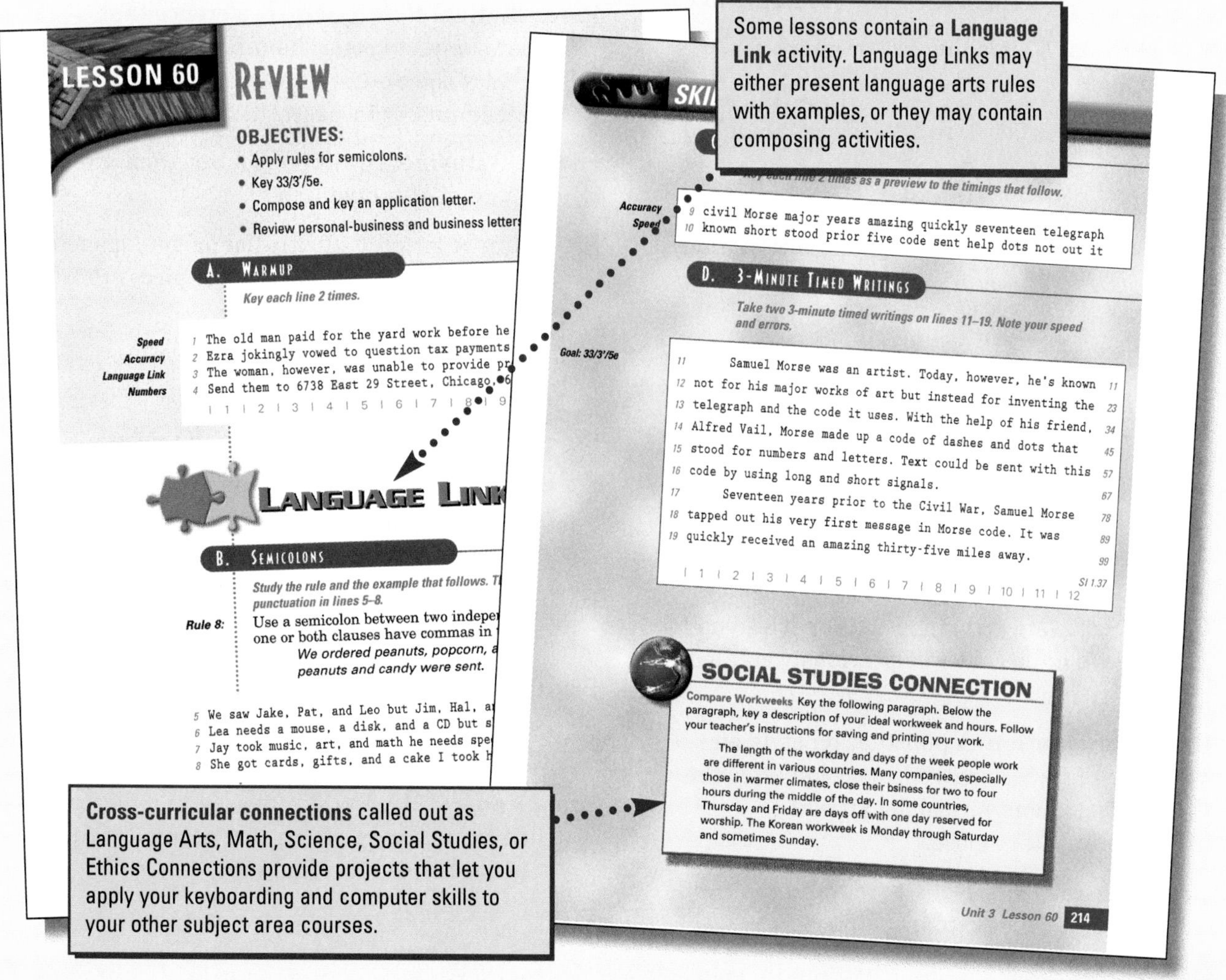

GLOSSARY *(continued)*

Line Spacing A software command that enables you to set the amount of space between lines of type.

M

Mail Merge A process of combining information from two documents to produce personalized documents.

Margins The blank space at the top, bottom, left, and right sides of a document.

Memo Written messages sent from one person to another in the same organization or business. Memos are less formal than letters and do not have salutations or closing lines.

Merge Cells To combine two or more cells in a table.

Minutes The official record of what happened at a meeting.

MLA Style A format for citing sources developed by the Modern Language Association.

N

Nonprinting Character A character or symbol that appears on the screen but does not print.

O

Open A software command that enables you to retrieve a file that was previously created and saved.

Open Punctuation A punctuation style for letters in which there is no colon after the salutation and no comma after the complimentary close.

Orphan A single line of a paragraph that appears at the bottom of a page.

Outline A plan for the organization of a document. It identifies the topics with the document and the sequence in which those topics are presented.

P

Page Numbering A software command that automatically numbers the pages of a document.

Page Orientation The direction in which you can print on a page.

Paragraph Headings Minor subdivisions of a report.

Parenthetical Reference A reference that follows a quotation. The MLA format includes the author or source's name and a page number in parentheses.

Personal Business Letter A letter from an individual to a business.

Pie Chart A graphic illustration of spreadsheet data that compares the sizes of pieces to a whole.

Point Size A reference to the size of text; 72 points equal one inch.

Portrait Page orientation in which the data prints across the narrower portion of a page.

Postscript An additional message at the end of a letter, placed below the close.

Primary Key A field that assigns a special identification for each record in a table.

Print Preview A software feature that enables you to view an entire document before it is printed.

Proofreaders' Marks Marks used to indicate changes and corrections in a document that is being revised for final copy.

REFERENCE SECTION *Table of Contents*

Function Keys Special keys located at the top of the keyboard (F1, F2, F3, etc.) that are used alone or with the Ctrl, Alt, and Shift keys to execute software commands.

G

Graphics Pictures, clip art, bar graphs, pie charts, or other images available on or created on a computer.

Gridlines The lines appearing around the cells in a table.

H

Hanging Indent A temporary left margin that indents all lines but the first line of the text.

Hard Page Break A manually inserted page break that does not change regardless of the changes made within the document.

Hard Return A code entered into a document by pressing the ENTER key that indicates the end of a paragraph or section.

Header Repetitive information or text that is repeated at the top of each page of a section or a document.

Help On-screen information about how to use a program and its features.

Home Keys The A S D F J K L keys in the center row of the keyboard, named for the specific key each finger controls.

Homonym Words spelled and pronounced alike.

Homophone Words pronounced alike but spelled differently.

I

Indent A temporary left margin that is used to align text at a set position to the right of the margin.

Insert A software command that enables you to add a variety of items to a document, such as text, page and column breaks, graphics, tables, charts, cells, rows, columns, formulas, dates, time, and fields.

Insertion Mode An input mode in which the existing text moves to the right as new text is added.

Insertion Point A vertical blinking bar on the computer screen that indicates where an action will begin.

Italic A special font attribute used to highlight text.

J

Justification A feature that aligns text to the center, right, or left. Full justification aligns text to both the right and the left margins by adding spaces between characters.

L

Labels Words entered into a spreadsheet.

Landscape Page orientation in which data prints across the wider portion of the page.

Leaders A row of characters that leads the reader's eye across a page.

Left Tab A tab setting that moves the insertion point to the left when the tab key is pressed.

Letterhead Stationery that has information such as the company name, address, and telephone number printed at the top.

OUTLINE

HOW TO MAKE DECISIONS ON THE JOB

1) DETERMINE WHAT CHOICES YOU HAVE.
   a) Make use of all available reference materials.
      i) Check company policy manuals.
      ii) Go to the company library or files.
   b) Ask your coworkers and your supervisors questions.
   c) Be observant and pay close attention in meetings.
2) DO NOT MAKE DECISIONS HASTILY.
   a) Postpone any doubtful decisions.
   b) Decisions based on emotions are usually not the best ones.
      i) If you are angry, allow enough time to consider things calmly.
      ii) You will risk losing the respect of others if you act impulsively.
3) EVALUATE YOUR DECISIONS OBJECTIVELY.
   a) Keep an open mind about the consequences of your decisions.
   b) Learn from past decisions you have made.
      i) Evaluate the results of each decision you make.
      ii) Learn something good from a poor decision.

Database Table The collection of related records within a database.

Date Insert A software feature that enables you to insert the current date into a document.

Data Source The information unique to each person receiving a form letter.

Decimal Tab A tab setting used to align a column of numbers at the decimal point.

Default Settings that are preset by the software and that remain in effect until the user changes them.

Descending Sort A sort of data in descending alphabetical (Z–A) or numerical (9–0) order.

Desktop Publishing Special software or software features that enable you to design and create documents such as newsletters, flyers, and brochures.

Discrimination Reaches Keys that are commonly substituted and easily confused, such as **W** and **E**.

Dot Leader Tab A tab setting that inserts leaders (a line of dots or other characters) between one column and another.

Drop Cap A large first letter that drops below the regular text.

Drop Shadows Shading that makes text look three dimensional.

E

Endnotes A list of sources or reference notations at the end of a report.

F

Field A category of information in a database.

Field Name A name used to identify the contents of a field.

File A document or a collection of related records.

File Name A unique name given to a document so that it can be saved and retrieved.

Fill Shading or patterns used to fill an area. In a spreadsheet, to enter common or repetitive values into a group of cells.

Fill Handle The small box in the lower right corner of an active spreadsheet cell that can be dragged to create the desired fill.

Filtering The process of finding and selecting information from a database.

Find and Replace A software command that enables you to search for and replace specific text, formatting commands, or special attributes.

Font A set of type characters of a particular design and size.

Footers Repetitive information or text that is repeated at the bottom of a page throughout a section or a document.

Footnote A software feature that automatically positions reference notations at the bottom of the page on which the footnote number appears.

Form File The main document or form letter to which variable information must be added.

Form Letter A letter that is keyed only once but can be sent to many different people.

Formula A mathematical expression that solves a problem (for example, adding, subtracting, multiplying, dividing, or averaging).

Function A pre-existing formula built into a spreadsheet that lets you make calculations quickly and easily.

TITLE PAGE

↓center vertically

HOW TO MAKE DECISIONS ON THE JOB ↓12x

By Allen J. Springer ↓12x

Mr. Joseph Simka
Business Communications I
March 4, {year}

GLOSSARY

A

Agenda A list of topics to be discussed at a meeting, or a formal program for a meeting.

Alignment The horizontal positioning (such as left, right, or center) of text.

Anchor A home-key position that helps bring each finger back to its home-key position. Also indicates what a text box is attached (anchored) to.

Ascending Sort A sort of data in alphabetical (A–Z) order or numerical (0–9) order.

Autofit A feature that automatically adjusts column width to what best fits the text.

AVERAGE A built-in spreadsheet formula that adds and divides numbers.

B

Bar Chart A graphic illustration of spreadsheet data.

Bibliography An alphabetical listing of all the books and articles consulted by the author of a report.

Bold A print enhancement used to make characters appear darker than other text to add emphasis.

Boolean Operators A series of symbols or words used to create a query in a database.

Borders Frames around text or pages.

Bullets and Numbering A word processing feature used to arrange items in a list with each item beginning with a bullet or a number.

Business Letter A letter that represents a company, not an individual. Business letters are usually printed on company stationery called letterhead.

Byline The name of the author of a report typed a double space below the title.

C

Cell The box formed at the intersection of a row and a column.

Cell Address The column letter and row number referring to a specific cell in a spreadsheet.

Center Page A software command that automatically centers copy vertically on a page.

Center Tab A type of tab used to horizontally center text at a particular position on a line.

Clip Art Graphic images that can be inserted into documents.

Close File A software command that enables you to exit the current document without exiting from the program.

Column Heading A heading at the top of a table column that describes the data in the column.

Columns Information arranged vertically.

Constants Unchanging values that are used in formulas.

Cut/Copy/Paste A feature that enables you to move or copy text from one place to another.

D

Data File The document that contains the variable information, such as names and addresses, used to personalize a form document.

Database A software program used to organize, find, and display information.

TABLE OF CONTENTS

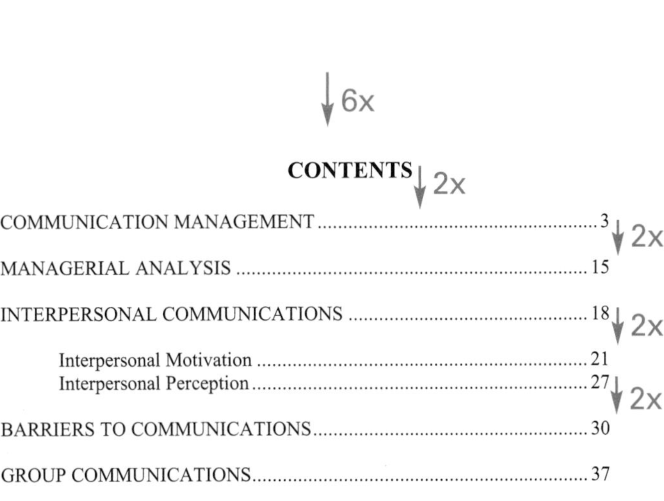
6x

CONTENTS 2x

Storage Devices Continued

If you have problems using a storage device, try the basic troubleshooting procedures below.

For Floppy Disks:

Make sure the write-protect tab is in the locked position. Look at the bottom right and bottom left corners of the disk. If there is a hole in both corners, turn the disk over. Then move the tab in the bottom right corner to cover the hole.

Make sure there is not a disk in the drive already.

Make sure the disk is right side up and the metal side is facing the drive. The disk being inserted in this photo is not facing the correct way. The bottom disk is facing the correct way.

Put a different floppy disk into the drive. If neither floppy works, the disk drive may be broken.

For Optical Disks:

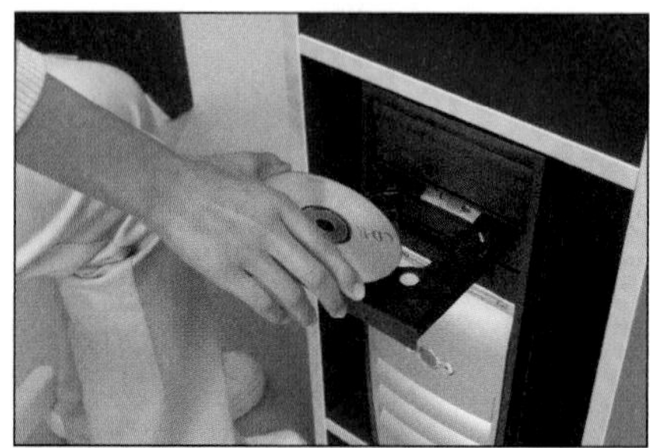

Make sure the CD or DVD is seated right side up in the disk tray. The shiny side should be on the bottom. Make sure there is not more than one CD or DVD in the tray.

If a CD will not work, as a last resort, wipe it with a very soft cloth. Wipe the shiny side gently from the center of the disk outward. Ask your teacher or a parent before attempting this.

TECH CHECK

1. **Evaluate** If you wanted to save a copy of a short story you wrote, could you use a floppy disk? Why or why not?
2. **Identify** What are the storage capacities of floppy disks, ZIP disks, and hard drives?
3. **Describe** Describe three things you can do if your CD-ROM is not working.

MULTIPAGE BUSINESS REPORT, PAGE 1

(with side and paragraph headings)

↓6x

THE INFORMATION EXPLOSION ↓2x

By Ann A. Minichiello ↓2x

Whatever your position, in today's business world you will find yourself at the center of an information explosion. Today's offices are equipped with many technologies, such as:

- High-speed networks
- Wireless networks
- Fax machines
- E-mail
- Voice mail

All of these technologies are designed to make the flow of communication faster and more effective. As a result, you must have excellent information skills to succeed in the business world. The following guidelines will help you to improve your information management skills. ↓2x

KNOW YOUR PRODUCT ↓2x

Every worker should know the product for which he or she is responsible. If you work in an office, your product is information. Your primary responsibility will be to handle information—to receive it and store it for future use, to research information and share it with others inside or outside of the company, or to evaluate the information and report on your evaluation.

Be sure that you understand the communication responsibilities of your position. Ask your manager for clarification if necessary.

COMMUNICATION

The role of communication is receiving a great deal of attention. The need to write and speak effectively is critical to success. Equally important to communication is the individual's ability to plan and organize information. ↓2x

Planning. It is important to plan and organize information. Every office worker must plan ahead to determine information needs. The first step in communicating is to anticipate needs.

Storage Devices Continued

All of the storage devices you have read about so far use electric charges to store information. **Optical disks,** another type of storage device, use lasers to read and write information. Four types of optical disks are explained below.

A **CD-R,** which stands for **C**ompact **D**isk-**R**ecordable, is a CD-ROM disk that does not yet contain any information. A CD-R drive writes information onto the CD-R disk. A CD-R can hold about the same amount of information that the CD-ROM can hold.

Information can only be put on CD-ROM and CD-R disk once. A **CD-RW** is an optical disk that can record information many times. CD-RW disks are useful for making copies of important information for backup.

A **flash drive** is a portable storage device that plugs directly into a computer's USB port. Some are as small as a pen or keychain and hold 32 MB to 256 MB of information or more.

A **CD-ROM** is an optical disk that can hold up to 1 gigabyte of information. One gigabyte of information is equal to 700 floppy disks or 300,000 pages of text. CD-ROM drives are very common in PCs because the CD-ROM is a cheap way to store lots of information.

Like the CD-ROM, a **DVD-ROM** is an optical disk. However, the DVD-ROM can hold up to 17 gigabytes of information. It would take 17 CD-ROMs to hold the information in one DVD-ROM. DVD-ROM disks are commonly used to store movies.

MULTIPAGE BUSINESS REPORT, PAGE 2

(with enumeration)

2

Organizing. Your ability to organize all notes, letters, memos, e-mails, reports, electronic documents, faxes, and other information will determine your success. No matter what your specific job title or duties may be, you will be surrounded with information. The key to handling that information overload effectively is to stay organized. To stay organized, follow these steps: ↓2x

1. Before leaving work each day, write your to-do list for the next day. This will help you to begin each day productively.
2. Set aside some time each day for setting up files and filing documents that have accumulated on your desk. Once you develop a system and use it consistently, you will find it easy to organize information right away instead of allowing it to build up on your desk.
3. Use a daily planner to keep track of the following items to ensure that they are all in one place and easily accessible:
   - Appointments
   - Deadlines
   - Important telephone numbers
   - Other important information

↓2x

Handling the flow of information to and from coworkers, clients, executives, and others can be done well if you analyze, plan, and prioritize.

Storage Devices

Key Terms
CD-R
CD-ROM
CD-RW
DVD-ROM
Flash drive
Flash memory
Floppy disk
Hard drive
Optical disk
ZIP disk

As you have already learned, computers change data into useful information. Computers are also useful for storing information. In this section, you will learn about some of the devices that are used to store information.

A **hard drive,** also called a hard disk, is the most widely used storage device. A hard drive can be internal or external. Hard drives today can usually hold 10 to 100 gigabytes (GB) of data. One GB equals one million kilobytes (KB). A five-page research paper uses about 40 KB.

A **floppy disk** contains a small portable disk inside a plastic cover. Floppy disks can hold up to 1.4 megabytes of information, which is about enough space to store the words in a small book.

A **ZIP disk,** like a floppy disk, has a portable disk inside a plastic case. A ZIP disk can hold 100 to 250 megabytes. Two hundred fifty megabytes is roughly equal to five volumes of an encyclopedia!

Flash memory is used in digital cameras, some MP3 players, portable storage drives, and other devices. It uses chips to hold information.

LEFT-BOUND 1-PAGE BUSINESS REPORT

(with footnotes)

↓6x

HOW TO PREPARE A REPORT ↓2x

A Review of Some Basic Guidelines ↓2x

Prepared by Abby Leonard ↓2x

When you are preparing the final copy of a paper, you should be sure that it is of the highest quality and that your best efforts have been put into the project.[1] ↓2x

SELECTION OF SUPPLIES ↓2x

The following supplies are considered essential for an attractive report: ↓2x

Paper. Only high-quality paper is appropriate for the final report. Also, most reports should be prepared on white paper. ↓2x

> Many report writers believe that 20-pound paper should be used for reports; 15-pound paper would be the minimum quality. In addition, the minimum rag content used for reports should be no lower than 50 percent.[2] ↓2x

Printing. Always print your report using the best printer you have available. A laser printer or an ink-jet printer is a good choice. Be sure that once your report is printed that the pages are free of smudges and that the type looks crisp and clean. Print the report in black ink.

Covers. Selecting a cover for your report is another very important decision to make. You want to be certain that your report is as attractive on the outside as you can make it so that it will enhance the overall appearance of the report. Choose a report cover that will not detract attention from the material contained within. You only have one chance to make a positive first impression.

FORMATTING THE REPORT

There are many styles for formatting a report. A common format for academic reports is MLA (Modern Language Association) style. Business reports follow a different style. Be sure you know which style is expected for your report.

---

[1] Samara Jaeger, *Guidelines for Reports*, Orange Grove Press, Los Angeles, 2006, p. 84.
[2] Ibid.

Processing Components

Key Terms

- CPU
- Memory
- Microprocessor
- Motherboard
- RAM
- ROM
- Process
- Storage devices

A computer uses hardware to **process** data into useful information. The part of the computer that processes information has many parts that work together. The **microprocessor** is the brain of a computer. A computer makes almost all of its calculations in the microprocessor. Not all microprocessors are the same. Some can perform more calculations per second than others. Today's handheld PDAs process data many times faster than the early mainframe computers.

Computers use **memory** to hold information and perform tasks:

- Random-access memory (**RAM**) holds information temporarily, when you are working in a particular file. It is erased when you turn off the computer.
- Read-only memory (**ROM**) is permanent information on your computer that cannot be changed. It holds your computer's built-in instructions and works when you turn on or shut down your computer.

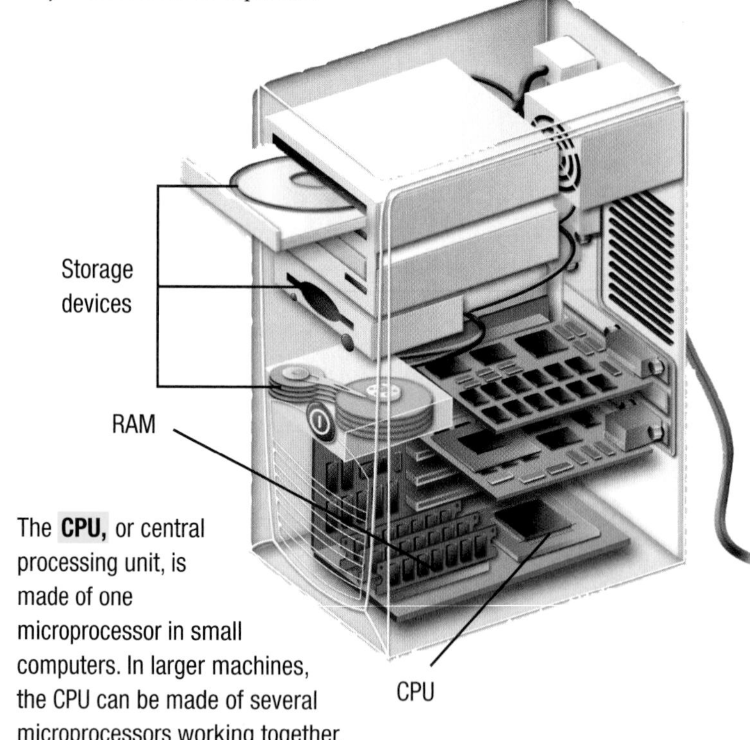

The **CPU,** or central processing unit, is made of one microprocessor in small computers. In larger machines, the CPU can be made of several microprocessors working together.

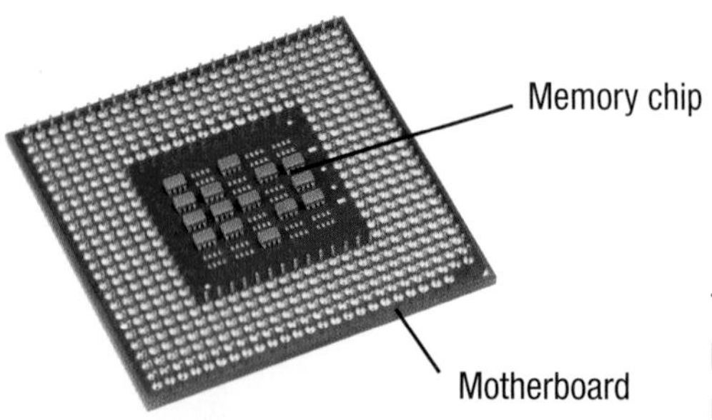

The **motherboard** is the main circuit board in a computer. All of the other circuit boards connect to the motherboard. In many computers, the microprocessor and memory can be found on the motherboard.

TECH CHECK

1. **Describe** List three processing components in a computer and explain what each does.
2. **Evaluate** What does the CPU have to do with the speed of a computer?
3. **Compare** What is the difference between RAM and ROM?

LEFT-BOUND MULTIPAGE BUSINESS REPORT, PAGE 1

(with endnotes)

↓6x

DESIGNING A COMPUTER SYSTEM↓2x

Designing a computer system involves a variety of different operations, including word processing, data processing, communications, printing, and other office-related functions. These areas can be integrated into a very powerful computer system.↓2x

DESIGNING THE SYSTEM↓2x

One of the first steps is to determine what information is going to be computerized and what personnel will need these resources.[i] This decision should involve all departments in the planning stage of system design. If necessary, you may have to invite input from those departments that are going to be closely involved in computer use after the system has been designed.↓2x

There may also be a need to acquire the system design experience of outside experts—people whose careers consist primarily of planning and developing computer systems for management.[ii]

SELECTING HARDWARE AND SOFTWARE

Bailey believes that "the selection of software precedes any hardware choices. Too many people, however, select the hardware first and then try to match their software with the computer."[iii] After the software has been selected, a decision must be made as to whether hardware should be purchased or leased. Although many firms decide to purchase their own hardware, others have taken the route of time-sharing or remote processing whereby the costs of processing data can be shared with other users.

TRAINING OPERATORS

Many firms neglect this important phase of designing a computer system. It is not enough to offer a one-week training course in an applications package and then expect proficiency from a worker.[iv] Training must occur over time to help those who will be using computers every day on the job.

Finally, it should be recognized that training is an ongoing responsibility. As technology, software, hardware, and procedures change, training must occur regularly and on a continuing basis. When additional training will be needed, plan for it well in advance. This will give workers time to learn the new technology while remaining

Output Devices

Key Terms
Monitor
Output device
Printer
Speaker

You have learned that input devices put information *into* a computer. **Output devices** carry information *out* of a computer. First, the computer changes the information into a useable format. Then, the output devices present the information to the computer user.

A **monitor,** which is also called a computer screen, displays information visually, just like a television set. An LCD (liquid crystal display) monitor is much thinner than a CRT (cathode ray tube) monitor.

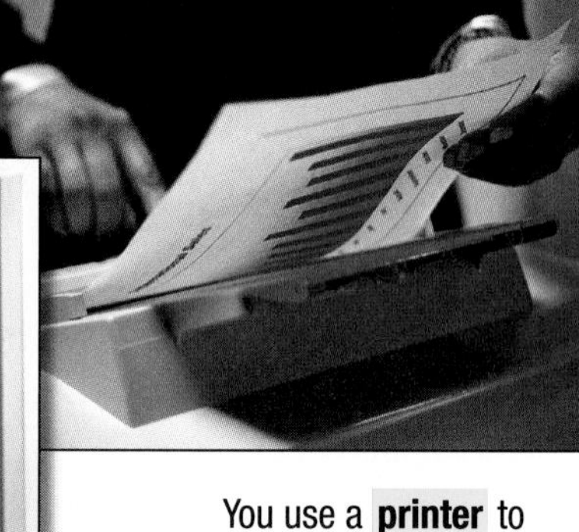

You use a **printer** to transfer images from a monitor to paper. For instance, when you key an essay on a computer, you can then print it out to turn in for class. You can also use a printer to print pictures.

Speakers carry information in the form of sound. They can output music, speech, and noises.

TECH CHECK

Illustrate Information flows out of a computer through output devices. Create a diagram that shows information flowing from a computer to three different output devices. Write a brief explanation next to each output device that explains what sort of information the device outputs.

LEFT-BOUND MULTIPAGE BUSINESS REPORT, PAGE 2

(with endnotes)

2

productive. Workers will also have time to discover and resolve any issues within the new software. It is likely that any new software product or major upgrade will have a small bug somewhere within the system.

UPDATING THE SYSTEM

The system and software should be evaluated at least once a year to see if updates are needed. Employees will be able to provide valuable feedback on the effectiveness of the current system. Send out a survey to all employees or ask key employees for their opinions.[v]

Plan ahead by budgeting for updates and upgrades well in advance. Remember to provide training about any changes in the system. Let employees know when the changes will be taking effect as soon as possible to allow them to plan their work efficiently.

You will find that if you design the system carefully, updates will go smoothly as well. Follow the guidelines above, keep communication open, and evaluate your system needs. If you remember the importance of training, your system is sure to be used efficiently for years to come.

---

[i] Neil Brent, *Information Management*, Systems Press, Westerville, Ohio, 2005, p. 172.
[ii] Laura Cuellar, "The Ins and Outs of System Design," *Processing and Design Monthly*, September 2005, p. 53.
[iii] Amanda Bailey, *System Management*, Northwestern University Press, Evanston, Illinois, 2004, p. 393.
[iv] Omar Rocha, *Administrative Management*, Proactive Publishing Corporation, Atlanta, Georgia, 2006, p. 320.
[v] Christina Pezzuti, "Tech Feedback," *Software Express*, May 2005, p. 138.

Input Devices

Key Terms
Input device
Joystick
Keyboard
Microphone
Mouse
Peripheral
Port
Scanner

Anything connected to your computer is considered a **peripheral.** In order for a computer to work, it must first have data. You can use peripherals called **input devices** to put information into a computer.

A **keyboard** is used to enter information in the form of words, numbers, and punctuation. You can also use a keyboard to give commands to some programs.

A **scanner** collects information in the form of pictures and sends the information to the computer.

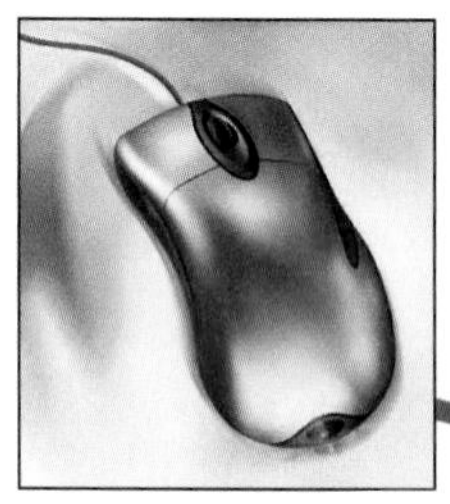

A **mouse** is used to control objects seen on a computer screen. A mouse can be used as an alternate to the keyboard for inputting instructions.

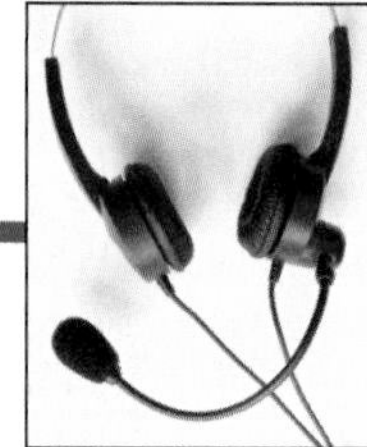

A **microphone** can be used to input audio such as music into a computer.

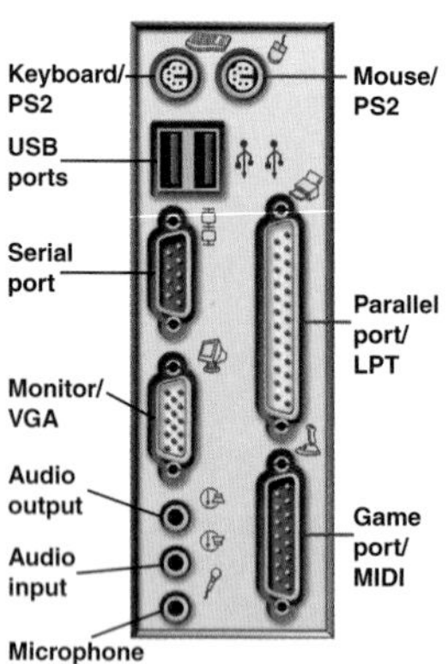

A **port** allows users to connect external input and output devices to the computer system.

A **joystick** is an input device used for playing games. The buttons send instructions to the computer.

A digital camera captures photographs as digital files that can be uploaded directly to a computer. A digital camcorder is used to create original video files.

TECH CHECK

1. **Describe** What type of information would you enter into a computer using a keyboard?
2. **Identify** In this topic, you learned about keyboards, mice, and scanners. Name three other devices that can be used as input devices.

BIBLIOGRAPHY

5

↓6x

BIBLIOGRAPHY ↓2x

Beauducel, Christie, *Create a Successful Interview*, Gaudium Press, New York, 2005. ↓2x

Dolfeld, Kim B., and Lisa Simmons, *Interview to Get the Job*, Figureroa Books, Monrovia, California, 2006.

Gokaraju, Chris, "After the Interview," *Communications*, Vol. XXVII, No. 8, May 2005, pp. 15-22.

Lymanski, Quentin, et al., "Keys to Interviewing: Style and Organization," *HR Expert*, Vol. LXVII, No. 7, October 2005, pp. 50-58.

"Prepare for the Interview," *Marketing Today*, Vol. XXXV, No. 3, August 19, 2005, pp. 102-105.

Tafoya, Jake, "Get the Job! Top Ten Interview Tips for Grads," *College of Georgia Career Center Online*, June 2005, College of Georgia, July 6, 2005 <http://www.collegeofgeorgia.edu/students/careercenter.html>.

Types of Computers and Computer Systems

Key Terms
Desktop
Laptop
Macintosh
Mainframe
Personal computer (PC)
Personal digital assistant (PDA)

In today's world, computers are everywhere. They come in different shapes and sizes, and they serve vastly different purposes.

Windows PC

A **desktop** computer is designed to remain in one location. The **personal computer (PC)** and the **Macintosh** support one user at a time. A company called Apple makes Macintosh computers. Many different companies make PCs.

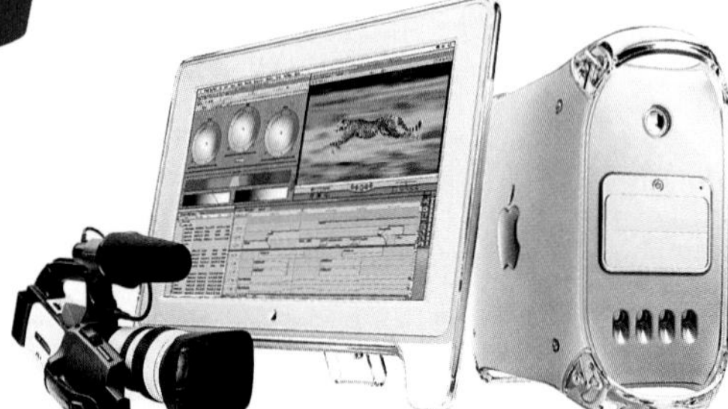

Macintosh PC

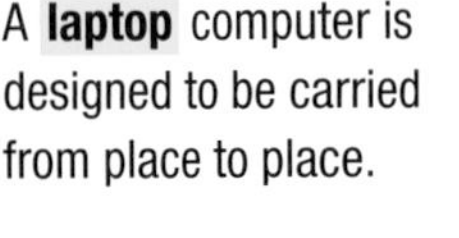

A **laptop** computer is designed to be carried from place to place.

Mainframes are very powerful computers that can do many things at once. While only one person at a time can use a PC or Macintosh, hundreds of people can use a mainframe at once.

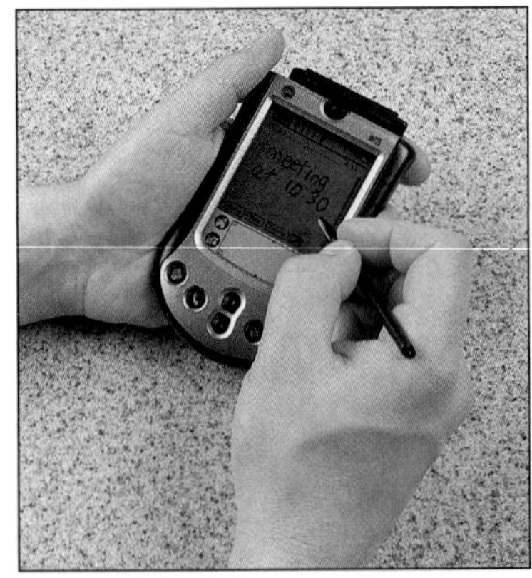

A **personal digital assistant (PDA)** is a computer that is small enough to hold in one's hand.

TECH CHECK

Vhat is the difference between a laptop and a desktop?

ve three reasons why a person might prefer a laptop to a desktop computer.

are PCs and a mainframe different? Which type of computer might be used by a large ?

ACADEMIC REPORT IN MLA STYLE, PAGE 1

↓1 inch Acacio 1

Cynthia Acacio ↓1x

Professor Roberts ↓1x

Business Communication 300 ↓1x

2 February {year} ↓1x

Communication Skills Needed in International Business ↓1x

International business plays an increasingly important role in the U.S. economy, and U.S. companies recognize that to be competitive nationally, they must be competitive internationally. Reflecting this trend, direct investment by U.S. private enterprises in foreign countries increased from $409 billion in 1994 to $528 billion in 1999, an increase of 29 percent in four years (N'Sonde 253). Today, more than 3,000 U.S. corporations have over 25,000 subsidiaries and affiliates in 125 foreign countries, and more than 25,000 American firms are engaged in international marketing (Berenholc 139, 143). ↓1x

International business is dependent on communication. According to Cara LaCuesta, chief executive officer of Amstrand Industries, an international supplier of automotive parts: ↓1x

> If a company cannot communicate with its foreign subsidiaries, customers, suppliers, and government, it cannot achieve success. The sad fact is that most American managers are not equipped to communicate with their international counterparts. (143-144) ↓1x

Because excellent business communication skills are one of the most important components for success in international business affairs, a survey instrument was designed to explore the importance of, level of competence in, and methods of developing four types of international business speaking skills. The survey was sent to over 5,000 international companies with staff members located around the world. Each company was asked to share the survey with

TECHNOLOGY HANDBOOK

COMPUTERS AND COMPUTER HARDWARE

How Have Computers Changed the World?

Key Terms
Computer
Technology

A **computer** is an electronic device that processes data and converts it into information that people can use. Chances are you cannot imagine a world without computers!

Common conveniences such as fast food restaurants and ATMs use computers to provide quick, easy service to customers.

Some computer-created games are so realistic that it seems as if you can see, hear, and sometimes even feel the action around you!

Doctors and medical technicians depend on heart ›onitors, full-body scanners, ›ther computer-based ˀ.

The term **technology** refers to the practical application of an art or skill. Nearly every part of the globe has been touched by technology.

E-mail and cell phones make it easy to contact friends and family—even if they live on the other side of the world!

TECH CHECK

...at aspects of your life do not involve computers?

...tions What would life be like without computers? How would your life change if computers ...peared from the world?

... to someone who is older than you, such as a parent or a grandparent. Did they use ... they were young? How was their life different from the way you live now?

WORKS CITED PAGE

Acacio 5

Works Cited ↓1x

Berenholc, Fatima. "Reading Body Language Cues." Management In Depth Feb. 2006: 138-153, 184. ↓1x

LaCuesta, Cara. Grow a True International Corporation. Philadelphia: Business International Press, 2006.

N'Sonde, Corrinne J. "Developing Global Business Implications: Now Is the Time." Market Research Monthly 78 (2005): 236-281.

Stadnyk, Douglas S., and Theda Rao. "Lost in Translation: A Growing Issue." Daily Times Herald 24 Oct. 2005: 4A+.

"Truth-Telling: Conducting Business Efficiently in Today's Russia." New International Journal 28 Jan. 2006: 47.

"Twenty Ways to Grow Your International Partnership." UW-UG Business Department Online. 2005. University of Wisconsin-Union Grove. 14 Dec. 2005 <http://www.uwug.edu/business/international.html>.

SKILLBUILDING *(continued)*

TIMED WRITING 19

Some specialists who work in memory training tell us 11
to think of memory as something we can control through the 23
use of strategies and organization. If you are trying to 34
remember a new name, spend a few seconds creating a mental 46
image to go along with the name. For example, to remember 57
the name Morehouse, you could make a quick mental image of 69
a person standing by a growing house. If you often misplace 81
your keys or your glasses, you could keep these objects in 93
one specific location. Then, make a conscious effort to 104
always return them to their same location. 113

Anxiety is the number one cause of slips of memory. 123
There are several strategies that can help with recall. You 135
can reduce anxiety block by not drawing attention to it. 147
For example, if a word is at the tip of your tongue, keep 158
talking while your brain keeps searching for it. A helpful 170
way to remember numbers is by connecting them to a phrase, 182
such as the old adage about Columbus sailing the ocean blue 194
in fourteen hundred and ninety-two. You might also try to 206
remember numbers by connecting them with a birthday or by 217
making number patterns. Another approach to improve memory 229
could be aerobic exercising, which speeds the flow of blood 241
to the brain and also sharpens memory performance. 251

| 1 | 2 | 3 | 4 | 5 | 6 | 7 | 8 | 9 | 10 | 11 | 12 |

AGENDA

NETWARE INCORPORATED EXECUTIVE COMMITTEE ↓2x

Meeting Agenda ↓2x

August 7, {year}, 2 p.m. ↓2x

1. Call to order
2. Approval of minutes of July 8 meeting
3. Progress report on building addition and parking lot restrictions (Satbir Bedi and Janelle Graham)
4. May 15 draft of Five-Year Plan
5. Review of National Computer Technology annual convention
6. Employee grievance filed by Leticia Burrows (Johann Lundstrom)
7. New expense-report form (John Constantino)
8. Announcements
9. Adjournment

SKILLBUILDING *(continued)*

TIMED WRITING 18

Do you live beyond your means? Are your expenses more 11
than your income? Are you quick to borrow money to pay off 23
debts? If you are, you are just like many other people. Our 35
government consistently operates on a deficit. In fact, it 47
runs two different deficits: one with its citizens, and the 59
other with the rest of the world. Some economists believe 70
these two deficits are related because if one of them were 82
not so large, the other would not be either. 91

Is all debt bad? No, deficit spending, within reason, 102
is healthy. It fuels the economy. When you buy a new car on 114
credit, you support the autoworkers. A problem arises when 126
the government borrows money to spend beyond its means. It 138
borrows from its citizens—you and me. It also borrows from 149
foreigners. Foreign countries purchase our treasury debt. 161
These investors certainly want to be compensated properly 173
for assuming the debt. The almost daily borrowing that the 184
government has to do often overwhelms credit markets. This 196
keeps interest rates high, which in turn creates appealing 208
investments. 211

Government debt is somewhat like individual debt. 221
The difference is that the government debt is much larger. 233
The moral of this story is that a little debt is okay, but 245
a lot of debt is not. 249

| 1 | 2 | 3 | 4 | 5 | 6 | 7 | 8 | 9 | 10 | 11 | 12 |

MINUTES OF A MEETING

↓6x

RESOURCE COMMITTEE ↓2x

Minutes of the Meeting ↓2x

March 13, {year} ↓2x

ATTENDANCE ↓2x

The Resource Committee met on March 13, {year}, at the Airport Sheraton in Portland, Oregon, in conjunction with the western regional meeting. Members present were Michael Davis, Cynthia Giovanni, Don Madsen, and Edna Pointer. Michael Davis, chairperson, called the meeting to order at 2:30 p.m. ↓2x

OLD BUSINESS ↓2x

The members of the committee reviewed the sales brochure on electronic copyboards. They agreed to purchase an electronic copyboard for the conference room. Cynthia Giovanni will secure quotations from at least two vendors.

NEW BUSINESS

The committee reviewed a request from the Purchasing Department for three new computers. After extensive discussion regarding the appropriate use of the computers in the Purchasing Department and software to be purchased, the committee approved the request.

ADJOURNMENT

The meeting was adjourned at 4:45 p.m. The next meeting has been scheduled for May 4, in the headquarters conference room. Members are asked to bring with them copies of the latest resource planning document. ↓2x

Respectfully submitted, ↓4x

D. S. Madsen, Secretary

SKILLBUILDING *(continued)*

TIMED WRITING 17

Taking tests can be an ordeal. Even for students who 11
are well prepared and aware of the teacher's goals, testing 23
can be stressful. They can become victim to test anxiety. 34
It is perfectly natural for people to feel some anxiety 46
when confronted with a test. Anxiety can work as a positive 58
motivational factor. It can improve your concentration, 69
encourage you to do well, and sharpen your performance. 81
However, if it does cause stress, try to rid yourself of 92
sweaty palms, the fear of failure, and the tight knot in 104
your stomach. 107

It might help to realize that most teachers want their 118
students to do well on tests. They might discuss a test 129
ahead of time. Pay attention to such discussions. There are 141
strategies you can use to help reduce anxiety in a test 152
situation. You might use relaxation techniques before and 164
during a test when you feel yourself becoming anxious. You 176
could visualize yourself as being successful and keep a 187
confident attitude during the test. Also, you could remind 198
yourself that the test is not a life-threatening situation 210
and you can survive it. You need to recognize that the test 222
is important, but you might ask yourself just how much of 233
an effect it will have on your life five years from now. 244

| 1 | 2 | 3 | 4 | 5 | 6 | 7 | 8 | 9 | 10 | 11 | 12 |

RESUME

Terry M. Martina
250 Maxwell Avenue, Apt. 8
Boulder, CO 80304
303-555-9331
tmm@netex.com ↓2x

OBJECTIVE ↓2x

To obtain a position as a resort manager in Colorado. ↓2x

EDUCATION ↓2x

Edgewood Community College, Boulder, Colorado 80304
Associate of Arts degree awarded May 2005
Major: Hotel Administration
Overall grade point average of 3.1 (on 4.0 scale)
Received Board of Regents' tuition scholarship.

Durango High School, Durango, Colorado 81301
Graduated May 2003

EXPERIENCE

Fastburger, 4404 Foxhound Road, Boulder, Colorado 80305
Position: Assistant Manager

July 2002 to present (full time during summers, part time during school year)
Developed work schedules for 19 part-time employees.
Supervised employees and handled daily receipts.

Ski Valley Haven, Aspen, Colorado 81612
Position: Assistant to the Night Manager of a 200-room ski resort

September-December 2004
Gained practical experience in operating First-Guest management system.
Produced daily occupancy reports.

ACTIVITIES

Secretary of Hospitality Services Association
Special Olympics volunteer—summer 2005

REFERENCES

References available upon request.

SKILLBUILDING *(continued)*

TIMED WRITING 16

Although heavy campaigning for a number of months now 11
leads up to a national convention for both parties, this 22
was not practiced in the early days of elections in our 34
country. Originally, candidates were selected by members of 46
their party congress. Selecting candidates in this manner 57
is called the caucus method. Caucusing was later dropped, 69
and nominations were made informally by state officials. 80

When the national convention process first started, it 91
brought much more national participation into the selection 103
process. When the first television camera was used, the 115
exposure increased even more. More citizens began to get 126
actively involved in politics. The use of the camera made 137
it seem as though they were at the convention. It has been 149
judged that over seventy million people watched during the 161
early years when conventions were televised. Today, most 172
Americans have likely watched at least one convention. 183

The expense of a national convention is quite high. 194
Citizens who are delegates feel that their participation is 206
worth whatever it costs to go. The parties do not pay for 218
television time. Sponsors pay for the commercials, and any 229
difference is paid for by the media itself. 238

| 1 | 2 | 3 | 4 | 5 | 6 | 7 | 8 | 9 | 10 | 11 | 12 |

APPLICATION LETTER

↓6x

March 2, {year} ↓4x

Ms. Lauren MacMillan, Director
Human Resources Department
Wilderness Lodge
P.O. Box 214
Denver, CO 80214 ↓2x

Dear Ms. MacMillan: ↓2x

Please consider me an applicant for the position of registration clerk for Wilderness Lodge as advertised in last Sunday's *Denver Times*. ↓2x

I will receive my A.A. degree in hotel administration from Edgewood Community College in May and will be available for full-time employment immediately. As you will see on my enclosed resume, in addition to extensive coursework in hospitality services and business, I've had experience in working for a ski lodge in Aspen similar to Wilderness Lodge.

As a lifelong resident of Colorado and an avid skier, I understand the needs of guests and how they should be treated. I would also be able to provide your guests with any information they request.

After you have reviewed my enclosed resume, I would appreciate having an opportunity to discuss with you in person why I believe I have the right qualifications and personality to serve as your registration clerk. I can be reached at 303-555-9311 after 4 p.m. daily. ↓2x

Sincerely, ↓4x

Chris L. Katroubis
250 Maxwell Avenue, Apt. 8
Boulder, CO 83035 ↓2x

Enclosure

SKILLBUILDING *(continued)*

TIMED WRITING 15

Before the middle of the twentieth century, workers 11
were treated as just additional elements of the production 22
process. Men and women worked under dismal conditions. Most 34
often, they were required to work twelve to sixteen hours a 46
day; and the work week was six days long. Wages were low. 58
Health and safety hazards were mostly ignored by employers. 70
When an employer provided any fringe benefits, they were 81
meager. Though workers were exploited, they were grateful 93
to have their jobs. Eventually, working conditions and the 105
treatment of workers have improved. 112

Effective management is a focus in today's work world. 123
A scientific approach in the management of employees may be 135
used. The scientific tool permits managers to motivate 146
workers by offering pay incentives to improve both product 158
quality and product quantity. For example, if a project 169
usually took an employee ten minutes to complete, a wage 181
incentive plan would pay a bonus for work finished in less 193
than ten minutes. Management has learned that workers will 204
produce more products as well as better products when the 216
working conditions are improved and wage incentives are 227
provided. 229

| 1 | 2 | 3 | 4 | 5 | 6 | 7 | 8 | 9 | 10 | 11 | 12 |

FOLLOW-UP LETTER

↓6x

Tab to center point May 10, {year} ↓4x

Mr. Herbert A. Juneau
Director of Personnel
Apex Products Inc.
6532 Turtle Creek Boulevard
Dallas, TX 75205 ↓2x

Dear Mr. Juneau: ↓2x

Thank you for the time you spent telling me about the billing clerk position with Apex Products. The interview you gave me yesterday definitely reaffirmed my interest in working for your company. ↓2x

I was especially impressed with the Payroll Department at Apex. The people and equipment in that department make this position very appealing to me.

The combination of my bookkeeping experience and the in-house training you provide for all new employees convinces me that this position is precisely the job that I have been seeking. When you have reached your decision, I will be most eager to hear from you. If you desire a second interview, I would be available after 12 noon any weekday. ↓2x

Tab to center point Sincerely yours, ↓4x

Eleanor G. Corsi
672 Wesley Street
Greenville, TX 75401

SKILLBUILDING *(continued)*

TIMED WRITING 14

The Hawaiian Islands have much to offer the tourist. 11
One attraction is the amazing parks. The flora, fauna, and 23
buildings are all protected by federal law. Hawaii's state 34
bird, the nene, is endangered. When visitors feed these 46
birds, they attract them to parking lots and roadsides. 57
This puts the birds in danger from auto traffic that may 68
injure or kill them. Visitors must avoid feeding the birds 80
and animals. 83

The volcanoes of the Hawaiian Islands add mystery and 94
exotic scenery. A wonderful way to observe the raw power of 106
a volcano is by taking a helicopter tour. The helicopter is 118
well-suited for the air maneuvers needed to get a closer 129
view. Pilots usually fly directly over areas with the most 141
volcanic activity. They often dip low over huge lava pools, 153
skim still-glowing flows, and circle towering steam clouds 165
rising from where the lava enters the sea. You might like 176
to spend a full day at Kilauea enjoying the sights. Atop 188
Kilauea, you can quietly appreciate the absolute beauty of 199
this impressive volcano. It is four thousand feet above sea 211
level and about ten degrees cooler than on the coast. 222

| 1 | 2 | 3 | 4 | 5 | 6 | 7 | 8 | 9 | 10 | 11 | 12 |

PERSONAL-BUSINESS LETTER IN BLOCK STYLE

(For an alternate style, see page 169)

↓6x

January 3, {year} ↓4x

Mr. Luis Fernandez, Manager
Arvon Industries, Inc.
21 St. Claire Avenue East
Toronto, Ontario M4T 1L9
CANADA ↓2x

Dear Mr. Fernandez: ↓2x

As a former employee and present stockholder of Arvon Industries, I protest the planned sale of the Consumer Products Division to Browning Manufacturing Company. ↓2x

According to published reports, consumer products accounted for 19 percent of last year's corporate profits, and they are expected to account for at least as much this year. In addition, Dun & Bradstreet predicts that consumer products nationwide will outpace the general economy for the next five years.

I am concerned about the effect the planned sale of the division will have on overall corporate profits, on cash dividends for investors, and on the economics of Louisville and Paducah, where the two consumer products plants are located.

Please ask your board of directors to reconsider this matter. ↓2x

Sincerely, ↓4x

Roger J. Michaelson
901 East Benson, Apt. 3
Ft. Lauderdale, FL 33310

TIMED WRITING 13

It is quite possible that Ellis Island is part of your 11
family history. For years, Ellis Island was an immigration 23
station. In the early part of the twentieth century, it 34
served as the main gateway to our country. Amazingly, over 46
twelve million foreigners had passed through its doors by 58
the middle of the twentieth century, when it closed. Ships 69
unloaded their passengers at the docks in New York. Then, 81
the passengers quickly transferred to boats and barges for 93
the trip to Ellis Island in New York Harbor. It was the 104
first place many of our forebears saw when they arrived in 116
America. 118

This country is comprised of immigrants, along with 128
native American Indians. An immigrant is someone who moves 140
from one country to another. An immigrant usually plans to 152
make the new country home. Millions of Americans can trace 163
their family history to ancestors who first arrived in the 175
United States through Ellis Island. Today, it is a museum. 187
Millions of dollars were raised to fix up the neglected 198
building. The museum is located only one mile from New York 210
City and a few hundred yards from the docks of New Jersey. 222

| 1 | 2 | 3 | 4 | 5 | 6 | 7 | 8 | 9 | 10 | 11 | 12 |

BUSINESS LETTER IN MODIFIED-BLOCK STYLE

(with subject line, enclosure notation, copy notation, and numbered list)

The Home Construction Associates
3218 Swiftwater Boulevard, Baltimore, OH 43105
Phone 740- TO B HOME Fax 740-862-4663
HomeConstructionAssoc@greenapple.com

↓6x

Tab to center point September 6, {year} ↓4x

Mr. Dennis Maryott
Maryott Associates
One Parklands Drive
Darien, CT 06820-3214 ↓2x

Dear Mr. Maryott: ↓2x

Subject: Remodeling Contract ↓2x

I am returning a signed contract to begin the remodeling job on your offices beginning the first of next month. I understand that this work must be done with a minimum amount of disruption to your staff. ↓2x

To ensure the quality of workmanship and materials, we have made the following changes to the contract: ↓2x

1. We revised Section 4.2 to state that only premium grade materials will be used for all new construction related to remodeling. ↓2x

2. We added Section 10.2 to change the length of time to complete this job to four months rather than five. We feel this will provide us with ample time to complete the work to your satisfaction. ↓2x

If these revisions are satisfactory, please sign and return one copy of the contract for our files. We look forward to this opportunity to work with you. ↓2x

Tab to center point Sincerely, ↓4x

Laurice Mitchell
Senior Consultant ↓2x

jea
Enclosure
c: Roger J. Michaelson, CEO

SKILLBUILDING *(continued)*

TIMED WRITING 12

Productivity measurement techniques are frequently 10
used in word processing installations today to evaluate the 22
output that is produced. This technique allows management 34
to compare workload effort in order to improve scheduling 46
and work dispersal. 50

Productivity measurement also can help a company by 60
recording, calculating, and tracking employee production 72
over a period of time. Supervisors are then able to create 83
performance standards designed for their organization. This 95
method of measurement can be used to assist managers in 107
making reliable decisions regarding salary increases and 118
promotion of word processing personnel. 126

A measure of production might also assist those who 136
are more capable in a number of ways. For example, when 148
compared to their peers, their abilities and skills will be 160
highlighted. Using this particular technique, all employees 172
can be evaluated on a parallel basis. Very talented workers 184
can be rewarded. Lastly, this measurement technique can 195
assist you in removing the subjectivity that is found in 206
company measurement systems used for evaluating employees. 218

| 1 | 2 | 3 | 4 | 5 | 6 | 7 | 8 | 9 | 10 | 11 | 12 |

BUSINESS LETTER IN MODIFIED-BLOCK STYLE, PAGE 1

(with open punctuation and table)

METRO BROADCASTING	200 South Main Salt Lake City, UT 84101-8967 Phone: 801-555-3917 Fax: 801-555-3998

↓6x

Tab to center point May 5, {year} ↓4x

British Mutual Broadcasting
24 Portland Place
London, WIN 4BB
ENGLAND ↓2x

Attention: Program Director ↓2x

Ladies and Gentlemen ↓2x

I have been invited by the Federal Communications Commission to participate in a study of television news programming in European countries. The invitation came from Jill Andrews, FCC vice-chair, and I am, of course, delighted to take part in this project. ↓2x

As noted on the enclosed report, one function of this study will be to compare the news programming in countries that have a long history of free-access broadcasting with the programming in newly developed countries. I have been assigned to lead a study group to six European countries to gather first-hand information on this topic. We will be visiting England, France, Germany, Poland, Italy, and Switzerland on August 24 through September 3. In addition to myself, our group will consist of the following members: ↓2x

Name	Organization	Location
Katherine Grant	KPQR-TV	Los Angeles, CA
Arkady Gromov	National Public Radio	Washington, DC
Richard Logan	Miami Herald	Miami, FL
Manuel Cruz	Cable News System	New York, NY
Barbara Brooks	Federal Comm. Commission	Washington, DC

↓2x

Our initial plans are to spend at least one full day in each of the countries meeting with the news programming staff of one or two of the major networks, touring their facilities, viewing recent broadcasts, and in general, getting a first-hand view of actual news organizations and decision-making.

TIMED WRITING 11

If you love mystery, you would certainly be amazed by 11
the speculation over how plants and animals first arrived 23
in Hawaii. Most people's thoughts of a Hawaiian paradise 34
include swaying palms, dense jungles, and luscious fruit 45
ready to be picked. For millions of years, the chain of 57
Hawaiian Islands were raw and barren places where no plants 69
or birds existed. These lush Pacific Ocean islands are a 80
geological mystery. They formed spontaneously more than two 92
thousand miles from any continental land, isolated from the 104
normal spread of plants and animals. Flora and fauna that 116
did reach them found a foreign ecosystem. They had to adapt 128
or perish in this environment. Many of the birds and plants 140
became so specialized that they were not only limited to 151
specific islands but also to specific isolated valleys. It 163
was fortunate that the soil was very rich. There were no 174
other plants or animals with which to compete. The climate 186
was nearly perfect for most of the entities growing on the 198
islands. The evolution of plants and animals on these tiny 210
islands took place quickly. 215

| 1 | 2 | 3 | 4 | 5 | 6 | 7 | 8 | 9 | 10 | 11 | 12 |

BUSINESS LETTER IN MODIFIED-BLOCK STYLE, PAGE 2

(with enumeration, attachment, delivery notation, and postscript)

British Mutual Broadcasting
Page 2
May 5, {year}

Our tentative itinerary calls for us to arrive at Heathrow Airport at 7:10 p.m. on Tuesday evening, August 24. Would it be possible for us to do the following: ↓2x

1. Meet with various members of your staff on August 25. We would be available from 8:30 a.m. until 1:30 p.m. ↓2x

2. Receive a copy of your programming log for the week of August 24 through September 3, and especially a minute-by-minute listing of the programming sequence for your national news reporting. ↓2x

I would appreciate your contacting Barbara Brooks, our liaison at the Federal Communications Commission (1919 M Street, NW, Washington, DC 20554; phone 202-555-3894), to let us know whether we may study your operation on August 25. ↓2x

So that we can finalize our plans and make the necessary arrangements, may we please hear from you by May 15. If your decision is positive, I will work directly with you in coordinating the details of our visit. ↓2x

Tab to center point — Sincerely ↓2x

METRO BROADCASTING ↓4x

Denise J. Watterson
General Manager ↓2x

jea
Attachment: FCC Report
By International Express Mail
c: Barbara Brooks ↓2x

PS: The Federal Communications Commission will reimburse your organization for any expenses associated with our visit, including phone calls, duplicating, and the like.

SKILLBUILDING *(continued)*

TIMED WRITING 10

If you are not a classical music fan and do not often 11
go to the theater, you probably think, as do most concert 23
goers, that music before Bach is a mystery. Many music fans 35
see classical music as intensely lyrical, with madrigals 46
and dances that are accompanied by various horns, bells, 57
drums, violins, and other instruments. But, music and opera 69
have been listened to for almost five centuries. One way to 81
effectively approach this music is to just relax and enjoy 93
its strangeness. While you are listening, recognize what 105
sounds are pleasing to your ear and what sounds seem like 116
irradiating noise. You can train your ear to pick up the 128
music of the violin, cello, trumpet, harp, clarinet, piano, 140
piccolo, xylophone, tuba, and flute. Melodies played as 151
intended by the composer may sound quite peculiar to the 162
untrained ears of today's listeners. One reason for this 174
might be that the tuning of instruments has changed. Also, 185
the listeners of the fifteenth century likely had their own 197
ideas of what was considered enjoyable music, and their 209
preferences were different. 214

| 1 | 2 | 3 | 4 | 5 | 6 | 7 | 8 | 9 | 10 | 11 | 12 |

REFERENCE SECTION *(continued)*

FORMATTING ENVELOPES

A standard large (No. 10) envelope is 9½ by 4⅛ inches. A standard small (No. 6¾) envelope is 6½ by 3⅝ inches. Either address format shown below is acceptable. The all-capitalized format shown for the large envelope uses no punctuation.

George Ellis
1553 Oak Lane
Muncie, IN 47302
Ms. Louise Tye
P.O. Box 770
Shreveport, LA 71101
Cape Cod Resorts
1408 Oceanside
Sandwich, MA 02563
DR MIA JENNINGS
9019 LAYTON AVENUE
LUBBOCK TX 79041-9019

FOLDING LETTERS

To fold a letter for a small envelope:

1. Place the letter *face up* and fold up the bottom half to 0.5 inch from the top edge of the paper.
2. Fold the right third over to the left.
3. Fold the left third over to 0.5 inch from the right edge of the paper.
4. Insert the last crease into the envelope first, with the flap facing up.

To fold a letter for a large envelope:

1. Place the letter *face up* and fold up the bottom third.
2. Fold the top third down to 0.5 inch from the bottom edge of the paper.
3. Insert the last crease into the envelope first, with the flap facing up.

TIMED WRITING 9

One of the many unique features of a democracy is that 11
everyone of legal age has the right to vote. Voting must be 23
taken seriously because it is our responsibility. It is 34
obvious that a government might not be representative if 46
citizens do not take an active part in choosing the people 58
who represent them. It is simple to pass judgment on our 69
leaders, but we also have to assume some responsibility 80
ourselves and participate in the voting process. 90

Citizens can vote for varying levels of government. 101
Federal, state, county, and city elections must be planned 112
for every year in which the terms of officials have ended. 124
Primaries are held to narrow the number of candidates. The 136
year in which a president is chosen can create a lot of 147
excitement, but citizens must be interested in and vote for 159
their choice each time. 164

A good voter should pay careful attention to the main 175
issues and the candidates. Newspapers, public debates, and 187
interviews are good sources of information. Choose those 198
officials who share your views and are best qualified. 209

| 1 | 2 | 3 | 4 | 5 | 6 | 7 | 8 | 9 | 10 | 11 | 12 |

MEMO (TEMPLATE)

Memorandum

To: Elizabeth Barnett

CC: Catherine Argetes

From: Jack Stanley

Date: Current

Re: Flexible Scheduling

Several of our employees who have certain family obligations have asked us to explore the possibility of flexible scheduling. These staff members feel that a flexible schedule will help to increase morale and productivity and reduce absenteeism and turnover.

We are now considering several options, which include flextime, job sharing, and compressed workweeks.

Flextime is the most popular option. Employees would work a set number of hours per day with flexible start and finish times. However, employees would be required to be on the job during particular hours of the day.

Job sharing involves two employees sharing the same job. The employees might have divided job responsibilities, or they might have totally unrelated responsibilities. The two employees involved in sharing a job would need to work out the hours that each would work so that we have full coverage of the position at all times.

Compressed workweeks are those in which employees work the same number of total hours, but they do so over a shorter number of days. Using a compressed workweek would enable us to extend our business hours and provide employees with an opportunity to handle their personal obligations during the week.

I have attached more complete descriptions for your review and will schedule a meeting before the end of the month to discuss all of the options with you.

urs

Attachment

SKILLBUILDING *(continued)*

TIMED WRITING 8

Genealogy has become a fascinating science to some 10
people. You do not need to be a scientist to get involved 22
in genealogy. You do not need a college degree to trace 33
your roots. There was a time when you may have wanted to 45
trace your family tree to prove that one or more of your 56
ancestors came over from Europe on the Mayflower. However, 68
today we often trace our roots as expressions of personal 79
and cultural pride and identity, no matter how humble a 91
person's origins may be. 96

There are many genealogical societies recognized in 106
this country. We all want to know where we came from and 118
how we arrived here. Genealogy can be a complex field. It 129
can include religion, demographics, geography, ethnic and 141
women's studies, legal history, photographic imaging, and 152
library research. Getting started at tracing your roots 164
does not have to be complicated. You just start with what 175
you know and then move toward the unknown. Inquire at your 187
school or city library to get you going with some research 199
you would like to do. 203

| 1 | 2 | 3 | 4 | 5 | 6 | 7 | 8 | 9 | 10 | 11 | 12 |

OPEN TABLE

(with blocked column heads)

↓center page vertically

SALES ANALYSIS
Borden Manufacturing Company
June 30, {year} ↓1x

Salesperson	**Units**	**Gross Sales ($)**
Brazinski, Robert	10	427.70
Dawkins, Carol	18	769.86
Greene, Janice	20	855.40
Herrera, Jose	17	727.09
Kessler, Diane	15	641.55
Yeung, Joe	19	812.63

SKILLBUILDING *(continued)*

TIMED WRITING 7

Did you ever look up at the sky during the night and 11
see a shooting star? Do you realize that what you saw was a 23
meteor racing across the sky? Sometimes meteor showers are 35
visible to the naked eye. At such times you do not need 46
special glasses or binoculars to view these space voyagers. 58
Between midnight and dawn is the best time to watch for 69
them. If you are watching outdoors, you get a much better 81
view. 82

Every year meteor showers are caused by extra scrap 92
matter of comets. When the comets are quite close to the 104
sun, more debris accumulates and there are likely to be 115
more meteors. Each summer, from around the middle of July 127
through the middle of August, a meteor show may light up 138
the night sky. At peak times, you may be able to see as 149
many as a hundred meteors in a night. In the city, a bright 161
meteor shower has to compete with the bright city lights. 173
From the ground, the meteors look as though they might be 184
coming from a constellation. 190

| 1 | 2 | 3 | 4 | 5 | 6 | 7 | 8 | 9 | 10 | 11 | 12 |

BOXED TABLE

(with shading and braced headings)

↓center page vertically

SALES ANALYSIS Borden Manufacturing Company June 30, {year} ↓1x				
↓1x	1st Quarter		2nd Quarter	
Salesperson	**Units**	**Gross Sales ($)**	**Units**	**Gross Sales ($)**
Brazinski, Robert	10	427.70	29	1,240.33
Dawkins, Carol	18	769.86	17	727.09
Greene, Janice	20	855.40	28	1,197.56
Herrera, Jose	17	727.09	24	1,026.48
Kessler, Diane	15	641.55	25	1,069.25
Yeung, Joe	19	812.63	32	1,368.64
TOTAL	99	4,234.23	155	6,629.35

SKILLBUILDING *(continued)*

TIMED WRITING 6

Many people have wondered what might possibly be the 11
greatest structure on earth. The tallest buildings, the 22
longest bridges, or the mightiest dams may all be examined 34
to find the answer to this difficult question. In the minds 46
of many people, one of the greatest structures ever built 57
was the Great Wall of China. It is a well-known fact that 69
its features are so impressive that astronauts have even 80
viewed the wall from their spaceships. 88

The structure was built primarily by mixing just earth 99
and bricks. It is wide enough at the top for several people 111
to walk abreast on it. It winds for miles through a large 123
part of the country, over mountains and across valleys. It 135
was constructed to keep out unwelcome tribes, and it is 146
believed that building the wall required the labor of many 158
thousands of persons for dozens of decades. The very first 170
sections of the Great Wall were built in the Age of Warring 182
States. 183

| 1 | 2 | 3 | 4 | 5 | 6 | 7 | 8 | 9 | 10 | 11 | 12 |

BOXED TABLE

(with multiline heads and footnote)

↓center page vertically

RETIREMENT CALCULATION* ↓1x				
↓1x **Age**	↓1x **Annual Salary**	**1 Percent of Earnings ($)**	↓1x **Year**	**Annual Benefit Times Years**
35-39	$15,000	$150	5	$750.00
40-49	$20,000	$200	10	$2,000.00
50-59	$30,000	$300	10	$3,000.00
60-64	$50,000	$500	5	$2,500.00
Annual Retirement Payment				$8,250.00
*Based on joining the plan at age 35.				

SKILLBUILDING *(continued)*

TIMED WRITING 5

Have you ever felt rundown, tired, and fatigued? The 11
symptoms listed above are common to many of us today. They 23
affect our job performance; they limit the fun we have with 35
our family and friends; and they can even affect our good 46
health. Here are a few of the ways by which we can quickly 58
minimize the problem and become more active in the things 70
we do daily. 72

It is critical that we get plenty of rest so that we 83
are rested when we get up each morning. We must eat a good 95
breakfast so that we can build up energy for the day that 106
follows. Physical exercise is a necessity, and it might be 118
the one most important ingredient in building up our energy 130
reserves. We must engage in vigorous exercise to make our 142
hearts beat faster and cause our breathing rate to increase 154
appreciably. These are things that can help us increase our 166
energy and make us much healthier people. 174

| 1 | 2 | 3 | 4 | 5 | 6 | 7 | 8 | 9 | 10 | 11 | 12 |

RULED TABLE

center page vertically

SALES ANALYSIS
Borden Manufacturing Company
June 30, {year} 1x

Salesperson	Units	Gross Sales ($)
Brazinski, Robert	10	427.70
Dawkins, Carol	18	769.86
Greene, Janice	20	855.40
Herrera, Jose	17	727.09
Kessler, Diane	15	641.55
Yeung, Joe	19	812.63

SKILLBUILDING *(continued)*

TIMED WRITING 3

Businesses and individuals are free to write letters 11
to officials in Washington. There are dozens of people to 22
whom you might send a letter. These include the President, 34
senators, or representatives. People who are elected to go 46
to Washington take along their staff who answers most of 57
the mail from their constituents. Using the mail is just 69
one way legislators keep in touch with what is happening in 81
their individual congressional districts. 89

People send inquiries on many topics. They may want to 101
express a positive position or they may want to complain 113
about taxes, pollution, and foreign policy. Some letters 124
influence how lawmakers make their decisions. 133

| 1 | 2 | 3 | 4 | 5 | 6 | 7 | 8 | 9 | 10 | 11 | 12 |

TIMED WRITING 4

Autumn in the “northland” is very exciting. You jump 11
up in the early morning; walk out under a clear, blue sky; 23
and feel the strong chill in the air. The leaves have lost 34
their brilliant green. It appears that they may have been 46
tinted by someone passing by. The truth is that during the 58
night hours a frost has painted the green to hues of brown, 70
yellow, orange, and scarlet. It is a breathtaking panorama 82
in Technicolor. The leaves seem not to move in the quiet 92
breeze. Then, suddenly, a brisk puff lifts them from the 104
limbs and carries them gently like feathers to the ground 116
below. You watch as legions of leaves jump free and float 128
to the earth, covering it like a quilted blanket that looks 140
much like moss. When you walk on top of the blanket, it 151
cushions each step you take as though you were walking on 162
air. 163

| 1 | 2 | 3 | 4 | 5 | 6 | 7 | 8 | 9 | 10 | 11 | 12 |

PROOFREADERS' MARKS

Proofreaders' Marks	Draft	Final Copy
Omit space	data base	database
V or ^ Insert	if hes going	if he's not going,
Capitalize	Maple street	Maple Street
Delete	a final draft	a draft
# Insert space	allready to	all ready to
Change word	and if you	and when you
/ Use lowercase letter	our President	our president
¶ Paragraph	¶ Most of the	Most of the
••• Don't delete	a true story	a true story
O Spell out	the only 1	the only one
Transpose	they all see	they see all
SS Single-space	SS first line second line	first line second line
ds Double-space	ds first line second line	first line second line
Move right	Please send	Please send
Move left	May I	May I
Bold	Column Heading	**Column Heading**
ital Italic	ital Time magazine	*Time* magazine
u/l Underline	u/l Time magazine	Time magazine readers
Move as shown	readers will see	will see

SKILLBUILDING *(continued)*

SUPPLEMENTARY TIMED WRITINGS

TIMED WRITING 1

Raising dogs can be a combination of both fun and hard 11
work. Before you even start, you should realize just which 23
breed can best adapt to your lifestyle. If you need a dog 35
to protect your house, a poodle will not give you enough 46
protection. If you are in your own apartment, a collie may 58
be too large. When you have chosen a dog for you, expect to 70
have to train it. This can be done quickly with a new puppy 82
that is willing to learn. 87

| 1 | 2 | 3 | 4 | 5 | 6 | 7 | 8 | 9 | 10 | 11 | 12 |

TIMED WRITING 2

For students who can speak a foreign language, there 11
is an amazing job market today. Many major companies in 22
other countries have been buying control of or investing in 34
American firms. The need for workers with foreign language 46
skills is seen in the large number of help wanted ads for 57
experts with language skills. 63

The fact that so many Americans cannot speak, read, or 75
write another language is tragic because the countries of 86
the world today are closely linked. International trade is 98
very important to business and government, and young people 110
cannot afford to be unequipped to meet the many changes and 122
challenges of the future. 127

| 1 | 2 | 3 | 4 | 5 | 6 | 7 | 8 | 9 | 10 | 11 | 12 |

LANGUAGE LINKS

ALWAYS SPACE ONCE...

- After a comma.
  We ordered two printers, one computer, and three monitors.
- After a semicolon.
  They flew to Dallas, Texas; Reno, Nevada; and Rome, New York.
- After a period following someone's initials.
  Mr. A. Henson, Ms. C. Hovey, and Mrs. M. Syzmanski will attend the meeting.
- After a period following the abbreviation of a single word.
  We will send the package by 7 p.m. next week. [Note: space once after the final period in the "p.m." abbreviation, but do not space after the first period between the two letters.]
- Before a ZIP code.
  Send the package to 892 Maple Street, Grand Forks, ND 58201.
- Before and after an ampersand.
  We were represented by the law firm of Argue & Johnson; they were represented by the law firm of Crandall & Humphries.
- After a period at the end of a sentence.
  Don't forget to vote. Vote for the candidate of your choice.
- After a question mark.
  When will you vote? Did you vote last year?
- After an exclamation point.
  Wow! What a performance! It was fantastic!
- After a colon.
  We will attend on the following days: Monday, Wednesday, and Friday.

60 wpm

Many standard dictionaries give brief essays on topics such as the history of English, what is good usage, and the different dialects of English. Usage refers to how words are used in speaking and writing. A regional way of pronouncing a word is considered dialect. Quite frequently, a dictionary will give instructions on how to use the word. The most obvious information appears first. It is correct syllable division and spelling. When you key a paper, you need to be razor sharp on the correct way to hyphenate a word. Do not be lax in your writing. Use a dictionary to help check every report.

PUNCTUATION

COMMAS:

1. Use a comma between independent clauses joined by a conjunction. (An independent clause is one that can stand alone as a complete sentence.)
We requested Brown Industries to change the date, and they did so within five days.

2. Use a comma after an introductory expression (unless it is a short prepositional phrase).
Before we can make a decision, we must have all the facts.
In 2004 our nation elected a president.

3. Use a comma before and after the year in a complete date.
We will arrive at the plant on June 2, 2005, for the conference.

4. Use a comma before and after a state or country that follows a city (but not before a ZIP Code).
Joan moved to Vancouver, British Columbia, in September.
Send the package to Douglasville, GA 30135, by express mail.

5. Use a comma between each item in a series of three or more.
We need to order paper, toner, and font cartridges.

6. Use a comma before and after a transitional expression (such as *therefore* and *however*).
It is critical, therefore, that we finish the project on time.

7. Use a comma before and after a direct quotation.
When we left, James said, "Let us return to the same location next year."

8. Use a comma before and after a nonessential expression. (A nonessential expression is a word or group of words that may be omitted without changing the basic meaning of the sentence.)
Let me say, to begin with, that the report has already been finalized.

9. Use a comma between two adjacent adjectives that modify the same noun.
We need an intelligent, enthusiastic individual for this job.

SEMICOLONS:

1. Use a semicolon to join two closely related independent clauses that are not connected by a conjunction (such as *and, but,* or *nor*).
Management favored the vote; stockholders did not.

2. Use a semicolon to separate three or more items in a series if any of the items already contain commas.
Region 1 sent their reports in March, April, and May; and Region 2 sent their reports in September, October, and November.

SKILLBUILDING *(continued)*

56 wpm

Each June, July, or August, some firms put a closed sign at the front[1] door. They let their employees have the entire month off. All of them[2] like to zip out of town for a nice relaxing vacation. During this month,[3] everyone can enjoy a little time in the sun, or in a boat. Some head[4] for the mountains for a camping or hiking trip. In the summer, most[5] of us usually do less indoors and spend quite a lot of time outside.[6] Many winter resorts have summer activities. Their activities can be enjoyable[7] and quite varied. They do a lot of business during the summer.[8]

58 wpm

It has been more than a hundred years since the phone first touched our[1] lives. It has modified the way all of us around the world converse. There[2] are more ways than just a phone to help us quickly stay in touch with[3] others. A computer connected to a modem or fax machine or a pager can be[4] used to carry messages from place to place. The use of these carriers can[5] be quicker and more cost-efficient than the use of the telephone. Today,[6] using more than one of these communication devices is a common practice.[7] We can choose to stay in touch by phone, fax, e-mail, page, or letter.[8]

REFERENCE SECTION *(continued)*

HYPHENS:

1. Hyphenate compound adjectives that come before a noun (unless the first word is an adverb ending in *-ly*).
   We reviewed an up-to-date report on Wednesday.
   We attended a highly rated session on multimedia software.

2. Hyphenate compound numbers (between twenty-one and ninety-nine) and fractions that are expressed as words.
   We observed twenty-nine infractions during the investigation.
   Bancroft Industries reduced their sales force by one-third.

3. Hyphenate words that are divided at the end of a line. Do not divide one-syllable words, contractions, or abbreviations; divide other words only between syllables.
   To appreciate the full significance of our actions, you must review the entire docu-
   ment that was sent to you.

APOSTROPHES:

1. Use *'s* to form the possessive of singular nouns.
   The hurricane caused major damage to Georgia's coastline.

2. Use only an apostrophe to form the possessive of plural nouns that end in *s*.
   The investors' goals were outlined in the annual report.

3. Use *'s* to form the possessive of indefinite pronouns (such as *someone's* or *anybody's*); do not use an apostrophe with personal pronouns (such as *hers, his, its, ours, theirs,* and *yours*).
   She was instructed to select anybody's paper for a sample.
   Each computer comes carefully packed in its own container.

COLONS:

Use a colon to introduce explanatory material that follows an independent clause. (An independent clause is one that can stand alone as a complete sentence.)

The computer satisfies three criteria: speed, cost, and power.

DASHES:

Use a dash instead of a comma, semicolon, colon, or parenthesis when you want to convey a more forceful separation of words within a sentence. (If your keyboard has a special dash character, use it. Otherwise, form a dash by typing two hyphens, with no space before, between, or after.)

At this year's meeting, the speakers—and topics—were superb.

PERIODS:

Use a period, rather than a question mark, to end a sentence that is a polite request. (Consider a sentence a polite request if you expect the reader to respond by doing as you ask rather than by giving a yes-or-no answer.)

Will you please call me if I can be of further assistance.

SKILLBUILDING *(continued)*

50 wpm

The Inca Indians lived hundreds of years ago near what is now called Peru. They were a great nation known for their many unique buildings. These buildings, in fact, are still visible in ruins deep in the jungle. The temples that remain can be scrutinized for clues about their religion, beliefs, culture, and way of life. Some knowledge already exists, for we have learned that they were a people of numerous skills. Perhaps in time we can uncover the answer to the secret of why the Incas vanished.

52 wpm

The brain controls conscious behavior like walking and thinking. It also controls involuntary behavior like the heartbeat and breathing. In humans, it is known to be the site of emotions, memory, and thought. It functions by receiving information through nerve cells from every part of the body. When the brain receives an influx of data, it needs to evaluate the data and then zip off commands to an area of the body like a muscle. Or, the brain might simply store the data. Neurons can process a large amount of data.

54 wpm

Working in a place where everyone gets along would be great. However, we all know that the chance of finding a job in a place like that really seldom happens. Each of us has a different personality. When we mix together all of those personalities, the results are quite varied. There will be those who get along with everyone and find no fault with anything. But, by and large, each of us can and will have a difference of opinion with someone at some point. We need to bring qualities like zeal and a good attitude to every job situation.

QUOTATION MARKS:

1. Use quotation marks around the titles of newspaper articles, magazine articles, chapters in a book, reports, conferences, and similar items.
The best article I found in my research was entitled "Multimedia for Everyone."

2. Use quotation marks around a direct quotation.
Harrison responded by saying, "This decision will not affect our merger."

ITALIC (OR UNDERLINE):

Italicize (or underline) the titles of books, magazines, newspapers, and other complete published works.
I read *The New York Times* yesterday. I read The New York Times yesterday.

GRAMMAR

AGREEMENT:

1. Use singular verbs and pronouns with singular subjects and plural verbs and pronouns with plural subjects.
I was pleased with the performance of our team.
Reno and Phoenix were selected as the sites for our next two meetings.

2. Some pronouns (*anybody, each, either, everybody, everyone, much, neither, no one, nobody,* and *one*) are always singular and take a singular verb. Other pronouns (*all, any, more, most, none,* and *some*) may be singular or plural, depending on the noun to which they refer.
Each employee is responsible for summarizing the day's activities.
Most of the workers are going to get a substantial pay raise.

3. Disregard any intervening words that come between the subject and verb when establishing agreement.
The box containing the books and pencils has not been found.

4. If two subjects are joined by *or, either/or, nor, neither/nor,* or *not only/but also,* the verb should agree with the subject nearer to the verb.
Neither the players nor the coach is in favor of the decision.

5. The subject *a number* takes a plural verb; *the number* takes a singular verb.
The number of new students has increased to six.
We know that a number of students are in sports.

6. Subjects joined by *and* take a plural verb unless the compound subject is preceded by *each, every,* or *many a (an).*
Every man, woman, and child is included in our survey.

7. Verbs that refer to conditions that are impossible or improbable (that is, verbs in the *subjunctive* mood) require the plural form.
If the total eclipse were to occur tomorrow, it would be the second one this year.

44 wpm

Most successful newspapers are large businesses with an extensive staff and several readers. Now, though, there is a growing number of smaller papers. Their aim is to focus on a community or one subject. A small paper that is well produced will concentrate on and promote a local public. In addition, for those who are in the business, operating it is challenging and rewarding. Moreover, papers provide everyone a vehicle for free speech.

46 wpm

Results of a citizenship test taken by a selected group of high school students were surprising. The test was conducted to determine how much knowledge young people have about our system of government. Also, it questioned whether they know how to split their ballot when they vote. Only one-third of the students participating in the program knew that a voter could divide his or her party choice. The majority was ignorant of the political system altogether.

48 wpm

Veterinarians are doctors who are trained to treat and to prevent disease in animals. Although they attend different medical schools than doctors trained to treat people, their program of study and training are similar. Vets can limit their practice to one kind of animal. If they choose to specialize in horses, they can be highly paid because the patients might be priceless race horses. Some vets, on the other hand, would rather work with or conduct research on wild animals.

REFERENCE SECTION *(continued)*

PRONOUNS:

1. Use nominative pronouns (such as *I, he, she, we,* and *they*) as subjects of a sentence or clause.
They traveled to Minnesota last week but will not return until next month.

2. Use objective pronouns (such as *me, him, her, us,* and *them*) as objects in a sentence or clause.
The package has been sent to her.

ADJECTIVES AND ADVERBS:

1. Use comparative adjectives and adverbs (*-er, more,* and *less*) when referring to two nouns; use superlative adjectives and adverbs (*-est, most,* and *least*) when referring to more than two.
Of the two movies you have selected, the shorter one is the more interesting.
The highest of the three mountains is Mt. Everest.

WORD USAGE:

1. Do not confuse the following pairs of words:

- *Accept* means "to agree to"; *except* means "to leave out."
  *We **accept** your offer for developing the new product.*
  *Everyone **except** Sam and Lisa attended the meeting.*

- *Affect* is most often used as a verb meaning "to influence"; *effect* is most often used as a noun meaning "result."
  *Mr. Smith's decision will not **affect** our programming plans.*
  *It will be weeks before we can assess the **effect** of this action.*

- *Farther* refers to distance; *further* refers to extent or degree.
  *Did we travel **farther** today than yesterday?*
  *We need to discuss our plans **further**.*

- *Personal* means "private"; *personnel* means "employees."
  *The letters were very **personal** and should not have been read.*
  *We hope that all **personnel** will comply with the new regulations.*

- *Principal* means "primary"; *principle* means "rule."
  *The **principal** means of research were interviewing and surveying.*
  *They must not violate the **principles** under which our company was established.*

- *Passed* means "went by"; *past* means "before now."
  *We **passed** another car from our home state.*
  *In the **past**, we always took the same route.*

- *Advice* means "to provide guidance"; *advise* means "help."
  *The **advice** I gave her was simple.*
  *I **advise** you to finish your project.*

- *Council* is a group; *counsel* is a person who provides advice.
  *The student **council** met to discuss graduation.*
  *The court asked that **counsel** be present at the hearing.*

SKILLBUILDING *(continued)*

36 wpm

An interesting and exciting hobby for you could be working with plants. You have missed a joy if you have never waited with expectation for a tiny sprig to sprout into a plant. Actually, plants make wonderful pets for apartment dwellers. They neither bark nor meow, and the neighbors don't grumble about being kept awake or about being annoyed by a noisy pet.

38 wpm

Have you ever been on a fairly long trip by car only to find yourself bored because you didn't have much to do? You, the passenger, can engross yourself in a great book. This answer to the boredom can make time appear to pass more rapidly. You could purchase several paperbacks at a local bookstore; and as you read, you can capture numerous hours of entertainment and enjoyment.

40 wpm

Today, a quick way to get from one destination to another is by plane. For your flight, you can choose from among many airlines. In addition, airlines throughout the nation offer daily service to many cities here and abroad. Passengers on domestic and international flights should allow enough time before departure to secure seats on board the plane and to check in baggage at the airport terminal.

42 wpm

Every year when winter approaches, you might look up at the sky and see hundreds and maybe even thousands of birds flying toward warmer weather. Quite simply, they migrate south just to escape the severe days that come so soon. Some experts hypothesize that birds migrate because they physically cannot last in the harsh winters of the frigid north. Other experts think that birds migrate to locate better food sources.

- *Then* means "at that time"; *than* is used for comparisons.
  He read for a while; ***then*** *he turned out the light.*
  She reads more books ***than*** *I do.*

- *Its* is the possessive form of it; *it's* is a contraction for it is.
  We researched the country and ***its*** *people.*
  It's *not too late to finish the project.*

- *Two* means "one more than one"; *too* means "also"; *to* means "in a direction."
  There were ***two*** *people in the boat.*
  We wished we were on board ***too.***
  The boat headed out ***to*** *sea.*

- *Stationery* means "paper"; *stationary* means "fixed position."
  Please buy some ***stationery*** *so that I can write letters.*
  The ***stationary*** *bike at the health club provides a good workout.*

MECHANICS

CAPITALIZATION:

1. Capitalize the first word of a sentence.
Please prepare a summary of your activities for our next meeting.

2. Capitalize proper nouns and adjectives derived from proper nouns. (A proper noun is the official name of a particular person, place, or thing.)
Judy Hendrix drove to Albuquerque in her new automobile, a Pontiac.

3. Capitalize the names of the days of the week, months, holidays, and religious days (but do not capitalize the names of the seasons).
On Thursday, November 25, we will celebrate Thanksgiving, the most popular fall holiday.

4. Capitalize nouns followed by a number or letter (except for the nouns *line, note, page, paragraph,* and *size*).
Please read Chapter 5, but not page 94.

5. Capitalize compass points (such as *north, south,* or *northeast*) only when they designate definite regions.
The Crenshaws will vacation in the Northeast this summer.
We will have to drive north to reach the closest Canadian border.

6. Capitalize common organizational terms (such as *advertising department* and *finance committee*) when they are the actual names of the units in the writer's own organization and when they are preceded by the word *the*.
The quarterly report from the Advertising Department will be presented today.

7. Capitalize the names of specific course titles but not the names of subjects or areas of study.
I have enrolled in Accounting 201 and will also take a marketing course.

28 wpm When shopping in this country, we generally accept the price tag on merchandise for the final price the store will consider. If we really want an item, we pay the amount asked. In other nations, prices might vary each moment, depending on the ability of the purchaser to bargain.

30 wpm National parks are owned by the people of America, and they are preserves for wildlife and timber. The parks are cared for by the government to be sure they remain protected and guarded resources. The rangers help prevent forest fires, analyze weather conditions, and keep watch on the wild animals.

32 wpm You simply do not go rafting down the quick river flowing through the Grand Canyon without plenty of skill and help. The hazards can be just too severe. The beautiful canyon is rocky, thorny, and hot during summer months. At times, it is so windy that sand sprays may hit you in the face with a brisk and stinging jolt.

34 wpm A batik is a dyed cloth that has hot wax placed on it to form a design. First the artist melts wax, tints it various colors, paints a design, and then dyes the cloth. Some artists prefer to paint the cloth with a clear wax. Then the batik is dyed again and again with many colors. Only the portion not covered with the wax becomes colored.

NUMBER EXPRESSION:

1. In general, spell out numbers 1 through 10, and use figures for numbers above 10.
We have rented two movies for tonight.
The decision was reached after 27 precincts had sent in their results.

2. Use figures for:

- Dates (use *st, d,* or *th* only if the day precedes the month).
  We will drive to the camp on the 23d of May.
  The tax report is due on April 15.

- All numbers if two or more related numbers both above and below ten are used in the same sentence.
  Mr. Carter sent in 7 receipts; Ms. Cantrell sent in 22 receipts.

- Measurements (time, money, distance, weight, and percentage).
  At 10 a.m. we delivered the $500 coin bank in a 17-pound container.

- Mixed numbers.
  Our sales are up 9½ percent over last year.

3. Spell out:

- Numbers used as the first word in a sentence.
  Seventy people attended the conference in San Diego last week.

- The smaller of two adjacent numbers.
  We have ordered two 5-pound packages for the meeting.

- The words *millions* and *billions* in even amounts (do not use decimals with even amounts).
  The lottery is worth 28 million this month.

- Fractions.
  About one-half of the audience responded to the questionnaire.

ABBREVIATIONS:

1. In nontechnical writing, do not abbreviate common nouns (such as *dept.* or *pkg.*), compass points, units of measure, or the names of months, days of the week, cities, or states (except in addresses).
The Sales Department will meet on Tuesday, March 7, in Tempe, Arizona.

2. In lowercase abbreviations made up of single initials, use a period after each initial but no internal spaces.
We will be including several states (e.g., Maine, New Hampshire, Vermont, Massachusetts, and Connecticut).

3. In all-capital abbreviations made up of single initials, do not use periods or internal spaces. (Exception: Keep the periods in most academic degrees and in abbreviations of geographic names other than two-letter state abbreviations.)
You need to call the EEO office for clarification on that issue.

SKILLBUILDING *(continued)*

18 wpm

Each year, many Americans suffer a stroke. It can cause serious problems. For some, it can become difficult to walk or to use an arm. For others, a stroke can affect their speech.

20 wpm

Many people think angora is the wool of sheep but it comes from goats. The goats are sheared two times a year. The wool is washed through a special process. It can then be dyed and spun into strands.

20 wpm

The old woman who walks in the park always has a huge smile on her face. She talks to the people who cross her path. When she makes new friends, she offers assistance in her quiet way and is excited.

22 wpm

There is no substitute for the taste of ice cream on hot, humid days. Choices of all types are out to engage the eye, and the sharp clerks will fix just the mix and size to suit you best. A cup or a cone would be great.

24 wpm

To see the artists' pain is a joy. To watch the zeal with which they work to have the exact color show up on the pad is exciting. As they glide the new brush quickly across the pad, the radiant hues take form and bring smiles to our faces.

26 wpm

When you work with people every day, you get to know what it is that they like best. You also find out quickly what does make them frown. A bit of extra kind effort in a dozen little ways will make your office a pleasant place in which to complete all duties.

UNIT 1 KEYBOARDING

Lessons 1–20

OBJECTIVES

- Demonstrate which fingers control each key on the keyboard.
- Use home key anchors to assist in developing location security.
- Develop and practice correct keyboarding techniques.
- Key at a speed of 25 words per minute for 1 minute with 2 or fewer errors.
- Use proper spacing after common marks of punctuation.
- Compose single word or short phrase responses at the keyboard.

PACED PRACTICE

The Paced Practice routine builds speed and improves accuracy in short, easy steps, using individualized goals and immediate feedback. You can use this routine any time after completing Lesson 18.

This section contains a series of 2-minute timed writings for speeds ranging from 14 wpm to 60 wpm. The first time you use these timed writings, take a 1-minute entry timed writing. Then, select a passage that is 2 wpm higher than your current keyboarding speed. Use a two-stage practice pattern to achieve each speed goal—first concentrate on speed, and then work on accuracy.

SPEED GOAL: Take three 2-minute timed writings on the same passage until you can complete it in 2 minutes (do not worry about the number of errors).

When you have achieved your speed goal, work on accuracy.

ACCURACY GOAL: To key accurately, you need to slow down—just a little bit. To reach your accuracy goal, drop back 2 wpm to the previous passage. Take three 2-minute timed writings on this passage until you can complete it in 2 minutes with no more than 2 errors.

For example, if you achieved a speed goal of 30 wpm, you should work on an accuracy goal of 28 wpm. When you have achieved the 28 wpm goal for accuracy, you would then move up 4 wpm (for example, to the 32 wpm passage) and work for speed again.

ENTRY TIMED WRITINGS

If your mailbox is full of mail that you do not want, 11
your name is on a mailing list. Firms buy mailing lists so 23
that they can send you their ads. Unless you write and ask 34
each company to take your name off its list, you will keep 46
getting junk mail. 50

14 wpm

Tourists like to[1] meander through the[2] Boston Gardens[3]
during the summer.[4] They stroll the[5] shady paths and then[6]
stop to ride[7] on the swan boats.[8]

16 wpm

Pleasure boats and large[1] tankers pass through[2] the
Cape Cod[3] canal every day. The canal[4] is spanned by[5] two
high bridges for[6] auto traffic and by[7] a railroad bridge.[8]

WORDS TO LEARN

In the lessons, software, and Student Manual (SM), you will learn the following vocabulary terms for Unit 1.

anchor (p. 3)
default (p. 45)
discrimination reach (p. 64)
home keys (p. 2)
insertion point (p. 4)
word count (p. 21)
word scale (p. 21)

CAREER BYTE

NURSING Many modern hospitals use computers to store the medical records of their patients. Information from each patient's medical chart is entered into a computer file. Nurses update this file every time they give medications or check the patient's blood pressure, pulse rate, temperature, and overall progress.

When nurses change shifts, they need only to have a quick briefing with oncoming nurses because the essential information about the patient's care is already on the computer.

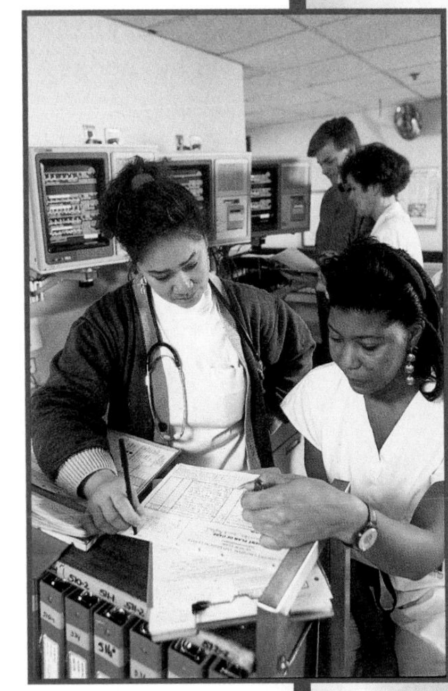

SKILLBUILDING *(continued)*

INDIVIDUAL REACHES

8

```
kik ki8k k8k 888 k8k 8/88 k8k 88.8 k8k ki8k 88.8 88,888 k8k
8 kegs, 88 kits, 888 kilns, 878 kickers, 876 knocks, or 8.8
The 8 keys fit 887 kits; Kim found 8,876 knots in the kits.
The 8 kind ladies got 882 kimonos for 188 kids in the play.
```

9

```
lol lo9l l9l 999 l9l 9/99 l9l 99.9 l9l lo9l 99.9 99,999 l9l
9 laps, 99 lots, 999 loops, 989 lilies, 987 lifters, or 9.9
Lillian said 9 times to leave 99 lilies for the 989 ladies.
My 9 lawyers had 19 leaky pens, 89 legal pads, and 9 limos.
```

10

```
;p; ;p0; ;0; 000 ;0; 0/00 ;0; 00.0 ;0; ;p0; 00.0 00,000 ;0;
10 pots, 20 pins, 300 parts, 400 plants, 500 parades or 0.0
The 10 party stores put 100 pots and 200 pans to pick from.
The 10 books had 23,000 pages in each; Paul read 500 pages.
```

All numbers

```
a1a s2s d3d f4f f5f j6j j7j k8k l9l ;0; Add 6 and 8 and 29.
That 534-page script called for 10 actors and 17 actresses.
After 1,374 miles in the car, she must then drive 185 more.
The 141 professors asked 4,690 sportscasters 230 questions.
```

All numbers

```
a1a s2s d3d f4f f5f j6j j7j k8k l9l ;0; Add 3 and 4 and 70.
They built 1,200 houses on 345 acres in just under 3 years.
Six boys arrived on May 26, 1994, and left on May 30, 1998.
Marlee bought 15 new books, 62 used books, and 47 new pens.
```

All numbers

```
a1a s2s d3d f4f f5f j6j j7j k8k l9l ;0; Add 5 and 7 and 68.
The 4 stores are open from 9:30 a.m. until 6:00 p.m. daily.
I gave away 2 pans, 4 plates, 8 glasses, and 25 containers.
She moved to 705 Garfield Street, not 507, on June 4, 2000.
```

NEW KEYS: A S D F J K L ; SPACE BAR ENTER

OBJECTIVE:

- Key the home keys, the SPACE BAR, and the ENTER key.

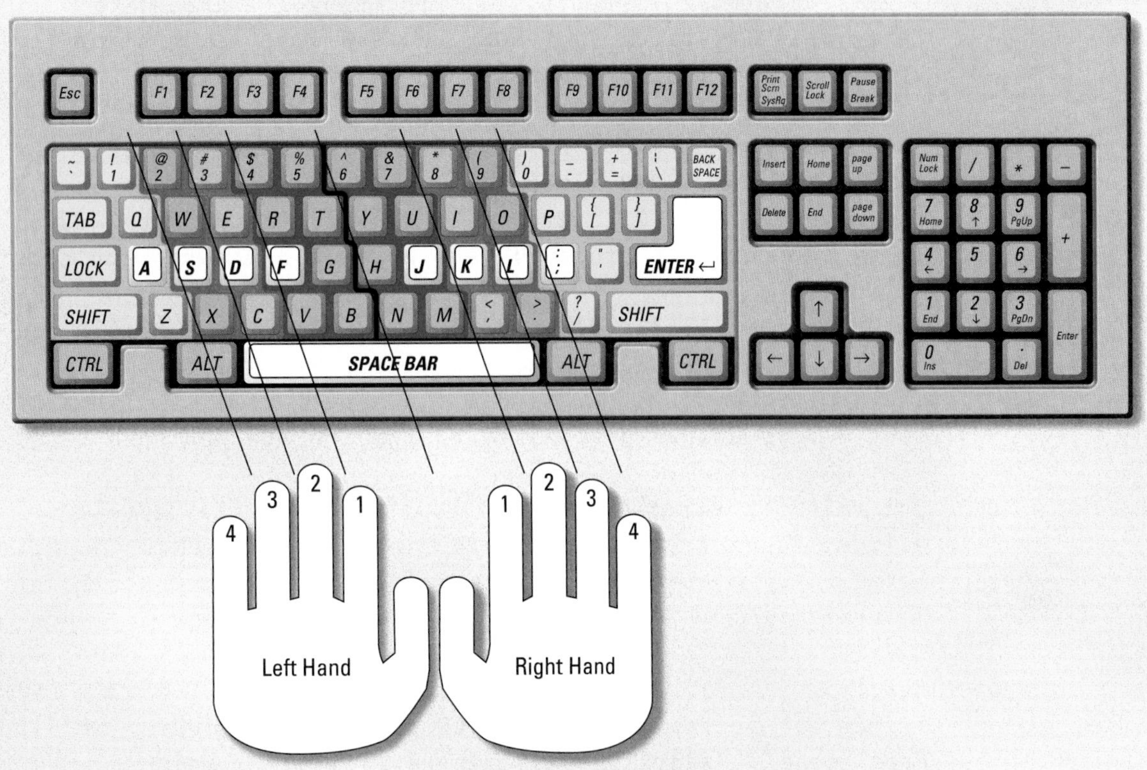

NEW KEYS

A. HOME-KEY POSITION

The A S D F J K L ; keys in the center row are called the **home keys**. Each finger controls a specific key and is named for its home key: A finger, S finger, D finger, and so on, ending with the Sem finger on the ; (semicolon) key.

1. Place the fingers of your left hand on A S D and F. Use the illustration as a guide.
2. Place the fingers of your right hand on J K L ;. Again, use the illustration as a guide.

INDIVIDUAL REACHES

1 aqa aq1a a1a 111 a1a 1/11 a1a 11.1 a1a aq1a 11.1 11,111 a1a
1 ant, 11 arms, 111 aunts, 101 apples, 131 animals, or 1.11
Henry read 111 pages in 1 hour and ate 1 apple in 1 minute.
Crystal wrote 1 story that was 1,111 pages long on 1 topic.

2 sws sw2s s2s 222 s2s 2/22 s2s 22.2 s2s sw2s 22.2 22,222 s2s
2 sips, 22 sets, 222 sites, 212 socks, 231 soldiers, or 2.2
She moved to Room 221 with 2,223 students for about 2 days.
Today 202 computer students were solving 322 math problems.

3 ded de3d d3d 333 d3d 3/33 d3d 33.3 d3d de3d 33.3 33,333 d3d
3 dots, 33 dogs, 333 drops, 323 dimes, 321 daisies, or 3.33
The 3 doctors and 3 nurses did the 3 surgeries in 33 hours.
Your 3 cats and 23 dogs liked to romp on the 330-acre farm.

4 frf fr4f f4f 444 f4f 4/44 f4f 44.4 f4f fr4f 44.4 44,444 f4f
4 figs, 44 fans, 444 farms, 434 finals, 431 friends, or 4.4
Meredith flew 444 miles to see 4 friends at 434 Oak Street.
Florence sold 41 fish dinners to the 44 customers at 4 p.m.

5 ftf ft5f f5f 555 f5f 5/55 f5f 55.5 f5f ft5f 55.5 55,555 f5f
5 foes, 55 facts, 555 foals, 545 fowls, 543 flights, or 5.5
Fred found 55 facts in 545 flights from 514 foreign places.
Theo found that flight 5253 leaves at 5 a.m. from gate 545.

6 jyj jy6j j6j 666 j6j 6/66 j6j 66.6 j6j jy6j 66.6 66,666 j6j
6 jaws, 66 jets, 666 jeeps, 656 jokes, 654 journals, or 6.6
She had 6 jobs to do in 66 hours. Julia worked 664 minutes.
Her 6 math tests had 165 problems to be done in 60 minutes.

7 juj ju7j j7j 777 j7j 7/77 j7j 77.7 j7j ju7j 77.7 77,777 j7j
7 jugs, 77 jars, 777 jumps, 767 joggers, 765 jewels, or 7.7
Joe saw 7 joggers run 177 miles across 7,777 acres of land.
The 7 suits were shipped to 7167 East 7th Avenue on July 7.

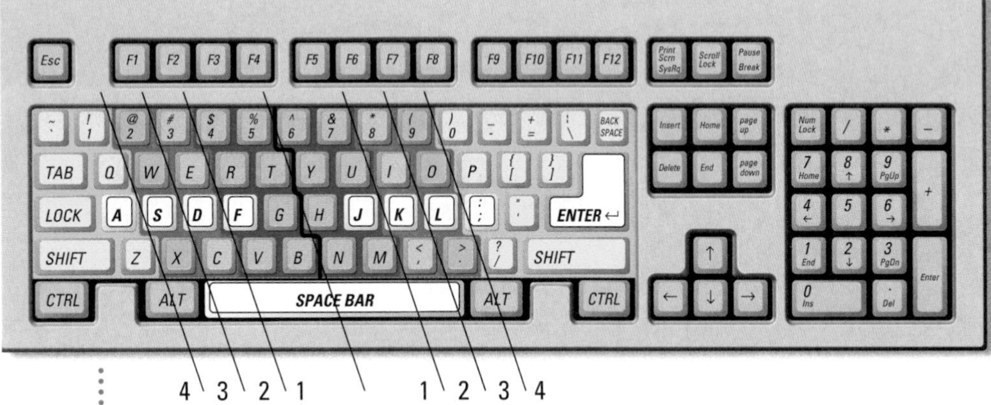

You will feel a raised marker on the F and J keys. These markers will help you keep your fingers on the home keys.

3. Curve your fingers.
4. Using the correct fingers, key each letter as you say it to yourself: `a s d f j k l ;`.
5. Remove your fingers from the keyboard and replace them on the home keys.
6. Key each letter again as you say it: `a s d f j k l ;`.

B. Using Anchors

An **anchor** is a home key that helps you return each finger to its home-key position after reaching for another key. When you do the activities in the following lessons, try to hold the anchor keys listed next to the activity. The anchor listed first is the most important.

C. Space Bar

The Space Bar, located at the bottom of the keyboard, is used to insert spaces between letters and words, and after punctuation. Use the thumb of your writing hand (left or right) to press the Space Bar.

1. With your fingers on the home keys, key the letters `a s d f`. Then press the Space Bar once.
2. Key `j k l ;`. Press the Space Bar once.
3. Key `a s d f`. Press the Space Bar once; then key `j k l ;`.
4. Repeat Steps 1–3.

DIAGNOSTIC PRACTICE: NUMBERS

The Diagnostic Practice: Numbers routine is designed to diagnose and then correct your keystroking errors. You may use this program at any time throughout the course after you complete Lesson 26.

DIRECTIONS:

1. Key one set of the Pretest/Posttest lines 1 time. Identify your errors.
2. Note your results—the number of errors you made on each key and your total number of errors. For example, if you keyed *24* for *25,* that would count as 1 error on the number *5*.
3. For any number on which you made 2 or more errors, select the corresponding drill lines, on p. SB5 and p. SB6, and key them 2 times. If you made only 1 error, key the drill 1 time. If you made no errors on the Pretest/Posttest lines, key the drills that contain all numbers on page SB6 and key each line 1 time.
4. Finally, rekey the Pretest/Posttest, and compare your performance with your Pretest.

PRETEST/POSTTEST

Set 1

```
ripe 4803, ire 843, wee 233, ore 943, pier 0834, wire 2843,
Silvio marked the chalkboard at 25, 30, and 45 centimeters.
Alice put markers at 10 km, 29 km, 38 km, 47 km, and 56 km.
Bob lost checks Nos. 234, 457, and 568. Mandy lost No. 901.
Please clean Rooms 340 and 380. Kerbey will clean Room 443.
Those five passengers are 25, 39, 42, 45, and 50 years old.
```

Set 2

```
wee 233, tie 583, toe 593, pure 0743, pour 0974, rout 4975,
Iva put 428 in group 1, 570 in group 2, and 396 in group 3.
The party governed during 1910, 1929, 1938, 1947, and 1956.
The total of 198, 384, 275, 470, and 672 is easy to figure.
They had 92 or 83. He has 10 or 74. We have 56 or maybe 57.
Check lockers 290, 471, 356, and 580 before school Tuesday.
```

Set 3

```
pie 083, rye 463, your 6974, tier 5834, eye 363, pipe 0803,
Read pages 100, 129, and 138; summarize Chapters 47 and 56.
By May 1, ship 29 seats, 38 stoves, 47 tents, and 56 coats.
The 29 females lived 180 days at 4387 South Parkview Court.
Janet read pages 105 through 120 and pages 387 through 469.
Marvin easily won the bulletins numbered 12,345 and 67,890.
```

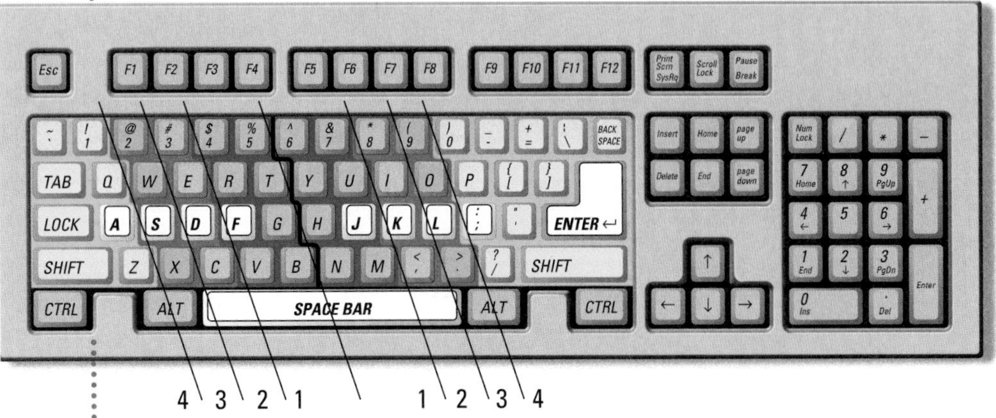

D. Enter Key

The Enter key moves the **insertion point** (the blinking line) to the beginning of a new line. Reach to the Enter key with the Sem finger. Lightly press the Enter key. Return the Sem finger to home position.

Practice using the Enter key. Key each line 1 time, pressing the Space Bar where you see a space and pressing the Enter key (represented by the ↵ symbol) at the end of a line.

```
asdf jkl; asdf jkl; asdf jkl;↵
asdf jkl; asdf jkl; asdf jkl;↵
asdf jkl; asdf jkl; asdf jkl;↵
asdf jkl; asdf jkl; asdf jkl;↵
```

E.  Keys

Key each line 1 time.

Use F and J fingers.

```
1 fff jjj fff jjj fff jjj ff jj ff jj f j↵
2 fff jjj fff jjj fff jjj ff jj ff jj f j↵
```

F.  Keys

Key each line 1 time.

Use D and K fingers.

```
3 ddd kkk ddd kkk ddd kkk dd kk dd kk d k↵
4 ddd kkk ddd kkk ddd kkk dd kk dd kk d k↵
```

SKILLBUILDING *(continued)*

TROUBLESOME PAIRS

A/S	Sal said he asked Sara Ash for a sample of the raisins.
B/V	Vera very bravely was verbose with a bevy of beverages.
C/D	Candie decided the December calendar decal could decay.
E/W	Weni knew in weekday weather weak weeds grew elsewhere.
F/G	Goeff goofed by finding the gulf for the grateful frog.
H/J	Judith wore jodhpurs; she joshed with John and Johanna.
I/O	Iona totally foiled Olin's spoiled oily ointment plans.
K/L	Karl liked to walk seven kilometers quickly with Kelly.
M/N	Many have names of maidens among the main mason manors.
O/P	Opal and Polly phoned three opera pollsters in Phoenix.
Q/A	Quin quickly qualified this quality quart quartz quota.
R/T	Robert tried trading rations to three terrific skaters.
U/Y	If you are busy, buy your supply of yucca Yule in July.
X/C	Cal expected the excitement to exceed all expectations.
Z/A	The five sizable, lazy zebras zigzagged as Eliza gazed.

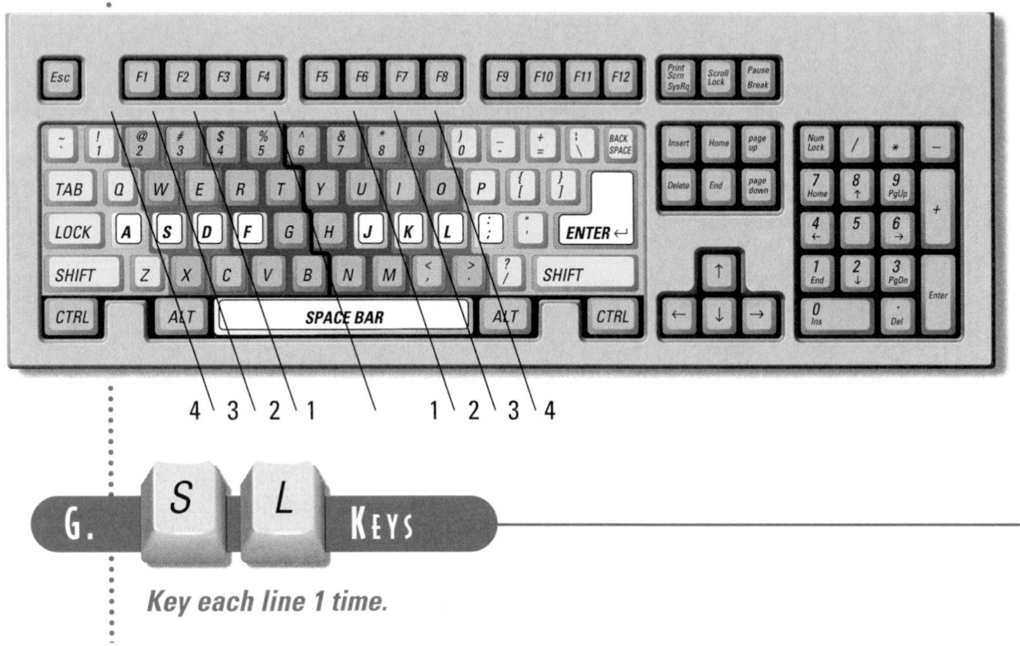

G. S L Keys

Key each line 1 time.

Use S and L fingers.

5 sss lll sss lll sss lll ss ll ss ll s l↵
6 sss lll sss lll sss lll ss ll ss ll s l↵

H. A ; Keys

Key each line 1 time.

Use A and Sem fingers.

7 aaa ;;; aaa ;;; aaa ;;; aa ;; aa ;; a ;↵
8 aaa ;;; aaa ;;; aaa ;;; aa ;; aa ;; a ;↵

SKILLBUILDING

I. Technique Checkpoint

Technique Checkpoints enable you to practice new keys. They also give you and your teacher a chance to evaluate your keyboarding techniques. Focus on the techniques listed in the margin, such as:

- Use correct fingers.
- Keep eyes on copy.
- Press Enter without pausing.
- Maintain correct posture.
- Maintain correct arm, hand, and finger position.

SKILLBUILDING *(continued)*

INDIVIDUAL REACHES

A Ada and Anna had an allowance and always had adequate cash.
B Barbara grabbed back the brown bag Bob bought at a bargain.
C Charles can accept and cash any checks the church collects.
D David drove down and deducted the dividends he had divided.
E Everyone here exerted extra effort each week we were there.

F Fred Ford offered to find fresh food for five fine fellows.
G Guy suggested getting eight guys to bring George's luggage.
H Hank hoped that she had withheld the cash they had to have.
I Iris insists their idea is simply idiotic in this instance.
J Jack and Jerry joined Joe just to enjoy a journey to Japan.

K Kathy asked Ken to take a blank checkbook back to her bank.
L Larry helped several little fellows learn to play baseball.
M Mr. Ammon made many mistakes in estimating minimum markets.
N Nan never knew when any businessman wanted an announcement.
O One or two of those older tool orders ought to go out soon.

P Please provide proper paper supplies for plenty of persons.
Q Quentin quietly inquired what sequences required questions.
R Run over for another order from the firm across the street.
S She says she sold us some shiny scissors sometime Saturday.
T Try to get the truth when they talk about better attitudes.

U Unless you pour out your mixture, you could hurt our stuff.
V Vivian raved over violets and even saved several varieties.
W William will work well whenever we know where we will work.
X X-rays exceed examinations except for external exploration.
Y Yes, any day they say you may be ready, you may try to fly.
Z Zenith Franz realizes that he idealized the zigzag friezes.

Key lines 9 and 10 one time.

Focus on these techniques:
- ***Keep eyes on copy.***
- ***Keep fingers on home keys.***

```
9  ff jj dd kk ss ll aa ;; f j d k s l a ;↵
10 ff jj dd kk ss ll aa ;; f j d k s l a ;↵
```

J. PRETEST

Key lines 11–12 for 1 minute. Repeat if time permits. Keep your eyes on the copy.

Hold Anchor Keys

```
11 sad sad fad fad ask ask lad lad dad dad↵
12 as; as; fall fall alas alas flask flask↵
```

K. PRACTICE

Key lines 13–24 one time. Repeat if time permits.

Leave a blank line after each set of lines (13–14, 15–16, and so on) by pressing ENTER 2 times.

```
13 aaa ddd sad sad aaa sss lll lll all all↵
14 aaa ddd sad sad aaa sss lll lll all all↵↵

15 aaa sss kkk ask ask fff aaa ddd fad fad↵
16 aaa sss kkk ask ask fff aaa ddd fad fad↵↵

17 aaa ddd ddd add add lll aaa ddd lad lad↵
18 aaa ddd ddd add add lll aaa ddd lad lad↵↵

19 aaa sss ;;; as; as; ddd aaa ddd dad dad↵
20 aaa sss ;;; as; as; ddd aaa ddd dad dad↵↵

21 f fl fla flas flask; l la las lass lass↵
22 f fl fla flas flask; l la las lass lass↵↵

23 f fa fal fall falls; a al ala alas alas↵
24 f fa fal fall falls; a al ala alas alas↵↵
```

L. POSTTEST

Key lines 11–12 for 1 minute. Repeat if time permits. Keep your eyes on the copy. Compare your Posttest results with your Pretest results.

M. END-OF-CLASS PROCEDURE

To keep hardware and software in good working order, treat them carefully. Your teacher will tell you what should be done at the end of each class period. You can also refer to the page Operating Your Computer, at the end of this book regarding the proper operation and care of your computer.

SKILLBUILDING

DIAGNOSTIC PRACTICE: ALPHABET

The Diagnostic Practice: Alphabet routine is designed to diagnose and then correct your keystroking errors. You may use this program at any time throughout the course after you complete Lesson 18.

DIRECTIONS:

1. Key one set of the Pretest/Posttest lines 1 time. Identify your errors.
2. Note your results—the number of errors you made on each key and your total number of errors. For example, if you keyed *rht* for *the,* that would count as 1 error on the letter *t.*
3. For any letter on which you made 2 or more errors, select the corresponding drill lines, on p. SB2, and key them 2 times. If you made only 1 error, key the drill 1 time.
4. If you made no errors on the Pretest/Posttest lines, turn to the practice on Troublesome Pairs on page SB3 and key each line 1 time. This section provides intensive practice on those pairs of keys commonly confused.
5. Finally, rekey the same set of Pretest/Posttest lines, and compare your performance with your Pretest.

PRETEST/POSTTEST

Set 1

```
Buzz quickly designed five new projects for the wax museum.
John's wacky quip amazed but also vexed his new girlfriend.
Zed quickly jumped five huge barrels to warn Max and Teddy.
Orville quickly objected to Wes dumping five toxic hazards.
From the tower Dave saw six big jet planes quickly zoom by.
Beverly, has John kept that liquid oxygen frozen with care?
```

Set 2

```
Did Robert move that psychology quiz to next week for John?
Stanley, cover this oozy liquid wax before Jack mops again.
The six heavy guys jumped for eighty waltzing quarterbacks.
Skip was quite vexed by the seventeen jazzmen from Cologne.
The eight taxi drivers quickly zip by the jumble of wagons.
While having Joel wait, Ben quickly fixed the many zippers.
```

Set 3

```
Last week Jed McVey was quite busy fixing the frozen pipes.
Vic quickly mixed frozen strawberries into the grape juice.
Five big jet planes zoomed quickly by the six steel towers.
Jeff amazed the audience by quickly giving six new reports.
Sixty equals only five dozen, but we promised Jackie eight.
Joel quietly picked sixteen razors from the blue woven bag.
```

LESSON 2 NEW KEYS: H E O

OBJECTIVE:

- Key H, E, and O by touch.

Hold Anchor Keys
For **H** anchor **; L K**
For **E** anchor **A**
For **O** anchor **J** or **;**

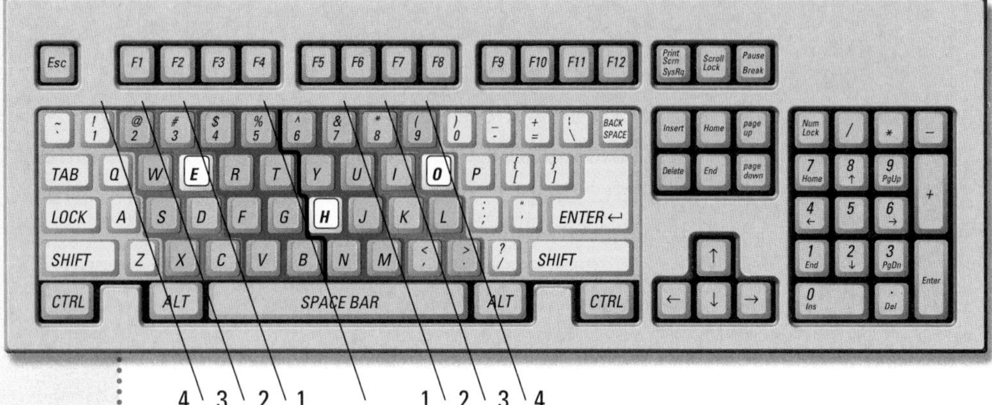

A. WARMUP

Key each line 2 times. Leave 1 blank line after each set of lines by pressing ENTER 2 times.

```
1 ff jj dd kk ss ll aa ;; f j d k s l a ;
2 adds adds fads fads asks asks lads lads
```

NEW KEYS

B. H KEY

Key each line 2 times. Repeat if time permits.

Use J finger.
For H anchor ; L K.

```
3 jjj jhj jhj hjh jhj jjj jhj jhj hjh jhj
4 jhj ash ash jhj has has jhj had had jhj
5 jhj a lass has; adds a half; a lad had;
6 has a slash; half a sash dad shall dash
```

(continued)

A wide variety of events ensured that students, teachers, parents, and community residents could each find something that interested them. The Sullivan High School and Waverly High School bake sales brought in many families from the local community. The Caldwell High School car wash appealed to parents and teachers. The River Run 5 km run/walk brought out athletes of all ages. The dance marathon sponsored by Moss High School attracted a youthful crowd. Every event helped to bring the community together in different ways.

The most popular event, the Baker High School pancake breakfast, was held on a Sunday morning in the Civic Center next to the library. Over 7,500 pancakes were sold over a four-hour period, according to James Allen of the Baker High School Fund-Raising Committee. The following table lists the final totals for all schools after the two-week fund-raising project.

PORTFOLIO Activity

Create a Database Think of a hobby that you have where it might be useful to put information into a database. For example, if you have a lot of music CDs, you might want to be able to sort them by different categories or keep a record of CDs you have borrowed or lent out.

Create a new database that you can use for your hobby to include as an example in your portfolio. Include at least four fields and five records. Follow your teacher's instructions for saving and printing your work.

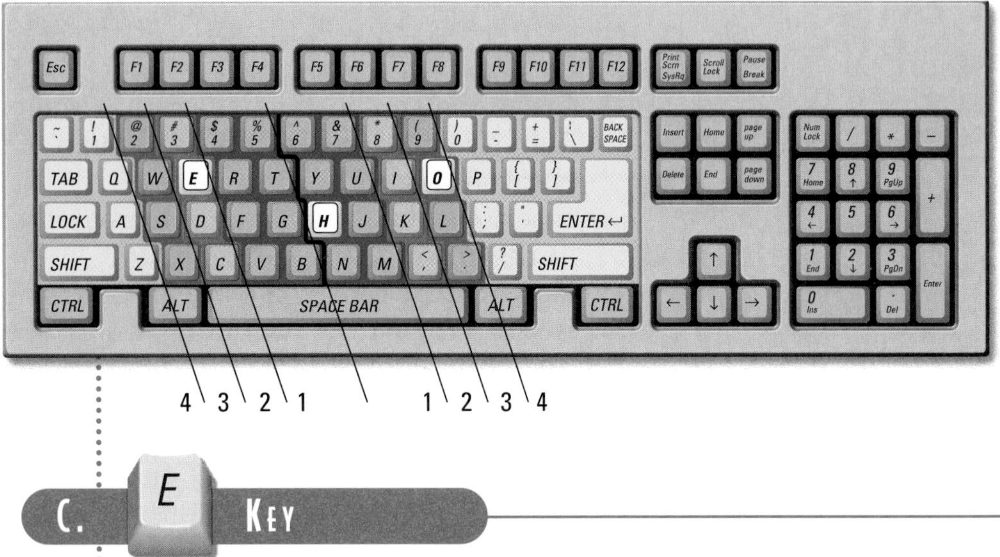

C. E Key

Key each line 2 times. Repeat if time permits.

Use D finger. For D anchor A S.

```
7  ddd ded ded ede ded ddd ded ded ede ded
8  ded led led ded she she ded he; ded he;
9  ded he led; she fell; he slashes sales;
10 he sees sheds ahead; she sealed a lease
```

D. O Key

Key each line 2 times. Repeat if time permits.

Use L finger. For L anchor J K.

```
11 lll lol lol olo lol lll lol lol olo lol
12 lol odd odd lol hoe hoe lol foe foe lol
13 load sod; hold a foe; old oak hoes; lol
14 she sold odd hooks; he folded old hoses
```

SOCIAL STUDIES CONNECTION

Non-English Keyboards If you were using a Spanish keyboard, it would have extra keys for accent marks and the letter ñ. Hebrew or Arabic computer users not only have keyboards with the alphabets for those languages, but on the monitor the cursor moves from right to left instead of left to right.

Go to the Online Learning Center at **KeyComps.glencoe.com>Social Studies Connection>Unit 1>Lesson 2** to find more examples of keyboards using different writing systems. Use a pen and paper to write a paragraph comparing the English keyboard to one of the examples on the Web page.

ACTIVITY 33

Report 72
2-Page Academic Report

Format and key the following 2-page report in MLA style. Follow these steps to complete the report:

1. Insert the spreadsheet chart that you created in Activity 31 after the first paragraph of the report.
2. Horizontally center the chart.
3. Insert the database table you created in Activity 32 at the end of the report.
4. Horizontally center the table.
5. Insert a row at the beginning of the table. Key the table title, FUND-RAISER TOTALS, in all caps and a 14-point font. Center and bold the title.
6. Where possible, modify the appearance of the database table to resemble the format of a word processing table.
7. Size the chart as necessary to keep the report to two pages.
8. Save the report as R72.
9. Follow your teacher's instructions for printing your report.

Library Fund-Raiser

School fund-raisers can be a great way to bring students, teachers, and the community together to raise money for worthy causes. This year, the district fund-raising committee issued a challenge to each high school to come up with a way to raise money to buy new books and equipment for the district's library. Student committees within each school coordinated the organization for their school's event. The first week got off to a good start, with sales increasing throughout most of the week, as shown in the following chart.

The library houses a growing collection of books designed to meet the needs of students who are learning how to complete research projects in all subject areas. The funds raised by each school will be used to buy books in the subject area picked by that school. After the fund-raisers are completed and the money raised by each school is totaled, students will be asked to help select the books and equipment that will be purchased. The district librarians will also be available to aid in the selection process. Once all of the books are purchased and received by the library staff, students will be invited to view all of them at a ceremony at the library.

(continued on next page)

E. Technique Checkpoint

Key each line 2 times. Repeat if time permits. Focus on the technique at the left.

Focus on this technique: Press and release each key quickly.

```
15 ddd ded ded ede ded ddd ded ded ede ded
16 lll lol lol olo lol lll lol lol olo lol
17 jjj jhj jhj hjh jhj jjj jhj jhj hjh jhj
18 she has old jokes; he has half a salad;
```

F. PRETEST

Key lines 19–20 for 1 minute. Repeat if time permits. Keep your eyes on the copy.

Hold anchor keys.

```
19 heed jade hoof elf; hash folk head hole
20 seed lake look jell sash hold dead half
```

G. PRACTICE

Key each line 2 times. Repeat if time permits.

When you repeat a line:
- ***Speed up as you key the line.***
- ***Key it more smoothly.***
- ***Leave a blank line after the second line (press ENTER 2 times).***

```
21 heed heed feed feed deed deed seed seed
22 jade jade fade fade fake fake lake lake
23 hoof hoof hood hood hook hook look look
24 elf; elf; self self sell sell jell jell

25 hash hash lash lash dash dash sash sash
26 folk folk fold fold sold sold hold hold
27 head head heal heal deal deal dead dead
28 hole hole hale hale hall hall half half
```

H. POSTTEST

Key lines 19–20 for 1 minute. Repeat if time permits. Keep your eyes on the copy. Compare your Posttest results with your Pretest results.

DATABASE APPLICATIONS

ACTIVITY 31
Spreadsheet 49

Create a spreadsheet using the following data. Save the spreadsheet as SS49.

Week 1	Sales in Dollars
Mon	$2,491
Tue	$3,258
Wed	$2,757
Thu	$3,423
Fri	$3,782

1. Create a vertical bar chart.
2. Title the chart Week 1 Results.
3. Title the x-axis Week 1.
4. Title the y-axis Sales.
5. Minimize the spreadsheet program.

ACTIVITY 32
Database Table 6

Follow these steps to create Database Table 6 and name it DT6:

1. Define the five fields as shown in the illustration below. Define the Enrollment field as a number field and the Amount Raised field as a currency field.
2. Specify the size of each field as shown.
3. Enter the records.
4. Close the table window.

20		25	18	
High School	**Enrollment**	**Event**	**Subject Area**	**Amount Raised**
Baker	1976	Pancake breakfast	History	$6,147
Sullivan	1466	Bake sale	Careers	$5,420
Waverly	1836	Bake sale	Literature	$4,722
Moss	928	Dance marathon	Events	$3,944
Caldwell	1494	Car wash	Science	$3,488
Wyndham	640	Recycling drive	Art	$2,775
River Run	1130	5 km run/walk	Music	$2,463

LESSON 3 NEW KEYS: M R I

OBJECTIVE:

- Key M, R, and I by touch.

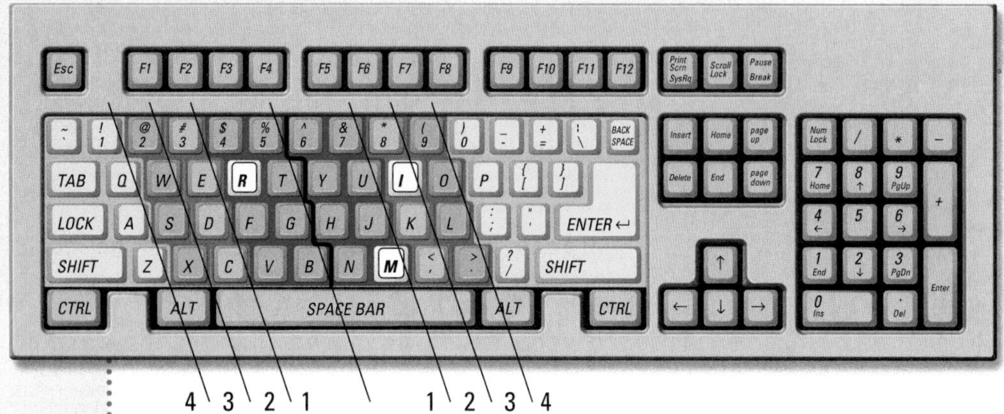

A. WARMUP

Key each line 2 times. Leave 1 blank line after each set of lines.

```
1 asdf jkl; heo; asdf jkl; heo; asdf jkl;
2 jade jade fake fake held held lose lose
```

NEW KEYS

B. M KEY

Key each line 2 times. Repeat if time permits.

Use J finger. For M anchor ; L K.

```
3 jjj jmj jmj mjm jmj jjj jmj jmj mjm jmj
4 jmj mom mom jmj mad mad jmj ham ham jmj
5 jmj make a jam; fold a hem; less flame;
6 messes make some moms mad; half a dome;
```

C. 5-Minute Timed Writings

Take two 5-minute timed writings on the paragraphs. Note your speed and errors.

Goal: 40/5'/5e

As this world shrinks daily, we become neighbors to 11
people who live in nations across the oceans. One major 22
issue now facing the United States and the world is that of 34
global competition. Some college students will soon realize 46
that work in a global environment is a large part of their 58
lives. 59

American students are less apt to be ready to work and 70
conduct business with those from different nations than are 82
students from other cultures. As countries continue to work 94
together, there is more and more demand to build skills for 106
this global marketplace. 111

More than half of the schools in the United States now 122
include the study of a foreign language as a requirement 134
for a degree, especially for students enrolled in schools 145
of business. A research study completed by the Department 157
of Education found that some American corporations expected 169
their new employees to have a background in international 181
affairs. This knowledge is essential for those who may be 192
employed in banking and communications. 200

SI 1.57

| 1 | 2 | 3 | 4 | 5 | 6 | 7 | 8 | 9 | 10 | 11 | 12

FORMATTING

D. Software Features

STUDENT MANUAL

Inserting Spreadsheet Charts into Documents
Inserting Database Tables into Documents

Study Lesson 150 in your Student Manual. Complete all the practice activities while at your computer. Then complete the tasks that follow.

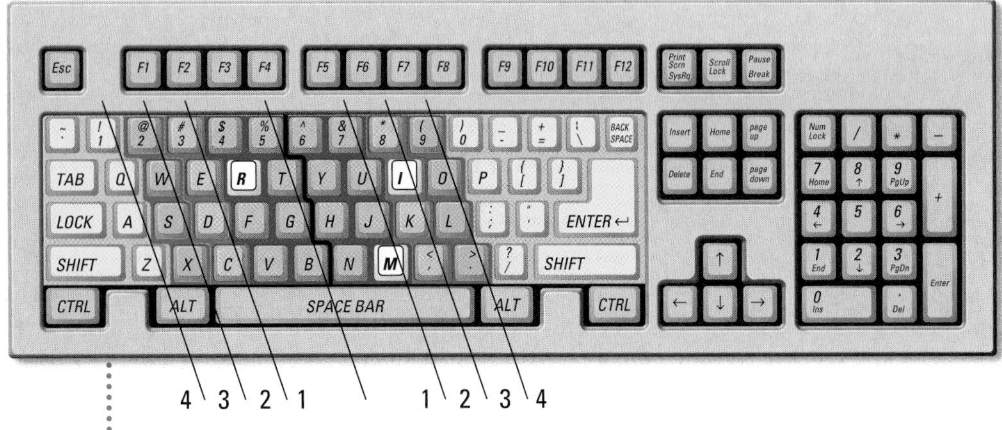

C. R KEY

Key each line 2 times. Repeat if time permits.

Use F finger. For R anchor A S D.

```
7  fff frf frf rfr frf fff frf frf rfr frf
8  frf far far frf for for frf err err frf
9  frf more rooms; for her marks; from me;
10 he reads ahead; more doors are far ajar
```

D. I KEY

Key each line 2 times. Repeat if time permits.

Use K finger. For I anchor L and ;.

```
11 kkk kik kik iki kik kkk kik kik iki kik
12 kik dim dim kik lid lid kik rim rim kik
13 kik if she did; for his risk; old mill;
14 more mirrors; his middle silo is filled
```

interNET CONNECTION

Use Online Dictionaries If you are not sure how to spell a word or need to find a definition, you can use an online dictionary. Go to the Online Learning Center at **KeyComps.glencoe.com> Internet Connection>Unit 1>Lesson 3** to find links to online dictionaries and other online reference tools.

LESSON 150 DATABASES: SIMULATION

OBJECTIVES:

- Key 40/5'/5e.
- Insert database tables and charts.

A. WARMUP

Key each line 2 times.

Speed	1	Gloria has to read the pages of this book before she stops.
Accuracy	2	Paula rejoiced at the amazing reviews of six quality books.
Language Link	3	The new computer desks came with easy-to-follow directions.
Numbers	4	I set tabs at 6, 15, 20, 35, 40, 60, 78, and 96 on the job.

| 1 | 2 | 3 | 4 | 5 | 6 | 7 | 8 | 9 | 10 | 11 | 12

SCIENCE CONNECTION

Identify Scientific Uses for Databases Scientists have many ways to use databases as they record and analyze data from experiments. Think of one of the experiments that you have done in science class. Compose and key at least one paragraph explaining how a database would be helpful to future students completing the experiment. Explain in detail what fields the new database table would contain and what queries or sorts a student could use when analyzing the data from the experiment. Follow your teacher's instructions for saving and printing your work.

SKILLBUILDING

B. PREVIEW PRACTICE

Key each line 2 times as a preview to the timed writings on page 551.

Accuracy	5	competition environment marketplace requirement corporations
Speed	6	foreign conduct banking people become world study major work

SKILLBUILDING

E. Technique Checkpoint

Key each line 2 times. Repeat if time permits. Focus on the techniques at the left.

Focus on these techniques:
- ***Fingertips touching home keys.***
- ***Wrists up, off keyboard.***

```
15 jjj jmj jmj mjm jmj jjj jmj jmj mjm jmj
16 fff frf frf rfr frf fff frf frf rfr frf
17 kkk kik kik iki kik kkk kik kik iki kik
18 he did; his firm red desk lid is a joke
```

F. PRETEST

Key lines 19–20 for 1 minute. Repeat if time permits. Keep your eyes on the copy.

```
19 joke ride sale same roam aims sire more
20 jars aide dark lame foal elms hire mare
```

G. PRACTICE

Key each line 2 times. Repeat if time permits.

Keep eyes on copy. It will be easier to keep your eyes on the copy if you:
- ***Review the charts for key positions and anchors.***
- ***Maintain an even pace.***
- ***Resist looking up from your copy.***
- ***Keep fingers on keys.***

```
21 joke joke jade jade jams jams jars jars
22 ride ride hide hide side side aide aide
23 sale sale dale dale dare dare dark dark
24 same same fame fame dame dame lame lame

25 roam roam loam loam foam foam foal foal
26 aims aims arms arms alms alms elms elms
27 sire sire dire dire fire fire hire hire
28 more more mire mire mere mere mare mare
```

H. POSTTEST

Key lines 19–20 for 1 minute. Repeat if time permits. Keep your eyes on the copy. Compare your Posttest results with your Pretest results.

(continued)

Title	Wholesale Price
Out of the Dust	$9.57
View From Saturday	$2.70
The Midwife's Apprentice	$6.57
Walk Two Moons	$2.97
Sarah, Plain and Tall	$8.97
The Bridge to Terabithia	$2.97
Roll of Thunder, Hear My Cry	$9.57
Mrs. Frisby and the Rats of NIMH	$10.20
Summer of the Swans	$2.97
Sounder	$8.97
Island of the Blue Dolphins	$3.30
Johnny Tremain	$12.00

ACTIVITY 30

Database Table 5, Report 3

Create a report using Database Table 5 (DT5), and name it DR3. Complete the following steps to format the report and perform the calculations. (The exact sequence of steps might vary depending on the software program you are using.)

1. Change the print orientation to landscape.
2. Include only the Code, Title, Inventory, Retail Price, Wholesale Price, Difference, and Inventory Value fields in the report.
3. Select a tabular format.
4. Select a format/style.
5. In the header, left-align the title Newbery Titles, and right-align your name.
6. Select a font size for the title and your name that is larger than the data text.
7. Enter a formula in the Difference field that will calculate the difference between the retail and wholesale prices of each book.
8. Enter a formula in the Inventory Value field that will calculate the total value of the inventory for each book.
9. Preview/run the report.
10. Follow your teacher's instructions for printing your report.
11. Close the report.

REVIEW

OBJECTIVE:

- Improve keyboarding skills.

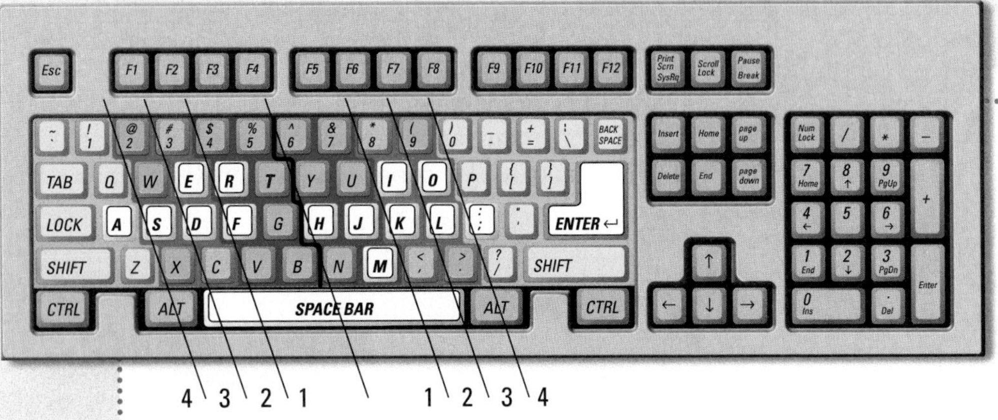

A. WARMUP

Key each line 2 times. Leave 1 blank line after each set of lines.

```
1 joke fade home jade mom lads lose less;
2 jell sods from jars adds half ash lead;
```

SKILLBUILDING

B. ENTER KEY

Key each line 1 time. Repeat if time permits.

Press ENTER after each semicolon and continue to type smoothly.

```
3 dad adds a home;↵ a sad lass sees ahead;↵
4 he led her here;↵ she folded old flames;↵
5 some lasses are moms;↵ he had less jade;↵
6 he sold old hooks;↵ she had jade flakes;↵
```

SKILLBUILDING

C. 12-Second Sprints

Take three 12-second timed writings on each line. Try to increase your speed each time.

```
9  Six men plan to take the boat trip to the side of the lake.
10 We must be ready when it is time for us to go to the shore.
11 This is what she said about it when she wanted to meet him.
12 Our real wish will come true many days from this very hour.
   |||| 5 |||| 10 |||| 15 |||| 20 |||| 25 |||| 30 |||| 35 |||| 40 |||| 45 |||| 50 |||| 55 |||| 60
```

FORMATTING

D. Software Features

STUDENT MANUAL

Formulas in Database Reports

Study Lesson 149 in your Student Manual. Complete all the practice activities while at your computer. Then complete the tasks that follow.

DATABASE APPLICATIONS

ACTIVITY 29

Database Table 5

Open the file DT5 and make the following changes:

1. Add three new fields in this order at the end of the table: Wholesale Price, Difference, Inventory Value.
2. Enter the wholesale prices for the titles as shown in the illustration on p. 549.
3. Close the table window.

(continued on next page)

C. Space Bar

Key each line 1 time. Repeat if time permits.

Space between words without pausing.

```
7  as a sad lass; ask a lad; as a sad dad;
8  he had old sod; she made me mad; a door
9  mom hems; dad marked rare oak; mash ash
10 see her; make me; a sad lad; ash doors;
```

D. Concentration

Fill in the missing vowels shown at the left as you key each line 1 time.

Keep eyes on copy.

```
e  11 h- s--s s-al-d l-as-s; sh- h-ars a r--d
a  12 al-s - s-d l-d h-d - lo-d of f-ke smoke
o  13 ask her f-r a l-ad -f s-me -ld -ak m-ld
i  14 she sa-d d-m m-rrors make h-m look sl-m
```

E. Technique Checkpoint

Key each line 2 times. Repeat if time permits. Focus on the techniques at the left.

Focus on:
- ***Fingertips touching home keys.***
- ***Wrists up.***

```
15 his dark oak desk lid is a joke; he did
16 make a firm door from some rare red ash
17 a lad made a shed; he slashed odd sales
18 foals roam a farm; she sees a small elm
```

LANGUAGE ARTS CONNECTION

Solve a Puzzle See if you can use the keys you have learned to solve the following puzzle. Start with the word **fade** and change one letter at a time to get to the word **mark**. For example, to go from **ride** to **farm**, you could use the sequence: ride, **h**ide, hi**r**e, **f**ire, f**a**re, far**m**. (The bold letter is the only change from word to word.)

LESSON 149 DATABASES: FORMULAS

OBJECTIVES:

- Improve keyboarding skills.
- Apply rules for hyphenating compound adjectives.
- Create and use formulas in database tables.

A. WARMUP

Key each line 2 times.

Speed	1	We will try as hard as we can to start the car in the cold.
Accuracy	2	Two sax players in the jazz band gave a quick demo for Tom.
Language Link	3	The speed limit on Highway Eighty-Four is seventy-five MPH.
Numbers/Symbols	4	Our guess was 15% off. Abe had #66; Vi had #77--nobody won.

| 1 | 2 | 3 | 4 | 5 | 6 | 7 | 8 | 9 | 10 | 11 | 12

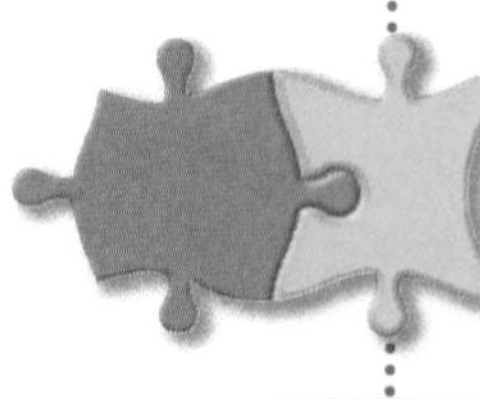

LANGUAGE LINK

B. HYPHENATED COMPOUND ADJECTIVES

Study the rule and examples below. Then edit lines 5–8 by inserting hyphens where needed.

Rule 48: Hyphenate compound adjectives that come before a noun (unless the first word is an adverb ending in ly).

We reviewed an up-to-date report on Wednesday.

We attended a highly rated session on multimedia software.

5 As stated in the above mentioned letter, she went to court.
6 You can order our products by calling our toll free number.
7 Their new, easy to operate recorder goes on sale next week.
8 She drove behind a slow moving vehicle for seventeen miles.

F. PRETEST

Key lines 19–20 for 1 minute. Repeat if time permits. Keep your eyes on the copy.

```
19 more sire aims roam same sale ride joke
20 mare hire elms foal lame dark aide jars
```

G. PRACTICE

Key each line 2 times. Repeat if time permits. Keep your eyes on the copy.

It is easier to keep your eyes on the copy if you:

- ***Review the charts for key positions and anchors.***
- ***Maintain an even pace.***
- ***Resist looking up from the copy.***
- ***Keep hands in position.***

```
21 more more mire mire mere mere mare mare
22 sire sire dire dire fire fire hire hire
23 aims aims arms arms alms alms elms elms
24 roam roam loam loam foam foam foal foal

25 same same fame fame dame dame lame lame
26 sale sale dale dale dare dare dark dark
27 ride ride hide hide side side aide aide
28 jade jade made made mode mode mole mole
```

H. POSTTEST

Key lines 19–20 for 1 minute. Repeat if time permits. Keep your eyes on the copy. Compare your Posttest results with your Pretest results.

LANGUAGE ARTS CONNECTION

Applying Keyboard Skills Use pen and paper to list the ways that keyboarding can help you in other classes and in your career. Then use your list to write a five-sentence paragraph explaining why keyboarding is a valuable skill.

Use a topic sentence and give at least two supporting examples. Do not just think about using computers to write papers. How else are they used in your classes? How do people use keyboarding in different types of employment?

ACTIVITY 27

Database Table 4, Report 1

Create a report using Database Table 4 and name it DR1. Complete the following steps to format the report. (The exact sequence of steps might vary depending on the software program you are using.)

1. Select a column format for the report.
2. Select a format/style.
3. In the header, left-align the title *Salary Ranges*, and right-align your name.
4. Select a font size for the title and your name that is larger than the data text.
5. Preview/run the report.
6. Follow your teacher's instructions for printing the report.
7. Close the report.

ACTIVITY 28

Database Table 2, Report 2

Create a report using Database Table 2 and name it DR2. Complete the following steps to format the report. (The exact sequence of steps might vary depending on the software program you are using.)

1. Select a tabular format for the report.
2. Select a format/style.
3. In the header, left-align the title *Olympic Tryouts*, and right-align your name.
4. Select a font size for the title and your name that is larger than the data text.
5. Preview/run the report.
6. Follow your teacher's instructions for printing the report.
7. Close the report.

Activity

Explain Reports You have learned how to create reports from database tables. In a new word processing document, compose and key two paragraphs that explain in your own words what reports are and how they are useful. Follow your teacher's instructions for saving and printing this file.

With your teacher's permission, print one of the reports that you completed in Activities 27 and 28 above. Include the printed report in your portfolio as an example to illustrate the paragraphs that you composed above.

LESSON 5 NEW KEYS: T N C

OBJECTIVE:

- Key T, N, and C by touch.

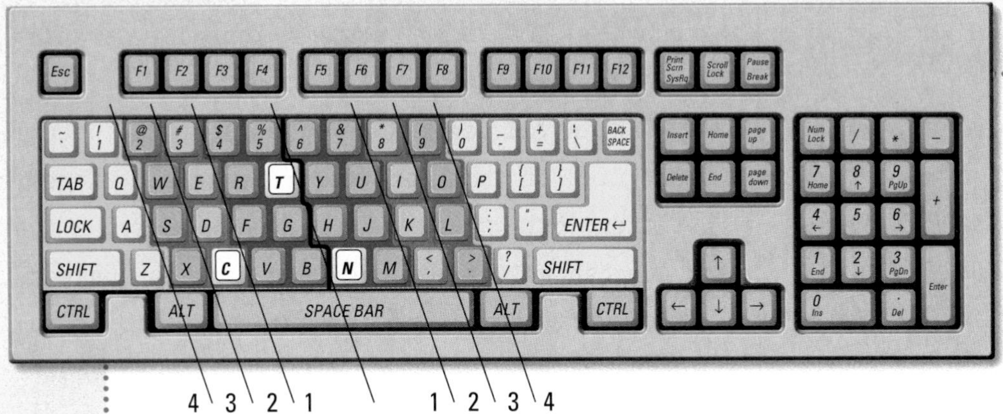

A. WARMUP

Key each line 2 times. Leave 1 blank line after each set of lines.

```
1 asdf jkl; heo; mri; asdf jkl; heo; mri;
2 herd herd mild mild safe safe joke joke
```

NEW KEYS

B.  KEY

Key each line 2 times. Repeat if time permits.

Use F finger. Anchor A S D.

```
3 fff ftf ftf tft ftf fff ftf ftf tft ftf
4 ftf kit kit ftf toe toe ftf ate ate ftf
5 ftf it is the; to them; for the; at it;
6 that hat is flat; it ate at least three
```

D. 5-Minute Timed Writings

Take two 5-minute timed writings on the paragraphs. Note your speed and errors.

Goal: 40/5'/5e

People with technical skills are in demand for dozens 11
of jobs. Once on the job, however, you will need more than 23
technical skills to survive. You must be able to deal with 35
all the unwritten company rules. 41

When you begin a new job, you will need to learn about 52
the rules of that particular workplace. Some rules will be 64
written, but others will not be. Observing these unwritten 76
rules can be vital to your success in business. 86

Every office has its own way of doing some things, yet 97
there are some basic rules of etiquette that are common in 109
all places of business. There are distinct behaviors that 120
seem to be required of each person who becomes an expert at 132
succeeding in business. For example, knowing the rules for 144
dressing appropriately and being well-groomed always helps. 156
In addition, if you are honest, courteous, well-mannered, 168
and punctual, you will probably be seen in a favorable way 179
by your peers. 182

Each employee should quickly become familiar with the 193
standard protocol of the company. 200

| 1 | 2 | 3 | 4 | 5 | 6 | 7 | 8 | 9 | 10 | 11 | 12 SI 1.49

FORMATTING

E. Software Features

STUDENT MANUAL

Creating Reports from Database Tables

Study Lesson 148 in your Student Manual. Complete all the practice activities while at your computer. Then complete the tasks that follow.

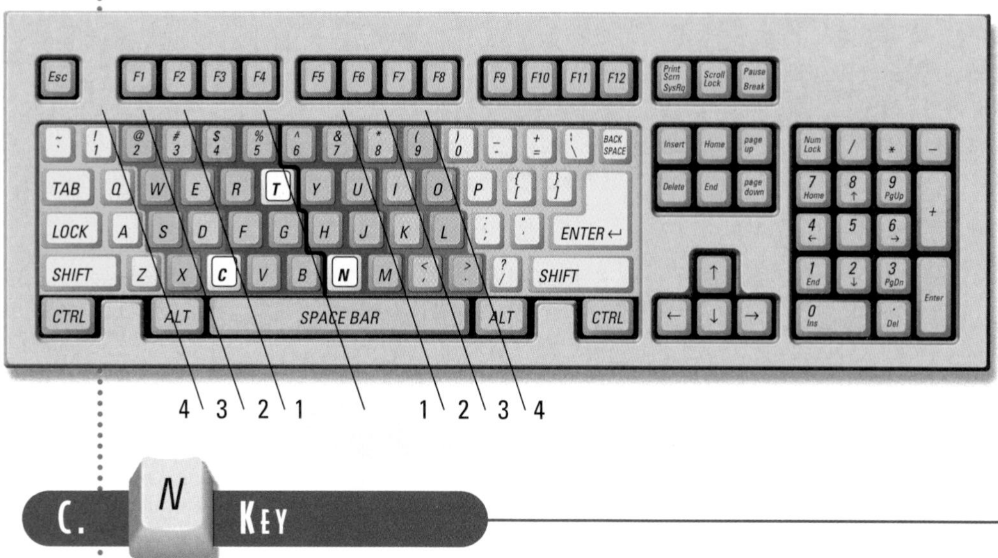

C. N Key

Key each line 2 times. Repeat if time permits.

Use J finger. Anchor ; L K.

7 jjj jnj jnj njn jnj jjj jnj jnj njn jnj
8 jnj ten ten jnj not not jnj and and jnj
9 jnj nine tones; none inside; on and on;
10 nine kind lines; ten done in an instant

D. C Key

Key each line 2 times. Repeat if time permits.

Use D finger. Anchor A.

11 ddd dcd dcd cdc dcd ddd dcd dcd cdc dcd
12 dcd ace ace dcd can can dcd arc arc dcd
13 dcd on a deck; in each car; cannot act;
14 act at once; call to cancel the tickets

SCIENCE CONNECTION

Use a Search Engine Use a search engine like Google to do a search. Key the words **earth to mars** into the search box. Click on the first five search results and evaluate the sites. Choose the one that you think is the most informative and reliable.

On a separate sheet of paper, write down the name of the site, its URL (Web address), and a paragraph explaining why you thought it was a better site than the other four you evaluated.

DATABASES: REPORTS

OBJECTIVES:

- Improve keyboarding skills.
- Key 40/5'/5e.
- Create reports based on database tables.

A. WARMUP

Key each line 2 times.

Speed	1	The paper might run low before we can finish that next job.
Accuracy	2	Judi's dog jumps over major hurdles to beat Max for prizes.
Language Link	3	Forty-two members scored over sixty-one points in the game.
Numbers/Symbols	4	On 10/14/05 Steven ran 38 laps; on 10/25/05 he ran 67 laps.

| 1 | 2 | 3 | 4 | 5 | 6 | 7 | 8 | 9 | 10 | 11 | 12

SKILLBUILDING

B. 30-SECOND OK TIMED WRITINGS

Take two 30-second OK (error-free) timed writings on lines 5–6. Then take two 30-second OK timed writings on lines 7–8. Goal: no errors.

5 Hazel hurt an elbow when she bumped into the chair as 11
6 she was quickly running through the room to avoid the fire. 23

7 The six jet-black vans zipped quietly through the wet 11
8 grass, but they could not finish the entire course in time. 23

| 1 | 2 | 3 | 4 | 5 | 6 | 7 | 8 | 9 | 10 | 11 | 12

C. PREVIEW PRACTICE

Key each line 2 times as a preview to the timed writings on page 545.

Accuracy	9	honest business etiquette particular appropriately punctual
Speed	10	common things demand doing learn about vital jobs seem deal

SKILLBUILDING

E. Technique Checkpoint

Key each line 2 times. Repeat if time permits. Focus on the techniques at the left.

Hold anchor keys. Eyes on copy.

```
15 fff ftf ftf tft ftf fff ftf ftf tft ftf
16 jjj jnj jnj njn jnj jjj jnj jnj njn jnj
17 ddd dcd dcd cdc dcd ddd dcd dcd cdc dcd
18 the carton of jam is here on this dock;
```

F. PRETEST

Key lines 19–20 for 1 minute. Repeat if time permits. Keep your eyes on the copy.

```
19 sail farm jets kick this none care ink;
20 rain hand jots tick then tone came sink
```

G. PRACTICE

Key each line 2 times. Repeat if time permits.

To increase skill:
- ***Keep eyes on copy.***
- ***Maintain good posture.***
- ***Speed up on the second effort.***

```
21 sail sail said said raid raid rain rain
22 farm farm harm harm hard hard hand hand
23 jets jets lets lets lots lots jots jots
24 kick kick sick sick lick lick tick tick

25 this this thin thin than than then then
26 none none lone lone done done tone tone
27 care care cake cake cane cane came came
28 ink; ink; link link rink rink sink sink
```

H. POSTTEST

Key lines 19–20 for 1 minute. Repeat if time permits. Compare your Posttest results with your Pretest results.

ACTIVITY 23

Database Table 3, Query 7

Create the following query on Database Table 3:

1. Select the *State* and *State Bird* fields, and sort the data on the *State Bird* field in ascending order.
2. Follow your teacher's instructions for printing the results of the query table.
3. Close the query window(s).
4. Name the query Q7.

ACTIVITY 24

Database Table 3, Query 8

Create the following query on Database Table 3:

1. Select the *State* and *State Bird* fields, and sort the data on the *State Bird* field in ascending order.
2. In the *State Bird* field, specify selection of those states with the cardinal, mockingbird, or robin as the state bird.
3. Follow your teacher's instructions for printing the results of the query table.
4. Name the query Q8.

ACTIVITY 25

Database Table 3, Query 9

Create the following query on Database Table 3:

1. Select the *State* and *State Bird* fields, and sort the data on the *State* field in ascending order.
2. In the *State Bird* field, specify selection of those states with the cardinal, mockingbird, or robin as the state bird.
3. Follow your teacher's instructions for printing the results of the query table.
4. Close the query window(s).
5. Name the query Q9.

ACTIVITY 26

Database Table 3, Query 10

Create the following query on Database Table 3:

1. Select the *State* and *Highest Point* fields, and sort the data on the *Highest Point* field in ascending order.
2. In the *Highest Point* field, specify selection of those states with elevations of 10,000 feet or higher.
3. Follow your teacher's instructions for printing the results of the query table.
4. Close the query window(s).
5. Name the query Q10.

LANGUAGE ARTS CONNECTION

Create and Explain a Query Open Database Table 1 (Lessons 142-143), which listed e-mail addresses, area codes, and zip codes. Think of a query that would be useful for this table. Create and run your query. In a new word processing document, compose and key a sentence that explains what your query does. Follow your teacher's instructions for saving and printing your work.

New Keys: V Right Shift Period (.)

OBJECTIVES:

- Key V, Right Shift, and period by touch.
- Apply proper spacing with the period.
- Compute speed (keying rate in words per minute).

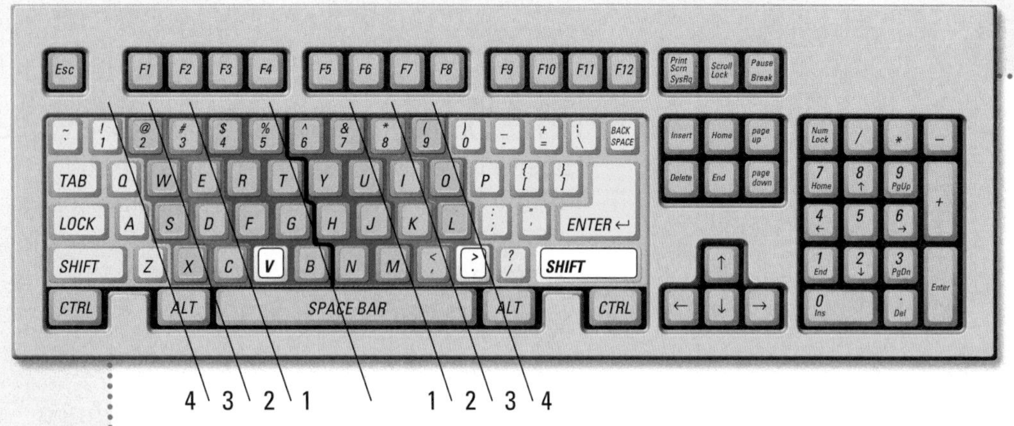

A. Warmup

Key each line 2 times.

```
1 asdf jkl; jh de lo jm fr ki ft jn dc ;;
2 cash free dine jolt milk iron trim star
```

NEW KEYS

B. V Key

Key each line 2 times. Repeat if time permits.

Use F finger. Anchor A S D.

```
3 fff fvf fvf vfv fvf fff fvf fvf vfv fvf
4 fvf vie vie fvf eve eve fvf via via fvf
5 fvf vie for love; move over; via a van;
6 vote to move; even vitamins have flavor
```

ACTIVITY 18

Database Table 3, Query 2

Create the following query on Database Table 3:

1. Select the *State* and *Date of Statehood* fields, and sort the data on the *Date of Statehood* field in ascending order.
2. In the *Date of Statehood* field, specify selection of those states that acquired statehood in the 1700s.
3. Follow your teacher's instructions for printing the results of the query table.
4. Close the query window(s).
5. Name the query Q2.

ACTIVITY 19

Database Table 3, Query 3

Create the following query on Database Table 3:

1. Select the *State* and *Date of Statehood* fields, and sort the data on the *Date of Statehood* field in ascending order.
2. In the *Date of Statehood* field, specify selection of those states that acquired statehood in the 1800s.
3. Follow your teacher's instructions for printing the results of the query table.
4. Close the query window(s).
5. Name the query Q3.

ACTIVITY 20

Database Table 3, Query 4

Create the following query on Database Table 3:

1. Select the *State* and *Date of Statehood* fields, and sort the data on the *Date of Statehood* field in ascending order.
2. In the *Date of Statehood* field, specify selection of those states that acquired statehood in the 1900s.
3. Follow your teacher's instructions for printing the results of the query table.
4. Close the query window(s).
5. Name the query Q4.

ACTIVITY 21

Database Table 3, Query 5

Create the following query on Database Table 3:

1. Select the *State* and *Capital* fields, and sort the data on the *Capital* field in ascending order.
2. Follow your teacher's instructions for printing the results of the query table.
3. Close the query window(s).
4. Name the query Q5.

ACTIVITY 22

Database Table 3, Query 6

Create the following query on Database Table 3:

1. Select the *State* and *Capital* fields, and sort the data on the *Capital* field in ascending order.
2. In the *Capital* field, specify selection of those states with capitals that begin with the letter *C*.
3. Follow your teacher's instructions for printing the results of the query table.
4. Close the query window(s).
5. Name the query Q6.

C. Right  Key

Key each line 2 times. Repeat if time permits.

Use Sem finger. Anchor J.

The Right Shift key capitalizes letters keyed with the left hand.

```
7  ;;; T;; T;; ;;; C;; C;; ;;; S;; S;; ;;;
8  ;;; Ted Ted ;;; Cal Cal ;;; Sam Sam ;;;
9  ;;; Ed likes Linda; Rick ran; save Tom;
10 Vera loved Florida; Aaron and Sam moved
```

D. . Key

Key each line 2 times. Repeat if time permits.

Use L finger. Anchor ; or J.

```
11 lll l.l l.l .l. l.l lll l.l l.l .l. lll
12 l.l Fr. Fr. l.l Sr. Sr. l.l Dr. Dr. l.l
13 l.l std. ctn. div. Ave. Rd. St. Co. vs.
14 Calif. Conn. Tenn. Colo. Fla. Del. Ark.
```

SKILLBUILDING

E. Spacing After Punctuation

Key each line 2 times. Repeat if time permits.

Space once after:
- *A period at the end of a sentence.*
- *A period used with an abbreviation.*
- *A semicolon.*

```
15 The draft is too cold. Close this door.
16 Ask Vera to start a fire. Find a match.
17 Dr. T. Vincent sees me; he made a cast.
18 Ash Rd. is ahead; East Ave. veers left.
```

ACTIVITY 12
Database Table 3

Open the file DT3 and follow these steps:

1. Sort the table on the *State Bird* field in ascending order.
2. Follow your teacher's instructions for printing the table.
3. Do not save your changes for this or the following activities.

ACTIVITY 13
Database Table 3

Using Database Table 3, perform the following sort:

1. Sort the table on the *Date of Statehood* field in ascending order.
2. Follow your teacher's instructions for printing the table.

ACTIVITY 14
Database Table 3

Using Database Table 3, perform the following sort:

1. Sort the table on the *Highest Point* field in descending order.
2. Follow your teacher's instructions for printing the table.

ACTIVITY 15
Database Table 3

Continue using Database Table 3 and perform the following sort:

1. Sort the table on the *State Bird* field in ascending order, and then sort the *State* field in descending order. Be sure the *State Bird* field is listed first.
2. Follow your teacher's instructions for printing the table.
3. Compare your results with Activity 12 results.

ACTIVITY 16
Database Table 3

Perform the following sort to return Database Table 3 to its original format:

1. Sort the table on the *State* field in ascending order.
2. Close the table window.

ACTIVITY 17
Database Table 3, Query 1

Create the following query on Database Table 3:

1. Select the *State* and *Date of Statehood* fields, and sort the data on the *Date of Statehood* field in ascending order.
2. Follow your teacher's instructions for printing the results of the query table.
3. Close the query window(s).
4. Name the query Q1.

F. Technique Checkpoint

Key each line 2 times. Focus on the technique at the left.

Hold anchor keys. Eyes on copy.

```
19 fff fvf fvf vfv fvf fff fvf fvf vfv fvf
20 ;;; T;; T;; ;;; C;; C;; ;;; S;; S;; ;;;
21 lll l.l l.l .l. l.l lll l.l l.l .l. lll
22 Dee voted for vivid vases on her visit.
```

G. Figuring Speed

Keying speed is measured in words per minute (wpm). To determine your keying speed:

- Key for 1 minute.
- Determine the number of words you keyed. Every 5 strokes (characters and spaces) count as 1 word. Therefore, a 40-stroke line equals 8 words. Two 40-stroke lines equal 16 words.
- Use the cumulative **word count,** the number at the end of each line, to determine the number of words in a complete line.

To determine the number of words in an incomplete line:

- Use the **word scale**, which is the number grid below the last line (below line 24 on this page).
- The number over which you stopped keying is the number of words for that line. For example, if you keyed line 23 and completed up to the word *task* in line 24, you have keyed 15 words per minute (8 + 7 = 15).

```
23 fold hide fast came hold ride mast fame    8
24 hone rice mask fade none vice task jade   16
   | 1 | 2 | 3 | 4 | 5 | 6 | 7 | 8
```

MATH CONNECTION

Calculating Words per Minute (wpm) Practice calculating the number of words you key per minute if you keyed lines 23–24 up to the following words:

- mast
- jade
- mask
- fame (the 2nd time, after keying both lines once)

(continued)

5 Two thirds of the membership must be present to enact a rule.
6 We observed twenty nine infractions during the investigation.
7 Bancroft Industries reduced their sales force by one fourth.
8 After we add all the numbers, we must increase it by fifty five.

SKILLBUILDING

C. 30-Second Timed Writings

Take two 30-second timed writings on lines 9–10. Then take two 30-second timed writings on lines 11–12. Try to increase your speed each time.

9 Presentation software will enable you to create some 11
10 colorful, animated, and visually exciting presentations. 22

11 You can include photos, clip art, sound, animation, 11
12 and a variety of colors, which will make a great impact. 22

| 1 | 2 | 3 | 4 | 5 | 6 | 7 | 8 | 9 | 10 | 11 | 12

LANGUAGE ARTS CONNECTION

Illustrate Hyphenation Rules In the Language Link on p. 539, you learned to hyphenate compound numbers and fractions that are expressed in words. Compose and key two sentences that contain compound numbers expressed in words and two sentences that contain fractions expressed in words. Follow your teacher's instructions for saving and printing your work.

FORMATTING

D. Software Features

STUDENT MANUAL

Sorting Database Tables Creating a Database Query

Study Lesson 147 in your Student Manual. Complete all the practice activities while at your computer. Then complete the tasks that follow.

H. PRETEST

Key lines 23–24 for 1 minute. Repeat if time permits. Note your speed. Keep your eyes on the copy.

```
23 fold hide fast came hold ride mast fame   8
24 hone rice mask fade none vice task jade  16
   | 1 | 2 | 3 | 4 | 5 | 6 | 7 | 8
```

I. PRACTICE

Key each line 2 times. Repeat if time permits.

Build speed on repeated word patterns.

```
25 fold fold hold hold sold sold told told
26 hide hide ride ride rice rice vice vice
27 fast fast mast mast mask mask task task
28 came came fame fame fade fade jade jade

29 last last vast vast cast cast case case
30 mats mats mars mars cars cars jars jars
31 fell fell jell jell sell sell seal seal
32 dive dive five five live live love love
```

J. POSTTEST

Repeat the Pretest. Compare your Posttest results with your Pretest results.

LANGUAGE ARTS CONNECTION

Rhyming Words Couplets are two lines that have the same end sound to create a rhyme. For example:

When asked to complete a difficult task,
His face became an unhappy mask.

or

After the seal took a dive,
It gave the man a wet high five.

Select five pairs of words from lines 25–32 above. Use these words to write by hand at least two couplets. With your teacher's permission, share your rhymes with your class.

DATABASES: SORT AND QUERY

OBJECTIVES:

- Apply rules for hyphenating words.
- Improve keyboarding skills.
- Sort database tables.
- Query database tables.

A. WARMUP

Key each line 2 times.

Speed	1	The dog and cat went to eat their food from the round dish.
Accuracy	2	Liza gave Max and Becky a quaint photo of a jar of flowers.
Language Link	3	Trina's GPA was found to be higher than that of her sister.
Numbers/Symbols	4	I concluded that 1/3 of $39 = $13, and that 20% of $10 = 2.

| 1 | 2 | 3 | 4 | 5 | 6 | 7 | 8 | 9 | 10 | 11 | 12

B. HYPHENATED WORDS

Study the rule and examples that follow. Then edit lines 5–8 on p. 540 by inserting hyphens where necessary.

Rule 47: Hyphenate compound numbers (between *twenty-one* and *ninety-nine*) and fractions that are expressed in words.

> *Seventy-five of the members voted to repeal the law—this was nearly two-fifths of the membership.*
>
> *Thirty-five letters were sent to Mr. Alexander to thank him for his excellent service.*

(continued on next page)

LESSON 7

NEW KEYS: W COMMA (,) G

OBJECTIVES:

- Key W, comma, and G by touch.
- Count errors.

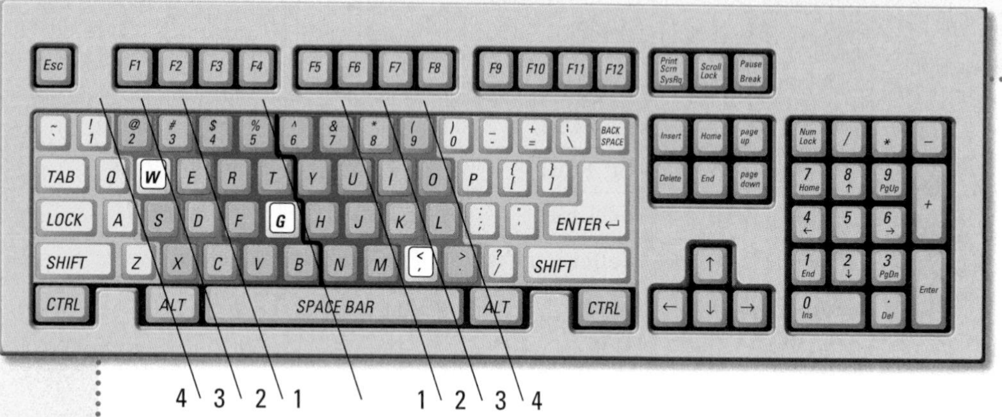

A. WARMUP

Key each line 2 times.

```
1 fail not; jest mist chin Rev. card sake
2 Rick did not join; Val loves that fame.
```

NEW KEYS

B. W KEY

Key each line 2 times. Repeat if time permits.

Use S finger. Anchor F.

```
3 sss sws sws wsw sws sss sws sws wsw sws
4 sws was was sws own own sws saw saw sws
5 sws white swans swim; sow winter wheat;
6 We watched some whales while we walked.
```

(continued)

State	Capital	Date of Statehood	State Bird	Highest Point
Kansas	Topeka	1/29/1861	Western meadowlark	4,039
Kentucky	Frankfort	6/1/1792	Cardinal	4,145
Louisiana	Baton Rouge	4/30/1812	Eastern brown pelican	535
Maine	Augusta	3/15/1820	Chickadee	5,268
Maryland	Annapolis	4/28/1788	Baltimore oriole	3,360
Massachusetts	Boston	2/6/1788	Chickadee	3,491
Michigan	Lansing	1/26/1837	Robin	1,980
Minnesota	St. Paul	5/11/1858	Common loon	2,301
Mississippi	Jackson	12/10/1817	Mockingbird	806
Missouri	Jefferson City	8/10/1821	Bluebird	1,772
Montana	Helena	11/8/1889	Western meadowlark	12,799
Nebraska	Lincoln	3/1/1867	Western meadowlark	5,424
Nevada	Carson City	10/31/1864	Mountain bluebird	13,143
New Hampshire	Concord	6/21/1788	Purple finch	6,288
New Jersey	Trenton	12/18/1787	Eastern goldfinch	1,803
New Mexico	Santa Fe	1/6/1912	Chaparral bird	13,161
New York	Albany	7/26/1788	Bluebird	5,344
North Carolina	Raleigh	11/21/1789	Cardinal	6,684
North Dakota	Bismarck	11/2/1889	Western meadowlark	3,506
Ohio	Columbus	3/1/1803	Cardinal	1,550
Oklahoma	Oklahoma City	11/16/1907	Scissor-tailed flycatcher	4,973
Oregon	Salem	2/14/1859	Western meadowlark	11,233
Pennsylvania	Harrisburg	12/12/1787	Ruffed grouse	3,213
Rhode Island	Providence	5/29/1790	Rhode Island red	812
South Carolina	Columbia	5/23/1788	Carolina wren	3,560
South Dakota	Pierre	11/2/1889	Red-necked pheasant	7,242
Tennessee	Nashville	6/1/1796	Mockingbird	6,643
Texas	Austin	12/29/1845	Mockingbird	8,749
Utah	Salt Lake City	1/4/1896	Sea gull	13,528
Vermont	Montpelier	3/4/1791	Hermit thrush	4,393
Virginia	Richmond	6/25/1788	Cardinal	5,729
Washington	Olympia	11/11/1889	Willow goldfinch	14,410
West Virginia	Charleston	6/20/1863	Cardinal	4,863
Wisconsin	Madison	5/29/1848	Robin	1,952
Wyoming	Cheyenne	7/10/1890	Western meadowlark	13,804

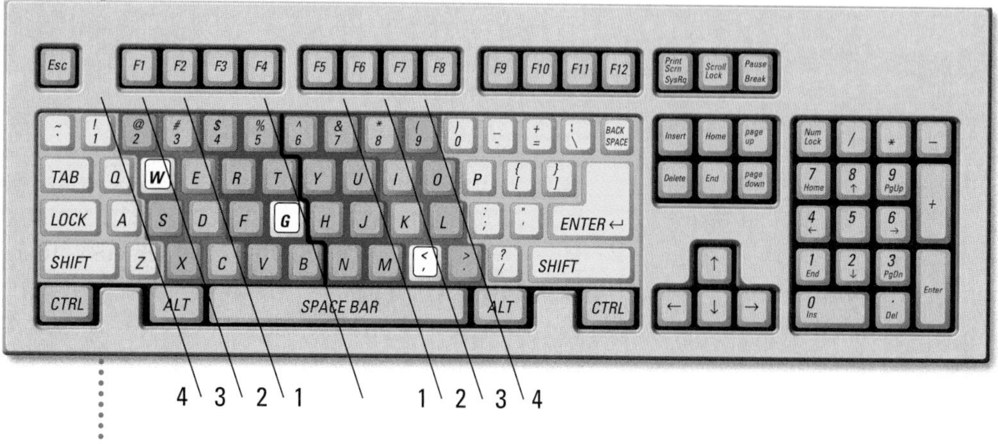

C. , Key

Key each line 2 times. Repeat if time permits.

Use K finger. Anchor ;. Space once after a comma.

7 kkk k,k k,k ,k, k,k kkk k,k k,k ,k, k,k
8 k,k it, it, k,k or, or, k,k an, an, k,k
9 k,k if it is, two, or three, as soon as
10 Vic, his friend, lives in Rich, Alaska.

D. G Key

Key each line 2 times. Repeat if time permits.

Use F finger. Anchor A S D.

11 fff fgf fgf gfg fgf fff fgf fgf gfg fgf
12 fgf leg leg fgf egg egg fgf get get fgf
13 fgf give a dog, saw a log, sing a song,
14 Gen gets a large sagging gift of games.

interNET CONNECTION

QWERTY Keyboards The keyboard on which you are working is known as the QWERTY keyboard. Go to the Online Learning Center at **KeyComps.glencoe.com> Internet Connection>Unit 1> Lesson 7** to find out more about the QWERTY keyboard and complete a short activity.

ACTIVITY 11

Database Table 3

Open the file DT3 and make the following changes:

1. Add a new field named *Highest Point;* specify it as a number field and format the field with commas.
2. Position the field *Highest Point* as the last field of the table.
3. Enter the elevations for the states as shown in the illustration below.
4. Add the records shown in the illustration on p. 538 to Database Table 3.
5. Print the table according to your teacher's instructions.
6. Close the table window.

Alabama	2,407
Alaska	20,320
Arizona	12,633
Arkansas	2,753
California	14,494
Colorado	14,433
Connecticut	2,380
Delaware	442
Florida	345
Georgia	4,784
Hawaii	13,796
Idaho	12,662
Illinois	1,235
Indiana	1,257
Iowa	1,670

(continued on next page)

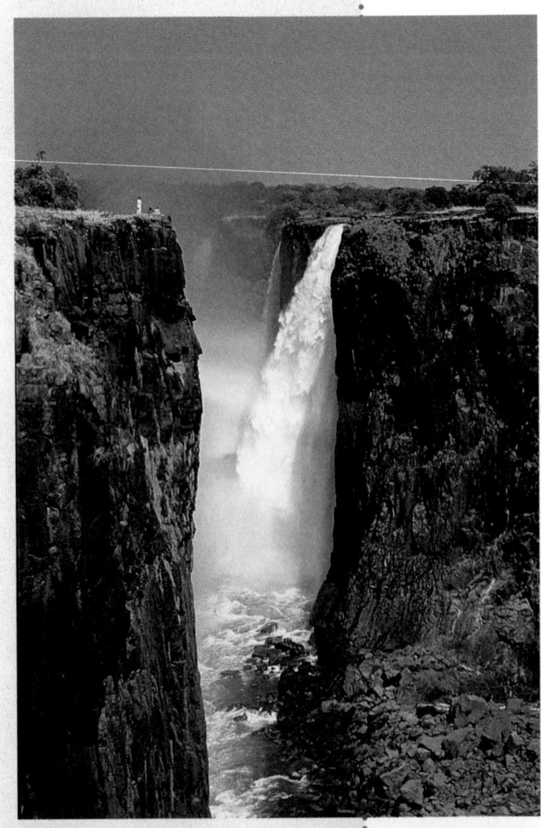

SKILLBUILDING

E. Technique Checkpoint

Key each line 2 times. Repeat if time permits. Focus on the techniques at the left.

Hold anchor keys. Keep elbows in.

```
15 sss sws sws wsw sws sss sws sws wsw sws
16 kkk k,k k,k ,k, k,k kkk k,k k,k ,k, k,k
17 fff fgf fgf gfg fgf fff fgf fgf gfg fgf
18 Wanda watched the team jog to the glen.
```

F. Counting Errors

Count 1 error for each word, even if it contains several errors. Count as an error:

- A word with an incorrect character (misspelling).
- A word with incorrect spacing after it.
- A word with incorrect punctuation after it.
- Each mistake in following directions for spacing or indenting.
- A word with a space within the word.
- An omitted word.
- A repeated word.
- Transposed (switched in order) words.

Compare these incorrect lines with the correct lines (19–21). Each error is highlighted in color.

```
Frank sold sold Dave old an washing mshcone .
     Carl joked with Al ice, Fran, Edith.
Wamda wore redsocks; Sadie wore green,
```

Key each line 2 times. Proofread carefully and note your errors.

```
19 Frank sold Dave an old washing machine.
20 Carl joked with Alice, Fran, and Edith.
21 Wanda wore red socks; Sadie wore green.
```

F. 5-Minute Timed Writings

Take two 5-minute timed writings on the paragraphs. Note your speed and errors.

Goal: 40/5'/5e

Do you realize that calendars begin with an epoch, a 11
span of time marked by a notable event? From the start, the 23
method of tracking time was based on one of three major 34
cycles. The cycles included the orbit of the sun, orbit of 46
the moon, and a combination of both of their paths. 56

Due to errors and omissions of the calendars of the 67
sixteenth century, a French chronologist by the name of 78
Joseph Scaliger proposed a new plan. He suggested a time 90
prior to any event in history. 96

Scaliger based his work on three unique cycles. One of 107
these was the twenty-eight-year cycle, the time after which 119
weekdays and days of the month repeat in the exact same 130
order. Another cycle was the nineteen-year Metonic orbit, 142
the time after which moon phases repeat on the same day of 154
the year. The third cycle was the fifteen-year indication, 165
which is also the Roman business and tax cycle. 175

He used these cycles to calculate a start date earlier 186
than all written events. His calendar was called the Julian 198
calendar. 200

SI 1.47

| 1 | 2 | 3 | 4 | 5 | 6 | 7 | 8 | 9 | 10 | 11 | 12

COMMUNICATION FOCUS

Summarize Netiquette Did you know that there are general guidelines of etiquette for using e-mail? These guidelines are called netiquette. Go to the Online Learning Center at **KeyComps.glencoe.com> Communication Focus>Unit 8>Lesson 146** and read the information provided. Complete the activity.

Then compose and key a short paragraph that explains what you learned about each of the following issues. Follow your teacher's instructions for saving and printing your work.

1. Keying everything in capital letters
2. Attaching files
3. Sending chain letters
4. Sending personal messages via office e-mail

G. PRETEST

Take a 1-minute timed writing on lines 22–23. Note your speed and errors. Keep your eyes on the copy.

```
22 sag, mow, crew elf, down well scow king    8
23 hag, jot, glow ink, tows west snow ring   16
   | 1 | 2 | 3 | 4 | 5 | 6 | 7 | 8
```

H. PRACTICE

Key each line 2 times. Repeat if time permits.

Focus on:

- ***Wrists up; do not rest palms on keyboard.***
- ***Fingers curved; move from home position only when necessary.***

```
24 sag, sag, wag, wag, rag, rag, hag, hag,
25 mow, mow, how, how, hot, hot, jot, jot,
26 crew crew grew grew grow grow glow glow
27 elf, elf, elk, elk, ilk, ilk, ink, ink,

28 down down gown gown town town tows tows
29 well well welt welt went went west west
30 scow scow stow stow show show snow snow
31 king king sing sing wing wing ring ring
```

I. POSTTEST

Repeat the Pretest. Compare your Posttest results with your Pretest results.

MATH CONNECTION

Calculate Averages It is fun to see how fast you can key, but if your errors go up with your speed, then you are not really keying faster. To see how your accuracy is affected by your speed, key lines 24–27 on this page three times. Try to increase your speed each time.

Calculate the words per minute for each of your attempts, and then count the number of errors you made. Find the average number of errors you made by adding the number of errors for all three practices, then dividing by 3. For example, if you made 0, 2, and 4 errors, the average would be 2 (0+2+4=6, then 6÷3=2).

SKILLBUILDING

B. PRETEST

Take a 1-minute timed writing on the paragraph. Note your speed and errors.

5 The way the computer works is quite a mystery to some, 11
6 for it is able to execute its tasks at a speed difficult to 23
7 comprehend. To perceive how a computer operates is not that 35
8 complicated when you realize that it is like a light switch. 47

| 1 | 2 | 3 | 4 | 5 | 6 | 7 | 8 | 9 | 10 | 11 | 12

C. PRACTICE

In the following chart, find the number of errors you made on the Pretest. Then key each of the designated drill lines two times.

Pretest Errors	0–1	2	3	4+
Drill Lines	12–16	11–15	10–14	9–13

Accuracy

9 quite appears charged realize mystery electrical comprehend
10 some however capable millions complete character understand
11 able tedious special numbers execute processing electricity
12 switch current difficult computer's complicated five letter

Speed

13 appears turned moving speed works light data like when that
14 holding letter wanted store cells which used such with each
15 seconds symbol called tasks being would five need word only
16 matters stored memory works takes bytes take slow time work

D. POSTTEST

Repeat the Pretest. Compare your Posttest results with your Pretest results.

E. PREVIEW PRACTICE

Key each line 2 times as a preview to the timed writings on page 536.

Accuracy 17 events written calculate combination sixteenth chronologist
Speed 18 calendars tracking notable cycles errors unique epoch orbit

LANGUAGE ARTS CONNECTION

Develop a Life List Think about some of the things that you might want to accomplish in your life. Key three goals for your "life list." After each goal, compose and key a short paragraph that explains why you listed that goal. Follow your teacher's instructions for saving and printing your work.

LESSON 8 REVIEW

OBJECTIVES:

- Increase speed and improve accuracy.
- Strengthen reaches to third, home, and bottom rows.

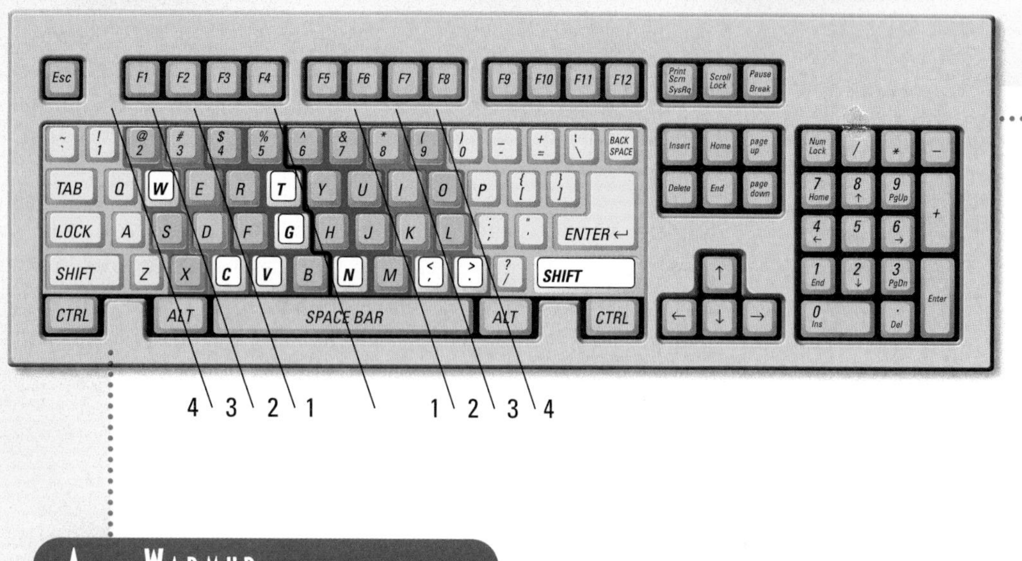

A. Warmup

Key each line 2 times.

1 memo dock sink wave heed crag jolt jest
2 Tommi Ra has two free carnival tickets.

SKILLBUILDING

B. Right Shift Key

Key each line 2 times. Repeat if time permits.

Anchor Right Shift with J.
Keep your rhythm steady as you reach to the Shift key and back to home position.

3 Wade Dana Alda Sami Cata Devo Wane Glen
4 Vera Edie Fran Seth Adam Cara Rene Dave
5 Gene Vick Rick Coel Fran Dave Carl Sadi
6 Anna Wade Gino Sali Vida Theo Dean Eric

Databases: Review

OBJECTIVES:

- Improve keyboarding skills.
- Key 40/5'/5e.
- Review database tables.

A. Warmup

Key each line 2 times.

Speed	1	These short, easy words help you when you build your speed.
Accuracy	2	Even Jacques may gaze up to find six crows in the blue sky.
Language Link	3	James anchored the swim event; his time was fastest of all.
Numbers	4	If we need 56 points, then 47, 29, 38, or 10 will not help.

| 1 | 2 | 3 | 4 | 5 | 6 | 7 | 8 | 9 | 10 | 11 | 12

ETHICS CONNECTION

Explore Digital Citizenship Digital citizenship is an emerging set of rules and norms meant to guide users of technology. Go to the Online Learning Center at **KeyComps.glencoe.com>Ethics Connection>Unit 8> Lesson 146** to learn more about digital citizenship. Complete the activity.

After you complete the activity, open a new word processing document and key the list below of the nine general areas of behavior that make up digital citizenship. Then compose and key a description of when you might need to use each of these areas in your daily activities. Follow your teacher's instructions for saving and printing your work.

Digital Citizenship

1. Etiquette: Electronic standards of conduct or procedure
2. Communication: Electronic exchange of information
3. Education: The process of teaching and learning about technology and the use of technology
4. Access: Full electronic participation in society
5. Commerce: Electronic buying and selling of goods
6. Responsibility: Electronic responsibility for actions and deeds
7. Rights: Those freedoms extended to everyone in a digital world
8. Safety: Physical well-being in a digital technology world
9. Security (self-protection): Electronic precautions to guarantee safety

C. Concentration

Fill in the missing letters shown at the left as you key each line 1 time.

Keep eyes on copy.

```
o   7 S-me w-rk s- we make the w-rld cleaner.
e   8 W- hav- th-m saf-; V-ra l-ft to s-- it.
r   9 See, the -ive-s and st-eams a-e -ising.
h  10 A damaging c-emical mig-t -arm t-e men.
m  11 Their -o- -akes ja- and so-e sew ite-s.
i  12 W-ll-am -s -ll and w-ll l-ve -n Alaska.
```

D. Technique Checkpoint

Key lines 13–16 twice. Remember to space once after a comma. Focus on the technique at the left.

Right Shift key. Keep your rhythm steady as you reach to the Shift key and back to home position.

```
13 Deloris sold red, tan, and orchid ties.
14 Dana had dogs, cats, and a tan hamster.
15 Todd ate mangoes, kiwis, and an orange.
16 Alicia worked on math, French, and law.
```

E. Technique Timed Writings

Take two 30-second timed writings on each line. Focus on the techniques at the left.

Sit up straight and keep both feet flat on the floor.

```
17 Edie Victor saw the Alo Reed dress too.
18 Tom Salt and Arti Wiggs saw Sam and Di.
19 Rick saw Chris at three Eastmoor games.
20 Donna wrote to Anna, Ellen, and Rachel.
   | 1 | 2 | 3 | 4 | 5 | 6 | 7 | 8
```

F. 12-Second Sprints

Take three 12-second timed writings on each line. Try to increase your speed on each timed writing.

Each stroke in a 12-second timed writing is counted as 1 word. If you complete a line, your speed is 40 words per minute.

```
21 Al had one good mark and told me later.
22 We want to go west to work in the rain.
23 The snow fell one dark night last fall.
24 Watch the river flow over the dark dam.
   ||||5||||10||||15||||20||||25||||30||||35||||40
```

ACTIVITY 10

Database Table 5

Open the file DT5 and make the following changes:

1. Add a new field named *Code;* specify *5* as the field size.
2. Position the field *Code* at the beginning of the table.
3. Add a new field named *Purchase Date,* and specify it as a date field; position it between the fields *Binding* and *Retail Price.*
4. Enter the codes and purchase dates (with the current year) for the titles shown in the illustration below.
5. Follow your teacher's instructions for saving and printing the table.
6. Close the table window.

Code	Title	Purchase Date
H29	Out of the Dust	4/4/--
S15	View From Saturday	4/4/--
H25	The Midwife's Apprentice	4/4/--
S33	Walk Two Moons	4/4/--
H48	Sarah, Plain and Tall	4/11/--
S36	The Bridge to Terabithia	4/11/--
H59	Roll of Thunder, Hear My Cry	4/11/--
H16	Mrs. Frisby and the Rats of NIMH	4/11/--
S45	Summer of the Swans	4/18/--
H22	Sounder	4/18/--
S61	Island of the Blue Dolphins	4/18/--
H57	Johnny Tremain	4/18/--

PORTFOLIO Activity

Create a Career Contacts Database Think of five people you know who have jobs that you find interesting. Create a new database, and enter each person's name, his or her job, and a way that you would prefer to contact him or her. In a new field, compose a question that you could ask about his or her career. Follow your teacher's instructions for saving and printing your work.

G. PRETEST

Take a 1-minute timed writing on lines 25–26. Note your speed and errors.

```
25 ring snow west tows ink, glow jot, hag,    8
26 king scow well down elf, crew mow, sag,   16
   | 1 | 2 | 3 | 4 | 5 | 6 | 7 | 8
```

H. PRACTICE

Key each line 2 times. Repeat if time permits.

Wrists up—do not rest palms on keyboard.

Fingers curved—move from the home position only when necessary.

```
27 ring ring wing wing sing sing king king
28 snow snow show show stow stow scow scow
29 west west went went welt welt well well
30 tows tows town town gown gown down down

31 ink, ink, ilk, ilk, elk, elk, elf, elf,
32 glow glow grow grow grew grew crew crew
33 jot, jot, hot, hot, how, how, mow, mow,
34 hag, hag, rag, rag, wag, wag, sag, sag,
```

I. POSTTEST

Repeat the Pretest. Compare your Posttest results with your Pretest results.

*inter*NET CONNECTION

Compare Keyboards There are many types of personal computers on the market today. Besides desktop and laptop computers, people use personal digital assistants (PDAs) and even cell phones to send, receive, and store information. All of these devices have different types of keyboards for inputting information. To find out more about these keyboards, go to the Online Learning Center at **KeyComps.glencoe.com>Internet Connection>Unit 1>Lesson 8**. Complete the activity.

(continued)

40	20		
Position	**Minimum Credentials**	**Low-End Salary**	**High-End Salary**
Accountant	Bachelor's Degree	$30,320	$40,500
Administrative Services Manager	Associate Degree	$36,190	$74,590
Budget Analyst	Bachelor's Degree	$42,000	$66,180
Education Administrator (Elementary)	Master's Degree	$60,340	$75,291
Food Services Manager	Associate Degree	$21,760	$67,490
Medical Social Worker	Bachelor's Degree	$23,840	$56,320
Paralegal	Associate Degree	$30,020	$48,760

ACTIVITY 9

Database Table 5

Follow these steps to create Database Table 5 and name it DT5.

1. Define the five fields as shown in the illustration below; identify the fourth field as a monetary field and the fifth field as a number field.
2. Specify the size of each text/alpha field as shown above the column.
3. Enter the records.
4. Print the table according to your teacher's instructions.
5. Close the table window.

34	22	11		
Title	**Author**	**Binding**	**Retail Price**	**Inventory**
Out of the Dust	Karen Hesse	hardcover	$15.95	14
View From Saturday	E. L. Konigsburg	paperback	$7.50	20
The Midwife's Apprentice	Karen Cushman	hardcover	$10.95	25
Walk Two Moons	Sharon Creech	paperback	$4.95	18
Sarah, Plain and Tall	Patricia MacLachlan	hardcover	$14.95	17
The Bridge to Terabithia	Katherine Paterson	paperback	$8.95	22
Roll of Thunder, Hear My Cry	Mildred D. Taylor	hardcover	$15.99	30
Mrs. Frisby and the Rats of NIMH	Robert C. O'Brien	hardcover	$17.00	28
Summer of the Swans	Betsy Byars	paperback	$7.99	32
Sounder	William H. Armstrong	hardcover	$14.95	35
Island of the Blue Dolphins	Scott O'Dell	paperback	$9.50	15
Johnny Tremain	Esther Forbes	hardcover	$20.00	12

LESSON 9

New Keys: B U Left Shift

OBJECTIVE:

- Key B, U, and the Left Shift by touch.

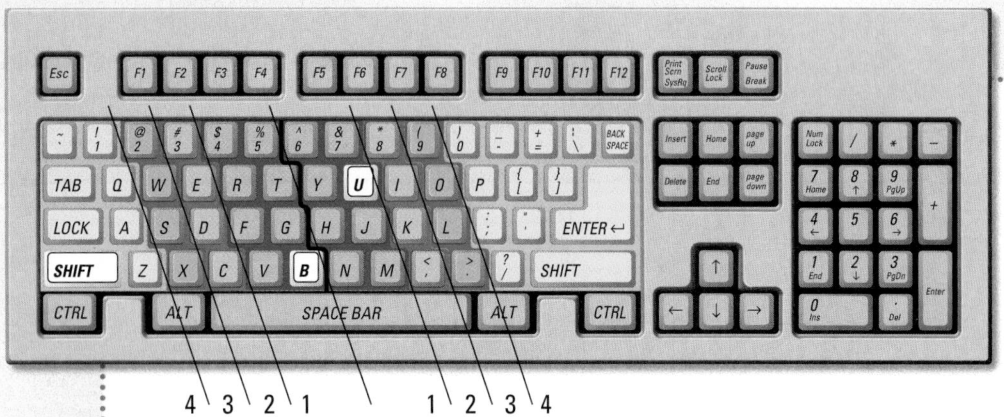

A. Warmup

Key each line 2 times.

1 dim logo wags jive foal corn them wags,
2 Wanda mailed the jewels that Carl made.

NEW KEYS

B.  Key

Key each line 2 times. Repeat if time permits.

Use F finger. Anchor A and S.

3 fff fbf fbf bfb fbf fff fbf fbf bfb fbf
4 fbf rob rob fbf ebb ebb fbf bag bag fbf
5 fbf a bent bin, a back bend, a big bag,
6 That boat had been in a babbling brook.

SKILLBUILDING

C. Diagnostic Practice: Numbers

Turn to the Diagnostic Practice: Numbers routine on page SB4. Key one of the Pretest/Posttest paragraphs and identify any errors made. Then key the corresponding drill lines 2 times for each number on which you made 2 or more errors and 1 time for each number on which you made only 1 error. Finally, repeat the same Pretest paragraph and compare your performance.

FORMATTING

D. Software Features

STUDENT MANUAL

Formatting Numeric Database Fields
Formatting the Current Date or Time

Study Lesson 145 in your Student Manual. Complete all the practice activities while at your computer. Then complete the tasks that follow.

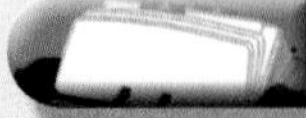

DATABASE APPLICATIONS

ACTIVITY 8

Database Table 4

Follow these steps to create Database Table 4 and name it DT4:

1. Define the four fields as shown in the illustration on p. 532.
2. Identify the third and fourth fields as monetary fields.
3. Specify the size of each text/alpha field as shown above the column.
4. Enter the records.
5. Print the table according to your teacher's instructions.
6. Close the table window.

(continued on next page)

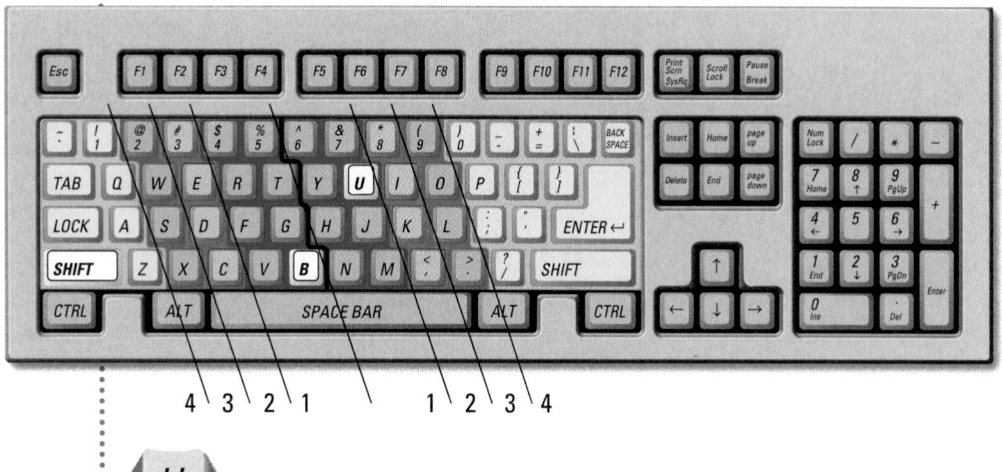

C. U KEY

Key each line 2 times. Repeat if time permits.

Use J finger. Anchor ; L and K.

7 jjj juj juj uju juj jjj juj juj uju juj
8 juj jug jug juj urn urn juj flu flu juj
9 juj jungle bugs, just a job, jumbo jets
10 Students show unusual business success.

Key each line 2 times. Repeat if time permits.

Use A finger. Anchor F.

The LEFT SHIFT key capitalizes letters keyed with the right hand.

11 aaa Kaa Kaa aaa Jaa Jaa aaa Laa Laa aaa
12 aaa Kim Kim aaa Lee Lee aaa Joe Joe aaa
13 aaa Jan left; Nora ran; Uncle Lee fell;
14 Mari and Ula went to Kansas in October.

SKILLBUILDING

E. TECHNIQUE CHECKPOINT

Key each line 2 times. Repeat if time permits. Focus on the technique at the left.

Keep F or J anchored when shifting.

15 fff fbf fbf bfb fbf fff fbf fbf bfb fbf
16 jjj juj juj uju juj jjj juj juj uju juj
17 aaa Kaa Kaa aaa Jaa Jaa aaa Laa Laa aaa
18 Jo told Mike and Nel that she would go.

LESSON 145 Databases: Monetary and Numeric Fields

OBJECTIVES:

- Compose a story at the keyboard.
- Build skills in keying numbers.
- Format monetary and numeric fields in a database.

A. Warmup

Key each line 2 times.

Speed	1	Hard rain came down very fast, so I could not see the road.
Accuracy	2	Everybody expected Jack's golf technique to win him prizes.
Language Link	3	We were told that it may be colder Friday than it is today.
Numbers/Symbols	4	Chris & David earned $7.75/hour loading 1,234# of #4 pines.

| 1 | 2 | 3 | 4 | 5 | 6 | 7 | 8 | 9 | 10 | 11 | 12

Language Link

B. Composing at the Keyboard

Compose a one-page story to complete the following paragraph:

I was watching the Super Bowl on television when the doorbell rang. Since I was the only one at home, I went to the door to see who would be interrupting my football game. Much to my surprise, I found a man carrying a giant check, flowers, and balloons. I could hardly believe my ears when he said, "Congratulations, you are the $10 million winner!" Since that day, my life has changed, and now...

F. PRETEST

Take a 1-minute timed writing on lines 19–20. Note your speed and errors.

```
19 bran gist vast blot sun, bout just beef    8
20 craw just rest bran sum, dole hunk bear   16
   | 1 | 2 | 3 | 4 | 5 | 6 | 7 | 8
```

G. PRACTICE

Key each line 2 times. Repeat if time permits.

Place your feet:
- ***In front of the chair.***
- ***Firmly on the floor, square, flat.***
- ***Apart, with 6 or 7 inches between the ankles.***
- ***One foot a little ahead of the other.***

```
21 bran brad bred brew brow crow crew craw
22 gist list mist must gust dust rust just
23 vast vest jest lest best west nest rest
24 blot blob blow blew bled bred brad bran

25 sun, nun, run, bun, gun, gum, hum, sum,
26 bout boat boot blot bold boll doll dole
27 just dust dusk dunk bunk bulk hulk hunk
28 beef been bean bead beak beam beat bear
```

H. POSTTEST

Repeat the Pretest. Compare your Posttest results with your Pretest results.

interNET CONNECTION

Explore an Online Bookstore Did you know that one of the largest "bookstores" in the world is not a real store, but a Web site? Instead of having shelves where customers can browse, online bookstores have their own search engine that lets customers find books and other merchandise in their databases.

Go to the Online Learning Center at **KeyComps.glencoe.com>Internet Connection>Unit 1>Lesson 9** to visit an online bookstore. In the site's search box, key **Mark Twain**. Write down ten books or products that are displayed in the search results. Choose one book, then write the following information from the site: the book's title, the cost, number of pages, publisher, and a short quote from a customer review.

(continued)

Alabama	Yellowhammer
Alaska	Willow ptarmigan
Arizona	Cactus wren
Arkansas	Mockingbird
California	California valley quail
Colorado	Lark bunting
Connecticut	Robin
Delaware	Blue hen chicken

State	Capital	Date of Statehood	State Bird
Florida	Tallahassee	3/3/1845	Mockingbird
Georgia	Atlanta	1/2/1788	Brown thrasher
Hawaii	Honolulu	8/21/1959	Nene
Idaho	Boise	7/3/1890	Mountain bluebird
Illinois	Springfield	12/3/1818	Cardinal
Indiana	Indianapolis	12/11/1816	Cardinal
Iowa	Des Moines	12/28/1846	Eastern goldfinch

SOCIAL STUDIES CONNECTION

List Historical Events Look up the date of statehood for your state in the tables on p. 525, p. 529, and p. 538. In a new word processing document, key each of the historical events below. Determine where your state's date of statehood falls in the list, and add that event in the correct place. Follow your teacher's instructions for saving and printing your work.

1776: The American Revolution begins.
1788: The U.S. Constitution is ratified.
1804: Lewis and Clark begin their expedition.
1835: Samuel Morse develops Morse code.
1879: Thomas Edison invents the electric light bulb.
1895: The Lumiere brothers show the first projected motion picture films.
1903: Orville and Wilbur Wright fly the first motor-driven airplane.
1928: Television broadcasts begin in the United States.
1947: Chuck Yeager is the first man to fly faster than the speed of sound.
1969: American astronauts are the first humans to walk on the moon.

LESSON 10

NEW KEYS: Q /

OBJECTIVE:

- Key Q and / (slash or diagonal) by touch.

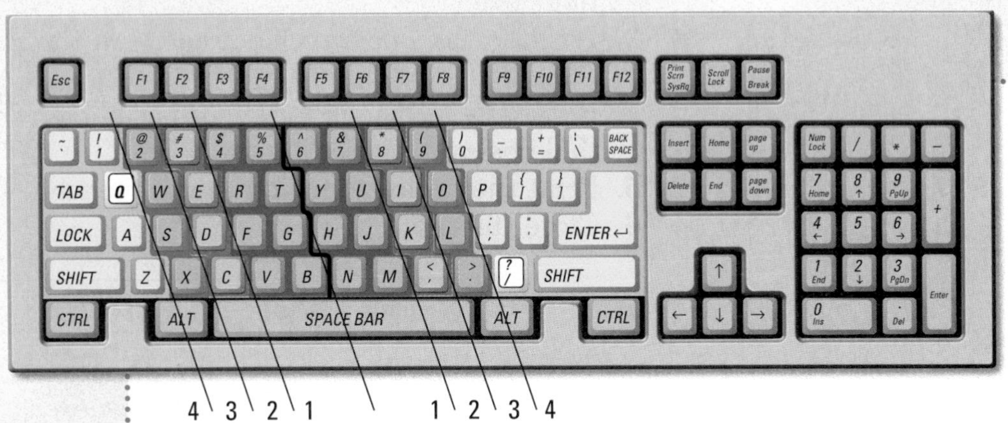

A. WARMUP

Key each line 2 times.

1 club face when silk mold brag java blue
2 Jana went biking, and Cila waved flags.

NEW KEYS

B. Q KEY

Key each line 2 times. Repeat if time permits.

Use A finger. Anchor F.

3 aaa aqa aqa qaq aqa aaa aqa aqa qaq aqa
4 aqa quo quo aqa qui qui aqa que que aqa
5 aqa quail, quit quick quid, half quest,
6 The quints squabbled on a square quilt.

ACTIVITY 6

Database Table 2

Open the file DT2 and make the following changes:

1. Change the field name *Competition* to *Event*.
2. Add a new field named *Location;* specify 16 as the field size.
3. Position the *Location* field between the *Event* and *Start Time* fields.
4. Enter the locations for events as shown in the table below.
5. Print the table according to your teacher's instructions.
6. Close the table window.

Speed Skating	The Oval
Luge	Metro Park
Figure Skating	Olympic Arena
Curling	The Coliseum
Ice Hockey	Moose Mountain

ACTIVITY 7

Database Table 3

Open the file DT3 and make the following changes:

1. Change the field name *State Name* to *State.*
2. Change the field name *Capital City* to *Capital.*
3. Add a new field named *State Bird*; specify 28 as the field size.
4. Position the field *State Bird* as the last field.
5. Enter the birds for the states displayed in the top illustration on p. 529.
6. Add the records from the bottom illustration on p. 529.
7. Print the table according to your teacher's instructions.
8. Close the table window.

(continued on next page)

LANGUAGE ARTS CONNECTION

Evaluate Databases Since databases are such a versatile way to store and search for information, they can be used with any topic. Think about each of the classes that you are taking right now. Key a sentence that describes how you could use a database to organize information that you have learned in each class. Follow your teacher's instructions for saving and printing your work.

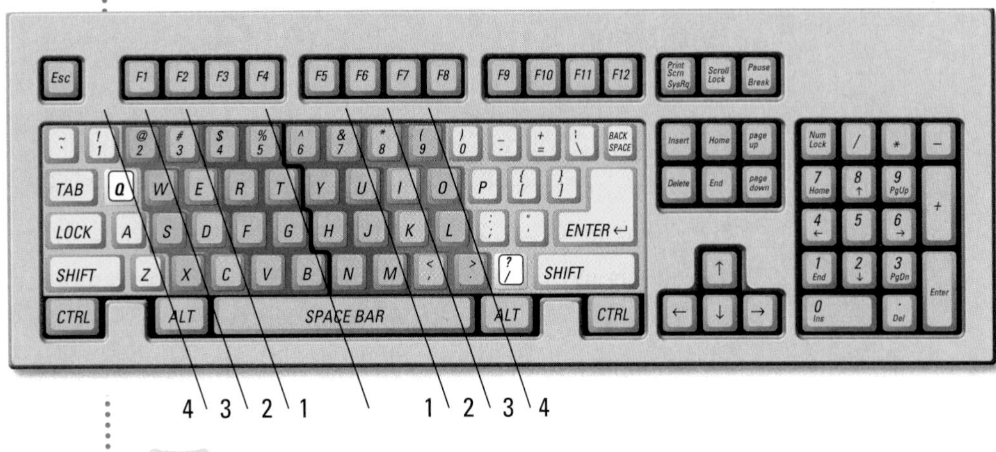

C. / Key

Key each line 2 times. Repeat if time permits.

Use Sem finger. Anchor J. Do not space before or after a slash (diagonal).

```
7  ;;; ;/; ;/; /;/ ;/; ;;; ;/; ;/; /;/ ;/;
8  ;/; her/him ;/; us/them ;/; his/her ;/;
9  ;/; slow/fast, walk/ride, debit/credit,
10 The fall/winter catalog has new colors.
```

SKILLBUILDING

D. Technique Checkpoint

Key each line 2 times. Repeat if time permits. Focus on the technique at the left.

Keep fingers curved and wrists level.

```
11 aaa aqa aqa qaq aqa aaa aqa aqa qaq aqa
12 ;;; ;/; ;/; /;/ ;/; ;;; ;/; ;/; /;/ ;/;
13 The quick squash squad requested quiet.
14 He/she said that we could do either/or.
```

E. Technique Timed Writings

Take two 30-second timed writings on each line. Focus on the technique at the left.

Keep your eyes on the copy.

```
15 Louise will lead if she makes the team.
16 Their bands will march at the quadrant.
17 Brad just had time to finish his goals.
18 I was quiet as he glided over the wave.
   | 1 | 2 | 3 | 4 | 5 | 6 | 7 | 8
```

C. 5-Minute Timed Writings

Take two 5-minute timed writings on the paragraphs. Note your speed and errors.

Goal: 40/5'/5e

The cost of attending college is quickly rising. Have 11
you thought about how you will pay for your training after 23
high school? Will you earn a scholarship or a grant? Would 35
you be willing to take out loans that must be paid back? 46
These are some of the sources of financial aid students 57
think of first. If you give it some thought, you may find 69
additional ways to earn money for school. 77

Many students earn money for education while working 88
at part-time jobs. Others find they can start their own 99
businesses. These students often provide services that are 111
in demand by fellow students. 117

Analyze your existing level of expertise to see if 127
your keyboarding skills could earn you money. Print flyers 139
to advertise your interest in providing fast, reliable help 151
with term papers for pay. If you have the equipment and a 163
collection of music, you could sell your services as a disk 175
jockey and provide the music for campus parties. 184

A creative student can probably think of other ways to 195
earn money for college. 200

SI 1.43

| 1 | 2 | 3 | 4 | 5 | 6 | 7 | 8 | 9 | 10 | 11 | 12

FORMATTING

D. Software Features

STUDENT MANUAL

Renaming Fields
Inserting New Fields
Rearranging Fields

Study Lesson 144 in your Student Manual. Complete all the practice activities while at your computer. Then complete the tasks that follow.

F. PRETEST

Take a 1-minute timed writing on lines 19–20. Note your speed and errors.

Hold those anchors.

```
19 find/seek boat fate jail cube brad swat    8
20 walk shut quid mile vane aqua slot quit   16
   | 1 | 2 | 3 | 4 | 5 | 6 | 7 | 8
```

G. PRACTICE

Key each line 2 times. Repeat if time permits.

To build skill:
- ***Key each line two times.***
- ***Speed up the second time you key the line.***

```
21 find/lose cats/dogs hike/bike walk/ride
22 seek/hide soft/hard mice/rats shut/ajar
23 boat goat moat mode rode rude ruin quid
24 fate face race rice nice Nile vile mile

25 jail fail fall gall mall male vale vane
26 cube Cuba tuba tube lube luau quad aqua
27 brad brat brag quag flag flat slat slot
28 swat swam swim slim slid slit suit quit
```

H. POSTTEST

Repeat the Pretest. Compare your Posttest results with your Pretest results.

FACT FILE

Using Slash Marks Slash marks are frequently used for entering information such as URLs into computers. For example, Google's image search engine has the URL: http://www.google.com/imghp.

The *http* before the double slashes identifies the protocol, or rules, used to transmit the information. The address, or domain name, of the Web site comes after the double slashes (www.google.com). The single slash indicates a subpage of the Web site (imghp).

Practice keying the following URLs:

www.glencoe.com/sec/index

www.smithsonianeducation.org/students/

www.reference.com/Dir/Reference/Almanac/

LESSON 144 Databases: Rename, Add, and Position Fields

OBJECTIVES:

- Key 40/5'/5e.
- Rename, add, and position fields in a database table.

A. Warmup

Key each line 2 times.

Speed	1	I hope to have the first check by the second of next month.
Accuracy	2	Jack Bowman was very excited when my quilt won first prize.
Language Link	3	His job record is the most impressive of the three interns.
Numbers	4	Read pages 17, 20, 35, 46, and 89 to see the right answers.

| 1 | 2 | 3 | 4 | 5 | 6 | 7 | 8 | 9 | 10 | 11 | 12

MATH CONNECTION

Create a Sports Database Look in the sports section of your local newspaper, and choose one sport which lists statistics. Choose the statistics that you feel are the most important. It might be the team statistics for one or more games, or it can be individual statistics for each of the athletes who are competing. Enter the statistics in a new database. Include at least four fields in the database. Follow your teacher's instructions for saving and printing your work.

SKILLBUILDING

B. Preview Practice

Key each line 2 times as a preview to the 5-minute timed writings that follow.

Accuracy	5	own analyze college probably creative equipment scholarship
Speed	6	grant could print still money their music start while think

LESSON 11 NEW KEYS: ' "

OBJECTIVES:

- Key the apostrophe (') and quotation mark (") by touch.
- Increase speed and improve accuracy.

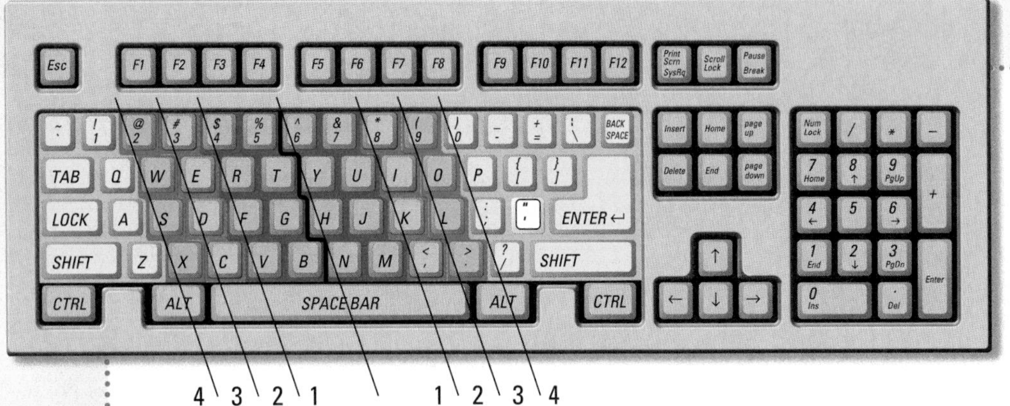

A. WARMUP

Key each line 2 times.

```
1 quill wagon cabin valued helms, and/or;
2 Jake is quite good in math but not Val.
```

NEW KEYS

B. ' KEY

Key each line 2 times. Repeat if time permits.

Use Sem finger. Anchor J. Do not space before or after an apostrophe within a word.

```
3 ;;; ;'; ;'; ';' ;'; ;;; ;'; ;'; ';' ;';
4 ;'; he's he's ;'; where's ;'; it's it's
5 ;'; ';' Kit's barn ;'; Ed's car ;'; ';'
6 Bill's car isn't running; it's at Li's.
```

(continued)

16	16	
State Name	**Capital City**	**Date of Statehood**
Alabama	Montgomery	12/14/1819
Alaska	Juneau	1/3/1959
Arizona	Phoenix	2/14/1912
Arkansas	Little Rock	6/15/1836
California	Sacramento	9/9/1850
Colorado	Denver	8/1/1876
Connecticut	Hartford	1/9/1788
Delaware	Dover	12/7/1787

Social Studies
Connection

ACTIVITY 5

Database Table 2

Open the file DT2 and make the following changes:

1. Change the date for speed skating to February 12.
2. Change the start time for luge to 11:50 a.m.
3. Change the date for ice hockey to February 14.
4. Add the following new records as shown in the illustration below.
5. Print the table according to your teacher's instructions.
6. Close the table window.

Date	Competition	Start Time
February 15	Speed Skating	9:15 a.m.
February 15	Luge	11:00 a.m.
February 16	Figure Skating	10:30 a.m.
February 17	Curling	7:00 p.m.
February 17	Ice Hockey	1:15 p.m.

SCIENCE CONNECTION

Create a Periodic Table Database Create a new database for some of the elements in the periodic table. Look up each of the elements below in a print or online periodic table. Enter each element's symbol, full name, and atomic number in the database. Follow your teacher's instructions for saving and printing your work.

No	Ra
Rh	S
Pt	Zn
He	Na

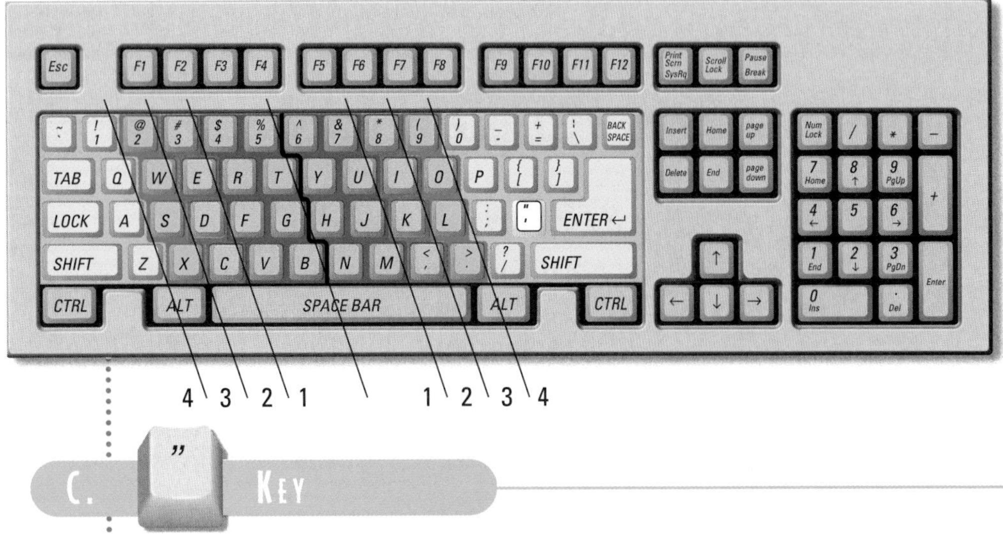

C. " KEY

Key each line 2 times. Repeat if time permits.

Shift of apostrophe. Use Sem finger. Anchor J.

```
7  ;;; ;"; ;"; ";" ;"; ;;; ;"; ;"; ";" ;";
8  ;"; "win" "win" ;"; "big" "big" ;"; ";"
9  ;"; "mew" "oink" "woof" "moo" "baa" ";"
10 "Green" means "go"; "red" means "wait."
```

SKILLBUILDING

D. TECHNIQUE CHECKPOINT

Key each line 2 times. Repeat if time permits. Focus on the technique at the left.

Key periods and commas inside the closing quotation mark.

```
11 ;;; ;'; ;'; ';' ;'; ;;; ;'; ;'; ';' ;';
12 ;;; ;"; ;"; ";" ;"; ;;; ;"; ;"; ";" ;";
13 He said "no thanks," but it was "lame."
14 Rita "forgot," but Tim added "flavors."
```

E. TECHNIQUE TIMED WRITINGS

Take two 30-second timed writings on each line. Focus on the technique at the left.

Keep your eyes on the copy.

```
15 Robb's clothes and image don't "match."
16 Mr. Quill said, "Wait." Lee did not go.
17 Jane's visit was "quick"; she ran back.
18 I haven't enough time to "quibble" now.
   | 1 | 2 | 3 | 4 | 5 | 6 | 7 | 8
```

FORMATTING

F. Software Features

STUDENT MANUAL

Editing Database Records
Adding New Database Records
Formatting Database Date/Time Fields

Study Lesson 143 in your Student Manual. Complete all the practice activities while at your computer. Then complete the tasks that follow.

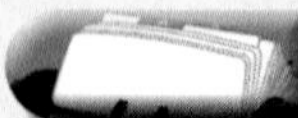

DATABASE APPLICATIONS

ACTIVITY 3

Database Table 1

Open the file DT1 and make the following changes:

1. Change the e-mail address for Jung Kim to *jkim6542@aol.com.*
2. Change the first name for Jay J. Baldwin to *James,* and change his e-mail address to *jbaldwin@csn.com.*
3. Change the first name for Carla Davis to *Karly,* and change the e-mail address to *karlyd@aol.com.*
4. Change the e-mail address for Felix Gonzales to *felixg@buffalo.net* and change the ZIP Code to *90145.*
5. Print the table according to your teacher's instructions.
6. Close the table window.

ACTIVITY 4

Database Table 3

Follow these steps to create Database Table 3 and name it DT3:

1. Define the three fields shown in the illustration on p. 525; identify the third field as a date field.
2. Specify the size of each field as shown above the columns.
3. Enter the records.
4. Print the table according to your teacher's instructions.
5. Close the table window.

(continued on next page)

F. 12-Second Sprints

Take three 12-second timed writings on each line. Try to increase your speed on each timed writing.

19 Go to the cabin and get us the dog now.
20 Now is the time to call all men for me.
21 She made a face when she lost the race.
22 Ask them if the vase is safe with them.
| | | | 5 | | | | 10 | | | | 15 | | | | 20 | | | | 25 | | | | 30 | | | | 35 | | | | 40

G. Pretest

Take a 1-minute timed writing on lines 23–24. Note your speed and errors.

23 We can't "remember" how Bo got bruised. 8
24 Burt's dad "asked" Kurt to assist Ross. 16
| 1 | 2 | 3 | 4 | 5 | 6 | 7 | 8

H. Practice

Key each line 2 times.

25 made fade face race lace lice nice mice
26 Burt Nora Will Mame Ross Kurt Olaf Elle
27 he's I've don't can't won't we've she's
28 Bo's dogs Lu's cows Mo's cats Di's rats

29 "mat" "bat" "west" "east" "gone" "tone"
30 He "quit"; she "tried." I hit a "wall."
31 sand/land vane/cane robe/lobe quit/suit
32 asks bask base vase case cast mast last

I. Posttest

Repeat the Pretest. Compare your Posttest results with your Pretest results.

LANGUAGE ARTS CONNECTION

Using Single Quotes A quotation within a quotation will use single, rather than double, quotation marks. Find the quotation within the quotation in the following sentence: "President Kennedy," said Tina, "told the nation, 'If we cannot end our differences, at least we can help make the world safe for diversity.'" Write two more sentences that use a quotation within a quotation.

(continued)

5 Which of these three carpets is the (more/most) practical?
6 Your layouts are the (more/most) appealing of any others in the display.
7 Both mountains have fantastic ski slopes; however, I prefer the slopes on the (higher/highest) one.
8 Of the two computers, the one that is networked is the (newer/newest).
9 Of the two movies you chose, the (shorter/shortest) one is the (more/most) interesting.
10 All three classes were difficult; however, math was the (lesser/least) challenging.

SKILLBUILDING

C. PRETEST

Take a 1-minute timed writing on the paragraph. Note your speed and errors.

```
11      You cannot build good skills while keying if you don't  12
12 practice various reaches on your keyboard. Practice all the  24
13 reaches that are especially difficult for you when you take  36
14 your timed writings. More practice will improve your speed.  48
   | 1 | 2 | 3 | 4 | 5 | 6 | 7 | 8 | 9 | 10 | 11 | 12
```

D. PRACTICE

SPEED: If you made 2 or fewer errors on the Pretest, key lines 15–22 two times each.

ACCURACY: If you made more than 2 errors on the Pretest, key lines 15–18 as a group two times. Then key lines 19–22 as a group two times.

Up Reaches

```
15 daily card early away date earn fear fold argue baked cargo
16 page plus rise seat voted theft tape stand rules vary plead
17 meant gift large hold hours jury grade lets films made nest
18 reach hard build good don't your skill more timed takes key
```

Down Reaches

```
19 very scope axle heavy cable value back calm cars sack bales
20 jobs each about disc badly cage cakes balk coach avid frank
21 taxi link packs rack reach palm score snack lack knee teach
22 wind vine blind came bland clans oxen column balm calm mine
```

E. POSTTEST

Repeat the Pretest. Compare your Posttest results with your Pretest results.

REVIEW

OBJECTIVE:

- Improve keyboarding skills.

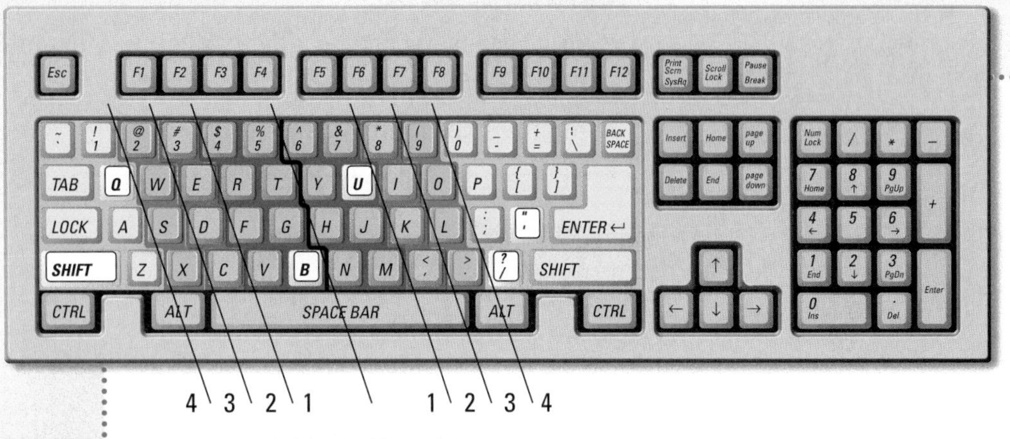

A. WARMUP

Key each line 2 times.

```
1 java blue club face when brag silk mold
2 Geof went sailing, but Lin was at home.
```

SKILLBUILDING

B. SHIFT KEYS

Key each line 2 times. Repeat if time permits.

Keep your rhythm steady as you reach to the SHIFT keys. Anchor LEFT SHIFT with F. Anchor RIGHT SHIFT with J.

```
3 Seth Kebo Otis Fran Iris Edie Jose Dave
4 Hans Cara Nita Rene Uris Vera Mark Adam
5 Theo Jean Saul Hugh Eric Noel Vida Ivan
6 Gino Leah Burt Olla Anna Kris Wade Mike
```

C. CONCENTRATION

Fill in the missing letters shown at the left as you key each line 1 time.

```
r    7 Ou- -ivers and oceans a-e being -uined.
eo   8 W- must w-rk t- mak- -ur w-rld cl-an-r.
h    9 -armful c-emicals fill muc- of t-e air.
es  10 W- hav- lo-t u-ag- of -om- of our -oil.
```

LESSON 143

Databases: Revise and Add Records

OBJECTIVES:

- Apply rules for comparative and superlative adjectives and adverbs.
- Improve keyboarding skills.
- Revise and add records to database tables.

A. Warmup

Key each line 2 times.

Speed	1	Jill has to take her time if she wants to do her best work.
Accuracy	2	Max quickly amazed Joan Bishop with five magic card tricks.
Language Link	3	Amy came at 10 a.m. to pick me up; I had left much earlier.
Numbers/Symbols	4	We ordered 130# of #8 stock @ $42.65 on April 7 and July 9.

| 1 | 2 | 3 | 4 | 5 | 6 | 7 | 8 | 9 | 10 | 11 | 12

Language Link

B. Comparative and Superlative Adjectives and Adverbs

Study the rule and examples below. Then edit lines 5–10 on p. 523 by choosing the correct word.

Rule 46: Use **comparative** adjectives and adverbs, which use *-er, more,* and *less,* when referring to two nouns; use **superlative** adjectives and adverbs, which use *-est, most,* and *least,* when referring to more than two nouns.

Of the two players, Sam is more skillful at free-throw shooting.

She is looking for the most beautiful state to visit this summer.

(continued on next page)

D. Technique Checkpoint

Key each line 2 times. Repeat if time permits. Focus on the techniques at the left.

Sit up straight and keep your feet on the floor.

```
11 The cook went to work with cork boards.
12 Four foul jugs were left at the stream.
13 Toil in the weeds to get the seeds now.
14 Tell a joke, then gather other jesters.
```

E. Technique Timed Writings

Take two 30-second timed writings on each line. Focus on the techniques at the left.

Keep your feet on the floor and sit up straight.

```
15 Ulan told Brian she would be glad to go.
16 In Boston one can see vast fish markets.
17 Bruce had this I/O switch changed again.
18 Treena saw quite a flock of "odd" birds.
   | 1 | 2 | 3 | 4 | 5 | 6 | 7 | 8
```

F. PRETEST

Take a 1-minute timed writing on lines 19–20. Note your speed and errors.

```
19 Walter took a ride to the quiet street.     8
20 Quakes threw her around the trick door.    16
   | 1 | 2 | 3 | 4 | 5 | 6 | 7 | 8
```

G. PRACTICE

SPEED: If you made 2 or fewer errors on the Pretest, key lines 21–28 two times each.
ACCURACY: If you made more than 2 errors on the Pretest, key lines 21–24 as a group two times; then key lines 25–28 as a group two times.

Third Row Keys
Check hands:
- ***Curve fingers***
- ***Hold home-key anchors.***

```
21 rook took cook cork work word ford fold
22 full fill file fire fore four foul fowl
23 jolt joke jets jerk jest just jugs jute
24 wire were went west jest quit quid quad

25 weed reed seed seat seal soil toil foil
26 dour sour sort tort tore wore sore lore
27 told hold sold sole hole role real teal
28 tire fire sire site suit quit whit with
```

H. POSTTEST

Repeat the Pretest. Compare your Posttest results with your Pretest results.

ACTIVITY 2
Database Table 2

Follow these steps to create Database Table 2 and name it DT2:

1. Define the three fields as shown in the illustration below; do not identify the first field as a date field.
2. Specify the size of each field as shown above the columns.
3. Enter the records.
4. Print the table according to your teacher's instructions.
5. Close the table window.

15	18	12
Date	**Competition**	**Start Time**
February 9	Speed Skating	10:30 a.m.
February 12	Luge	11:45 a.m.
February 13	Figure Skating	9:15 a.m.
February 14	Curling	3:30 p.m.
February 24	Ice Hockey	2:45 p.m.

*inter*NET CONNECTION

Explore Olympic Sports Go to the Online Learning Center at **KeyComps.glencoe.com>Internet Connection>Unit 8> Lesson 142** to find information about the Olympic sports listed in the table above. Complete the activity. Save your work according to your teacher's instructions.

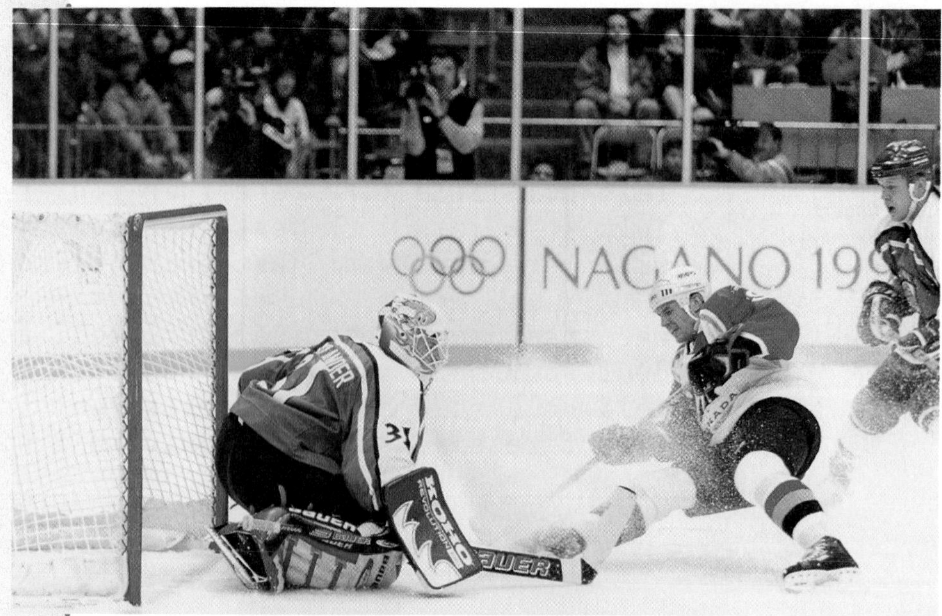

LESSON 13

NEW KEYS: P X

OBJECTIVE:

- Key the P and X keys by touch.

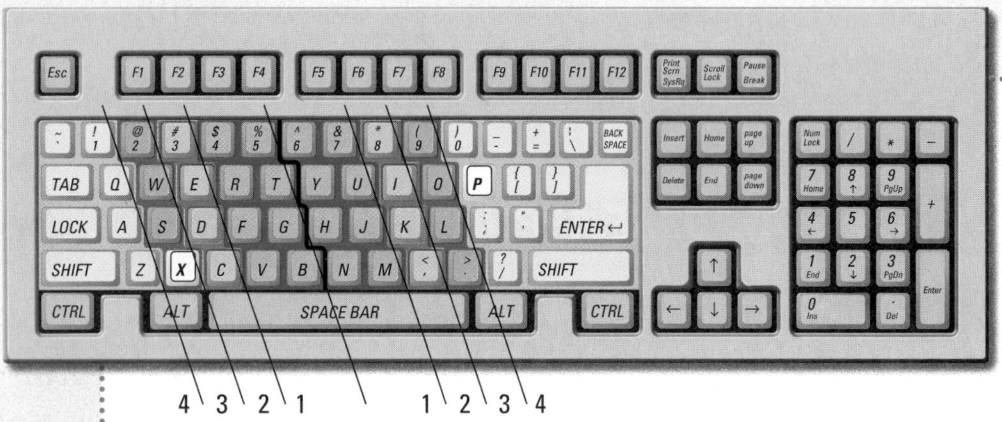

A. WARMUP

Key each line 2 times.

1 fade cave what swim quad blot king jars
2 Black liquids vanish from the jug I saw.

NEW KEYS

B. P KEY

Key each line 2 times. Repeat if time permits.

Use Sem finger. Anchor J and K.

3 ;;; ;p; ;p; p;p ;p; ;;; ;p; ;p; p;p ;p;
4 ;p; nap nap ;p; pen pen ;p; ape ape ;p;
5 ;p; perfect plot, a pale page, pen pal,
6 Pam pulled a pouting pup past a puddle.

FORMATTING

C. Software Features

STUDENT MANUAL

Creating a Database Table
Entering Data

Study Lesson 142 in your Student Manual. Complete all the practice activities while at your computer. Then complete the tasks that follow.

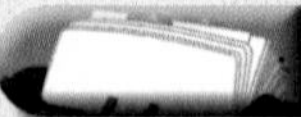

DATABASE APPLICATIONS

ACTIVITY 1

Database Table 1

Note: Paradox users simply create a table; name the table DT1.

Follow these steps to create Database Table 1. Name the file DT1.

1. Create a database and name it *Activities.*
2. Define the five fields as shown below.
3. Specify the size of each field as indicated by the numbers above the columns.
4. Enter the records.
5. Print the table according to your teacher's instructions.
6. Close the table window.

12	12	32	5	7
First Name	**Last Name**	**E-mail Address**	**Area Code**	**ZIP Code**
Jung	Kim	jkim5642@aol.com	303	80015
Steven	Stein	steven-stein@ccsdl.shhs.k12.com	719	80012
Jay J.	Baldwin	jjbald@csn.com	790	82211
Carla	Davis	cdavis547@aol.com	303	80013
Jentry P.	Mitchell	jpmitchell@nesd.sbhs.k12.com	303	80215
Karey	Fletcher	12946@netserve.net	719	82211
Felix	Gonzales	felixg@landnet.com	818	90144
Osana	Kiux	ok5466@wallnet.com	818	90128

LANGUAGE ARTS CONNECTION

Identify Databases A database is a large collection of data organized for rapid search and retrieval. They can be on computers or paper. Some examples of databases are online shopping sites, dictionaries, and library catalogs. Think of five kinds of databases that you have used. Key a sentence that describes how you used each database. Follow your teacher's instructions for saving and printing your work.

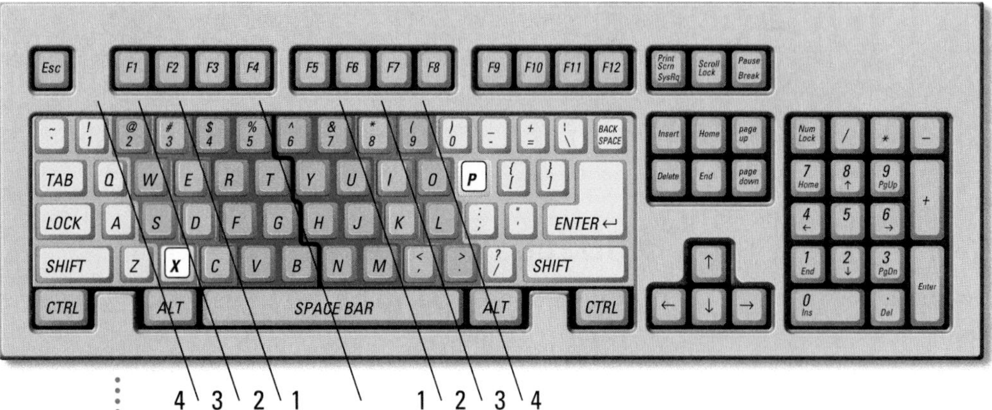

C.  Key

Key each line 2 times. Repeat if time permits.

Use S finger. Anchor A or F.

```
7  sss sxs sxs xsx sxs sss sxs sxs xsx sxs
8  sxs tax tax sxs mix mix sxs axe axe sxs
9  sxs lax taxes, vexed vixen, six Texans,
10 Fix the next six boxes on next weekend.
```

LANGUAGE ARTS CONNECTION

Use a Print Dictionary Very few words start with the letter *x*. Use a print dictionary to find words that begin with *x*. Key five words that start with *x* and use other letters you have learned to key. Then write their definitions.

SKILLBUILDING

D. Technique Checkpoint

Key each line 2 times. Focus on the techniques at the left.

Remember to keep:
- **Wrists up.**
- **Fingers curved.**
- **Feet flat on the floor.**

```
11 ;;; ;p; ;p; p;p ;p; ;;; ;p; ;p; p;p ;p;
12 sss sxs sxs xsx sxs sss sxs sxs xsx sxs
13 Phil will fix ripped carpets alone now.
14 Go see that duplex before next weekend.
```

LESSON 142 DATABASES: CREATE DATABASE TABLES

OBJECTIVES:

- Improve keyboarding skills.
- Create database tables.

A. WARMUP

Key each line 2 times.

Speed	1	I went to visit my aunt who lives down the street from Sue.
Accuracy	2	Max had a zest for quiet living and placed work before joy.
Language Link	3	Leo and Jan enrolled in an M.B.A. program at MSU last year.
Numbers/Symbols	4	Do it now! Pay Bruce *(Adams) 10% and Pauline *(Drake) 15%.

| 1 | 2 | 3 | 4 | 5 | 6 | 7 | 8 | 9 | 10 | 11 | 12

SKILLBUILDING

B. 12-SECOND SPRINTS

Take three 12-second timed writings on each line. Try to increase your speed each time.

5 Take time to drop in on us if you are now in town sometime.
6 The girl is in the third grade and does fine work for them.
7 You have made the best use you could of all that free time.
8 If he visits with us, we shall call them at once from town.

|||| 5 |||| 10 |||| 15 |||| 20 |||| 25 |||| 30 |||| 35 |||| 40 |||| 45 |||| 50 |||| 55 |||| 60

COMMUNICATION FOCUS

Share Foreign Language Tips Learning another language takes practice and study. Think of at least three tips that have helped you to learn another language. If you are not enrolled in a foreign language class, ask some classmates for tips. Key your tips in a new document. Follow your teacher's instructions for saving and printing your work.

E. Technique Timed Writings

Take two 30-second timed writings on each line. Press Enter at the end of each sentence. Focus on the technique at the left.

Keep your rhythm steady as you reach to the Enter key and back to home position.

```
15 Pull on the tabs.↵ The box will open.↵
16 Speed is good.↵ Errors are not good.↵
17 Glue the picture.↵ The book is done.↵
18 Get the clothes.↵ Bring me their caps.↵
   | 1 | 2 | 3 | 4 | 5 | 6 | 7 | 8
```

F. PRETEST

Take a 1-minute timed writing on lines 19–20. Note your speed and errors.

```
19 slag chop gate plop tops bows veal dart   8
20 apex slab gave quit fix, hoax text jell  16
   | 1 | 2 | 3 | 4 | 5 | 6 | 7 | 8
```

G. PRACTICE

Key each line 2 times.

To key faster:

- ***Read copy before keying.***
- ***Key with smooth strokes.***

```
21 slag flag flap flax flux flex Alex apex
22 chop clop clap clan claw slaw slap slab
23 gate gale pale page pave have cave gave
24 plop flop flip slip ship whip quip quit

25 tops tips sips sits sit, six, mix, fix,
26 bows bowl jowl howl cowl coal coax hoax
27 veal real seal meal meat neat next text
28 dart part park bark balk ball bell jell
```

H. POSTTEST

Repeat the Pretest. Compare your Posttest results with your Pretest results.

E. 5-Minute Timed Writings

Take two 5-minute timed writings on the paragraphs . Note your speed and errors.

Goal: 40/5'/5e

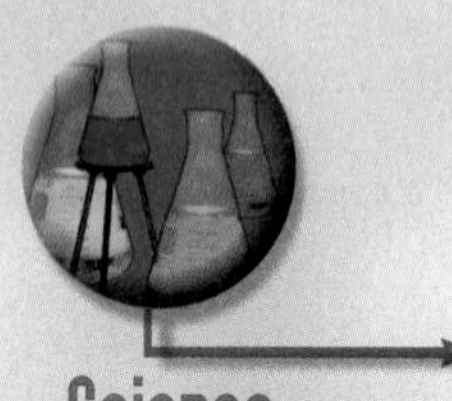

Science Connection

Comets, composed of frozen particles of water, can be 11
many miles long. As they travel through our solar system 22
from space and become visible, they put on quite a display. 34
The head of a comet is somewhat spherical, and it is 45
surrounded by a fuzzy halo called a coma. Comets also have 57
sleek tails that are made up of just gas and dust that fan 69
out behind the comet. Each comet can have as many as three 81
tails that extend miles from the head of the comet. 91
The white dust tail is the most visible. It is created 102
as heat from the sun causes frozen particles of the comet 114
to evaporate. As the particles evaporate, they create gas 126
molecules that stream off and carry dust with them. 136
A bluish tail is created as the energy from the sun 147
ionizes some of the gases of the comet. This tail streams 158
directly away from the sun. 164
The tail between the other two is formed at the head 175
of the comet by chemical reactions. It is made of hydrogen 187
and is not seen from Earth, since the atmosphere absorbs 198
its light. 200

SI 1.41

| 1 | 2 | 3 | 4 | 5 | 6 | 7 | 8 | 9 | 10 | 11 | 12

FORMATTING

F. Software Features

STUDENT MANUAL

Looking at a Database
Opening a Database File

Study Lesson 141 in your Student Manual. Complete all the practice activities while at your computer.

LESSON 14 NEW KEYS: Y TAB

OBJECTIVE:

- Key the Y and the TAB keys by touch.

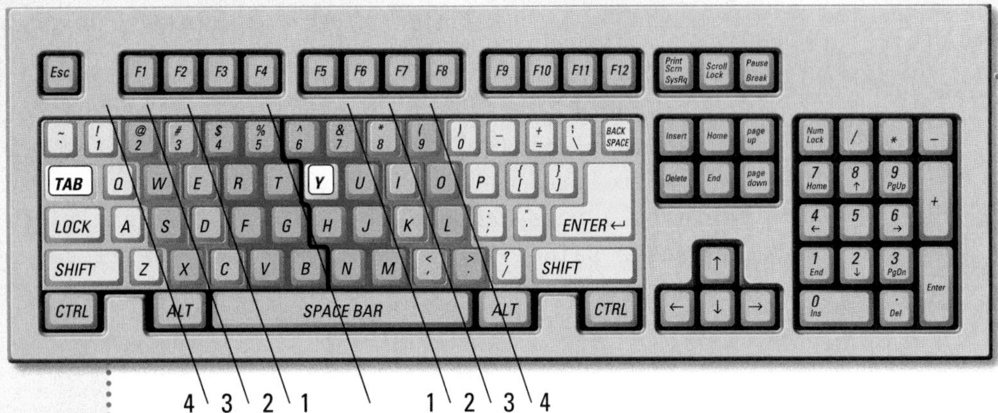

A. WARMUP

Key each line 2 times.

1 jibe wing more vase deft lack hex; quid
2 Max just put a pale slab over the gate.

NEW KEYS

B.  KEY

Key each line 2 times. Repeat if time permits.

Use J finger. Anchor ; L, and K.

3 jjj jyj jyj yjy jyj jjj jyj jyj yjy jyj
4 jyj yes yes jyj joy joy jyj aye aye jyj
5 jyj yard of yarn, July joy, yellow yam,
6 Shelley yearns to yodel but only yells.

(continued)

Rule 45: In all-capital abbreviations made up of single initials, do not use periods or internal spaces. (Exception: Keep the periods in most academic degrees and in abbreviations of geographic names other than two-letter state abbreviations.)

You will need to call the EEO office for clarification on that issue.

He earned an M.A. in business administration.

5 The meeting has been changed to 1 pm because of room conflicts.
6 Auditors said sales were understated in the June eom statement.
7 She enlisted in the U.S.M.C. after she received her PhD degree.
8 His old research paper deals with the early history of N A T O.
9 Denise said I should call about the paralegal position A.S.A.P.
10 We have consulted with A.A.A. about our upcoming European trip.

LANGUAGE ARTS CONNECTION

List Acronyms All-capital abbreviations made up of single initials, like the ones that you keyed in the activity above, are called acronyms. Each letter in the acronym stands for a word in a phrase. For example, U.S.M.C. stands for United States Marine Corps.

Key as many acronyms as you can in three minutes. Then key the phrase that each acronym represents. Follow your teacher's instructions for saving and printing your work.

SKILLBUILDING

C. Paced Practice

Turn to the Paced Practice routine beginning on page SB7. Take three 2-minute timed writings, starting at the point where you left off the last time.

D. Preview Practice

Key each line 2 times as a preview to the timed writings on page 518.

Accuracy
Speed

11 chemical evaporate atmosphere hydrogen spherical surrounded
12 from heat made other since tail sun seen dust most them and

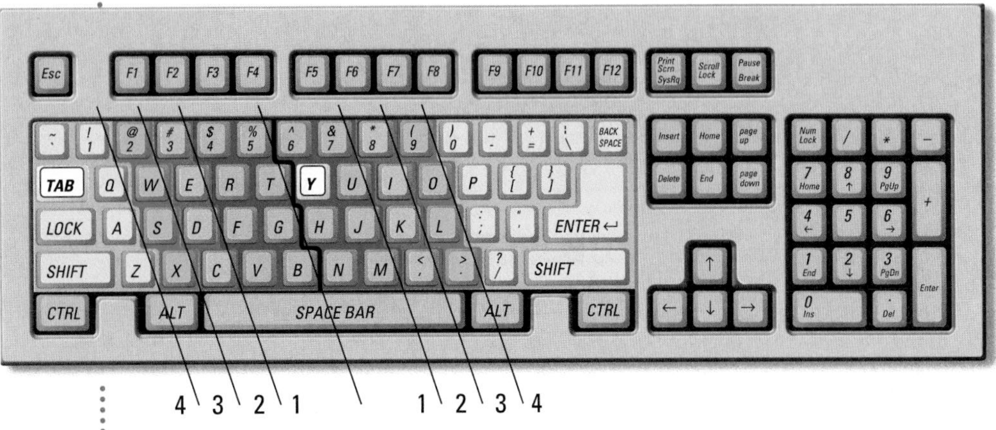

C. Tab Key

The TAB key is used to indent paragraphs. The TAB key is located to the left of the Q key. Reach to the TAB key with the A finger. Keep your other fingers on the home keys as you quickly press the TAB key.

Pressing the TAB key will move the insertion point 0.5 inch (the preset, or **default**, setting) to the right. This is the standard indentation for a paragraph.

Word wrap ***automatically moves a word that does not fit on one line down to the next line.***

Key each paragraph 2 times. Let lines wrap, but press ENTER at the end of a paragraph. Repeat if time permits.

```
7       If you are happy, you will be able
8  to set goals. You will also smile more.
9       The jury was back and no one could
10 leave the room. We all had to stay put.
```

SKILLBUILDING

D. Technique Checkpoint

Key each line 2 times. Repeat if time permits.

Keep your eyes on the copy.

```
11 jjj jyj jyj yjy jyj jjj jyj jyj yjy jyj
12 I saw yards of yellow fabric every day.
13 They happily played in the lonely yard.
14 Yes, the daily reports are ready today.
```

LESSON 141

Databases: Database Orientation

OBJECTIVES:

- Apply rules of abbreviation.
- Improve keyboarding skills.
- Key 40/5'/5e.
- Navigate and select text within a database.

A. Warmup

Key each line 2 times.

Speed	1	She wanted low rates but did not want to lose any services.
Accuracy	2	I quickly explained that few big jobs involve many hazards.
Language Link	3	Al's dad received 53 pages inside of the two-pound package.
Numbers/Symbols	4	Tell each student to get his/her parents/guardians on 9/17.

| 1 | 2 | 3 | 4 | 5 | 6 | 7 | 8 | 9 | 10 | 11 | 12

Language Link

B. Abbreviations

Study the rules and examples that follow. Then edit lines 5–10 on p. 517 to correct any abbreviation errors.

Rule 44: In lowercase abbreviations made up of single initials, use a period after each initial but no internal spaces.

We will include several states in our tour (e.g., Maine, New Hampshire, and Vermont).

We will begin our travel at 8 a.m. so that we can see everything.

(continued on next page)

E. TECHNIQUE TIMED WRITINGS

Take two 30-second timed writings on each line. Focus on the technique at the left.

Keep your eyes on the copy as you take each timed writing.

```
15 Push your fingers to find the keys now.
16 Keyboarding speed will rapidly improve.
17 Your goal is to key faster than before.
18 Try every day to achieve that new goal.
   | 1 | 2 | 3 | 4 | 5 | 6 | 7 | 8
```

F. PRETEST

Take a 1-minute timed writing on lines 19–22. Note your speed and errors.

Remember: Press ENTER only at the end of the paragraph (line 22).

```
19      A jury will meet next January to        7
20 get a verdict. People stole costly fuel     15
21 from the boys. We found bags of cards       22
22 next to the mops in the broom closet.       30
   | 1 | 2 | 3 | 4 | 5 | 6 | 7 | 8
```

G. PRACTICE

Key each line 2 times.

```
23 fuel duel duet suet suit quit quip quid
24 gape nape cape cave wave wage wags bags
25 mops pops maps hops tops toys joys boys
26 rope lope lops laps lips lids kids kiss

27 card cart curt hurt hurl furl fury jury
28 cost most lost lest best test text next
29 slab flab flap flaw flay slay clay play
30 pan, fan, tan, man, can, ran, Dan, Jan,
```

H. POSTTEST

Repeat the Pretest. Compare your Posttest results with your Pretest results.

WORDS TO LEARN

In the lessons, software, and Student Manual (SM), you will learn the following vocabulary terms for Unit 8.

Boolean operators (SM Lesson 147)
database (SM Lesson 141)
database table (SM Lesson 141)
field (SM Lesson 141)
primary key (SM Lesson 142)
query (SM Lesson 147)
record (SM Lesson 141)
report (SM Lesson 148)

CAREER BYTE

COMPOSER Composers create original music such as popular songs; music for films, TV, or advertisements; and classical music such as symphonies and operas. They transcribe ideas into musical notations using melody, harmony, rhythm, and tonal structure. Many songwriters now compose and edit music using computers. They can also use computers to record music, add electronic effects, and even convert the score into written notations. An arranger is a type of composer who adapts music to fit a particular style. For example, an arranger might transcribe a pop tune so that it can be played by a marching band or be suitable for a commercial. Arrangers can use computer software to cut and paste pieces of music and make many types of changes in musical elements such as tempo or the instruments that are used.

LESSON 15 New Keys: Z Colon (:)

OBJECTIVE:

- Key the Z and colon keys by touch.

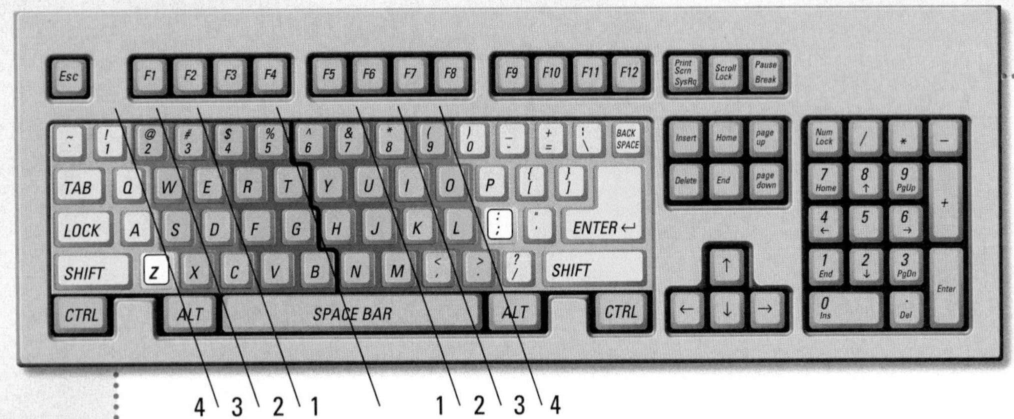

4 3 2 1 1 2 3 4

A. Warmup

Key each line 2 times.

1 bake chin jogs wave quip dome onyx left
2 His soft big lynx quickly jumped waves.

NEW KEYS

B. Z Key

Key each line 2 times. Repeat if time permits.

Use A finger. Anchor F.

3 aaa aza aza zaz aza aaa aza aza zaz aza
4 aza zip zip aza zoo zoo aza zap zap aza
5 aza dozing zebu, he zags, dazed zebras,
6 Zachary ate frozen pizza in the gazebo.

UNIT 8 DATABASES

Lessons 141–150

OBJECTIVES

- Demonstrate keyboarding speed and accuracy on straight copy with a goal of 40 words per minute for 5 minutes with 5 or fewer errors.
- Demonstrate the ability to create, navigate, and sort databases.
- Demonstrate the ability to create charts and tables and incorporate them into other applications.
- Apply rules for using abbreviations and hyphens.
- Identify proper use of comparative and superlative adverbs and adjectives.
- Compose a one-page story at the keyboard.

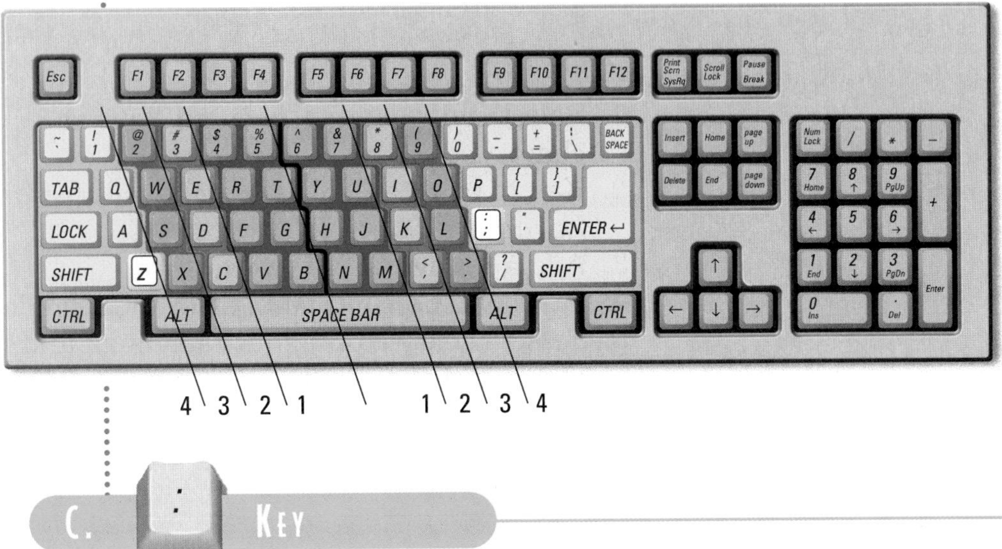

C. : Key

Key each line 2 times. Repeat if time permits.

Shift of ;
Use LEFT SHIFT key.
Anchor J.
Space once after a colon.

```
7  ;:; ;:; ;:; :;: ;:; ;:; ;:; ;:; :;: ;:;
8  Dr. Webb: Mr. Que: Mrs. Downs: Ms. Lia:
9  Mr. Dode: Mrs. Chin: Ms. Finn: Dr. Mai:
10 To: From: Date: Subject: Attention: To:
```

LANGUAGE ARTS CONNECTION

Write an Analogy Colons are used in analogies, or comparisons. For example, the analogy "water : liquid :: ice : solid" means "Water is to liquid as ice is to solid." Key the following sentence as an analogy with colons, following the format above: "March is to spring as September is to fall." Follow your teacher's instructions for saving and printing your work.

SKILLBUILDING

D. Technique Checkpoint

Key each line 2 times. Repeat if time permits. Focus on the technique at the left.

Keep your elbows close to your body.

```
11 aaa aza aza zaz aza aaa aza aza zaz aza
12 ;;; ;:; ;:; :;: ;:; ;;; ;:; ;:; :;: ;:;
13 Zach and zany Hazel visited local zoos.
14 They saw: lazy zebras, apes, and lions.
```

ACTIVITY 55
Spreadsheet 48

Open the file SS47, save it as SS48, and create a pie chart by doing the following:

1. Select cell range A4 through B12, and create a pie chart.
2. Key in bold the title *A Sample of Median Occupational Earnings.*
3. Add a border to the chart.
4. Display a percentage in each section/slice of the chart.
5. Select the slice of highest earnings and set it off from the rest of the chart.
6. Preview the chart and make any necessary changes.
7. If your teacher has given you instructions for printing, print the spreadsheet. Otherwise, save the changes and close the file.

interNET CONNECTION

Create a Career Spreadsheet Learn about different careers at the Online Learning Center at **KeyComps.glencoe.com> Internet Connection>Unit 7>Lesson 140**. Choose three careers that are interesting to you, then compile information for each career, using the following categories:

- Description of the work
- Salary range
- Training and qualifications

Create a table, using the categories above as column headers for the information that you enter. Follow your teacher's instructions for saving and printing your work.

PORTFOLIO Activity

Choose and Print Spreadsheets Choose one of the spreadsheets and the related chart you have created in this unit. With your teacher's permission, print the spreadsheet and chart and add them to your portfolio as a sample of your work.

E. Technique Timed Writings

Take two 30-second timed writings on each line. Focus on the technique at the left.

Keep your elbows in by your sides.

15 Key fast to reach the end of that line.
16 Keep your eyes on your copy as you key.
17 Tests are easy if you know the answers.
18 If they go to the zoo, invite them too.
| 1 | 2 | 3 | 4 | 5 | 6 | 7 | 8

F. PRETEST

Take a 1-minute timed writing on the paragraph. Note your speed and errors.

Remember to press ENTER only at the end of the paragraph.

19 As Inez roamed the ship, she told 7
20 fond tales. She slipped on that waxy 14
21 rung and fell to the deck. She hurt her 22
22 face and was dazed, but felt no pain. 30
| 1 | 2 | 3 | 4 | 5 | 6 | 7 | 8

G. PRACTICE

Key each line 2 times.

Check your posture.

23 waxy wavy wave save rave raze razz jazz
24 ship whip whop shop stop atop atoms At:
25 rung rang sang sing ring ping zing zinc
26 cure pure sure lure lyre byre bytes By:

27 tale kale Kate mate late lace face faze
28 fond pond bond binds bins inns Inez In:
29 gaze game fame same sale dale daze haze
30 roam loam loom zoom boom books took To:

H. POSTTEST

Repeat the Pretest. Compare your Posttest results with your Pretest results.

ACTIVITY 53
Spreadsheet 46

Open the file SS45, save it as SS46, and create a chart following these steps:

1. Select cell range A4 through E8 and create a horizontal bar chart.
2. Key in bold the title *Appliance Bids.*
3. Key the labels for each appliance and each store.
4. Be sure the chart is easy to understand; a separate legend is optional.
5. Add a border and gridlines.
6. Preview the spreadsheet and check for any errors.
7. If your teacher has given you instructions for printing, print the spreadsheet. Otherwise, save your changes and close the file.

ACTIVITY 54
Spreadsheet 47

Create a new spreadsheet and save it as SS47.

1. Enter the data as shown in the table below. Remember *not* to enter commas in the numbers.
2. Format the spreadsheet in a style similar to the illustration.
3. Select cell range A5 through B12, and sort by column A in ascending order.
4. Save your changes and close the file.

	A	B
1	***A Sample of***	
2	***Median Occupational Earnings***	
3		
4	*Occupations*	*Salaries*
5	Air Traffic Controller	91,600
6	Civil Engineer	60,700
7	Computer Programmer	60,290
8	Lawyer	90,290
9	Musician, Singer	36,290
10	Administrative Assistant	33,410
11	Teacher	44,340
12	Urban Planner	49,880

LESSON 16 REVIEW

OBJECTIVES:

- Refine keyboarding skills.
- Key 25/1'/2e (25 wpm for 1 minute with no more than 2 errors).
- Compose at the keyboard.

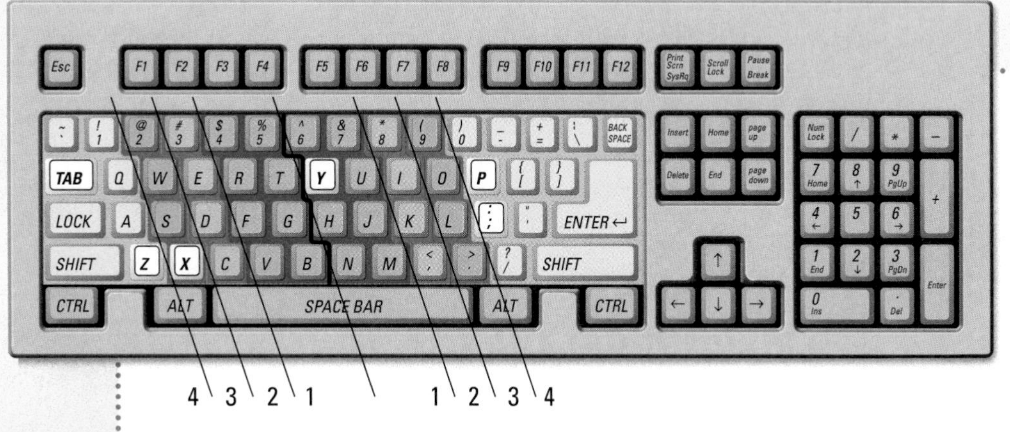

A. WARMUP

Key each line 2 times.

```
1 nest vote farm hail quid gaze coal waxy bake jeep
2 Gail must hold two jobs; she has had a hard life.
3 Kim, Ted has kept liquid oxygen frozen with care.
```

SKILLBUILDING

B. THIRD-ROW KEYS

Key each line 2 times. Repeat if time permits.

```
4 pest west test rest guest roast yeast toast totes
5 yarn yard ward word worry hurry query quirt quilt
6 Try to get an aqua shirt to wear for the picture.
7 We took your tire to the shop, but it was ruined.
```

C. PRACTICE

SPEED: *If you made 2 or fewer errors on the Pretest, key lines 9–16 two times each.*

ACCURACY: *If you made more than 2 errors on the Pretest, key lines 9–12 as a group two times. Then key lines 13–16 as a group two times.*

Up Reaches

```
 9 away card date earn fear fold argue baked cargo daily early
10 gift hold jury lets made nest films grade hours large meant
11 page plus rise seat tape vary plead rules stand theft voted
12 jump pink join pump limp join polka feats mumps kilts mints
```

Down Reaches

```
13 avid balk cage disc each jobs about badly cakes coach frank
14 knee lack palm rack slab taxi packs reach score snack teach
15 vary axle back calm cars sack value bales cable heavy scope
16 vice face save vase bear beat civic valor baker print copes
```

D. POSTTEST

Repeat the Pretest. Compare your Posttest results with your Pretest results.

SPREADSHEET APPLICATIONS

ACTIVITY 52

Spreadsheet 45

Create a new spreadsheet, and save it as SS45.

1. Enter the data as shown in the table below. Do not enter the commas in the numbers.
2. Insert blank rows 3 and 9.
3. Format the spreadsheet in a style similar to the illustration.
4. Use SUM and Fill Right to enter totals in cells B10 through E10.
5. Select cell range A5 through E8, and sort by column B in descending order.
6. Save your changes and close the file.

	A	B	C	D	E
1	***Appliance Bid Sheet for [Your Name]***				
2	***Young Quality Construction***				
3					
4	**Appliances**	**TJ's Place**	**Home Store**	**Winston's**	**Kitchens**
5	Double Oven	1,095.99	1,047.89	1,337.00	1,217.79
6	Cooktop	529.95	539.95	549.99	469.95
7	Dishwasher	519.99	559.00	479.00	439.00
8	Microwave	169.99	219.00	199.00	159.00
9					
	Totals	**2,315.92**	**2,365.84**	**2,564.99**	**2,285.74**

C. Punctuation Spacing

Key lines 8–12 two times. Note the spacing before and after each punctuation mark. Repeat if time permits.

Space once after a colon, a semicolon, a period at the end of a sentence, initials, and titles.
Do not space after a period used within abbreviations.

8 Robb passed the test; he studied about two hours.
9 These courses are open: marketing, band, and art.
10 Rachel wishes to key. Her cat is on the computer.
11 Dr. E. O. Anton was given the award in the U.S.A.
12 Gretchen received her B.S. and M.B.A. in the a.m.

D. Technique Timed Writings

Take two 30-second timed writings on each line. Focus on the technique at the left.

Press Enter at the end of each line and continue keying smoothly.

13 Ask Brenda about the summer sale. It's in Tucson.
14 Will could buy socks there. The price is minimal.
15 Today, stationery is half off. Help me buy paper.
16 Even the books are reduced. We want to read more.
| 1 | 2 | 3 | 4 | 5 | 6 | 7 | 8 | 9 | 10

E. PRETEST

Take a 1-minute timed writing on the paragraph. Note your speed and errors.

17 My cousin, Vera, has been exercising for at 8
18 least seven weeks. I did my best to keep up with 16
19 her for at least one hour today, but it was much 24
20 too difficult. She is very strong and very quick. 32
| 1 | 2 | 3 | 4 | 5 | 6 | 7 | 8 | 9 | 10

F. PRACTICE

SPEED: If you made 2 or fewer errors on the Pretest, key lines 21–28 two times each.

ACCURACY: If you made more than 2 errors on the Pretest, key lines 21–24 as a group two times. Then key lines 25–28 as a group two times.

***Adjacent reaches** are consecutive letters that are next to each other on the same row, such as* w *and* e.
***Jump reaches** are consecutive letters on the top and bottom rows keyed with one hand, such as* e *and* x.

21 as base vases lasts haste taste fasts waste paste
22 po pole polar poems point poker polka spore spots
23 tr trade trips trace strut treat trend stray tray
24 re read real ream reel reeds breeds freed decreed

25 br bran brush brute broth bring break bread brain
26 mu must munch murky mushy musty music mumps mulch
27 ze amaze gauze dozen prize blaze craze glaze size
28 cr crate crater create crack crab crib crow croak

LESSON 140 SPREADSHEETS: REVIEW

OBJECTIVES:

- Improve keyboarding skills.
- Reinforce skill on up and down reaches.
- Reinforce spreadsheet concepts.

A. WARMUP

Key each line 2 times.

Speed	1	Lee felt he could read five books by the end of this month.
Accuracy	2	Five or six dozen clubs may sign up with Karl for jonquils.
Language Link	3	Will you please order 20 pounds for the February 8 meeting.
Numbers/Symbols	4	Within 5% error, I can guess the prices of #32 and #48 now.
		| 1 | 2 | 3 | 4 | 5 | 6 | 7 | 8 | 9 | 10 | 11 | 12

SOCIAL STUDIES CONNECTION

Match Spreadsheets and Charts Use an almanac or a social studies book to find at least five statistics about a country or event that you are studying. Enter those statistics into a new spreadsheet. Then create a simple pie or bar chart from the spreadsheet. With your teacher's permission, print the chart and spreadsheet on separate sheets of paper. Mix up your sheets with your classmates', and hang them on a wall. Work together as a class to match each chart to the correct spreadsheet.

SKILLBUILDING

B. PRETEST

Take a 1-minute timed writing on the paragraph. Note your speed and errors.

5 You cannot build good skills while keying if you don't 11
6 practice various reaches on the keyboard. Practice all the 23
7 reaches that are especially difficult for you when you are 35
8 taking timed writings. 39

| 1 | 2 | 3 | 4 | 5 | 6 | 7 | 8 | 9 | 10 | 11 | 12

G. POSTTEST

Repeat the Pretest. Compare your Posttest results with your Pretest results.

H. 1-Minute Timed Writings

Take two 1-minute timed writings on the paragraph. Note your speed and errors.

Goal: 25/1'/2e

```
29      It is good that you have learned all of the     9
30 alphabet keys. With just some extra practice, you   19
31 will zip through work quickly.                      25
   | 1 | 2 | 3 | 4 | 5 | 6 | 7 | 8 | 9 | 10   SI 1.22
```

I. Composing at the Keyboard

Keep your eyes on the screen as you key; do not worry about errors.

Composing at the keyboard enables you to create documents without having to write them by hand. As you compose at the keyboard, key at a comfortable pace. Do not look at your hands, and do not worry about errors. Get your thoughts recorded.

Answer each question with a single word.

32 Who is your best friend?
33 What is your favorite sport?
34 What type of pet would you like?
35 Have you ever ridden a horse?
36 What is your favorite color?

(continued)

7. Format the date in cell A7 as *MM/DD/YY*.
8. Automatically set the width of columns A4 through E11.
9. Fill the following: from cell A7, fill down through cell A11. The dates should increase by 1. From cell B7, fill down through B11; from cells D7 through D8, fill down through cell D11.
10. In cell E7, enter a formula to multiply C7 by D7; then fill down through cell E11.
11. In cell C13, use SUM to add cell range C7 through C11; then copy the formula to cell E13.
12. In cell E15, enter a formula to subtract E13 from C13.
13. Format numbers as follows: in columns C and E, format numbers for 2 decimal places; in column D, format numbers as percentages with no decimal places.
14. Place a double line under cell range A3 through E3 and a single line under cell range A5 through E5.
15. Shade rows 7, 9, and 11.
16. Add a border around cell range A15 through E15, and bold the cells.
17. If your instructor has given you instructions for printing, print the spreadsheet. Otherwise, save your changes and close the file.

MATH CONNECTION

Create a Spreadsheet from a Pie Chart Look at the pie chart below. If there are 100 students in the school, how many students prefer each subject? Create a spreadsheet that contains each subject and the number of students who prefer that subject. Include a title. Follow your teacher's instructions for saving and printing your work.

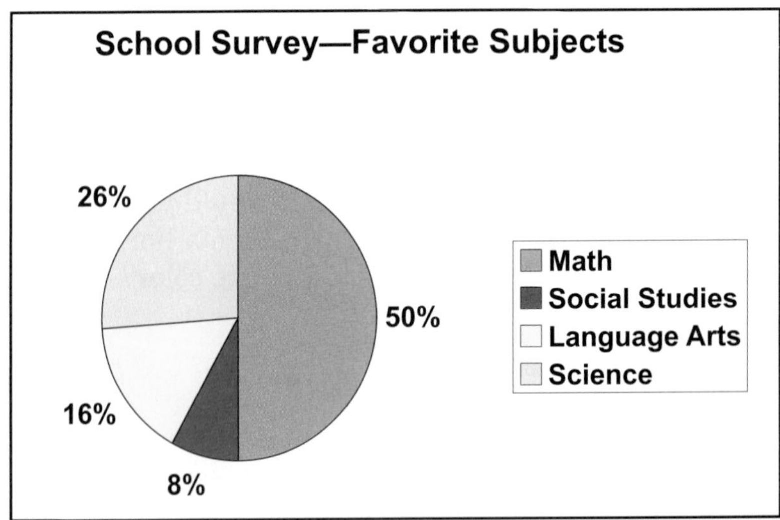

LESSON 17 New Keys: ? Caps Lock

OBJECTIVES:

- Key the ? (question mark) by touch.
- Apply the Caps Lock key to key all-capital letters.
- Compose at the keyboard.

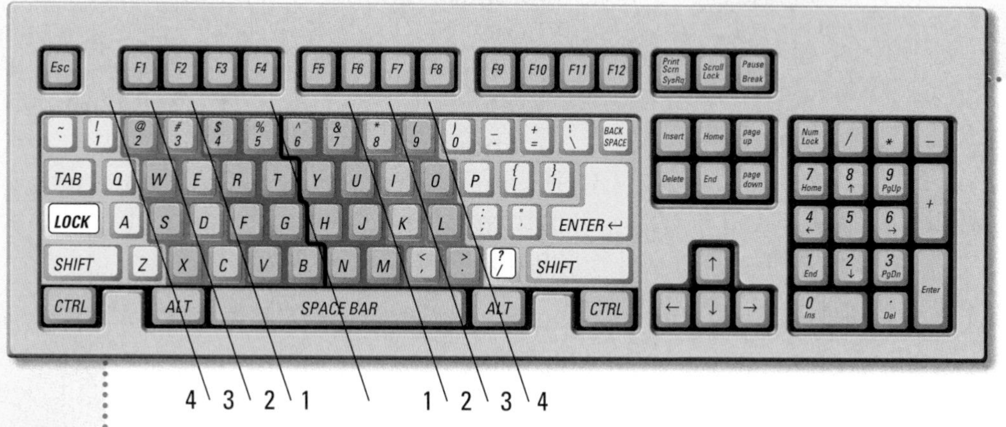

4 3 2 1 1 2 3 4

A. Warmup

Key each line 2 times.

Hold those anchors.

1 herbs jinx gawk miff vest zinc ploy quad best zoo
2 Dozy oryx have quit jumping over the huge flocks.
3 Lax folks quickly judged the lazy dogs unfit now.

NEW KEYS

B. ? Key

Key each line 2 times. Repeat if time permits.

Shift of /.
Use Sem finger and Left Shift key.
Anchor J.
Space once after a question mark.

4 ;;; ;/; ;/? ;?; ;?; ;;; ;/; ;/? ;?; ;?; ;;; ;/ ;?
5 ;/; ;?; now? now? ;?; how? how? ;?; who? who? ;?;
6 Who? What? Why? Where? When? Next? How many? Now?
7 How can Joe get there? Which way are the outlets?

(continued)

5. Select cells A6 through E14, and sort column B in descending order.
6. Select cells A4 through E14 and automatically widen the columns.
7. Change the following fonts: cell A1 to 14-point bold; cell A2 to 12-point bold.
8. Center cells A1 and A2 across the spreadsheet.
9. Shade cells A1 through E5. Place a line under row 5.
10. Shade the odd rows beginning with row 7.
11. Place a border around the spreadsheet and interior gridlines in A6 through E14.
12. Preview the spreadsheet; then change the orientation to landscape.
13. If your instructor has given you instructions for printing, print the spreadsheet. Otherwise, save your changes and close the file.

ACTIVITY 51

Spreadsheet 44

Create a new spreadsheet and save it as SS44. Then complete the following steps:

1. Enter the data as shown in the table below.

	A	B	C	D	E
1	Comprehensive Healthcare				
2	Statement of Benefits for [Your Name]				
3			Benefits	Amount	Payment
4	Dates	Procedures	Paid	Submitted	Rate
5	1/12	X-Ray/Testing		187	0.8
6				96	0.8
7				242	
8				23	
9				117	
10	Totals				
11	Patient's Responsibility				

2. Insert blank rows 3, 6, 12, and 14.
3. Make the following font changes: cell A1, 16-point; cell A2, 12-point italic.
4. Move cell range C4 through C5 to F4 through F5.
5. Move cell range D4 through F11 to C4 through E11.
6. Italicize cell range A4 through E5, and align cell range C4 through E5 at the right.

(continued on next page)

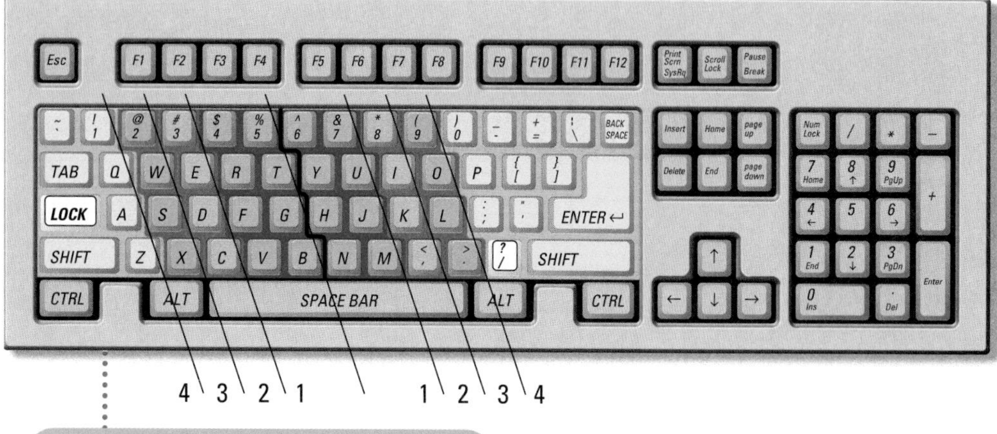

C. Caps Lock Key

Use A finger.

Press the Caps Lock key to turn all-capital letters (all caps) on and off. You must still press the Shift key to key the symbols that are on the top half of the number keys.

Key each line 2 times. Repeat if time permits.

```
8  A COMPUTER rapidly scanned most AIRMAIL packages.
9  Another START/STOP safety lever was stuck lately.
10 Was JOSE elected CLASS PRESIDENT today or sooner?
11 You should not answer my door WHEN YOU ARE ALONE.
```

SKILLBUILDING

D. Technique Checkpoint

Key each line 2 times. Repeat if time permits.

Quickly return fingers to home keys after reaching to other keys.

```
12 ;;; ;/; ;/? ;?; ;?; ;;; ;/; ;/? ;?; ;?; ;;; ;/ ;?
13 Did you see HELEN? Did you learn about her crash?
14 Her car was hit from BEHIND. She broke BOTH arms.
15 HOW will she manage while both arms are in casts?
```

E. Technique Timed Writings

Take two 30-second timed writings on each line. Focus on the technique at the left.

Hold those anchors. Quickly return your fingers to home-key position.

```
16 Tony was a better friend than Hope was to Salena.
17 Lu and I were at Camp Piney Forest in early fall.
18 I rode the Rocky Ford train to San Juan in March.
19 Maya, Sue, and Grace were there. It was exciting.
   | 1 | 2 | 3 | 4 | 5 | 6 | 7 | 8 | 9 | 10
```

SKILLBUILDING

C. 30-Second Timed Writings

Take two 30-second timed writings on lines 9–10. Then take two 30-second timed writings on lines 11–12. Try to increase your speed on each paragraph.

```
 9      One of the best ways to learn from past mistakes is to  11
10 study what has taken place in the journal of man's history.  23

11      It is a wise person who can learn from the mistakes of  11
12 others and not have to learn those lessons from experience.  23
   | 1 | 2 | 3 | 4 | 5 | 6 | 7 | 8 | 9 | 10 | 11 | 12
```

SPREADSHEET APPLICATIONS

ACTIVITY 50

Spreadsheet 43

Create a new spreadsheet. Save it as SS43. Then complete these steps:

1. Enter the data as shown in the table below.

	A	B	C	D	E
1	Great Music Composers				
2	Prepared by [Your Name]				
3	Tchaikovsky, Piotr Ilych	1840–1893	Russia	Russian Folk Songs	
4	Haydn, Franz Joseph	1732–1809	Austria	Classical	Voice
5	Beethoven, Ludwig van	1770–1827	Germany		Organ
6	Chopin, Frederic	1810–1849	Poland	Polish Dances	Piano
7	Debussy, Claude	1862–1918	France	Impressionism	
8	Gershwin, George	1898–1937	America	Musical Comedy	
9	Mozart, Wolfgang Amadeus	1756–1791			Violin
10	Schubert, Franz	1797–1828			
11	Bach, Johann Sebastian	1685–1750		Baroque	

2. Insert blank rows 3, 4, and 5.

3. Center and key in bold the following column headings beginning in cell A4: *Composer, Life Span, Country, Music, Specialty.*

4. Copy the following cells to these locations: C7 to C12 and C13; C8 to C14; D7 to D8, D12, and D13; E9 to E6, E10, E11, and E13; E8 to E14.

(continued on next page)

F. PRETEST

Take a 1-minute timed writing on the paragraph. Note your speed and errors.

20 The blind slats are broken. Can you fix the 9
21 broken ones? My WILY dog jumped out of the window 19
22 which is how this happened. There should be some 29
23 way to stop him. For a young dog, he is AMAZING. 38

| 1 | 2 | 3 | 4 | 5 | 6 | 7 | 8 | 9 | 10

G. PRACTICE

Key each line 2 times.

24 slat slit skit suit quit quid quip quiz whiz fizz
25 LASS bass BASE bake CAKE cage PAGE sage SAGA sags
26 maze mare more move wove cove core cure pure pore
27 mix; fix; fin; kin; kind wind wild wily will well

28 cape cane vane sane same sale pale pals pats bats
29 jump pump bump lump limp limb lamb jamb jams hams
30 slow BLOW blot SLOT plot PLOP flop FLIP blip BLOB
31 mite more wire tire hire hide hive jive give five

H. POSTTEST

Repeat the Pretest. Compare your Posttest results with your Pretest results.

I. COMPOSING AT THE KEYBOARD

Key answers to the following questions with a single word.

Keep your eyes on the screen as you key.

32 What day of the week is today?
33 What is your favorite subject?
34 What is your favorite food?
35 What is your favorite ice cream flavor?
36 What month is your birthday?

LESSON 139 SPREADSHEETS: REVIEW

OBJECTIVES:

- Apply abbreviation rules for common nouns.
- Improve keyboarding skills.
- Reinforce spreadsheet skills.

A. WARMUP

Key each line 2 times.

Speed	1 Our school band played in the show for four years in a row.
Accuracy	2 Our squad was amazed that Xenia would quarrel with a judge.
Language Link	3 He enjoys three types of music: popular, country, and jazz.
Numbers/Symbols	4 My check on 11/30 for $279.81 should have been for $305.06.

| 1 | 2 | 3 | 4 | 5 | 6 | 7 | 8 | 9 | 10 | 11 | 12

LANGUAGE LINK

B. ABBREVIATIONS

Study the rule and examples that follow. Then edit lines 5–8 to correct any abbreviation errors.

Rule 43: In nontechnical writing, do not use abbreviations for common nouns (such as *dept.* or *pkg.*), compass points, and units of measure, or for the names of months, days of the week, cities, or states (except in addresses).

Our sales department will meet on Tuesday, March 7, in Tempe, Arizona.

5 The new co. fleet cars are averaging about 21 miles per gal.
6 The remaining men will be transferred in Jan. to Athens, Ga.
7 On Mon., the trustee and auditor will meet with the co. pres.
8 The new product pkg. was colorful; the book was over 33 pgs.

LESSON 18 NEW KEYS: - _

OBJECTIVES:

- Key the hyphen (-) and underscore (_) by touch.
- Key 25/1'/2e.

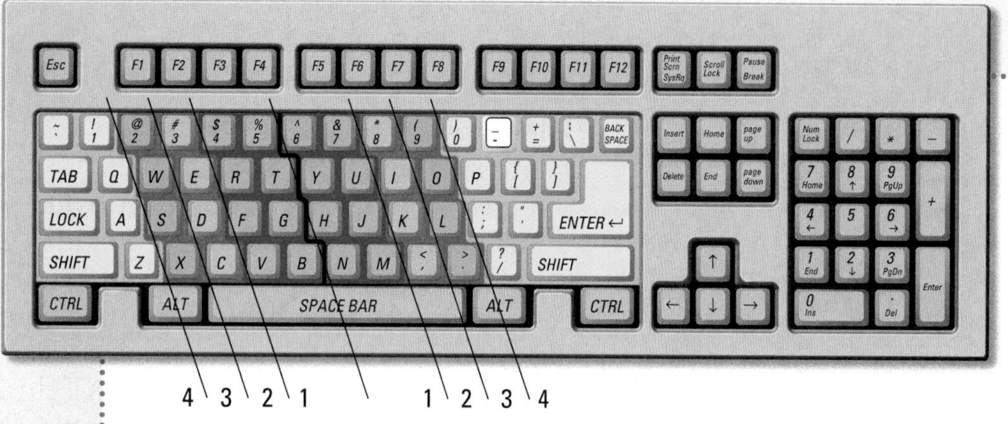

A. WARMUP

Key each line 2 times.

```
1 rave jinx tact safe mind glib quit yelp hawk doze
2 We all must be good friends to have good friends.
3 We have quickly gained sixty prizes for best jam.
```

NEW KEYS

B. - KEY (HYPHEN)

Key each line 2 times. Repeat if time permits.

Use Sem finger. Anchor J. Do not space before or after hyphens.

```
4 ;;; ;p; ;p-; ;-; -;- ;;; ;p; ;p-; ;-; -;- ;;; ;-;
5 ;p- ;-; self-made ;-; one-third ;p- one-sixth ;-;
6 ;p- ;-; part-time ;-; one-tenth ;p- two-party ;-;
7 Self-made Jim stopped at an out-of-the-way place.
```

(continued)

7. Change the page orientation to landscape and preview the document.
8. Adjust the size of the chart or make any other changes that are necessary so that all titles and labels can be read.
9. If your teacher has given you instructions for printing, print the spreadsheet. Otherwise, save your changes and close the file.

ACTIVITY 48

Spreadsheet 41

Open the file SS29, save it as SS41, and then follow these steps:

1. Delete rows 3 and 4.
2. Delete columns C, D, E, and F.
3. Change rows 1 and 2 to 10-point bold.
4. Adjust column A so that it is 20 points wide.
5. Align cell A4 at the left; align cell B4 at the right.
6. Place interior and exterior gridlines on cells A4 through B10.
7. Place a border around cell range A1 through B10.
8. Change the print orientation to landscape.
9. Save your changes, and close the file.

ACTIVITY 49

Spreadsheet 42

Open the file SS41, save it as SS42, and create a pie chart following these steps:

1. Select cell range A6 through B10 and create a pie chart.
2. Key in bold the title *Size of Small Caribbean Islands.*
3. Key in bold the subtitle *In Square Miles.*
4. Add the series labels as shown in column A. Have the actual values displayed on the chart instead of percentages.
5. Add a border around the chart.
6. Place the chart to the right of the spreadsheet if your software has that capability.
7. Preview the file and make any necessary adjustments.
8. If your teacher has given you instructions for printing, print the spreadsheet. Otherwise, save your changes and close the file.

MATH CONNECTION

Convert Feet to Inches Using the data from Spreadsheet 39, create a formula to calculate the amount of snow in feet rather than inches. Follow your teacher's instructions for saving and printing your work.

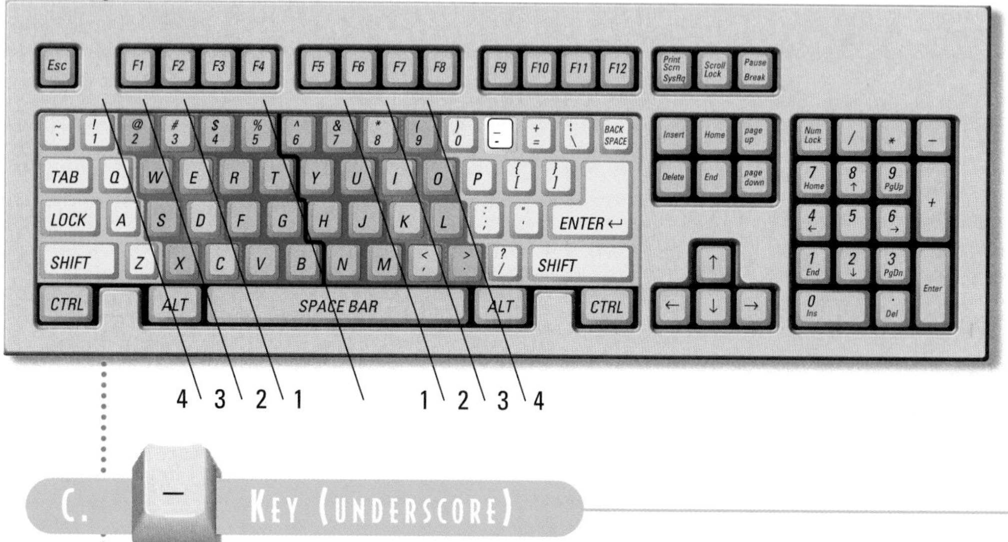

C. _ Key (Underscore)

Key each line 2 times. Repeat if time permits.

Use the Sem finger and the Left Shift key. Anchor J.

```
8  ;p; ;p- ;-; ;-_; ;-_; ;p-_ _;_ ;p-_ ;-_; ;_; ;p-_
9  ;;; ;p; ;p_; ;_; _;_ ;;; ;p; ;p_; ;_; _;_ ;;; ;_;
10 Quick, create this seven-character line: _______.
11 Be sure to use her e-mail name, jennifer_cochran.
```

SKILLBUILDING

D. Technique Checkpoint

Key each line 2 times. Repeat if time permits. Focus on the techniques at the left.

Keep your feet on the floor, back straight, elbows in.

```
12 ;;; ;p; ;p-; ;-; -;- ;;; ;p; ;p-; ;-; -;- ;;; ;-;
13 ;;; ;p; ;p_; ;_; _;_ ;;; ;p; ;p_; ;_; _;_ ;;; ;_;
14 Are you an easy-going person who gets along well?
15 The new name he now uses for e-mail is jute_rope.
```

E. Technique Timed Writings

Take two 30-second timed writings on each line. Focus on the techniques at the left.

Sit up straight, keep your elbows in, and keep your feet flat on the floor.

```
16 Steward and Phon drove a car down to the shelter.
17 Ten people helped serve meals to thirty children.
18 They said it was hard work. Jung felt happy then.
19 This might help solve these problems in our city.
   | 1 | 2 | 3 | 4 | 5 | 6 | 7 | 8 | 9 | 10
```

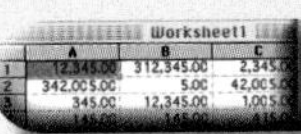

SPREADSHEET APPLICATIONS

ACTIVITY 46
Spreadsheet 39

Create a new spreadsheet, and save it as SS39. Then follow these steps to complete the spreadsheet and a correlated pie chart.

1. Key the data as shown in the illustration.
2. Bold cells A1 through B4.
3. Align cell B4 at the right.
4. Adjust column A to be 30 points wide.
5. Center cells A1 through A2 across the spreadsheet.
6. Sort cells A5 through B10 alphabetically in ascending order (A–Z).
7. Shade rows 6, 8, and 10.
8. Place 1 line under row 4.
9. Place an outline border around cell range A1 through B10.
10. Save your changes and close the file.

	A	B	C
1	Annual Snowfall at Popular Ski Resorts		
2	Prepared by Your Name		
3			
4	Resort	Inches	
5	Squaw Valley, Calif.	450	
6	Taos, N.M.	312	
7	Aspen, Colo.	400	
8	Jackson Hole, Wyo.	400	
9	Snowbird, Utah	500	
10	Sun Valley, Idaho	220	

ACTIVITY 47
Spreadsheet 40

Open the file SS39, save it as SS40, and then follow these steps to create a pie chart:

Math
Connection

1. Select cell range A5 through B10, and create a pie chart similar to the illustration that appears on page 503. Note that your spreadsheet may not create a separate legend.
2. Key in bold the title *Annual Snowfall at Popular Ski Resorts.*
3. Key in bold the subtitle *Inches Per Year.*
4. Add the series labels as shown in cells A5 through A10. Have the actual values displayed on the chart instead of percentages.
5. Add a border around the chart.
6. Place the chart to the right of the spreadsheet if your software has that capability.

(continued on next page)

F. PRETEST

Take a 1-minute timed writing on the paragraph. Note your speed and errors.

```
20      Look up in the western sky and see how it is       9
21 filled with magnificent pinks and reds as the sun      19
22 begins to set. As the sun sinks below the clouds,      29
23 you will see an amazing display of great colors.       39
   | 1 | 2 | 3 | 4 | 5 | 6 | 7 | 8 | 9 | 10
```

G. PRACTICE

SPEED: If you made 2 or fewer errors on the Pretest, key lines 24–31 two times each.

ACCURACY: If you made more than 2 errors on the Pretest, key lines 24–27 as a group two times. Then, key lines 28–31 as a group two times.

***Left and right reaches are a sequence of at least three letters keyed by fingers on either the left or the right hand. Two examples are* lease *and* think.**

```
24 was raged wheat serve force carts bears cages age
25 tag exact vases rests crank enter greet moves ear
26 was raged wheat serve force carts bears cages age
27 tag exact vases rests crank enter greet moves ear

28 get table stage hired diets gears wages warts rat
29 hop mouth union input polka alone moors tunic joy
30 him looms pumps nouns joked pound allow pours hip
31 lip mopes loose equip moods unite fills alike mop
```

H. POSTTEST

Repeat the Pretest. Compare your Posttest results with your Pretest results.

I. 1-Minute Timed Writings

Take two 1-minute timed writings on the paragraph. Note your speed and errors.

Goal: 25/1'/2e

```
32      We saw where gray lava flowed down a path.          9
33 At the exit, Justin saw trees with no bark and a        19
34 quiet, fuzzy duck looking at me.                        25
   | 1 | 2 | 3 | 4 | 5 | 6 | 7 | 8 | 9 | 10  SI 1.23
```

C. Creating Pie Charts

A **pie chart** uses a circle divided into pieces or slices to visually show the relationship among values in a spreadsheet. Each piece of the pie represents one of the values in the spreadsheet; the whole circle represents the total. Pie charts are especially appropriate for displaying percentages of a whole, and the software will automatically calculate the percentages for you.

In the following illustration, each slice of the pie chart represents a percentage of the total acres used for planting the top five crops in Texas. The labels and percentages make it easy to see which are the largest crops.

Top Five Crops Planted in Texas	
Crops	**Acres**
Cotton	6,400,000
Wheat	5,800,000
Grain Sorghum	2,700,000
Corn	2,100,000
Oats	650,000
Total	**17,650,000**

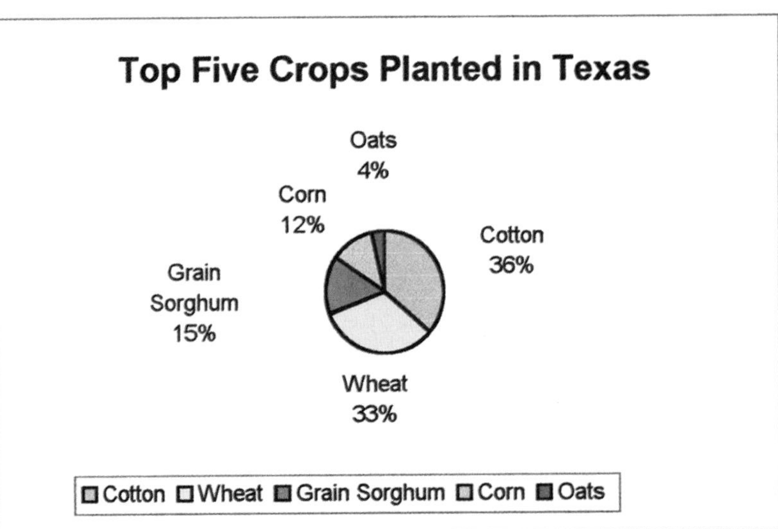

D. Software Features

STUDENT MANUAL

Pie Charts

Study Lesson 138 in your Student Manual. Complete all the practice activities while at your computer. Then complete the tasks that follow.

SKILLBUILDING

OBJECTIVES:

- Refine keyboarding skills.
- Use correct spacing before and after punctuation.

A. WARMUP

Key each line 2 times.

Words 1 fuzz busy flat apex gash avow junk quad czar mink
Speed 2 We should try to make a call before the day ends.
Accuracy 3 Rob moved a psychology quiz to next week for Jay.

SKILLBUILDING

B. SPACE BAR

Key each line 2 times. Repeat if time permits.

Space between words without pausing.

4 up by rod hub cue dry mow zip elk jaw van era ark
5 do we fad wet tab boy hid lug mug zap box kid fog
6 in my car zoo tag pop vat jar lid yam fix war qua
7 so to add fun joy run sew lad man did nip was hop

C. SHIFT KEYS

Key each line 2 times. Repeat if time permits.

Key smoothly as you use the SHIFT keys.

8 Quinton Robert Farris Cheryl Eunice Xavier George
9 Juliet Noelle Ulysses Ingmar Hunter Yasmin Melvin
10 Tamara Zachary Quenna Aurora Bryant Dawson Salome
11 Mignon Jeffrey Yvette Olinda Harold Joanna Lionel

LESSON 138 SPREADSHEETS: CREATING PIE CHARTS

OBJECTIVES:

- Improve keyboarding skills.
- Create pie charts.

A. WARMUP

Key each line 2 times.

Speed	1	The boy ran for the toys as fast as his short legs let him.
Accuracy	2	Squeeze that liquid gel into an opaque jar sealed with wax.
Language Link	3	The computer now works--she finally had it repaired Friday.
Numbers/Symbols	4	Horses #29, #35, #17, and #48 are racing at 2:30 Wednesday.

| 1 | 2 | 3 | 4 | 5 | 6 | 7 | 8 | 9 | 10 | 11 | 12

SKILLBUILDING

B. 30-SECOND TIMED WRITINGS

Take two 30-second timed writings on lines 5–6. Then take two 30-second timed writings on lines 7–8. Try to increase your speed on each paragraph.

5 Some kinds of birds sleep with one half of their brain 11
6 at a time, with one eye closed and one open to spy enemies. 23

7 Dolphins sleep with only half their brains, also. They 11
8 need to remember to surface for air since they are mammals. 23

| 1 | 2 | 3 | 4 | 5 | 6 | 7 | 8 | 9 | 10 | 11 | 12

COMMUNICATION FOCUS

Evaluate Labels It is important to label the X axis and Y axis of a chart clearly. An unclear label will confuse the reader. Choose two spreadsheets that you have not turned into charts. Create labels for the X and Y axes and create the charts. Trade your charts with a partner. Ask him or her for suggestions to make your labels easier to understand. Follow your teacher's instructions for saving and printing your work.

D. Tab Key

Key each paragraph 2 times. Press the Tab key to indent the first line; press Enter only at the end of lines 13 and 15.

12 We read the daily newspaper to learn what is
13 going on in other countries. Do you also read it?

14 Do you read or watch the news? If you don't,
15 you should. How will you learn what is happening?

E. Concentration

Fill in the missing vowels as you key each line 1 time. Repeat if time permits.

16 E-ch d-y thos- fing-rs w-ll m-ve a l-ttl- f-st-r.
17 Y-u m-st le-rn to th-nk wh-re all thos- k-ys ar-.
18 D- y-u ke-p yo-r ey-s on th- c-py y-u ar- key-ng?
19 On- d-y so-n yo-r f-ng-rs w-ll fly ov-r th- k-ys.

F. Punctuation Spacing

Key lines 20–24 one time. Note the spacing before and after each punctuation mark. Repeat if time permits.

20 Accounting is a good course. I am taking it soon.
21 Dr. Tim Bellio, Ph.D., is in the U.S. or the U.K.
22 Please turn on the TV; my favorite program is on.
23 Mr. C. L. Brickmann and his son, T. J., are home.
24 We must talk to two people: Anthony and Consuela.

G. Technique Timed Writings

Take two 30-second timed writings on each line. Focus on the techniques at the left.

Lines 25 and 26: Concentrate on efficient, smooth operation of the Shift keys. Lines 27 and 28: Space quickly without pausing.

25 Jay and Ed were on time. Iva liked doing Tai Chi.
26 Both Y. O. Fox and T. C. Ole had a Ph.D. in math.
27 Alberto, set the clock. It is good to be on time.
28 Mr. Vasquez and Mr. Mayer were not in the office.
| 1 | 2 | 3 | 4 | 5 | 6 | 7 | 8 | 9 | 10

ACTIVITY 45
Spreadsheet 38

Open the file SS37, save it as SS38, and create a chart by following these steps:

1. Select cell range A6 through D13 and create a vertical bar chart.
2. Key in bold the title *Baseball Game Attendance.*
3. Key in bold the subtitle *June 5–6, [Year].*
4. Key the Y-axis label *Attendance.*
5. Key the X-axis label *Stadiums.*
6. Add the legend labels *Capacity; June 5; June 6.*
7. Place the chart to the right of the spreadsheet if your software has that capability. Otherwise, the spreadsheet and chart will be two separate documents.
8. Preview the file in landscape orientation. You may need to adjust the size of the chart or make changes in the font sizes so that all titles and labels can be read. For example, the font size of the stadium names may need to be smaller.
9. If your teacher has given you instructions to print, print the chart. Otherwise, save your changes and close the file.

PORTFOLIO Activity

Create a Bar Chart Choose a spreadsheet that you created in a previous activity or Portfolio Project. Create a bar chart from the spreadsheet. Be sure to include a title, a legend, and labels for the X axis and Y axis. Adjust the formatting of the chart as necessary to ensure that it is easy to read. Follow your teacher's instructions for saving and printing your work.

H. PRETEST

Take a 1-minute timed writing on the paragraph. Note your speed and errors.

```
29      Have you tried to get a project completed by     9
30 a deadline only to realize that you simply will      19
31 not be able to finish it? What you do next will      28
32 depend on the project and how soon you need it.      38
   | 1 | 2 | 3 | 4 | 5 | 6 | 7 | 8 | 9 | 10
```

I. PRACTICE

***SPEED:** If you made 2 or fewer errors on the Pretest, key lines 33–40 two times each.*

***ACCURACY:** If you made more than 2 errors on the Pretest, key lines 33–36 as a group two times. Then key lines 37–40 as a group two times.*

***Up reaches** are consecutive letters on the home row and third row keyed by one hand, such as* **at**.

***Down reaches** are consecutive letters on the home row and bottom row keyed by one hand, such as* **ax**.

```
33 se seats seal pulse lease seams eases sedan mouse
34 gr great gray grows grain grade grass groan grave
35 lo love glove ploys clock locks flock block lobes
36 dr draft drift drive dress drama drums drab drape

37 av lava paved avert favor shave avoid brave raven
38 nk drink pink links crank plank sinks honks blank
39 sc scar scare scant scrap scent scoot scold scone
40 ba barks bare barns barb baby back bang bald bath
```

J. POSTTEST

Repeat the Pretest. Compare your Posttest results with your Pretest results.

K. COMPOSING AT THE KEYBOARD

Answer each question with a few words or a short phrase.

41 What do you like about your best friend?
42 Who are two people who have been in the news this week?
43 When is your birthday?
44 What is your favorite type of music?
45 What is your favorite song?

ACTIVITY 44

Spreadsheet 37

Create a new spreadsheet, and save it as SS37.

1. Key the data as shown in the illustration below. Enter the dates in cells C6 and D6 as labels. To do this, key an apostrophe before the date (*'June 5*). The apostrophe indicates that the value is to be treated like a label; it will not be visible in the cell after you press ENTER.
2. Bold cell range A1 through D6.
3. Center cells A1 through A3 across the spreadsheet.
4. Center cells A5 through D6.
5. Automatically change the column width in cell range A5 through D12.
6. Place a border under A6 through D6.
7. Format all numbers to have commas and no decimal places.
8. Sort cell ranges A7 through D12 to alphabetize the park names in ascending order (A–Z).
9. Insert a blank row 12.
10. Key the following information beginning in cell A12: *The Ball Park; 48100; 43917; 34866.*
11. Shade the odd-numbered rows beginning with row 7 through row 13.
12. Place a border around cell range A1-D13.
13. Save your changes and close the file.

	A	B	C	D
1	Baseball Game Attendance			
2	June 5-6, {year}			
3	Prepared by [Your Name]			
4				
5		Stadium	Attendance	Attendance
6	Park	Capacity	June 5	June 6
7	Shea Stadium	55600	15872	53210
8	Fenway Park	33870	20187	18992
9	Wrigley Field	38760	17438	38760
10	Dodger Stadium	56000	55110	30031
11	Jacobs Field	42400	42310	22764
12	Angel Stadium	64590	27321	58542

LESSON 20 SKILLBUILDING

OBJECTIVES:

- Refine keyboarding skills.
- Use correct spacing before and after punctuation.
- Key 25/1′/2e.

A. WARMUP

Key each line 2 times.

Words	1 itch plum jilt waxy fizz next clod quad brag skit
Speed	2 It is good to meet new people as soon as you can.
Accuracy	3 Cover the cozy liquid wax before Jack mops again.

SKILLBUILDING

B. ALPHABET REVIEW

Key each line 2 times. Repeat if time permits.

4 baffle quartz toxic veins major whack gaudy equip
5 banjo wizard rhyme heaven steep affix laugh quack
6 matrix shady squat venom jacket spill zebra fudge
7 Be quick to move them up/down; jinx lazy fingers.

C. SHIFT KEYS

Key each line 2 times. Repeat if time permits.

Key smoothly as you use the SHIFT keys.

8 Querida Arthur Donata Regina Gwynne Warden Samuel
9 Leilani Ursula Javier Margot Phoebe Irving Oliver
10 Timothy Carlos Elliot Felice Zenina Vernon Winona
11 Nokomis Isabel Hayley Pascal Justin Latham Kameko

(continued)

A bar chart uses vertical or horizontal bars to represent the values in the spreadsheet. In the illustration below, the **Y axis,** or vertical scale, displays the values from the spreadsheet, enrollment numbers that range from 0 to 6,000. The **X axis,** or horizontal scale, displays the labels, in this case the names of the schools. The legend on the right uses color and shading to identify the year the data is being charted. This chart makes it very easy to see the enrollment changes in each school over a three-year period.

This illustration displays the enrollment using numbers.

Three-Year Student Enrollment
Barker County Schools

Schools	2004	2005	2006
Buffalo	2,165	2,298	3,147
Edna	1,834	1,054	1,576
Santa Rosa	3,009	3,641	3,880
Seminole	5,316	5,203	4,921

This illustration displays the enrollment visually, which is easier to understand.

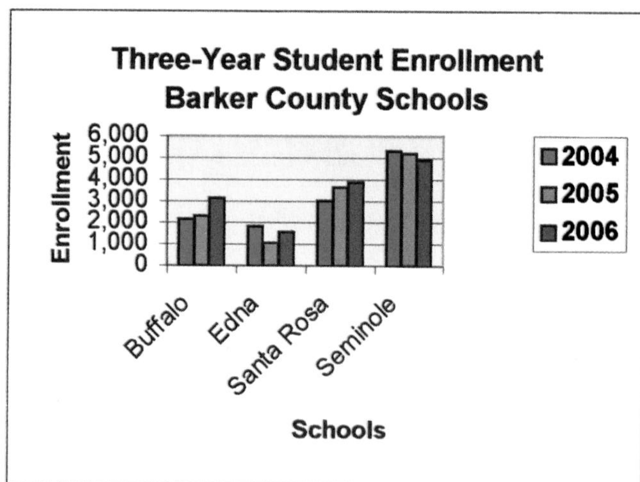

F. Software Features

STUDENT MANUAL

Bar Charts

Study Lesson 137 in your Student Manual. Complete all the practice activities while at your computer. Then complete the tasks that follow.

D. Tab Key

Key each line 1 time. Each line has three sentences. Before each sentence in the line, press the Tab key. After each sentence, press Enter. Repeat if time permits.

Press the Tab key to begin each sentence, and press Enter at the end of each sentence.

12 Did you meet your goals? I did not. They all did.
13 My car is stuck. I need it towed. Will you do it?
14 Let's see a movie. What's playing? I do not know.
15 Look at that. It is quite amazing. I am thrilled.

E. Concentration

Fill in the missing vowels as you key each line 1 time. Repeat if time permits.

16 K--p all f-ng-rs curv-d -nd y--r wr-sts up a b-t.
17 Ke-p yo-r b-ck er-ct, b-t le-n yo-r b-dy forw-rd.
18 Ke-p y-ur elb-ws r-lax-d and cl-se to y-ur s-des.
19 K-ep y-ur h-ad up -nd t-rned tow-rd th- textb--k.
20 K-ep b-th fe-t on th- flo-r, on- aft-r th- oth-r.

F. Punctuation Spacing

Key lines 21–25 one time. Note the spacing before and after each punctuation mark. Repeat if time permits.

21 Tom's flowers--especially the tulips--are lovely.
22 Have you seen her gloves? Are they in the drawer?
23 If Leilani can go tomorrow, we will go then also.
24 Estes Park has roads as well as hike/bike trails.
25 That fly-by-night business was selling old disks.

D. 5-Minute Timed Writings

Take two 5-minute timed writings on the paragraphs. Note your speed and errors.

Goal: 40/5'/5e

Social Studies Connection

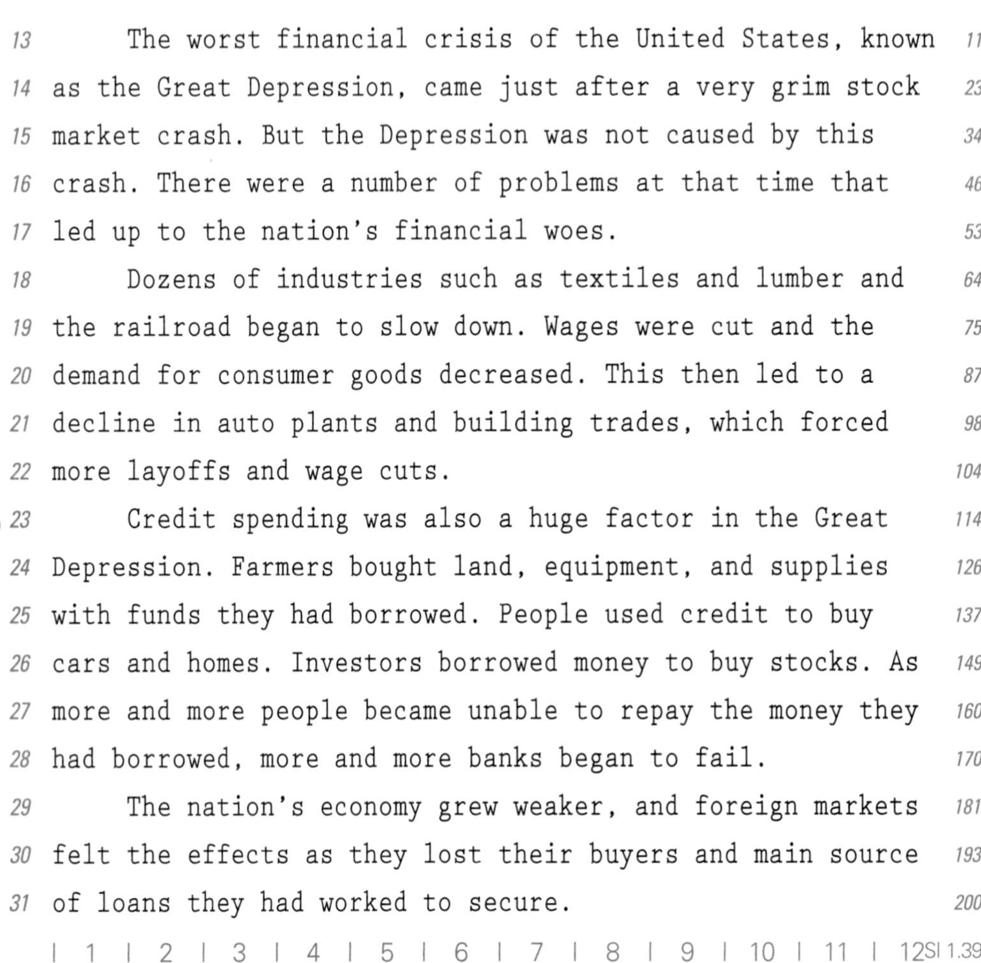

The worst financial crisis of the United States, known 11
as the Great Depression, came just after a very grim stock 23
market crash. But the Depression was not caused by this 34
crash. There were a number of problems at that time that 46
led up to the nation's financial woes. 53

Dozens of industries such as textiles and lumber and 64
the railroad began to slow down. Wages were cut and the 75
demand for consumer goods decreased. This then led to a 87
decline in auto plants and building trades, which forced 98
more layoffs and wage cuts. 104

Credit spending was also a huge factor in the Great 114
Depression. Farmers bought land, equipment, and supplies 126
with funds they had borrowed. People used credit to buy 137
cars and homes. Investors borrowed money to buy stocks. As 149
more and more people became unable to repay the money they 160
had borrowed, more and more banks began to fail. 170

The nation's economy grew weaker, and foreign markets 181
felt the effects as they lost their buyers and main source 193
of loans they had worked to secure. 200

| 1 | 2 | 3 | 4 | 5 | 6 | 7 | 8 | 9 | 10 | 11 | 12 SI 1.39

FORMATTING

E. Bar Charts

Information in a spreadsheet can be used to create bar charts. A **bar chart** is a type of picture or graph that shows the relationships among values. The bars may be different colors or patterns. In some programs the spreadsheet and chart are two separate documents; other programs let you place the chart inside the spreadsheet.

(continued on next page)

G. Technique Timed Writings

Take two 30-second timed writings on each line. Focus on the technique at the left.

Key smoothly as you operate the SHIFT ***keys.***

26 Oliver let Margo answer the TCP/IP Internet quiz.
27 Connecting with the World Wide Web was difficult.
28 Janice learned about URLs, FTP, and TCP/IP sites.
29 Sam, Jo, and Di were fluent in German and French.
| 1 | 2 | 3 | 4 | 5 | 6 | 7 | 8 | 9 | 10

H. PRETEST

Take a 1-minute timed writing on the paragraph. Note your speed and errors.

30 There are fewer golf courses in Clark County 9
31 than in Milton County. One reason is the need for 19
32 rich soil to grow grass. Clark County has mostly 29
33 clay soil, which does not absorb water well. 38
| 1 | 2 | 3 | 4 | 5 | 6 | 7 | 8 | 9 | 10

I. PRACTICE

SPEED: If you made 2 or fewer errors on the Pretest, key lines 34–41 two times.

ACCURACY: If you made more than 2 errors on the Pretest, key lines 34–37 as a group two times. Then key lines 38–41 as a group two times.

***Discrimination reaches** are keys that are commonly substituted and easily confused, such as* w *and* e.

34 asa aside sadly flask sails saved trash masks sas
35 fgf fight goofs golfs fugue gaffe foggy frogs gfg
36 wew weans sweet swell sweat sewer fewer weeks ewe
37 rtr art part port sort fort worth trade title rtr

38 klk kilns kilts kelts keels flock block locks lkl
39 nmn means lemon minor numbs names money hymns mnm
40 oio boils soils joins coins lions toils spoil ioi
41 jhj joy jewels judge huge hugs jugs just jury jhj

J. POSTTEST

Repeat the Pretest. Compare your Posttest results with your Pretest results.

(continued)

Rule 41: Use a dash instead of a comma, semicolon, colon, or parentheses when you want to convey a more forceful separation of words within a sentence.

At the meeting, the speakers—and topics—were superb.

The icy road—slippery as a fish—was a hazard.

Rule 42: Use a period, rather than a question mark, at the end of a sentence that is a polite request. (Consider a sentence a polite request if you expect the reader to act or do as you ask rather than give you a yes-or-no answer.)

Will you please fax us a copy of the insurance policy today.

Will you please close the door before you are seated.

```
5  Her birthday present a World Atlas was finally delivered.
6  Since you are going to the pharmacy, will you buy vitamins.
7  Will you please send Guy your resume by e-mail before 11 a.m.
   today?
8  Several brands of soaps are on sale Zest, Dial, and Ivory.
9  The radio station not my favorite was giving the weather.
10 Living in the country has advantages quiet, calm, and tranquil
   days.
```

LANGUAGE ARTS CONNECTION

Explain Punctuation Rules Compose and key two sentences for each of the rules explained in the Language Link above. Exchange your examples with a classmate and make any corrections. Save your work according to your teacher's instructions.

SKILLBUILDING

C. Preview Practice

Key each line 2 times as a preview to the timed writings on page 498.

```
11 slow Dozens textile borrowed equipment financial Depression
12 layoffs markets lumber demand crash grew main cars fail pay
```

K. 1-Minute Timed Writings

Take two 1-minute timed writings on the paragraph. Note your speed and errors.

Goal: 25/1'/2e

```
     Paul bought five quartz watches. He expects    9
to give me one just to show his thanks. He will    19
also give me a large dog today.                    25
| 1 | 2 | 3 | 4 | 5 | 6 | 7 | 8 | 9 | 10   SI 1.16
```

PORTFOLIO *Activity*

Create a Portfolio A portfolio is a collection of the best documents and projects that you have created to showcase your abilities and document the progress you have made. Items in a portfolio can be saved on the computer or on paper. Portfolios can be used in a class to show the range of work you have done and the skills you have acquired. It is also common to create a portfolio to show your best work to a potential employer.

If your teacher allows you to print your work, save your favorites in a folder to use as your portfolio. Make sure to choose different types of projects to display a range of skills.

*inter*NET CONNECTION

Explore the Online Learning Center Go to the Online Learning Center (OLC) at **KeyComps.glencoe.com.** Click on at least five of the links that you find. Key a short phrase that describes what you find when you click on each link. Follow your teacher's instructions for saving and printing your work.

LESSON 137

Spreadsheets: Creating Bar Charts

OBJECTIVES:

- Apply rules for colons, dashes, and periods.
- Key 40/5'/5e.
- Create a bar chart.

A. Warmup

Key each line 2 times.

Speed	1	`A friend would like to go to the school play with me later.`
Accuracy	2	`The banquet speaker, James Carvings, analyzed a few hoaxes.`
Language Link	3	`The flight attendant got huge, soft pillows for her and me.`
Numbers/Symbols	4	`Flight #1389 arrived late--7 p.m. (It was due at 6:45 p.m.)`
		| 1 | 2 | 3 | 4 | 5 | 6 | 7 | 8 | 9 | 10 | 11 | 12

Language Link

B. Colons, Dashes, and Periods

Study the rules and examples that follow. Then edit lines 5–10 to correct any errors in the use of colons, dashes, and periods.

Rule 40: Use a colon to introduce explanatory material that follows an independent clause. (An **independent clause** is one that can stand alone as a complete sentence.)

> *The computer satisfies three criteria: speed, cost, and power.*
>
> *There are many fine poets: Shelley, Keats, and Frost.*

(continued on next page)

UNIT 2 KEYBOARDING

Lessons 21–40

OBJECTIVES

- Demonstrate which fingers control the number and symbol keys.
- Refine and improve keyboarding techniques.
- Demonstrate proficiency on the numeric keypad.
- Use proper spacing before and after special symbols.
- Key at a speed of 27 words per minute for 2 minutes with 4 or fewer errors.
- Compose short phrases at the keyboard.
- Apply capitalization rules.

ACTIVITY 43
Spreadsheet 36

Create a new spreadsheet, save it as SS36, and then follow these steps to create a multiplication table.

1. Key the data as shown in the illustration below.
2. Use Fill Series to fill in the numbers in cells B4 and C4 to M4. The last number should be *12*.
3. Bold the numbers.
4. Use Fill Series to fill in the numbers in cells A5 and A6 to A16. The last number should be *12*.
5. Bold the numbers.
6. Use Fill Series to fill in the numbers in cells B5 through C6 to D5 through M6.
7. Use Fill Series to fill in the numbers in cells B5 through M6 to B7 through M16. The number in M16 should be *144*.
8. Change cell A1 to 16-point bold.
9. Change cell A2 to 12-point bold.
10. Center cells A1 through A2 across the spreadsheet.
11. Shade cells B4 through M4 and A5 through A16.
12. Select cell range B5 through M16. Place a thin-line border around each cell.
13. Place a heavy-line border around the entire spreadsheet.
14. Change to landscape orientation.
15. If your teacher has given you instructions on how to print, print the spreadsheet. Otherwise, save your changes and close the file.

Math Connection

	A	B	C
1	Multiplication Tables		
2	Prepared by Your Name		
3			
4		1	2
5	1	1	2
6	2	2	4

MATH CONNECTION

Apply the Fill Series Command As you have learned, the Fill Series command is used to create data with a pattern. You used the Fill Series command in the activity above to create multiplication tables. Think about other types of mathematical data that could be completed with the Fill Series command. Key a short paragraph that describes three types. Follow your teacher's instructions for saving and printing your work.

WORDS TO LEARN

In the lessons, software, and Student Manual (SM), you will learn the following vocabulary terms for Unit 2.

homonym (p. 129) **homophone (p. 129)**

CAREER BYTE

GEOLOGIST Geologists use technology to study the physical aspects and history of Earth. They identify and examine rocks, study information collected by remote sensing instruments in satellites, conduct geological surveys, construct field maps, and use instruments to measure Earth's gravity and magnetic field.

Many geologists and geophysicists search for oil, natural gas, minerals, and groundwater. Some geologists use two- or three-dimensional computer modeling to portray water layers and the flow of water or other fluids through rock cracks and porous materials. Other geological scientists use computers to analyze conditions and develop solutions to environmental problems.

ACTIVITY 42

Spreadsheet 35

Open the file SS34, save it as SS35, and then follow these steps:

1. In row 4, use Fill Series to complete the months through June, which should be in column G.
2. In column A, complete the days through Sunday which will be in row 12.
3. Use Fill Down to copy cells B6 through C7 to B8 through C10.
4. Use Fill Right to copy cell range C6 through C10 to D6 through D10.
5. Use Fill Down to copy cells E6 through F7 to E8 through F10.
6. Use Fill Down to copy cells G6 through G7 to G8 through G9.
7. Use Fill Right to copy cell B11 to C11 through G11.
8. Use Fill Down to copy cell range B11 through G11 to B12 through G12.
9. Bold and center the names of the months.
10. Bold the names of the days.
11. Select cell range A6 through G12 and automatically widen the columns.
12. Change cells A1 and A2 to 12-point bold and center each line above the block A1 through G1 and A2 through G2.
13. Shade cell range A1 through G2. Add a border at the bottom of cell range A2 through G2.
14. Shade cell ranges B3 through B12; D3 through D12; and F3 through F12.
15. Place a border around cell range A1 through G12.
16. Save your changes and close the file.

COMMUNICATION FOCUS

Create a Tutorial When you are teaching someone how to do something new, it is important to communicate clearly. If you wanted to teach a family member or friend to use Fill Series, Fill Right, and Fill Down, and you did not have your textbook, how would you do it?

Create a tutorial that explains in your own words how to use Fill Series, Fill Right, and Fill Down. Divide the tutorial into steps so that it is easy to follow. Follow your teacher's instructions for saving and printing your work.

LESSON 21 NEW KEYS: 4 $ 7 &

OBJECTIVES:

- Key the 4, $, 7, and & by touch.
- Refine keyboarding techniques.
- Key 27/2'/4e.

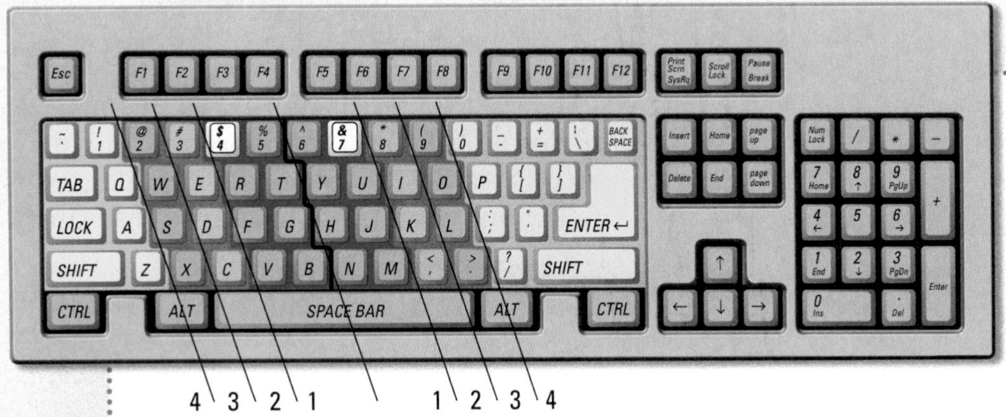

A. WARMUP

Key each line 2 times.

Words 1 shot idea jobs corn quip give flex whey maze elks
Speed 2 It is not a good idea to play ball in the street.
Accuracy 3 My joke expert amazed five huge clowns in Quebec.

NEW KEYS

B. 4 AND $ KEYS

Key each line 2 times. Repeat if time permits.

Use F finger. Anchor A.

4 frf fr4f f4f 444 f4f 4/44 f4f 44.4 f4f 44,444 f4f
5 44 films, 44 foes, 44 flukes, 44 folders, or 4.44
6 I saw 44 ducks, 4 geese, and 4 swans on the lake.
7 Today, our team had 4 runs, 4 hits, and 4 errors.

$ is the shift of 4. Do not space between the $ and the number.

8 frf fr4 f4f f4$f f$f f$f $4 $44 $444 f$f f4f $444
9 $444, 44 fish, 4 fans, $44, 444 fellows, $4, $444
10 Jo paid $44 for the oranges and $4 for the pears.
11 They had $444 and spent $44 of it for 4 presents.

FORMATTING

C. Fill Right, Fill Down, and Fill Series

Spreadsheet fill commands reproduce or copy the same data down a column (**Fill Down**) or across a row (**Fill Right**). Fill commands can be used with text and values, including formulas.

The **Fill Series** command is used to create data with a pattern. For example, if you key *Monday* and *Tuesday* in cells A1 and B1, you can use the fill command to fill cells C1 through G1 with the rest of the days. The same is true for months and numbers that have a pattern such as *5, 10, 15* or *15, 12, 9*. The fill commands generate data quickly and accurately and are great time-savers.

D. Software Features

STUDENT MANUAL

Fill Right/Fill Down
Fill Series

Study Lesson 136 in your Student Manual. Complete all the practice activities while at your computer. Then complete the tasks that follow.

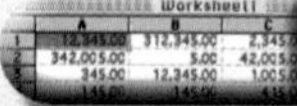

SPREADSHEET APPLICATIONS

ACTIVITY 41

Spreadsheet 34

Create a new spreadsheet and save it as SS34. Then follow these steps:

1. Key the data as shown in the illustration below, using Copy and Paste where applicable.

	A	B	C	D	E	F	G
1		January	February				
2							
3	Monday	8 a.m.-5 p.m.	8 a.m.-5 p.m.		7 a.m.-4 p.m.	7 a.m.-4 p.m.	7 a.m.-6 p.m.
4	Tuesday	8 a.m.-5 p.m.	8 a.m.-5 p.m.		7 a.m.-4 p.m.	7 a.m.-4 p.m.	7 a.m.-6 p.m
5							
6							
7							Closed
8		Closed					

2. Insert 3 blank rows above row 1.
3. In cell A1, key the label *Proposed Work Schedule for Carlton, Inc.*
4. In cell A2, key *Prepared by* followed by your name.
5. Save your changes and close the file.

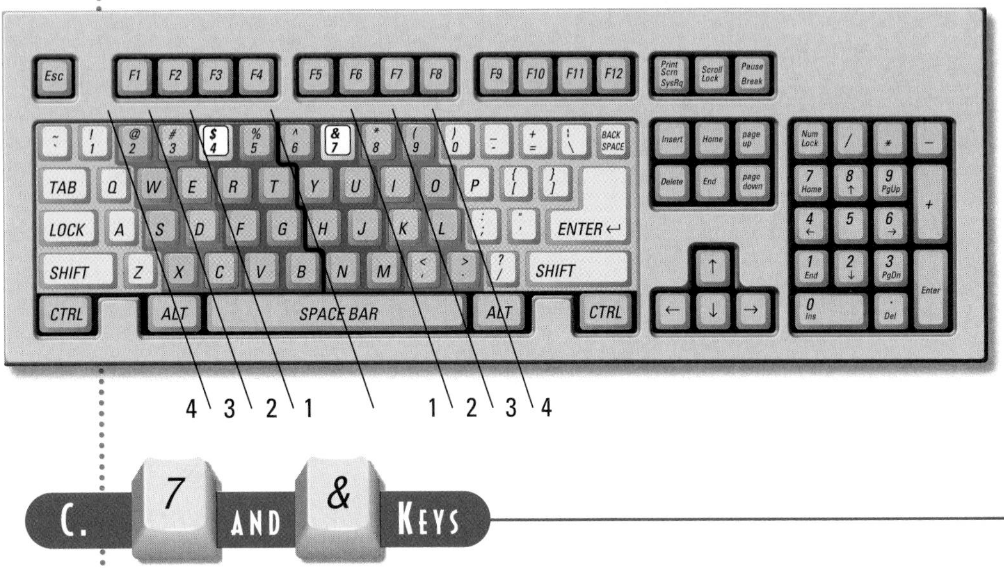

C. 7 AND & KEYS

Key each line 2 times. Repeat if time permits.

Use J finger. Anchor ;.

12 juj ju7j j7j 777 j7j 7/77 j7j 77.7 j7j 77,777 j7j
13 77 jokers, 77 joggers, 77 jets, or 7.77, 77 jumps
14 Hank will perform July 4 and 7, not June 4 and 7.
15 On July 4, we celebrated; on August 7, we rested.

Use J finger and LEFT SHIFT. Anchor ;. Space before and after the ampersand.

16 juj ju7 j7j j7&j j&j j&j j& &j& ju7& j&j j7j ju7&
17 7 jugs & 7 jars & 7 jewels & 7 jurors & 7 jungles
18 He thinks he paid $44 & $77 instead of $47 & $74.
19 B & C ordered 744 from Dixon & Sons on January 7.

SKILLBUILDING

D. TECHNIQUE TIMED WRITINGS

Take two 30-second timed writings on each line. Focus on the techniques at the left.

Lines 20 and 21: Keep your eyes on the copy. Lines 22 and 23: Space without pausing.

20 Kara saw a ship as she was walking over the hill.
21 Ned says he can mend the urn that fell and broke.
22 The five of us had to get to the bus before noon.
23 Lou said he would be at the game to see us later.

| 1 | 2 | 3 | 4 | 5 | 6 | 7 | 8 | 9 | 10

Spreadsheets: Fill Right/Fill Down Commands

OBJECTIVES:

- Improve keyboarding skills.
- Use Fill Right and Fill Down commands in a spreadsheet.
- Use Fill Series command in a spreadsheet.

A. Warmup

Key each line 2 times.

Speed	1	The boys will not go to the zoo as was said at the meeting.
Accuracy	2	Liza quit her job, packed six new bags, and moved far away.
Language Link	3	It was she who thought she could get seats at today's game.
Numbers/Symbols	4	You will set tabs for these jobs at 18, 24, 37, 42, and 54.

| 1 | 2 | 3 | 4 | 5 | 6 | 7 | 8 | 9 | 10 | 11 | 12

SKILLBUILDING

B. 30-Second OK Timed Writings

Take two 30-second OK (error-free) timed writings on lines 5–6. Then take two 30-second OK timed writings on lines 7–8. Goal: no errors.

5 Quinn was in a daze after watching six rented movies; 11
6 she wanted to jot down the plots before she forgot them. 23

7 Marvin went to buy zippers to fix the jeans, but then 11
8 he could not squeeze his vehicle into the parking place. 23

| 1 | 2 | 3 | 4 | 5 | 6 | 7 | 8 | 9 | 10 | 11 | 12

E. PRETEST

Take a 1-minute timed writing on the paragraph. Note your speed and errors.

24 Each of us should try to eat healthful food, 9
25 get proper rest, and exercise moderately. All of 19
26 these things will help each of us face life with 29
27 more enthusiasm and more energy. 35

| 1 | 2 | 3 | 4 | 5 | 6 | 7 | 8 | 9 | 10

F. PRACTICE

SPEED: ***If you made 2 or fewer errors on the Pretest, key lines 28–35 two times.***

ACCURACY: ***If you made more than 2 errors on the Pretest, key lines 28–31 as a group two times. Then key lines 32–35 as a group two times.***

Adjacent Reaches

28 tr train tree tried truth troop strum strip stray
29 op open slope opera sloop moped scoop hoped opine
30 er were loner every steer error veers sewer verge
31 po port porter pole pods potter potion pound pout

Jump Reaches

32 on onion ozone upon honor front spoon phone wrong
33 ex exams exist exact flex exits exalt vexed Texas
34 ve even veers vests verbs leave every verge heave
35 ni nine ninth night nimble nifty nice nickel nigh

G. POSTTEST

Repeat the Pretest. Compare your Posttest results with your Pretest results.

H. 1-MINUTE ALPHANUMERIC TIMED WRITING

Take a 1-minute timed writing on the paragraph. Note your speed and errors.

36 Luke sent a $47 check to Computers & Such to 9
37 get a disk with 44 games & 4 special programs for 19
38 7 friends. He saw 47 of his friends at 4 p.m. 28

| 1 | 2 | 3 | 4 | 5 | 6 | 7 | 8 | 9 | 10

ACTIVITY 39

Spreadsheet 32

Open the file SS18, save it as SS32, and follow these steps to clear formatting properties:

1. Select cell range A1 through E16 and clear the formatting. Note what happens to your spreadsheet.
2. If the format of the numbers in column C did not change, change them to numeric, general.
3. Move the contents of cells C1 and C2 to A1 and A2.
4. Change rows 1 and 2 to 10-point bold, and center cells A1 and A2 across the spreadsheet.
5. Clear the contents of cell range A7 through A16; then key these numbers: *7, 15, 30, 37, 45, 51, 68, 77, 93, 105.*
6. Center and bold cell range A4 through E5.
7. Change the font in cells B5 and D5 to Wingdings®.
8. Format cell range C7 through C16 for no decimal places.
9. Shade cell range A1 through E5 in a shade of your choice.
10. Shade the data in rows 7, 9, 11, 13, and 15 in a shade of your choice.
11. Add a border around the entire spreadsheet.
12. Save your changes and close the file.

ACTIVITY 40

Spreadsheet 33

Open the file SS24, save it as SS33, and follow these steps:

1. Delete column C. Notice that the grade averages are either recalculated or you get an error message indicating that you must recalculate or rewrite the formula.
2. Delete the rows containing data for Robin Flewharty, Logan Pfiel, and Priscilla Swafford.
3. Shade the data in rows 4, 6, 8, 10, 12, and 14 in a shade of your choice.
4. Place a border around the entire spreadsheet.
5. Place a line at the bottom of cell range A2 through F2.
6. Save your changes and close the file.

I. 2-Minute Timed Writings

Take two 2-minute timed writings on lines 39–44. Note your speed and errors.

Goal: 27/2'/4e

39 Have you been to see our zoo? It is a fun 9
40 thing to do in the summer. Bring your lunch to 18
41 eat in the park by the lake. You can watch a bear 28
42 cub perform or just view the zebras. Then explore 38
43 this place and see all the quail and ducks. Take 48
44 some photos to capture the day. 54

| 1 | 2 | 3 | 4 | 5 | 6 | 7 | 8 | 9 | 10 SI 1.10

MATH CONNECTION

Convert Currencies Different countries use different systems of money, or currencies. Each kind of currency has its own symbol, such as £ for the British pound, € for the Euro, and ¥ for the Japanese yen. If a currency's symbol is not available on the keyboard or in a software application, you can use a three-letter abbreviation for the currency. Go to the Online Learning Center at **KeyComps.glencoe.com>Math Connection> Unit 2>Lesson 21**. Learn more about currencies and complete the activity.

E. Clearing Cells

When you press delete or backspace in a cell or cell range, the contents of the cell are removed, but the formatting remains. To remove formatting properties from cells, use the **clear** commands. Clear usually removes basic formatting commands such as bold, italics, underline, and fonts. Some clear commands also remove shading, borders, alignments, and numeric formats. An option in the clear command is to remove both the contents and the formatting properties at the same time.

F. Deleting Rows and Columns

Spreadsheet rows and columns can be deleted by selecting the row number or column letter and using the delete command. If the spreadsheet contains formulas and a row or column is deleted, the software will adjust the addresses of the shifted cells. However, if a formula depends upon a cell that has been deleted, an error message will be displayed.

G. Software Features

STUDENT MANUAL

Clearing Cells
Deleting Rows and Columns

Study Lesson 135 in your Student Manual. Complete all the practice activities while at your computer. Then complete the tasks that follow.

LANGUAGE ARTS CONNECTION

Illustrate Pronoun Use Review the Language Link on p. 488. Create a spreadsheet with three columns. In the first column key four nominative pronouns and in the second column key their related objective pronouns. For example, *I* would be paired with *me*.

For each set of pronouns, compose a sentence in which both pronouns are used correctly (for example: *I think that belongs to me*). Enter the sentences in the third column. Follow your teacher's instructions for saving and printing your work.

NEW KEYS: 3 # 8 *

OBJECTIVES:

- Key the 3, #, 8, and * by touch.
- Key 27/2'/4e.
- Compose short phrases at the keyboard.

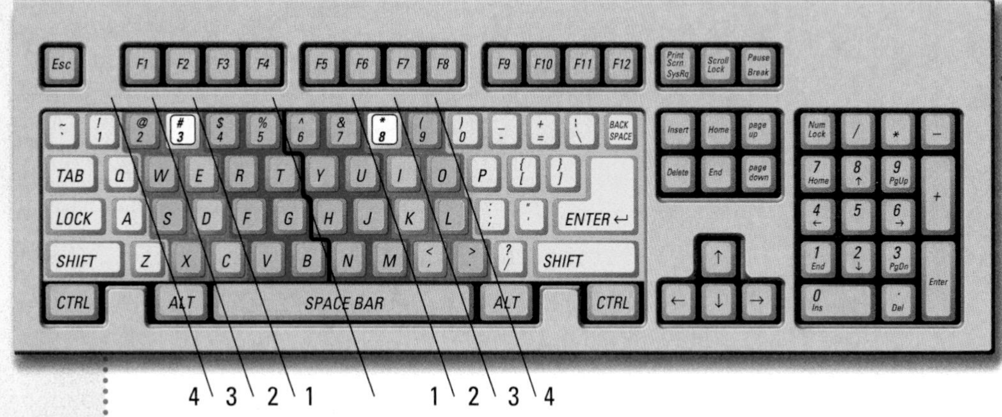

A. WARMUP

Key each line 2 times.

Speed	1 The time for Andrew to stop is when the sun sets.
Accuracy	2 Ten foxes quickly jumped high over twelve zebras.
Numbers	3 Lines 47, 77, and 44 were right; line 74 was not.
Symbols	4 Bakes & Deli pays $4, $4.77, and $7.44 for dimes.

NEW KEYS

B. 3 AND # KEYS

Key each line 2 times. Repeat if time permits.

Use D finger. Anchor A or F.

```
5 ded de3d d3d 333 d3d 3/33 d3d 33.3 d3d 33,333 d3d
6 33 dimes, 33 dishes, 33 dots, 33 daisies, or 3.33
7 Draw 33 squares, 3,333 rectangles, and 3 circles.
8 They had 333 dogs in 33 kennels for over 3 weeks.
```

The # (number or pound sign) is the shift of 3. Anchor A or F. Do not space between the number and #.

```
9 ded de3 d3d d3#d d#d d#d #3 #33 #333 d#d d3d #333
10 #3, 3 dots, #33, 33 dogs, #333, 333 ditches, #333
11 Is Invoice #373 for 344#, 433#, or 343# of fruit?
12 The group used 43# of grade #3 potatoes at lunch.
```

C. Preview Practice

Key each line 2 times as a preview to the timed writings that follow.

Accuracy United dispute quality criticize organization international
Speed fixing other over were most keep with came and not is to up

D. 5-Minute Timed Writings

Take two 5-minute timed writings on the paragraphs. Note your speed and errors.

Goal: 39/5'/5e

Social Studies Connection

During the Second World War, world leaders knew that 10
something had to be done to prevent another war. They met 22
and came up with the idea for the United Nations, which has 34
served as a forum for many international disputes. 44

Almost all the countries in the world have joined this 55
organization. The United Nations has several groups that 66
help to solve crises and keep peace among countries. 76

Even though this quality organization does not pass 87
laws, it has worked for over fifty years to help keep world 99
peace, offer a place where people can meet and work out 110
their problems, and help nations cooperate among themselves 122
in fixing the problems that bother them. The members of the 134
United Nations work to protect human rights and improve 145
standards of living all over the world. 153

Like any big family, this one is not without problems. 165
The United Nations has some money woes and is denounced for 177
the way it spends money. But while there are problems, most 189
people agree that we do need it. 195

SI 1.45

| 1 | 2 | 3 | 4 | 5 | 6 | 7 | 8 | 9 | 10 | 11 | 12

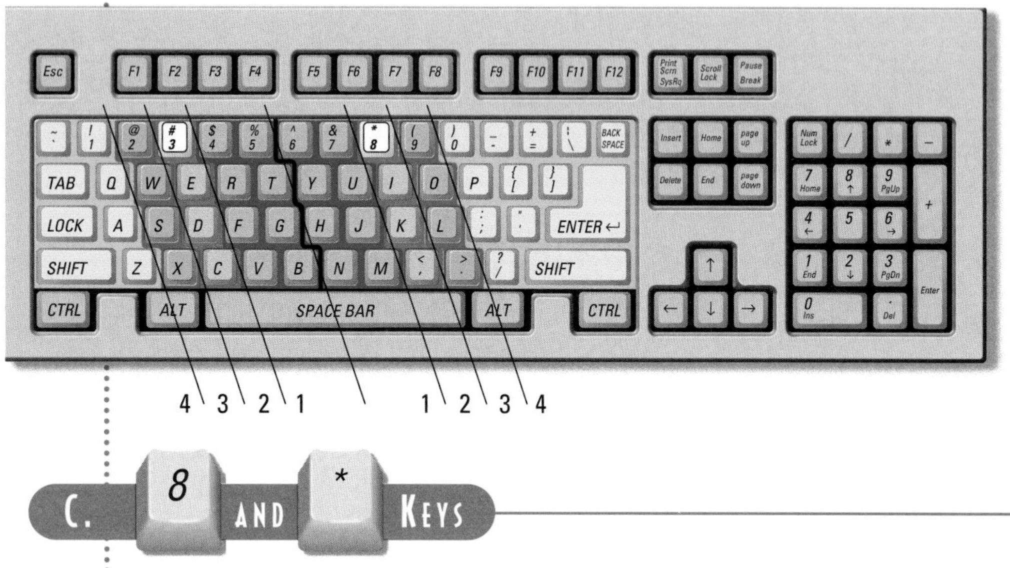

C. 8 AND * KEYS

Key each line 2 times. Key smoothly as you use the SHIFT keys. Repeat if time permits.

Use K finger. Anchor ;.

13 kik ki8k k8k 888 k8k 8/88 k8k 88.8 k8k 88,888 k8k
14 88 kegs, 88 kilns, 88 knocks, 88 kickers, or 8.88
15 Our zoo has 88 zebras, 38 snakes, and 33 monkeys.
16 The house is at 88 Lake Street, 8 blocks farther.

*The * (asterisk) is the shift of 8. Do not space between the word and *.*

17 kik ki8 k8k k8*k k*k k*k *8 *88 *888 k*k k8k *888
18 *8, 88 kits, *88, 88 keys, *888, 88 kimonos, *888
19 This manual* and this report* are in the library.
20 Reports* are due in 8 weeks* and should be keyed.

SKILLBUILDING

D. PRETEST

Take a 1-minute timed writing on the paragraph. Note your speed and errors.

21 Do you brood when you make errors on papers? 9
22 It would be better to figure out what causes the 19
23 errors and to look for corrective drills to help 29
24 you make fewer errors in the future. 36

| 1 | 2 | 3 | 4 | 5 | 6 | 7 | 8 | 9 | 10

LESSON 135 SPREADSHEETS: CLEAR CELLS, DELETE ROWS AND COLUMNS

OBJECTIVES:

- Apply rules for nominative and objective pronoun use.
- Key 39/5'/5e.
- Clear cells and delete rows and columns in a spreadsheet.

A. WARMUP

Key each line 2 times.

Speed	1	That round key that you gave me will not fit into the door.
Accuracy	2	Buzz was pleased to qualify in the men's bike extravaganza.
Language Link	3	Everybody in this school is invited to attend the ceremony.
Numbers/Symbols	4	Just 4% of the #156 ($2.36) on 3% of #78 ($1.90) were used.

| 1 | 2 | 3 | 4 | 5 | 6 | 7 | 8 | 9 | 10 | 11 | 12

LANGUAGE LINK

B. PRONOUN USE

Study the rules and examples that follow. Then edit lines 5–8 to correct any errors in pronoun use.

Rule 38: Use **nominative** pronouns (such as *I, he, she, we,* and *they*) as subjects of a sentence or clause. Subjects perform an action.

The programmer and he are reviewing that.

It is she who likes this software.

Rule 39: Use **objective** pronouns (such as *me, him, her,* and *them*) as objects in a sentence or clause. Objects receive an action.

The folders are for Susan and him.

She went out with him and me.

5 Rob knows art better than (she/her), but (she/her) can't add.
6 (She/Her) and (I/me) saw the new movie before (they/them) did.
7 My friends and (I/me) do not like (he/him) when (he/him) brags.
8 I'm sure (he/him) has more knowledge of cultures than (I/me).

E. PRACTICE

SPEED: ***If you made 2 or fewer errors on the Pretest, key lines 25–32 two times.***

ACCURACY: ***If you made more than 2 errors on the Pretest, key lines 25–28 as a group two times. Then key lines 29–32 as a group two times.***

Double Reaches

```
25 rr errs hurry error furry berry worry terry carry
26 ll bill allay hills chill stall small shell smell
27 tt attar jetty otter utter putty witty butte Otto
28 ff stuff stiff cliff sniff offer scuff fluff buff
```

Alternate Reaches

```
29 is this list fist wish visit whist island raisins
30 so sons some soap sort soles sound bosses costume
31 go gone goat pogo logo bogus agora pagoda doggone
32 fu fun fume fund full fuel fuss furor furry fuzzy
```

F. POSTTEST

Repeat the Pretest. Compare your Posttest results with your Pretest results.

G. Number and Symbol Practice

Key each line 1 time. Repeat if time permits.

```
33 83 doubts, 38 cubs, 37 shrubs, 33 clubs, 34 stubs
34 87 aims, 83 maids, 88 brains, 73 braids, 84 raids

35 78 drinks, 48 brinks, 43 inks, 83 minks, 33 links
36 88 canes, 78 planes, 73 manes, 34 cans, 84 cranes

37 #7 blue, 4# roast, $3 paint, 77 books,* 3 & 4 & 8
38 7# boxes, 38 lists, $4 horse, #8 tree,* 7 & 3 & 4

39 Seek & Find Research sells this book* for $37.84.
40 The geometry test grades were 88, 87, 84, and 83.
```

ACTIVITY 38
Spreadsheet 31

Open the file SS30, save it as SS31, and make the following changes:

1. Fill cell range A1 through G5 with a light shading or light horizontal lines.
2. Add a medium border at the top of cell range A15 through G15.
3. Using the same fill you used in step 1, shade the following cell ranges: A7 through G7; A9 through G9; A11 through G11; A13 through G13.
4. Save your changes and close the file.

LANGUAGE ARTS CONNECTION

Analyze Shading and Borders Examine the shading and borders used in Spreadsheet 31 that you created above. Key a paragraph that discusses how the shading and borders make the information easier to understand. Include two tips for using borders and shading. Follow your teacher's instructions for saving and printing your work.

PORTFOLIO Activity

Apply Shading and Borders Use a spreadsheet to create a weekly calendar for planning your schedule. Have columns for each day of the week. Have rows for each hour of the day from 7:00 A.M. to 7:00 P.M.

In your planner, key in all the important items you need to schedule for the week. Add borders and shading to make the information easier to enter and read at a glance. Follow your teacher's instructions for saving and printing your work.

H. 1-Minute Alphanumeric Timed Writing

Take a 1-minute timed writing on the paragraph. Note your speed and errors.

```
41      B. Warmsly & J. Barnet paid the $847 charges    9
42 for the closing costs of their home at 3487 Cliff   19
43 Road; claim #47* shows the charge.                   26
   | 1 | 2 | 3 | 4 | 5 | 6 | 7 | 8 | 9 | 10
```

I. 2-Minute Timed Writings

Take two 2-minute timed writings on lines 44–49. Note your speed and errors.

Goal: 27/2'/4e

```
44      We just want to stay all day in the store to     9
45 see the very new shoe styles. Sue quickly saw the    19
46 mix of zany colors. Jo put on a yellow and green     29
47 pair and looked in a mirror. The shoes had wide      39
48 strips on the soles. We were certain of the good     48
49 brand, so I bought two pair.                         54
                                                     SI 1.12
   | 1 | 2 | 3 | 4 | 5 | 6 | 7 | 8 | 9 | 10
```

Language Link

J. Composing at the Keyboard

Key a short phrase to answer each of the following questions. Follow your teacher's directions for printing and/or sharing your response.

50 What do you want to do after graduating from high school?
51 What is your favorite class and why?
52 Why do you/do you not participate in extra-curricular activities?
53 In what city and state would you like to live and why?
54 What do you like most about your school?

ACTIVITY 36
Spreadsheet 29

Open the file SS12, save it as SS29, and then follow these steps to change the spreadsheet:

1. Insert a blank column D.
2. In cell D6, center and key in bold the label *Transportation.*
3. In cell range D8 through D12, key the following entries: *Antilles Air; Ferry; Isle Air; Mailboat; Ferry.*
4. Automatically widen column D.
5. Select cell range A8 through F12, and sort column B in descending (high to low) order.
6. Follow your teacher's instructions for printing.
7. Save your changes and close the file.

ACTIVITY 37
Spreadsheet 30

Open the file SS20, save it as SS30, and then follow these steps to change the spreadsheet:

1. Insert a blank column F.
2. In cell F5, key the label *Our Store.*
3. In cell range F7 through F12, key the following values: *1.97; 1.03; 2.88; 0.99; 3.11; 1.78.*
4. Copy the formula in cell E14 to F14.
5. Select cell range A5 through G14, and automatically change the column width.
6. Insert a blank row 9.
7. In cell range A9 through G9, key the following data: *Holstein Milk; 1 gal.; 1.56; 1.78; 1.89; 1.65; 1.49.*
8. Select cell range A7 through G13 and sort column A in ascending order.
9. If necessary, center cells A1 through A3 across the spreadsheet again.
10. Add a heavy border around cell range A1 through G15.
11. Add a border at the bottom of cell range A1 through G5.
12. Save your changes and close the file.

LESSON 23 NEW KEYS: 2 @ 9 (

OBJECTIVES:

- Key the 2, @, 9, and (by touch.
- Refine keyboarding skills.
- Key 27/2'/4e.

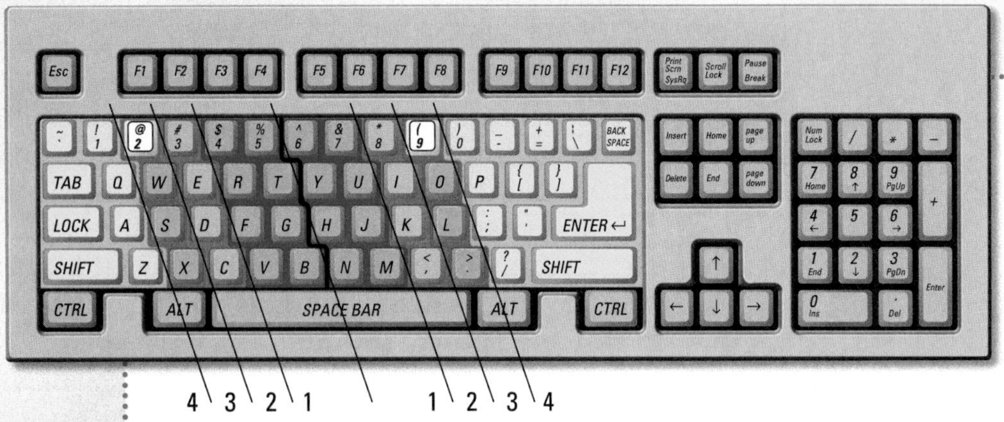

4 3 2 1 1 2 3 4

A. WARMUP

Key each line 2 times.

Speed	1	The big lake was filled with many ducks and fish.
Accuracy	2	Lazy Jaques picked five boxes of oranges with me.
Numbers	3	The answer is 78 when you add 44 and 34 together.
Symbols	4	Invoices #73 and #48 from C & M Supply were $438.

NEW KEYS

B. 2 AND @ KEYS

Key each line 2 times. Repeat if time permits.

Use S finger. For 2 and @, anchor F.

5 sws sw2s s2s 222 s2s 22.2 s2s 2/22 s2s 22,222 s2s
6 22 sips, 22 swings, 22 signals, 22 sites, or 2.22
7 Our class used 22 pens, 23 disks, and 24 ribbons.
8 There were 22 people waiting for Bus 22 on May 2.

@ (at) is the shift of 2. Space once before and after @ except when it is used in an e-mail address.

9 sws sw2 s2s s2@s s@s s@s @2 @22 @222 s@s s2s @222
10 @2, 2 sons, @22, 22 sets, @222, 222 sensors, @222
11 Paul said his e-mail address was smith@acc.co.us.
12 She bought 2 @ 22 and sold 22 @ 223 before 2 p.m.

C. Inserting Columns Into a Spreadsheet

Sometimes it may be necessary to insert additional columns into a spreadsheet. When you insert a column, all the columns following the insertion will be relettered automatically, and formulas in the spreadsheet will be readjusted.

D. Adding Borders and Shading

Spreadsheets can be made more attractive and readable by using lines, or **borders,** both in and around the worksheet and darker or color backgrounds called **shading.** Choose shading that does not interfere with reading the text. Also, do not use too many special treatments in a single spreadsheet. You may need to experiment with available options to find what works best.

Borders *Lines placed around spreadsheet cells and/or cell ranges.*

Shading *Darkened or colored background of cells or cell ranges.*

CONCESSION STAND ROSTER
Tuesday, September 12

5:30-6:30	6:30-7:30	7:30-8:30	8:30-9:30	9:30-Cleanup
Gray, Aubrey	Bessonett, Teri	Diener, Darren	Corbin, Curt	Daehn, Sonja
Maddox, Roy	Horvath, Jessie	Katchinska, Ken	Estes, Edith	Feddon, Lee
McNeal, Mike	Ottwell, Dionne	Roark, Randa	Geitner, Gail	Gustafson, Gunther
Owen, Beverly	Rubio, Nan	Vega, Oscar	Hosea, Jim	Nix, Nita

E. Software Features

STUDENT MANUAL

Insert Columns
Add Borders and Shading

Study Lesson 134 in your Student Manual. Complete all the practice activities while at your computer. Then complete the tasks that follow.

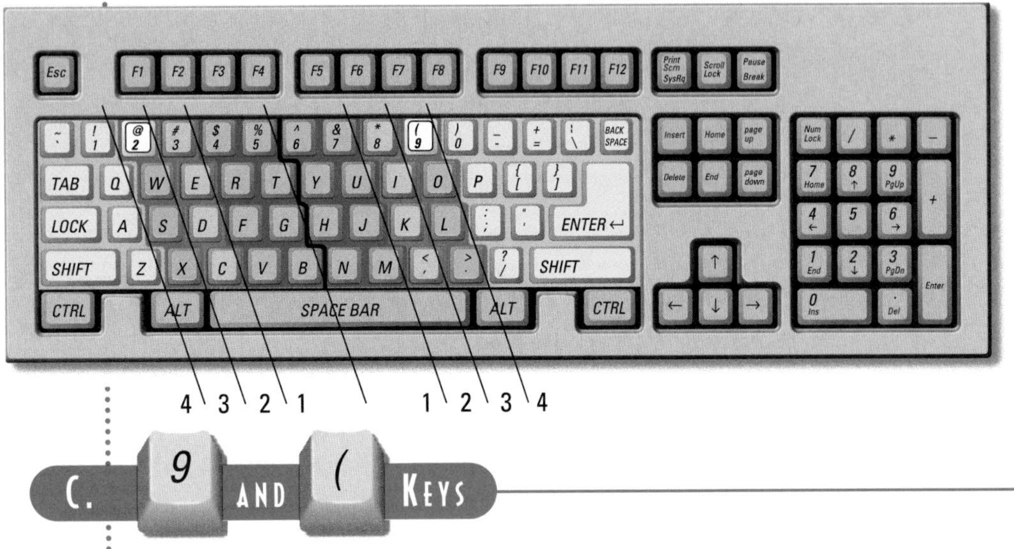

C. 9 AND (KEYS

Key each line 2 times. Repeat if time permits.

Use L finger. For 9 and (, anchor J.

```
13 lol lo91 191 999 191 9/99 191 99.9 191 99,999 191
14 99 laps, 99 loops, 99 lilies, 99 lifters, or 9.99
15 He said 99 times not to ask for the 99 fair fans.
16 They traveled 999 miles on Route 99 over 9 weeks.
```

The ((opening parenthesis) is the shift of 9. Space once before an opening parenthesis; do not space after it.

```
17 lol lo9 191 19(1 1(1 1(1 (9 (99 (999 1(1 191 (999
18 (9, 9 lots, (99, 99 logs, (999, 999 latches, (999
19 lo9( (99( (9 lo9(1 lo( 9( 9(9 (9( 9(9 1( lo9(1 9(
20 lo9( 19(1 9(91 1((1 (9ol 99 lambs, (999, 999 lads
```

SKILLBUILDING

D. TECHNIQUE CHECKPOINT

Key each line 2 times. Focus on the technique at the left.

Keep your eyes on the copy when keying numbers and symbols.

```
21 sws sw2s s2s 222 s2s 22.2 s2s 2/22 s2s 22,222 s2s
22 sws sw2 s2s s2@s s@s s@s @2 @22 @222 s@s s2s @222
23 lol lo91 191 999 191 9/99 191 99.9 191 99,999 191
24 lol lo9 191 19(1 1(1 1(1 (9 (99 (999 1(1 191 (999
```

E. PRETEST

Take a 1-minute timed writing on the paragraph. Note your speed and errors.

```
25      Were you in the biology group that mixed the    9
26 ragweed seeds with some vegetable seeds? Jon and    19
27 Kim sneezed all month because of that. All of us    29
28 agreed that we must be more careful in the lab.     38
   | 1 | 2 | 3 | 4 | 5 | 6 | 7 | 8 | 9 | 10
```

LESSON 134 Spreadsheets: Inserting Columns, Borders, and Shading

OBJECTIVES:

- Improve keyboarding skills.
- Insert columns into a spreadsheet.
- Add borders and shading to a spreadsheet.

A. Warmup

Key each line 2 times.

Speed	1	The four women spent the day on the lake in a fishing boat.
Accuracy	2	Ximenez may jeopardize the quality of those antique quilts.
Language Link	3	None of the parents wanted their children out in the storm.
Numbers/Symbols	4	Those answers are: (a) $135, (b) $46, (c) $128, (d) $97.03.

| 1 | 2 | 3 | 4 | 5 | 6 | 7 | 8 | 9 | 10 | 11 | 12

SKILLBUILDING

B. Paced Practice

Turn to the Paced Practice routine beginning on page SB7. Take three 2-minute timed writings, starting at the point where you left off the last time.

SOCIAL STUDIES CONNECTION

Study with a Spreadsheet A spreadsheet can help you to study by allowing you to sort information in different ways. For example, if you had a spreadsheet listing all of the presidents and the years that they were in office, you could sort the presidents alphabetically and quiz yourself on the years each was in office.

Think of three other topics that you have studied in Social Studies class that would be helpful to have in a spreadsheet. Key a sentence that describes each topic and explains how a spreadsheet could be helpful. Follow your teacher's instructions for saving and printing your work.

F. PRACTICE

SPEED: ***If you made 2 or fewer errors on the Pretest, key lines 29–36 two times each.***

ACCURACY: ***If you made more than 2 errors on the Pretest, key lines 29–32 as a group two times. Then key lines 33–36 as a group two times.***

Left Reaches

29 tab wards grace serve wears farce beast crate car
30 far weeds tests seeds tread graze vexed vests saw
31 bar crest feast refer cease dated verge bread gas
32 car career grasses bread creases faded vested tad

Right Reaches

33 you Yukon mummy ninon jolly union minim pylon hum
34 mom nylon milky lumpy puppy holly pulpy plink oil
35 pop oomph jumpy unpin nippy imply hippo pupil nip
36 you union bumpy upon holly hill moon pink ill mop

G. POSTTEST

Repeat the Pretest. Compare your Posttest results with your Pretest results.

H. 1-Minute Alphanumeric Timed Writing

Take a 1-minute timed writing on the paragraph. Note your speed and errors.

37 The planned ski tour #4 begins at 2:43 p.m., 9
38 and tour #3 begins at noon. Every tour costs $43, 19
39 and every one will end at 7:38 p.m. 26

| 1 | 2 | 3 | 4 | 5 | 6 | 7 | 8 | 9 | 10

I. 2-Minute Timed Writings

Take two 2-minute timed writings on lines 40–45. Note your speed and errors.

Goal: 27/2'/4e

40 It is a joy to end a term with good grades. 9
41 Fall term could be very nice if it were not for 19
42 exams and quizzes. Jan, though, likes to study to 29
43 show how much she has learned. She places great 38
44 value in having high marks. She knows her peers 48
45 admire the grades she achieved. 54

SI 1.17

| 1 | 2 | 3 | 4 | 5 | 6 | 7 | 8 | 9 | 10

ACTIVITY 35

Spreadsheet 28

Open the file SS24, save it as SS28, and then follow these steps to change the spreadsheet by inserting rows and sorting data:

1. Insert a blank row 1.
2. In cell A1, key in 12-point bold the label *Fifth-Period Junior English Class.*
3. Insert a blank row 2.
4. In cell A2, key in bold the label *Prepared by* followed by your name.
5. Insert a blank row 3.
6. In cell A3, key in bold the label *Beginning February 10,{year}.*
7. Center A1 across the spreadsheet. Repeat for A2 and A3.
8. Insert a blank row 4.
9. Bold and center cell range A5 through G6.
10. Select any cell in column A, and sort the names in column A in ascending order.
11. Format all numbers to have no decimal places.
12. Insert gridlines and change the print orientation to landscape.
13. Follow your teacher's instructions for printing.
14. Save your changes and close the file.

PORTFOLIO Activity

Sort Data In the Language Arts Connection on p. 482, you thought of three situations in which it would be useful to sort data in a spreadsheet. Choose one of those situations, and create a new spreadsheet with data that relates to that situation. You can use real data or make up realistic data.

Sort the data different ways. For example, you might want to organize your friends' birthdays by alphabetizing their names or by the dates of their birthdays. Then key a short paragraph that explains which sort works best to display the information you want. Follow your teacher's instructions for saving and printing your work.

LESSON 24 REVIEW

OBJECTIVES:

- Improve keyboarding skills.
- Key 27/2'/4e.
- Compose at the keyboard.

A. WARMUP

Key each line 2 times.

Speed	1	The first time Alf drove a car, he hit a pothole.
Accuracy	2	Zigzag through the zebu with zip to avoid injury.
Numbers	3	Room 43 holds 87 people, but only 29 are present.
Symbols	4	Buy 78 gross* of #2 pencils @ $3.94 at the store.

SKILLBUILDING

B. TAB KEY

Key each paragraph 2 times. Press the TAB to indent the first line; press ENTER only at the end of lines 6 and 8. Repeat if time permits.

5 We found 99 gnats, 44 flies, 33 fleas, and
6 77 seals beside the 33 trees at the 2-acre beach.

7 Bo & Son bought 88 axles @ $42.98. They said
8 Rule #37 on page 88 was now Rule #42 on page 93.

C. ENTER KEY

Key each line 2 times. Press ENTER at the end of every sentence. Continue keying smoothly. Repeat if time permits.

Remember to press ENTER at the end of every sentence.

9 Study all of Chapter 29. It covers pages 234-249.
10 Chelsea lives at 778 Cherokee. That's in Paducah.
11 Write Jo at pets@coyote.com. Jo's address is new.
12 That text* is at B & B Printing. It is makeready.

ACTIVITY 32
Spreadsheet 25

Open the file SS1, save it as SS25, and follow these steps:

1. Insert a blank row 1.
2. In cell A1, key in 14-point bold the label *Fund-Raising Report.*
3. Insert a blank row 2.
4. In cell A2, key in 12-point bold the label *Prepared by* followed by your name.
5. Insert a blank row 3.
6. Save your changes and close the file.

ACTIVITY 33
Spreadsheet 26

Open the file SS25, save it as SS26, and follow these steps:

1. In cell A3, key in 12-point bold, the label *October 12-30, {year}.*
2. Insert a blank row 4.
3. Center cell range A1 through A3 across the spreadsheet.
4. Bold the contents of rows 19 and 20.
5. Change the print orientation to landscape.
6. If the contents of any column are not visible, adjust the width.
7. Save your changes and close the file.

ACTIVITY 34
Spreadsheet 27

Open the file SS26, save it as SS27, and follow these steps:

1. Select cell range A7 through E17.
2. Sort column E in descending order (from high to low). The names are no longer in alphabetic order but are arranged in order of highest to lowest total sales.
3. Follow your teacher's instructions for printing.
4. Save your changes and close the file.

LANGUAGE ARTS CONNECTION

Identify Ways to Use Sorted Data In your own words, key definitions of ascending order and descending order. Think about how the ability to sort the data in a spreadsheet in ascending and descending order could be useful to you. For example, what would be the best way to sort a spreadsheet showing your friends' birthdays? Key descriptions of three situations in which you might need to sort data in ascending or descending order. Follow your teacher's instructions for saving and printing your work.

D. Technique Timed Writings

Take two 30-second timed writings on each line. Focus on the technique at the left.

Keep elbows in.

13 She works for Mr. D. N. Logan at Logan Locksmith.
14 Is the May/June issue late? My copy has not come.
15 Find these colors: pink, blue, green, and purple.
16 My hoity-toity behavior was rude, extremely rude.
| 1 | 2 | 3 | 4 | 5 | 6 | 7 | 8 | 9 | 10

E. PRETEST

Take a 1-minute timed writing on the paragraph. Note your speed and errors.

17 Ed's prize-winning ewe stays on Mario's farm 9
18 until the petting zoo opens. Every day Skip takes 19
19 that ewe and her lamb to the fair. It's amazing 29
20 to see how much time is spent caring for animals. 39
| 1 | 2 | 3 | 4 5 | 6 | 7 | 8 | 9 | 10

F. PRACTICE

SPEED: ***If you made 2 or fewer errors on the Pretest, key lines 21–28 two times each.***

ACCURACY: ***If you made more than 2 errors on the Pretest, key lines 21–24 as a group two times. Then key lines 25–28 as a group two times.***

Adjacent Reaches	21 io trio riot pious Mario ew ewes mews sewer views
Jump Reaches	22 un tune dune under bound ze zeal zest prize seize
Double Reaches	23 ss hiss boss dress gloss ll fall tall small jolly
Up Reaches	24 dr drip drive dream drab hi hill hike hide hidden
Alternate Reaches	25 ro rode rote crows throw do doze judo kudos docks
Left Reaches	26 fa farm fast favor fazed er errs were erase terms
Right Reaches	27 ki kiln skip skill skimp pl plot plum plows plugs
Down Reaches	28 ca call caps cards caper ni niece nine nick night

G. POSTTEST

Repeat the Pretest. Compare your Posttest results with your Pretest results.

SKILLBUILDING

C. 30-Second Timed Writings

Take two 30-second timed writings on lines 5–6. Then take two 30-second timed writings on lines 7–8. Try to increase your speed each time.

5 One type of report is an agenda; it is used to inform 11
6 people of items that may be discussed at a future meeting. 23

7 Minutes of a meeting are another kind of report; they 11
8 are records of reference for what takes place in meetings. 23

| 1 | 2 | 3 | 4 | 5 | 6 | 7 | 8 | 9 | 10 | 11 | 12

FORMATTING

D. Inserting Rows

Even when you carefully plan a spreadsheet, there will be times when you need to insert additional rows. When you insert a row, all of the rows after the insertion will be renumbered, and any formulas in the spreadsheet will be readjusted.

E. Sorting Data

To **sort** data is to arrange it in a certain order, such as alphabetic or numeric. You can sort data in **ascending order** (from A to Z or low to high) or in **descending order** (from Z to A or high to low). You can also choose which column to sort first, second, and third. Before you sort data, it is a good idea to save your file. Your sort may not turn out the way you intended.

F. Software Features

STUDENT MANUAL

Inserting Rows Sorting Data

Study Lesson 133 in your Student Manual. Complete all the practice activities while at your computer. Then complete the tasks that follow.

H. 1-Minute Alphanumeric Timed Writing

Take a 1-minute timed writing on lines 29–31. Note your speed and errors.

```
29      Our black cat, Beauty, weighed 9#. She had a    9
30 checkup at Paws & Claws on June 23. Her shots and   19
31 exam cost $84, but she's worth it all.               27
   | 1 | 2 | 3 | 4 | 5 | 6 | 7 | 8 | 9 | 10
```

I. 2-Minute Timed Writings

Take two 2-minute timed writings on lines 32–37. Note your speed and errors.

Goal: 27/2'/4e

```
32      Why use proper grammar when you speak? One       9
33 of the best reasons is that others will judge you   19
34 by your speech. Fair or not, people examine words   29
35 you use and how you use them. You have to speak     38
36 well daily. Avoid buzzwords and slang. People       48
37 will be very quick to judge you.                     54
                                                   SI 1.23
   | 1 | 2 | 3 | 4 | 5 | 6 | 7 | 8 | 9 | 10
```

Language Link

J. Composing at the Keyboard

Key a short phrase to answer each of the following questions. Follow your teacher's directions for printing and/or sharing your response.

38 What are your greatest strengths as a student?
39 What are your greatest challenges as a student?
40 If you could, how would you change the town/city you live in?
41 What do you look for in a friend?
42 In what ways have you contributed to your community?

LESSON 133 SPREADSHEETS: INSERTING ROWS/SORTING DATA

OBJECTIVES:

- Compose a story at the keyboard.
- Improve keyboarding skills.
- Insert rows into a spreadsheet.
- Sort data in a spreadsheet.

A. WARMUP

Key each line 2 times.

Speed	1	Three workers left early and were paid for only half a day.
Accuracy	2	Del and Wanda Quaid are great examples of quality citizens.
Language Link	3	Everybody was warned to stay home due to the freezing rain.
Numbers/Symbols	4	18, 290, 27, 38, 851, 63, 94, 704, 91, 48, 532, 10, 76, 495

| 1 | 2 | 3 | 4 | 5 | 6 | 7 | 8 | 9 | 10 | 11 | 12

LANGUAGE LINK

B. COMPOSING AT THE KEYBOARD

Compose the body of a one-page story which begins as follows:

"The last thing I remember was taking the dog for a walk. When I awoke, I found myself in a hospital room, but I couldn't remember..."

When you finish your story, proofread it carefully and correct any errors that you find.

LESSON 25 NEW KEYS: 1 ! 0)

OBJECTIVES:

- Key the 1, !, 0, and) by touch.
- Refine keyboarding skills.
- Key 27/2'/4e.

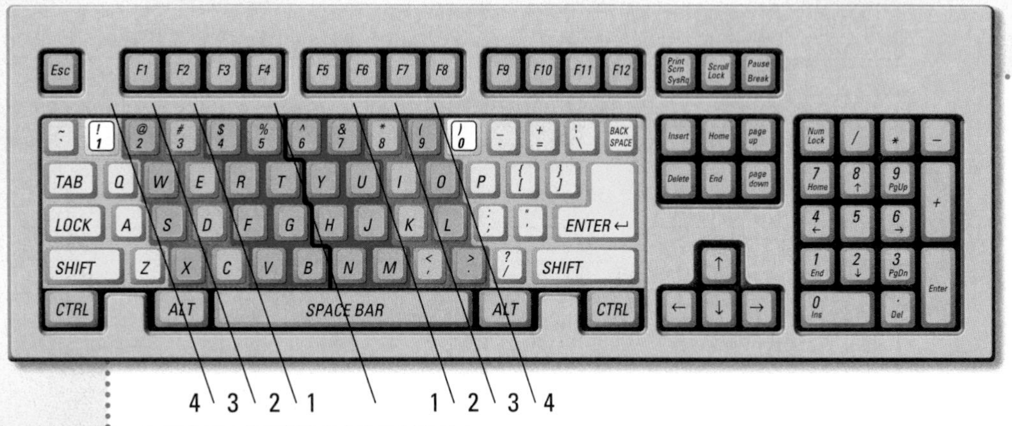

A. WARMUP

Key each line 2 times.

Speed	1 The goal of trade schools is to teach job skills.
Accuracy	2 Jess Mendoza quickly plowed six bright vineyards.
Numbers	3 Nate took this new order: 78, 74, 83, 29, and 23.
Symbols	4 Purchase 32# of grass seed today @ $2.98 a pound.

NEW KEYS

B. 1 AND ! KEYS

Key each line 2 times. Repeat if time permits.

For 1 and !, anchor F. Use A finger. Do not use the lowercase letter l (el) for 1.

5 aqa aq1a a1a 111 a1a 1/11 a1a 11.1 a1a 11,111 a1a
6 11 arms, 11 areas, 11 adages, 11 animals, or 1.11
7 My 11 aides will key 111 pages within 11 minutes.
8 Joann used 11 gallons of gas to travel 111 miles.

! is the shift of 1. Space once after an exclamation point.

9 aqa aq1 a1a a1!a a!a a!a 1! 11! 111! a!a a1a 111!
10 1!, 1 ant, 11! 11 acres, 111! 111 adverbs, 1 area
11 Listen! There was a cry for help! They need help!
12 Look! It's moving! I'm frightened! Run very fast!

ACTIVITY 31

Spreadsheet 24

Create a new spreadsheet and save it as SS24. Then follow these steps:

1. Key the data as shown in the following table.
2. In cell G4, use the AVERAGE function to average Howard Joslin's grades.
3. Copy the contents of cell G4 to cell range G5 through G17.
4. Widen columns A, D, and F and the titles, so that you can read the names easily.
5. Save your changes and close the file.

	A	B	C	D	E	F	G
1	Students	Author	Portfolios	Persuasive	Narrative	Descriptive	Grade
2		Projects		Essays	Essays	Essays	Averages
3							
4	Joslin, Howard	88	92	78	83	75	
5	Calavan, Casey	97	99	91	93	89	
6	Petropoulos, Cheryl	73	81	80	65	77	
7	Figueroa, Miguel	79	90	87	82	80	
8	Vititow, Megan	75	55	81	73	69	
9	Mathis, Monica	98	94	88	95	96	
10	Quintero, Luis	84	76	66	89	92	
11	Kizer, Paula	90	87	94	88	91	
12	Yankey, Ottis	79	74	78	77	83	
13	Pfiel, Logan	95	89	96	92	87	
14	Locks, Andrea	100	97	99	98	100	
15	Flewharty, Robin	99	89	90	87	98	
16	Jimmerson, Gennifer	85	71	82	78	84	
17	Swafford, Priscilla	87	69	83	76	68	

interNET CONNECTION

Practice Good Ergonomics Ergonomics is the science of designing and arranging work equipment so that people can work efficiently and safely. Go to the Online Learning Center at **KeyComps.glencoe.com>Internet Connection>Unit 7>Lesson 132** to find out about the latest ergonomic equipment available for computer users. Then complete the activity. Follow your teacher's instructions for saving and printing your work.

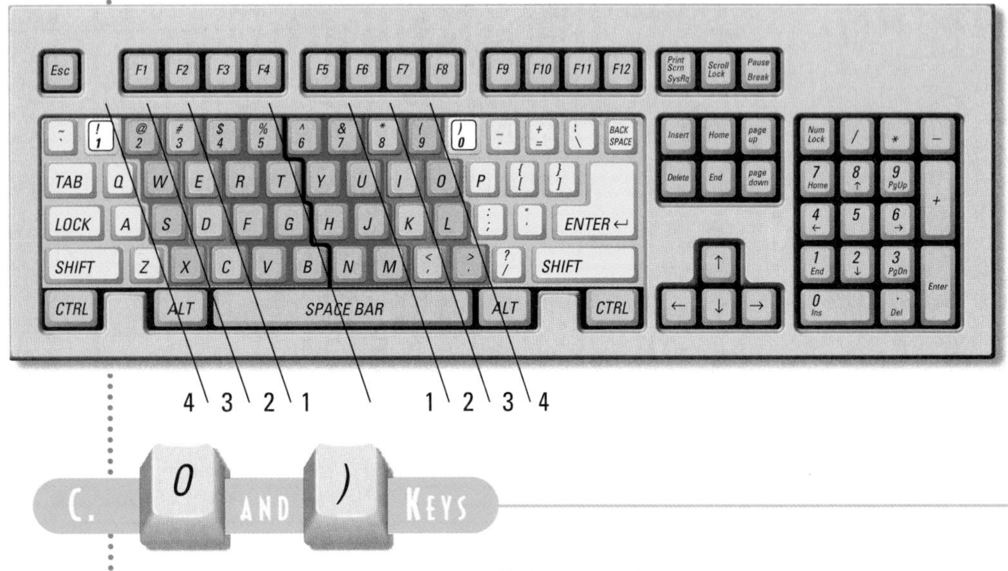

C. 0 AND) KEYS

Key each line 2 times. Repeat if time permits.

Use Sem finger. For 0 and), anchor J. Do not use the capital letter O for 0.

```
13 ;p; ;p0; ;0; 000 ;0; 1.00 ;0; 20.0 ;0; 30,000 ;0;
14 300 parts, 700 planks, 800 parades, 900 particles
15 Can you add these: 80, 10, 90, 40, 20, 70, & 130?
16 Some emoticons such as :-( or :( use parentheses.
```

) is the shift of 0 (zero). Space once after a closing parenthesis except when it is followed by punctuation; do not space before it.

```
17 ;p; ;p0 ;0; ;0); ;); ;); );; );;; ;); ;0; );;; ;)
18 ;0; ;0) ;); ;); 10) 20) 30) 40) 70) 80) 90) 1001)
19 The box (the big red one) is just the right size.
20 My friend (you know which one) is arriving early.
```

SKILLBUILDING

D. TECHNIQUE CHECKPOINT

Key each line 2 times. Focus on the techniques at the left.

Keep eyes on copy; hold home-key anchors.

```
21 aqa aq1a a1a 111 a1a 1/11 a1a 11.1 a1a 11,111 a1a
22 aqa aq1 a1a a1!a a!a a!a 1! 11! 111! a!a a1a 111!
23 ;p; ;p0; ;0; 000 ;0; 1.00 ;0; 20.0 ;0; 30,000 ;0;
24 p;p p;0 ;0; ;0); ;); ;); );; );;; ;); ;0; );;; ;)
```

E. PRETEST

Take a 1-minute timed writing on the paragraph. Note your speed and errors.

```
25      Dave and I took our backpacks and started up    9
26 the old mountain trail. Around sunset, we stopped   19
27 to set up camp and have a hot meal. We were very    29
28 tired after such a long day hiking uphill.          37
   | 1 | 2 | 3 | 4 | 5 | 6 | 7 | 8 | 9 | 10
```

STUDENT MANUAL

Using an AVERAGE Function

Study Lesson 132 in your Student Manual. Complete all the practice activities while at your computer. Then complete the tasks that follow.

MATH CONNECTION

Calculate Averages Create a spreadsheet that lists three types of numeric data from your classmates. Follow your teacher's instructions when you interview 10–20 classmates to find out their ages, their height in inches, and the number of people in their families. Then use the AVERAGE function to find out the average age, height, and family size of the students in your class. Follow your teacher's instructions for saving and printing your work.

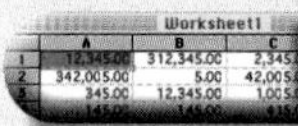

SPREADSHEET APPLICATIONS

ACTIVITY 29

Spreadsheet 22

Open the file SS1 and save it as SS22. Then follow these steps to change a spreadsheet by inserting the AVERAGE function.

1. Move cell range E1 through E16 to F1 through F16.
2. In cell E1, center and key in bold the label *Averages*.
3. In cell E3, find the average for weeks 1, 2, and 3.
4. Save your changes and close the file.

ACTIVITY 30

Spreadsheet 23

Open the file SS22 and save it as SS23. Then make the following changes:

1. In cell E4, find the average by keying the function name and selecting the cells to be averaged.
2. In cell E5, find the average by keying the function name and cell range.
3. Copy the contents of cell E5 to cell range E6 through E13.
4. Format all numbers to have two decimal places where necessary.
5. In cell E16, find the average of cell range E3 through E13.
6. Set the gridlines to print.
7. Automatically format the column width of cells E1 and F1.
8. Save your changes and close the file.

F. PRACTICE

SPEED: ***If you made 2 or fewer errors on the Pretest, key lines 29–36 two times each.***

ACCURACY: ***If you made more than 2 errors on the Pretest, key lines 29–32 as a group two times. Then key lines 33–36 as a group two times.***

Up Reaches

```
29 hu hush hull hunt human humid humor humble hurdle
30 st stair guest stone blast nasty start casts step
31 il lilac filed drill build spill child trail pail
32 de dear redeem warden tide render chide rode dead
```

Down Reaches

```
33 ab squab labor habit cabin cable abate about able
34 ca pecan recap catch carve cable scale scamp camp
35 av ravel gavel avert knave waved paved shave have
36 in ruin invent winner bring shin chin shrink pine
```

G. POSTTEST

Repeat the Pretest. Compare your Posttest results with your Pretest results.

H. 1-Minute Alphanumeric Timed Writing

Take a 1-minute timed writing on lines 37–39. Note your speed and errors.

```
37      Joy wanted to get a dozen (12) baseball bats    9
38 @ $4.29 from the sports store at 718 Miner Place.   19
39 When I went, only 10 bats were left.                26
   | 1 | 2 | 3 | 4 | 5 | 6 | 7 | 8 | 9 | 10
```

I. 2-Minute Timed Writings

Take two 2-minute timed writings on lines 40–45. Note your speed and errors.

Goal: 27/2'/4e

```
40      As you look for jobs, be quite sure that the    9
41 way you dress depicts the position that you want.   19
42 If you desire to obtain an office job, a zippy      29
43 fashion is not for you. Expect to arrive in a       38
44 clean, pressed business suit. Your clothes should   49
45 match that job you are seeking.                     54
   | 1 | 2 | 3 | 4 | 5 | 6 | 7 | 8 | 9 | 10  SI 1.23
```

C. PRETEST

Take a 1-minute timed writing on the paragraph. Note your speed and errors.

9 It is essential that we get plenty of sleep so that we 11
10 are rested when we get up each morning. We must eat a good 23
11 breakfast to build up energy for the day. Physical exercise 35
12 is a must for stronger hearts and greater endurance. 45

| 1 | 2 | 3 | 4 | 5 | 6 | 7 | 8 | 9 | 10 | 11 | 12

D. PRACTICE

In the chart below, find the number of errors you made on the Pretest. Then key each of the designated drill lines 2 times.

Pretest Errors	0–1	2	3	4+
Drill Lines	16–20	15–19	14–18	13–17

Accuracy

13 by friends families stronger breakfast minimize experienced
14 many rested problems run-down physical fatigued performance
15 build plenty energy increases endurance essential adversely
16 we quality morning exercise symptoms mentioned increasingly

Speed

17 hearts become energy there lives time each that when run we
18 levels active plenty tired these they good must felt our is
19 affect making crease limit spend with ways have down and it
20 friend affect rested sleep break days many just ever job of

E. POSTTEST

Repeat the Pretest. Compare your Posttest results with your Pretest results.

FORMATTING

F. Using the AVERAGE Function

The **AVERAGE** (or AVG) function is a formula that automatically adds the values in a range of cells and divides by the number of values to find the average. The average can then be formatted to have the desired number of decimal places.

LESSON 26

NEW KEYS: 5 % 6 ^

OBJECTIVES:

- Key the 5, %, 6, and ^ by touch.
- Refine keyboarding skills.
- Key 27/2'/4e.

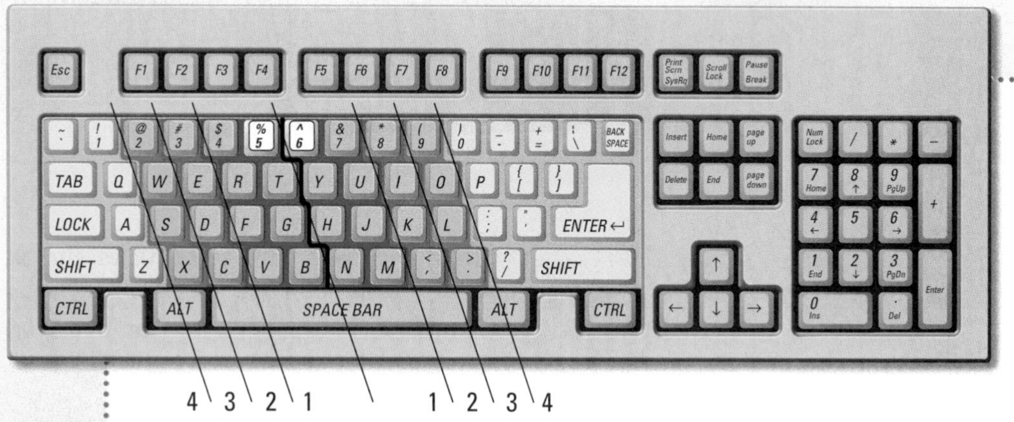

A. WARMUP

Key each line 2 times.

Speed	1	Our team at band camp did a new drill for guests.
Accuracy	2	Two jobs require packing five dozen axes monthly.
Numbers	3	Mark read the winning numbers: 190, 874, and 732.
Symbols	4	The shop (J & B) has #10 envelopes* @ $.24 a doz.

NEW KEYS

B. 5 AND % KEYS

Key each line 2 times. Repeat if time permits.

Use F finger. For 5 and %, anchor A.

5 ftf ft5f f5f 555 f5f 5/55 f5f 55.5 f5f 55,555 f5f
6 55 fins, 55 facts, 55 fields, 55 futures, or 5.55
7 Jo saw 55 bulls, 14 cows, 155 sheep, and 5 goats.
8 I just sold 55 items; his total for today is 555.

% is the shift of 5. The % (percent) is used in statistical data. Do not space between numbers and %.

9 ftf ft5 f5f f5%f f%f f%f 5% 55% 555% f%f f5f 555%
10 5%, 5 foes, 55%, 55 fees, 555%, 555 fiddles, 555%
11 The meal is 55% protein, 20% starch, and 25% fat.
12 On June 5, 55% of the students had 5% more skill.

SPREADSHEETS: AVERAGE FUNCTION

OBJECTIVES:

- Improve keyboarding skills.
- Apply the AVERAGE function in a spreadsheet.

A. WARMUP

Key each line 2 times.

Speed	1	Ruth sets her alarm so that she will wake up on time daily.
Accuracy	2	Zelda squeezed the six bouquets into a quaint antique vase.
Language Link	3	Each artist is responsible for cleaning his own work tools.
Numbers/Symbols	4	I ordered #6, #7, and #34 at discounts of 5%, 15%, and 20%.

| 1 | 2 | 3 | 4 | 5 | 6 | 7 | 8 | 9 | 10 | 11 | 12

LANGUAGE ARTS CONNECTION

Identify Time Management Tips Workers often find that they have too much to do and too little time to do it. Students, too, often feel the same time crunch. Have a class discussion about effective ways to manage time. After the discussion, compose a short paragraph that summarizes the discussion and includes three time management tips. Follow your teacher's instructions for saving and printing your work.

SKILLBUILDING

B. 12-SECOND SPRINTS

Take three 12-second timed writings on each line. Try to increase your speed each time.

5 The new desk and chair will be put in the back of the room.
6 Those boys were asked to cut and water the dry, brown lawn.
7 At long last I have a pen that will not leak on my fingers.
8 We need to turn off the light before they tell us to do it.

| | | | 5 | | | | 10 | | | | 15 | | | | 20 | | | | 25 | | | | 30 | | | | 35 | | | | 40 | | | | 45 | | | | 50 | | | | 55 | | | | 60

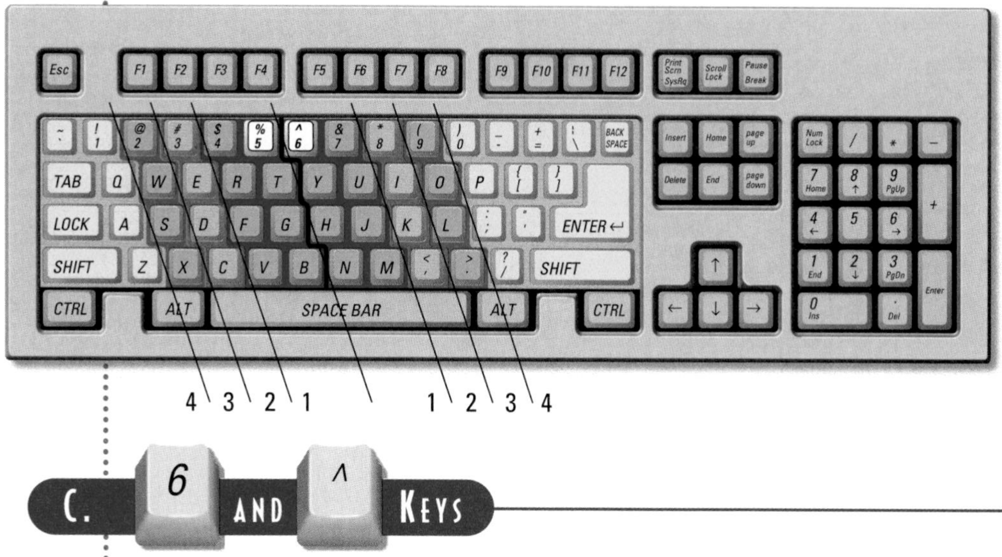

C. 6 AND ^ KEYS

Key each line 2 times. Repeat if time permits.

Use J finger. For 6 and ^, anchor ;.

13 jyj jy6j j6j 666 j6j 6/66 j6j 66.6 j6j 66,666 j6j
14 66 jaws, 66 jokes, 66 jewels, 66 jackets, or 6.66
15 Her averages were 76.46, 81.66, 86.56, and 96.36.
16 Multiply .66 by .51; the correct answer is .3366.

^ is the shift of 6. The ^ (caret) is used in some programming languages. Do not space between the caret and numbers.

17 jyj jy6 j6j j6^j j^j j^j ^j ^jj ^jjj j^j j6j ^jjj
18 6^, 6 jams, 66^, 66 jets, 666^, 666 jingles, 666^
19 The test problems included these: 75^2, 4^3, 8^6.
20 The ^ (caret) appeared 6 times in a line of code.

SKILLBUILDING

D. TECHNIQUE TIMED WRITINGS

Take two 30-second timed writings on each line. Focus on the technique at the left.

Sit up straight with your feet flat on the floor.

21 Snow leopards are graceful animals with soft fur.
22 They live in the high, rugged mountains of Tibet.
23 These big cats are adept at climbing and leaping.
24 They use their tails to balance on narrow ledges.

| 1 | 2 | 3 | 4 | 5 | 6 | 7 | 8 | 9 | 10

(continued)

	A	B	C	D	E	F
5	Item	Size	Cost Cutter	Family Foods	Food Queen	Paul Bunyon
6						
7	Egg Subs	16 oz	2.17	2.34	1.99	2.25
8	Bully Paper Towels	80.6 sq ft	0.96	1.07	1.14	0.99
9	Zippy Pasta Sauce	26 oz	2.89	2.53	2.67	2.73
10	Fizzy Cola	2 L	1.24	1.29	1.19	1.36
11	Fruit Crunch Cereal	16 oz	2.98	3.18	3.06	3.24
12	Buzzy Bee Honey	12 oz	1.98	1.99	1.83	1.91
13						
14	Total					

ACTIVITY 27
Spreadsheet 20

Open the file SS19, save it as SS20, and then make the following changes:

1. Select cell C14, and use AutoSum/QuickSum to get the total.
2. Select cell D14, and use Insert, Function to get the total.
3. Select cell E14, key = *SUM*, and select the cell range to be added to get the total.
4. Select cell F14, key = *SUM*, and select the cell range to be added to get the total.
5. Format cell range C14 through F14 with dollar signs and two decimals.
6. Save your changes and close the file.

ACTIVITY 28
Spreadsheet 21

Open the file SS20, save it as SS21, and then make the following changes:

1. Bold and center row 5.
2. Select cell range A5 through F14, and automatically change the column width.
3. Align cell range B7 through B12 at the right.
4. Change cell A1 to 16-point bold.
5. Change cell A2 to 12-point bold.
6. Add gridlines so they will print.
7. Select cell range A1 through F3; center horizontally across the selection.
8. Change the height of row 4 to approximately 1.5 times the default height.
9. If your teacher has given you instructions for printing, print the spreadsheet. Otherwise, save your changes and close the file.

E. PRETEST

Take a 1-minute timed writing on lines 25–28. Note your speed and errors.

25 As a flock, the crows flew to some clumps of 9
26 stalks near the eddy. They seemed to eat the pods 19
27 joyfully as they fed in the field. We like to 28
28 watch them, especially in the morning. 36

| 1 | 2 | 3 | 4 | 5 | 6 | 7 | 8 | 9 | 10

F. PRACTICE

SPEED: ***If you made 2 or fewer errors on the Pretest, key lines 29–36 two times each.***

ACCURACY: ***If you made more than 2 errors on the Pretest, key lines 29–32 as a group two times. Then key lines 33–36 as a group two times.***

Adjacent	29	po pods poem point poise lk hulk silk polka stalk
Jump	30	mp jump pump trump clump cr cram crow crawl creed
Double	31	dd odds eddy daddy caddy tt mitt mutt utter ditto
Consecutive	32	un unit punk funny bunch gr grab agree angry grip
Alternate	33	iv give dive drive wives gl glad glee ogled gland
Left/Right	34	fe fear feat ferns fetal jo joys join joker jolly
Up/Down	35	sw swan sway sweat swift k, ark, ask, tick, wick,
In/Out	36	lu luck blunt fluid lush da dash date sedan panda

G. POSTTEST

Repeat the Pretest. Then compare your Posttest results with your Pretest results.

H. 1-MINUTE ALPHANUMERIC TIMED WRITING

Take a 1-minute timed writing on lines 37–39. Note your speed and errors.

37 Kim ran the 7.96-mile race last week. Yanni 9
38 ran 14.80 miles. Zeke said the next 5K run will 19
39 be held on August 14 or August 23. 25

| 1 | 2 | 3 | 4 | 5 | 6 | 7 | 8 | 9 | 10

FORMATTING

E. Using Functions

A **function** is a pre-existing formula built into a spreadsheet that lets you make calculations or text changes quickly and easily. The following list shows some of the most common functions available with most spreadsheets.

SUM (Σ)	Adds values in a cell range	=SUM(A5:A16)
AVERAGE	Averages values in a cell range	=AVERAGE(D1:D9)
MAX	Finds largest value in a cell range	=MAX(F3:F91)
MIN	Finds smallest value in a cell range	=MIN(C12:C55)
ROUND	Rounds to a specified number of digits	=ROUND(SUM(B1:B3),2)
MEDIAN	Finds middle value in a cell range	=MEDIAN(L17:Q17)
SQRT	Finds square root of the value in a cell	=SQRT(Y54)
PROPER	Changes text to initial caps	=PROPER("kathy reeves")
UPPER	Changes text to all caps	=UPPER("jamal h. fowler")
NOW	Displays current time and/or date	=NOW()

F. Software Features

STUDENT MANUAL

Using a SUM Function
Centering Across Cell Ranges

Study Lesson 131 in your Student Manual. Complete all the practice activities while at your computer. Then complete the tasks that follow.

SPREADSHEET APPLICATIONS

ACTIVITY 26

Spreadsheet 19

Create a new spreadsheet, save it as SS19, then follow the steps below to create a spreadsheet similar to the example on p. 475.

1. In cell A1, key the label *Grocery Store Price Comparisons.*
2. In cell A2, key *Prepared by* followed by your name.
3. In cell A3, key the date as *February 14 {year}*, or 14 Feb., {year} in bold. Note that your spreadsheet may automatically change the format of the date.
4. Key the data into the cells as shown below.
5. Save your changes and close the file.

(continued on next page)

1. 2-Minute Timed Writings

Take two 2-minute timed writings on lines 40–45. Note your speed and errors.

Goal: 27/2'/4e

In the fall of the year, I find pleasure in 9
zipping up to the foothills to quietly view the 19
trees changing colors. Most all aspens turn to 28
shades of gold. Oak trees exude tones of red and 38
orange. The plants change colors each fall, but 47
all the changes are just amazing. 54

| 1 | 2 | 3 | 4 | 5 | 6 | 7 | 8 | 9 | 10 SI 1.27

MATH CONNECTION

Calculate Percentages The percent sign, %, is used to show a part of a whole. For example, if 50% of your class is girls, that means of the whole class (100%), half are girls. To calculate a percentage, divide the number of items you are evaluating by the total number of items. Then move the decimal point two places to the right.

For example, say that you received 15 votes in your class election, and there are 20 students in your class. To calculate the percentage of votes that you received, divide the number of votes that you received (15) by the total number of votes (20). 15 divided by 20 is 0.75. Move the decimal point two places to the right to get the percentage, which is 75%.

Calculate the percentage for each of the following problems. Key each percentage.

6/12 6/24 8/40

(continued)

5 All of the books in our catalog (is/are) categorized by subject.
6 Each of you (is/are) to bring two pencils to the test.
7 Neither one of us (is/are) likely to win the nomination.
8 One of the new cases storing books and tapes (was/were) damaged.

SKILLBUILDING

C. Preview Practice

Key each line 2 times as a preview to the timed writings that follow.

Accuracy 9 how extent impaired Alexander equipment surprised telephone
Speed 10 hearing speech moved wires help soon just grew live but was

D. 5-Minute Timed Writings

Take two 5-minute timed writings on the paragraphs. Note your speed and errors.

Goal: 39/5'/5e

11 Throughout its history America has prospered and grown 11
12 with the help of countless inventions. Although he could 23
13 not have realized the full extent of its effects at that 34
14 time, Alexander Graham Bell invented a device that led to a 46
15 change in the way we communicate not just in our country 57
16 but also in the entire world. 63
17 Bell grew up in a family that had a deep interest in 74
18 speech and deafness. He moved from Scotland to the United 86
19 States where he learned how to teach the hearing impaired 97
20 to speak. He also began to work with equipment that could 109
21 send several telegraph messages over one line. From this 120
22 interest, he started to try to send voices over electrical 132
23 wires. Soon the telephone was born. 139
24 Bell might be surprised at how his work has linked our 151
25 world together, but we can be sure he would be most proud 163
26 of the strides that have been made in helping the hearing 174
27 impaired. Bell's inventions have assisted those who cannot 186
28 hear to live richer lives in a hearing world. 195

| 1 | 2 | 3 | 4 | 5 | 6 | 7 | 8 | 9 | 10 | 11 | 12 SI 1.41

LESSON 27 SPECIAL SYMBOLS

OBJECTIVES:

- Employ the <, >, \, +, =, {, }, [,], and ~ keys.
- Refine keyboarding skills.
- Key 27/2'/4e.

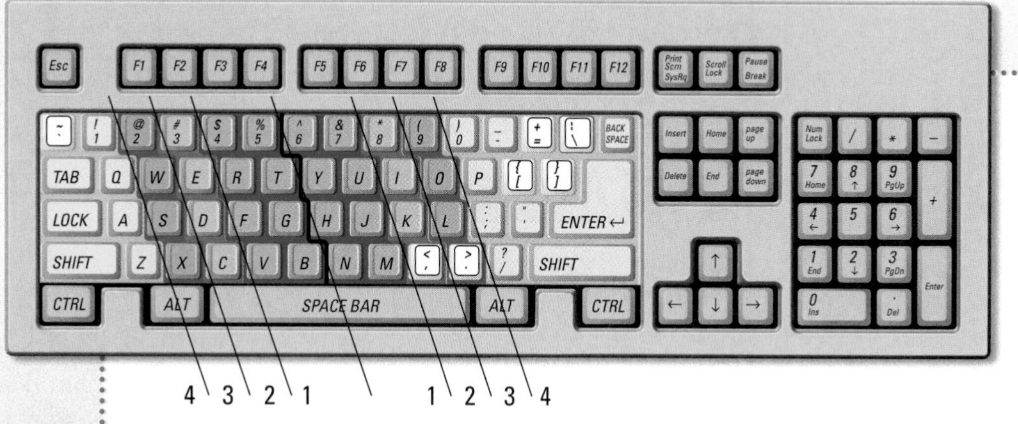

A. WARMUP

Key each line 2 times.

Speed	1	Brent hurt his arm today and is in a lot of pain.
Accuracy	2	The tax is zero on these dozen tax-exempt pizzas.
Numbers	3	The population of Cooper is 216,974, not 326,815.
Symbols	4	Stop & Shop has 25% off reams of 24# paper @ $13.

NEW KEYS

B. SPECIAL SYMBOLS

You have learned to key many frequently used symbols by touch. Other less frequently used symbols also appear on the keyboard. Although it is not necessary to learn these symbols by touch, you should know what they are, how they are used, where they are located, and what fingers to use.

(continued on next page)

LESSON 131 SPREADSHEETS: SUM FUNCTION, CENTER DATA

OBJECTIVES:

- Apply rules for using verbs with pronouns.
- Key 39/5'/5e.
- Apply the SUM function.
- Center data across a spreadsheet selection.

A. WARMUP

Key each line 2 times.

Speed	*1*	The loan form asked for two proofs of a good credit record.
Accuracy	*2*	If prizes were given for anxiety, Ms. Jaquan would qualify.
Language Link	*3*	An old adage says that a dog's bark is worse than its bite.
Numbers/Symbols	*4*	7/8, 4/5, 11/12, 1/2, 8/9, 10/11, 3/4, 6/7, 12/13, 5/6, 2/3

| 1 | 2 | 3 | 4 | 5 | 6 | 7 | 8 | 9 | 10 | 11 | 12

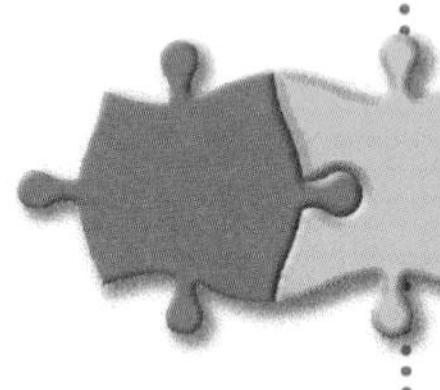

LANGUAGE LINK

B. SINGULAR AND PLURAL PRONOUNS

Study the rules and examples that follow. Then edit lines 5–8 by choosing the correct verb.

Rule 37: Some pronouns (*anybody, each, either, everybody, everyone, much, neither, no one, nobody,* and *one*) are always singular and take a singular verb. Other pronouns (*all, any, more, most, none,* and *some*) may be singular or plural, depending on the noun to which they refer.

Everybody was glad to hear that we could leave early.

Most of the workers are going to get a large raise.

Each employee is responsible for summarizing reports.

Some of the gas is being pumped into the tank.

(continued on next page)

(continued)

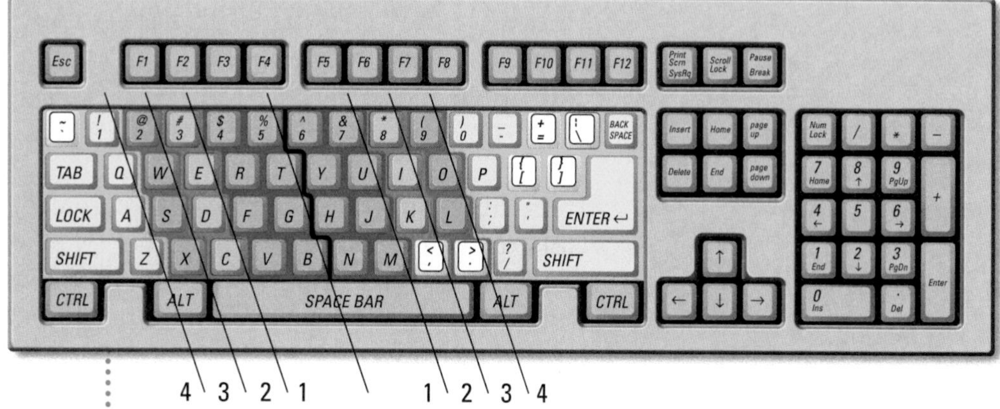

Find each of the symbols shown below on your keyboard. Note which finger controls each key and the spacing used with the symbol. In the example column, study how the symbol is used.

Key	Name	Use	Finger	Spacing	Example
\	Back-slash	Naming files/ directories	Sem	No space before and after.	`a:\Medical\ Doctor.cgs`
<	Less Than	Math	K	One space before and after.	`15 < 25`
>	Greater Than	Math	L	One space before and after.	`31 > 19`
=	Equal	Math	Sem	One space before and after.	`A = 27`
+	Plus	Math	Sem	One space before and after.	`3 + 3 = 6`
[ ]	Left and Right Brackets	Enclose special text	Sem	No space after [or before].	`"He [Twain] wrote . . . "`
{ }	Left and Right Curly Braces	Math and Internet searches	Sem	No space after { or before }.	`{4, 2, 6}`
~	Tilde	Internet addresses	A	No space before and after.	`www.isp.com/~jon`

(continued on next page)

(continued)

6. In cell C4, key *Celsius.* Enter the following numbers below as shown from low to high (ascending order) into cell range A7 through A16.

   0, 10, 24, 32, 43, 57, 70, 86, 95, 100

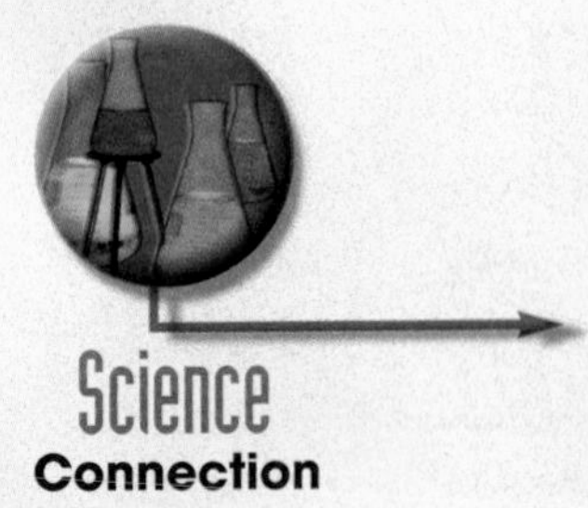

7. In cell C7, enter the formula to convert Fahrenheit to Celsius: (A7-32)*5/9.
   (To convert Fahrenheit to Celsius, you subtract 32 from Fahrenheit degrees, multiply by 5, and divide by 9, or F-32*5/9.)
8. Copy the formula from cell C7 into cell range C8 through C16.
9. Save your changes and close the file.

ACTIVITY 25

Spreadsheet 18

Open file SS17, save the file as SS18, and make the following changes:

1. In cell E7, enter the formula to convert Celsius to Fahrenheit: C7*9/5+32.
   (To convert Celsius to Fahrenheit, you multiply Celsius by 9, divide by 5, and add 32. Since the order of operations is correct, no parentheses are necessary.)
2. Copy this formula to cell range E8 through E16.)
3. Format the numbers in column C to have 1 decimal place.
4. Format the rest of the spreadsheet so that it is attractive and easy to read. Use Print Preview to see what adjustments are necessary.
5. Save your changes and close the file.

	A	B	C	D	E
1	Temperature Conversions				
2	Prepared by	[Your Name]			
3					
4	Fahrenheit		Celsius		Fahrenheit
5	Temperatures	➔	Temperatures	➔	Temperatures
6					
7	0		-17.8		0
8	10		-12.2		10
9	24		-4.4		24
10	32		0.0		32
11	43		6.1		43
12	57		13.9		57
13	70		21.1		70
14	86		30.0		86
15	95		35.0		95
16	100		37.8		100

(continued)

Key each line 2 times. Repeat if time permits.

5 Dakota keyed "C:\DATABASE\FRESHMEN\OFFICERS.SEP."
6 If X < Z and Y > X but < Z, then Z > X and Z > Y.
7 Please see if 7.13 + 5.21 = 12.34 and 9 + 2 = 11.

8 "They [Americans] captured Trenton [New Jersey]."
9 Search for these: {New York}, Ohio, {New Mexico}.
10 Use this format: http://www.server.com/~username.

SKILLBUILDING

C. PRETEST

Take a 1-minute timed writing of lines 11–14. Note your speed and errors.

11 A news report said that the trash will be 9
12 collected next week. Many county roads are still 19
13 covered with too much snow. The county officials 29
14 will discuss this problem for a few more days. 38

| 1 | 2 | 3 | 4 | 5 | 6 | 7 | 8 | 9 | 10

D. PRACTICE

SPEED: ***If you made 2 or fewer errors on the Pretest, key lines 15–22 two times each.***

ACCURACY: ***If you made more than 2 errors on the Pretest, key lines 15–18 as a group two times. Then key lines 19–22 as a group two times.***

Discrimination reaches ***are keys that are commonly substituted and easily confused, such as*** **w** ***and*** **e.**

15 asa flask aside sails saved masks sadly trash sas
16 fgf frogs foggy gaffe fugue golfs goofs fight gfg
17 ewe weeks fewer sewer sweat swell sweet weans wew
18 ded deal heeded dent need debate feed student ede

19 ioi spoil toils lions coins joins soils boils oio
20 mnm hymns money names numbs minor lemon means nmn
21 klk locks block flock keels kelts kilts kilns lkl
22 yuy yule young unduly pulley bully ruby jumpy uyu

E. POSTTEST

Repeat the Pretest. Compare your Posttest results with your Pretest results.

C. PRACTICE

In the chart below, find the number of errors you made on the Pretest. Then key each of the following designated drill lines two times.

Pretest Errors	0–1	2	3	4+
Drill Lines	12–16	11–15	10–14	9–13

Accuracy

```
 9 men money enjoy living buffalo trapping moccasins Americans
10 fur spent called Oregon wearing adopted collected mountains
11 gun alone settle coffee trading because buckskin rendezvous
12 set would summer lodges friends country companies exchanged
```

Speed

```
13 native skins these traps call many wild quit try joy fur in
14 trader would Rocky times most time year with can for way of
15 friend first pelts their hers guns meet most end men and at
16 living where pants their buck good were they sum set met or
```

D. POSTTEST

Repeat the Pretest. Compare your Posttest results with your Pretest results.

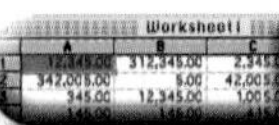

SPREADSHEET APPLICATIONS

E. ENTERING FORMULAS

When you work with formulas, you may need to use several operators. Spreadsheet formulas are completed in a specific order called the **order of operations**. For example, multiplication and division are performed before addition and subtraction. If the operators are equal (such as + and −), they will be completed in the order in which they appear in the formula. To change the order, enclose what you want calculated first in parentheses.

ACTIVITY 24
Spreadsheet 17

Create a new spreadsheet and save it as SS17. Then, follow these steps:

1. In cell A1, key the label *Temperature Conversions.*
2. In cell A2, key *Prepared by* and your name.
3. In cell A4, key *Fahrenheit;* copy this label into cell E4.
4. In cell A5, key *Temperatures;* copy this label into cells C5 and E5.
5. In cell B5, change the font to Wingdings®. Hold down the Alt key and enter *0232* on the numeric keypad. This character should appear: →. Copy this to cell D5.

(continued on next page)

F. Alphabet Review

Key each line 1 time. Repeat if time permits.

```
23 aa alas also again after bb bake blow begin black
24 cc came coat charm clear dd drop door dream dated

25 ee ever each eager enemy ff five foal frame flute
26 gg game give grate guard hh hope hall heavy human

27 ii iced into ideal ionic jj jail joke jewel juice
28 kk keep kick knife knock ll long lace lower lever

29 mm mope mail merit music nn name none never night
30 oo over open order occur pp pure pain piece plump

31 qq quit quad quest quote rr roar rain rhyme rural
32 ss sing soap saber sense tt time talk tooth trait

33 uu us urge upon vv via vase vine ww wag west warm
34 xx ox axis exit yy yen year yank zz zoo zany zinc
```

G. Number and Symbol Review

Key each line 1 time. Repeat if time permits.

```
35 46 maps, 69 snaps, 65 traps, 15 drapes, 63 grapes
36 57 lots, 85 plots, 16 slots, 50 floats, 86 clocks

37 53 hams, 46 trams, 95 slams, 62 flames, 67 blames
38 58 ails, 60 sails, 96 nails, 45 snails, 47 trails

39 (1) 32% of $17, (2) 2^9, (3) 15 @ $.81, (4) Wait!
40 (5) the key,* (6) A & W, (7) 56 @ $.10, (8) 40^3*

41 Tony said 3^2 and 20% of 40 have the same answer.
42 He rented 56 vases, 239 tables, and 4,078 chairs.

43 A & Z billed us for 79 pens @ $.23 on Invoice #8.
44 Dan collected 98 flowers, 39 bugs, and 47 leaves.

45 Nice & Clean (formerly #1 Laundry) is in Memphis.
46 The 743 people were served 980 rolls by 12 girls.
```

LESSON 130 SPREADSHEETS: ENTERING FORMULAS

OBJECTIVES:

- Improve keyboarding skills.
- Enter formulas into a spreadsheet.

A. WARMUP

Key each line 2 times.

Speed	Do not try to blame anyone else when you are late for work.
Accuracy	Mr. Jakman found exactly a quarter in the woven zipper bag.
Language Link	The towels in the Mallens' house said his and hers on them.
Numbers/Symbols	Olo saw apples @ $1.09, pears @ $1.29, and oranges @ $1.49.
	| 1 | 2 | 3 | 4 | 5 | 6 | 7 | 8 | 9 | 10 | 11 | 12

SCIENCE CONNECTION

Develop a Scientific Spreadsheet Think of an experiment that you have conducted in science class. How could you have used a spreadsheet to track your data and calculate the results? Design and create a spreadsheet that could be used for the experiment. Follow your teacher's instructions for saving and printing your work.

SKILLBUILDING

B. PRETEST

Take a 1-minute timed writing on the paragraph. Note your speed and errors.

Fur traders were the first Americans to settle in the 11
part of the country we now call Oregon. Because they spent 23
most all of their time in the mountains, they were called 34
mountain men. Many adopted the ways of Native Americans. 46

| 1 | 2 | 3 | 4 | 5 | 6 | 7 | 8 | 9 | 10 | 11 | 12

H. 1-Minute Alphanumeric Timed Writing

Take a 1-minute timed writing of lines 47–49. Note your speed and errors.

Jason paid Invoice #75 with Check #2301. He 9
mailed it June 24, but he forgot the $.39 stamp. 19
Stop & Go's bill needs to be paid July 1. 27
| 1 | 2 | 3 | 4 | 5 | 6 | 7 | 8 | 9 | 10

I. 2-Minute Timed Writings

Take two 2-minute timed writings of lines 50–55. Note your speed and errors.

Goal: 27/2'/4e

The Cherokee had no desire to leave the land 9
of their fathers. Troops required them to move to 19
the west. Many of them froze to death during the 29
brutal winter journey. They were not equipped to 39
exist through the cold winter as they moved along 49
the tragic Trail of Tears. 54
| 1 | 2 | 3 | 4 | 5 | 6 | 7 | 8 | 9 | 10 SI 1.25

MATH CONNECTION

Evaluate Inequalities Solve each of the problems below. Then replace each question mark with the *greater than* (>) symbol, the *less than* (<) symbol, or an equal sign (=). Key each problem and its solution. Follow your teacher's instructions for saving and printing your work.

Example: To solve the problem 30 + 5 ? 40 − 6, follow these steps:

1. Add 30 + 5 to get 35.
2. Subtract 6 from 40 to get 34.
3. Since 35 is greater than 34, insert the *greater than* symbol in place of the question mark: 35>34.

37 + 13 ? 35 + 16
100 − 30 ? 95 − 35
88 − 44 ? 22 + 11
40 × 2 ? 4 × 20
33 / 3 ? 33 × 0

ACTIVITY 21
Spreadsheet 14

Open the file SS13, save it as SS14, and make the following changes:

1. Select cell E10 and enter a formula to multiply cells C10 and D10.
2. Select cell E11 and enter a formula to multiply cells C11 and D11.
3. Select cell E15 and enter a formula to multiply cells C15 and D15.
4. Select cell E16 and enter a formula to multiply cells C16 and D16.
5. Select cell F7 and enter a formula to add cells E5 and E6.
6. Select cell F12 and enter a formula to add cells E10 and E11.
7. Save your changes and close the file.

ACTIVITY 22
Spreadsheet 15

Open the file SS14, save it as SS15, and then do the following:

1. Select cell F17 and enter a formula to add cells E15 and E16.
2. Select cell F19 and enter a formula to add cells F7, F12, and F17. Change the font to 12-point bold.
3. Format the numbers in columns E and F for currency with the dollar sign and 2 decimals.
4. Increase the height of row 3 until it is about 1.5 times the default height.
5. Select column E and change the width to 12.
6. Save your changes and close the file.

ACTIVITY 23
Spreadsheet 16

Open the file SS15, save it as SS16, and then do the following:

1. Preview the spreadsheet.
2. Change the page orientation to landscape.
3. Set the gridlines to print.
4. Preview the spreadsheet again.
5. If your teacher has given you instructions for printing, print the spreadsheet. Otherwise, save your changes and close the file.

MATH CONNECTION

Design a Spreadsheet Design and create a spreadsheet that you could use to calculate expenses for your favorite hobby. Include at least one formula. Then compose a short paragraph that explains how your spreadsheet works and how it will help you with your hobby. Follow your teacher's instructions for saving and printing your work.

LESSON 28 NUMERIC KEYPAD: 4 5 6 ENTER

OBJECTIVES:

- Apply capitalization rules.
- Key the 4, 5, 6, and ENTER keys on the numeric keypad.
- Refine keyboarding skills.
- Key 30/2'/4e.

A. WARMUP

Key each line 2 times.

Speed	1	We will be out for spring break in two more days.
Accuracy	2	Skip was quite vexed by the jazzman from Cologne.
Numbers	3	Your fingers can now find 10, 29, 38, 47, and 56.
Symbols	4	If T > Z, then explain (please!) why {T + H = Z}.

ACTIVITY 20

Spreadsheet 13
Expense Report

Create a new spreadsheet and save it as SS13. Then follow the steps below to create an expense report.

1. In cell A1, key the label *Expense Report for November.*
2. In cell A2, key *Prepared by* and your name.
3. Key the data as shown in the illustration. Use the copy feature when it is appropriate.
4. Change the font in cells A1 and A2 to 12-point bold.
5. Move A1 through A2 to C1 through C2. Center the text in rows 1 and 2.
6. Bold and center the data in rows 4, 9, and 14.
7. Select cell range A4 through E17, and automatically widen the columns.
8. Align cells A7, A12, and A17 at the right.
9. Change the font in cell A19 to 12-point bold.
10. Select cell E5 and enter a formula to multiply cells C5 and D5 (C5*D5).
11. Select cell E6 and enter a formula to multiply cells C6 and D6.
12. Save the changes and close the file.

	A	B	C	D	E
4	Travel	Dates	Miles	Per Mile	Mileage
5		November 7-9	500	0.31	
6		November 18-19	175	0.31	
7	Total Travel				
8					
9	Lodging	Dates	Nights	Per Night	Total
10		November 7-9	3	75	
11		November 18-19	2	80	
12	Total Lodging				
13					
14	Meals	Dates	Days	Per Day	Total
15		November 7-9	3	40	
16		November 18-19	2	40	
17	Total Meals				
18					
19	Total Expenses for November				

LANGUAGE LINK

B. Capitalization

Study the rules and the examples below. Then edit lines 5–8 to correct any errors in capitalization.

Rule 1: Capitalize the first word of a sentence.

The weather bureau predicted a winter storm. It was severe.

Rule 2: Capitalize the names of the days of the week, months, holidays, and religious days. Do not capitalize the names of the seasons.

In the fall, we celebrate Thanksgiving on Thursday, November 24.

Edit the lines to correct any errors in capitalization.

```
5 memorial day this year will fall on monday, may 27.
6 why wait until wednesday? we can leave later today.
7 during the Winter, they skied and skated every day.
8 Offices are closed on memorial day and on thursday.
```

NEW KEYS

C. Keypad Home-Key Position

The NUM LOCK key (usually located at the top left of the number keypad) must be active before you can key numbers on the keypad. If the NUM LOCK light is not on, press the NUM LOCK key.

The 4, 5, and 6 are the home keys for the numeric keypad.

1. Place your J, K, and L fingers on 4, 5, and 6 on the numeric keypad. You will feel a raised marker on the 5 key. This marker will help you keep your fingers on the home keys.
2. Place your Sem finger over the ENTER key. The ENTER key on the numeric keypad functions just like the ENTER key on the alphabetic keyboard.

(continued)

Cell Reference
Displays the address of the active cell.

Entry Bar
Displays the contents of the active cell.

B9 = =B4+B5+B6+B7

Formula in Active Cell B9
Adds the contents of four cells.

	A	B
1	**The Ellis Family**	
2	**Monthly Fixed Expenses**	
3		
4	Cass Telephone Cooperative	$65.00
5	Citizen's Electric	$185.00
6	Farmers' Insurance	$245.96
7	Titus Mortgage Company	$327.05
8		
9	**Total Fixed Expenses**	**$823.01**

Active Cell
Displays the formula results.

Formula Results
Gives the sum of the contents of cells B4 through B7.

E. Software Features

STUDENT MANUAL

Formulas

Study Lesson 129 in your Student Manual. Complete all the practice activities while at your computer. Then complete the tasks that follow.

*inter*NET CONNECTION

Develop Budgeting Skills Many college graduates who earn good salaries begin their adult lives in financial trouble because of mismanagement of credit and poor budgeting habits during their college years. Developing good budgeting habits now will start you on the path to healthy money management. Go to the Online Learning Center at **KeyComps.glencoe.com>Internet Connection> Unit 7>Lesson 129** and read the information about creating budgets. Then complete the activity. Follow your teacher's instructions for saving and printing your work.

D. 4 5 6 Keys

Key the following numbers column by column. Use the proper finger for each key. Press Enter after the final digit of each number. Repeat if time permits.

Use J finger to key 4. Use the K finger to key 5. Use the Sem finger to press Enter.

Keep your eyes on the copy.

Accuracy is very important when keying numbers.

9	444	456	454
10	555	654	464
11	666	445	546
12	455	446	564
13	466	554	654
14	544	556	645
15	566	664	666
16	644	665	555
17	655	456	444
18	456	654	456

SKILLBUILDING

E. Keypad Practice

Key the following numbers column by column. Press Enter after the final digit of each number. Keep your eyes on the copy. Repeat if time permits.

Use J, K, and L fingers.

Keep your eyes on the copy.

Accuracy is very important when keying numbers.

19	444	455	464	555	466	646	666	544	456	445	644
20	546	554	556	454	645	664	545	654	665	565	465
21	445	446	455	466	456	454	465	464	554	556	544
22	644	655	645	646	654	656	666	464	555	665	456
23	654	456	564	465	646	656	464	456	546	564	465

SKILLBUILDING

C. 30-Second OK Timed Writings

Take two 30-second OK (error-free) timed writings on lines 9–10. Then take two 30-second OK timed writings on lines 11–12. Goal: no errors.

```
 9      A quick leap from a taxi caused Gavez to hurt his arm.   11
10 He fell down and hurt his shoulder, which was already sore.   23

11      Jay's six long vans zipped quickly down the wet roads,   11
12 but they were not able to finish the entire route in time.    23
   | 1 | 2 | 3 | 4 | 5 | 6 | 7 | 8 | 9 | 10 | 11 | 12
```

FORMATTING

D. Spreadsheet Formulas

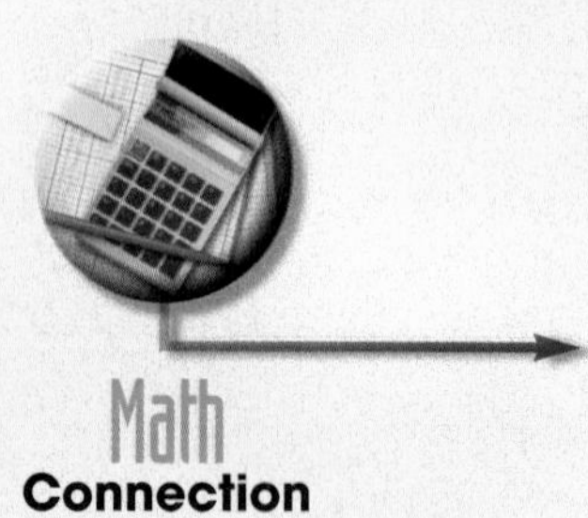

A spreadsheet **formula** simply instructs the spreadsheet to perform various calculations. For example, if you create a spreadsheet for your budget, you can enter formulas to automatically add your income, add your expenses, and subtract your expenses from your income.

To enter a formula in a spreadsheet, you must use the cell names and the following **mathematical operators:**

+ (plus sign) for addition
- (hyphen) for subtraction
* (asterisk) for multiplication
/ (slash) for division
^ (caret) for exponentiation

When you enter a formula into a cell and press ENTER, only the answer appears in the cell. The formula is displayed in the entry bar. (See the example page 466.)

To enter a formula, select the cell where you want the formula. Begin formulas with an equal sign (=) to indicate that you are going to enter a value, not a label. Formulas are keyed without spaces.

Study the formula displayed in the entry bar on the next page. It adds the contents of cells B4 through B7 and displays the answer in the active cell, B9.

(continued on next page)

F. Technique Timed Writings

Take two 30-second timed writings of each line. Focus on the techniques at the left.

Lines 24 and 25: Efficient and smooth operation of the SHIFT keys. Lines 26 and 27: Efficient and smooth operation of the ENTER key.

```
24 Will Zeb and Vern work Zone Two with Cam and Nic?
25 Miriam and Dolores saw Broadway and Main Streets.
26 Did Ben Milo fix that off/on switch? Did it work?
27 Ivan is grateful that it is ready for the winter.
   | 1 | 2 | 3 | 4 | 5 | 6 | 7 | 8 | 9 | 10
```

G. Diagnostic Practice: Alphabet

Turn to the Diagnostic Practice: Alphabet routine on page SB1. Key one of the Pretest/Posttest paragraphs and identify any errors. Then key the corresponding drill lines on p. SB2 2 times for each letter on which you made 2 or more errors and 1 time for each letter on which you made only 1 error. Finally, rekey the Pretest and compare your performance.

H. 12-Second Sprints

Take three 12-second timed writings of each line. Try to increase your speed on each timed writing.

```
28 Walking can pick you up if you are feeling tired.
29 Your heart and lungs can work harder as you walk.
30 It may be that a walk is often better than a nap.
31 You will keep fit if you walk each and every day.
   ||||5||||10||||15||||20||||25||||30||||35||||40||||45||||50
```

I. 2-Minute Timed Writings

Take two 2-minute timed writings of lines 32–38. Note your speed and errors.

Goal: 30/2'/4e

```
32      Good workers will be quick to discover what    9
33 others on the job like or dislike. Just a bit of   19
34 extra effort by them will make the office a more   29
35 pleasing place in which to work. A cheerful card   38
36 once in a while can bring a smile to one in need   49
37 of support at work. It is amazing how one kind     59
38 act spreads.                                       60
   | 1 | 2 | 3 | 4 | 5 | 6 | 7 | 8 | 9 | 10     SI 1.21
```

LESSON 129 SPREADSHEETS: ENTERING FORMULAS

OBJECTIVES:

- Apply rules for apostrophes and possessives.
- Improve keyboarding skills.
- Enter formulas into a spreadsheet.

A. WARMUP

Key each line 2 times.

Speed	1	Bill has worked as a short order cook in a small town cafe.
Accuracy	2	Ziggy James quickly paid us for the five new Rambler taxis.
Language Link	3	Sara's car required four hundred dollars' worth of repairs.
Numbers	4	Old Models 75, 83, and 96 are now Models 121, 344, and 500.

| 1 | 2 | 3 | 4 | 5 | 6 | 7 | 8 | 9 | 10 | 11 | 12

LANGUAGE LINK

B. APOSTROPHE

Study the rules and examples below. Then edit lines 5–8 by inserting apostrophes where appropriate.

Rule 35: Use apostrophe *s* (*'s*) to form the possessive of indefinite pronouns.

She was instructed to select anybody's paper for a sample.

Rule 36: Do not use an apostrophe with possessive personal pronouns.

Each computer comes carefully packed in its own container.

5 The new house was hers, but now it is yours.
6 Somebodys lottery ticket is going to be worth millions.
7 Our company recycles its paper, and everyones support is needed.
8 No ones desktop is running, so the laptops are ours for today.

LESSON 29 NUMERIC KEYPAD: 7 8 9

OBJECTIVES:

- Key 7, 8, 9 on the numeric keypad.
- Refine keyboarding skills.
- Key 30/2'/4e.

1 2 3 4

A. WARMUP

Key each line 2 times.

Speed	1	No one can say that he is not giving full effort.
Accuracy	2	Alex was puzzled by the czar's quip about oxygen.
Language Link	3	Molly saw Alex on a Sunday, Easter Day, in March.
Numbers	4	Without looking he can key 67, 89, 23, 14, and 5.

MATH CONNECTION

Determine Leap Years A standard year is equal to 365 days. That is the time the earth takes to complete one orbit around the sun. However, the earth actually takes 365 and one-fourth days to complete an orbit. To make up for this extra quarter day, an extra day is added to the calendar once every four years. A year with this extra day is called a leap year.

The years 2000 and 2004 were leap years. Use the numeric keypad to key 2008, which is also a leap year. Add 4 to 2008 to determine the next leap year to key, which is 2012. Key the next five leap years after 2012, adding 4 each time. Save your work according to your teacher's instructions.

ACTIVITY 16
Spreadsheet 5-B

Open the file SS5-B; then follow these steps:

1. Preview the file using Print Preview. Notice that the page orientation is portrait and there are no gridlines in the spreadsheet.
2. Change the page orientation to landscape.
3. Set the gridlines to print.
4. Preview the file, and note the changes that you made.
5. If your teacher has given you instructions for printing, print the spreadsheet. Otherwise, close the file without saving your changes.

ACTIVITY 17
Spreadsheet 3-B

Open the file SS3-B; then follow these steps:

1. Preview the file.
2. Change the orientation to landscape.
3. Select cell range A13 through G13, and print-preview that range.
4. Set the gridlines and row and column headings to print, and preview the spreadsheet again.
5. If your teacher has given you instructions for printing, print the selected cell range. Otherwise, close the file without saving your changes.

ACTIVITY 18
Spreadsheet 6

Open the file SS6; then follow these steps:

1. Preview the file.
2. Select cell range A1 through E8, and preview that range.
3. Deselect the cell range.
4. Close the file without saving your changes.

ACTIVITY 19
Spreadsheet 7

Open the file SS7; then follow these steps:

1. Change the page orientation to landscape.
2. Set the gridlines and row and column headings to print.
3. Preview the spreadsheet.
4. If your teacher has given you instructions for printing, print the spreadsheet. Otherwise, close the file without saving your changes.

NEW KEYS

B. 7 8 9 Keys

Key the following numbers column by column. Use the proper finger for each key. Press Enter after the final digit of each number. Keep your eyes on the copy. Repeat if time permits.

Use the J finger to key 7. Use the K finger to key 8. Use the L finger to key 9.

Be sure Num Lock is on.

Concentrate on accuracy as you key the numbers.

5	474	585	696
6	747	858	969
7	774	885	996
8	447	558	669
9	744	855	966
10	477	588	699
11	444	555	666
12	747	858	969
13	774	885	996
14	747	858	969

SKILLBUILDING

C. Keypad Practice

Key the following numbers column by column. Press Enter after the final digit of each number. Keep your eyes on the copy. Repeat if time permits.

Keep eyes on copy. Use correct fingers. Concentrate on accuracy.

15	456	556	474	699	477	577	677	748	847	947
16	654	664	585	747	488	588	688	749	849	948
17	445	665	696	858	499	599	699	758	857	957
18	446	456	477	969	478	578	678	759	859	958
19	554	654	588	789	489	589	689	767	868	969

D. Printing Spreadsheets

Many spreadsheets are too wide to print on a standard 8.5-inch-wide page. However, spreadsheets can be printed on an 11-inch-wide page. **Page orientation** is the direction of the page on which the spreadsheet is printed. The default page orientation (standard 8.5 × 11 inches) is called **portrait**. When the orientation is changed to print across the 11-inch width of a page, it is called **landscape**.

Portrait

	A	B	C	D	E	F
1	Small Caribbean Islands					
2	Prepared by Student's Name					
3	10/25/98					
4	2:35 PM					
5						
6	Name	Square Miles	Population	Transportation	Lodging	Cost
7						
8	Anegada	15.0	250	Antilles Air	Coral Reef Estate	$180
9	Little Cayman	10.0	100	Isle Air	The Farm House	$120
10	Bequia	7.0	5,000	Ferry	Parrots' Roost	$75
11	Saba	5.0	1,200	Ferry	The Gang Plank	$240
12	Mayreau	1.5	250	Mailboat	Pirates' Hideaway	$90

Landscape

	A	B	C	D	E	F
1	Small Caribbean Islands					
2	Prepared by Student's Name					
3	10/25/98					
4	2:35 PM					
5						
6	Name	Square Miles	Population	Transportation	Lodging	Cost
7						
8	Anegada	15.0	250	Antilles Air	Coral Reef Estate	$180
9	Little Cayman	10.0	100	Isle Air	The Farm House	$120
10	Bequia	7.0	5,000	Ferry	Parrots' Roost	$75
11	Saba	5.0	1,200	Ferry	The Gang Plank	$240
12	Mayreau	1.5	250	Mailboat	Pirates' Hideaway	$90

Spreadsheets often consist of multiple pages. However, you can print only a portion of a spreadsheet. In addition, you can print spreadsheets with or without the gridlines and with or without the row and column headings. Before you print a spreadsheet, use Print Preview to ensure you are printing what you want.

E. Software Features

STUDENT MANUAL

Printing Worksheets
Printing Cell Ranges
Print Gridlines, Row, and Column Headings

Study Lesson 128 in your Student Manual. Complete all the practice activities while at your computer. Then complete the tasks that follow.

D. Paced Practice

Turn to the Paced Practice routine beginning on page SB7. Take a 1-minute timed writing on the Entry Timed Writing paragraph. Then follow the directions at the top of page SB7 for completing the activity.

E. 30-Second OK Timed Writings

Take two 30-second OK timed writings on lines 20–21. Then take two 30 second OK timed writings on lines 22–23. Goal: no errors.

```
20      He wants to work for a company that provides
21 benefits to workers. Jay's benefits are terrific.

22      Flat computer screen means that I can set up
23 my computer on my desk because the parts all fit.
   | 1 | 2 | 3 | 4 | 5 | 6 | 7 | 8 | 9 | 10
```

F. PRETEST

Take a 1-minute timed writing on the paragraph. Note your speed and errors.

```
24      Jenny loved most all of the opera music that   9
25 the kids sang. No one could deny how funny they    19
26 looked in muffs and emu feathers. Everyone had a   29
27 very good time that day.                           33
   | 1 | 2 | 3 | 4 | 5 | 6 | 7 | 8 | 9 | 10
```

G. PRACTICE

SPEED: *If you made 2 or fewer errors on the Pretest, key lines 28–35 two times each.*

ACCURACY: *If you made more than 2 errors on the Pretest, key lines 28–31 as a group two times. Then key lines 32–35 as a group two times.*

Adjacent Reaches

```
28 as mast blast phase clash ashes atlas brash hasty
29 op crop opera flops opens poppy drops opals mopes
30 ds kids spuds grids bonds birds brads leads holds
31 lk milk talks walks balks milky silky bulky sulky
```

Jump Reaches

```
32 mu mute music muffs munch murky mulls musty muddy
33 ve cove verse serve curve verve wives chive sieve
34 ny deny funny phony shiny sunny irony corny agony
35 in sink blink slink whine shine winds pines inlet
```

H. POSTTEST

Repeat the Pretest. Compare your Posttest results with your Pretest results.

LESSON 128 SPREADSHEETS: PRINTING

OBJECTIVES:

- Increase keyboarding speed and improve accuracy.
- Print a worksheet and cell ranges.
- Print with and without gridlines.
- Print with and without row and column headings.

A. WARMUP

Key each line 2 times.

Speed 1 The girls had fun playing games in the park near our house.
Accuracy 2 A sequence of jobs, or queue, is held in auxiliary storage.
Language Link 3 The building's exterior was so worn, he questioned its age.
Symbols 4 less than = <; greater than = >; backslash = \; a tilde = ~

| 1 | 2 | 3 | 4 | 5 | 6 | 7 | 8 | 9 | 10 | 11 | 12

SKILLBUILDING

B. 30-SECOND TIMED WRITINGS

Take two 30-second timed writings on lines 5–6. Then take two 30-second timed writings on lines 7–8. Try to increase your speed each time.

5 A resume must be entirely free of errors; an employer 11
6 will view it as a reflection of how you will do on the job. 23

7 Before you go to an interview, learn all you can about 11
8 that company by spending some time in your public library. 23

| 1 | 2 | 3 | 4 | 5 | 6 | 7 | 8 | 9 | 10 | 11 | 12

C. DIAGNOSTIC PRACTICE: ALPAHBET

Turn to the Diagnostic Practice: Alphabet routine on page SB1. Key one of the Pretest/Posttest paragraphs and identify any errors made. Then key the corresponding drill lines 2 times for each letter on which you made 2 or more errors and 1 time for each letter on which you made only 1 error. Finally, repeat the same Pretest and compare your performance.

1. 2-Minute Timed Writings

Take two 2-minute timed writings on lines 36–42. Note your speed and errors.

Goal: 30/2'/4e

36 The end of a school program is a great feat 9
37 for most students. Some believe it might be the 19
38 last time for a test. This may not be so, as a 28
39 number of exams may be taken in their lifetime. 38
40 It is quite puzzling to some why tests should be 47
41 given when they have already been judged by their 57
42 achievements. 60

| 1 | 2 | 3 | 4 | 5 | 6 | 7 | 8 | 9 | 10 SI 1.22

COMMUNICATION FOCUS

List Teamwork Tips The ability to work well as part of a team is an important communication skill. Think of a time when you were part of a team that worked well together. Consider why you made a good team. Key three short tips that you think could help other teams to work well together. Follow your teacher's instructions for saving and printing your work.

(continued)

	A	B	C	D	E
8	Name	Square Miles	Population	Lodging	Cost
9					
10					
11					
12	Anegada	15	250	Coral Reef Estate	180
13	Beguia	7	5000	Parrot's Roost	78
14	Little Cayman	10	100	The Farm House	120
15	Mayreau	1.5	250	Pirate's Hideaway	90
16	Saba	5	1200	The Gang Plank	240

ACTIVITY 14
Spreadsheet 11

Open the file SS10, save it as SS11, and make the following changes:

1. Select row 1, and change the point size to 16.
2. Move cell A5 to A2.
3. Select cell A3, and format the date as *MM/DD/YY*.
4. Select cell A4, and format the time as *H:MM PM*.
5. Change rows 3 and 4 to 12-point size.
6. Move cell range A8 through E8 to A6 through E6.
7. Save your changes and close the file.

ACTIVITY 15
Spreadsheet 12

Open the file SS11, save it as SS12, and make the following changes:

1. Bold row 6.
2. Move cell range A12 through E16 to A8 through E12.
3. Format cell range B8 through B12 to have 1 decimal place.
4. Format cell range C8 through C12 to have commas and no decimals.
5. Format cell range E8 through E12 to have dollar signs and no decimals.
6. Select cell range A6 through E12, and automatically widen the columns.
7. Horizontally center the text in rows 1 through 4 between columns A through E.
8. Change row 5 to double the default height.
9. Change row 7 to 1.5 times the default height.
10. Save your changes and close the file.

MATH CONNECTION

Convert Fractions to Decimals You might prefer to use decimals rather than fractions to display data. To convert a fraction, you simply divide the numerator (the top number) by the denominator (the bottom number).

For example: 1/2 = 1 ÷ 2 = .50

Convert the following fractions to decimals: 3⁄4; 1⁄8; 1 1⁄2; 3 1⁄4

REVIEW

OBJECTIVES:

- Refine numeric keypad skills.
- Refine keyboarding skills.
- Key 30/2'/4e.
- Compose short phrases at the keyboard.

A. WARMUP

Key each line 2 times.

Speed	1	Tish dances with grace and seems to float on air.
Accuracy	2	Zudora and Javan are amazed by the tranquil pool.
Language Link	3	I went to an April spring flower show on Tuesday.
Numbers/Symbols	4	Movies 7 (on Highway 59) charges $2 on Thursdays.

SKILLBUILDING

B. KEYPAD REVIEW

Key the following numbers column by column. Press ENTER after the final digit of each number. Keep your eyes on the copy. Repeat if time permits.

Use the correct fingers as you key each set of numbers. Operate the numeric keypad smoothly.

5	444	999	657	547	557	985	968	897	766	687
6	555	489	658	548	558	986	969	898	768	697
7	666	589	659	549	559	964	894	899	769	567
8	777	689	654	554	987	965	895	764	684	459
9	888	789	655	556	984	967	896	765	685	648

C. TECHNIQUE CHECKPOINT

Key each line 2 times. Focus on the technique at the left.

Concentrate on smooth operation of the SHIFT keys.

10 Benji keyed a report on New Guinea and Australia.
11 Kodi said that all of us should meet after class.
12 I bought yards of flannel at Sew Easy this month.
13 Oren donated his profit to the Find-a-Child Fund.

E. Formatting Spreadsheet Values

A **value** is a spreadsheet entry that begins with a number or a mathematical sign. Because spreadsheets are designed to work with values, you can format numbers, dates, and times in many different ways. For example, the number *15.75* can be formatted as 15¾, *$15.75, 15.8*, or *16*. The date *November 13, 2006,* can be formatted *11/13/06*. Remember that if a value is too wide to fit in a column, you will see only number signs (#####). When you widen the column, the value will be displayed.

F. Software Features

STUDENT MANUAL

Formatting Values

Study Lesson 127 in your Student Manual. Complete all the practice activities while at your computer. Then complete the tasks that follow.

MATH CONNECTION

Formatting Values Excel provides many options for formatting numbers. In the Format Cells screen, click on the categories to see how the formatting options change. Then create a spreadsheet titled **Value Formatting Options**. Enter ten categories in the first column. In the second column describe the formatting options for each category. In a third column, add examples for each category. Follow your teacher's instructions for saving and printing your work.

SPREADSHEET APPLICATIONS

ACTIVITY 13
Spreadsheet 10

Create a new spreadsheet and save it as SS10. Then follow these steps to format the values:

1. In cell A1, key the label *Small Caribbean Islands*.
2. In cell A3, key the date as *10/25*.
3. In cell A4, key the time as *2:35:49 PM*.
4. In cell A5, key *Prepared by* and your name.
5. Enter the data as shown in the illustration on page 460 into the correct cells.
6. Save your changes and close the file.

(continued on next page)

D. Alphabet Review

Key each line 1 time. Concentrate on efficient and smooth operation of the SHIFT keys. Repeat if time permits.

14 A Anna Aram Alan B Bel Bern Beth C Curt Chan Cleo
15 D Desi Dino Dona E Ean Erin Egan F Fifi Finn Faye
16 G Gaby Gian Gena H Ham Hank Hedy I Ilse Ilya Iris

17 J Jess Jori Jojo K Kia Kern Kwan L Luke Lars Lyda
18 M Miki Marc Mara N Noe Niki Noel O Olin Otto Olga
19 P Pace Pita Powa Q Qam Quin Quan R Rani Reid Rory

20 S Suni Saul Shan T Tov Taio Tobi U Ulma Urie Ushi
21 V Vera Vick Vala W Web Wren Wilt X Xann Xela Xuxa
22 Y Yoki York Ynez Yusif Z Zizi Zane Zena Zeke Zara

E. Technique Timed Writings

Take two 30-second timed writings on each line. Focus on the technique at the left.

Concentrate on smooth operation of the SHIFT keys.

23 David and Ian still work at B. K. Dry Goods, Inc.
24 Mrs. R. K. Dunn taught Spanish at Jefferson High.
25 Rory, Anna, and Han ran the Mile-High Race today.
26 She is at the top in her new job at the car wash.

| 1 | 2 | 3 | 4 | 5 | 6 | 7 | 8 | 9 | 10

F. PRETEST

Take a 1-minute timed writing on the paragraph. Note your speed and errors.

27 Buzz did research about the history of tidal 9
28 waves. The doom and gloom of his essay threw our 19
29 class into a tizzy. The wild storm outside didn't 29
30 help matters. We were all upset that day. 37

| 1 | 2 | 3 | 4 | 5 | 6 | 7 | 8 | 9 | 10

SKILLBUILDING

C. Preview Practice

Key each line 2 times as a preview to the timed writings that follow.

Accuracy trend amazing relaxed quickly powerful employee communicate
Speed leisure office small trend home with that room work made by

D. 5-Minute Timed Writings

Take two 5-minute timed writings on the paragraphs. Note your speed and errors.

Goal: 39/5'/5e

Businesses that are based in the home are booming as a 11
way to earn a good living. Also, more and more workers can 23
choose to stay at home and communicate with the company by 35
computer. An office in the home saves time and money spent 47
traveling to and from the office. 53

This trend is now possible because of the ease with 64
which workers can make use of small, powerful computers. 75
This means that the workplace does not need to be in the 87
corporate office building itself. Computers can fit into a 99
small part of a room in the home, and they have an amazing 110
power to communicate with each other. This ability has had 122
a huge impact on where people do work. Projects worked on 134
by an employee on the computer at home can be sent quickly 146
over phone lines to the office through the use of modems, 157
faxes, and e-mail. 161

Today's workers want to have a more relaxed life and 172
to enjoy more leisure time than they could in the past. 183
Thanks to powerful computers, millions of people can do so. 195

SI 1.38

| 1 | 2 | 3 | 4 | 5 | 6 | 7 | 8 | 9 | 10 | 11 | 12

G. PRACTICE

SPEED: ***If you made 2 or fewer errors on the Pretest, key lines 31–38 two times each.***

ACCURACY: ***If you made more than 2 errors on the Pretest, key lines 31–34 as a group two times. Then key lines 35–38 as a group two times.***

Double Reaches

```
31 ss pass floss guess essay lasso fussy abyss issue
32 oo doom gloom igloo roomy roost afoot bloom scoot
33 zz buzz pizza dizzy jazzy fuzzy dizzy tizzy fizzy
34 ll will silly hello jelly wells drill tells walls
```

Alternate Reaches

```
35 ti tidy ticks tight optic title tidal stick stiff
36 or fork odors storm world coral works adorn stork
37 wi wiry wield twice widow swift wicks swish twirl
38 sl slap slick isles aisle slant slams slips slows
```

H. POSTTEST

Repeat the Pretest. Compare your Posttest results with your Pretest results.

I. 2-Minute Timed Writings

Take two 2-minute timed writings on lines 39–45. Note your speed and errors.

Goal: 30/2'/4e

```
39      Poachers hunt and kill game against the law.    9
40 Many species such as big cats, caimans, quetzal     19
41 birds, and whales may become extinct from being     28
42 killed for their fur, hides, or feathers. Laws      38
43 have been passed to save wildlife. Parks have       47
44 been jointly set up in all parts of the world to    57
45 serve as havens.                                    60
   | 1 | 2 | 3 | 4 | 5 | 6 | 7 | 8 | 9 | 10     SI 1.22
```

SCIENCE CONNECTION

Research Animal Diets Choose five animals and key their names. Use a print or online resource, such as an encyclopedia, to look up each animal. Key two items that are part of each animal's diet. Follow your teacher's instructions for saving and printing your work.

LESSON 127 SPREADSHEETS: FORMATTING VALUES

OBJECTIVES:

- Compose a letter at the keyboard.
- Format values in a spreadsheet.
- Key 39/5′/5e.

A. WARMUP

Key each line 2 times.

Speed	1	If you find the small blue ball, please toss it to our dog.
Accuracy	2	Gwyn exceeds the speed limit by zigzagging through traffic.
Language Link	3	The teacher's day was full of her children's fun and games.
Numbers	4	Dale should use cars 47, 38, 29, or 10 if 56 laps are left.

| 1 | 2 | 3 | 4 | 5 | 6 | 7 | 8 | 9 | 10 | 11 | 12

LANGUAGE LINK

B. COMPOSING AT THE KEYBOARD

Compose the body of a letter to the Public Relations department of a large computer or software company and ask them for information on their latest developments. Explain that you are studying the future of technology and that you need the information to write a report on how new technology will affect education in the future.

COMMUNICATION FOCUS

Organize Information A letter requesting information should be easy to follow so that the receiver can include all the requested information quickly. One way to make it easy is to bullet each item to be checked off by the receiver.

In the letter that you wrote in Activity B above, add bullets so that each item of information that you requested is a separate item. Rewrite your sentences if necessary. Save your work according to your teacher's instructions.

J. Composing at the Keyboard

Answer each question with a few words or a short phrase. Keep your eyes on the screen as you compose; do not look at your hands.

46 What career interests you?
47 What is your favorite book?
48 What are two states you would like to visit?
49 What are three things you like about yourself?
50 Who are three people who have been in the news recently?

PORTFOLIO *Activity*

Evaluate Your Progress Select two of the timed writings you have completed in Unit 2. Compare your speed and accuracy from those timed writings to your speed and accuracy in a timed writing from Lesson 20.

Key two short phrases explaining how your keyboarding skills have improved. Then key two short phrases about what you can do to improve even more during the weeks ahead. Follow your teacher's instructions for saving and printing your work.

SOCIAL STUDIES CONNECTION

Identify States That Border Water Many states have borders along major bodies of water. Locate a map of the United States in an atlas, encyclopedia, textbook, or online source. Key the names of five states that border an ocean or a lake. Follow your teacher's instructions for saving and printing your work.

ACTIVITY 11
Spreadsheet 8

Open the file SS7 and save it as SS8. Then follow these steps:

1. Select cell range A3 through F3, and center the cell contents.
2. While cell range A3 through F3 is still selected, move the contents to cells A4 through F4.
3. Select cell range A16 through F16, and move the contents to A8 through F8.
4. Select cell range A8 through F15, and move the contents to A6 through F13.
5. Select cell range C4 through C13, and move the contents to B4 through B13.
6. Select row 4, and change the point size to 16.
7. Change row 3 to approximately 2 times the default height.
8. Change row 5 to approximately 1.5 times the default height.
9. Select row 4, and automatically widen the columns.
10. Save your changes and close the file.

ACTIVITY 12
Spreadsheet 9

Open the file SS8 and save it as SS9. Then follow these steps to move cell contents and change row heights:

1. Select cell range E4 through E13, and move the contents to C4 through C13.
2. Select cell range F4 through F13, and move the contents to E4 through E13.
3. Select cell range B6 through E13, and align the cell contents on the right.
4. Select cell range A4 through E13, and automatically widen the columns.
5. In cell A1, delete the words *for Tours of Summer.*
6. Select row 1, and change the point size to 20.
7. Select row 2, and change the point size to 18.
8. Select cell range A1 through A2, and move the contents to C1 and C2. Then center the column data.
9. Save your changes and close the file.

COMMUNICATION FOCUS

Communicate with Spreadsheets Spreadsheets are useful tools for communicating information such as schedules, budgets, inventories, and directories. Think of two ways that your school might use spreadsheets. Then key two paragraphs describing each type of spreadsheet, how it would be used, and who would benefit from it.

LESSON 31 NUMERIC KEYPAD: 1 2 3

OBJECTIVES:

- Key 1, 2, and 3 on the numeric keypad.
- Refine numeric keypad skills.
- Key 30/2'/4e.
- Compose short phrases at the keyboard.

A. WARMUP

Key each line 2 times.

Speed	1	The rain will stop soon; then the sun will shine.
Accuracy	2	Zeke exhibits exuberance on quizzes about quakes.
Language Link	3	Louise will meet us in May on the first Saturday.
Numbers/Symbols	4	Paige added 7 + 1 + 24 + 13 + 22 + 11 and got 78.

MATH CONNECTION

Create a Math Quiz Think of and key five multiplication problems, such as 6 x 30. Key the answers in a separate document. Follow your teacher's instructions for saving and printing your work.

Trade quizzes with another student, and complete the quiz that you receive. When you have completed the quiz, trade it back to the student who created it. Score the quiz using the answer key that you created, and show the results to your partner.

STUDENT MANUAL

Moving Spreadsheet Data
Changing Row Height

Study Lesson 126 in your Student Manual. Complete all the practice activities while at your computer. Then complete the tasks that follow.

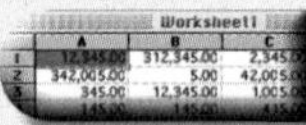

SPREADSHEET APPLICATIONS

ACTIVITY 10

Spreadsheet 7

Create a new spreadsheet and save it as SS7. Add the necessary data by following these steps.

1. In cell A1, key the label *Flight Departure Schedule for Tours of Summer.*
2. In cell A2, key the label *Prepared by* and your name.
3. Key the data shown in the illustration into the correct cells.
4. Select cell range A1 through F3, and bold the cell contents.
5. Save your changes and close the file.

	A	B	C	D	E	F
1	Flight Departure Schedule for Tours of Summer					
2	Prepared by [Your Name]					
3	Carrier		Boston	Phoenix	Omaha	Seattle
4						
5						
6						
7						
8						
9	American		4:50 p.m.	3:25 p.m.	3:10 p.m.	6:20 p.m.
10	Continental		7:10 p.m.	4:30 p.m.	2:45 p.m.	3:35 p.m.
11	Delta		6:25 p.m.	2:50 p.m.	4:17 p.m.	5:50 p.m.
12	Northwest		NA	3:50 p.m.	5:30 p.m.	NA
13	Southwest		NA	4:15 p.m.	2:15 p.m.	4:15 p.m.
14	United		5:45 p.m.	6:45 p.m.	2:15 p.m.	5:55 p.m.
15	US Airways		4:40 p.m.	7:25 p.m.	3:55 p.m.	5:55 p.m.
16	America West		NA	6:30 p.m.	NA	5:35 p.m.

NEW KEYS

B. 1 2 3 Keys

Key the following numbers column by column. Use the proper finger for each key. Press ENTER after the final digit of each number. Keep your eyes on the copy. Repeat if time permits.

Use the J finger to key 1. Use the K finger to key 2. Use the L finger to key 3.

Concentrate on accuracy.

5	444	555	666
6	111	222	333
7	144	225	336
8	441	552	663
9	144	255	366
10	411	522	633
11	444	555	666
12	414	525	636
13	141	252	363
14	411	525	636

SKILLBUILDING

C. Keypad Practice

Key the following numbers column by column. Press ENTER after the final digit of each number. Keep your eyes on the copy. Repeat if time permits.

Keep your eyes on the copy. Concentrate on accuracy.

15	476	167	754	531	746	334	568	829	957	146
16	372	426	193	942	853	712	149	637	486	329
17	551	789	592	726	962	365	438	218	582	381
18	983	238	812	861	147	819	129	341	673	247
19	421	945	638	397	285	654	247	759	149	655

C. PRETEST

Take a 1-minute timed writing on the paragraph. Note your speed and errors.

9 You may get a better grade in your courses if you will 11
10 allow enough time to find and fix any errors in a paper as 23
11 you prepare the final draft. A neat paper will impress most 35
12 people who read it. 39

| 1 | 2 | 3 | 4 | 5 | 6 | 7 | 8 | 9 | 10 | 11 | 12

D. PRACTICE

SPEED: ***If you made 2 or fewer errors on the Pretest, key lines 13–20 two times each.***

ACCURACY: ***If you made more than 2 errors on the Pretest, key lines 13–16 as a group two times. Then key lines 17–20 as a group two times.***

Left Reaches

13 fad bar bag era few best data acted beads brass cards caves
14 get raw sat sea tea cage case debts defer edges erase faces
15 bed beg eve fat war debt rest fewer grade refer seats state
16 cat fed tar tab rat vest star gages water fever waste taxes

Right Reaches

17 him hop ill boil clip coil cool fill full allow ample ankle
18 ink inn joy gulp hill hold hole hook hope built child chips
19 mop oil pin hung hunt jump like lime lips clips color drill
20 pin pop hop kiln pump poll joke loan lump plump jolly plums

E. POSTTEST

Repeat the Pretest. Compare your Posttest results with your Pretest results.

FORMATTING

F. Moving Spreadsheet Data

At times, you may need to move the contents of a cell to a different location within a spreadsheet. Unlike copying, which duplicates the cell contents, moving removes the contents from the original cell and inserts the contents into the new cell. Moving replaces the contents of the new cell. Be careful not to overwrite data that you still need.

G. Changing Row Height

The height of a spreadsheet row automatically adjusts to fit the size of the font being used. If you change from 12-point to 18-point, the row height will automatically adjust. You may also want to adjust the height of a row manually, which will not affect font size.

SKILLBUILDING

D. Technique Timed Writings

Take two 30-second timed writings on each line. Focus on the technique at the left.

Keep your eyes on the copy.

```
20 The high school students will visit other places.
21 I toured an art museum that was west of the city.
22 Twenty letters were addressed to the three of us.
23 My car (the blue convertible) is hard to keep up.
   | 1 | 2 | 3 | 4 | 5 | 6 | 7 | 8 | 9 | 10
```

E. PRETEST

Take a 1-minute timed writing on the paragraph. Note your speed and errors.

```
24      Molly and Abe took water to the barn for the    9
25 horses to drink. Half an hour later, Ralph filled   19
26 the hay racks. It was he who discovered Star, our   29
27 very best horse, was ill.                           30
   | 1 | 2 | 3 | 4 | 5 | 6 | 7 | 8 | 9 | 10
```

F. PRACTICE

SPEED: ***If you made 2 or fewer errors on the Pretest, key lines 28–35 two times each.***

ACCURACY: ***If you made more than 2 errors on the Pretest, key lines 28–31 as a group two times. Then key lines 32–35 as a group two times.***

Left Reaches

```
28 Abe purse bases debts large match ocean nurse Tad
29 red urban water yearn Jerry trays racks horse set
30 war rated tubes upset verbs Xerox quart image cad
31 car fears raven carts froze graze exact grave sad
```

Right Reaches

```
32 Lon pilot linen Molly hours Louis zooms films Jim
33 mop jumps knows plugs Naomi quill flint drink hum
34 nip human flood Ralph mound joins yolks co-op poi
35 mop polka plums homey plump mound limps money Lou
```

G. POSTTEST

Repeat the Pretest. Compare your Posttest results with your Pretest results.

SPREADSHEETS: MOVING DATA, CHANGING ROW HEIGHT

OBJECTIVES:

- Reinforce left and right reaches.
- Move data in a spreadsheet.
- Change row heights in a spreadsheet.

A. WARMUP

Key each line 2 times.

Speed	1	The road to the left is the right one to take on our drive.
Accuracy	2	Wolf gave Jake an extra dozen quarts, but he can't pay him.
Language Link	3	Ruth's sister went to the Women's Center to look for a job.
Numbers/Symbols	4	I can guess the prices for #32 and #48 within 5% error now!

| 1 | 2 | 3 | 4 | 5 | 6 | 7 | 8 | 9 | 10 | 11 | 12

SKILLBUILDING

B. 12-SECOND SPRINTS

Take three 12-second timed writings on each line. Try to increase your speed on each timed writing.

5 We will stop to rest as soon as we finish the last section.
6 The roof on our old shed is in need of repair at this time.
7 The cafe down the road has both good food and good service.
8 Chuck says rain is likely during the early part of the day.

| | | | 5 | | | | 10 | | | | 15 | | | | 20 | | | | 25 | | | | 30 | | | | 35 | | | | 40 | | | | 45 | | | | 50 | | | | 55 | | | | 60

H. 2-Minute Timed Writings

Goal: 30/2'/4e

Take two 2-minute timed writings on lines 36–42. Note your speed and errors.

36	Some senior students realize that once they	9
37	leave school, they must plan for more education.	19
38	Most might not know exactly what their first job	28
39	will be or what skills will equip them to move	38
40	ahead in a job or to change to another job. You	47
41	should make plans for your future now while you	57
42	have the time.	60
	| 1 | 2 | 3 | 4 | 5 | 6 | 7 | 8 | 9 | 10	*SI 1.25*

I. Composing at the Keyboard

Answer each question with a short phrase. Keep your eyes on the screen as you compose.

43 What are three things you should know before you agree to baby-sit?
44 Why should you keep your eyes on the copy when you key?
45 What three things do you admire most about your best friend?

JOURNAL ENTRY

Analyze Career Options Think about careers that you might like to have. Key five careers that you find interesting. For each career, key a short phrase that explains why you might like that career. Follow your teacher's instructions for saving and printing your work.

ACTIVITY 9
Spreadsheet 6

Create a new spreadsheet file and save it as SS6. Then follow these steps:

1. In cell A1, key the label *Favorite Amusement Parks.*
2. In cell A2, key *Prepared by* and your name.
3. Enter the remaining data as shown in the illustration, copying cell contents whenever possible.
4. Select cell range A1 through D4 and bold the cell contents.
5. Select cell range A4 through D4 and center the cell contents.
6. Select cell range A6 through D14 and change the width of columns so that all information is displayed.

	A	B	C	D
1	**Favorite Amusement Parks**			
2	**Prepared by [Your Name]**			
3				
4	**State**	**City**	**Park**	**Attraction**
5				
6	California	Anaheim	Disneyland	Indiana Jones Adventure
7	California	Hollywood	Universal Studios	Back to the Future—The Ride
8	Florida	Orlando	Universal Studios	Back to the Future—The Ride
9	Florida	Orlando	Universal Studios	Terminator 2 3-D
10	New York	Lake George	The Great Escape	Comet
11	Ohio	Sandusky	Cedar Point	Raptor
12	Pennsylvania	Elysburg	Knoebels Amusement Resort	Haunted House
13	Pennsylvania	Hershey	Hersheypark	Wildcat
14	Texas	Arlington	Six Flags Over Texas	Texas Giant

LANGUAGE ARTS CONNECTION

Alphabetize Data It is easier to find data if labels are alphabetized. In Spreadsheet 6 above, the State column is in alphabetical order, which makes it easier to find a park by location. If you preferred finding amusement parks by name rather than location, it would be better to arrange the data so that the Park column is in alphabetical order.

Practice your alphabetizing skills by arranging the park names in alphabetical order. Later, in Lesson 133, you will learn how to do this automatically using the Excel sort feature. Follow your teacher's instructions for saving and printing your work.

NUMERIC KEYPAD: 0 .

OBJECTIVES:

- Key 0 and decimal point (.) on the numeric keypad.
- Refine numeric keypad skills.
- Refine keyboarding skills.
- Key 30/2'/4e.

A. WARMUP

Key each line 2 times.

Speed	1	To have more pep, walk one or two miles each day.
Accuracy	2	Zorba has cichlids imported from Lake Tanganyika.
Language Link	3	We thought May 1 was on Sunday instead of Monday.
Numbers/Symbols	4	S & A closed at 3 7/16, up 5/8, a +14.71% change.

interNET CONNECTION

Analyze the Numeric Keypad The numeric keypad is a separate set of keys on some keyboards that contains the numbers 0 through 9 and a decimal point arranged as on an adding machine. It also contains common mathematical symbols and an ENTER key. Go to the Online Learning Center at **KeyComps.glencoe.com> Internet Connection>Unit 2>Lesson 32** and read the information about using numeric keypads, then complete the activity.

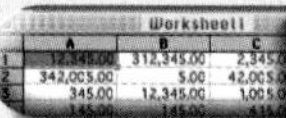

ACTIVITY 8

Spreadsheet 5

Open the file SS5, save it as SS5-B, and follow these steps:

1. Key your name after the words *Prepared by* in cell A2. Autofit the text in this column.
2. Center and bold the column headings (*Teachers*, *Period 1*, *Period 2*, and so on).
3. Key the names in column A as shown in the illustration below.
4. Copy the name in cell B6 to the other columns as shown.
5. Copy other names that are repeated in other columns.
6. Proofread your work carefully.

	A	B	C	D	E	F	G
1	**Teacher Assistant Schedule**						
2	**Prepared by [Your Name]**						
3							
4	**Teachers**	**Period 1**	**Period 2**	**Period 3**	**Period 4**	**Period 5**	**Period 6**
5							
6	Akins, Jason	Bunnell, N.					
7	Bailey, Karen			Graham, T.			
8	Brawner, Seth					Graham, T.	
9	Carter, Crystal					Walker, O.	
10	Clawson, Anna		Graham, T.				
11	Cowley, Rhonda			Bunnell, N.			
12	Green, Brad				Graham, T.		
13	Holloway, Nicholas	Graham, T.					
14	Ivie, Karla				Bunnell, N.		
15	Lane, Kathleen						Bunnell, N.
16	Morrison, Molly		Walker, O.				
17	Parish, James				Walker, O.		
18	Quillian, Harris		Bunnell, N.				
19	South, Suzette						Graham, T.
20	Sprock, Daniel			Walker, O.			
21	Turner, Wilson						Walker, O.
22	Williams, Virginia					Bunnell, N.	
23	Zobel, Adrian	Walker, O.					

NEW KEYS

B. 0 KEY

Key the following numbers column by column. Press ENTER after the final digit of each number. Keep your eyes on the copy. Repeat if time permits.

Use the right thumb to key 0.

Keep your eyes on the copy.

Concentrate on accuracy.

5	404	470	502
6	505	500	603
7	606	690	140
8	707	410	250
9	808	520	360
10	909	630	701
11	101	407	802
12	202	508	903
13	303	609	405
14	505	401	506

C. . KEY

Key the following numbers column by column. Press ENTER after the final digit of each number. Keep your eyes on the copy. Repeat if time permits.

Use L finger to key a decimal point. Keep K finger anchored on the 5 key as you reach down to the decimal point.

15	4.5	7.8	1.2
16	6.5	9.8	3.2
17	4.4	7.7	1.1
18	4.4	7.7	1.1
19	5.5	8.8	2.2
20	5.5	8.8	2.2
21	6.6	9.9	3.3
22	6.5	9.9	3.3
23	4.5	7.8	1.2
24	6.5	8.9	1.3

E. Copying Spreadsheet Data

Sometimes it is necessary to enter the same information in several cells. Copying a cell's contents is faster and more accurate than keying the same information repeatedly. However, you must be sure that the information you are going to copy is correct before you copy it.

F. Changing Column Widths

When you key data into a spreadsheet, some data may be hidden because the column is too narrow to display the data. When this occurs, you will have to adjust the width of the column to fit the data.

G. Software Features

STUDENT MANUAL

Copying Data   Changing Column Widths

Study Lesson 125 in your Student Manual. Complete all the practice activities while at your computer. Then complete the tasks that follow.

MATH CONNECTION

Create a Budget Imagine that you are planning a birthday party for a friend. You have $50 to spend and there will be ten people, including yourself and your friend. Create a spreadsheet that lists the food and decorations that you plan to buy for the party. Use the list below to determine what you should buy. Remember that you must buy enough for ten people and you cannot spend more than $50. Follow your teacher's instructions for saving and printing your work.

- Cake with 12 servings — $15
- 1 dozen cans of soft drink — $ 4
- 1 bag of chips — $ 2
- Pizza with 8 slices — $12
- 24 decorated paper plates — $ 5
- 24 paper cups — $ 3
- 24 plastic forks — $ 3
- 1 Happy Birthday sign — $ 8

SKILLBUILDING

D. Keypad Practice

Key the following numbers column by column. Press ENTER after the final digit of each number. Keep your eyes on the copy. Repeat if time permits.

25	1.7	7.5	7.6	5.0	6.2	6.0	6.7	4.5	3.0	6.4
26	5.8	2.4	2.3	2.8	3.5	9.1	5.1	3.0	7.6	2.8
27	1.6	8.3	1.7	9.9	5.0	2.7	1.6	9.3	1.3	5.9
28	3.0	4.2	3.4	8.1	7.4	1.8	2.8	8.0	8.2	5.1
29	6.9	9.0	6.5	4.0	4.6	8.9	7.2	4.9	4.7	9.0

E. 12-Second Sprints

Take three 12-second timed writings on each line. Try to increase your speed each time.

30 If nothing nice can be said, do not say anything.
31 Be kind if you want others to be kind toward you.
32 You won't smell like roses if you play with pigs.
33 Keep the dog away from the cats to avoid a fight.

| | | | | 5 | | | | | 10 | | | | | 15 | | | | | 20 | | | | | 25 | | | | | 30 | | | | | 35 | | | | | 40 | | | | | 45 | | | | | 50

F. PRETEST

Take a 1-minute timed writing on lines 34–37. Note your speed and errors.

34 George asked Zoe to bring along five boxed 9
35 lunches, and Quincy was to find just seven mugs 18
36 that could be used for the snacks to be served to 28
37 the group later on that day. 34

SI: 1.15

| 1 | 2 | 3 | 4 | 5 | 6 | 7 | 8 | 9 | 10

LANGUAGE ARTS CONNECTION

Identify Maxims A maxim is a common saying about a general truth or rule of conduct, such as "Practice makes perfect" or "A stitch in time saves nine." Think of two maxims and key them. Be sure that they are complete sentences. Then key a short explanation of each maxim. Follow your teacher's instructions for saving and printing your work.

(continued)

5 At the customers request, she sent a copy of the companys report.
6 The mens watches and the womens shoes are on sale today.
7 The childs boots were a gift from her friends parents.
8 The secretaries computers were purchased with funds from the governments retraining program.

SKILLBUILDING

C. Preview Practice

Key each line 2 times as a preview to the timed writings that follow.

Accuracy 9 include quality favorable vacations experience achievements
Speed 10 their might start when late cite firm job few for can up by

D. 5-Minute Timed Writings

Take two 5-minute timed writings on the paragraphs. Note your speed and errors.

Goal: 39/5'/5e

11 Job seekers can get a head start by starting their 10
12 search in late summer. This can be a good time to start a 22
13 job hunt because by late August, most managers have taken 34
14 their vacations and are back at work, sizing up the quality 46
15 of their staff. It also might be easier to get an interview 58
16 in the late summer when business is somewhat slower. Most 69
17 job openings are found by referrals or through personal 81
18 contacts. Meeting someone in person will sometimes give you 93
19 the best chance to make the most favorable impression. 104
20 When you search for a job, you will need a resume. It 115
21 should include a list of what you have done in your career. 127
22 Realize that you are trying to make a positive impact. You 138
23 can cite a few of your achievements. Also, you should send 150
24 a cover letter with a resume to the person who does the 161
25 hiring for the firm where you wish to work. Your letter and 173
26 resume should list each of your unique abilities and skills 185
27 and include all of your experience and training. 195

SI 1.38

| 1 | 2 | 3 | 4 | 5 | 6 | 7 | 8 | 9 | 10 | 11 | 12

G. PRACTICE

SPEED: ***If you made 2 or fewer errors on the Pretest, key lines 38–45 two times each.***

ACCURACY: ***If you made more than 2 errors on the Pretest, key lines 38–41 as a group two times. Then key lines 42–45 as a group two times.***

Up Reaches

38 hu hunt shuts churn hunch human husky huffs hulls
39 de deck bride depth order wader adept video decay
40 fr free frock frame frost fryer fruit frail fresh
41 li line flies blind click slick limes light flier

Down Reaches

42 ac acre poach whack acrid actor tract slack enact
43 l. pal. hill. jail. nail. yowl. dial. peel. till.
44 az raze graze craze glaze dazed blaze gazed jazzy
45 on once ponds fonts stone clone alone don't front

H. POSTTEST

Repeat the Pretest. Compare your Posttest results with your Pretest results.

I. 2-Minute Timed Writings

Take two 2-minute timed writings on lines 46–52. Note your speed and errors.

Goal: 30/2'/4e

46 Zebras are members of the horse family and 9
47 are well known for their unique stripes. They 18
48 enjoy life on the plains and foothills of Africa 28
49 where they feed on grass and trees. Attempts to 37
50 use them for work and to ride have failed. The 47
51 quagga, which is now extinct due to hunting, was 57
52 kin to the zebra. 60

| 1 | 2 | 3 | 4 | 5 | 6 | 7 | 8 | 9 | 10 *SI 1.25*

Spreadsheets: Copying Data, Changing Column Widths

OBJECTIVES:

- Apply the rules for apostrophes and possessives.
- Key 39/5'/5e.
- Copy data within a spreadsheet and change column width.

A. Warmup

Key each line 2 times.

Speed	1	The usual signal by this lagoon made the birds take flight.
Accuracy	2	Jody keyed white requisitions for moving large-sized boxes.
Language Link	3	Follow the advice of your legal counsel to sign the papers.
Numbers	4	Read Chapters 129 and 374 and summarize Chapters 48 and 56.
		| 1 | 2 | 3 | 4 | 5 | 6 | 7 | 8 | 9 | 10 | 11 | 12

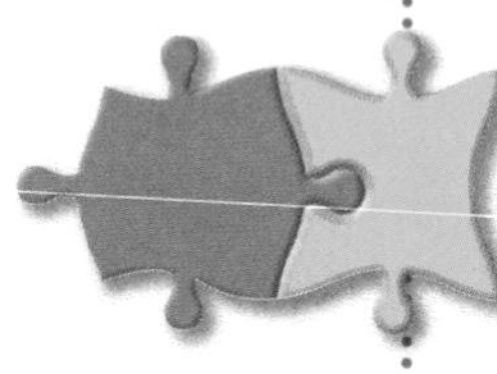

Language Link

B. Apostrophes and Possessives

Study the rules and examples below. Then edit lines 5–8 by deciding whether an apostrophe or an apostrophe and s ***are needed.***

Rule 32: Use *'s* to form the possessive of singular nouns.

The hurricane caused major damage to Georgia's crops.

Rule 33: Use only an apostrophe to form the possessive of plural nouns that end in *s*.

The investors' goals were outlined in the annual report.

Rule 34: Use *'s* to form the possessive of plural nouns that do not end in *s*.

The women's offices were next door to the gym.

(continued on next page)

LESSON 33 REVIEW

OBJECTIVES:

- Refine numeric keypad and keyboarding skills.
- Key 30/2′/4e

A. WARMUP

Key each line 2 times.

Speed	1	Think about this: If it is to be, it is up to me.
Accuracy	2	Vladimir Kosma Zworykin made the television tube.
Language Link	3	I think Passover begins in early April this year.
Numbers/Symbols	4	Nashville has *985,026 people; Miami, *1,192,582.

SKILLBUILDING

B. KEYPAD PRACTICE—3-DIGIT NUMBERS

Key the following numbers column by column. Press ENTER after the final digit of each number. Repeat if time permits.

Key numbers smoothly. Use correct fingers. Keep eyes on copy.

5	136	964	806	295	597	628	728	627	959	172
6	940	250	275	407	426	519	546	341	241	859
7	852	173	394	718	618	537	639	730	862	931
8	710	982	180	363	304	405	410	859	730	604
9	788	829	903	120	311	441	349	555	668	776

C. KEYPAD PRACTICE—DECIMAL NUMBERS

Key the following numbers column by column. Press ENTER after the final digit of each number. Repeat if time permits.

Key numbers smoothly. Use correct fingers. Keep eyes on copy.

10	1.97	5.08	6.19	3.52	4.33	17.44	52.28	68.61
11	3.85	6.44	9.37	8.10	2.19	14.20	23.85	60.97
12	6.55	6.65	7.87	9.00	3.10	20.49	88.47	19.39
13	2.10	2.81	2.33	7.06	7.68	67.99	44.53	45.54
14	8.83	7.90	4.16	8.20	1.49	55.20	15.62	37.39

(continued)

	A	B	C	D	E
1	Budget for the Month of July				
2	Prepared by Your Name				
3					
4	Income				
5		Allowance	$30.00		
6		Baby-sitting	$80.00		
7		Lawn Care	$20.00		
8				$130.00	
9					
10	Expenses				
11		Clothes	$50.00		
12		Movies	$20.00		
13		Loan from Dad	$10.00		
14		Savings	$15.00		
15					
16	Total Expenses			$95.00	
17					
18	Money for Misc. Expenses			$35.00	
19					

ACTIVITY 7

Spreadsheet 4

Open SS3-B and save it as SS4. Key the data from the following "what if" questions and see what changes result in the spreadsheet.

1. What if your allowance was increased to $55? (Your total income increases to $155, and miscellaneous money increases to $60.)
2. Key the original amount of $30 in cell C5 before continuing.
3. What if you do extra baby-sitting and earn $95?
4. What if rain reduces your lawn care income to $10?
5. What if you spend $75 on clothes?
6. What if you put $30 in savings?
7. Save the file.
8. Now try some of your own "what if" situations.
9. Close the file without saving your changes.

MATH CONNECTION

Evaluate Budgets Look at the spreadsheet you created in Activity 6 and notice that the income is higher than the expenses. If there were no left-over money, or expenses were greater than the income, this budget would need to be reevaluated.

Key one paragraph explaining what should happen to expenses if they exceed the income, and for what "miscellaneous expenses" any leftover money can be used. Follow your teacher's instructions for saving and printing your work.

D. Technique Timed Writings

Take two 30-second timed writings on each line. Focus on the techniques at the left.

Lines 15–16: Key without pauses.

Lines 17–18: Key end-of-sentence punctuation smoothly.

```
15 Roy and Bob did their best to study for the test.
16 My two cats are eager to sit in my lap as I work.
17 If you are to make friends, you must be friendly.
18 Who me? Oh no! I can. What time? Look out! Did I?
   | 1 | 2 | 3 | 4 | 5 | 6 | 7 | 8 | 9 | 10
```

E. PRETEST

Take a 1-minute timed writing on lines 19–22. Note your speed and errors.

```
19      Joy's niece darted in front of a car, but        8
20 the driver was able to stop quickly. She was only    18
21 dazed. She did not want us to cheer or make a        27
22 fuss over her.                                       30
   | 1 | 2 | 3 | 4 | 5 | 6 | 7 | 8 | 9 | 10
```

F. PRACTICE

SPEED: ***If you made 2 or fewer errors on the Pretest, key lines 23–30 two times each.***

ACCURACY: ***If you made more than 2 errors on the Pretest, key lines 23–26 as a group two times. Then key lines 27–30 as a group two times.***

Adjacent Reaches	23	rt sort part heart start ui quit suit quiet quick
Jump Reaches	24	mo most move among money ce aced race cease niece
Double Reaches	25	ee glee weed keeps cheer ss sass fuss grass cross
In Reaches	26	st stay stop stray state pi pint pile pines spine
Alternate Reaches	27	to tofu torn storm torso pa paid pals pause pants
Left/Right Reaches	28	da dart dabs dazed dates jo joys join enjoy jolly
Up/Down Reaches	29	st star stop first coast h? ash? huh? Noah? dish?
Out Reaches	30	fa fall sofa loofa farms ho hose hone hoist phone

G. POSTTEST

Repeat the Pretest. Compare your Posttest results with your Pretest results.

ACTIVITY 5
Spreadsheet 2

Create a new spreadsheet and save it as SS2.

1. In cell A1, key the label *Paint Inventory*. Notice that the portion of the label that doesn't fit in cell A1 displays in cell B1 because that cell is empty.
2. In cell A2, type *Prepared by* followed by your full name.
3. Key the labels and values shown in the illustration.
4. Select cells A1 through C4 and bold the contents.
5. Select cells A4 through C4 and center the contents.

	A	B	C	D
1	**Paint Inventory**			
2	**Prepared by [Your Name]**			
3				
4	**Colors**	**Gallons**	**Cost**	
5	Black	8	5.79	
6	Blue	13	3.99	
7	Green	9	6.88	
8	Pink	11	9.75	
9	Red	7	4.89	
10	White	5	5.95	
11	Yellow	6	4.97	
12				

ACTIVITY 6
Spreadsheet 3

Open the file SS3. Save it as SS3-B. Then complete the following steps:

1. In cell A2, key your name after *Prepared by*.
2. The illustration on page 447 shows new information that is missing from the spreadsheet. Key the new data into the correct cells. (The amounts in column D will change because formulas have been entered into these cells. The column has been automatically formatted to insert dollar signs and decimals.)
3. When you finish keying the data, proofread carefully and correct any errors. If you have entered the correct numbers, cell D18 will show $35.00.
4. Save the file with your changes.

(continued on next page)

H. 1-Minute Alphanumeric Timed Writings

Take a 1-minute timed writing on lines 31–34. Note your speed and errors.

31	In 1929 stock prices passed $350 per share.	9
32	By 1932, they had dropped under $100, forcing	18
33	9,000 banks to close. People without jobs climbed	28
34	above 25%.	30
	| 1 | 2 | 3 | 4 | 5 | 6 | 7 | 8 | 9 | 10	

I. 2-Minute Timed Writings

Take two 2-minute timed writings on lines 35–41. Note your speed and errors.

Goal: 30/2'/4e

35	A good way to earn extra money is by taking	9
36	care of children. It is not a job for the lazy.	18
37	Being in charge of small children requires hard	28
38	work and savvy. You can take workshops to learn	37
39	the basics of child care, and you should take a	47
40	course in first aid so you are prepared for any	57
41	medical crisis.	60
	| 1 | 2 | 3 | 4 | 5 | 6 | 7 | 8 | 9 | 10	SI 1.27

LESSON 124 SPREADSHEETS: CREATE, ALIGN COLUMNS

OBJECTIVES:

- Increase keyboarding speed.
- Create a spreadsheet and align columns.
- Enter data into a spreadsheet.

A. WARMUP

Key each line 2 times.

Speed	1	Jane and the man got five fish and kept them on the island.
Accuracy	2	Maizie quickly paid Jane for the five new taxis she bought.
Language Link	3	If you follow your counsel's advice, you will plea-bargain.
Technique	4	Saul Kent Dora Mary Alva Paul Ruth Kate Zora Lena Rick Juan

| 1 | 2 | 3 | 4 | 5 | 6 | 7 | 8 | 9 | 10 | 11 | 12

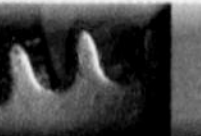

SKILLBUILDING

B. PACED PRACTICE

Turn to the Paced Practice routine beginning on page SB7. Take three 2-minute timed writings, starting at the point where you left off the last time.

FORMATTING

C. SOFTWARE FEATURES

STUDENT MANUAL

Create a Spreadsheet   Align Columns

Study Lesson 124 in your Student Manual. Complete all the practice activities while at your computer. Then complete the tasks that follow.

SKILLBUILDING

OBJECTIVES:

- Refine numeric keypad skills.
- Refine keyboarding skills.
- Key 31/3′/5e.

A. WARMUP

Key each line 2 times.

Speed	1	All of us have bad days now and then, but they do not last.
Accuracy	2	The quetzal, a superb green and gold bird, lives in Mexico.
Language Link	3	This auto race on Labor Day was on Monday at Memorial Park.
Numbers/Symbols	4	When Tip & Toe has a sale, buy 24 pairs of socks @ 25% off.

SKILLBUILDING

B. KEYPAD PRACTICE—4-DIGIT NUMBERS

Key the following numbers column by column. Press ENTER after the final digit of each number. Repeat if time permits.

Use correct fingers. Keep eyes on copy. Concentrate on accuracy.

5	8964	8073	6182	8090	2401	3159	5361	6047
6	3103	2619	5079	9324	5561	8252	6873	7984
7	5295	5302	6416	7451	8564	2785	9790	1021
8	7206	6195	2840	5327	4963	7548	2080	1976
9	1847	8443	3594	1686	1378	9029	4303	4267

SOCIAL STUDIES CONNECTION

Research Populations Think of three countries that you would like to visit. Use an atlas, encyclopedia, almanac, or other resource in your classroom to look up the population of each country. Key the name of the country and its population. Follow your teacher's instructions for saving and printing your work.

(continued)

The positioning of data at the left, center, or right of a cell is called **alignment**. The default alignment for labels is left, and the default alignment for values is right. Alignment can be changed easily.

Study the spreadsheet illustration below. Note that the contents of cells A1 through E1 are displayed in bold. Labels (words) are aligned at the left. Values (numbers) are aligned at the right. A formula was entered into cells B15–E15 to calculate the total sales.

	A	B	C	D	E
1	**Class Members**	**Week 1**	**Week 2**	**Week 3**	**Total Sales**
2					
3	Finzer, Nick	$15.35	$22.00	$32.89	$70.24
4	Follman, Jadie	$21.98	$18.55	$29.98	$70.51
5	Fowler, Eric	$13.50	$29.19	$24.35	$67.04
6	Glosup, Margaret	$20.00	$14.75	$28.05	$62.80
7	Grimes, Kelley	$19.00	$23.80	$18.15	$60.95
8	McCoy, Andres	$24.25	$18.85	$33.97	$77.07
9	Parker, Kent	$29.88	$28.10	$23.54	$81.52
10	Spoeder, Dustin	$25.79	$21.95	$20.65	$68.39
11	Spradlin, Sherry	$11.15	$16.65	$35.50	$63.30
12	Stanley, Ronnie	$33.35	$27.99	$19.94	$81.28
13	Wright, Mary	$16.50	$31.00	$22.75	$70.25
14					
15	Total Sales	$230.75	$252.83	$289.77	$773.35
16	Average Sales	$20.98	$22.98	$26.34	$70.30

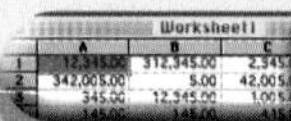

SPREADSHEET APPLICATIONS

ACTIVITY 4

Spreadsheet 1

Open the file SS1 and save it as SS1-B. Then do the following:

1. In cell A1, change the label to *Students*.
2. In cell A7, change the name *Grimes, Kelley* to *Grimes, Kerry*.
3. In cell A10, key the name *Soeder, Dean*.
4. In cell A12, key *Stanley, Robert*.
5. In cell A13, key *Wright, Wendy*.
6. Key the following numbers in cells C3 through C13: C3, *15.05*; C4, *22.37*; C5, *13.75*; C6, *20.02*; C7, *17.54*; C8, *24* (notice what happens after you press ENTER); C9, *31.53*; C10, *23.88*; C11, *18.51*; C12, *22.52*; C13, *26.60*. You do not need to key the dollar sign. Notice how the numbers in cells C15, C16, E15, and E16 change as you key the new numbers. Formulas have been entered into these cells to recalculate the sums and averages. If you enter the numbers correctly, cell E16 will show 68.75.

C. Keypad Practice—Decimal Numbers

Key the following numbers column by column. Press **ENTER** ***after the final digit of each number. Repeat if time permits.***

Use correct fingers. Keep your eyes on the copy.

10	80.5	9.72	67.04	4387.90	98.10	86.17
11	724.16	15.39	904.32	128.50	6524.01	349.05
12	7512.41	4607.09	583.55	95.63	141.16	2508.96
13	1204.78	672.80	808.23	379.94	6.39	677.28
14	339.45	453.92	1.62	4.63	7813.25	1.96

D. 12-Second Sprints

Take three 12-second timed writings on each line. Try to increase your speed each time.

15 You must repress your fears, or you will not be in control.
16 Our failures can teach us good lessons if we will let them.
17 When you have a dream, you must never, never give up on it.
18 You should give your best effort to everything that you do.

| | | | | 5 | | | | | 10 | | | | | 15 | | | | | 20 | | | | | 25 | | | | | 30 | | | | | 35 | | | | | 40 | | | | | 45 | | | | | 50 | | | | | 55 | | | | | 60

E. Technique Timed Writings

Take two 30-second timed writings on each line. Focus on the technique at the left.

Keep your eyes on the copy.

19 Lau went to the cafe in the city to have a good dinner out.
20 She and Travis left the band and saw the parade in Detroit.
21 Isau moved the desk over to my right side during our class.
22 People who work at the desk like to keep paper on the left.

| 1 | 2 | 3 | 4 | 5 | 6 | 7 | 8 | 9 | 10 | 11 | 12

COMMUNICATION FOCUS

Identify Positive Body Language Body language is the gestures, posture, and eye contact that you use to express yourself. Go to the Online Learning Center at **KeyComps.glencoe.com>Communication Focus>Unit 2>Lesson 34** and read the information provided. Complete the activity.

(continued)

5 The student sought (advise/advice) from the school's (counsel/council) president.

6 I (advise/advice) you not to answer until you have retained reputable (counsel/council).

7 The AMA (Counsel/Council) on Aging (advises/advices) people to stop smoking.

8 Her (advise/advice) is based on years of experience giving (advise/advice) to others.

9 The archeologist (advised/adviced) the town (counsel/council) to take action quickly.

10 The Tribal (Counsel/Council) gave the group good (advise/advice).

SKILLBUILDING

C. 30-Second OK Timed Writings

Take two 30-second OK (error-free) timed writings on lines 11–12. Then take two 30-second OK timed writings on lines 13–14. Goal: no errors.

11 It is not just the size of fingers but their quickness 11
12 that builds every extra word per minute in a timed writing. 23

13 Exercise maintains good health and gives you zest when 11
14 you adjust for the pace required to keep your body healthy. 23

| 1 | 2 | 3 | 4 | 5 | 6 | 7 | 8 | 9 | 10 | 11 | 12

FORMATTING

D. Entering Spreadsheet Data

Words entered into a spreadsheet are called **labels**. Numbers, dates, or times entered into a spreadsheet are called **values**. Mathematical calculations that are entered into a spreadsheet cell are called **formulas**. You can use formulas to add, subtract, multiply, or average the contents of cells.

You can format a spreadsheet to change how information is displayed. Data can be displayed in bold or italics and with different font styles and sizes. Numbers, times, and dates can also be displayed in a variety of formats.

(continued on next page)

F. Alphabet Review

Key each line 1 time. Repeat if time permits.

23 Alf is able to add; Bill bikes by Beth; Cal can call Carli.
24 Darla's dad is Dale; Evi eats eggs; Flo's farm is far away.
25 Gary's grass is green; Hans has his hats; Ilse is innocent.

26 Just jump, Jeff; Kylie knows knives; Lyle loves Louisville.
27 Marta manages a mall; Nona noted nothing; Orion owns opals.
28 Pat pinches pennies; Quinn quietly quit; Rez reads rapidly.

29 Suni serves sushi; Tara tells tall tales; Uriah uses umber.
30 Val visits Vermont; Wilma washes windows; Xan x-rays Xylia.
31 Yvonne yearns for a yellow yo-yo; Zachariah's zest is zero.

G. Paced Practice

Turn to the Paced Practice routine beginning on page SB7. Take three 2-minute timed writings, starting at the point where you left off the last time.

H. 3-Minute Timed Writings

Take two 3-minute timed writings on lines 32–40. Note your speed and errors.

Goal: 31/3'/5e

32 Those five members of the basketball team hope to be 11
33 chosen as part of the main team. They will need a lot of 22
34 practice to attain their goal. However, they know what the 34
35 excitement will be if they are chosen for the finals. 45
36 They expect that their team will be in first place in 56
37 its conference when the season ends. The team has shown a 67
38 lot more zip since February. Just eight more away games 79
39 have yet to be played. They must not lose the last game to 90
40 Quaker State. 93

| 1 | 2 | 3 | 4 | 5 | 6 | 7 | 8 | 9 | 10 | 11 | 12 *SI 1.22*

LANGUAGE ARTS CONNECTION

Alphabetize Book Titles Key the titles of five books that you have read or would like to read. Arrange your book titles in alphabetical order. Follow your teacher's instructions for saving and printing your work.

LESSON 123 SPREADSHEETS: ENTERING DATA

OBJECTIVES:

- Identify frequently confused words.
- Improve keyboarding accuracy.
- Enter and change spreadsheet data.

A. WARMUP

Key each line 2 times.

Speed	1	Their firm is paid to paint half the signs for those towns.
Accuracy	2	Jacqueline of Hainaut lost Zeeland and Holland to a cousin.
Language Link	3	You need these personal traits: tact, quick wit, and humor.
Numbers/Symbols	4	Certain sales are 15% or 20% off and one is $10 or $15 off.

| 1 | 2 | 3 | 4 | 5 | 6 | 7 | 8 | 9 | 10 | 11 | 12

LANGUAGE LINK

B. CONFUSING WORDS

Study the confusing words and their meanings shown below. Then edit lines 5–10 by choosing the correct word.

advice (n.) An opinion, recommendation, information, or notice given

advise (v.) To give information or advice to; to counsel

council (n.) An organization or group

counsel (v.) To give advice as a result of a consultation
(n.) A policy or plan of action or behavior; a lawyer

(continued on next page)

LESSON 35 SKILLBUILDING

OBJECTIVES:

- Apply capitalization rules.
- Refine numeric keypad skills.
- Refine keyboarding skills.
- Key 31/3′/5e.

A. WARMUP

Key each line 2 times.

Speed	1	Set your goals, and then make plans to achieve those goals.
Accuracy	2	The bombastic flibbertigibbit was bedizened in a bombazine.
Language Link	3	We plan to travel via airplane on Tuesday for Thanksgiving.
Numbers/Symbols	4	Try this: 1 1/3 cup milk, 4/5 cup bananas, 1/8 cup raisins.

LANGUAGE LINK

B. CAPITALIZATION

Study the rule and the examples below. Then edit lines 5–8 to correct any errors in capitalization.

Rule 3: A proper noun is the name of a particular person, place, or thing. Capitalize proper nouns and adjectives derived from proper nouns.

Tara and I always watch the Thanksgiving Day parade in Chicago.

Our supervisor, Mrs. Jazarian, is going to Tibet next year.

5 lou and darian saw chicago from the top of the sears tower.
6 we saw the american flag flying at our embassy in scotland.
7 mr. and mrs. haber wrote that they had visited san antonio.
8 president abraham lincoln did write the gettysburg address.

ACTIVITY 1
Spreadsheet 1

Open the file SS1 and practice selecting and deselecting cells.

1. Click on cell A3, *Finzer, Nick.*
2. Use the arrow keys to move to cell A7, *Grimes, Kelly.* Check the entry bar at the top of the spreadsheet to be sure you are in the correct cell.
3. Use the arrow keys to move to cell C1, *Week 2.*
4. Select a group of cells by clicking cell D3 and dragging down through cell D13. Note that the entry bar shows only cell D3 and its contents.
5. Deselect cells D3 through D13 by clicking outside the shaded area.

ACTIVITY 2
Spreadsheet 1

Continue in or, if necessary, open the file SS1, and follow these steps:

1. Select cells A3 through E3.
2. Deselect cells A3 through E3.
3. Select cells A3 through E9.
4. Deselect cells A3 through E9.
5. Move the cell pointer to cell E5. Note the formula in the entry bar and the results in cell E5.

ACTIVITY 3
Spreadsheet 1

Continue in or, if necessary, open the file SS1, and do the following:

1. Move the cell pointer to cell C16 and note the formula in the entry bar.
2. Move the cell pointer to cell C15 and note the formula in the entry bar.
3. Select all of column D by clicking once on the letter D.
4. Deselect column D.
5. Select all of row 11 by clicking once on the number 11.
6. Deselect row 11.
7. Select the entire spreadsheet by clicking once on the Select All button in the upper-left corner where the row and column headings meet. Note what is displayed in the entry bar.
8. Deselect the spreadsheet.
9. Close the file.

SKILLBUILDING

C. Keypad Review

Key the following numbers column by column. Press Enter after the final digit of each number. Repeat if time permits.

Use correct fingers. Keep eyes on copy. Concentrate on accuracy.

```
9  3221  8997  5446  7114  2558  9336  5991  3775  4665  79.13
10 7987  6465  1323  4065  3120  9078  4005  7009  2003  10.05
11 5217  8469  1356  2007  3062  9940  1517  1492  1943  99.49
12 1541  1556  1603  1632  1689  1714  1763  1774  1775  18.04
13 6.59  2.58  37.4  20.0  9.48  7.11  30.6  51.2  8.83  25.67
```

D. PRETEST

Take a 1-minute timed writing on lines 14–17. Note your speed and errors.

```
14      The meadow is covered with sweet vetch and daisies. I   11
15 saw a covey of quail popping in and out of the shade and     22
16 a herd of cows foraging lazily among the bees. Soon it       38
17 will be too cold to walk in the meadow.                      41
   | 1 | 2 | 3 | 4 | 5 | 6 | 7 | 8 | 9 | 10 | 11 | 12
```

E. PRACTICE

SPEED: ***If you made 2 or fewer errors on the Pretest, key lines 18–25 two times each.***

ACCURACY: ***If you made more than 2 errors on the Pretest, key lines 18–21 as a group two times. Then key lines 22–25 as a group two times.***

Discrimination reaches are keys that are commonly substituted and easily confused, such as w *and* e*.*

```
18 dsd sides dense shade dress daisy squad sedan dispel sedate
19 pop poise opens poach optic power piano opals proper option
20 wew wedge sweet weave tweed wreck vowel elbow twelve wealth
21 klk klutz bulky milky kilns slick click block plucky lackey

22 yuy dusky yours bumpy juicy murky truly query purify luxury
23 fgf gifts feign graft fling foggy fight grief forage fringe
24 vcv civil cover vicar covey havoc evict vetch vacate victor
25 mnm mania money numbs mines woman mints gnome sampan nomads
```

F. POSTTEST

Repeat the Pretest. Compare your Posttest results with your Pretest results.

C. PRACTICE

In the chart below, find the number of errors you made on the Pretest. Then key each of the following designated drill lines 2 times.

Pretest Errors	0–1	2	3	4+
Drill Lines	12–16	11–15	10–14	9–13

Accuracy

```
9  those seize whether require advanced training opportunities
10 two- high capable colleges graduates finishing communicates
11 want watched getting complete employers carefully coworkers
12 up judged failing criterion four-year essential exceptional
```

Speed

```
13 degree demand others after often while open many for can go
14 finish judged worker there doors these wish also who but on
15 people person school right thing prime find jobs may the is
16 listed reason skills along going being will than one get of
```

D. POSTTEST

Repeat the Pretest. Compare your Posttest results with your Pretest results.

FORMATTING

E. Software Features

STUDENT MANUAL

Selecting and Deselecting Cells

Study Lesson 122 in your Student Manual. Complete all the practice activities while at your computer. Then complete the tasks that follow.

interNET CONNECTION

Compare Earning Potential A high school diploma or General Equivalency Diploma (GED) is required for almost every job you can name today. Each level of education completed thereafter pays a higher salary and leads to potential career advancement.

Go to the Online Learning Center at **KeyComps.glencoe.com>Internet Connection>Unit 7>Lesson 122** to compare potential salaries earned without graduating high school, with a high school diploma, and with a college degree. Then answer the questions at the end of the activity.

G. Punctuation Spacing

Key each line 2 times. Note the spacing before and after each punctuation mark. Repeat if time permits.

Keep your eyes on the copy.

26 The shift of number 9 is (; be sure to hold anchor fingers.
27 Joy shops at Mann & Sons; she spent $72.33 today on slacks.
28 Add these numbers: 22, 33, 44, 77, 88, and 99. Answer: 363.

29 Paula owes Kim these amounts: $2.78, $3.47, $19.82, $21.42.
30 Sonja bought 44# of seed from Mrs. R. G. Herrera yesterday.
31 Look up Route #9 on the U.S.A. map for Ms. Lucky instantly.

32 Have you seen Perry? I think he went to 738 Mainard Street.
33 I need some #2 pencils. Will you get them for me at Paul's?
34 Belle and/or Jay will go to the airport tomorrow afternoon.

H. 3-Minute Timed Writings

Take two 3-minute timed writings on lines 35–43. Note your speed and errors.

Goal: 31/3'/5e

35 A rain forest and a jungle are not quite the same. A 11
36 rain forest has very lofty trees that form a canopy for 22
37 shorter trees as well as vines and other plants that grow 34
38 in the shade. The floor is more or less open. A jungle, on 45
39 the other hand, is the dense, scrubby brush that exists on 57
40 the floor after a rain forest has been cut. 66
41 Large rain forests are found in the Amazon basin. Rain 78
42 forests give us timber and sites for crops like tea and 89
43 house many species. 93

| 1 | 2 | 3 | 4 | 5 | 6 | 7 | 8 | 9 | 10 | 11 | 12 *SI 1.26*

LESSON 122 SPREADSHEETS: NAVIGATING

OBJECTIVES:

- Increase keyboarding speed and improve accuracy.
- Navigate within a spreadsheet.

A. WARMUP

Key each line 2 times.

Speed	1	The firm sent the forms over an hour after she called them.
Accuracy	2	These women quietly gave back the prizes of the six judges.
Language Link	3	They're planning to eat there for their brother's birthday.
Numbers	4	Those five passengers are 10, 29, 38, 47, and 56 years old.

| 1 | 2 | 3 | 4 | 5 | 6 | 7 | 8 | 9 | 10 | 11 | 12

SCIENCE CONNECTION

Organize Information Science relies on logical evaluation of data to see relationships and draw conclusions. Spreadsheets and tables are useful ways to organize information so that data can be analyzed quickly and clearly. You may not realize it, but you see spreadsheets every day.

Look at a TV schedule or your report card. Key a short paragraph describing how the information is organized, then describe three other examples of spreadsheets or tables that you see in your daily life. Follow your teacher's instructions for saving and printing your work.

SKILLBUILDING

B. PRETEST

Take a 1-minute timed writing on the paragraph. Note your speed and errors.

5 Finishing high school can open up many doors for those *11*
6 who wish to go on to complete a two- or four-year degree in *23*
7 college. It may also open up opportunities for those who *35*
8 wish to find jobs after high school. *42*

| 1 | 2 | 3 | 4 | 5 | 6 | 7 | 8 | 9 | 10 | 11 | 12

LESSON 36

ORIENTATION TO WORD PROCESSING

OBJECTIVES:

- Refine numeric keypad skills.
- Improve keyboarding skills on adjacent and jump reaches.
- Apply word processing features.

A. WARMUP

Key each line 2 times.

Speed	1	Tom and Shelley may wish to sell this house if they own it.
Accuracy	2	While Sylvie waited, Jacques quickly fixed a dozen zippers.
Language Link	3	Winifred will accept delivery of paper from Brown Paper Co.
Numbers/Symbols	4	Joel Paxon got a 15% discount on the 24# of bread at B & B.

SKILLBUILDING

B. KEYPAD PRACTICE

Key the following numbers column by column. Press ENTER after the final digit of each number. Keep your eyes on the copy, and use the proper finger for each key. Do not key the commas.

Numbers with 4 or more digits often contain commas to make the numbers easier to read. When keying numbers with the keypad, do not key the commas.

5	45.12	56.89	8,505	1,303	.89	404	975	488	312	38
6	36.78	74.04	9,606	5,238	.24	101	606	577	250	56
7	56.23	52.38	1,404	2,953	.72	232	491	186	598	71
8	90.46	58.52	2,505	1,404	.94	494	638	904	756	32
9	69.63	87.42	3,606	2,505	.62	456	240	496	387	97

(continued)

will be taking a major test and want to know what your final grade would be if you received a test grade of 85. You could enter the 85 and have the spreadsheet recalculate your grade average.

Spreadsheets consist of rows and columns. Vertical columns are identified with letters of the alphabet. Horizontal rows are identified with numbers. The rectangle where a column and row meet is called a **cell**. A **cell** or **address** is the column letter and row number. For example, the cell name of the highlighted cell in the example is D10.

Entry Bar
Area where the text, number, or formula in the active cell is displayed. The entry bar is called the formula bar in some programs.

Cell name or address
Column and row of a cell; for example cell D10 means Column D, Row 10.

Row
Horizontal data identified by numbers.

Cell D10
Box where column D and row 10 intersect.

D10 | fx 20.65

	A	B	C	D	E
1	Class Members	Week 1	Week 2	Week 3	Total Sales
2					
3	Finzer, Nick	$ 15.25	$ 22.00	$ 32.99	$ 70.24
4	Follman, Jadie	$ 21.98	$ 18.55	$ 29.98	$ 70.51
5	Fowler, Eric	$ 13.50	$ 29.15	$ 24.35	$ 67.04
6	Glosup, Margaret	$ 20.00	$ 14.75	$ 28.05	$ 62.80
7	Grimes, Kelley	$ 19.00	$ 23.80	$ 18.15	$ 60.95
8	McCoy, Andres	$ 24.25	$ 18.85	$ 33.97	$ 77.07
9	Parker, Kent	$ 29.00	$ 28.10	$ 23.54	$ 81.52
10	Spoeder. Dustin	$ 25.79	$ 21.95	$ 20.65	$ 68.39
11	Spradlin, Sherry	$ 11.15	$ 16.65	$ 35.50	$ 63.30
12	Stanley, Ronnie	$ 33.35	$ 27.99	$ 19.94	$ 81.28
13	Wright, Mary	$ 16.50	$ 31.00	$ 22.75	$ 70.25
14					
15	Total Sales	$ 230.75	$ 252.83	$ 289.77	$ 773.35
16	Average Sales	$ 20.98	$ 22.98	$ 26.34	$ 70.30

Column
Vertical data identified by letters.

Active Cell
Cell currently in use or selected.

F. Software Features

STUDENT MANUAL

GO TO

Identifying Spreadsheet Components

Study Lesson 121 in your Student Manual. Complete all the practice activities while at your computer.

C. PRETEST

Take a 1-minute timed writing on lines 10–13. Note your speed and errors.

```
10      If they have any extra fruit and milk, can you please   11
11 deliver them to the annex? I must buy twenty stamps before   23
12 tomorrow to mail my food-drive flyers. If I don't get these  35
13 in the mail quickly, we will not meet our goal.              44
   | 1 | 2 | 3 | 4 | 5 | 6 | 7 | 8 | 9 | 10 | 11 | 12
```

D. PRACTICE

SPEED: ***If you made 2 or fewer errors on the Pretest, key lines 14–21 two times each.***

ACCURACY: ***If you made more than 2 errors on the Pretest, key lines 14–17 as a group two times. Then key lines 18–21 as a group two times.***

Adjacent Reaches

```
14 ui suits fruit guilt quilt quint squid fluid guide build ui
15 we weigh swept tweed tower power dowel jewel fewer vowel we
16 lk caulk yolks talks hulks sulks stalk balky silky chalk lk
17 as vases masts tasks lasts pasta gases aspen cases bases as
```

Jump Reaches

```
18 ex excel exact exert exile exist extra annex vexed index ex
19 mp skimp mumps stamp plump imply champ ample swamp crimp mp
20 mo lemon month money movie mouse emote smoke among model mo
21 ce cents mince paces cease piece slice fence place faces ce
```

E. POSTTEST

Repeat the Pretest. Compare your Posttest results with your Pretest results.

FORMATTING

F. Software Features

STUDENT MANUAL

Start Your Word Processor
Opening a File
Closing a File
New Documents
Closing Word

Study Lesson 36 in your Student Manual. Complete all of the steps while at your computer.

SKILLBUILDING

D. 5-Minute Timed Writings

Take two 5-minute timed writings on the paragraphs. Note your speed and errors.

Goal: 39/5'/5e

Social Studies
Connection

After the Civil War, the railroad played a vital role 11
in the growth of America. Expansion of the railroads helped 23
the iron and coal mining and lumber industries grow through 35
the need for iron tracks, engines, fuel, and wood railway 47
ties. New jobs were opened for people who built stations, 58
laid tracks, and produced equipment. 66

At the start, each train line built tracks of varied 76
widths. This made long-distance travel slow and difficult. 88
Later, rail widths were set to a standard size. This meant 100
that goods could be shipped more quickly using just one 111
train to cross the country. Trains shipped produce, raw 122
materials, and finished goods from place to place. 133

Four inventions improved rail transport a great deal. 144
Air brakes decreased the hazard of stopping a train. The 155
Janney car coupler made it simpler to link one car to the 167
next. Pullman sleeping cars increased the comfort of long 178
trips, and refrigerated cars allowed food to be shipped 189
without the risk of spoiling. 195

| 1 | 2 | 3 | 4 | 5 | 6 | 7 | 8 | 9 | 10 | 11 | 12 SI 1.36

FORMATTING

E. Spreadsheet Orientation

A **spreadsheet** is an electronic worksheet or grid that is used to organize and analyze information. The spreadsheet data can be calculated to make predictions.

For example, suppose you have your English grades entered and averaged in a spreadsheet. On Friday, you

(continued on next page)

Orientation to Word Processing

OBJECTIVES:

- Apply special symbols.
- Apply word processing features.
- Key 31/3'/5e.

A. Warmup

Key each line 2 times.

Speed	*1*	We may make a nice profit if all of the work is done right.
Accuracy	*2*	From the tower Dave saw six big jet planes quickly zoom by.
Language Link	*3*	May saw her uncle at the Ohio State football game Saturday.
Numbers	*4*	Please buy 50 paper clips, 9 pencils, 7 pens, and 4 stamps.

SKILLBUILDING

B. Special Symbols

Many keys on the keyboard can be used to represent special symbols. The most common of these special symbols are shown below.

Symbols	Keystrokes	Examples
Roman numerals	Capital letters: I, V, X, L, C, D, and M	Chapters VII-XV
Feet and inches	Apostrophe, feet; quotation mark, inches	Marion is 5′ 2″
Minutes and seconds	Apostrophe, minutes; quotation mark, seconds	My time: 3′ 15″
Multiply	Small letter x with a space before and after	What is 58 x 12?
Subtract	Single hyphen with a space before and after	240 – 106 = 134
Ellipsis	Three periods (space before, between and after); four periods if words are omitted at the end of the sentence.	He . . . and no

LESSON 121 SPREADSHEETS: ORIENTATION

OBJECTIVES:

- Compose at the keyboard.
- Key 39/5'/5e.
- Identify the basic parts of a spreadsheet.

A. WARMUP

Key each line 2 times.

Speed	1	Just see how well his fingers are flying over the keys now.
Accuracy	2	Kaz quickly mixed the two squeezed juices in the brown jug.
Language Link	3	The personal note he got said they were on their way there.
Technique	4	Do NOT type any CAPITAL in lowercase; always use UPPERCASE.

| 1 | 2 | 3 | 4 | 5 | 6 | 7 | 8 | 9 | 10 | 11 | 12

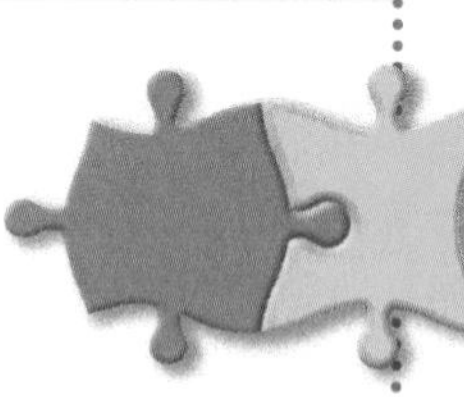

LANGUAGE LINK

B. COMPOSING AT THE KEYBOARD

Compose the body of a short letter requesting information from a nearby museum. Explain that you will be visiting the museum on a certain date. Ask for a program of scheduled events, the hours of operation, and the cost of admission.

SKILLBUILDING

C. PREVIEW PRACTICE

Key each line 2 times as a preview to the timed writings that follow.

Accuracy	5	hazard country quickly inventions industries refrigerated
Speed	6	Janney place food risk just link made from the set in of be

C. Symbol Practice

Key each line 1 time. Notice the spacing with the symbols and how the symbols are used.

5 Dr. Karl told us to read Chapters II and IV from Volume XX.
6 At 6' 3", Mike was able to beat the record time of 10' 32".
7 Does Satbir know the answer to this: 480 x 120 – 150 x 307?
8 During a long, hot summer . . . water was extremely scarce.

D. 12- Second Sprints

Take three 12-second timed writings on each line. Try to increase your speed each time.

9 As you read a map, bear in mind that the top part is north.
10 If the top of a map is north, then the right of it is east.
11 Maps have legends that tell what the symbols and codes are.
12 When you can read maps, you possess a skill of great value.
| | | | 5 | | | | 10 | | | | 15 | | | | 20 | | | | 25 | | | | 30 | | | | 35 | | | | 40 | | | | 45 | | | | 50 | | | | 55 | | | | 60

E. Preview Practice

Key each line 2 times as a preview to the 3-minute timed writings on page 127.

13 lightened pioneers quickly removing blocked journey endless
14 leave spring arrive young owned wagon have easy was not all

MATH CONNECTION

Interpreting Roman Numerals The basic Roman numerals are: I (1), V (5), X (10), L (50), C (100), D (500), and M (1000). These can be combined to form any number. For example:

III is 1 + 1 + 1 = 3
XVI is 10 + 5 + 1 = 16
CLXII is 100 + 50 + 10 + 1 + 1 = 162

Key the following Roman numerals, then convert them to our number system by using the technique shown above: VIII, XXVI, LV, CXII. Follow your teacher's instructions for saving and printing your work.

WORDS TO LEARN

In the lessons, software, and Student Manual (SM), you will learn the following vocabulary terms for Unit 7.

ascending order (p. 481; SM Lesson 133)

AutoFit (SM Lesson 125)

bar chart (p. 498, SM Lesson 137)

cell address (p. 438)

descending order (p. 481; SM Lesson 133)

formula (p. 443; SM Lesson 129)

function (p. 474; SM Lesson 131)

labels (p. 443)

pie chart (p. 503; SM Lesson 138)

sort (p. 481; SM Lesson 133)

spreadsheet/worksheet (p. 437; SM Lesson 121)

values (p. 443)

workbook (SM Lesson 121)

CAREER BYTE

METEOROLOGIST Meteorology is the study of the atmosphere. Meteorologists use computer technology to study the atmosphere's physical characteristics and the way it affects the rest of our environment. Weather forecasting is the best-known branch of meteorology. Meteorologists study information on air pressure, temperature, humidity, and wind velocity. Specialized software then allows them to apply physical and mathematical relationships to make short- and long-range weather forecasts. Data is analyzed from weather satellites, radar, and remote sensors and observers in many parts of the world. Weather data is valuable for air-pollution control, agriculture, air and sea transportation, defense, and studying trends in Earth's climate such as global warming or ozone depletion.

F. 3-Minute Timed Writings

Take two 3-minute timed writings on lines 15–23. Note your speed and errors.

Goal: 31/3'/5e

Life on the Oregon Trail was not easy. The pioneers 11
had to leave in the spring and arrive before the winter 22
freeze blocked the passes. They packed their wagons with 34
all they owned and then walked beside them. Only those who 45
were sick, old, or young rode on the journey. The plains 57
were endless, and the rivers that had to be crossed were 66
swift and raging. If a wagon fell behind, it may have to be 78
lightened quickly by removing excess goods and leaving them 89
there. 93

| 1 | 2 | 3 | 4 | 5 | 6 | 7 | 8 | 9 | 10 | 11 | 12 | SI 1.27

FORMATTING

G. Software Features

STUDENT MANUAL

Moving in a File
Backspacing
Using the Spelling and Grammar Check
Saving a File

Study Lesson 37 in your Student Manual. Complete all the practice activities while at your computer.

UNIT 7 SPREADSHEETS

Lessons 121–140

OBJECTIVES

- Demonstrate keyboarding speed and accuracy on straight copy with a goal of 39 words per minute for 5 minutes with 5 or fewer errors.
- Demonstrate knowledge of the basic parts of a spreadsheet.
- Demonstrate the ability to create a spreadsheet and manipulate the data.
- Demonstrate the ability to use spreadsheets to ask "what if" questions.
- Compose letters and short stories at the keyboard.
- Identify frequently confused words
- Apply rules for using apostrophes.

ORIENTATION TO WORD PROCESSING

OBJECTIVES:

- Identify confusing words.
- Refine techniques for keying symbols.
- Apply word processing features.

A. WARMUP

Key each line 2 times.

Speed	1	Tom kept his bank records for both last year and this year.
Accuracy	2	Braxton's wacky quip amazed but vexed his girlfriend, Thuy.
Language Link	3	Svetlana will change planes at Kennedy Airport in New York.
Symbols	4	He saw Jan's new car. It's not "up" but "down"! (I'm sure.)

FACT FILE

Describe Your Time Management System A time management system helps you to accomplish everything that needs to be done. How do you plan and organize your day? Do you use a calendar, a daily planner, or a simple list? Key five short sentences about the system or method that you use.

(continued)

Promoting Conservation
¶The Forest Service has restored millions of acres of forests used for outdoor recreation, for timber, and for wildlife habitats.
¶The federal government created the Environmental Protection Agency to help clean up our air, water, land, and other natural resources.
¶Recycling has now become more important than ever. Business and industry are finding new ways to recycle waste products such as paper, plastics, glass, oil, animal by-products, tires, and other trash. In many places, trash is being burned to create electricity.
¶There is a wealth of information available on global environmental changes. There are Web sites, software, and other materials available to help explore the various aspects of Earth's systems. Everyone needs to be aware of what he or she can do to help protect life on Earth.

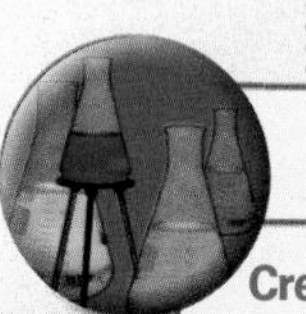

SCIENCE CONNECTION

Create a Newsletter Go to the Online Learning Center at **KeyComps.glencoe.com>Science Connection>Unit 6>Lesson 120** to find Web sites and learn more about what you can do to protect the environment. Then create a one-page newsletter about an environmental group or issue that interests you. Your newsletter should include:

- A brief description of the group or issue.
- Information for readers to find out more about the group or issue.
- Five environmental tips for readers to follow.
- A graphic such as a chart, table, or clip art.

Follow your teacher's instructions for saving and printing your work.

REPORT 71
Invitation

Create an invitation to a formal dinner dance using the desktop publishing features you have learned.

1. The dance is called the Washington Ball.
2. It will be held on September 23.
3. Dinner will begin at 7:30 p.m. and dancing will begin at 9 p.m.
4. The dance will be held at the Mt. Washington Hotel in Bretton, New Hampshire.
5. The cost is $60 per couple, and reservations must be made.
6. The telephone number is 603-555-0203, and all reservations must be received by September 1.

B. Confusing Words

Easily confused words include* homonyms *(words spelled and pronounced alike) and* homophones *(words pronounced alike but spelled differently). Homonyms do not affect spelling, but homophones do. Study the confusing words and their meanings shown below. Read each sentence carefully and determine which word should be used. Then edit lines 5–8 by choosing the correct word.

accept (v.)	to take willingly
except (prep.)	other than
stationary (adj.)	fixed, immovable
stationery (n.)	paper, writing materials

I will accept the award. Everyone attended except Jo.

The boat remained stationary while I wrote my letter on nautical stationery.

5 Why did she (except/accept) all of the programs (except/accept) the one entry?

6 Our motto will be, "We will (except/accept) nothing (except/accept) the best."

7 A (stationary/stationery) wall unit is used to store our new (stationary/stationery).

8 While he designed our new (stationary/stationery), he remained (stationary/stationery).

SKILLBUILDING

C. Technique Timed Writings

Take two 30-second timed writings on each line. Focus on the techniques at the left.

Keep your fingers curved and your elbows in.

9 You should know how you would use a computer before buying.

10 Decide what kinds of programs you will be using most often.

11 Will you be using database or spreadsheet programs with it?

12 Choose a computer that will meet all of your current needs.

| 1 | 2 | 3 | 4 | 5 | 6 | 7 | 8 | 9 | 10 | 11 | 12

REPORT 70
Newsletter

Create a newsletter by following these steps:

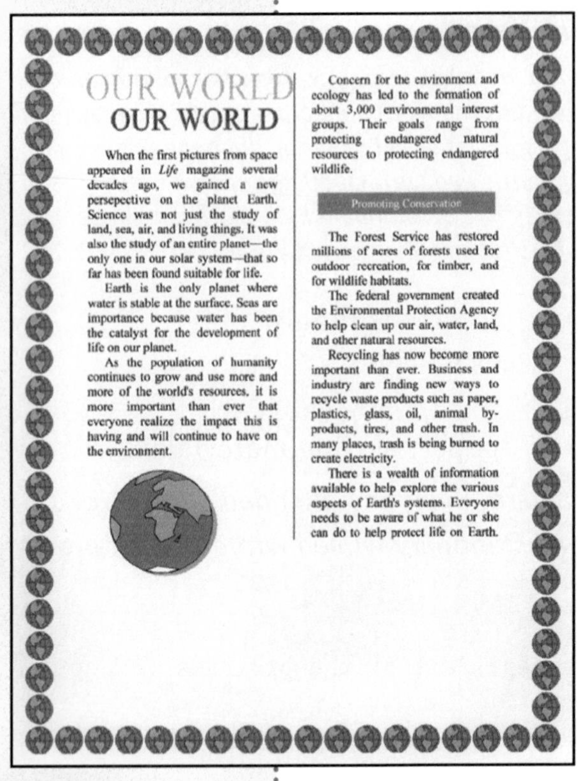
OUR WORLD

OUR WORLD

When the first pictures from space appeared in *Life* magazine several decades ago, we gained a new persepective on the planet Earth. Science was not just the study of land, sea, air, and living things. It was also the study of an entire planet—the only one in our solar system—that so far has been found suitable for life.

Earth is the only planet where water is stable at the surface. Seas are importance because water has been the catalyst for the development of life on our planet.

As the population of humanity continues to grow and use more and more of the world's resources, it is more important than ever that everyone realize the impact this is having and will continue to have on the environment.

Concern for the environment and ecology has led to the formation of about 3,000 environmental interest groups. Their goals range from protecting endangered natural resources to protecting endangered wildlife.

Promoting Conservation

The Forest Service has restored millions of acres of forests used for outdoor recreation, for timber, and for wildlife habitats.

The federal government created the Environmental Protection Agency to help clean up our air, water, land, and other natural resources.

Recycling has now become more important than ever. Business and industry are finding new ways to recycle waste products such as paper, plastics, glass, oil, animal by-products, tires, and other trash. In many places, trash is being burned to create electricity.

There is a wealth of information available to help explore the various aspects of Earth's systems. Everyone needs to be aware of what he or she can do to help protect life on Earth.

1. Use WordArt and Times New Roman 36-point to create the title *OUR WORLD.*
2. Key the body of the newsletter in two columns using Times New Roman 13-point and full justification. Insert a vertical line between the columns.
3. Indent paragraphs 0.25 inch.
4. Insert a graphic of a globe between the third and fourth paragraphs.
5. Key the heading *Promoting Conservation* so that the font color is white in a green box.
6. Add an appropriate page border to the newsletter.

¶When the first pictures from space appeared in *Life* magazine several decades ago, we gained a new perspective on the planet Earth. Science was not just the study of land, sea, air, and living things. It was also the study of an entire planet—the only one in our solar system—that so far has been found suitable for life.

¶Earth is the only planet where water is stable at the surface. Seas are important because water has been the catalyst for the development of life on our planet.

¶As the population of humanity continues to grow and use more and more of the world's resources, it is more important than ever that everyone realize the impact this is having and will continue to have on the environment.

¶Concern for the environment and ecology has led to the formation of about 3,000 environmental interest groups. Their goals range from protecting endangered natural resources to protecting endangered wildlife.

(continued on next page)

D. Symbol Review

Key each line 1 time. Repeat if time permits.

$	13 Buy 11 blue @ $.79, 43 purple @ $.85, and 17 green @ $1.19.
@	14 Our e-mail addresses are david@xyz.com or larry@netnow.com.
#	15 Carpet remnants #3, #16, and #37 sell for 25% and 35% less.
%	16 Their #7, #8, and #9 sizes are from 36% to 46% higher here.
&	17 Pair them as follows: 10 & 29, 38 & 47, 56 & 65, 135 & 780.
:	18 What is the correct date: 2001* or 2010* or 2008* or 2009*?
*	19 S & L* left at 10:30 and arrived at 11:45. Peter* was late.
=	20 The answers are: 91 + 82 = 173; 14 + 76 = 90; 24 + 36 = 60.
+	21 Lisa, did you know that (3 + 4)(2 + 6)(5 + 7) = 7 x 8 x 12?
()	22 Bella labeled items (10), (21), (65), (74), (83), and (92).
[]	23 Their [Aztec] houses were [very] old and expensive [$400K].
{}	24 Mrs. Gibson assigned this: ({7^2} {4^3}) + ({17^4} {13^5}).
<>	25 In ASCII, G < H and J < K. Are T > S and W > V and Z > A-Y?

FORMATTING

E. Software Features

STUDENT MANUAL

Changing Fonts and Font Sizes
Previewing a Document Before Printing
Printing a Document

Study Lesson 38 in your Student Manual. Complete all the practice activities while at your computer.

LANGUAGE ARTS CONNECTION

Using Symbols Key three short sentences using one or more of the symbols used in Activity D. Your sentences should show how the symbols can be used correctly. Follow your teacher's instructions for saving and printing your work.

DESKTOP PUBLISHING REVIEW

OBJECTIVES:

- Increase keyboarding speed and improve accuracy.
- Review desktop publishing features.

A. WARMUP

Key each line 2 times.

Speed	1	It is now time for all of us to take the time to save more.
Accuracy	2	Pat quickly froze the gold mixtures in five old brown jars.
Language Link	3	Do not discuss your personal problems with other personnel.
Numbers/Symbols	4	The total bill was $5.78 + $9.64 + $2.13, less 5% = $16.67.
		| 1 | 2 | 3 | 4 | 5 | 6 | 7 | 8 | 9 | 10 | 11 | 12

SKILLBUILDING

B. 12-SECOND SPRINTS

Take three 12-second timed writings on each line. Try to increase your speed each time.

5 They will be able to amend the votes that were taken today.
6 She sent a note about an issue to four kind men who helped.
7 When you take a tour, you may see four new members at work.
8 The first court passed one new law today that we must read.
| | | | 5 | | | | 10 | | | | 15 | | | | 20 | | | | 25 | | | | 30 | | | | 35 | | | | 40 | | | | 45 | | | | 50 | | | | 55 | | | | 60

C. DIAGNOSTIC PRACTICE: ALPHABET

Turn to the Diagnostic Practice: Alphabet routine beginning on page SB1. Key one of the Pretest/Posttest paragraphs and identify any errors made. Then key the corresponding drill lines 2 times for each letter on which you made 2 or more errors and 1 time for each letter on which you made only 1 error. Finally, repeat the same Pretest paragraph and compare your performance.

Orientation to Word Processing

OBJECTIVES:

- Define confusing words.
- Refine skills on double letters and alternate reaches.
- Apply word processing features.

A. Warmup

Key each line 2 times.

Speed	*1*	I did not see her take the pencil, but I know that she did.
Accuracy	*2*	Taxi drivers are quick to zip by the huge jumble of wagons.
Language Link	*3*	It's the secretary who accepted the stationery on Thursday.
Numbers/Symbols	*4*	Lee cut the pieces of twine 9 1/2, 7 3/4, and 6 5/8 inches.

COMMUNICATION FOCUS

Define Confusing Words To avoid confusing people, choose your words carefully. Some words are often misunderstood and misused. Use a dictionary to look up the definitions of the following words:

accept, except **access, excess** **than, then** **cite, sight, site**

Key each word and its definition. Use each word in a sentence. Follow your teacher's instructions for saving and printing your work.

(continued)

Headline: BRIGHTON HOSTS 70TH EAGLE CELEBRATION
Byline: By Collette Searle
¶Hugh Brighton, Welco Civic Affairs Director, hosted the 70th birthday festivities for the Golden Order of Eagles earlier this week in Baltimore. Brighton, who was recently elected president of the local chapter of the organization, hosted the order's national president, Milton Land. The highlight of the three-day celebration was the dedication of the New Eagle Wing of Children's Hospital. The 200-bed facility will provide free care to children who have been referred there from 12 eastern states.
Company Announcements:
You and Your W-2: Most employees should have received their W-2 forms by now. Employees who were on the accident and sickness program administered by Blue Banner will receive their forms this week. If you have questions about your W-2 forms, contact Gary Ashford in the Accounting Department at Ext. 589.
Short-Term Parking Passes: Because of road repairs near Wesley Tower and Building H, additional parking has been arranged for employees. If you work in either building, you can obtain a special parking permit from Roger Loucks, Mail Code 1209.
¶The permits are valid for spaces in Lot A on the northwest corner of Logan and Beaubien Streets.
Theater Tickets: If there is sufficient interest by Welco employees in seeing West Side Story, which is coming to the Palm City Theater, the company will purchase a block of discount tickets for the Friday, March 16, performance. The show begins at 8 p.m. If you are interested in purchasing tickets, please call Diane Cohen, Civic Affairs Dept., Ext. 479, before March 2.
Las Vegas Night: The Five-Year Club is sponsoring a Las Vegas Night fundraiser on April 26 at 8 p.m. at the Town Line House. All proceeds from this event will be donated to those charities supported by the club. Please call Helen Oldhoff at Ext. 291 for details.
Community Service: Welco continues to support the local school system by providing employees with release time to speak at schools or career fairs with students who are making career decisions. If you are interested, please contact Diane Cohen, Ext. 479.
Credits: THE REPORTER is published weekly by Welco. Letters should be addressed to the editor at New Center Building, 609 Griswold, Room 703, Detroit, Michigan 48030. Editor: Phillip S. DeRoy; Reporters: Gilbert Hall, Diane Novick, Anne Ricci, Collette Searle; Designer/Desktop Specialist: Betty Lynclyff.

B. Confusing Words

Study the confusing words and their meanings shown below. Read each sentence carefully to determine which word should be used. Then edit lines 5–8 by choosing the correct word.

principle (n.)	rule, code of conduct
principal (adj.)	chief, leading
(n.)	a person in a leading position
it's	contraction meaning "it is"
its	possessive pronoun, belonging to it

The students consider the coach a man of principle.
The school principal treats all students fairly.
It's a challenge to hold a job after school and study.
The coach praised the team for its leadership.

5 The (principle/principal) upon which this (principle/principal) was hired is clear.
6 Does the (principle/principal) know what (principle/principal) affected the choice?
7 (It's/Its) good to see that the firm is improving (it's/its) poor image.
8 (It's/Its) quiet movement is a sign that (it's/its) operating very well.

SKILLBUILDING

C. 30-Second OK Timed Writings

Take two 30-second OK (errorless) timed writings on lines 9–10. Then take two 30-second OK timed writings on lines 11–12. Goal: No errors.

9 The students begin to excel when they have peace and quiet.
10 Analyze your study habits and learn to be successful daily.
11 When you key, try moving your fingers speedily on the keys.
12 I think I have answered all of your questions at this time.

| 1 | 2 | 3 | 4 | 5 | 6 | 7 | 8 | 9 | 10 | 11 | 12

(continued)

4. Add a flag to the left of the title (Wingdings, O), and make it red, 36 points. Insert a space after the flag.
5. Key the article's byline on the next line in Times New Roman 10-point.
6. Key the body of the article on page 430 in Times New Roman 12-point.
7. Insert a text box with a black border and yellow fill, and key *COMPANY ANNOUNCEMENTS* in bold Times New Roman 14-point.
8. Center and key each announcement head in initial caps, bold, Times New Roman 14-point. Key the announcement text in 12-point Times New Roman, full-justified.
9. Use the Drawing toolbar to add a diamond on one side of *Las Vegas Night,* and add a heart on the other side.
10. Insert an appropriate graphic above the community service article.
11. Insert a text box for the credits at the end of the second column. Add a double-line border, shade the box light yellow, and key the credits in Times New Roman 11-point.
12. Adjust the columns, graphic images, and text boxes so that your page looks similar to the illustration.
13. Number the page (2) at the bottom center of the page.

BRIGHTON HOSTS 70TH EAGLE CELEBRATION
By Collette Searle

Hugh Brighton, Welco Civic Affairs Director, hosted the 70th birthday festivities for the Golden Order of Eagles earlier this week in Baltimore. Brighton, who was recently elected president of the local chapter of the organization, hosted the order's national president, Milton Land. The highlight of the three-day celebration was the dedication of the New Eagle Wing of Children's Hospital. The 200-bed facility will provide free care to children who have been referred there from 12 eastern states.

COMPANY ANNOUNCEMENTS

You and Your W-2

Most employees should have received their W-2 forms by now. Employees who were on the accident and sickness program administered by Blue Banner will receive their forms this week. If you have questions about your W-2 forms, contact Gary Ashford in the Accounting Department at Ext. 589.

Short-Term Parking Passes

Because of road repairs near Wesley Tower and Building H, additional parking has been arranged for employees. If you work in either building, you can obtain a special parking permit from Roger Loucks, Mail Code 1209. The permits are valid for spaces in Lot A on the northwest corner of Logan and Beaubien Streets.

Theater Tickets

If there is sufficient interest by Welco employees in seeing *West Side Story,* which is coming to the Palm City Theater, the company will purchase a block of discount tickets for the Friday, March 16, performance. The show begins at 8 p.m. If you are interested in purchasing tickets, please call Diane Cohen, Civic Affairs Dept., Ext. 479, before March 2.

Las Vegas Night

The Five-Year Club is sponsoring a Las Vegas Night fundraiser on April 26 at 8 p.m. at the Town Line House. All proceeds from this event will be donated to those charities supported by the club. Please call Helen Oldhoff at Ext. 291 for details.

Community Service

Welco continues to support the local school system by providing employees with release time to speak at schools or career fairs with students who are making career decisions. If you are interested, please contact Diane Cohen, Ext. 479.

THE REPORTER is published weekly by Welco. Letters should be addressed to the editor at New Center Building, 609 Griswold, Room 703, Detroit, Michigan 48030. Editor: *Phillip S. DeRoy*; Reporters: *Gilbert Hall, Diane Novick, Anne Ricci, Collette Searle*; Designer/Desktop Specialist: *Betty Lynoluff.*

2

(continued on next page)

D. PRETEST

Take a 1-minute timed writing on lines 13–16. Note your speed and errors.

13 When the food fight began, we all laughed. But Coach 11
14 Parr took one look and ushered all eight guilty students 22
15 to the office for mops and scrubbing supplies. All of them 31
16 were very quiet as they cleaned up the mess.

| 1 | 2 | 3 | 4 | 5 | 6 | 7 | 8 | 9 | 10 | 11 | 12

E. PRACTICE

SPEED: ***If you made 2 or fewer errors on the Pretest, key lines 17–24 two times each.***

ACCURACY: ***If you made more than 2 errors on the Pretest, key lines 17–20 as a group two times. Then key lines 21–24 as a group two times.***

Double Reaches

17 ff offer cliff stuff bluff affix scuff cliff sniff whiff ff
18 oo goose looks shoot loose noose scoop boost swoop roost oo
19 rr error carry tarry berry merry worry sorry furry hurry rr
20 ee cheer jeers trees sleep keeps weeps breed creek deeds ee

Alternate Reaches

21 tight fight hairy eight sight bland rigid girls laugh Blair
22 chair girls chant clams flame worms their maybe prowl Chris
23 signs usher heist other growl light gowns proxy prism Diana
24 vigor field anvil bugle dozen quake names right soaps Jamel

F. POSTTEST

Repeat the Pretest. Compare your Posttest results with your Pretest results.

FORMATTING

G. SOFTWARE FEATURES

STUDENT MANUAL

Selecting Text
Non-Printing Characters
Alignment

Study Lesson 39 in your Student Manual. Complete all the practice activities while at your computer.

SKILLBUILDING

C. PRETEST

Take a 1-minute timed writing on the paragraph. Note your speed and errors.

```
9      It is our civic duty to vote for the mayor of this      10
10  city. We may also need to audit the books so that we have   22
11  proof that the manner in which we do business is correct.   34
12  We will have to go through channels for this to work out.   45
    | 1 | 2 | 3 | 4 | 5 | 6 | 7 | 8 | 9 | 10 | 11 | 12
```

D. PRACTICE

SPEED: ***If you made 2 or fewer errors on the Pretest, key lines 13–20 two times each.***

ACCURACY: ***If you made more than 2 errors on the Pretest, key lines 13–16 as a group two times. Then key lines 17–20 as a group two times.***

```
13  nn funny cannon cannot dinner manner runner winner channels
14  oo good wood room soon proof spoon foods tooth groom booths
15  tt kitty bottle button attach cattle fitted attacks attends
16  mm rummy tummy drummer summer simmer summit yummy hammer mm

17  duck duty bush busy city clay audit blend civic cycle field
18  dock down both bowl buck burn flaps girls goals panel risks
19  dial corn cork body also auto rocks spend their tight vivid
20  dark pens kept coal gyms pent fight right tight burnt socks
```

E. POSTTEST

Repeat the Pretest. Compare your Posttest results with your Pretest results.

DESKTOP PUBLISHING APPLICATIONS

REPORT 69
Newsletter

Complete the second page of the newsletter you created in Lesson 118. Your page should look similar to the example on page 429. Follow these steps:

1. Set the top and bottom margins at 0.75 inch and the left and right margins at 1.2 inches.
2. Format the text in two columns, justify the text, and use automatic hyphenation.
3. At the left margin, key the headline for the article on page 430. Use Times New Roman 14-point, bold, in all caps.

(continued on next page)

Orientation to Word Processing

OBJECTIVES:

- Improve keyboarding skills.
- Key 32/3'/5e.
- Apply word processing features.

A. Warmup

Key each line 2 times.

Speed	1	I like to read about Lewis and Clark as they traveled west.
Accuracy	2	Sacagawea was the Shoshone who helped navigate the terrain.
Language Link	3	It's her fur. Jim will give the principle skiing rules now.
Numbers/Symbols	4	After 18 months and 4,000 miles, the journey ended in 1805.

SKILLBUILDING

B. Diagnostic Practice: Numbers

Turn to the Diagnostic Practice: Numbers routine on page SB4. Key one of the Pretest/Posttest paragraphs and identify any errors made. Then key the corresponding drill lines, on p. SB5 and p. SB6, 2 times for each number on which you made 2 or more errors and 1 time for each number on which you made only 1 error. Finally, repeat the Pretest and compare your performance.

C. Preview Practice

Key each line 2 times as a preview to the 3-minute timed writings on page 135.

5 in Civil maize Quapaw Arkansas smallpox Oklahoma eighteenth
6 migrate topped homes beans tribe clay went East and War the

LESSON 119 NEWSLETTERS

OBJECTIVES:

- Identify confusing words.
- Create the second page of a newsletter.

A. WARMUP

Key each line 2 times.

Speed	1	Andy may pay me for the bicycle if he is paid for the work.
Accuracy	2	Jacqueline was vexed by the folks who got the money prizes.
Language Link	3	My savings account pays low interest of only 4 5/8 percent.
Numbers	4	She sold 1,234 in June, 3,456 in July, and 7,890 in August.

| 1 | 2 | 3 | 4 | 5 | 6 | 7 | 8 | 9 | 10 | 11 | 12

LANGUAGE LINK

B. CONFUSING WORDS

Study the confusing words and their meanings shown below. Then edit lines 5–8 by selecting the correct word to complete each sentence.

personal (adj.)	private; of, relating to, or affecting a person;
personnel (n.)	employees; a staff making up a work-force; human resources workers
their (pron.)	possessive form of *they*
there (adv.)	at or in that place
(pron.)	used to introduce a clause

5 The letters are (personal/personnel) and should not be read at (there/their) party.

6 All of the teachers expressed (their/there) (personal/personnel) concerns about the problems.

7 Over (their/there) are our neighbors; (their/there) family is very pleasant.

8 The (personal/personnel) staff are (their/there) to help you.

D. 3-Minute Timed Writings

Take two 3-minute timed writings on lines 7–15. Note your speed and errors.

Goal: 32/3'/5e

```
 7      The Quapaw Indians first lived on the East Coast. They   11
 8 moved to the prairies of the Midwest and later went to the    23
 9 Arkansas River where they built and lived in homes of earth   35
10 topped with tree bark. They grew maize and beans and were     47
11 noted for their red and white clay jars.                      55
12      In the eighteenth century, much of the tribe was wiped   66
13 out by smallpox. Floods and the Civil War caused the Quapaw   78
14 to migrate many times. Today, although the tribe has few      89
15 members, they reside in Oklahoma.                             96
   | 1 | 2 | 3 | 4 | 5 | 6 | 7 | 8 | 9 | 10 | 11 | 12    SI 1.28
```

FORMATTING

E. Software Features

STUDENT MANUAL

Using Help

Study Lesson 40 in your Student Manual. Complete all the practice activities while at your computer.

LANGUAGE ARTS CONNECTION

Evaluate Uses for Types of Documents In this book, you will be using word processing skills to create many different types of documents. For each type of document listed below, key a short sentence that describes one situation at school in which you could use that type of document. Follow your teacher's instructions for saving and printing your work.

Report	Flyer
Agenda	Newsletter
Outline	Certificate
Letter	Invitation

(continued)

Article 1 headline: MORENCY TOPS ANNUAL ESP AWARDS
Byline: By Anne Ricci
Article 1 text: ¶Heather Morency's suggestion to send out-of-town requests for discharge information via facsimile won her the top prize in this year's Employee Suggestion Program (ESP). Morency, a Welco employee for nearly eight years, won $500 and, according to Caroline Harvey, the awards director, earned the gratitude of customer relations and records personnel throughout the country.
¶Eight other employees also received cash awards for their suggestions: John Vallejo ($300), to install an intercom system in the pump room; Linda Kane ($300), to place recycling bins for paper in the copy center; Trudy Fong ($200), to post no-parking signs on all ramps; James Sholes ($200), to film reports from tape instead of hard copy; Delois Jackson ($200), to obtain missing claims information by telephone or fax rather than regular mail; Susan Bonner ($200), to revise the Refund Computation Ticket; Patricia Kizarian ($200), to generate complete Inquiry and Open Claims Reports monthly; Rosalyn Gluck ($200), to revise the Data Conversion Control Form.
¶The winning suggestions were selected from more than 250 entries. This level of participation in the ESP marked an all-time high for the suggestion program.

Article 2 headline: SMART USERS KEEP PCs SECURE
Byline: By Gilbert Hall
Article 2 text: When the topic of computer theft comes up, most people think only of "hackers," clever PC users who break into large computer systems and steal or manipulate information. However, Dave Devaney, Computer Systems Manager, thinks that employees should be far more concerned with another kind of theft—the physical removal of their equipment from the office.
¶"Right now we don't have a problem, but the situation bears watching," says Devaney. "Other companies have had instances where equipment has just disappeared. Employees must learn to think of their computers and their software in the same manner as other valuable office items."
¶Devaney strongly recommends two measures:
- Physically lock down the equipment using a special device available from the Computer Systems Department.
- Lock all software in a drawer or specially designed case when not in use.

UNIT 3 WORD PROCESSING

Lessons 41–60

Objectives

- Demonstrate keyboarding speed and accuracy on straight copy with a goal of 33 words per minute for 3 minutes with 5 or fewer errors.
- Demonstrate correct use of word processing features.
- Demonstrate an understanding of proofreaders' symbols by editing copy marked for revision.
- Demonstrate basic formatting skills on a variety of reports, correspondence, and envelopes from a variety of copy—arranged, unarranged, rough draft, and handwritten.
- Compose sentences and paragraphs at the keyboard.
- Apply rules for subject/verb agreement.
- Apply rules for using commas and semicolons.

(continued)

5. Add the date line below the masthead. Align the volume number and date at the left; align the tag line at the right. Use Times New Roman 11-point italic. The line should read: *Volume 6, Number 3, January 20, {year} / The Welco Health System Weekly.*
6. Add a thin horizontal line from margin to margin below the date line.
7. Key the headline for article 1 in all capital letters at the left margin. Use bold Times New Roman 14-point.
8. Key the byline in Times New Roman 10-point.
9. Key the body of the article on page 426 in Times New Roman 12-point. Indent paragraphs approximately 0.25 inch, justify the text, and use automatic hyphenation.
10. Key the names of the eight other winners in bold.
11. Balance the columns.
12. Follow steps 7–9 for the second article on page 426.
13. Add an appropriate graphic at the top of the second column of the second article. Balance the columns.
14. Adjust the spacing and/or the size of the graphic image as necessary to fit everything on one page.

(continued on next page)

Volume 6, Number 3, January 20, {year} *The Welco Health System Weekly*

MORENCY TOPS ANNUAL ESP AWARDS
By Anne Ricci

Heather Morency's suggestion to send replies to out-of-town requests for discharge information via facsimile won her the top prize in this year's Employee Suggestion Program (ESP). Morency, a Welco employee for nearly eight years, won $500 and, according to Caroline Harvey, the awards director, earned the gratitude of customer relations and records personnel throughout the country.

Eight other employees also received cash awards for their suggestions: **John Vallejo** ($300), to install an intercom system in the pump room; **Linda Kane** ($300), to place recycling bins for paper in the copy center; **Trudy Fong** ($200) to post no-parking signs on all ramps; **James Sholes** ($200), to film reports from tape instead of hard copy; **Delois Jackson** ($200), to obtain missing claims information by telephone or fax rather than regular mail; **Susan Bonner** ($200), to revise the Refund Computation Ticket; **Patricia Kizarian** ($200), to generate complete Inquiry and Open Claims Reports monthly; **Rosalyn Gluck** ($200), to revise the Data Conversion Control Form.

The winning suggestions were selected from over 250 entries. This level of participation in the ESP marked an all-time high for this particular program.

SMART USERS KEEP PCs SECURE
By Gilbert Hall

When the topic of computer theft comes up, most people think only of "hackers," clever PC users who break into large computer systems and steal or manipulate information. However, Dave Devaney, Computer Systems Manager, thinks that employees should be far more concerned with another kind of theft—the physical removal of their equipment from the office.

"Right now we don't have a problem, but the situation bears watching," says Devaney. "Other companies have had instances where equipment has just dis-

appeared. Employees must learn to think of their computers and their software in the same light as other valuable office items."

Devaney strongly recommends two measures:

- Physically lock down the equipment using a special device available from the computer systems department.
- Lock all software in a drawer or specially designed case when not in use.

WORDS TO LEARN

In the lessons, software, and Student Manual (SM), you will learn the following vocabulary terms for Unit 3.

agenda (p. 156)
bold (SM Lesson 42)
bullets (SM Lesson 43)
business letter (p. 182)
hard page break (SM Lesson 46)
italic (SM Lesson 42)
letterhead (p. 182)
minutes (p. 160)
outline (p. 156)
paragraph (run-in) headings (p. 148)
personal-business letter (p. 168–169)
proofreaders' marks (p. 144)
reference initials (p. 182)
side headings (p. 148)
soft page break (SM Lesson 46)

CAREER BYTE

RESERVATION AGENT Reservation agents help people plan trips and make reservations. They offer suggestions on travel arrangements such as routes, time schedules, rates, and types of accommodation. Agents use computers and Internet connections to find fares and room rates, make and confirm transportation and hotel reservations, and sell tickets. With computerized systems, they can quickly obtain information needed to make, change, or cancel reservations for customers. Reservation agents can work for airlines, hotels, car rental services, and travel agencies.

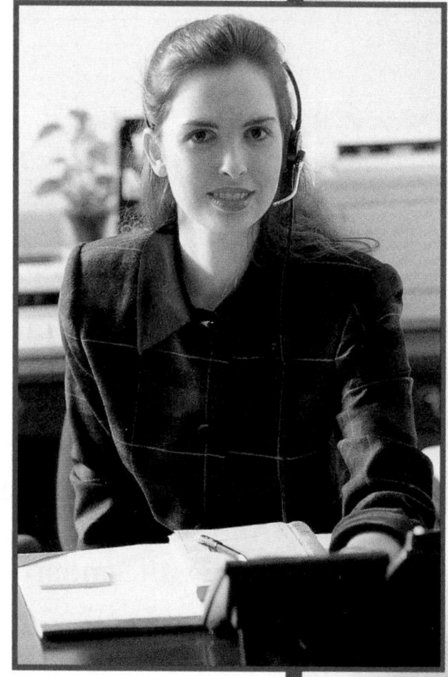

C. 5-Minute Timed Writings

Take two 5-minute timed writings on the paragraphs. Note your speed and errors.

Goal: 38/5'/5e

Many leaves change colors in the fall. The two main 11
types of trees are evergreens and broadleafs. Evergreen 22
trees have green needles all year round. The needles form a 34
quality heavy waxy cover that protects them. They also have 46
natural antifreeze inside that will usually protect them. 57

Broadleaf trees are just as the name implies. These 68
trees have leaves that are flat and wide. They lack the wax 80
covering or natural antifreeze that will protect them from 92
being zapped by winter's cold. When the weather gets cold 103
enough and the leaves die, they usually fall off. 113

Some broadleaf trees are considered to be evergreens, 124
such as holly. They are green all year. In warmer areas, 136
some broadleaf trees do not turn colors. Those trees that 147
turn beautiful fall colors are where the weather gets below 159
freezing. Usually, they turn fall colors just before the 171
leaves fall off the trees. The usual season to see fall 183
foliage is from September through October. 190

SI 1.45

| 1 | 2 | 3 | 4 | 5 | 6 | 7 | 8 | 9 | 10 | 11 | 12

DESKTOP PUBLISHING APPLICATIONS

REPORT 68

Newsletter

Follow these steps to create the first page of the newsletter on page 425.

1. Set the top and bottom margins at 0.75 inch and the left and right margins at 1.2 inches.
2. Press ENTER until you reach approximately 2.5 inches, then move the cursor to the top of the page.
3. Create the masthead, *THE REPORTER,* using colorful WordArt. Use Arial Black 36-point for the font.
4. Add a thick horizontal line from margin to margin under the masthead.

(continued on next page)

LESSON 41

ONE-PAGE ACADEMIC REPORTS

OBJECTIVES:

- Improve keyboarding skills.
- Format one-page academic reports with titles.
- Apply word processing features.

A. WARMUP

Key each line 2 times.

Speed	1 Nancy came into the room knowing that we were hiding there.
Accuracy	2 Voltaire wrote about Zadig, a Babylonian forced into exile.
Language Link	3 Terri thinks Bill will be accepted as the school principal.
Numbers/Symbols	4 Go to the store (M & W Feed) and buy 9# of #7 corn* @ $.43.
	| 1 | 2 | 3 | 4 | 5 | 6 | 7 | 8 | 9 | 10 | 11 | 12

SKILLBUILDING

B. 12-SECOND SPRINTS

Take three 12-second timed writings on each line. Try to increase your speed each time.

5 He did see my two dogs walk along the road to the red barn.
6 The dogs went into the barn to eat their meals and to rest.
7 The cat was in the barn and did not want the dogs in there.
8 It was calm in the barn while the cat hid in the dark silo.
| | | | 5 | | | | 10 | | | | 15 | | | | 20 | | | | 25 | | | | 30 | | | | 35 | | | | 40 | | | | 45 | | | | 50 | | | | 55 | | | | 60

LESSON 118 NEWSLETTERS

OBJECTIVES:

- Improve keyboarding skills.
- Key 38/5'/5e.
- Complete the first page of a two-page newsletter.

A. WARMUP

Key each line 2 times.

Speed	1	Both of the men may go soon if he pays them for their work.
Accuracy	2	Brown jars would prevent the mixture from freezing quickly.
Language Link	3	Her driver's license must be renewed by the 25th of August.
Numbers	4	There are 539 students and 68 faculty members at this camp.

| 1 | 2 | 3 | 4 | 5 | 6 | 7 | 8 | 9 | 10 | 11 | 12

MATH CONNECTION

Compare Columns Find five examples of printed works that use different column layouts. You can use newspapers, magazines, brochures, or textbooks. Measure the column widths and count the number of words per line.

Create a table comparing the publications, then use a red font to show which publication uses the maximum number of words in column, and a green font to show which shows the fewest words. Key 2–3 sentences evaluating which size column is easiest to read and why. Follow your teacher's instructions for saving and printing your work.

SKILLBUILDING

B. PREVIEW PRACTICE

Key each line 2 times as a preview to the timed writings on page 424.

Accuracy	5	waxy zapped needles quality September antifreeze broadleaf
Speed	6	enough leaves change types green where that name all the to

C. One-Page Academic Reports

There are many different formats for reports. Academic reports, however, are usually formatted in the MLA (Modern Language Association) style. To format a report in MLA style:

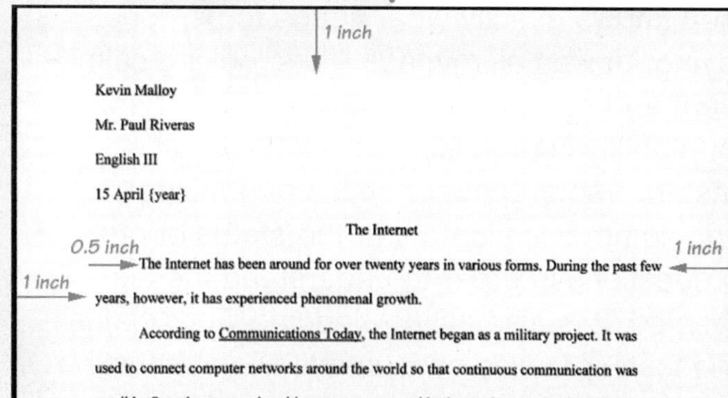

Kevin Malloy

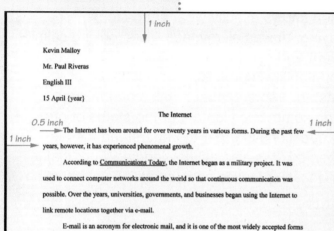

Mr. Paul Riveras

English III

15 April {year}

The Internet

The Internet has been around for over twenty years in various forms. During the past few years, however, it has experienced phenomenal growth.

According to Communications Today, the Internet began as a military project. It was used to connect computer networks around the world so that continuous communication was possible. Over the years, universities, governments, and businesses began using the Internet to link remote locations together via e-mail.

E-mail is an acronym for electronic mail, and it is one of the most widely accepted forms of business communication. With electronic mail, messages can be sent through computers to other users in various locations. Responses to the originator can be sent back by the computer in a fraction of the time that it would take to mail a letter or document.

Millions of users access the information and services offered on the Internet every day. Linking to the Internet requires little more than standard computer hardware. A keyboard, monitor, hard drive, modem, mouse, and basic Internet software are all that are necessary to hook up to one of the many consumer services on the Internet. Travel arrangements and financial services can be executed with the click of the mouse.

1. Use 1-inch top, bottom, and side margins.
2. Double-space the entire report, including the heading information.
3. Key the heading information (your name, your teacher's name, the class name, and the date) at the left margin.
4. Key the date in military style: 15 April {year}.
5. Center and key the title with initial capital letters for each important word.
6. Indent paragraphs 0.5 inch.

D. Software Features

STUDENT MANUAL

Setting Margins
Changing Line Spacing
Underlining Text

Study Lesson 41 in your Student Manual. Complete all the practice activities while at your computer. Then complete the tasks that follow.

REPORT 66

Newsletter Article

Open Report 65 and add the following text in two balanced columns as a separate section beginning below the first section. Double space between sections. Compare your work with the illustration on page 421.

¶Accountability involves asking for help when necessary to produce the desired results. It means knowing how to delegate and making sure each person knows exactly what needs to be done. Accountability is not saying, "It was all my fault." It is looking calmly at what caused a problem and determining how to prevent it from happening again. Accountability is promising only what can be delivered. It means constantly sorting out priorities and taking responsibility for ongoing communication about the status of projects. It involves asking questions in order to understand the big picture and what is expected. It is also acknowledging work that is well done. If your boss doesn't practice accountability, you must still be accountable.

REPORT 67

Newsletter

Open Report 66 and revise it as follows. Your final newsletter should look similar to the example on page 421.

1. Create a masthead using WordArt and Arial 36-point font. The name of the newsletter is *Professional Journal.*
2. Add a heavy line beneath the masthead.
3. Before you press ENTER, change the font to Times New Roman 12-point; then press ENTER once.
4. Key the volume and number at the left margin and the current date at the right margin. This newsletter is *Vol. 6, No. 3.*
5. Add a lighter line beneath the date line and leave some space between this line and the headline type.
6. To the second article, add the title *ACCOUNTABILITY* in Times New Roman 22-point.
7. Add a byline in Times New Roman 10-point. Use your name in the byline.
8. At the end of the first article, insert a graphic of people working in an office.
9. Size the graphic appropriately, and keep the columns balanced.

REPORT 1

One-Page MLA Format

Key this report in MLA format. Underline the magazine title in the second paragraph.

Kevin Malloy

Mr. Paul Riveras

English III

15 April {year}

The Internet

The Internet has been around for over twenty years in various forms. During the past few years, however, it has experienced phenomenal growth.

According to <u>Communications Today</u>, the Internet began as a military project. It was used to connect computer networks around the world so that continuous communication was possible. Over the years, universities, governments, and businesses began using the Internet to link remote locations together via e-mail.

E-mail is an acronym for electronic mail, and it is one of the most widely accepted forms of business communication. With electronic mail, messages can be sent through computers to other users in various locations. Responses to the originator can be sent back by the computer in a fraction of the time that it would take to mail a letter or document.

(continued on next page)

SKILLBUILDING

C. Paced Practice

Turn to the Paced Practice routine beginning on page SB7. Take three 2-minute timed writings, starting at the point where you left off the last time.

FORMATTING

D. Newsletters

Newsletters are a good way to provide information to a wide range of people. A well-planned newsletter is attractive and easy-to-read. It uses graphics and other DTP features to add visual interest and emphasize text.

Most newsletters have these standard elements:

1. **Masthead:** section located on the first page, giving the name of the newsletter, the name of the organization, and possibly a logo. It sometimes includes a tagline explaining the newsletter's purpose.
2. **Date line:** line under the masthead that includes the volume number, issue number, and date of publication.
3. **Headline:** large-font title stating the subject of an article. (Some articles may also have a byline giving the name of the writer.)
4. **Body text**: information in an article.
5. **Credits:** list of the newsletter's staff.

Professional Journal

Vol. 6, No. 3 *January 15, [year]*

THE EXCEPTIONAL ASSISTANT

For any organization to run smoothly, the organization must have a highly skilled, well-trained support staff. In today's fast-paced business world, executive secretaries and administrative assistants are an essential element. As businesses streamline their operations, executive secretaries and administrative assistants become increasingly important as they take on key managerial roles. In fact, according to a survey conducted several years ago, managers have now turned over more than 70 percent of their responsibilities to their support staff.

Support staff must have a combination of finely tuned management, interpersonal, and technical skills; a positive work attitude; and a willingness to promote change in order to advance the organization. Assistants now negotiate, manage projects, coordinate the office, and handle many other managerial responsibilities that used to be handled by their bosses.

Assistants must develop vital management skills. They must be able to manage priorities and projects, communicate more effectively, creatively solve problems, and much more. Assistants must be team players who can manage increasing responsibility and get things done.

ACCOUNTABILITY

By Andrea Meehan

Accountability also involves asking for help when necessary to produce the desired results. It means knowing how to delegate and making sure each person knows exactly what needs to be done. Accountability is not saying, "It was all my fault." It is looking calmly at what caused a problem and determining how to prevent it from happening again. Accountability is promising only what can be delivered. It means constantly sorting out priorities and taking responsibility for ongoing communication about the status of projects. It involves asking questions in order to understand the big picture and what is expected. It is also acknowledging work that is well done. If your boss doesn't practice accountability, you must still be accountable.

(continued)

Millions of users access the information and services offered on the Internet every day. Linking to the Internet requires little more than standard computer hardware. A keyboard, monitor, hard drive, modem, mouse, and basic Internet software are all that are necessary to hook up to one of the many consumer services on the Internet. Travel arrangements and financial services can be executed with the click of the mouse.

REPORT 2

One-Page MLA Format

Key this report in MLA format. Underline the book title in the last paragraph.

Lindy Alvarez

Mrs. Karen Schmidt

Computer Literacy II

13 November {year}

Software Ethics

Everyone who owns a computer uses software for various activities such as word processing, spreadsheets, and games.

That neat game your friend has would be great to add to your collection of games. Of course, you would also allow your friend to make a copy of one of your games. Before you copy software, be aware that you and your friend would be breaking the law.

(continued on next page)

LESSON 117

Desktop Publishing: Newsletters

OBJECTIVES:

- Apply rules for keying numbers.
- Create a newsletter.

A. Warmup

Key each line 2 times.

Speed	1	If they pay me for the emblem, I may make it to the social.
Accuracy	2	Six big men quickly won over Jeff despite his greater size.
Language Link	3	Our school's research team can, of course, solve the issue.
Numbers/Symbols	4	With the 8% increase, Ed bought 29# of #134 and #56 for $7.

| 1 | 2 | 3 | 4 | 5 | 6 | 7 | 8 | 9 | 10 | 11 | 12

Language Link

B. Number Expression

Study the rules and examples that follow. Then edit lines 5–8 to correct any errors in number usage.

Rule 30: Use figures for dates. (Use *st, d,* or *th* with a date only if it precedes the month.) If two or more related numbers with values above and below ten are used in a sentence, write them all as figures.

Rule 31: Use figures for measurements (time, money, distance, weight, and percentage) and mixed numbers.

She ordered 2 printers, 3 keyboards, and 12 printer cartridges on May 1 at 10 a.m.

On the 4th of July, we spent $65 to buy 20 pounds of meat for the picnic, which was held $3\frac{5}{8}$ miles away.

5 We bought 15 pairs of socks, seven jackets, and 23 scarves.
6 On the third of July, he made plans for the July 4th parade.
7 At nine a.m. we delivered the $500 rent check to the owner.
8 On the sixth of December, we got ten tickets for January 2.

(continued)

Illegal copying of software is called piracy. When you purchase software, you have the right to use the software only on your computer. New methods of preventing software piracy are being implemented every year. Soon every computer will have a "fingerprint" that will prevent a person from installing software on another person's computer.

The creators and writers of the software that you purchase in stores own what is called a copyright on their programs. A copyright is a legal right to exclusive publication, distribution, sale, or use of the copyrighted work. Musicians and authors own the same right for songs and books they write. The ease of copying software, even though it is illegal and unethical, has caused a real problem for the owners of software copyrights. Jane Ellis writes in her book, Don't Share That Software!, that what seems like a harmless thing to do is costing businesses and consumers millions, perhaps billions, of dollars.

ETHICS CONNECTION

Write a Skit In the report above, you learned that copying software is illegal and unethical. How would you persuade others to avoid copying software? Work with a partner. Compose and key a short skit of at least four lines in which one character persuades another that he or she should not copy software. Follow your teacher's instructions for saving and printing your work. Perform your skit for the class.

REPORT 65

Newsletter Article

Open Report 64 and revise it as follows:

1. At the top of the page, add the title *THE EXCEPTIONAL ASSISTANT* in a font that resembles a newspaper heading (for example, Times New Roman Bold Italic or Arial Black).
2. Increase the font size so that the title spans two columns.
3. Format the report into two balanced newspaper columns.
4. Add a line between the columns.

THE EXCEPTIONAL ASSISTANT

For any organization to run smoothly, the organization must have a highly skilled, well-trained support staff. In today's fast-paced business world, executive secretaries and administrative assistants are an essential element. As businesses streamline their operations, executive secretaries and administrative assistants become increasingly important as they take on key managerial roles. In fact, according to a survey conducted several years ago, managers have now turned over more than 70 percent of their responsibilities to their support staff.

Support staff must have a combination of finely tuned management, interpersonal, and technical skills; a positive work attitude; and a willingness to promote change in order to advance the organization. Assistants now negotiate, manage projects, coordinate the office, and handle many other managerial responsibilities that used to be handled by their bosses.

Assistants must develop vital management skills. They must be able to manage priorities and projects, communicate effectively, creatively solve problems, and much more. Assistants must be team players who can manage increasing responsibility and get things done.

LANGUAGE ARTS CONNECTION

Create a Two-Column Article If you owned a small business, what would you expect of your employees? For example, if your business were a small jewelry store, you would want your employees to dress and act a certain way to appeal to customers. You might need them to know how to change a watch band or monitor the inventory.

Key a two-column article describing the type of business you would run, the employees you would need to hire and their job duties, and the qualifications you would look for when interviewing for the positions. Follow your teacher's instructions for saving and printing your work.

LESSON 42 ONE-PAGE BUSINESS REPORTS

OBJECTIVES:

- Improve keyboarding skills.
- Apply proofreaders' marks.
- Apply word processing features.
- Format and key a one-page business report with a title and byline.

A. WARMUP

Key each line 2 times.

Speed	1 Have you been to the new cafe that is down on Marsh Street?
Accuracy	2 Egyptians carved the Sphinx to guard King Khafre's pyramid.
Language Link	3 Please accept the stationery that Principal White gave you.
Numbers/Symbols	4 Bill paid $85 for 3 shirts and $197.50 for 2 pair of pants.
	| 1 | 2 | 3 | 4 | 5 | 6 | 7 | 8 | 9 | 10 | 11 | 12

SKILLBUILDING

B. CONCENTRATION DRILLS

Key each line 1 time. Concentrate on keeping your eyes on the copy. Repeat if time permits.

5 accommodation lackadaisical weatherproofed environmentalist
6 objectionable bougainvillea characteristic hyperventilation
7 philosophical discombobulate identification thoughtlessness
8 filibustering noninvolvement reconnaissance departmentalize

C. TECHNIQUE CHECKPOINT

Key each line 2 times. Repeat if time permits. Focus on the technique at the left.

Do not hesitate before or after pressing the SPACE BAR.

9 I will not go to Joe Yen's home if he has gone to the mall.
10 You are the one to be at the home when all of us have gone.
11 It is a good idea to have me save all of my pay that I can.
12 Go get the cat and the dog so we can get to the park early.

FORMATTING

D. Columns

In desktop publishing, columns are often used to format documents such as brochures and newsletters. **Columns** are narrow sections of text arranged vertically on the page. Arranging text in columns often makes the text easier to read and provides more visual interest. In addition, the length and width of columns can be varied, and lines and boxes can be added to columns.

E. Software Features

STUDENT MANUAL

Using Columns

Study Lesson 116 in your Student Manual. Complete all the practice activities while at your computer. Then complete the tasks that follow.

DESKTOP PUBLISHING APPLICATIONS

REPORT 64

Newsletter Article

Single-space the following copy. Begin at the top margin, and indent paragraphs 0.5 inch. Do not leave a blank line between paragraphs.

¶For any organization to run smoothly, the organization must have a highly skilled, well-trained support staff. In today's fast-paced business world, executive secretaries and administrative assistants are an essential element. As businesses streamline their operations, executive secretaries and administrative assistants become increasingly important as they take on key managerial roles. In fact, according to a survey conducted several years ago, managers have now turned over more than 70 percent of their responsibilities to their support staff.
¶Support staff must have a combination of finely tuned management, interpersonal, and technical skills; a positive work attitude; and a willingness to promote change in order to advance the organization. Assistants now negotiate, manage projects, coordinate the office, and handle many other managerial responsibilities that used to be handled by their bosses.
¶Assistants must develop vital management skills. They must be able to manage priorities and projects, communicate effectively, creatively solve problems, and much more. Assistants must be team players who can manage increasing responsibility and get things done.

D. Proofreaders' Marks

Proofreaders' marks are used to indicate changes and corrections in a document (called a rough draft) that is being revised for final copy. Study the proofreaders' marks and examples that follow, and learn what each mark means.

Proofreaders' Marks	Draft	Final Copy
Omit space	data base	database
Insert	if hes going (insert ' not ,)	if he's not going,
Capitalize	Maple street	Maple Street
Delete	a final draft	a draft
Insert space	allready to (#)	all ready to
Change word	and if you (when)	and when you
Use lowercase letter	our President	our president
Paragraph	¶ Most of the	Most of the
Bold	He did say	He **did** say
Do not delete	a true story	a true story

E. One-Page Business Reports

The format of a business report is different from an academic report. To format a business report:

1. Use default side and bottom margins.
2. Single-space the entire report. Double-space (press ENTER twice) between paragraphs.
3. Leave an approximate 2-inch top margin (press ENTER 6 times).
4. Center and key the report title in all caps, bold, and a 14-point font.
5. Double space after the title to add a subtitle (a further description of the title) or byline (the author's name). Center and use a 12-point font and initial caps.
6. Press ENTER 2 times and begin keying the report. Indent each paragraph 0.5 inch.

LESSON 116 COLUMNS

OBJECTIVES:

- Improve keyboarding skills.
- Format text in columns.

A. WARMUP

Key each line 2 times.

Speed	1	Sue is to pay the man to fix the bicycle for the six girls.
Accuracy	2	Pete quickly froze the egg mixtures in five old brown jars.
Language Link	3	One student, however, rode the bus all the way from Boston.
Numbers	4	The 10 men lived 29 days at 3847 Bluff Way and 5 days here.

| 1 | 2 | 3 | 4 | 5 | 6 | 7 | 8 | 9 | 10 | 11 | 12

SKILLBUILDING

B. 30-SECOND TIMED WRITINGS

Take two 30-second timed writings on lines 5–6. Then take two 30-second timed writings on lines 7–8. Try to increase your speed each time.

5 Ida will go to the movie with Jay and take her small 11
6 dog to a vet today. Tom will also be there with his dog. 22

7 We had the box of new books in our office and got the 11
8 new pens before he did. My boss gave us a ride to the city. 23

| 1 | 2 | 3 | 4 | 5 | 6 | 7 | 8 | 9 | 10 | 11 | 12

C. DIAGNOSTIC PRACTICE: ALPHABET

Turn to the Diagnostic Practice: Alphabet routine on page SB1 near the end of the textbook. Key one of the Pretest/Posttest paragraphs and identify any errors made. Then key the corresponding drill lines 2 times for each letter on which you made 2 or more errors and 1 time for each letter on which you made only 1 error. Finally, repeat the same Pretest paragraph and compare your performance.

STUDENT MANUAL

Bold and Italic
Cutting, Copying, and Pasting Text

Study Lesson 42 in your Student Manual. Complete all the practice activities while at your computer. Then complete the tasks that follow.

WORD PROCESSING APPLICATIONS

REPORT 3

One-Page Business Report

Use the BACKSPACE key to delete a character to the left of the insertion point. Reach to the BACKSPACE key with the Sem finger.

Key the following one-page report. Use the format guidelines in Activity E on page 144. Make the corrections indicated by the proofreaders' marks.

THE AMAZING COMPUTER

by Gayle Todd

The computer is and amazing electronic device. It can compute complex calculations, store vast amounts of data, and process information with the stroke of a key. All this can take place within amatter of ~~minutes~~ seconds.

Computers are a significant part of our lives, and new and exciting uses are continuallly being developed. software is the fastest changing component ofthe computer. new and improved versions of Software are frequently introduced that improve the capability and functions ofthe computer.

according to one of the monthly computer magazines, *~~Education~~ ~~Software~~*, what and how we learn has also been affected by the computer. Interactive Software ~~allows~~ enables students and

(continued on next page)

(continued)

You are cordially invited
to join family and friends
in a celebration to honor
our graduate:
FAYE MARIE THEMUS

Date: Sunday, June 2, {year}
Time: 5 p.m. to 8 p.m.
Place: 21337 Kenwyck Circle
West Columbia, SC 29170

Please respond before May 22.
Call 803-555-3219.

4. Adjust the size of the WordArt so that it extends from the top margin to the bottom margin of the page.
5. Insert a text box below the clip art and horizontally center it.
6. Select an attractive, easy-to-read font style and size, then key the copy shown at the left into the text box.
7. Center the text horizonally, breaking the lines as shown in the illustration below.
8. Key the graduate's name in bold in a slightly larger font size. Double space before and after the graduate's name and between the separate sections. (See the illustration below.)
9. If you have additional clip art available, you may want to add it to the bottom of the invitation.
10. Size the box so that the bottom aligns evenly with the text on the right and left. If necessary, adjust the font style and/or size to fit all of the text in the box.

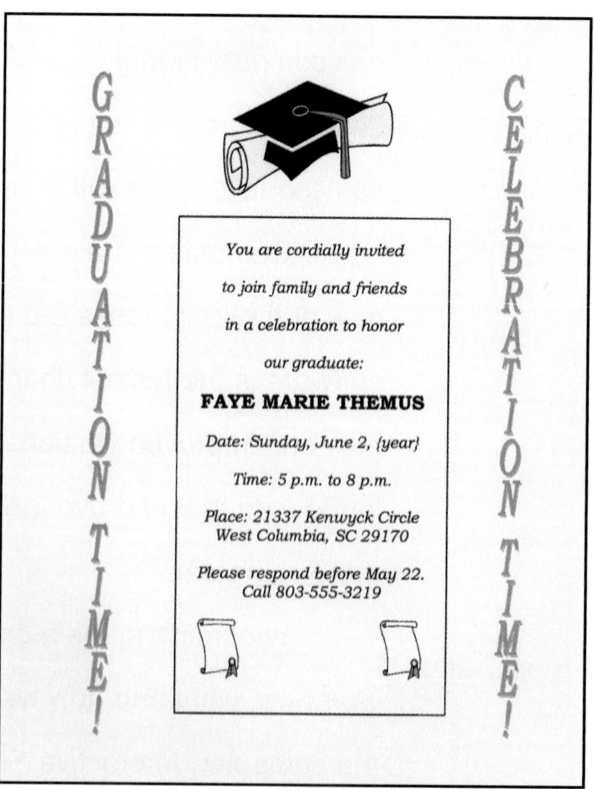

REPORT 63
Invitation

Design an invitation to your own birthday party, which will be held at your house.

(continued)

teachers to explore subject areas previously limited to text-books. Math and Science classes utilizes the computer to teach complex concepts using a hands-on approach. Language Arts and Literature classes write reports and creative assignments using computers. Business classes teach students to use the latest software currently being used in businessses and colleges. Computers continue to become an integrated part of our lives. It would be hard difficult, if not impossible, to name an area of our life lives that has not been affected by this amazing device.

REPORT 4

One-Page Business Report

Open Report 3 and revise it by moving the second paragraph to the beginning of the report. Move the last paragraph to before the third paragraph.

LANGUAGE ARTS CONNECTION

Review Proofreaders' Marks In this lesson, you learned about some proofreaders' marks. In your own words, key a short description of five of the marks listed below. Follow your teacher's instructions for saving and printing your work.

Omit space	Change word
Insert	Use lowercase letter
Capitalize	Paragraph
Delete	Bold
Insert space	Don't delete

D. 5-Minute Timed Writings

Take two 5-minute timed writings. Note your speed and errors.

Goal: 38/5'/5e

American companies used to be content with people who 11
showed up for work on time, performed their jobs, and did 23
as they were told. Now, managers want to find better ways 34
to run a business. 38

As they have in the past, we expect workers to have 49
solid skills such as being able to read, to write, and to 60
do math. But those skills alone are not enough. Employers 72
want to hire workers who have creative ideas, good manners, 84
and confidence. Workers must also be strong in a technical 96
skills area. Additional pluses are being a quick thinker, 108
a team player, and being willing to learn. 116

Although employers might provide training, they still 127
seek workers who have at least some of the above traits. 138
Employers also say that if they could hire enough bright, 150
able workers, middle management would not be needed. They 161
realize this can lead to more profits. American companies 173
looked at the success of foreign rivals and found ways to 185
improve how to do business. 190

| 1 | 2 | 3 | 4 | 5 | 6 | 7 | 8 | 9 | 10 | 11 | 12 SI 1.44

DESKTOP PUBLISHING APPLICATIONS

REPORT 62
Invitation

Follow these steps to create an invitation similar to the one in the illustration on page 416.

1. Select a piece of clip art that has something to do with either graduation or a celebration.
2. Adjust the size of the clip art to form a 2.5-inch square, and horizontally center it on the page.
3. Using WordArt and an attractive font set for 30 or 32 points, arrange the words *GRADUATION TIME!* vertically down the left side of the page. Then insert *CELEBRATION TIME!* vertically down the right side of the page.

(continued on next page)

LESSON 43 REPORTS WITH HEADINGS

OBJECTIVES:

- Improve keyboarding skills.
- Format reports with side headings and paragraph headings.

A. WARMUP

Key each line 2 times.

Speed	1	I am quite sure that we have had rain every day this month.
Accuracy	2	Zanzibar, a part of Tanzania, exports cassava and coconuts.
Language Link	3	The truck cannot keep its momentum; it's losing speed fast.
Numbers/Symbols	4	Pets & Paws will groom my dog for $45 (that's a lot) today.
		| 1 | 2 | 3 | 4 | 5 | 6 | 7 | 8 | 9 | 10 | 11 | 12

SKILLBUILDING

B. 12-SECOND SPRINTS

Take three 12-second timed writings on each line. Try to increase your speed each time.

```
5 We all like to be able to have fun and get the chores done.
6 While we work, we may find more work that needs to be done.
7 As we work at a job, we know what to do and it gets easier.
8 The more you do the same task, the better you become at it.
  ||||5||||10||||15||||20||||25||||30||||35||||40||||45||||50||||55||||60
```

C. PACED PRACTICE

Turn to the Paced Practice routine beginning on page SB7. Take three 2-minute timed writings, starting at the point where you left off the last time.

LESSON 115 DESIGNING AN INVITATION

OBJECTIVES:

- Compose a three-paragraph report at the keyboard.
- Key 38/5'/5e.
- Create a party invitation.

A. WARMUP

Key each line 2 times.

Speed	1	The profit she got for the corn and hay may make them rich.
Accuracy	2	Jim saw five dozen extra quilts by peeking under the truck.
Language Link	3	Did you know, Henry, that Carol's coat was found yesterday?
Symbols	4	Mr. Edward C. Jones joined Smith & Smythe, Inc., last June.

| 1 | 2 | 3 | 4 | 5 | 6 | 7 | 8 | 9 | 10 | 11 | 12

LANGUAGE LINK

B. COMPOSING AT THE KEYBOARD

Choose one of the following topics and compose a short, three-paragraph report. Use the topic as the report title.

5 My Most Embarrassing Moment
6 My Favorite Relative
7 My Favorite Memory

SKILLBUILDING

C. PREVIEW PRACTICE

Key each line 2 times as a preview to the 5-minute timed writings that follow.

8 lead improve profits foreign employers management technical
9 enough better middle quick still found seek area and how to

FORMATTING

D. Reports With Paragraph and Side Headings

Side Headings break a report into specific sections. Key side headings:

1. At the left margin in all caps and bold.
2. With a double space before and after.

Paragraph Headings (or **run-in** headings) are minor subdivisions of a report. Key paragraph headings:

1. Indented 0.5 inch.
2. In initial caps and bold.
3. Followed by a period (also in bold).
4. Followed by one space.

WORD PROCESSING APPLICATIONS

REPORT 5

One-Page Business Report With Side Headings

Key the following report. Single-space the report; press ENTER before and after side headings.

KENYA THE BEAUTIFUL

By Sharon Eldridge

The republic of Kenya is located near the equator on the east coast of Africa. One of the most beautiful places on earth, it's blessed with a rich assortment of wildlife and spectacular scenery. Kenya's most famous landmark, Mount Kilimanjaro, is located in Tanzania.

TOURISM

Visitors from all over the world come to see the variety of plant and animal species found here. Beautiful, uncrowded beaches are found along the coastline, with snorkeling and diving being popular recreation activities.

WILDLIFE

The wildlife of Kenya is among the most populous and diversified in the world. Large herds of zebras, giraffes, elephants, gazelles, and other grazing animals are seen

(continued on next page)

(continued)

8. Key the signer's title, *RCTC Training Specialist,* beneath the signature line, and key the word *Date* beneath the date line.

CERTIFICATE OF PROFICIENCY

This certifies that

Jonathan Riley

has successfully completed the requirements of the

Level 1 Desktop Publishing Training

offered by

Rodgers Career Technical Center

RCTC Training Specialist | *Date*

PORTFOLIO Activity

Create Certificates Certificates are given to people to acknowledge that they have completed training or coursework, but they also honor other accomplishments, such as volunteer work, sports achievements, and other types of success. They can even be used to thank people or commemorate special events, like birthdays or anniversaries.

Think of a certificate that you would like to give to someone who has done something special for you. It can be a friend, teacher, family member, or colleague. Then create a unique certificate just for that person. Follow your teacher's instructions for saving and printing your work.

(continued)

roaming the landscape in search of food. There is also an abundance of predator animals such as the leopard, the wild dog, and the cheetah.

LANDSCAPE

Both the deserts and highlands can be found in Kenya. The forests that once covered the highlands have been decreasing due to clearing the land for crops. The desert area has little in the way of trees, but grazing grasses cover the desert floor.

REPORT 6

One-Page Business Report With Paragraph Headings

Key the following report with paragraph headings. Single-space the report, and remember to turn off bold after keying the period in the paragraph heading.

BIRD WATCHING

By Thomas Chastain

Bird watching is the most popular and fastest growing outdoor activity for people of all ages. Both young and old delight in observing all kinds of birds from the common backyard bird to the majestic eagle. No special equipment is needed for bird watching; it is easily the most inexpensive outdoor activity today.

Birds are identified in two ways, either by sight or by sound. Learning to identify birds is challenging, educational, and fun. There is also a sense of accomplishment when the identification is correct.

Identification by Sight. When a bird is perched in a tree, it can be identified by its silhouette, by its movement, or by its flight pattern. The color and special markings of a bird also help to identify it.

Identification by Sound. Identifying birds by sound is an additional aid to identification and also adds fun to bird watching. Sound is also a way for the blind to participate in this fun activity. Birds sing for two reasons: to find a mate and to mark their territory. Many birds look alike, making positive identification difficult. Sound is one way to distinguish between look-alikes. Birds that look alike generally have very different songs. Knowing the song of a particular bird can aid in positive identification.

C. PRACTICE

In the chart below find the number of errors you made on the Pretest. Then key each of the designated drill lines 2 times.

Pretest Errors	0–1	2	3	4+
Drill Lines	12–16	11–15	10–14	9–13

Accuracy

```
 9 is exist message selection computer comparison presentation
10 are common variety software referred supported relationship
11 it's because writers although choosing recognize frequently
12 pie format written graphic excellent information understand
```

Speed

```
13 reader sliced number chart their order items they most line
14 manner pieces change kinds graph looks right will used work
15 better reveal period today three often makes that when want
16 support report choice print forms parts like this show over
```

D. POSTTEST

Repeat the Pretest. Compare your Posttest results with your Pretest results.

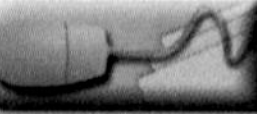

DESKTOP PUBLISHING APPLICATIONS

REPORT 61
Certificate

Create a certificate similar to the illustration on page 413.

1. Change the page orientation to landscape (11 × 8½ inches).
2. Vertically center the page.
3. Using WordArt, select a slightly curved style and an interesting font. Change the font size to 40-point.
4. Center and key the certificate title.
5. Below the certificate title, insert a graphic that relates to academic achievement, such as the seal in the illustration.
6. Center and key the text of the certificate using a script font set at 24 points. Key the name of the student in a heavier but complementary 24-point font.
7. Change to 12-point font. Approximately one inch below the last line of text, draw two lines for the signature and date.

(continued on next page)

LESSON 44

MULTIPAGE REPORTS

OBJECTIVES:

- Practice the top-row number keys.
- Apply word processing features.
- Format and key multipage reports.

A. WARMUP

Key each line 2 times.

Speed	1	Check our lists to be sure that we are ready for this trip.
Accuracy	2	Zachariah analyzed the situation and queried the witnesses.
Language Link	3	The principal investigator is concerned about the evidence.
Numbers/Symbols	4	Our seat assignments are 30-41, 56-72, 88-109, and 111-114.

| 1 | 2 | 3 | 4 | 5 | 6 | 7 | 8 | 9 | 10 | 11 | 12

LANGUAGE ARTS CONNECTION

Cut, Copy, and Paste In Lesson 42, you learned how to cut, copy, and paste text. Compose and key a short paragraph explaining why these tools are useful when writing and editing a report. Follow your teacher's instructions for saving and printing your work.

SKILLBUILDING

B. 30-SECOND TIMED WRITINGS

Take two 30-second timed writings on lines 5–6. Then take two 30-second timed writings on lines 7–8. Try to increase your speed each time.

5 Before you drive a car, adjust your seat and mirrors. 11
6 Lock the doors and buckle your seat belt. Drive with care. 23

7 Eating like a bird could mean drilling trees for ants 11
8 or diving in water for fish or probing mud for marine life. 23

| 1 | 2 | 3 | 4 | 5 | 6 | 7 | 8 | 9 | 10 | 11 | 12

LESSON 114 DESIGNING A CERTIFICATE

OBJECTIVES:

- Improve keyboarding skills.
- Design a certificate.

A. WARMUP

Key each line 2 times.

Speed	1	When did he go to the city and pay them for the world maps?
Accuracy	2	Five brown ibexes quickly zipped up among the jagged rocks.
Language Link	3	I think, Charlene, that you will like the new leather sofa.
Numbers/Symbols	4	Ronda knew that 3/4 of $84 = $63 and that 30% of $90 = $27.

| 1 | 2 | 3 | 4 | 5 | 6 | 7 | 8 | 9 | 10 | 11 | 12

LANGUAGE ARTS CONNECTION

Word Origins The word *diploma* is a Greek word that means "folded or doubled paper." It wasn't until the late 17th century that the word became associated with documents, or certificates, showing that a person had graduated from an educational institute. Use a print or online dictionary to look up the origins of the words *document* and *certificate*. Key both terms, the words and languages from which they are derived, and their original meanings. Follow your teacher's instructions for saving and printing your work.

SKILLBUILDING

B. PRETEST

Take a 1-minute timed writing on the paragraph. Note your speed and errors.

5 Information that is presented in a graph or a chart is 11
6 frequently referred to as graphics. Many writers like this 23
7 manner of presentation because they recognize that a reader 35
8 will best understand a message when it includes graphics. 46

| 1 | 2 | 3 | 4 | 5 | 6 | 7 | 8 | 9 | 10 | 11 | 12

C. PRETEST

Take a 1-minute timed writing on lines 9–12. Note your speed and errors.

Number diagnostic

We serviced 11 phones at 2:22 p.m. in offices 3-13 at 11
4455--the headquarters of Outlook 77. They had not replaced 23
their equipment since 1998. It was not difficult for them 34
to spend $9,000--$1,660 more than they had estimated. 45

| 1 | 2 | 3 | 4 | 5 | 6 | 7 | 8 | 9 | 10 | 11 | 12

D. PRACTICE

Key lines 13–22 one time. Then repeat any lines that stress the digits on which you made errors in the Pretest.

1 At 11 a.m. on 10-11-01, there were 11 ducks at 1011 Redbud.
2 Paul says that 1/2 of 2424 is 1212; now figure 1/2 of 1212.
3 Please get the names of players 33, 34, 38, 53, 73, and 93.
4 Lu made 14 copies of Chapter 4 in Volume 44, pages 424-443.
5 Timothy's number is 513-555-2505; Philip's is 513-555-5250.

6 The 6:15 train arrived at 6:56, so the 63 guests were late.
7 Tina is 7; Tia is 17; their mother is 37; her mother is 67.
8 Sue was born August 8, 1988, so write 8-8-1988 on the form.
9 This hat costs $9.99, but I have only $9. Do you have $.99?
0 He counts by tens: 10, 20, 30, 40, 50, 60, 70, 80, 90, 100.

E. POSTTEST

Repeat the Pretest. Compare your Posttest results with your Pretest results.

FORMATTING

F. Multipage Reports

To format a multipage business report:

1. Use default side margins for all pages of the report.
2. Single-space the report.
3. Leave a 2-inch top margin on page 1; leave a 1-inch top margin on continuing pages.
4. Leave a 1-inch bottom margin on all pages. A soft page break will be inserted automatically at the bottom of each page as you key the report.
5. Turn on widow/orphan protection.
6. Do not number the first page. However, number all continuing pages at the top right.
7. Indent each paragaph of the report 0.5 inch.

(continued)

6. Begin to key the information shown into the text box as follows: Use Times New Roman 36-point for the first line, and insert a space between the letters; change to italic for the second line.
7. Press ENTER 2 times, change the font size to 24-point, and key the next sentence.
8. Press ENTER 2 times, key *HSK* in bold (no italic), then complete the rest of the sentence in italic (no bold).
9. Press ENTER 2 times and key the next line.
10. Press ENTER 2 times and center and key the Internet address in regular type.
11. Add a blank line between each line of text at the left of the text box, and position the text box so that the copy appears to be vertically centered beside the box.
12. Create another text box at the lower left of the page, and insert the text in Times New Roman 10-point. Position the box so that the bottom of both boxes align. The text for the text box is Member of Retail Career Association.

REPORT 60

Flyer

Open Report 59 and make the following changes:

1. Change the color of the title to red, and add a shadow.
2. Change the text at the left of the text box to bold.
3. Add blue shading to the text box at the right.
4. Add a shadow to the first two lines of text in the text box at the right.

STUDENT MANUAL

Page Breaks
Page Numbering
Widows and Orphans

Study Lesson 44 in your Student Manual. Complete all the practice activities while at your computer. Then complete the following tasks.

WORD PROCESSING APPLICATIONS

REPORT 7

Multipage Business Report

Key the following multipage business report using single-spacing, with side and paragraph headings. Format the report according to the guidelines on pages 144, 148, and 151. Check to be sure that widow/orphan protection is turned on.

JAPANESE BUSINESS ETIQUETTE

By Chris Rocchio

Understanding quickly evolving Japanese business practices and the Japanese market has become a necessity for the American executive. Having a working knowledge of how Japanese business people think and what factors influence their decision-making is critical to your success. Japan is a country with a strong sense of hierarchy and honor.

UNWRITTEN CODES OF CONDUCT

There are many customs regarding etiquette and manners that apply to the business world. Although no one will expect a foreigner to know and abide by all of these "codes of conduct," knowing a few of the basics will help smooth the path to success in Japan.

(continued on next page)

SKILLBUILDING

C. 30-Second OK Timed Writings

Take two 30-second OK (error-free) timed writings on lines 9–10. Then take two 30-second OK timed writings on lines 11–12. Goal: no errors.

```
 9      Paula reviewed the subject before giving Raylynn and     11
10 Monte a quiz and quietly reviewed the next game with Buzz.   22

11      Even with all kinds of gripes, Maxine had a zest for     11
12 quiet living; Zeke examined all work and rejected most all.  22
   | 1 | 2 | 3 | 4 | 5 | 6 | 7 | 8 | 9 | 10 | 11 | 12
```

DESKTOP PUBLISHING APPLICATIONS

REPORT 59

Flyer

Create the flyer in the illustration following these steps:

HSK's ***Job Forum***

Linking

Marketing

Professionals

With

Retail Careers

Member of Retail Career Association.

H S K
Online

Your retail career center on the Net.

HSK *has the resources to help you find a rewarding job.*

Contact us at:

www.hsk.org

1. At the top right of a page, insert a graphic element similar to the one shown in the illustration.
2. Change the font to 48-point bold, and select a font style such as Garamond.
3. Approximately 2 inches from the top of the page, key the beginning of the title in regular font; key the remainder of the line in italic.
4. Change the font to 28-point italic, press ENTER 3 times, and key the copy at the left of the page with initial caps.
5. Create a text box similar in size to the one shown, position it at the right side of the page, and set the wrap to the left of the box.

(continued on next page)

(continued)

EXCHANGING BUSINESS CARDS

It is customary to exchange "meishi," or business cards. Always present yours to the receiver using both hands to hold on to the corners as you pass it forward while stating your name and the name of your company. When you receive a person's meishi, take it with both hands. Study it carefully. Often business cards will have Japanese on one side and English on the reverse. You should be able to understand what is on the card. Then put the meishi away—somewhere suitable. Do not drop the card into your pocket or purse, as this may be seen as rude.

VISITING THE OFFICE

Meeting Rooms. Possibly, you will wait in a meeting room. Most meeting rooms consist of four or more chairs set around a table. As the honored guest, you take the seat farthest from the door. You should stand up and bow or shake hands when someone comes in the room.

When you receive guests, reverse the process. You sit on the side closest to the door, with the senior member of your party farthest from the door on your side. This "farthest from the door" approach also applies in most other situations, including out of office gatherings.

What to Wear. When visiting a Japanese office, men should wear conservative suits, probably in a blue or gray color, with a white shirt and dark tie. It is also a good idea to take with you a decent supply of socks, since your socks will be seen more than usual. Women should dress conservatively as well. Jewelry, perfume, and makeup should be used sparingly. In today's business office, many Japanese women are comfortable wearing slacks or pant suits to work, depending on the type of job they have.

ADDITIONAL PROTOCOL

When you meet, should you bow or shake hands? A simple extended nod of the head followed by a short handshake is probably the easiest compromise. As long as you show the other person respect and politeness, everyone will be comfortable.

Desktop Publishing Designs

OBJECTIVES:

- Apply comma usage rules.
- Prepare documents using desktop publishing features.

A. Warmup

Key each line 2 times.

Speed	1 The man got a snap of an authentic whale by the big island.
Accuracy	2 I quickly explained that few big jobs involve many hazards.
Language Link	3 The twins' book had big, large print and its cover was red.
Numbers/Symbols	4 Ed had 789 birds there in 2002; but by 2006 there were 823.

| 1 | 2 | 3 | 4 | 5 | 6 | 7 | 8 | 9 | 10 | 11 | 12

Language Link

B. Comma Usage

Study the rule and the examples below. Then edit lines 5–8 to correct any errors in comma usage.

Rule 29: Use a comma *before* and *after* a nonessential expression. Use one comma if a nonessential element appears at the end or at the beginning of a sentence. Nonessential expressions include:

- words, phrases, or clauses that are not necessary for the meaning of a sentence
- the name of a person being addressed.

Therefore, the lease will be terminated next Thursday.
We are willing, as you know, to renegotiate the offer.
Lisa requested, however, that she retain her position.
You will be notified, Mr. Samuel, of our new location.

5 He will therefore, take all precautions before proceeding.
6 Can she however be certain that all the reports are there?
7 I would under most circumstances approve the merger today.
8 Hillary is as you can see the perfect candidate for them.

LESSON 45

LISTS, OUTLINES, AND AGENDAS

OBJECTIVES:

- Compose sentences at the keyboard.
- Key 33/3'/5e.
- Format and key outlines and agendas.

A. WARMUP

Key each line 2 times.

Speed	1	After the cats ate lunch, they bathed their paws and faces.
Accuracy	2	Quentin and Ynez Zbleski moved to Phoenix, Arizona, in May.
Language Link	3	It's just weird how the kitten lost its red leather collar.
Numbers/Symbols	4	On August 23-25, A.D. 79, 19-23 feet of ash buried Pompeii.

| 1 | 2 | 3 | 4 | 5 | 6 | 7 | 8 | 9 | 10 | 11 | 12

LANGUAGE LINK

B. COMPOSING AT THE KEYBOARD

Answer each question with a complete sentence.

5 Which season is your favorite?
6 What is the most recent movie you have seen?
7 Where would you like to go on summer vacation?
8 Who is your favorite recording artist?

SKILLBUILDING

C. DIAGNOSTIC PRACTICE: ALPHABET

Turn to the Diagnostic Practice: Alphabet routine on page SB1. Key one of the Pretest/Posttest paragraphs and identify any errors made. Then key the corresponding drill lines 2 times for each letter on which you made 2 or more errors and 1 time for each letter on which you made only 1 error. Finally, repeat the Pretest and compare your performance.

REPORT 58
Survey Form

Create a customer survey form similar to the one shown below.

1. Use Times New Roman 36-point italic with a shadow for the title.
2. Choose an appropriate graphic for the upper right corner of the page.
3. Use Times New Roman 16-point for the remaining text except for the bottom box.
4. Add a drop cap to the first line.
5. Draw three red check boxes that are large enough to write a number from 1 to 5 inside.
6. Leave an appropriate amount of space between the parts of the form.
7. Add a light shading to the bottom box and key the text in red Times New Roman 36-point italic bold.

What do you think?

Please rate our business today.

Excellent = 5   Poor = 1

You may use any number from 1 through 5. The higher the number, the more positive the rating. Use the boxes at the left to fill in your rating.

☐ How would you rate our overall service today?

☐ How friendly were our employees?

☐ Please rate the appearance of the store.

What can we do to make your next visit better?

____

____

Please write the names of any employees you feel were especially helpful to you.

____

____

Thank you for your help.

D. 30-Second OK Timed Writings

Take two 30-second OK (error-free) timed writings on lines 9–10. Then take two 30-second OK timed writings on lines 11–12. Goal: no errors.

9 Exercise your fingers on these drill lines every day, 11
10 and watch them zip and bound over all of the keys quickly. 23

11 Exercise such as walking gives your body the zest it 11
12 needs to adjust to the pace needed to maintain good health. 23

| 1 | 2 | 3 | 4 | 5 | 6 | 7 | 8 | 9 | 10 | 11 | 12

E. Preview Practice

Key each line 2 times as a preview to the timed writings that follow.

13 additional technical teamwork keyboard realize acquire work
14 know that must will need good plan some help your this just

F. 3-Minute Timed Writings

Take two 3-minute timed writings on the paragraphs. Note your speed and errors.

Goal: 33/3'/5e

15 Once you leave school, you should know that you must 11
16 acquire additional skills. On the job you will need good 23
17 work habits, teamwork skills, and technical skills. Plan to 34
18 take some courses that can help you advance in your career. 46
19 You should also realize that the skill you learn in 58
20 this class is but one example of the kind of skill you will 69
21 need on the job. Just about every job now requires use of a 81
22 keyboard. Learn the skill as well as you can so that you 93
23 can succeed in your career choice. 99

| 1 | 2 | 3 | 4 | 5 | 6 | 7 | 8 | 9 | 10 | 11 | 12 SI 1.23

LESSON 112 DESKTOP PUBLISHING REVIEW

OBJECTIVES:

- Improve keyboarding skills.
- Apply desktop publishing features.

A. WARMUP

Key each line 2 times.

```
Speed             1 The six forms she got from the firm may do for the problem.
Accuracy          2 Jack keyed four dozen requisitions for hollow moving boxes.
Language Link     3 He was always trying to be a helpful, courteous individual.
Numbers/Symbols   4 Key the problems: 100 - 74 = 26; 106 + 17 = 123; 4 - 3 = 1.
                    | 1 | 2 | 3 | 4 | 5 | 6 | 7 | 8 | 9 | 10 | 11 | 12
```

SKILLBUILDING

B. 30-SECOND TIMED WRITINGS

Take two 30-second timed writings on lines 5–6. Then take two 30-second timed writings on lines 7–8. Try to increase your speed each time.

```
5      Things seem to happen right for some people; they know   11
6 when a good chance comes along and can quickly seize it.      22

7      They are quick to get an exact vision of how this luck   11
8 can work for them; it may make their lives very different.    22
  | 1 | 2 | 3 | 4 | 5 | 6 | 7 | 8 | 9 | 10 | 11 | 12
```

G. Numbered and Bulleted Lists

Use numbers or bullets to display items in a list. Numbers and bullets are automatically indented, and carryover lines are automatically indented to align with the text in the line above.

1. If the order of the items is important, use numbers; otherwise, use bullets.
2. If the list is part of a single-spaced document, single-space the list (press ENTER 2 times before and after the list). If the list is part of a double-spaced document, double-space the list (press ENTER only 1 time before and after the list).

H. Outlines

An **outline** is a plan for the organization of a document. It identifies the topics within the document and the sequence in which those topics are presented. To format an outline:

1. Use default side and bottom margins. Leave an approximate 2-inch top margin (press ENTER 6 times).
2. Center and key the title of the outline in all caps, bold, and a 14-point font.
3. Press ENTER 2 times; then turn on the outline numbering command and key each item. Increase and decrease the indentations as needed.

I. Agendas

An **agenda** is a list of topics to be discussed at a meeting or a formal program of a meeting. To format an agenda:

1. Use default side and bottom margins. Leave an approximate 2-inch top margin (press ENTER 6 times).
2. Center and key the name of the committee or the company in all caps, bold, and a 14-point font.
3. Press ENTER 2 times; then center and key *Meeting Agenda* in initial caps.
4. Press ENTER 2 times; then center and key the date in initial caps.
5. Press ENTER 2 times; then turn on the numbering command and key each item.

REPORT 57

Academic Report

Open Report 51 and make the following changes:

1. Change the title to a vertical style at the left of the page.
2. Position the vertical text so that it extends from the top of the text to the bottom of the text.
3. Change the color of the text to green.
4. Move the graphic at the beginning of the first paragraph to the end of that same paragraph.
5. Change the wrap so that the text wraps to the left of the graphic.
6. Move the graphic at the end of the last paragraph to just below the vertical text.
7. Adjust the size of the graphic and copy and paste it so that three of them extend from the left margin to the right margin.

ANIMAL BEHAVIOR

Different animals behave in a variety of ways. An animal's behavior is dependent on a number of factors. One factor that affects its behavior is the environment. The environment consists not only of living things but also of physical characteristics such as temperature, types of soil, amount of rainfall, and amount of light.

Animal behavior is greatly affected by the temperature of the environment where the animal lives. Animals' body temperatures can vary greatly. Some animals are described as cold-blooded—such as snakes and frogs. *Cold-blooded* means that their body temperature changes as the temperature of their environment changes. Although the body temperature of cold-blooded animals is not always the same as the environment, it is usually close to it.

Warm-blooded animals—including tigers and humans—maintain the same body temperature nearly all the time. Warm-blooded animals usually maintain the temperature at which they function best. People, for example, maintain an average body temperature of 37 degrees Celsius.

Some warm-blooded animals hibernate during the winter. Groundhogs and woodchucks are examples of mammals that hibernate. Their body activities come to almost a complete halt. Bears are often thought, erroneously, to hibernate. However, they have been known to occasionally wake up and walk around.

STUDENT MANUAL

Bullets and Numbering

Study Lesson 45 in your Student Manual. Complete all the practice activities while at your computer. Then complete the tasks that follow.

WORD PROCESSING APPLICATIONS

REPORT 8
Agenda

Key the following agenda using the bullets and numbering feature for the numbered and bulleted items. Do not space before or after a slash.

ASSOCIATION OF COMPUTER USERS

Meeting Agenda

January 6, {year}

1. Access the World via the Internet/Alexander Room
   - Chris Melrose
   - Adam Chandler
2. Technology in the Workplace/Saturn Room
   - Karen Larsen
3. Lunch/Ballroom A
4. Virtual Reality: A Training Tool/Franklin Room
   - Willard Gallagher
   - Michael Laney
5. Teleconference Roundtables/Ballroom B

REPORT 9
Outline

Key this report using the outline feature.

PLAYING YOUR MUSIC

1) YOUR CHOICES
   a) CD players
   b) MP3 players
2) PERFORMANCE ISSUES
   a) Sound quality
   b) Shock resistance
   c) Battery life
      i) Chargeable or non-chargeable
      ii) AC adapter
3) PRICING

STUDENT MANUAL

Using Text as Art

Study Lesson 111 in your Student Manual. Complete all the practice activities while at your computer. Then complete the tasks that follow.

DESKTOP PUBLISHING APPLICATIONS

REPORT 56

Poster

Open Report 37 and make the following changes:

GOOD MANNERS FOR JOB INTERVIEWS

It is important to display good manners at all times. Manners are especially important during a job interview. Good manners show that you are sociable and civilized and may be a potentially good member of the company's team.

Arriving for an interview on time is one way to demonstrate your good manners. This indicates that you are reliable and will be on time for work. Being late for an interview could harm your chances of being hired.

Go to your interview alone. Even if someone must drive you to the interview, do not have him or her accompany you to the interview site. If possible, leave your hat and coat in the outer office. Carrying or wearing them into the interviewer's office may be awkward, and it may give the interviewer the impression that you are anxious to leave!

When you arrive for an interview, be sure to introduce yourself to the receptionist or assistant. Be pleasant and courteous. You can be assured that the manager will receive feedback on your manners and appearance from this person.

Once you are in the interviewer's office, wait until you are invited to sit. This shows that you have respect for the interviewer's position. If someone comes into the office during the interview, stand up and be prepared to shake hands with this person—it might be the interviewer's boss.

GET THE JOB YOU WANT!

1. Change the title to a wavy shape.
2. Adjust the width of the title to fit within the margins of the page.
3. Remove the bullets and begin each paragraph with a drop cap in a color that complements the title.
4. Add the following text to print vertically on the right side of the page: *GET THE JOB YOU WANT!* If necessary, change the color to complement the title and drop caps.
5. Add an appropriate graphic at the bottom center of the page and size it appropriately.

Minutes Of Meetings

OBJECTIVES:

- Apply the rule for subject-verb agreement.
- Apply additional proofreaders' marks.
- Format and key minutes of meetings.

A. Warmup

Key each line 2 times.

Speed	1	The Pilgrims were brave, but they did not know how to live.
Accuracy	2	Samoset and Squanto, a Wampanoag, helped the Pilgrims farm.
Language Link	3	The principle behind her actions was accepted; she was not.
Symbol	4	If ({X + Y} < {A - B}), then ({A - B} > {X + Y}), isn't it?

| 1 | 2 | 3 | 4 | 5 | 6 | 7 | 8 | 9 | 10 | 11 | 12

Language Link

B. Subject-Verb Agreement

Study the rule and examples below. Then edit lines 5–8 by choosing the correct verb to agree with the subject in each sentence.

Rule 4: Use singular verbs and singular pronouns with singular subjects and plural verbs and plural pronouns with plural subjects.

Singular subject and verb:

The doctor advised his patients to stay in bed.

She called her doctor to see if she should get a flu shot.

Plural subject and verb:

Several doctors were able to agree on the prognosis.

They were relieved that Dad's chest pains were gone.

5 The computer prices (has/have) greatly fallen in March.
6 Ed's past sales experiences (has/have) aided his growth.
7 Dan's method (was/were) not good for organizing supplies.
8 The volunteers' hard work (is/are) appreciated by all.

(continued)

5 Karen has what I would call a dynamic forceful presentation.
6 The sleek colorful tractor won first prize at the contest.
7 Last week they went to a long, boring movie at the theater.
8 The space shuttle is transported on a long sturdy vehicle.

SKILLBUILDING

C. 12-Second Sprints

Take three 12-second timed writings on each line. Try to increase your speed on each timed writing.

9 Mark can quickly key the words from, the, but, can, and go.
10 The four of them had to get to the bus by the time it left.
11 Sue says that she can fix the vase that fell from the desk.
12 Jane and the girl kept their title to the farm on the hill.

| | | | 5 | | | | 10 | | | | 15 | | | | 20 | | | | 25 | | | | 30 | | | | 35 | | | | 40 | | | | 45 | | | | 50 | | | | 55 | | | | 60

D. Diagnostic Practice: Numbers

Turn to the Diagnostic Practice: Numbers routine on page SB4. Key one of the Pretest/Posttest paragraphs and identify any errors made. Then key the corresponding drill lines 2 times for each number on which you made 2 or more errors and 1 time for each number on which you made only 1 error. Finally, repeat the same Pretest paragraph and compare your performance.

FORMATTING

E. WordArt

The design of a page can be made more exciting by creating special effects with text. **WordArt** (or **text art**) lets you curve, distort, and twist text into a variety of shapes and sizes. In addition, you can shade the text and make it three-dimensional. Treating text as art is useful in creating unique company or personal logos on letterhead and business cards.

SKILLBUILDING

C. Diagnostic Practice: Alphabet

Turn to the Diagnostic Practice: Alphabet routine on page SB1. Key one of the Pretest/Posttest paragraphs and identify any errors made. Then key the corresponding drill lines 2 times for each letter on which you made 2 or more errors and 1 time for each letter on which you made only 1 error. Finally, repeat the Pretest and compare your performance.

FORMATTING

D. Proofreaders' Marks

Study these proofreaders' marks and learn what each mark means.

Proofreaders' Marks	Draft	Final Copy
Transpose	how you can	how can you
Single-space	ss first line second line	first line second line
Double-space second line	ds first line second line	first line
Spell out	keep 1 copy	keep one copy
Move left	She fell	She fell
Move right	The final	The final
Move as shown	The two pages extra	The extra two pages
Italic	ital Vogue magazine	*Vogue* magazine
underline	u/l *Vogue* magazine	Vogue magazine

LESSON 111 WordArt

OBJECTIVES:

- Apply comma usage rules.
- Increase keyboarding speed.
- Apply WordArt.

A. Warmup

Key each line 2 times.

Speed	1	The six girls held a social to pay for a visit to the lake.
Accuracy	2	Why would quick brown foxes want to jump over any lazy dog?
Language Link	3	Brittney moved to Grand Forks, ND 58201, in late September.
Numbers/Symbols	4	Ed & Zoe sold 59# of sugar @ $1.67, for a total of $103.84.

| 1 | 2 | 3 | 4 | 5 | 6 | 7 | 8 | 9 | 10 | 11 | 12

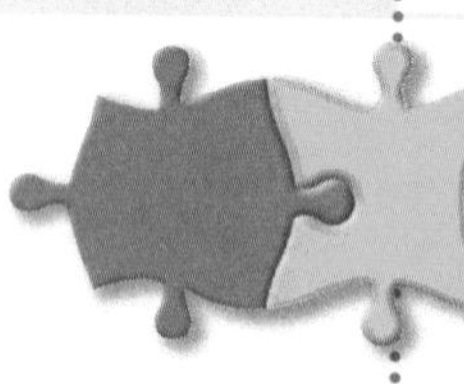

Language Link

B. Comma Usage

Study the rule and examples that follow. Then edit lines 5–8 to correct any errors in comma usage.

Rule 28: Use a comma between two adjacent adjectives that modify the same noun. To determine whether the adjectives do describe the same noun, use the following test.

Read the sentence, "Chris gave a *short, emotional* speech." Now change the order to say, "A speech was short *and* emotional." If it makes sense, it proves that both adjectives describe *speech,* and a comma is necessary.

Read the sentence, "She mailed a *new spring* schedule. Now change the order to say, "A schedule is new *and* spring." It doesn't make sense, so no comma is needed.

The soft Angora kitten slept peacefully near the fireplace.

Roger purchased a noise shield for the loud, rapid printer.

(continued on next page)

E. Minutes of Meetings

The secretary of an organization is responsible for taking and keeping minutes of meetings. **Minutes** are the official record of what happened at a meeting. To format minutes:

1. Use default side and bottom margins and single spacing.
2. Leave an approximate 2-inch top margin (press Enter 6 times).
3. Center and key the name of the committee or the company in all caps, bold, and a 14-point font.
4. Press Enter 2 times, then center and key *Minutes of the Meeting* in initial caps 2 lines below the title.
5. Press Enter 2 times, then center and key the date in initial caps.
6. Key the side headings in all caps and bold at the left margin. Leave a blank line above and below the side headings.
7. After the last section, press Enter 2 times and begin the closing at the left margin.
8. Then press Enter 4 times and key the secretary's name and title at the left margin.

WORD PROCESSING APPLICATIONS

REPORT 10

Minutes of Meeting

Key these minutes. Remember to leave a blank line before and after the side headings.

LINCOLN HIGH PARENT ORGANIZATION

Minutes of the Meeting

(Current Date)

ATTENDANCE

The monthly meeting of the Lincoln High School Parent Organization was held in the school library with Mario Palazollo presiding. The meeting was called to order at 7 p.m. Forty-seven parents attended. All officers were present.

APPROVAL OF MINUTES

The secretary read the minutes of the last meeting. They were approved as read. The treasurer reported that there was $790 in the treasury as of the end of the month.

(continued on next page)

REPORT 54

Personal Stationery

Create informal personal stationery for yourself. Be sure to include your full name, your address including ZIP Code, and your telephone number.

1. Insert a shape of your choice from the shapes available in your word processor.
2. Center the shape at the top of the page.
3. Choose a font to use for your initials, which will be keyed inside the shape.
4. Center your main initial (the first letter of your last name) between your first initial and your middle initial. Make the main initial twice as large as the others.
5. Center your name, address, telephone number, and e-mail address below the shape (either on one line with spaces between sections or on several lines).
6. Create a table in a footer and insert a series of shapes or symbols of your choice for the bottom of the page.

REPORT 55

Formal Letterhead

Create a more formal letterhead for yourself.

1. Use Times New Roman 16-point.
2. Center and key your name.
3. Press ENTER once.
4. Change the font to Times New Roman 12-point, and center your address on 2 lines. Use initial caps.
5. Press ENTER once.
6. Center and key your telephone number, beginning with your area code.
7. Press ENTER once.
8. Center and key your e-mail address.
9. Add a heavy line above and below your name and address.

interNET CONNECTION

Create Letterhead Stationery Go to the Online Learning Center at **KeyComps.glencoe.com>Internet Connection> Unit 6>Lesson 110** to find more examples of stationery layouts. Choose one and re-create it on your own. Match the example that you choose as closely as possible. Be sure that it contains your full name, address, and telephone number. Follow your teacher's instructions for saving and printing your work.

(continued)

ADJOURNMENT

There being no new business, the meeting was adjourned at 9 p.m.

Respectfully submitted,

Mary Upchurch, Secretary

REPORT 11

Minutes of Meeting

Key these minutes. Leave a blank line above and below the side headings.

Use the BACKSPACE key to delete a character to the left of the insertion point.

THE CHILDREN'S FOUNDATION
Minutes of the Meeting
November 16, {year}

CALL TO ORDER
The meeting was called to order by Elsie Russell at 11:30 a.m. in the Conference Room of the Foundation Building. The meeting was adjourned at 1 p.m. All members of the Board were present except Anne Laster.
UNFINISHED BUSINESS
The minutes of the October meeting were read ang approved. The Treasurer's report was reviewed an accepted as submitted. The proposed budget was presented and discussed. There was agreement that the amount listed in the budget from grants the budget as income should be should be decreased from $40,000 to $20,000. The proposed budget was approved as revised.

The Executive Director's report was read and accepted. Ms. Russell shared that we need to expend our Big Brother/Big Sister outreach program. Suggestions for accomplishing this were discussed.
NEW BUSINESS
Mrs. Costa suggested that there is a need to establish a publicity Plan for the work being done by the foundation. This would help with fund-raising efforts.

Motion carried to accept 4 new prospective members as members of the Board of Directors--Richard Bates, Wanda Rudd, Florence Loucks and Melvin Hearns.
Respectfully submitted,
Arlene Porter, Secretary

C. 5-Minute Timed Writings

Take two 5-minute timed writings on the paragraphs. Note your speed and errors.

Goal: 38/5'/5e

```
     If you feel fortunate to have a job today, this might      11
not be in your best interest. In fact, this feeling may         22
prevent some individuals from taking the risks needed to        34
keep up with salary trends in their field.                      42
     You should realize that getting a raise is harder now      53
than it was ten years ago. When you believe you merit one,      65
do not be afraid to seek it out. Usually, a promotion comes     77
with a raise. In this case, your good work already is being     89
recognized and rewarded. However, there are times when an      101
employee must take the initiative to seek what is due.         112
     Take inventory of yourself. Be sure you know what your    123
strengths are and how your experience makes you a valuable     135
employee. Know why you deserve the raise so you can justify    147
it to your employer.                                           151
     Requesting a raise on your own may mean you need to       161
meet a different set of job standards. Your employer might     173
expect something more from you. You might want to think        184
about a response beforehand.                                   190
                                                           SI 1.40
| 1 | 2 | 3 | 4 | 5 | 6 | 7 | 8 | 9 | 10 | 11 | 12
```

FORMATTING

D. Designing Letterhead

When you are designing **letterhead**, which is stationery that includes your name and address, consider how it will be used. For example, if you are designing a letterhead for writing letters to friends, you can use a less formal font and style. If the letterhead is for a personal-business letter, such as a letter of application for employment, use a more traditional, formal style.

LESSON 47 REVIEW

OBJECTIVES:

- Apply the rules for correct subject-verb agreement.
- Key 33/3'/5e.
- Review reports and minutes of meetings.

A. WARMUP

Key each line 2 times.

Speed	1 The Sun is center of our solar system and our closest star.
Accuracy	2 The Aztecs built Tenochtitlan on an island in Lake Texcoco.
Language Link	3 The seas of Australia include the Tasman Sea and Coral Sea.
Technique	4 Ada Bob Cam Don Evi Fay Gil Hal Ian Joy Kay Lon Mya Nan Ola

| 1 | 2 | 3 | 4 | 5 | 6 | 7 | 8 | 9 | 10 | 11 | 12

LANGUAGE LINK

B. SUBJECT-VERB AGREEMENT

Study the rule and examples below. Then edit lines 5–8 by choosing the correct verb for subject/verb agreement.

Rule 5: The subject *the number* takes a singular verb; *a number* takes a plural verb.

The number of children riding in the bus was minimal.

The number of dogs and cats is astronomical.

A number of pages were missing from the file.

A number of women were to meet for lunch.

5 A number of students in the class (is/are) working on a project.
6 The number of men attending the convention (was/were) greater than expected.
7 The number of cars to be parked (exceeds/exceed) the number of spaces available.
8 A number of workers (was/were) waiting for word about that.

LESSON 110 PERSONAL STATIONERY

OBJECTIVES:

- Improve keyboarding skills.
- Key 38/5'/5e.
- Create personal stationery.

A. WARMUP

Key each line 2 times.

Speed	1 The home row keys are easy to use as you key all your work.
Accuracy	2 Why did Professor Black give you a quiz on the major texts?
Language Link	3 We will drive to Douglasville, Georgia, on August 21, 2005.
Numbers	4 I saw on page 38 that 47 times 29 was much less than 1,560.

| 1 | 2 | 3 | 4 | 5 | 6 | 7 | 8 | 9 | 10 | 11 | 12

FACT FILE

Personalizing Stationery Some versions of Word let you add a distinct background and text formatting to a document, which can be used to create your own stationery. Open a Word document, click the **Format** menu, and then choose **Theme**. Choose a theme that you like from the scroll box, and choose **OK** to apply it to your document.

SKILLBUILDING

B. PREVIEW PRACTICE

Key each line 2 times as a preview to the timed writings that follow.

Accuracy	5 fortunate individuals prevent recognized inventory employer
Speed	6 want meet more the are how you own not set it be so to in a

SKILLBUILDING

C. Preview Practice

Key each line 2 times as a preview to the timed writings that follow.

9 craftsmen Pilgrims equipped desired hunting journey weather
10 were poor they life knew fish when took them half four farm

D. 3-Minute Timed Writings

Take two 3-minute timed writings on the paragraphs. Note your speed and errors.

Goal: 33/3'/5e

11 The Pilgrims were a mix of people who desired freedom 10
12 to worship and poor farmers and craftsmen who hoped for a 23
13 better life. They had guns but knew little about hunting. 34
14 They planned to fish but knew nothing about fishing. 45
15 When their journey took them north of their target, it 56
16 was winter; and they found they were not equipped for the 68
17 harsh weather. Almost half of the Pilgrims froze or died of 80
18 hunger or disease. In the early spring, four native friends 92
19 taught them to farm, hunt, and fish. 99

| 1 | 2 | 3 | 4 | 5 | 6 | 7 | 8 | 9 | 10 | 11 | 12 SI 1.28

SOCIAL STUDIES CONNECTION

Create a Mnemonic A mnemonic is a sentence or phrase that can help you to remember important information. Each word in the mnemonic starts with the same letter as the words that you want to remember. For example, you can remember the names of the departments in the president's Cabinet by remembering this mnemonic: **S**ee **t**he **d**og **j**ump **v**igorously **i**n **a** **c**ircle; **l**eave **h**er **h**ere **t**o **e**ntertain **e**fficiently. (State, Treasury, Defense, Justice, Veterans Affairs, Interior, Agriculture, Commerce, Labor, Health and Human Services, Housing and Urban Development, Transportation, Energy, Education)

Compose a three-word mnemonic that will help you to remember the three branches of government: executive, legislative, and judicial. Follow your teacher's instructions for saving and printing your work.

REPORT 53

Notepad

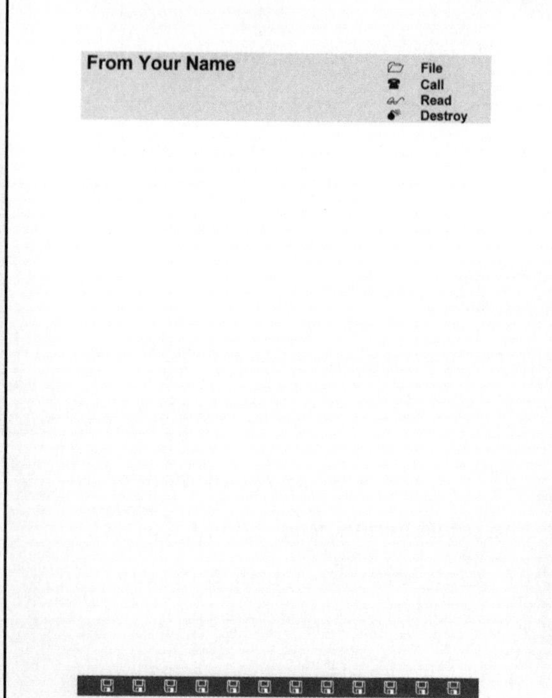

Create a different notepad following these steps:

1. At the top of the page, insert a boxed table with 1 column and 1 row, and apply a 20 percent color fill to the row.
2. Set tabs at 4.5 inches and 5 inches from the left margin.
3. Change the font to Arial Bold 20-point, and key *From* and your name. Then press CTRL + TAB to move to the first tab stop.
4. Change the font to Wingdings® 14-point, and key the number *1* to create the file folder.
5. Press CTRL + TAB, change the font to Arial Bold 14-point, and key *File.* Then, press ENTER once.
6. Repeat steps 4–6 for the remaining words and symbols: (= telephone; $ = glasses; M = bomb.
7. Create a footer, insert a 1-column, 1-row table, and apply a 100 percent color fill.
8. Change the font to Wingdings 18-point, space once, and key < to create a disk. Space once between each wingding. Key as many disks as needed to fill the row.
9. Reverse the text to white.

MATH CONNECTION

Calculate Color Fill Percentages A color fill that gradually increases or decreases its percentage of shading can add visual interest to documents. The effect will look best if the increases or decreases are consistent. For example, if you have a 3-column chart you may want to increase the fill shading by 30 percent each time; so the first column will be 0 percent, the second 30 percent, and the third 60 percent.

For each of the tables described below, calculate the color fill percentage for each row or column, increasing evenly to 100 percent.

1. A table with 5 columns
2. A table with 6 columns
3. A table with 11 columns

REPORT 12

One-Page Business Report With Numbered List

Key the following report using single spacing. Double-space before and after a group of single-spaced numbered items.

TELEPHONE TECHNIQUES FOR THE JOB

When you answer the telephone, remember that you represent the company. Make the first impression of your business a good one by following these techniques:

1. Greet the caller by identifying your company and yourself. Ask how you may assist or direct the call.
2. Use a friendly tone, speak clearly and distinctly, and avoid slang or mumbling.
3. Listen carefully to be sure you understand everything the caller is saying.
4. Be professional if you have to place a caller on hold while you get files or if you need to transfer the call to someone else.

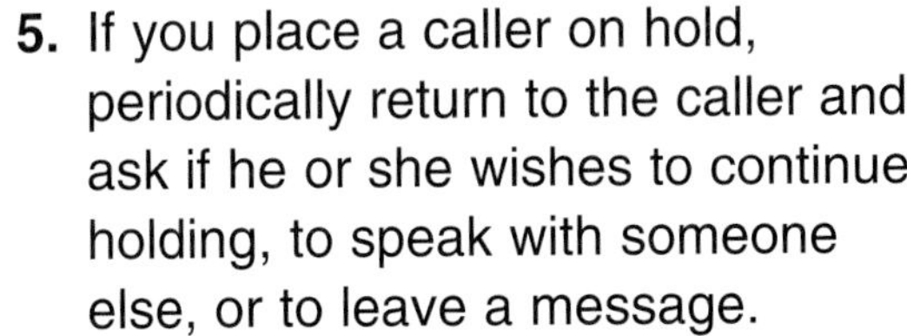

5. If you place a caller on hold, periodically return to the caller and ask if he or she wishes to continue holding, to speak with someone else, or to leave a message.
6. Offer to take a message or have someone return the phone call.
7. Record messages accurately. Include the caller's name and telephone number and any other important information such as when they called and why. Repeat the telephone number to be sure you wrote it correctly.
8. Close the call by expressing appreciation to the caller. Be sure you and the caller agree on what action is to be taken. Then say goodbye.

REPORT 52

Notepad

From the desk of Your Name . . .

- ❑ *Urgent*
- ❑ *Do Today*
- ❑ *Do As Soon As Possible*
- ❑ *Follow Up*

Create the notepad illustrated here by following these steps:

1. At the top of the page, insert a boxed table with 1 column and 1 row.
2. Change the font to Times New Roman Bold Italic 24-point.
3. Key *From the desk of* and your name followed by a space and then by three periods. Leave one space between each period.
4. Apply a 100 percent fill in the color of your choice to the box and reverse the text to white.
5. Create a footer.
6. Change the font to Wingdings® 16-point. Key the letter *q* to create a check box, and space once.
7. Change the font to Times New Roman Bold Italic 16-point. Key *Urgent,* and press ENTER once.
8. Repeat steps 6-7 to create three additional check boxes, accompanied by the following text:

   Do Today
   Do As Soon As Possible
   Follow Up
9. Change the color of the text in the footer to match the color you chose for the top section.

PORTFOLIO Activity

Create a Notepad Design a notepad that keeps track of your daily assignments. At the top of the notepad, include your name and a line on which you can write the date. Insert a table with one row for each class and three columns. In the first column, skip one row, then key the name of each class. In the first cell of the second column, key the heading "Assignment Details." Above the third column, key the heading "Due Date." Follow your teacher's instructions for saving and printing your work.

REPORT 13

Minutes of a Meeting

Key the following report.

PLANNING COMMITTEE

Minutes of Meeting

November 13, {year}

ATTENDENCE

The Plaing Committee met on Nov. 13, {year}, at the Board Room of the Douglas County Courthouse. Members present were Ronald Horton, Lakisha Lopez, Tonnetta McCoy, Chris Ngyen, Martha Ristau, and Steve Vanderhoff. Ronald Horton, chairperson, called the meeting to order at 7:15 p.m.

UNFINISHED BUSINESS

Arbor Mall Station construction began on Nov. 10. Martha Ristau moved that land parcels on the east side of the construction site be auctioned to prospective new businesses, since those parcels are zoned E-5. Chris Ngyen seconded the motion. After a lengthy discussion, the motion was passed unanimously.

NEW BUSINESS

Kendall Construction Company presented a blue print for developing the land parcels across Douglas boulevard from Arbor Station Mall. Mr. Kevin O'Rourke from Kendall Construction Company proposed the building of several "big box" stores in those parcels. After several questions arose concerning the environment impact of developing these parcels, a motion was made to table a vote until the corps of Engineers could conduct land impact studies on the area.

ADJOURNMENT

The meeting was adjourned at 9:30 p.m. The next meeting for December 10, is scheduled {year}, in the Conference Room at Douglas County High School. Respectfully submitted, J. D. Harper, Secretary

COMMUNICATION FOCUS

Taking Minutes Whether for student council or a business meeting, minutes maintain a record of the issues that were covered. They can then be distributed in hard copy, downloaded through the Internet, or read at the next meeting. Key a brief paragraph describing one type of meeting where minutes should be taken, who should receive a copy of the minutes, and the best way to distribute them. Follow your teacher's instructions for saving and printing your work.

SKILLBUILDING

C. PRETEST

Take a 1-minute timed writing on the paragraph. Note your speed and errors.

```
 8      Reading a book during a weekend is a wise choice. You       10
 9 can increase your word power even by reading popular books.    22
10 Enjoy yourself; join a number of those who choose to read a    33
11 good book. Invest your weekend time wisely by reading.          44
   | 1 | 2 | 3 | 4 | 5 | 6 | 7 | 8 | 9 | 10 | 11 | 12
```

D. PRACTICE

SPEED: ***If you made 2 or fewer errors on the Pretest, key lines 12–19 two times each.***

ACCURACY: ***If you made more than 2 errors on the Pretest, key lines 12–15 as a group two times. Then key lines 16–19 as a group two times.***

Adjacent Reaches

```
12 we weak wean wept weave wedge sweat weigh weary dowel sweet
13 oi soil toil boil hoist point joist poise spoil avoid noise
14 po pond port pour pound pouch poach point polka power polar
15 rt tort sort dart short court party warts sorts forth mirth
```

Jump Reaches

```
16 ce cede cell cent cease hence sauce grace niece cedar cello
17 um numb jump lump chump mumps crumb gummy stump thumb bumpy
18 in bind find grin brain cabin cling brink drain faint grain
19 om come pomp some bloom romps domes homes tombs zooms rooms
```

E. POSTTEST

Repeat the Pretest. Compare your Posttest results with your Pretest results.

FORMATTING

F. SOFTWARE FEATURES

STUDENT MANUAL

Reverse Text

Study Lesson 109 in your Student Manual. Complete all the practice activities while at your computer. Then complete the tasks that follow.

REPORT 14

One-Page Business Report With Paragraph Headings

CHOOSING THE RIGHT COLLEGE

By Carl Klees

Choosing a college is one of the big decisions a student makes in life. Careful planning and thoughtful consideration can make this decision easier for you.

Match Your Interests. Finding a college that matches your interests is an important factor in your choice. Several colleges, not just one, can offer you an opportunity to match your interests with those of other students. Choosing a college just because it's popular or because your parents went there could result in the loss of time spent at a college that best suits your needs.

Academic Programs. The offering of specific academic programs is one of the most important reasons for choosing a college. Some colleges specialize in particular majors while others offer a broad range of majors. Determine what your academic needs are in order to aid your decision.

Size. Consider the size of the college when making your decision. Perhaps you like small classes where you know the professor and other classmates rather than classes held in lecture hall situations with hundreds of other students. Many people do better in small situations as opposed to large ones.

Extracurricular Activities. The extracurricular offerings of a college deserve a special look. Consider whether the college offers activities that you enjoy and whether these activities are available to people of your skill level. Also determine whether these activities will interfere with your class and study obligations. The activities offered outside the college in the surrounding community should also be considered.

Financial Considerations. Cost, of course, is an important consideration in college choice. Public versus private school will impact cost as will attending school in state or out of state. Tuition for out-of-state students is double or triple the cost of in-state students.

Plan a Visit. Once you have narrowed the choice down to a few colleges, plan to visit the campus. A visit to the campus can give you a better picture of the college, the students, the community, and whether the overall picture suits you. The earlier you begin considering colleges, the more time you will have to visit them.

LESSON 109 Personal Notepads

OBJECTIVES:

- Compose at the keyboard.
- Improve keyboarding skills.
- Reverse text shading.
- Create personal notepads.

A. Warmup

Key each line 2 times.

Speed	1	Nan said she may go back to her job by the end of the week.
Accuracy	2	Jane quickly seized the wax buffer and removed a big patch.
Language Link	3	On August 15, 2005, we received a blue ribbon for our work.
Technique	4	q z p / w x o . e c I , r v u m t b y n a ; s l d k f j g h

| 1 | 2 | 3 | 4 | 5 | 6 | 7 | 8 | 9 | 10 | 11 | 12

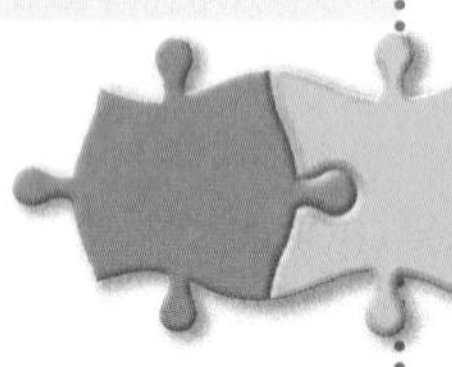

Language Link

B. Composing at the Keyboard

Choose one of the following topics and compose a short three-paragraph report.

5 My Greatest Fear
6 My Proudest Moment
7 My Future Plans

ETHICS CONNECTION

Evaluate Office Ethics Studies show that common violations of office ethics include using the office computer and telephone for personal business, using office supplies and copiers for personal business, and using office computers to play games. Write three short paragraphs about what you might do as an office manager if you saw employees performing these actions. Write one paragraph for each of the examples in the first sentence. Follow your teacher's instructions for saving and printing your work.

LESSON 48 PERSONAL-BUSINESS LETTERS

OBJECTIVES:

- Improve keyboarding accuracy.
- Apply word processing features.
- Format personal-business letters.

A. WARMUP

Key each line 2 times.

Speed	1	Check our lists to be sure that we are ready for this trip.
Accuracy	2	Zachariah analyzed the situation and queried the witnesses.
Language Link	3	A number of students were excused from their science class.
Numbers/Symbols	4	Buy 2# of pears (#1 Bartlett*) @ $1.98 at the Fruit & More.

SKILLBUILDING

B. 30-SECOND OK TIMED WRITINGS

Take two 30-second OK (error-free) timed writings on lines 5–6. Then take two 30-second OK timed writings on lines 7–8. Goal: no errors.

5 Extend a burst of energy to your fingers as you force 11
6 them to zoom over the keys. Enjoy the rush of rapid keying. 23
7 People who routinely succeed squeeze value out of each 11
8 minute. They judge the best way to do a task and act on it. 23

| 1 | 2 | 3 | 4 | 5 | 6 | 7 | 8 | 9 | 10 | 11 | 12

C. PRETEST

Take a 1-minute timed writing on lines 9–12. Note your speed and errors.

9 Wyoming was the first state to give women the right to 11
10 vote. The other states in the West joined the cause in the 23
11 next two decades. After New York and Illinois gave women 34
12 the right to vote, Congress began to debate the issue. 45

(continued)

Much has been said about the effect of smiles on human beings. Perhaps you have heard some of the following well-known sayings. "A smile is an expression your face wears when your heart is happy." "A smile is your umbrella during stormy times." "A smile is a frown turned upside down." "Smile, it gives your face something to do." "Frowns cause wrinkles; smile now—avoid wrinkles later." "Smile—everyone will wonder what you are up to." "Smile and the world smiles with you—cry and you cry alone." "Smiles beget smiles." "It takes fewer face muscles to smile than to frown." Why not give smiling a try?

REPORT 51

Essay

Open Report 49 and make the following changes:

1. Change the border of the title to a heavy line.
2. Resize the graphic at the top of the page to approximately 1.5 by 1.5 inches, and add a thin border the same color as the title border.
3. Move the graphic to the beginning of the first paragraph, and wrap the text to the right of the graphic.
4. Move the graphic at the end of the report to the end of the second paragraph, and size it to approximately 2 inches wide.
5. Wrap the text around both sides of the graphic.
6. Add a page border that relates to the content of the report.

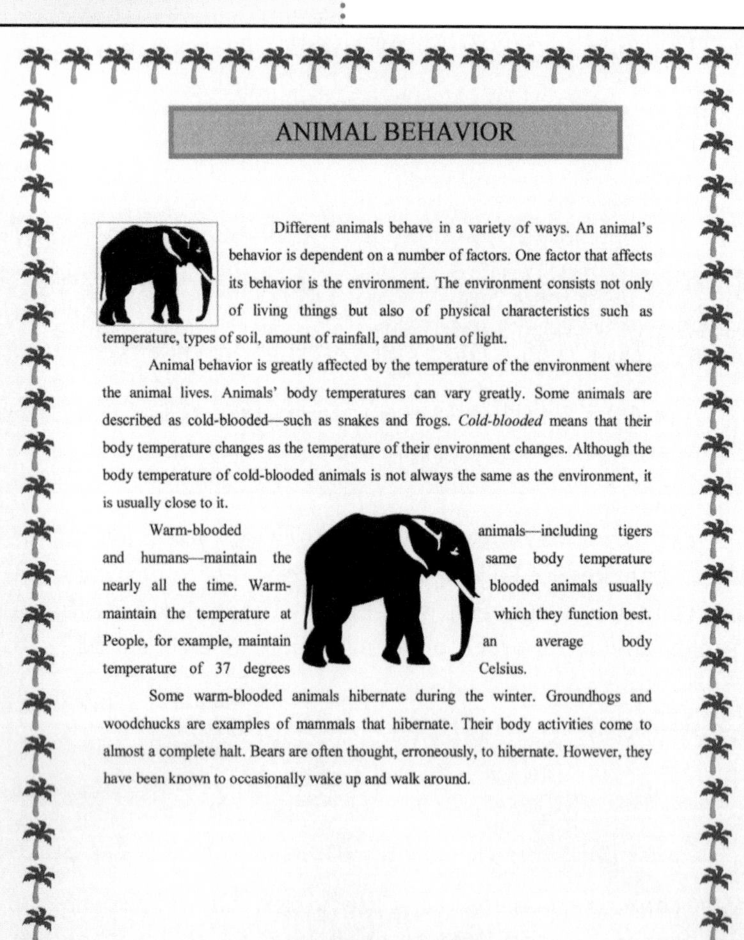

ANIMAL BEHAVIOR

Different animals behave in a variety of ways. An animal's behavior is dependent on a number of factors. One factor that affects its behavior is the environment. The environment consists not only of living things but also of physical characteristics such as temperature, types of soil, amount of rainfall, and amount of light.

Animal behavior is greatly affected by the temperature of the environment where the animal lives. Animals' body temperatures can vary greatly. Some animals are described as cold-blooded—such as snakes and frogs. *Cold-blooded* means that their body temperature changes as the temperature of their environment changes. Although the body temperature of cold-blooded animals is not always the same as the environment, it is usually close to it.

Warm-blooded animals—including tigers and humans—maintain the same body temperature nearly all the time. Warm-blooded animals usually maintain the temperature at which they function best. People, for example, maintain an average body temperature of 37 degrees Celsius.

Some warm-blooded animals hibernate during the winter. Groundhogs and woodchucks are examples of mammals that hibernate. Their body activities come to almost a complete halt. Bears are often thought, erroneously, to hibernate. However, they have been known to occasionally wake up and walk around.

D. PRACTICE

Key each line 2 times.

Build speed on repeated word patterns.

```
13 road toad load loam loan moan moat goat coat coal cowl cows
14 vows bows rows tows tons tone zone cone come comb tomb bomb

15 quip quit suit suet sued sues cues cued coed toed toes does
16 dogs bogs cogs logs lots loss boss moss most cost lost post

17 noon soon loon boon boot soot spot spat scat swat swam swim
18 swum scum scup scud stud stun shun shin chin thin then them

19 Tex. text test rest west lest lost last mast past fast cast
20 case vase base bask back tack pack hack hark mark dark dart

21 gaze haze faze daze raze race pace pate gate bate bade wade
22 ware hare mare more mode rode rote vote tote tope rope hope

23 Dora Lora Lara Mara Myra Myla Nyla Nola Nona Rona Rena Zena
24 Bill Will Wilt Walt Dalt Dale Kale Kole Cole Colt Cort Cory
```

E. POSTTEST

Repeat the Pretest. Compare your Posttest results with your Pretest results.

FORMATTING

F. PERSONAL-BUSINESS LETTERS

A letter from an individual to a business is called a **personal-business letter**. A personal-business letter should contain these parts:

Date Line The month, day, and year the letter is keyed.
Inside Address The name and address of the person to whom the letter is being sent.
Salutation An opening greeting such as *Dear Ms. Jones.*
Body The text of the letter.
Complimentary Closing A closing to the letter such as *Sincerely* or *Yours truly.*
Signature The writer's signature.
Writer's Identification The writer's keyed name and address.

(continued on next page)

FORMATTING

D. Wrapping Text

Once a text or graphic box is inserted into a document, it can be positioned anywhere on the page. In order to keep the original text on the page readable, you may want to **wrap** the text. When you wrap text, you are moving the text around the box or above, below, or beside the box.

E. Software Features

STUDENT MANUAL

Wrapping Text

Study Lesson 108 in your Student Manual. Complete all the practice activities while at your computer. Then complete the tasks that follow.

DESKTOP PUBLISHING APPLICATIONS

REPORT 50

Flyer

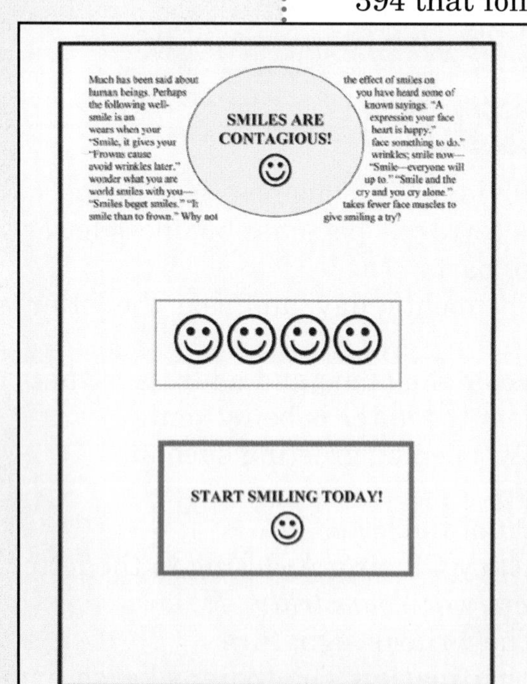

Open Report 46 and revise it as follows:

1. At the top of the report, key the paragraph on page 394 that follows these steps.
2. Wrap the text around the sides of the circle containing the words *SMILES ARE CONTAGIOUS.* Make any adjustments to lay out the text and circle attractively.
3. Add a 48-point smiley face centered below the text in the circle.
4. Delete the graphic in the text box.
5. Insert four 78-point smiley face symbols in the text box, horizontally center them, and adjust the size of the text box as necessary.
6. Add a 48-point smiley face centered below the text in the bottom text box.
7. Add a heavy black border to the page.

(continued on page 394)

[[Current Date]]

Ms. Louise Feigleson
Personnel Director
Smith and Kovacs Agency
7858 High Street
Columbus, OH 43216

Dear Ms. Feigleson:

I was told there were job opportunities in your agency this summer, and I would like to apply for a job in your accounting department.

I am completing my junior year as an accounting major at Ohio State University. I have completed basic, intermediate, and advanced accounting. I will be available for employment from May 15 through August 1. During the year, I have been employed as a part-time bookkeeper at the Buckeye Lodge in Westerville. Mr. John Forte, manager of the lodge, has indicated that he would send you a letter of recommendation. My academic advisor, Dr. Josephine Craig, will be happy to make a recommendation if you wish.

You may, at your convenience, call me at my dorm telephone number, 555-0677, after 3:30 p.m. Monday through Friday. If you would like for me to come in for an interview, please let me know.

Yours truly,

May Kent
234B Hayes Hall
Ohio State University
Columbus, OH 43210

2314 Oak Street
Scottsdale, AZ 85257
(Current Date)

Mrs. Joan L. Locke
2356 North Central Avenue
Phoenix, AZ 85004

Dear Mrs. Locke:

Thank you for helping our sponsor by assisting on our trip to Flagstaff last week. It was a pleasure to meet you and hear about the various trips you have made in southwestern United States. As you know, we just moved to Arizona. It's my intention to learn about and see more of my new state.

I was particularly interested in Flagstaff and its importance as a vacation area. The presentation by the Chamber of Commerce was very worthwhile. It surprised me to learn that skiing is one of Flagstaff's top winter tourist attractions. No one would think that skiers would come from such states as California, New Mexico, or Texas to ski in Arizona. I would have thought it was too warm in Arizona for such a winter sport.

My parents and I plan to go to the Grand Canyon this coming summer; I told them that Flagstaff was the gateway to the Canyon. They indicated to me that my grandparents had taken a train to Flagstaff and then, taken a bus to the Canyon. I hope I can do something similar.

Thanks again for helping us on our trip.

Sincerely yours,

Ms. Alice L. L'Huillier

(continued)

To format a personal-business letter in block style:

1. Use the default margins.
2. Press ENTER 6 times to leave a 2-inch top margin.
3. Key all lines beginning at the left margin.
4. Key the date.
5. After the date, press ENTER 4 times and key the inside address. Space once between the state and the ZIP code.
6. After the inside address, press ENTER 2 times and key the salutation.
7. Press ENTER 2 times and begin the body of the letter. Single-space the body, but press ENTER 2 times between paragraphs.
8. After the last paragraph, press ENTER 2 times and key the complimentary closing.
9. Press ENTER 4 times. Key the writer's name and address.

Alternate: Block Style Personal-Business Letter

Instead of keying the writer's address after the signature, it can be added before the date. To format a letter in this style:

1. Use the same margins as described above.
2. Key the writer's address beginning at the left margin; then key the date below it.
3. Follow the steps above to key the body of the letter and the complimentary closing.
4. Press ENTER 4 times and key the writer's name. Do not key the address again.

G. SOFTWARE FEATURES

STUDENT MANUAL

Date Insert   Center Page

Study Lesson 48 in your Student Manual. Complete all the practice activities while at your computer. Then complete the following tasks.

LESSON 108 BOXES: WRAPPING TEXT

OBJECTIVES:

- Improve keyboarding skills.
- Wrap text around boxes.

A. WARMUP

Key each line 2 times.

Speed	1	Show her what a nice day it is so that she may take a walk.
Accuracy	2	Expert jockeys quickly led a horse away from a blazing van.
Language Link	3	Diane drove all the way to Tucson, Arizona, on May 7, 2006.
Numbers/Symbols	4	Jon & Bev paid for 674# of #95 glue @ $2.50 at Quill & Ink.
		| 1 | 2 | 3 | 4 | 5 | 6 | 7 | 8 | 9 | 10 | 11 | 12

SKILLBUILDING

B. 12-SECOND SPRINTS

Take three 12-second timed writings on each line. Try to increase your speed each time.

Keep your eyes on the copy.

5 Irene was to make the cake for the office party this month.
6 He bought a new computer from the dealer at the mall today.
7 My courses were given in the rooms of the old school house.
8 When you go to the dance, be sure to take her some flowers.
||||5||||10||||15||||20||||25||||30||||35||||40||||45||||50||||55||||60

C. PACED PRACTICE

Turn to the Paced Practice routine beginning on page SB7. Take three 2-minute timed writings, starting at the point where you left off the last time.

LETTER 1

Block Style Personal-Business

Key the following personal-business letter in block style. Insert the current date. Use standard punctuation: a colon after the salutation and a comma after the complimentary closing.

(Current Date)

Mrs. Joan L. Locke
2356 North Central Avenue
Phoenix, AZ 85004

Dear Mrs. Locke:

Thank you for helping our sponsor by assisting on our trip to Flagstaff last week. It was a pleasure to meet you and hear about the various trips you have made in southwestern United States. As you know, we just moved to Arizona. It's my intention to learn about and see more of my new state.

I was particularly interested in Flagstaff and its importance as a vacation area. The presentation by the Chamber of Commerce was very worthwhile. It surprised me to learn that skiing is one of Flagstaff's top winter tourist attractions. No one would think that skiers would come from such states as California, New Mexico, or Texas to ski in Arizona. I would have thought it was too warm in Arizona for such a winter sport.

My parents and I plan to go to the Grand Canyon this coming summer; I told them that Flagstaff was the gateway to the Canyon. They indicated to me that my grandparents had taken a train to Flagstaff and then taken a bus to the Canyon. I hope I can do something similar.

Thanks again for helping us on our trip.

Sincerely yours,

Ms. Alice L. L'Huillier
2314 Oak Street
Scottsdale, AZ 85257

REPORT 48

Essay

Open Report 47 and modify it as follows:

1. Beginning with the first paragraph, change the line spacing to 1.5.
2. Add the page number at the bottom center.
3. Change the body of the report to full justification.
4. Create a text box at the beginning of the first paragraph.
5. Choose an animal graphic and insert it into the box.
6. Resize the graphic and the text box so that the graphic remains proportional.
7. Position the text box so that it does not cover any text.
8. Delete the text box border.

REPORT 49

Essay

Open Report 48 and make the following changes:

1. Create a text box at the top of the report.
2. Horizontally center the text box.
3. Inside the text box, center and key *ANIMAL BEHAVIOR* in Times New Roman 20-point bold.
4. Shade the text box with a 15-percent fill in a color that complements the graphic.
5. Add the same animal graphic that appears at the beginning of the page after the last line of text.
6. Position the graphic so that it does not cause text to shift, and delete the border.
7. Change the alignment so the body of the report is aligned left.

ANIMAL BEHAVIOR

Different animals behave in a variety of ways. An animal's behavior is dependent on a number of factors. One factor that affects its behavior is the environment. The environment consists not only of living things but also of physical characteristics such as temperature, types of soil, amount of rainfall, and amount of light.

Animal behavior is greatly affected by the temperature of the environment where the animal lives. Animals' body temperatures can vary greatly. Some animals are described as cold-blooded—such as snakes and frogs. *Cold-blooded* means that their body temperature changes as the temperature of their environment changes. Although the body temperature of cold-blooded animals is not always the same as the environment, it is usually close to it.

Warm-blooded animals—including tigers and humans—maintain the same body temperature nearly all the time. Warm-blooded animals usually maintain the temperature at which they function best. People, for example, maintain an average body temperature of 37 degrees Celsius.

Some warm-blooded animals hibernate during the winter. Groundhogs and woodchucks are examples of mammals that hibernate. Their body activities come to almost a complete halt. Bears are often thought, erroneously, to hibernate. However, they have been known to occasionally wake up and walk around.

1

LETTER 2

Key the following letter in block style, using the alternate format. The slash marks in the inside address and closing lines indicate line endings. Do not key the slashes.

The ¶ symbol indicates the start of a new paragraph. Do not indent a new paragraph. However, leave one blank line before beginning a new paragraph.

Alternate
Block Style
Personal-Business

To prepare this personal-business letter in alternate block style, key the writer's address before the date.

Do not key the address after the sender's name.

Refer to page 169, if needed.

347 Main Street / Topeka, KS 67209 / Current Date / Ms. Caroline Davis / 5200 Roselawn Avenue / Topeka, KS 67218 / Dear Ms. Davis: /

¶Your presentation at the Kentwood Business Club was one of the most enjoyable our club has ever had.

¶It is always a pleasure to have a professional like you speak on ways a graduate can seek a job. The follow-up question-and-answer period as well as your handouts were well received.

¶On the advice of our teacher, our accounting class has decided that one way we can follow up your presentation is to bring to class employment ads, and then write letters of application. Already the class has prepared twelve letters, which were sent to our teacher as the employer; thirteen more are all ready to be signed.

¶I believe this is one of the most interesting projects I have ever been assigned. Members of the class have learned to critique the letters without feeling self-conscious about their work.

¶Would you consider reviewing some of our letters and advise us which you think are the best? We hope you will say yes! I will call you next Monday to discuss the details. Sincerely yours, / Brian K. Long

LANGUAGE ARTS CONNECTION

Evaluate Personal-Business Letters Make a list of the various kinds of personal-business letters you may need to send in the future. Then compose and key a short paragraph explaining the differences between a personal letter and a personal-business letter. Next, describe why it is important to know how to correctly format a personal-business letter. Follow your teacher's instructions for saving and printing your work.

FORMATTING

E. Software Features

STUDENT MANUAL

Fill and Borders

Study Lesson 107 in your Student Manual. Complete all the practice activities while at your computer. Then complete the tasks that follow.

DESKTOP PUBLISHING APPLICATIONS

REPORT 47

Essay

Key the following report single-spaced. Press Enter 6 times to leave an approximately 2-inch margin at the top. Do not include a title. Indent paragraphs, but do not leave a blank line between paragraphs.

Science Connection

¶Different animals behave in a variety of ways. An animal's behavior is dependent on a number of factors. One factor that affects its behavior is the environment. The environment consists not only of living things but also of physical characteristics such as temperature, types of soil, amount of rainfall, and amount of light.

¶Animal behavior is greatly affected by the temperature of the environment where the animal lives. Animals' body temperatures can vary greatly. Some animals are described as cold-blooded—such as snakes and frogs. Cold-blooded means that their body temperature changes as the temperature of their environment changes. Although the body temperature of cold-blooded animals is not always the same as the environment, it is usually close to it.

¶Warm-blooded animals—including tigers and humans—maintain the same body temperature nearly all the time. Warm-blooded animals usually maintain the temperature at which they function best. People, for example, maintain an average body temperature of 37 degrees Celsius.

¶Some warm-blooded animals hibernate during the winter. Groundhogs and woodchucks are examples of mammals that hibernate. Their body activities come to almost a complete halt. Bears are often thought, erroneously, to hibernate. However, they have been known to occasionally wake up and walk around.

LESSON 49 Reinforcement

OBJECTIVES:

- Improve keyboarding skills.
- Reinforce formatting personal-business letters.

A. Warmup

Key each line 2 times.

Speed	1	If being good at keyboarding is vital, then practice daily.
Accuracy	2	Xavier is amazed by the two jazz artists' expert qualities.
Language Link	3	The number of students involved in intramural sports is up.
Numbers	4	We are scheduled for April 29, May 14, June 30, and July 7.

| 1 | 2 | 3 | 4 | 5 | 6 | 7 | 8 | 9 | 10 | 11 | 12

SKILLBUILDING

B. Technique Timed Writings

Take two 30-second timed writings on each line. Focus on the technique at the left.

Key without hesitation.

5 We would find life very different in a world without trees.
6 Trees provide us food, fuel, fibers, lumber, and chemicals.
7 Trees keep our soil from eroding and provide us windbreaks.
8 Even dead trees are useful by providing homes for wildlife.

| 1 | 2 | 3 | 4 | 5 | 6 | 7 | 8 | 9 | 10 | 11 | 12

SKILLBUILDING

C. Preview Practice

Key each line 2 times as a preview to the timed writings that follow.

Accuracy everything technology examine competitive foreigners abroad
Speed They We in the and our for are get has how job sell with

D. 5-Minute Timed Writings

Take two 5-minute timed writings on the paragraphs. Note your speed and errors.

Goal: 38/5'/5e

Almost everything we use today is made with the help 11
of machines. Technology has caused a great change in how we 23
produce our goods. People first invent and then run the 34
machines. They also come up with new ideas for all of the 46
quality items these machines can produce. 54

Human hands never examine some goods. In some cases, 65
all workers have to do is push a button. But, employees do 77
need to know which button to push so that they can get the 88
job done right. 92

The producers in our country realize they must sell 102
their goods abroad to stay competitive. It is said that we 114
are the world's biggest exporter. Our country offers a huge 126
market for producers in other countries as well. For that 138
reason, foreigners want to sell their goods here. There is 149
strong competition from foreign products. We are reported 161
also to have the most productive workers in the world. Our 173
product worth has improved because our workers are skilled, 185
diverse, and well-trained. 190

| 1 | 2 | 3 | 4 | 5 | 6 | 7 | 8 | 9 | 10 | 11 | 12 SI 1.36

C. Concentration Drills

Key each line 2 times. Concentrate on keeping your eyes on the copy.

```
9  A proficient secretary manipulates microcomputers expertly.
10 Authorized institutions substitute experimental techniques.
11 The Mississippi and Missouri Rivers provide transportation.
12 Agricultural goods surpass manufactured industrial gadgets.
```

D. Paced Practice

Turn to the Paced Practice routine beginning on page SB7. Take three 2-minute timed writings, starting at the point where you left off the last time.

WORD PROCESSING APPLICATIONS

LETTER 3

Block Style
Personal-Business

Key this letter in block style with standard punctuation. Insert the current date.

(Current Date) / Ms. Louise Feigleson / Personnel Director / Smith and Kovacs Agency / 7858 High Street / Columbus, OH 43216 / Dear Ms. Feigleson:
¶I was told there were job opportunities in your agency this summer, and I would like to apply for a job in your accounting department.
¶I am completing my junior year as an accounting major at Ohio State University. I have completed basic, intermediate, and advanced accounting. I will be available for employment from May 15 through August 1. During the year, I have been employed as a part-time bookkeeper at the Buckeye Lodge in Westerville. Mr. John Forte, manager of the lodge, has indicated that he would send you a letter of recommendation. My academic advisor, Dr. Josephine Craig, will be happy to make a recommendation if you wish.
¶You may, at your convenience, call me at my dorm telephone number, 555-0677, after 3:30 p.m. Monday through Friday. If you would like for me to come in for an interview, please let me know.
Yours truly, / May Kent / 234B Hayes Hall / Ohio State University / Columbus, OH 43210

LESSON 107 BOXES: FILL, BORDERS

OBJECTIVES:

- Key 38/5'/5e.
- Apply rules for commas.
- Add borders and fill.

A. WARMUP

Key each line 2 times.

Speed	1	I came to work for this firm and have been here since then.
Accuracy	2	Jacques picked five boxes of oranges while Diz stayed home.
Language Link	3	Dave asked, "Are you aware of the changes we have to make?"
Numbers	4	Please clean Rooms 4, 6, and 7 but not Rooms 9, 29, and 38.

| 1 | 2 | 3 | 4 | 5 | 6 | 7 | 8 | 9 | 10 | 11 | 12

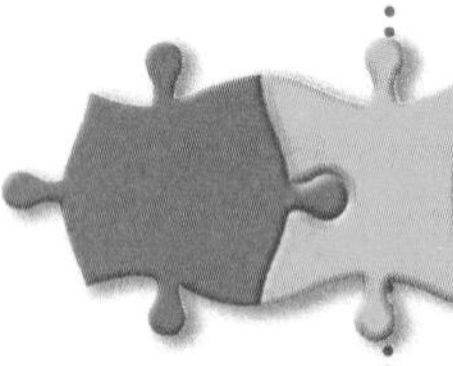

LANGUAGE LINK

B. COMMAS

Study the following rules and examples for comma usage. Then edit lines 5–8 to correct any errors.

Rule 26: Use a comma before and after the year in a complete date.

On December 7, 2005, the Tribune reviewed the Pearl Harbor events.

BUT: *The News Monthly printed December 2005 reviewed the same events.*

Rule 27: Use a comma before and after a state or country that follows a city, but not before a ZIP Code.

Sioux City, Iowa, is a lovely place in which to live.

BUT: *Sioux City, IA 51102, is where she plans to live.*

5 The warehouse buildings will be ready in September, 2007.
6 The lawyer told the clerk to use May 3, 2004 as the date.
7 The reports were sent to Nagoya, Japan on March 14, 2005.
8 The move to Toledo, Ohio, was scheduled for August, 2006.

LETTER 4

Block Style Personal-Business

Key this letter in block style with standard punctuation. Make the corrections indicated by the proofreaders' marks.

(Current Date)

Mr. Jacob Ries, Manager
Longhorn Department Store
1366 South State St.
Chicago, IL 60616

Dear Mr. Reis:

Thank you for sending me an application for the position of a part-time clerk in your store.

I am currently working part time as a clerk at the One-A Supermarket. My cooperative education teacher assisted me in obtaining this position and I have been on this job for 2 years.

As is requested on the form, I am asking that the letters of recomendation be sent to you. You will receive letters from my cooperative teacher, current employer, and scout leader within the next few days. The high school office administration will send you a transcript of my grades.

As I indicated in my letter of application, I will be completeing high school in June, and will enroll at Northern Illinois University in September. I am pleased with the position you are offering me, and I know the position will assist me in financing my college education.

I look forward to meeting you, my fellow employees, and our customers in July.

Sincerely yours,

Kyle Long
4578 Chicago Road
Evanston, IL 62242

D. Software Features

STUDENT MANUAL

Text Boxes
Sizing Boxes
Positioning Boxes
Graphic or Figure Boxes

Study Lesson 106 in your Student Manual. Complete all the practice activities while at your computer. Then complete the tasks that follow.

DESKTOP PUBLISHING APPLICATIONS

REPORT 45
Flyer

Create a flyer following these steps:

1. Create a circle at the top of the page and horizontally center it.
2. In the circle, center and key in Times New Roman 18-point bold, *SMILES ARE CONTAGIOUS!,* and size the circle to fit the text on 2 lines.
3. Approximately 1 inch below the circle, insert a text box that is 3 inches wide and 3 inches high.
4. In the text box, vertically and horizontally center and key in Times New Roman 18-point bold, *SPREAD SMILES IN YOUR NEIGHBORHOOD.*
5. Approximately 1 inch below the text box, insert another text box and center and key in Times New Roman 18-point bold, *START SMILING TODAY!*

REPORT 46
Flyer

Open Report 45 and revise it following these steps:

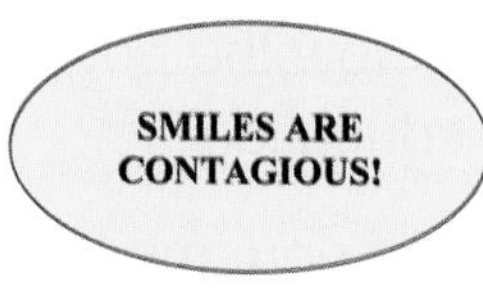

START SMILING TODAY!

1. Change the background of the circle to light yellow.
2. Replace the text in the first text box with an appropriate graphic.
3. Adjust the size of the graphic and/or the text box so that the graphic looks proportionally correct and fills the text box without increasing the size of the text box.
4. Change the border of the bottom text box to a thick green border.

LESSON 50 ENVELOPES

OBJECTIVES:

- Improve keyboarding skills.
- Apply word processing features.
- Format and key envelopes.

A. WARMUP

Key each line 2 times.

Speed	1	The true beauty of that diamond was brought out by its cut.
Accuracy	2	Aquilla told Bix the difference in a xylophone and marimba.
Language Link	3	A number of fields of cotton and milo haven't been planted.
Technique	4	Paul Quan Rand Stan Trev Ulan Vern Ward Xerxes Yohann Zared
		| 1 | 2 | 3 | 4 | 5 | 6 | 7 | 8 | 9 | 10 | 11 | 12

SKILLBUILDING

B. 30-SECOND OK TIMED WRITINGS

Take two 30-second OK (error-free) timed writings on lines 5–6. Then take two 30-second OK timed writings on lines 7–8. Goal: no errors.

5	The students decided today what they wanted to eat for	11
6	breakfast. Amazingly, just six bravely asked for ham quiche.	23
7	Both the dog and the fox were fat and lazy. They never	11
8	ran or jumped quickly. All they ever did was eat and sleep.	23
	| 1 | 2 | 3 | 4 | 5 | 6 | 7 | 8 | 9 | 10 | 11 | 12	

LESSON 106

BOXES: TEXT AND GRAPHIC BOXES

OBJECTIVES:

- Improve keyboarding accuracy.
- Insert text boxes and add text and graphics.

A. WARMUP

Key each line 2 times.

Speed	1	All my friends met Tom at the mall and went on to the play.
Accuracy	2	Judy gave a quick jump as the zebra and lynx fought wildly.
Language Link	3	Please summarize the article, "School Safety is Important."
Technique	4	Anne saw RCA, BBS, US, and MTV written on the PTO brochure.

| 1 | 2 | 3 | 4 | 5 | 6 | 7 | 8 | 9 | 10 | 11 | 12

SKILLBUILDING

B. 30-SECOND OK TIMED WRITINGS

Take two 30-second OK (error-free) timed writings on lines 5–6. Then take two 30-second OK timed writings on lines 7–8. Goal: no errors.

5	Roxie picked yellow jonquils as Delbert watched; then	12
6	he zipped off to the cavern to tell of the amazing event.	24
7	Holly received a prize for jumping over six feet, and	12
8	Mac quickly explained that some big jumps involved risks.	24

| 1 | 2 | 3 | 4 | 5 | 6 | 7 | 8 | 9 | 10 | 11 | 12

FORMATTING

C. INSERTING BOXES

Text boxes are boxes that hold text or **graphics**, images such as clip art, photographs, or charts. Text boxes make it easy to format, move, resize, or highlight text or graphics without affecting the rest of the document. You can also add borders or fill to a text box.

C. PRETEST

Take a 1-minute timed writing on lines 9–12. Note your speed and errors.

9 Andrew Jackson, seventh President of our country, was 11
10 known as Old Hickory by his friends and King Andrew by his 23
11 foes. Born in Waxhaw, South Carolina, Jackson was left an 34
12 orphan in his teens and grew up poor. 41

| 1 | 2 | 3 | 4 | 5 | 6 | 7 | 8 | 9 | 10 | 11 | 12

D. PRACTICE

In the chart below, find the number of errors you made on the Pretest. Then key each of the following designated drill lines 2 times.

Pretest Errors	0–1	2	3	4+
Drill Lines	16–20	15–19	14–18	13–17

Accuracy

13 Old grew votes orphan fought common Andrew Jackson Carolina
14 King East Adams seventh federal citizens settlers self-made
15 known liked South workers instead Hickory country President
16 West fired plain teens bitter Waxhaw Quincy friends farmers

Speed

17 hired made race from dent poor drew king left our the in he
18 seven plain work jobs beat grew east foes was who try an of
19 liked farms self born when fire west mean and son for by up
20 south know those teen came held like vote most his old as a

E. POSTTEST

Repeat the Pretest. Compare your Posttest results with your Pretest results.

PORTFOLIO Activity

Revise a Letter Decide which of the letters that you created in this unit is your best one. Key the letter again, but this time use your name and address in place of the writer's name and address.

Correct any errors that you find. Then have a classmate examine the new letter for errors and use proofreader marks to correct any errors that he or she finds. Revise the letter. Follow your teacher's instructions for saving and printing your work.

STUDENT MANUAL

Inserting/Drawing Shapes
Sizing, Moving, and Deleting Objects

Study Lesson 105 in your Student Manual. Complete all the practice activities while at your computer. Then complete the tasks that follow.

DESKTOP PUBLISHING APPLICATIONS

REPORT 43

Picture

Follow these directions to create a snowman similar to the illustration at the left.

1. Draw an oval approximately 3 inches wide and 2.5 inches high.
2. Drag the oval to the lower half of the page.
3. Create a circle and size it so that it is approximately 2 inches in diameter.
4. Place this circle on the top of the oval (slightly overlapping it) and center it.
5. Create another circle and size it so that it is approximately 1 inch in diameter.
6. Place this circle on top of the second circle in the approximate horizontal center.
7. Add the face, arms, and other features using drawing tools.

REPORT 44

Essay

Open Report 35 and make the following changes:

1. Insert a right arrow beside the title. Size the arrow so that it is approximately the height of the title and does not overlay the text.
2. Add red fill to the arrow.
3. Insert a rounded rectangle at the end of the document approximately 4 inches wide and 0.25 inch high.
4. Change the rectangle's border to red.

F. Envelopes

There are two commonly used envelope sizes: a No. 10 (large envelope) and a No. 6: (small envelope). The No. 10, which is the standard size for business letters, is 9 ½ by 4 ⅛ inches. A correctly addressed No. 10 envelope should be keyed as follows:

1. **Return Address.** The writer's name and address keyed or printed in the upper left corner of the envelope (see the illustration that follows).
2. **Mailing Address.** The recipient's name and address beginning at least 2 inches from the top edge and 4 inches from the left edge of the envelope. The mailing address may be keyed either in initial caps with punctuation (see the small envelope), or in all caps with no punctuation (see the large envelope).

HiTech Construction Associates
4200 Cedar Avenue, Minneapolis, MN 55404-1839

MS JOAN R HUNTER
BOLWATER ASSOCIATES
ONE PARKLANDS DRIVE
DARIEN CT 06820-3214

Roger J. Michaelson
901 East Benson, Apt. 3
Ft. Lauderdale, FL 33301

Mr. Joseph G. Jenshak
17032 Stewart Avenue
Augusta, GA 30904

SKILLBUILDING

C. PRETEST

Take a 1-minute timed writing on the paragraph. Note your speed and errors.

```
 9      Regardless of the type of job you have or the work you   12
10 do, it is most important that you manage your time so that    24
11 you can get more work accomplished. It is not possible for    36
12 us to reuse time; therefore, we should organize our days.     47
   | 1 | 2 | 3 | 4 | 5 | 6 | 7 | 8 | 9 | 10 | 11 | 12
```

D. PRACTICE

In the chart below find the number of errors you made on the Pretest. Then key each of the designated drill lines 2 times.

Pretest Errors	0–1	2	3	4+
Drill Lines	16–20	15–19	14–18	13–17

Accuracy

```
13 possible organize important beginning accomplish regardless
14 remember employed recognize improving particular prioritize
15 activity powerful therefore essential difficult suggestions
16 quite borrows maximum example another critical accomplished
```

Speed

```
17 manage should reuse can't type have work that the you of or
18 stolen others never first your time more from can not do it
19 moment saving write items once gone back good for may so us
20 placed employ those above down jobs wish this top use to we
```

E. POSTTEST

Repeat the Pretest. Compare your Posttest results with your Pretest results.

FORMATTING

F. CIRCLES, ELLIPSES (OVALS), AND OTHER SHAPES

By using a variety of shapes such as circles, rectangles, and ellipses (ovals), you can make page layouts more interesting. Once these shapes are inserted into a document, they can be repositioned and resized.

G. Folding Letters

To fold a letter for a large (No. 10) envelope:

1. Place the letter face up and fold up the bottom third.
2. Fold the top third down to approximately 0.5 inch from the bottom edge.
3. Insert the last crease into the envelope first with the flap facing up.

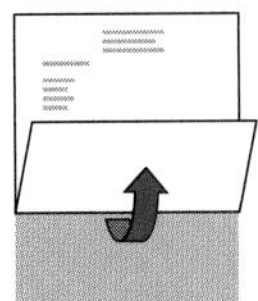

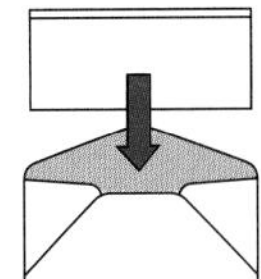

To fold a letter for a small (No. 6) envelope:

1. Place the letter face up and fold up the bottom half to 0.5 inch from the top.
2. Fold the right third over to the left.
3. Fold the left third over to 0.5 inch from the right edge.
4. Insert the last crease into the envelope first with the flap facing up.

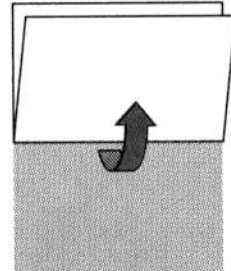
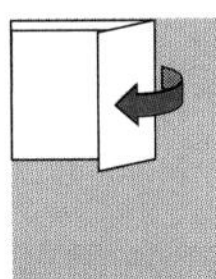
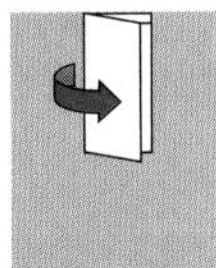
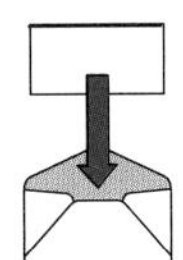

H. Software Features

STUDENT MANUAL

Envelopes

Study Lesson 50 in your Student Manual. Complete all the practice activities while at your computer. Then complete the tasks that follow.

WORD PROCESSING APPLICATIONS

ENVELOPE 1

Open the file for Letter 2, and prepare a No. 10 envelope. Use the correct return address and add the envelope to the letter.

ENVELOPE 2

Open the file for Letter 3, and prepare a No. 10 envelope. Use the correct return address and add the envelope to the letter.

LESSON 105 DRAWING

OBJECTIVES:

- Apply quotation marks and italics.
- Insert and manipulate shapes in a document.

A. WARMUP

Key each line 2 times.

Speed	1	Norma may go for a walk on this nice day to visit that boy.
Accuracy	2	A dozen big witches quickly jumped over six long red sofas.
Language Link	3	"I think," said Phil, "the football is over in Sam's yard."
Numbers/Symbols	4	They bought #2 lead pencils @ $.24 each at Penzey's Papers.

| 1 | 2 | 3 | 4 | 5 | 6 | 7 | 8 | 9 | 10 | 11 | 12

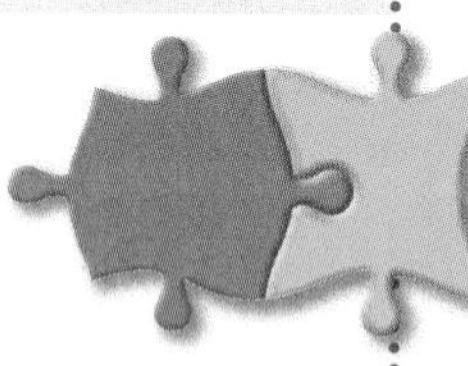

LANGUAGE LINK

B. QUOTATION MARKS AND ITALICS

Study the following rules and examples. Then edit lines 5–8 to correct any errors in the use of quotation marks and italics.

Rule 24: Use quotation marks around the titles of newspaper or magazine articles, chapters in a book, and reports.

The next assignment is to read the chapter entitled "The Kennedy Years."

Kurt read and reread the article "An Interview With Tom Brady."

Rule 25: Italicize (or underline) the titles of books, magazines, newspapers, and other complete published works.

The Fifties by David Halberstam gives an excellent portrait of the decade.

The article in Sports Illustrated covered the new basketball rules changes.

5 The interest rates were discussed in the November 24 Tribune.
6 Types of Life Insurance is an excellent chapter in your text.
7 Her proposed title for the report was Vacations Versus Trips.
8 The December 2 issue of "Newsweek" had most excellent coverage.

ENVELOPE 3

Open the file for Letter 4, and prepare a No. 10 envelope. Use the correct return address and add the envelope to the letter.

LETTER 5

Block Style
Personal-Business
With Envelope

ENVELOPE 4

Key the following letter in block style, and prepare a large envelope for the letter.

(Current Date) / Ms. Kaye Lincoln / Waldo Travel Bureau / 8900 Longwood Avenue / Suite 1304 / Boston, MA 02115 / Dear Ms. Lincoln:
¶I am interested in a trip to England, Holland, France, and Germany this coming summer. Do you have special packaged tours for students?
¶My financial resources are limited. I am looking for a trip that would take less than a month and cost less than $2,000. Currently, I am working as a waiter in a local restaurant; and I hope to save additional money for the trip.
¶What is the round trip airfare from Boston to London? Can I use trains from London to Amsterdam, Paris, and Frankfurt? Can you recommend a hostel in each city and give me some idea of the daily costs? I would appreciate your sending me brochures on airlines, railroads, and hostels you recommend. I plan to apply for my passport, and I am aware that it takes more than a week for processing.
¶If you have further questions concerning my proposed trip, please let me know. You may call me at 781-555-2535. I can get released time from work to see you, and I can see you at your convenience.
Sincerely yours, / William Stoneman / 678 Main Street / Milton, MA 02186

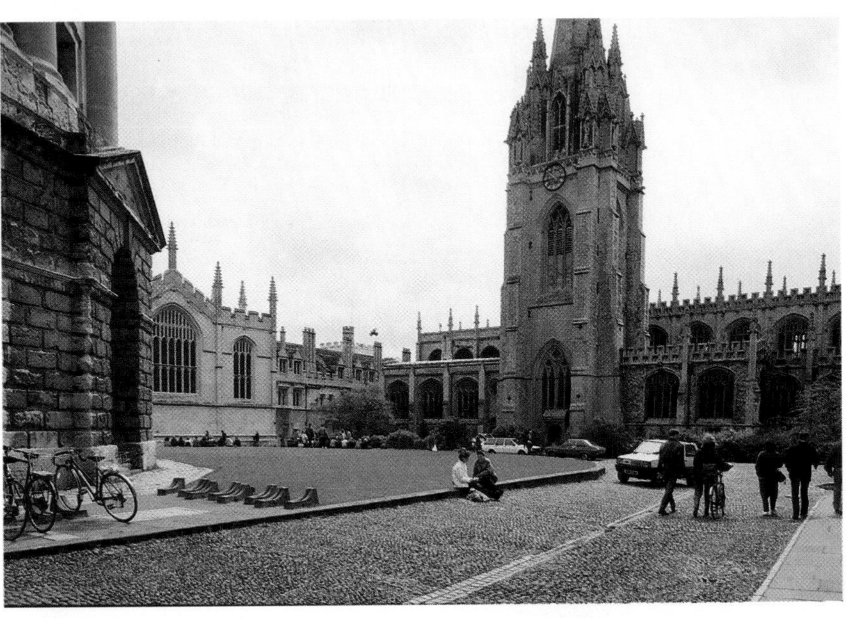

REPORT 42

Flyer

Open Report 40 and make the following changes.

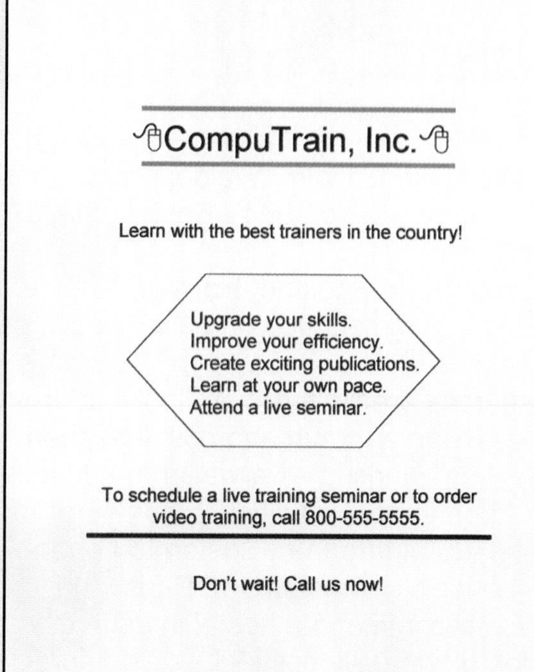

CompuTrain, Inc.

Learn with the best trainers in the country!

Upgrade your skills.
Improve your efficiency.
Create exciting publications.
Learn at your own pace.
Attend a live seminar.

To schedule a live training seminar or to order video training, call 800-555-5555.

Don't wait! Call us now!

1. Change the listed items so that they left-align approximately 1.5 inches from the margin.
2. Adjust the geometric shape so that it still wraps around the list.
3. Delete the line at the bottom of the page.
4. Add a thick horizontal line from margin to margin below the section containing the telephone number.
5. Change the color of the rules above and below the title to red.
6. Change the border of the geometric shape to red.

*inter*NET CONNECTION

Compare Desktop Publishing Software If you create a lot of specialized documents, like flyers and newsletters, you should use software that is created specifically for desktop publishing, such as Microsoft Publisher. To find out about different desktop publishing products, go to the Online Learning Center at **KeyComps.glencoe.com>Internet Connection>Unit 6>Lesson 104**. Complete the activity.

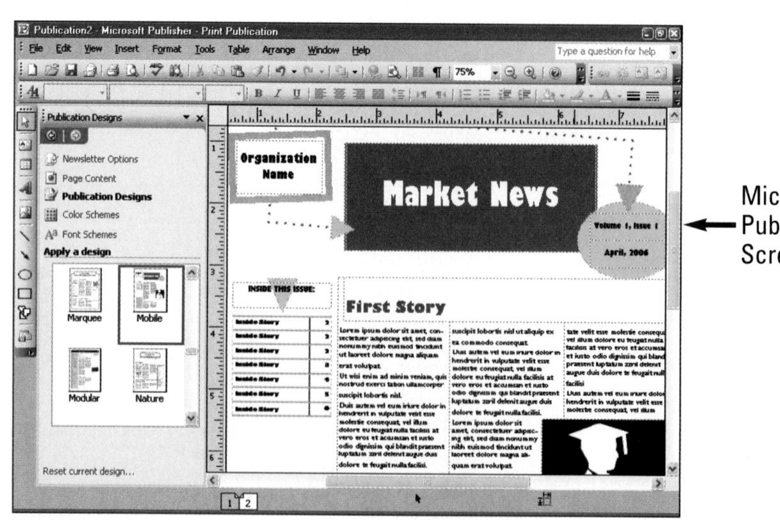

Microsoft Publisher Screen

LESSON 51 BUSINESS LETTERS

OBJECTIVES:

- Compose a paragraph at the keyboard.
- Key 33/3′/5e.
- Format and key business letters.

A. WARMUP

Key each line 2 times.

Speed	1	We will be happy to see the sun after so many days of rain.
Accuracy	2	Janita and six friends quickly zipped by the two villagers.
Language Link	3	The number of farmers helping their sick neighbor was huge.
Numbers/Symbols	4	Our 9 cakes, 45 pies, 60 doughnuts, and 72 cookies arrived.

| 1 | 2 | 3 | 4 | 5 | 6 | 7 | 8 | 9 | 10 | 11 | 12

B. COMPOSING AT THE KEYBOARD

Answer one of the following questions with a short paragraph.

5 Why is it important to have friends?
6 Why are hurricanes dangerous?
7 What historical person would you most like to meet? Why?
8 Do you prefer team or individual sports? Why?
9 Why is music important to you?

FORMATTING

C. Graphic Lines/Rules

Vertical and/or horizontal lines, or rules, can be used to enhance the appearance of a printed page or to separate text to make it more readable. There are many line styles from which to choose. Lines may be light, heavy, solid, broken, double, and so on. In addition, lines can be positioned in different ways to make your document visually appealing.

D. Software Features

STUDENT MANUAL

Lines	Line Position
Line Size	Line Style

Study Lesson 104 in your Student Manual. Complete all the practice activities while at your computer. Then complete the tasks that follow.

DESKTOP PUBLISHING APPLICATIONS

REPORT 40

Flyer

Open and revise Report 33 as follows:

1. Add a heavy line that is the length of the heading, above and below the heading.
2. Add a heavy line the length of the longest text line approximately 0.5 inch below the last line of text.
3. Delete the Wingdings® diamonds and extra spaces from both sides of each item in the list.
4. Draw a geometric shape around the items in the list.

REPORT 41

Flyer

Open Report 38. Give it a new look by following these steps:

1. Delete the border around the title.
2. Delete the page border.
3. Change the page layout so that the title starts approximately 2 inches from the top of the page.
4. Change the title to Times New Roman 20-point blue.
5. Add a thick horizontal blue line beneath the title.
6. Change the bullets to 20-point red.
7. Add a 5-inch horizontal double blue line 0.5 inch below the last line of text.

SKILLBUILDING

C. 12-Second Sprints

Take three 12-second timed writings on each line. Try to increase your speed each time.

```
Ray looks nice in his new jacket, but he does not think so.
He finds it hard to accept nice words being said about him.
He should smile and thank the one who said the nice things.
Do you find you are ill at ease when a nice remark is made?
||||5||||10||||15||||20||||25||||30||||35||||40||||45||||50||||55||||60
```

D. Preview Practice

Key each line 2 times as a preview to the timed writings that follow.

```
opportunity experience qualify amazed problem training work
this look work have will give seem high earn they some stay
```

E. 3-Minute Timed Writings

Take two 3-minute timed writings on the paragraphs. Note your speed and errors.

Goal: 33/3′/5e

```
     Picture this. You go to look for work, but you do not   11
qualify for the job since you have no work experience. You   23
cannot get work experience, and no one will give you the     34
opportunity. You may seem a bit amazed by the problem, but   46
students who enroll in a co-op work class have solved it.    58
While still in high school, they earn as they learn. Some    69
stay on the job full time. Some go on to college or other    81
training. In any case, they have work experience to put on   93
their resumes after high school.                             99
                                                      SI 1.29
| 1 | 2 | 3 | 4 | 5 | 6 | 7 | 8 | 9 | 10 | 11 | 12
```

LESSON 104 GRAPHIC LINES/RULES

OBJECTIVES:

- Refine keyboarding skills.
- Use the Drawing toolbar.
- Select, size, and position lines.
- Apply line styles.

A. WARMUP

Key each line 2 times.

Speed	1	Clair may wish to blame me for both of these big work jams.
Accuracy	2	By quietly giving back six tops, we amazed the four judges.
Language Link	3	The French student will visit the Grand Canyon in February.
Numbers/Symbols	4	Rick sold 64 tickets on 10/23/05, and then he sold 75 more.

| 1 | 2 | 3 | 4 | 5 | 6 | 7 | 8 | 9 | 10 | 11 | 12

SKILLBUILDING

B. 30-SECOND TIMED WRITINGS

Take two 30-second timed writings on lines 5–6. Then take two 30-second timed writings on lines 7–8. Try to increase your speed each time.

5 I think that we might cut down our staff loss if you *11*
6 will make a pay scale that shows all are being paid fairly. *23*

7 We have not been able to cut costs. We do not know how *11*
8 a boss set up the pay scale to show we are all paid fairly. *23*

| 1 | 2 | 3 | 4 | 5 | 6 | 7 | 8 | 9 | 10 | 11 | 12

FORMATTING

F. Business Letters

The Home Construction Associates
3218 Swiftwater Boulevard, Baltimore, OH 43105
Phone 740- TO B HOME Fax 740-862-4663
HomeConstructionAssoc@greenapple.com

September 6, {year}

Mr. Dennis Maryott
Maryott Associates
One Parklands Drive
Darien, CT 06820-3214

Dear Mr. Maryott:

I am returning a signed contract to begin the remodeling job on your offices beginning the first of next month. I understand that this work must be done with a minimum amount of disruption to your staff.

To ensure the quality of workmanship and materials, we have made several changes to the contract. These are the changes that we discussed over the phone, so they should be familiar to you. They are summarized below.

We revised Section 4.2 to state that only premium grade materials will be used for all new construction related to remodeling. We also added Section 10.2 to change the length of time to complete this job to four months rather than five. We feel this will provide us with ample time to complete the work to your satisfaction.

If these revisions are satisfactory, please sign and return one copy of the contract for our files. We look forward to this opportunity to work with you.

Sincerely,

Laurice Mitchell
Senior Consultant

jea

A **business letter** is a letter that represents a company, not an individual. Business letters are usually printed on company stationery called **letterhead**. The letterhead usually includes the company's name, address, and telephone number. The differences between a business letter and a personal-business letter are these:

1. The writer's company name and address appear in the letterhead; therefore, they are not keyed in the closing lines.
2. The writer's business title is keyed below the name. A short title may be placed on the same line as the name, separated by a comma. The name and title are called the writer's identification.
3. The initials of the person keying the letter (called **reference initials**) are keyed a double space below the writer's identification.

WORD PROCESSING APPLICATIONS

Key the following letter in block style. Use your own initials for the reference initials. Address a No. 10 envelope. Do not include a return address. Add the envelope to the letter.

LETTER 6

Block-Style Business with Envelope

ENVELOPE 5

November 23, {year} / Mr. Keith MacPhee / Indiana State Insurance Company / 2500 Wabash Avenue / Terre Haute, IN 47803 / Dear Mr. MacPhee:
¶I would like to invite you to speak at our business club meeting on December 14.

(continued on next page)

(continued)

¶When you arrive for an interview, be sure to introduce yourself to the receptionist or assistant. Be pleasant and courteous. You can be assured that the manager will receive feedback on your manners and appearance from this person.

¶Once you are in the interviewer's office, wait until you are invited to sit. This shows that you have respect for the interviewer's position. If someone comes into the office during the interview, stand up and be prepared to shake hands with this person—it might be the interviewer's boss.

REPORT 37

Essay

Open Report 36 and make the following changes:

1. At the top of the page, insert the title *GOOD MANNERS FOR JOB INTERVIEWS* centered, in all caps, and bold. Leave space between the title and first paragraph.
2. Add a thin border around the title.
3. Add a drop shadow to the title border.
4. Add a 10 percent fill inside the border.
5. Add a thick border to the entire page.
6. Change the paragraphs to a bulleted list.

REPORT 38

Essay

Open Report 37 and revise it following these steps:

1. Change the border around the title to a double line.
2. Change the page border to a heavy double line.
3. Delete the fill inside the title border.
4. Change the justification of the paragraphs to full justification.
5. Vertically center the page.

REPORT 39

Flyer

Open Report 33 and make these changes:

1. Add a heavy border around the heading.
2. Add a heavy, double-line border around the page.
3. Add a broken-line border to the last line.
4. Add a 5 percent fill/shading to the last line.

(continued)

¶The Terre Haute High School Business Club is over 20 years old and has been recognized by the State Department of Education as one of the most active in the state. At the national level, our club is a member of both the Future Business Leaders of America and Business Professionals of America associations.
¶The membership is composed of more than 65 students who have chosen to pursue a career in business. Most of the students have taken many courses in the business department; however, some members have taken just a few business courses.
¶Many students have had courses in accounting, keyboarding, word processing, and office technology. Since many of the students could eventually work in the insurance industry, they have asked for a speaker from that field. We would like you to speak on "Careers in the Insurance Industry."
¶We hope that you can be with us in the high school cafeteria on December 14 at 4:30 p.m. We look forward to your acceptance of this invitation. You may call me at 555-7450 any school day after 3:30 p.m.
Sincerely yours, / Alex Kielbaso / Secretary / urs

Key the following letter in block style. Use your initials for the reference initials. Use the current date.

LETTER 7

Block-Style Business

(Current Date) / Ms. Elyse Demers / 2101 Market Street / York, PA 17404 / Dear Ms. Demers:
¶You have been scheduled for surgery next month by the Orthopedic Unit of St. Ann's Hospital. Within the next few days, you will receive a form that authorizes your physician to provide us with information on your medical history. This information is vital to us. It will help us to eliminate repeat tests and take into consideration any additional health problems you may have.
¶Please provide the name of your physician and your date of birth on the form. Then, sign and date the form and give it to your physician so that your medical history will be forwarded to us before your surgery.
¶If you have more than one physician from whom we need records or if you have any questions or concerns, please call us at 717-555-9000 and request additional forms.
Sincerely, / Marsha Cunningham / Administrator / urs

FORMATTING

F. Borders, Drop Shadow, Fill

In addition to different fonts and colors, there are other special formatting techniques that will make documents more eye-catching. For example, you can use **borders** (frames), around text or pages; **drop shadows** (shading), to make text look three-dimensional; or **fill** (shading), options to call attention to text.

G. Software Features

STUDENT MANUAL

Borders Fill

Study Lesson 103 in your Student Manual. Complete all the practice activities while at your computer. Then complete the tasks that follow.

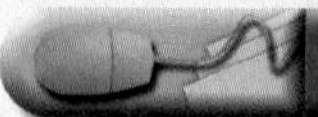

DESKTOP PUBLISHING APPLICATIONS

REPORT 36

Essay

Key the following report single-spaced. Use the default top margin. Leave a blank line between paragraphs and indent.

¶It is important to display good manners at all times. Manners are especially important during a job interview. Good manners show that you are sociable and civilized and may be a potentially good member of the company's team.

¶Arriving for an interview on time is one way to demonstrate your good manners. This indicates that you are reliable and will be on time for work. Being late for an interview could harm your chances of being hired.

¶Go to your interview alone. Even if someone must drive you to the interview, do not have him or her accompany you to the inter-view site. If possible, leave your hat and coat in the outer office. Carrying or wearing them into the interviewer's office may be awkward, and it may give the interviewer the impression that you are anxious to leave!

(continued on next page)

LESSON 52

Business Letters

OBJECTIVES:

- Apply word processing features.
- Format business letters.

A. Warmup

Key each line 2 times.

Speed	1	It will help to put away worry and doubt about your skills.
Accuracy	2	The dozen extra blue jugs were quickly moved from the pool.
Language Link	3	The number of items to remember to pick up is overwhelming.
Numbers/Symbols	4	(it is) [to the] {of a} 5 < 9 (in at) [by it] {be on} 7 > 1

| 1 | 2 | 3 | 4 | 5 | 6 | 7 | 8 | 9 | 10 | 11 | 12

SKILLBUILDING

B. Diagnostic Practice: Alphabet

Turn to the Diagnostic Practice: Alphabet routine on page SB1. Key one of the Pretest/Posttest paragraphs and identify any errors made. Then key the corresponding drill lines 2 times for each letter on which you made 2 or more errors and 1 time for each letter on which you made only 1 error. Finally, repeat the Pretest and compare your performance.

C. Paced Practice

Turn to the Paced Practice routine beginning on page SB7. Take three 2-minute timed writings starting at the point where you left off the last time.

LANGUAGE ARTS CONNECTION

Evaluate Types of Letters For each of the following types of letters, key one sentence describing a situation in which you might want to send:

- a personal letter
- a personal-business letter
- a formal business letter

Follow your teacher's instructions for saving and printing your work.

SKILLBUILDING

C. PRETEST

Take a 1-minute timed writing on the paragraph. Note your speed and errors

```
15      You should join those who have learned how to utilize    11
16 their keyboarding skill on the job. This skill can be used    23
17 in many walks of life, and it is just what you need to help   35
18 you succeed. Most jobs now require computer keyboarding.      46
   | 1 | 2 | 3 | 4 | 5 | 6 | 7 | 8 | 9 | 10 | 11 | 12
```

D. PRACTICE

SPEED: If you made 2 or fewer errors on the Pretest, key lines 19–26 two times each.

ACCURACY: If you made more than 2 errors on the Pretest, key lines 19–22 as a group two times. Then key lines 23–26 as a group two times.

Left-Hand Reaches

```
19 ded den dear deaf dread greed horde stead adept defer dried
20 wew wet week weed weave swear where worse weigh wheat wheel
21 cdc cod clad cord cedar crowd cloud cadet child crude cider
22 rtr art wart cart track train start trail tramp parts troop
```

Right-Hand Reaches

```
23 uyu your duly yule duty lucky young youth dusty yucca murky
24 jhj just huge join harm joist hunch jumpy house judge heart
25 klk milk folk walk silk silky balky milky links polka stalk
26 opo pop poor stop snoop whoop spoon ponds pound polka scope
```

E. POSTTEST

Repeat the Pretest. Compare your Posttest results with your Pretest results.

COMMUNICATION FOCUS

Evaluate Design When you look at a newspaper, magazine, or book, you expect to find the same design applied throughout. The page layout, the fonts, and the colors are usually the same from page to page, so that the reader knows what to expect and where to find things.

Look through this textbook. Compare fonts and graphics in the different headings, the timed writings, and the boxed features. Then key a paragraph describing your observations and why you think this textbook's design is or is not effective.

FORMATTING

D. Software Features

STUDENT MANUAL

Find and Replace

Study Lesson 52 in your Student Manual. Complete all the practice activities while at your computer. Then complete the tasks that follow.

WORD PROCESSING APPLICATIONS

LETTER 8

Business Letter in Block Style

Key the following letter in block style. Use your own initials for the reference initials. Address a No. 10 envelope. Do not include a return address, and add the envelope to the letter.

(Current Date) / Mrs. Alma Louise Yeu / President / Yeu & Yeu Associates / 4500 Elk Grove Avenue / Arlington Heights, IL 60004 / Dear Mrs. Yeu:

¶It is a pleasure to accept the task of chairperson for the United Fund campaign this fall.

¶As you are aware, I have been on the local United Fund board for the past eight years. I have had a great eight years; I look forward to at least four more years with the fund. Will I, as the new chairperson, have the responsibility of selecting the campaign committee? Jason Lewis, last year's chairperson, told me that it would be best if I could. He selected a committee composed of representatives from the business, industrial, educational, and lay communities. Last year's drive was the best yet; I think the results were due in large part to the committee.

¶Jason Lewis, Marsha Hunt, and Alex Garcia were on the committee last year; they were outstanding members. I plan to retain them if they are willing to serve again.

¶If you have questions about the proposed committee, please call me.

Sincerely yours, / Louise K. Fletcher / Production Engineer / urs

LESSON 103 Borders and Fill

OBJECTIVES:

- Compose at the keyboard.
- Improve keyboarding skills.
- Apply borders, drop shadows, and fill.

A. Warmup

Key each line 2 times.

Speed	The six forms she got from the firm may do for the problem.
Accuracy	The judge quickly gave six of the prizes to the able woman.
Language Link	"Do not ask personal things," warned the personnel manager.
Technique	I need TWO or THREE or FOUR, but ONE or FIVE are good also.

| 1 | 2 | 3 | 4 | 5 | 6 | 7 | 8 | 9 | 10 | 11 | 12

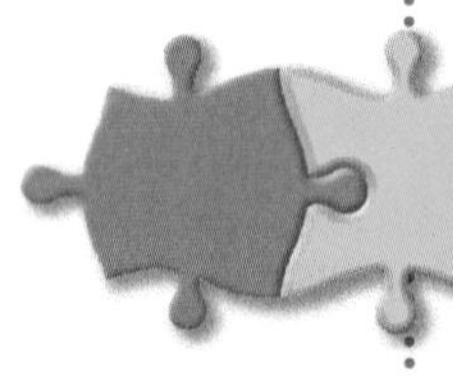

Language Link

B. Composing at the Keyboard

To make your writing easier to read and understand, use concise wording. Replace lengthy phrases such as *due to the fact that* with *because.*

Revise the following paragraph to eliminate the redundant wording.

Last week I completed my term paper in a satisfactory manner. The paper was six pages in length and was written for the purpose of describing what happened during the Civil War. For the simple reason that I had done my research for the purpose of completing this report, I know that my grade will meet with my approval. It would appear that my instructor plans to extend to me an invitation to read the report to the class. Due to the fact that I am not a good speaker, I am experiencing nervousness about doing this.

LETTER 9

Business Letter in Block Style

Key the following letter in block style. Use your own initials for the reference initials. Address a No. 10 envelope. Do not include a return address, and add the envelope to the letter.

(Current Date) / Mrs. Lottie Alexander / Personnel Director / Minneapolis Manufacturing Co. / 1700 University Avenue / Minneapolis, MN 55104-3020 / Dear Mrs. Alexander:
¶It is a pleasure to write a recommendation for John Saum for the position of word processor specialist with your company. John was in my accounting, computer, and multimedia classes; he was an outstanding student. He has an excellent background in grammar and spelling. He consistently received high grades in his production work on the computer.
¶Our advisory committee recommended him as the top student in the cooperative education program his senior year. John worked for the Miller Manufacturing Company as a word processor trainee in the mornings and attended afternoon classes. His supervisor consistently gave him exceptional ratings.
¶I am sure that John has asked the school to send you a copy of his transcript; it is outstanding. He indicates that he would like to attend a university once he has a job. I know that John Saum will be an excellent employee.
Sincerely yours, / Jose Sauceda / Business Instructor / urs

LETTER 10

Business Letter in Block Style

Open Letter 8 and make these revisions: Use find and replace to change Yeu to Yeun and Jason Lewis to Leonard Whilhite.

LETTER 11

Business Letter in Block Style

Open Letter 9 and make the following changes:

1. *Use find and replace to change John Saum to Maria Suma.*
2. *Use find and replace to change all the masculine pronouns to feminine pronouns (***he, his, him*** to ***she, her***).*
3. *Be sure to change all instances of John's given name with Maria's name.*

(continued)

¶The next step is to prepare a draft of your resume. Start with your name, address, and telephone number. You may want to include an objective such as "Obtain a position that utilizes my skills and provides an opportunity for growth." Next, include your educational background. Include school names, dates, special courses, and your grade point average.
¶Next, list your work experience, if any. This list should be arranged in chronological order, with the most recent experience first. Include the name and address of your employer, your supervisor's name, and a brief description of your duties. If you have no work experience, you may want to describe activities in which you participated that have provided you with valuable skills.
¶Finally, develop a list of references. Before doing so, ask people for permission to use their names. References should consist of teachers, employers, supervisors, or other people who can vouch for your work ethics and other important traits.
¶Once you determine what should be on your resume, key the final copy. Be sure to proofread carefully. Your resume will often make the first impression an employer will have of you, and you want it to be perfect. Then, print your resume on high-quality paper that matches the paper you will use for your cover letter and the envelope.
¶While sending a perfect resume will maximize your chances of securing a job, it does not guarantee that everyone to whom you send your resume will interview you.

LANGUAGE ARTS CONNECTION

Outline Your Resume Even before you need a resume, you can start preparing the information you will use to create one. This information should be updated every few months so that contact information is correct and details are fresh in your mind.

Create an informal outline that lists your experience, skills, and references. (See Lesson 43 in the Student Manual to review outlining.) Use the following as your main headings and supporting details.

Education: List any diplomas, honors, or special courses you have taken that are relevant to your employment. Include the dates.

Experience: List companies you have worked for, the dates of employment, descriptions of the company, job duties, and skills you used.

References: Include the contact's name, title, contact information (phone, e-mail, and address), and a brief description of the information they might provide employers.

Follow your teacher's instructions for saving and printing your work.

REVIEW

OBJECTIVES:

- Use commas in a series and with transitional expressions.
- Format personal-business letters, envelopes and business letters.

A. WARMUP

Key each line 2 times.

Speed	1 Emi would like to buy the dress if it comes in green denim.
Accuracy	2 Karl may sign up with five or six dozen clubs for jonquils.
Language Link	3 When our order arrived, a number of lightbulbs were broken.
Symbols	4 My brother-in-law gave Trev that you-know-what-I-mean look.
	| 1 | 2 | 3 | 4 | 5 | 6 | 7 | 8 | 9 | 10 | 11 | 12

LANGUAGE LINK

B. COMMAS

Study the rules and examples below. Then edit lines 5–8 to correct any errors in comma usage.

Rule 6: Use a comma between each item in a series of three or more.

I walked the beach, read novels, and ate well while on vacation.

Rule 7: Use a comma before and after a transitional expression (such as *therefore* or *however*).

Our account, therefore, is current.

5 The ball bat and glove were in the garage beside the car.
6 Meg told about big cities tall buildings and busy people.
7 Raking the yard therefore should be completed by Tuesday.
8 Lowering gas prices however does not affect costs of cars.

STUDENT MANUAL

Font Color   Drop Caps

Study Lesson 102 in your Student Manual. Complete all the practice activities while at your computer. Then complete the tasks that follow.

DESKTOP PUBLISHING APPLICATIONS

REPORT 35

Essay

Follow these directions to format the report that follows:

1. Turn on widow/orphan control.
2. Center and key the title in a 20-point sans serif font, such as Arial, approximately 2 inches from the top of the page.
3. Add a diamond symbol to either side of the title with Wingdings. (Use the t key.)
4. Change the title color to red.
5. Leave a blank line after the title. Then center and key your name in a 16-point sans serif font.
6. Key the body of the report in Times New Roman 16-point, single-spaced with full justification. Leave a blank line between paragraphs, but do not indent the paragraphs.
7. Use a blue drop cap for the first letter of each paragraph.
8. Number the pages at the bottom center.

AN EFFECTIVE RESUME / By [Your Name]

¶The main goal of a resume is to create enough interest to secure an interview for a job. A resume should be brief—no more than one page. It should reflect your education, skills, accomplishments, and experience in a positive way.

¶Before you begin writing your resume, do a self-evaluation. Determine your abilities and your goals and ensure that they are compatible. Know what you want to do, why you want to do it, and why someone should hire you to do this.

(continued on next page)

SKILLBUILDING

C. 30-Second Timed Writings

Take two 30-second timed writings on lines 9–10. Then take two 30-second timed writings on lines 11–12. Try to increase your speed each time.

```
9       When you talk to customers on the phone, here are some   12
10  tips. Answer on the first ring, and identify the company.    24

11      Speak courteously. If you wear a smile, it will help     11
12  you have a friendly tone of voice. Try to be friendly.       22
    | 1 | 2 | 3 | 4 | 5 | 6 | 7 | 8 | 9 | 10 | 11 | 12
```

WORD PROCESSING APPLICATIONS

LETTER 12

Business Letter in Block Style

Key the following rough-draft business letter. Make the corrections indicated by the proofreaders' marks. Use your initials as the reference initials.

(Current Date)

Mrs. Stephany Ackerman

3257 Lake Side Drive

Lake Oswago, OR 97053

Dear Mrs. Ackerman:

Thank you for asking for Pleasure Isalnd Tavel to plan your overseas trip. While we finalize you itenerary, you may want to apply for your passport. Often it takes weeks before you receive it in the mail.

your passport

A passport application can be oytained from you post office or form any federal or state court. There is a required fee, and two current, identical photos of you are needed to help prove who you are. You will also need a document, such as a

(continued on next page)

C. 5-Minute Timed Writings

Take two 5-minute timed writings on the paragraphs. Note your speed and errors.

Goal: 38/5'/5e

```
     You can realize many benefits from using a computer      11
calendar program. At times, however, even with computers,     22
there still might be a need for a desk calendar. A desk       33
calendar can be quite useful if entries are neatly written    45
in pencil so that you can change them quickly as you need     57
to. If your calendar is visible on the desk and your notes    69
are clear, your coworkers and your boss can extract needed    80
details of your schedule when you are out of the office. Do   92
not jot your private notes on the calendar.                  101
     A daily planner can also help you manage your time.     112
This record might have ruled or blank paper with room to     123
mark each hour of your day. Some people prefer to use a      134
weekly planner that shows the schedule for a whole week.     146
The pages are split into parts and may have a blank space    157
for routine entries.                                         162
     Another daily reminder tool is a tickler file. The      172
tickler file uses dated index cards. You can then place      183
reminders behind the correct date.                           190
                                                         SI 1.39
| 1 | 2 | 3 | 4 | 5 | 6 | 7 | 8 | 9 | 10 | 11 | 12
```

FORMATTING

D. Font Colors and Drop Caps

In addition to changing font sizes and styles, you can add visual effect by changing font color or using drop caps. A **drop cap** is an effect in which the first letter of a paragraph is larger and lower than the rest of the text. Keep in mind that you should limit the number of font styles and colors to keep your document readable.

(continued)

certificate birth, to prove that you are a U.s. citizen.

Instructions on the application detail the types of proof of citizenship that are accpetable. once your passport is issued, it will remain valid for five or ten years, depending on your age.

¶We would like to have your itinerary finalized in about two weeks. If there is any thing else we can do during that time to assist you, please give us a call.

Sincerely

Margret Sagan

Agent

urs

LETTER 13

Business Letter in Block Style

Key the following business letter in block style. Use your initials.

(Current Date) / Ms. Alexia Wilcox / 956 Second Avenue/ Seattle, WA 98101 / Dear Ms. Wilcox:

¶Thank you for your telephone call requesting information about the clothing we carry at Easygoing Wear. Under separate cover we have sent you a catalog which contains all of our clothing lines.

¶Our sales representative, Ms. Nelda Gomez, has received your name and address; she will be calling on you within the next few days. Ms. Gomez will answer any questions you have concerning purchases, credit, and deliveries. In addition, she will have an array of products we are featuring this year.

¶This week's ad for Jacobson's, a store that carries our line and advertises in The Seattle Inquirer, features clothing that could be worn this fall; the ad displays clothing for football games and hiking. Jacobson's tells us that our fall line is one of their best-selling lines.

¶We hope that you will be impressed with our line and that you will consider purchasing some of our clothing. We believe that you will be pleased with the quality, the styling, and the price.

Sincerely yours, / Mr. Alexander Long / Sales Manager / urs

LESSON 102 Font Colors and Features

OBJECTIVES:

- Change font color.
- Add drop caps.
- Key 38/5'/5e.

A. Warmup

Key each line 2 times.

Speed	1 They may go to town for the pens if they are not both busy.
Accuracy	2 We amazed six judges by quietly giving back the four pages.
Language Link	3 He said, "Aunt Joan, go buy Major Roanett a birthday gift."
Numbers/Symbols	4 Jo & Don bought 20 cookies @ $.40 from the You & Me Bakery.
	| 1 | 2 | 3 | 4 | 5 | 6 | 7 | 8 | 9 | 10 | 11 | 12

Choosing Fonts When might you want to use a Times New Roman font and when is it better to use Arial? How are the fonts used on a Web page different from those used in a document? To learn more about font design, go to the Online Learning Center at **KeyComps.glencoe.com>Internet Connection>Unit 6>Lesson 102**.

SKILLBUILDING

B. Preview Practice

Key each line 2 times as a preview to the timed writings that follow.

Accuracy	5 quickly planner realize penciled calendar reminder benefits
Speed	6 on if of as may day for use the can jot your each with help

LESSON 54 MODIFIED-BLOCK LETTERS

OBJECTIVES:

- Strengthen reaches.
- Apply word processing features.
- Format business letters in modified-block style.

A. WARMUP

Key each line 2 times.

Speed	1	The boys will miss swim class for the first time this term.
Accuracy	2	The lazy judge was quick to pay my taxes on the five barns.
Language Link	3	Please proofread five reports, one letter, and two timings.
Numbers/Symbols	4	$76.01 $13.02 $83.03 $92.04 $62.05 $30.06 $65.07 $82.08 $10
		| 1 | 2 | 3 | 4 | 5 | 6 | 7 | 8 | 9 | 10 | 11 | 12

SKILLBUILDING

B. PRETEST

Take a 1-minute timed writing on the paragraph. Note your speed and errors.

5	The blazing paint gave off toxic odors which gagged	11
6	the nearby runners and joggers. Quickly the sunny sky grew	22
7	dimmer as it filled with the acrid smoke. Everyone ran	33
8	even faster to get away from the spreading flames.	43
	| 1 | 2 | 3 | 4 | 5 | 6 | 7 | 8 | 9 | 10 | 11 | 12	

C. PRACTICE

SPEED: If you made 2 or fewer errors on the Pretest, key lines 9–16 two times each.

ACCURACY: If you made more than 2 errors on the Pretest, key lines 9–12 as a group two times. Then key lines 13–16 as a group two times.

Double Reaches	9	mm comma gamma gummy mummy dummy yummy jimmy tummy hammy mm
	10	gg baggy leggy foggy soggy doggy muggy piggy buggy jaggy gg
	11	nn inner annoy sunny funny bunny bonny gunny nanny runny nn
	12	tt kitty ditty bitty catty nutty witty vitta patty motto tt

(continued on next page)

REPORT 34

Paragraph

Follow these steps to key a paragraph using special characters:

1. Change the font size to 24, Times New Roman.
2. Key the following paragraph:

   When my alarm clock rang, I was unhappy. I turned on some music to make me happy; then I read the paper. There were several articles I cut out to send to my friends. Of course, that meant I had to write to them first. As someone pointed out, letters may be the sunshine in someone's day.
3. Delete the words listed below and replace them with special characters. To do this, delete the word, then change the font from Times New Roman to Wingdings®. Use the indicated keystrokes to insert the symbols in place of the deleted word.

Word to delete	Keystroke to Use
Unhappy	Capital *L*
Happy	Capital *J*
Cut	#
Write	@
Letters	+
Sunshine	Capital *R*

When my alarm clock rang, I was ☹. I turned on some music to make me ☺; then I read the paper. There were several articles I ✂ out to send to my friends. Of course, that meant I had to ✍ to them first. As someone pointed out, 🖃 may be the ☼ in someone's day.

LANGUAGE ARTS CONNECTION

Apply Picture Symbols Symbols are often used instead of words because people can understand the concept conveyed in a picture more quickly than they can interpret text. Symbols also work as an international language. For example, people from most countries understand what a red or green light means; they might add smiley (☺) or frowning (☹) faces to a message; and they know not to do something if a sign shows a picture with a circle and a slash.

Microsoft® Word has a variety of picture symbols and characters that can be used to emphasize specific content or add visual interest to a document. Look through the symbols that are available in Word's Webdings® and Wingdings fonts. Then key a paragraph that uses at least 6 of these picture characters.

With your teacher's permission, print your work or switch seats with a classmate. Then re-key each other's paragraphs, adding in the text that is represented by the pictures. See if you interpreted each other's visual clues correctly.

(continued)

Alternate Reaches

```
13 toxic blame paint their towns bland panda theme tucks blend
14 panel throb turns flame pause throw tusks bogus proxy title
15 tutor boric prism tithe ticks bowls prowl tight bugle psych
16 rigor slept vigor quake chant flair shame snake right thigh
```

D. POSTTEST

Repeat the Pretest. Compare your Posttest results with your Pretest results.

E. 12-Second Sprints

Take three 12-second timed writings on each line. Try to increase your speed each time.

```
17 He bought the buns at the store for my friends in the park.
18 We went to the park to have a good time and play some ball.
19 The ball got lost in the water, and we had to find another.
20 None of us wanted to leave when it got dark, but we had to.
   ||||5||||10||||15||||20||||25||||30||||35||||40||||45||||50||||55||||60
```

FORMATTING

F. Modified-Block Style Letters

In the **modified-block style** letter, the date and closing lines (complimentary closing, writer's name, and title) begin at the center point of the writing line. Paragraphs in a modified-block style letter may be blocked at the left margin (the preferred style) or indented 0.5 inch.

Current Date

Mr. William J. Gross, President
National Training and Development Association
3500 Collingwood Boulevard
Toledo, OH 43624

Dear Mr. Gross:

It is a pleasure to accept your invitation to speak at the National Training and Development Association's Annual Convention in Cleveland next April. I will be glad to speak either on the current status of word processing or the skills needed by a beginning word processor.

As you know, I have spent considerable time in advising various firms on how a quality word processing center affects the total communication system of the firm. The effects of a good center bring increased revenues and also result in a better image of the firm.

If you wish, I would be most happy to discuss with your members the importance of hiring well-trained word processors. I have taught technology administration at the local university as well as developed in-house training programs for firms. I could include in the speech the need for highly developed technical, human relations, and personal skills.

You or your members may desire another topic in the area of word processing or its personnel; if so, please let me know.

Again, thank you for an invitation to speak at your annual meeting.

Sincerely yours,

David G. Moran
Consultant

urs

G. Software Features

STUDENT MANUAL

Ruler Tab Set

Study Lesson 54 in your Student Manual. Complete all the practice activities while at your computer. Then complete the tasks that follow.

REPORT 33

Flyer

Create the flyer in the illustration following these steps:

1. Center the text vertically and horizontally.
2. Key the heading using Arial 36-point.
3. Add the mouse symbols on either side of the heading using Wingdings® 36-point. (Use the 8 key.)
4. Double-space after the heading.
5. Change to Arial 20-point and key the remaining text. Quadruple-space before and after the list; double-space before keying the last line.
6. Add the diamond shapes to the listed items using Wingdings. (Use the T key.) Leave a space after the symbol at the beginning of a line and before the symbol at the end of a line.

🖰CompuTrain, Inc.🖰

Learn with the best trainers in the country!

♦ Upgrade your skills. ♦
♦ Improve your efficiency. ♦
♦ Create exciting publications. ♦
♦ Learn at your own pace. ♦
♦ Attend a live seminar. ♦

To schedule a live training seminar or to order video training, call 800-555-5555.

Don't wait! Call us now!

LETTER 14

Business Letter in Modified-Block Style

Key the following letter in modified-block style. Use your initials.

(Current Date) / Mr. Weijun Zhao, President / All-Star Appliances / 2200 South Maybelle Avenue / Tulsa, OK 74107-2000 / Dear Mr. Zhao: / Welcome to the select group of Apex television dealers. ¶Your application has been approved, and we look forward to many years of successful business for both your firm and ours. ¶We take pride in the fact that we have never rescinded a dealership agreement in our 40 years of manufacturing quality television sets. Every dealer will tell you that we are a family working together to improve the industry —both the manufacturing and servicing industry. ¶We are aware of the fine reputation of your company for service and sales in the greater Tulsa area; therefore, it would be a pleasure to have you visit our offices and plant at our expense as soon as you have an opportunity to do so. / Sincerely yours, / Amos Morgan / President / urs

LETTER 15

Business Letter in Modified-Block Style

Key the following letter in modified-block style. Use your initials.

(Current Date) / Mr. William J. Gross, President / National Training and Development Association / 3500 Collingwood Boulevard / Toledo, OH 43624 / Dear Mr. Gross: / It is a pleasure to accept your invitation to speak at the National Training and Development Association's Annual Convention in Cleveland next April. I will be glad to speak either on the current status of word processing or the skills needed by a beginning word processor. ¶As you know, I have spent considerable time in advising various firms on how a quality word processing center affects the total communication system of the firm. The effects of a good center bring increased revenues and result in a better image of the firm. ¶If you wish, I would be most happy to discuss with your members the importance of hiring well-trained word processors. I have taught technology administration at the local university as well as developed in-house training programs for firms. I could include in the speech the need for highly developed technical, human relations, and personal skills. ¶You or your members may desire another topic in the area of word processing or its personnel; if so, please let me know. ¶Again, thank you for an invitation to speak at your annual meeting. / Sincerely yours, / David G. Morgan / Consultant / urs

FORMATTING

C. Orientation to Desktop Publishing

Desktop publishing (DTP) is the application of special word processing features to make your documents visually appealing. By using different font styles, colors, boxes, and graphics, you can create a variety of documents such as stationery, flyers, and newsletters.

To create effective documents, keep the layout fairly simple. Use a limited number of font styles and do not make the page too crowded.

D. Software Features

STUDENT MANUAL

Special Characters

Study Lesson 101 in your Student Manual. Complete all the practice activities while at your computer. Then complete the tasks that follow.

DESKTOP PUBLISHING APPLICATIONS

REPORT 32

Follow these steps to key a paragraph using special characters.

1. Change the font size to 20 points, Times New Roman.
2. Key the following paragraph:

   I wrote a letter and rushed to get it into the mailbox. I was sending it by air to get it delivered quickly. Once the letter was sent, I telephoned my friend, who was happy to learn it was coming.

3. Delete the words listed below and replace them with special characters. To do this, change the font from Times New Roman to Wingdings® font. (**Wingdings** are special characters or symbols.) Use the indicated keystrokes to insert the symbols in place of the deleted word.

> I wrote a 🖃 and rushed to get it into the 📫. I was sending it by ✈ to get it delivered quickly. Once the 🖃 was sent, I ☎ my friend, who was ☺ to learn it was coming.

Word to delete	Keystroke to Use
letter	+ (plus)
mailbox	- (hyphen)
air	Capital *Q*
telephoned	((left parenthesis)
happy	Capital *J*

LESSON 55 LETTERS WITH INDENTED PARAGRAPHS

OBJECTIVES:

- Compose sentences at the keyboard.
- Format letters with indented paragraphs.

A. WARMUP

Key each line 2 times.

Speed	1	I could not read the small print on the map she sent to me.
Accuracy	2	A dozen jumpy zebras quickly zipped over the six big gates.
Language Link	3	My good grades, therefore, led to my scholarship's renewal.
Symbols	4	it's hasn't we'll aren't they'll couldn't you've don't I've

| 1 | 2 | 3 | 4 | 5 | 6 | 7 | 8 | 9 | 10 | 11 | 12

LANGUAGE LINK

B. COMPOSING AT THE KEYBOARD

Ethics Connection

Read the following passage, then use a print or online dictionary to help answer the questions that follow. Answer each question with a complete sentence.

Workplace Ethics Unethical behavior in a business causes loss of profits and productivity. For example, when an employee uses the company's e-mail for personal use, the employee is being paid for time that should be used for work. The employee is also using the company's equipment and resources.

5 What does *ethics* mean?
6 What does *unethical* mean?
7 What does *productive* mean?
8 Why is it unethical for an employee not to be productive?

LESSON 101 DESKTOP PUBLISHING: SPECIAL CHARACTERS

OBJECTIVES:

- Increase keyboarding speed.
- Apply desktop publishing skills.
- Key special characters.

A. WARMUP

Key each line 2 times.

Speed	1	The goal of the rich girls is to fix a bike for an old man.
Accuracy	2	Dave froze the mixtures in the deep brown jugs too quickly.
Language Link	3	The runner asked, "Is June 7 the last day we can register?"
Numbers	4	Fabra will mark the board at 10, 29, 38, 47, and 56 inches.

| 1 | 2 | 3 | 4 | 5 | 6 | 7 | 8 | 9 | 10 | 11 | 12

SKILLBUILDING

B. 12-SECOND SPRINTS

Take three 12-second timed writings on each line. Try to increase your speed each time.

5 She said the four girls can swim across the lake with ease.
6 Please take one of these big boxes down to the post office.
7 May we go to the game with you, or do you have other plans?
8 The short words are often keyed faster than the long words.

||||5||||10||||15||||20||||25||||30||||35||||40||||45||||50||||55||||60

SKILLBUILDING

C. Preview Practice

Key each line 2 times as a preview to the 3-minute timed writing that follows.

```
 9 check crucial analyze quality equipped processed acceptable  12
10 rates today tool work just data sure help job can fix at is  24
   | 1 | 2 | 3 | 4 | 5 | 6 | 7 | 8 | 9 | 10 | 11 | 12
```

D. 3-Minute Timed Writing

Goal: 33/3′/5e

Take two 3-minute timed writings on lines 11–20. Note your speed and errors.

```
11      Computers used today will help produce work that is     11
12 free from errors. These machines are equipped to work with   22
13 data at high rates of speed. This means that errors are      34
14 processed at high speeds as well. For this reason, it is     45
15 crucial that computer users have skills to analyze and fix   57
16 errors.                                                      58
17      In every job, it is important to check your work to be  70
18 sure that what you have is what you wanted and that the      81
19 quality is acceptable. The computer is just a tool, but it   93
20 can make your job a simpler one.                             99
                                                           SI: 1.32
   | 1 | 2 | 3 | 4 | 5 | 6 | 7 | 8 | 9 | 10 | 11 | 12
```

Proofread and Revise Choose one of the business letters you have written in this unit. Print and proofread the letter. Make corrections on the printed copy using proper proofreaders' marks, then key the corrections in your document. Save the revised version of the letter with a new name, such as Letter 15_Rev. With your teacher's permission, print a copy of the corrected letter, and save copies of both the original and revised letters in your portfolio.

WORDS TO LEARN

In the lessons, software, and Student Manual (SM), you will learn the following vocabulary terms for Unit 6.

borders (p. 378)
desktop publishing (p. 369)
drop cap (p. 373; SM Lesson 102)
drop shadows (p. 378)
fill (p. 378)
graphics (p. 386)
letterhead (p. 400)
text boxes (p. 386; SM Lesson 106)
WordArt/text art (p. 403; SM Lesson 111)
Wingdings® (p. 369)
wrap text (p. 393)

CAREER BYTE

GRAPHIC ARTIST Graphic artists may create brochures or ads for new products, visual designs for annual reports and other corporate literature, or distinctive logos for products or businesses. Graphic artists use a variety of print, electronic, and film media to create art. Most graphic artists today use computer software to design new images; some of this work appears on the Internet and CD-ROMs. Artists may be assigned to create the overall layout and design of magazines, newspapers, journals, and other publications. They may also be asked to create computer-generated media, such as special effects used in movies and television, and visuals in video games.

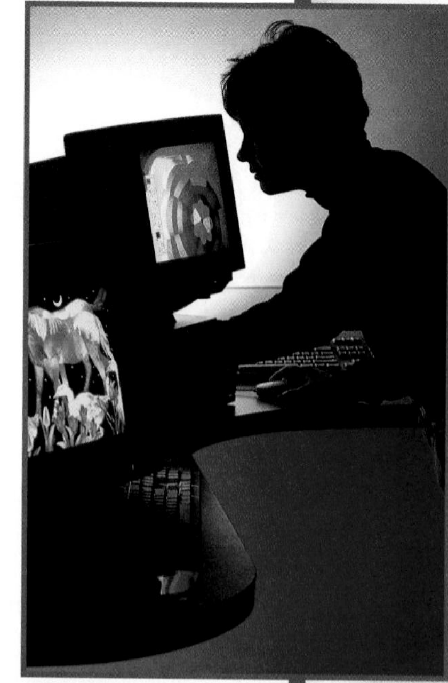

FORMATTING

E. Letters With Indented Paragraphs

Current Date

Ms. Barbara Cole
One North 79 Avenue
Chicago, IL 60635

Dear Ms. Cole:

Congratulations on completing the requirements for your undergraduate degree! As you look forward to joining the workforce on a full-time basis, you are probably trying to determine how you can stretch your budget to include reliable transportation. We can be of help to you!

During the next three months, we are offering a special discount package. This package is available only to members of this year's college graduating class who will be purchasing a new car for the first time. In addition, we can arrange financing at a rate lower than the rates available at most banks.

Call us toll free at 1-800-555-5295. Our customer service representative will put you in touch with your nearest Astra dealer. Act now! This special offer will be available for a limited time.

Sincerely,

Madonna Chavez
Marketing Manager

urs

The modified-block style letter can be varied by indenting the first line of each paragraph, usually 0.5 inch.

When using the indented paragraph style, set two tabs—one for the paragraph (at 0.5 inch from the left margin) and one for the date and closing lines (at the center point of the line).

WORD PROCESSING APPLICATIONS

LETTER 16

Business Letter in Modified-Block Style with Indented Paragraphs

Key the following business letter in modified-block style with indented paragraphs. Remember to set 2 tabs.

(Current Date) / Ms. Barbara Cole / One North 79 Avenue / Chicago, IL 60635 / Dear Ms. Cole:

¶Congratulations on completing the requirements for your undergraduate degree! As you look forward to joining the workforce on a full-time basis, you are probably trying to determine how you can stretch your budget to include reliable transportation. We can be of help to you!

¶ During the next three months, we are offering a special discount package. This package is available only to members of this year's college graduating class who will be purchasing a new car for the first time. In addition, we can arrange financing at a rate lower than the rates available at most banks.

¶Call us toll free at 1-800-555-5295. Our customer service representative will put you in touch with your nearest Astra dealer. Act now! This special offer will be available for a limited time.

Sincerely, / Madonna Chavez / Marketing Manager / urs

UNIT 6

LESSONS 101–120

DESKTOP PUBLISHING

OBJECTIVES

- Demonstrate keyboarding speed and accuracy on straight copy with a goal of 38 words per minute for 5 minutes with 5 or fewer errors.
- Demonstrate correct use of word processing features.
- Demonstrate basic design and formatting skills on a variety of reports including flyers, invitations, stationery, certificates, and newsletters.
- Compose short reports at the keyboard.
- Apply rules for using commas, citing titles, and noting figures.
- Identify redundancies and confusing words.

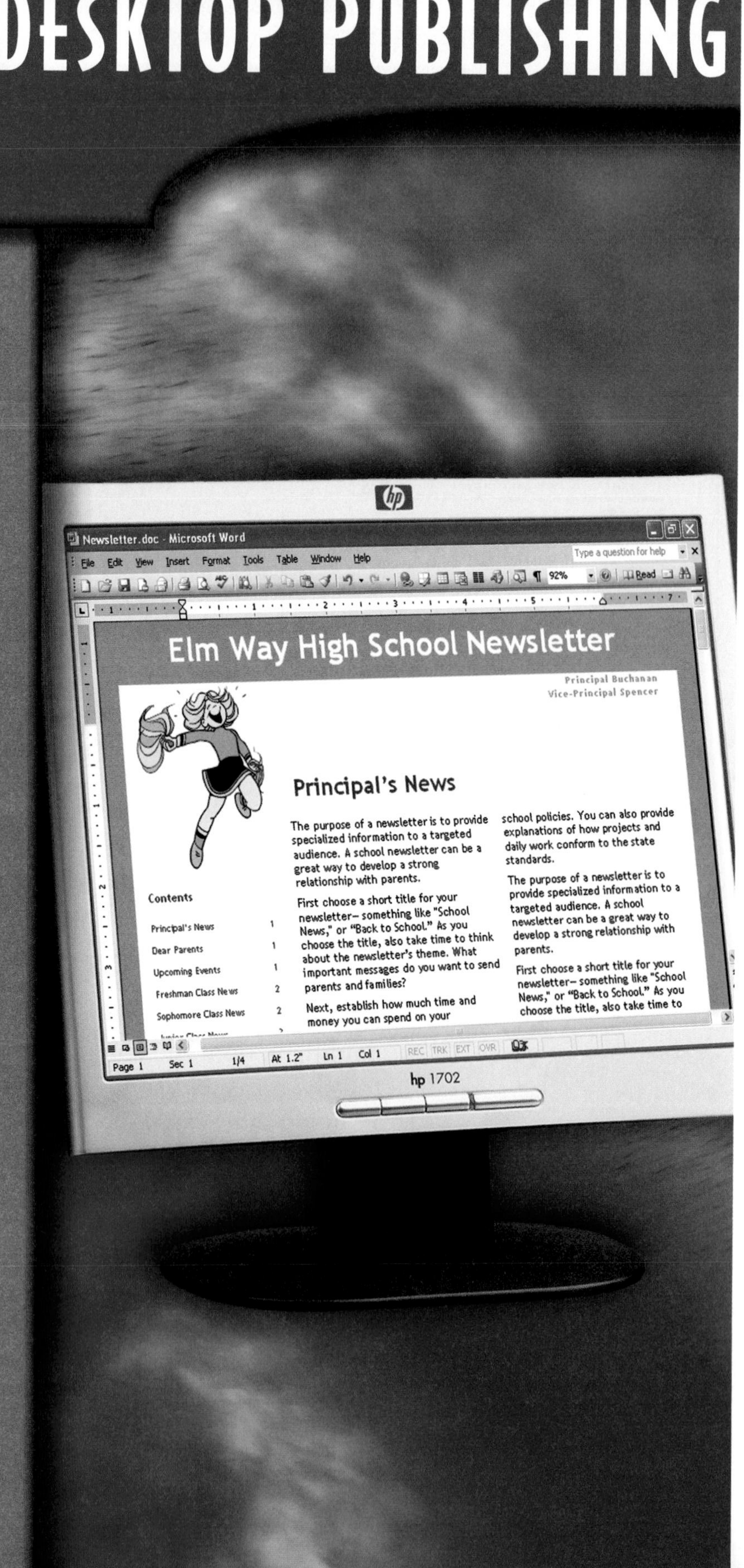

LETTER 17

Business Letter in Modified-Block Style with Indented Paragraphs

Key the following letter in modified-block style with indented paragraphs, making the corrections indicated by the proofreaders' marks. Use your initials for reference.

(Current Date)

↓4

Mr. Marvin Estawick
Lawton Industries
5492 warren Avenue
Detroit, MI 48207-9602

Dear Mr. Estawick:

Mrs. Barbara Cole, who was an employee by your company as a summer intern, has applied for credit. Since Ms. Cole does not have a credit record, we will need a data sheet to be completed by her most recent employer.

Will you please fill out and return the form that was sent to you so we that we may process Ms. Cole's request for an automobile loan. A release statment has been signed giving you permision to disclose the requested informations.

If you have any questions regarding this form can be answered by calling me at 312-555-9672, Ext. 40. Please FAX the form to me at 312-555-9677.

Sincereley,

Ms. Madonna Chavez
Marketing Manager

urs

TABLE 42

Boxed Table

Change the page orientation to landscape. Create a 5-column, 10-row boxed table. Automatically adjust the column widths. Center the table vertically and horizontally. Add 10 percent shading to the braced column headings. Use the SUM formula to calculate totals for columns 2–5.

SALES ANALYSIS Borden Manufacturing Company June 30, {year}				
	1st Quarter		2nd Quarter	
Salesperson	**Units**	**Gross Sales ($)**	**Units**	**Gross Sales ($)**
Robert Brazinski	10	427.70	29	1,240.33
Carol Dawkins	18	769.86	17	727.09
Janice Greene	20	855.40	28	1,197.56
Carlos Bieseda	17	727.09	24	1,026.48
Diane Kessler	15	641.55	25	1,069.25
Charles Young	19	812.63	32	1,368.64
TOTAL				

MATH CONNECTION

Convert Currencies The euro is the currency of a growing number of countries in the European Union. Go to the Online Learning Center at **KeyComps.glencoe.com>Math Connection>Unit 5>Lesson 100** to find links to Web sites that will calculate the exchange rate from the dollar to the euro.

Create a table similar to the one below. From the list on the Online Learning Center, choose four additional items. Key the additional items and their prices in the blank rows. Convert each price in U.S. dollars to the price in euros. Use the SUM function to calculate the totals. Format the figures in two columns with a dollar sign or euro symbol (ALT+ 8364) and two decimal places. Follow your teacher's instructions for saving and printing your work.

U.S. DOLLAR/EURO CONVERSIONS

Item	Price in U.S. Dollars	Price in Euros
Wool Jacket	$49.99	€41.33
TOTALS		

LESSON 56 Letters With Enclosures and Attachments

OBJECTIVES:

- Improve keyboarding skills.
- Format modified-block letters with enclosures and attachments.

A. Warmup

Key each line 2 times.

Speed	1	James was not here when all of us signed the card for Rita.
Accuracy	2	Jacqueline was glad her family took five or six big prizes.
Language Link	3	We baked cakes, mowed lawns, and washed cars to make money.
Technique	4	Will students use the SHIFT LOCK to type in SOLID CAPITALS?

| 1 | 2 | 3 | 4 | 5 | 6 | 7 | 8 | 9 | 10 | 11 | 12

SKILLBUILDING

B. PRETEST

Take a 1-minute timed writing on the paragraph. Note your speed and errors.

5 The fight for women's suffrage took quite a few years. 11
6 One zealous leader of the battle was a Quaker named Alice 22
7 Paul who used protest marches and hunger strikes to fight 33
8 for the right to vote. 37

| 1 | 2 | 3 | 4 | 5 | 6 | 7 | 8 | 9 | 10 | 11 | 12

LETTER 62

Business Letter in Modified-Block Style

Key the following business letter in modified-block style. Use today's date.

Dr. David Rosenbloom / The Open University / Maks Rhoho Educational Center / 255 Klausner Street / Tel-Aviv 61392 / ISRAEL / Dear Dr. Rosenbloom:
¶The Board of Directors for the Atlanta International School, Atlanta, Georgia, (United States) is personally inviting you to become a member of their board. Your name was suggested at the summer meeting of the Foundation of International Schools in Geneva, Switzerland.
¶Your credentials contain most of what our personnel are seeking. We are impressed with your work as a Professor of Psychology in Tel-Aviv and notice that you have done extensive work with youth groups. Dr. Rosenbloom, we have a great need for someone with your talent and experience. We feel you could make an outstanding contribution as a member of the Board of Directors here in Atlanta.
¶Please respond as quickly as possible. You may telephone me at 404-555-1454 or send an e-mail to me at Aistalk@aol.com.
Yours truly, / Dr. Lien Vandermark, President / Atlanta International School / urs

MEMO 8

Template

Complete the following memo using the first memo template listed in your word processing software.

TO: Allison Wong / **CC:** Zachary Barkley / **FROM:** Rocio Cunningham / **DATE:** February 15, (year) / **SUBJECT:** Council Meeting
¶The office council meeting originally scheduled for Tuesday, February 23, has been changed to Thursday, February 25, upon the advice of Mr. Brown, our company's legal counsel. A revised agenda is attached.
¶There will be time for each person to voice his/her feelings on all major issues concerning changing personnel. Everyone's personal opinion will be taken into consideration before final decisions are made.
¶If you cannot attend the meeting, please send a representative who can speak for your department.
urs / Attachment

C. PRACTICE

In the chart below, find the number of errors you made on the Pretest. Then key each of the following designated drill lines 2 times.

Pretest Errors	0–1	2	3	4+
Drill Lines	12–16	11–15	10–14	9–12

Accuracy

```
9  not fight women named until marches battle zealous Illinois
10 did leader states joined strikes protest suffrage Amendment
11 was after begin issue quite hunger decades Wyoming Congress
12 New their first debate Alice woman thirty Quaker Nineteenth
```

Speed

```
13 decades state years next pass took nine York the and did in
14 protest right named vote last test mend gave for was but to
15 strikes cause first lead them West used teen win who few of
16 fight other march rage Paul join zeal give two one not at a
```

D. POSTTEST

Repeat the Pretest. Compare your Posttest results with your Pretest results.

FORMATTING

E. Enclosure and Attachment Notations

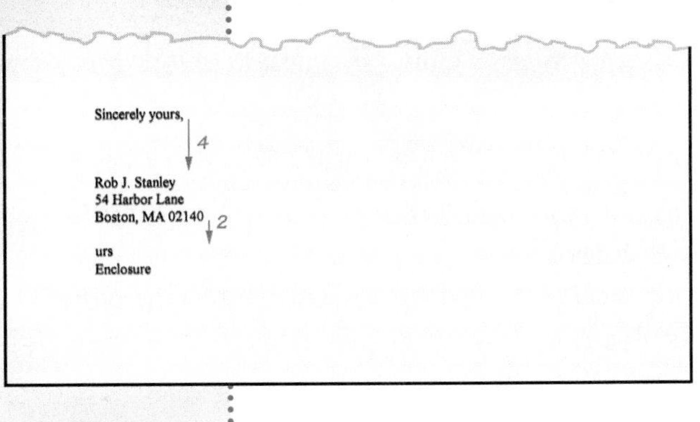
Sincerely yours,
↓ 4
Rob J. Stanley
54 Harbor Lane
Boston, MA 02140 ↓ 2
urs
Enclosure

Yours truly,

Laurice J. Mattingly
Assistant Treasurer

urs
Attachments

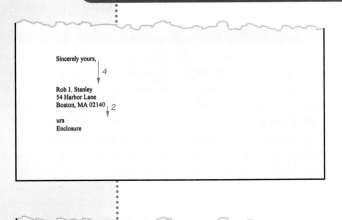

An **enclosure** is an item that is enclosed with a letter. An **attachment** is an item that is stapled or clipped to the letter.

To show that a letter contains an enclosure or attachment, key the word *Enclosure* or the word *Attachment* at the left margin on the line below the reference initials. If more than one item is enclosed or attached, key *Enclosures* or *Attachments*.

(continued)

"Remember" said Sara "turn off the lights when you leave."
Sharon asked "Would you like to have half of my sandwich?"
"If you have not eaten lunch yet" said Bev "let's eat."
"I can hardly believe it is afternoon" said the professor.

SKILLBUILDING

C. CONCENTRATION

***Key the following paragraph 1 time. Every time a number appears, replace it with a number that is two greater. For example, replace* two *with* four *and* five *with* seven.**

Three students wanted five notebooks, three calendars, six mechanical pencils, four black markers, seven sheets of poster paper, and eight ink pens for the school store. They planned to market these items to students to make a profit.

WORD PROCESSING APPLICATIONS

LETTER 61

Business Letter in Block Style

Key the following business letter in block style. Use today's date.

Ms. Wynona Foster / Owner / Frills & Fluff Fine Fashion /
560 James Naismith Drive / Gloucester, Ontario / CANADA /
K1B5N / Dear Ms. Foster:
¶Thank you for your clothing merchandise order. The New York Fashion Show was the best we have presented. We were delighted that you could attend.
¶Your purchase entitles you to a 25 percent discount on your next order. We know that our business relationship with Frills & Fluff Fine Fashion will be long-lasting. / Sincerely yours, / Yolanda McDonald / Merchandise Marketing / urs

LETTER 18

Business Letter in Modified-Block Style with Indented Paragraphs

Key this letter in modified-block style with indented paragraphs. Be sure to include an enclosure notation.

(Current Date) / Mr. and Mrs. Marvin Carson / Circle Route, Box 318 / Elk City, OK 73644 / Dear Mr. and Mrs. Carson: ¶Congratulations on becoming the owner of a Model L350 dishwasher! The TurboKleen name on your dishwasher identifies it as a top-quality kitchen appliance. ¶For the past 25 years, we have produced appliances that are reliable—products that will help America's busy families better manage their limited time. Because we are so certain of the reliability of our appliances, every TurboKleen appliance comes with a ten-year warranty. Your warranty is enclosed with this letter. If your dishwasher should need servicing before that time, a call to our dealer will bring a service technician to your door within 24 hours. ¶Welcome to our family of satisfied customers. When we can be of any assistance to you, please let us know. /Cordially yours, / William Clifford / President / urs

LETTER 19

Business Letter in Modified-Block Style with Indented Paragraphs

Key this letter in modified-block style with indented paragraphs. Remember to add your reference initials and an enclosure notation.

May 17, {year}
Mrs. Rosa Ortez
39 McFarland Lane
Madison, WI 53714
Dear Mrs. Ortez:

We are pleased to answer the question of your science students about allergy testing. The test takes two days. This includes food allergy tests as well as the usual tests for plants, animals, mold spores, and so on. Technicians in our labs must be able to conduct these tests.

You were interested in having your class visit our labs. This would be a good time to plan to have your students visit. I would be willing to come in early on the Thursday morning you specify to work with your students and you. When you have decided upon a date, please give me a call. Use the enclosed form to select the best time for your students to visit our labs.

Sincerely,
Hans Rosen
Clinic Manager

LESSON 100 FORMATTING REVIEW

OBJECTIVES:

- Apply rules for commas with direct quotations.
- Reinforce letter, memo, and table formatting.

A. WARMUP

Key each line 2 times.

Speed	1	Shaun keyed by touch in order to key at his fastest speed.
Accuracy	2	Viv poured a liquid that froze quickly into the beige jars.
Language Link	3	Alana asked, "Did you record that book on a separate disk?"
Numbers/Symbols	4	By October 10 you need to order 253# of Item #46 @ $798.15.

| 1 | 2 | 3 | 4 | 5 | 6 | 7 | 8 | 9 | 10 | 11 | 12

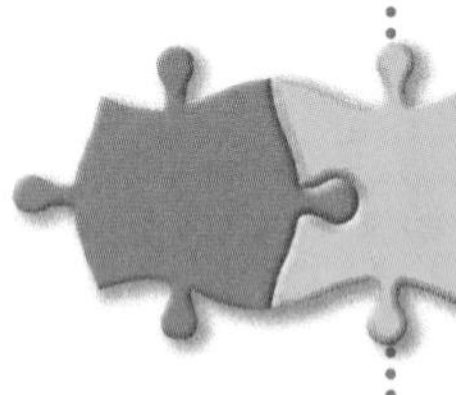

LANGUAGE LINK

B. COMMAS WITH DIRECT QUOTATIONS

Study the rules and examples below. Then edit lines 5–8 on p. 363 to correct any errors in punctuation. Note that the punctuation is placed inside the final quotation mark.

Rule 21: Use a comma before a direct quotation.

The magician said, "Hokus pokus."

The officer replied, "The fingerprints are in the lab for analysis."

Rule 22: Use a comma after a direct quotation.

"Over here," shouted the traffic officer.

"All books are to be returned within one week," the statement read.

Rule 23: Use a comma before and after a direct quotation.

"When you go outside," said Mom, "be sure to wear a coat."

"When you drive my car," said Dad, "be very careful!"

(continued on next page)

LETTER REINFORCEMENT

OBJECTIVE:

- Strengthen skills in formatting business letters.

A. WARMUP

Key each line 2 times.

Speed	1	It was a good idea to start to write your report this week.
Accuracy	2	My ax just zipped through the fine black wood quite evenly.
Language Link	3	Micah was, however, most apologetic for being tardy Monday.
Symbols	4	What a sight! Good luck! Watch out! At last! No way! Never!
		| 1 | 2 | 3 | 4 | 5 | 6 | 7 | 8 | 9 | 10 | 11 | 12

SKILLBUILDING

B. TECHNIQUE TIMED WRITINGS

Take two 30-second timed writings on each line. Focus on the techniques at the left.

Use the correct SHIFT keys. Key without pausing.

5 Dr. and Mrs. Wynans won tickets to the Hula Bowl in Hawaii.
6 The Gas & Go was first named Your Place and then Shop Stop.
7 Mr. Ulan is taking us to the Museum of Fine Arts in Boston.
8 I turned right on Lemon, left on Davis, and left on Fuller.
| 1 | 2 | 3 | 4 | 5 | 6 | 7 | 8 | 9 | 10 | 11 | 12

C. PACED PRACTICE

Turn to the Paced Practice routine beginning on page SB-7. Take three 2-minute timed writings, starting at the point where you left off the last time.

SOCIAL STUDIES CONNECTION

Compose a Letter Did you know that high school is not mandatory in Japan? Students are selected to attend high school based on their entrance exam scores. Compose a letter to a high school student in Japan. Describe how students are promoted in American high schools and why you prefer either Japan's or America's school policy. Follow your teacher's instructions for saving and printing your work.

MEMO 7

Template

Complete the following handwritten memo using the first memo template listed in your word processing software. Use today's date. Remember to add your reference initials.

TO: *Nina Lewis, Supervisor*

CC: *Marc Pak*

FROM: *Sam Roshdy*

SUBJECT: *Employees' Gym*

¶The new gym and the Olympic swimming pool are now open for employee use. Thanks to your support of this effort, the company has equipped this gym for their personnel with most of the exercise equipment needed for a good 30-minute workout.

¶You know that there is now an hour and a half for the lunch break. This will give employees time to work out, eat their lunches, and attend to personal matters before the afternoon shift begins.

¶Please encourage all those employees that you supervise to use this modern, new workout facility. It's free to employees during the week and open on Saturdays for employees and their families.

PORTFOLIO Activity

Review Memos with Copy Notation and Attachments Go to the Online Learning Center at **KeyComps.glencoe.com>Portfolio Activity>Unit 5>Lesson 99** to find information about the European Union and its members. Select a memo template in Word and address it to a teacher with a copy going to a friend briefly explaining the purpose of the European Union. Create a 2-column table as an attachment that lists the countries that make up the European Union and the year each country became a member. Add shading and borders of your choice. Follow your teacher's instructions for saving and printing your work.

LETTER 20

Personal-Business Letter in Block Style

Format the personal-business letter below in block style; prepare a No. 10 envelope. Use the writer's name and address for the return address on the envelope. Add the envelope to the letter.

(Current Date) / Ms. Zoe Albright / Merkel Realtors, Inc. / 150 E. Ponce De Leon / Decatur, GA 30032 /
Dear Ms. Albright: ¶My family and I are moving to Decatur from Indianapolis in October, and I would like your help in finding our new home. Friends in Decatur have told me that you know which homes best suit your clients; no one can do better. I am employed by the Albertson Corporation as an accountant, and I would like to drive less than 10 miles to work.
¶We are interested in a four-bedroom home with three and a half baths, a family room, a double-car garage, and a pool, if possible. We would like either a brick ranch or two-story colonial home. My wife prefers the ranch style, and I prefer the colonial style. I have attached some pictures of similar homes that appeal to us.
¶As we have two children, a boy and a girl, two of the four bedrooms would be for their use. One bedroom and bath would be for guests. We would like a large master bedroom overlooking the rear of the property.
¶Please send me any available information on such a home including the location, price, taxes, closing costs, and other such fees. As soon as we hear from you, we will make an appointment to visit you and see the homes you suggest.
¶You may call me at work at 317-555-2900 or my wife at home at 317-555-8957.
Sincerely yours, / Lewis K. Lincoln / 3350 Carson Avenue / Indianapolis, IN 46227/Attachments

LANGUAGE ARTS CONNECTION

Compose a Business Letter Review Letter 20 and note the type of house the writer is looking for and the information he is requesting. Then compose an answer as if you were a real estate agent who has found the ideal house. Use your town or neighborhood as the location of the house, and check online or print real estate listings to find a realistic price. Follow your teacher's instructions for saving and printing your work.

MEMO 6

Template

Complete this memo using the first memo template listed in your word processing software. Use today's date. Single space with a blank space between paragraphs. Make the corrections indicated by the proofreaders' marks.

TO: Daniel White buffalo

FROM: Ellen herrera

SUBJECT: Technology in education conference

The tie conference willbe held again this year in Snowmass.

There are rooms available at the Aspen Lodge for all of our personnel. I have asked that the management make our stay more personal by reserving the entire west wing of the lodge for our group of 21 people.

I have attached directions to the Lodge; however, the Company will provide us with a mini van. If you wish to ride along in the minivan please contact me via E-mail. The address is eherrera@ccds.k12.ca.us. The minivan will pick us up in front of the School. We will leave promptly at 8 a.m. exactly on Thursday, September 16.

I hope you will choose to join me in the ride to Snow mass. The fall tree colors at that time will be beautiful. I look forward to seeing you then.

urs

attachment

LETTER 21

Business Letter in Modified-Block Style

Format the business letter below in modified-block style with blocked paragraphs. Make the corrections indicated by the proofreaders' marks, and prepare a large envelope. Include the envelope with the document.

(Current Date)

Mr. William J. Gross President

National WordProcessing Association

3500 Collingwood Boulevard

Toledo, Oh 43624

Dear Mr. Gross:

Thank you for you letter of last week telling me that you believe a talk on the skills needed by a word processor would be a great intrest to your associatoin member.

I have taken the liverty of developing a talk and have entitled it "The Well-trained Word Processor." The talk will take approximate one hour. I will need an over head projector, a screen, and a mike. Its my intent to have them involve during the talk, and I will need assistance in distributing handouts to the audience. Would you please have two assistants available to help me?

Enclosed is an outline of my talk; also, I have enclosed a synopsis of the talk. I thought you might be interested in what I was planning to discuss. If you have suggestions for other points which should be included please let me know.

(continued on next page)

FORMATTING

D. Copy Notations

When you send a copy of a memo to someone in addition to the addressee, key a copy notation on the memo. Many memo templates already have a field where you can simply insert the names of the people to whom you want to send copies of the memo. If there is no field, then key the copy notation as follows:

1. Key the copy notation on the line below the reference initials or below the enclosure or attachment notation.
2. At the left margin, key a lowercase *c* followed by a colon (*c:*)
3. Key one space and then key the name of the person receiving the copy.

E. Attachments

When material is physically attached to a memo (either clipped or stapled), key an attachment notation below the reference initials. To key the attachment notation:

1. Press Enter once after keying your reference initials.
2. Key the word *Attachment* at the left margin.

WORD PROCESSING APPLICATIONS

MEMO 5

Template

Complete this memo using the first memo template listed in your word processing software. Use today's date.

TO:/ Katrina Stevens / **CC:** / Marshall McElreath **FROM:**/ Justine O'Neal / **SUBJECT:** / Evaluation Criteria
¶Please refer to the attachment as you develop your suggestions for the evaluation criteria for the new department personnel brochure. Please give thought to developing at least five suggestions.
¶Submit your suggestions to me via e-mail by October 1. My personal e-mail address is joneal@jobs.personnel.gov.co.us. I assure you that all of your suggestions will be kept confidential in my personal mailbox. We will meet on October 5 in the Spruce Conference Oval Room to review all of your suggestions, develop a list of 25 criteria for personnel evaluation, and plan the brochure. / urs / Attachment

(continued)

¶ I plan to make my air plane reservations next week.

Is there an exact time you would like me to arrive on the first day of the meeting. I plan to attend many sessions as possible.

Sincerely yours

David G. Moran

Consultant

urs

Enclosures

LETTER 22

Business Letter in Modified-Block Style with Indented Paragraphs

Open Letter 21, and revise it as follows:

1. Change the format to modified-block style with indented paragraphs.
2. Replace all instances of *talk* with *presentation*.

PORTFOLIO Activity

Create a Letter Think of the ideal trip that you would like to take and what you would need. For example, imagine that you were going to an amusement park for the weekend. You would need plane tickets for traveling on a specific date. At the park, you might want reservations at a hotel that is within walking distance. You would also need all-day passes for two days.

Key a personal-business letter to a travel agent. Your letter should have at least four paragraphs. Describe where you are going and what details you want the agent to take care of for you. Proofread your letter, then follow your teacher's instructions for saving and printing your work.

Memos With Copy Notations and Attachments

OBJECTIVES:

- Improve keyboarding skills.
- Format and key memos with copy notations and attachments.
- Reinforce keying from rough draft copy.

A. Warmup

Key each line 2 times.

Speed	1	The memo does not have any errors, so it can be sent today.
Accuracy	2	Pat quickly froze the gold mixtures in five old brown jars.
Language Link	3	The old woman in the shoe said, "No more children, please."
Numbers/Symbols	4	Kenny & April ordered 50# of potatoes (red) @ $.45 a pound.

| 1 | 2 | 3 | 4 | 5 | 6 | 7 | 8 | 9 | 10 | 11 | 12

SKILLBUILDING

B. Technique Timed Writings

Take two 30-second timed writings on lines 5–6. Then take two 30-second timed writings on lines 7–8. Focus on the technique at the left.

Keep your eyes on the copy.

5 We sit and toss rocks in the lake as the sun sets, but 11
6 we cannot see if they are going to skip over the big waves. 23

7 The lane that goes to the lake turns and goes to town, 11
8 but we do not know if you can use it all the way right now. 23

| 1 | 2 | 3 | 4 | 5 | 6 | 7 | 8 | 9 | 10 | 11 | 12

C. Diagnostic Practice: Alphabet

Turn to the Diagnostic Practice: Alphabet routine on page SB1. Key one of the Pretest/Posttest paragraphs and identify any errors made. Then key the corresponding drill lines 2 times for each letter on which you made 2 or more errors and 1 time for each letter on which you made only 1 error. Finally, repeat the Pretest and compare your performance.

RESUMES

OBJECTIVES:

- Refine keyboarding skills.
- Format resumes.

A. WARMUP

Key each line 2 times.

Speed	1	To build speed, work with short, easy words, not long ones.
Accuracy	2	Maxine will become eloquent over a zany gift like jodhpurs.
Language Link	3	The first deadline for the project, therefore, was not met.
Numbers/Symbols	4	She decided that 1/3 of $36 = $12 and that 20% of $30 = $6.

SKILLBUILDING

B. 30-SECOND OK TIMED WRITINGS

Take two 30-second OK (error-free) timed writings on lines 5–6. Then take two 30-second OK timed writings on lines 7–8. Goal: no errors.

5	Bea majored in zoology after she qualified for a large	12
6	research grant. She must speak with her adviser, Dr. Haver.	24
7	I am anxious because I have a dozen errands and cannot	12
8	be late for class. Have Paula adjourn this meeting quickly.	24

| 1 | 2 | 3 | 4 | 5 | 6 | 7 | 8 | 9 | 10 | 11 | 12

interNET CONNECTION

Electronic Resumes Resumes used to be sent by mail. Today, many companies prefer receiving resumes as e-mail attachments or through the company Web site. Go to the Online Learning Center at **KeyComps.glencoe.com>Internet Connection>Unit 3> Lesson 58** to learn more about applying for jobs through the Internet and complete an activity.

LETTER 60

Business Letter in Modified-Block Style With Indented Paragraphs

Key this business letter in modified-block style with indented paragraphs.

(Current Date) / Oksana Khizir / Elbrussky Prospekt 78-3 / Tyrnyanz, KBR 361600 / RUSSIA / Dear Ms. Khizir:
¶Careers in international marketing are everywhere, not only with firms involved directly with international business, but also with those that might be entering the global marketplace in the foreseeable future. Our firm, U.S. Industries, Inc., is one of those just entering the global market.
¶The CEO of our company met you last month when she was in Russia. She was impressed with your knowledge of politics, geography, and world history. Also, your sensitivity to the differences between cultures impressed her. You have mastered the English language, both written and spoken. These are all qualities necessary to have a successful career in international marketing.
¶We are hopeful that you will accept our offer of a position in our International Marketing Department.
Yours truly, / Joseph R. Murray / International Marketing Director / urs

SOCIAL STUDIES CONNECTION

List World Currencies Each kind of currency has its own symbol. For example, the symbol for the American dollar is the dollar sign: $. Create a boxed table like the one below. Key the text as shown. Fill in the symbols in column 3 by holding down the ALT key and keying the 4-digit number in column 4 on the numeric keypad. Format the table with shading and borders of your choice. Follow your teacher's instructions for saving and printing your work.

A SAMPLE OF WORLD CURRENCIES

Country	Currency	Symbol	Alt +
Costa Rica	Colon		8353
Germany	Euro		8364
Great Britain	Pound		0163
India	Rupee		8360
Israel	Sheqel		8362
Japan	Yen		0165
Laos	Kip		8365
Mexico	Peso		0036
Mongolia	Tugrik		8366
Netherlands Antilles	Guilder		0402
Nigeria	Naira		8358
Thailand	Baht		3647
Turkey	Lira		8356

C. Resumes

Once you decide to apply for a job, you will need to prepare a resume. A **resume** is a summary of your training, background, and qualifications for the job. There are many acceptable formats for resumes, but there is basic information that should be included no matter which format you choose.

1. **Heading.** Your name, address, telephone number (with area code), and e-mail address if you have one.
2. **Objective.** A statement about the type of job you are seeking.
3. **Education.** A list of your educational background beginning with the highest level of and most recent education first. Include the school name and address, any diplomas or degrees, the year you earned them, honors or awards, and your major area of study.
4. **Experience.** A list of your work experience beginning with the most recent. Include the name, address, and telephone number of the company; dates of employment; your job title(s); and the name and title of your supervisor. You may also want to include a brief description of your duties.
5. **Honors, Awards, and Activities.** Any special activities or achievements that relate to the position for which you are applying. (These may give you an "edge" over other applicants.)
6. **References.** A list of at least three people who can tell a prospective employer about what kind of worker you are. Include their names, job titles, addresses, and telephone numbers. You may want to use teachers, former supervisors, and former employers as references. Before you use a person's name as a reference, you *must* get permission from that person. Another option for references is to include the statement, "References will be furnished upon request."

(continued on next page)

LETTER 58

Business Letter in Block Style

Key the following business letter in block style.

(Current Date) / Mr. George Grinderemann / Arnoldstrabe 56 / 22256 Hamburg / GERMANY / Dear Mr. Grinderemann: /
¶The VanHughes School of Fine Arts is pleased to notify you of your acceptance into our program. George, you realize that only a select few new students are accepted each year.
¶We considered your outstanding scholastic record at your school in Hamburg, Germany, and looked favorably upon your many extracurricular activities. Our Board of Directors unanimously voted you to be our foreign exchange student of the year.
¶Next month we will be sending you more information regarding the VanHughes School of Fine Arts, its housing choices, courses of study, and the many extracurricular activities we have available. You'll find that our faculty and staff are skilled, knowledgeable, and interested only in helping you succeed in a career in fine arts.
¶We look forward to hearing from you soon.
Sincerely yours, / Dr. Paula Toddsworthy / President / urs

LETTER 59

Personal-Business Letter in Modified-Block Style

Key this personal-business letter in modified-block style.

(Current Date) / Michael Renard / EuroBureau Interim / Rue de Hesperange 5 / L-1731 / LUXEMBOURG / Dear Mr. Renard:
¶Please send me an application form for your organization. I am interested in applying for a job as a temporary office assistant/computer operator in Luxembourg during the summer months of June, July, and August.
¶I will graduate from Evergreen High School in May and will be available for employment on June 1. I speak fluent German as well as French and Italian. My clerical and computer skills are excellent. My keyboarding speed is 90 words per minute with 95 percent accuracy. I am proficient in word processing, spreadsheet, database, desktop publishing, and presentation applications.
¶I have spent the past three summers traveling in Europe, so I am familiar with the differences in culture, the various governments, and the transportation systems.
Sincerely, / Michele LaGare / 4810 South Longs Peak Road / Longmont, CO 80501

(continued)

This is one example of a formatted resume. There are many acceptable styles.

Martina Valdez
4101 Fuller Apartments
Clio, MI 48420
313-555-2714
E-mail: martina@valdez.net

OBJECTIVE

To obtain an office position with word processing responsibilities.

EDUCATION

Clio High School, Clio, MI 48420

Graduated: June 2006
Major: Computer Technology
Grade Point Average: 3.66

Business Subjects: Accounting, keyboarding (75 wpm), word processing

Honors and Activities: Student Council president during senior year; concert choir for four years; Business Student of the Year in 2006

EXPERIENCE

Rathjen Moving Co., 471 Vienna Road, Flushing, MI 48433
Telephone: 313-555-5420

June 2006 to present
Position: General Office Assistant
Supervisor: Joyce Wiesnewski, Administrative Assistant

Duties: Composing and keying routine correspondence; preparing invoices

REFERENCES

References will be furnished upon request.

E. International Addresses

International mailing addresses are similar to domestic mailing addresses. International addresses may also include:

1. Numbers, similar to our zip codes, to identify the routing of the correspondence.
2. The name of the country keyed in all capital letters as the final line of the address.

[Current Date]

Dr. David Rosenbloom
The Open University
Maks Rhoho Educational Center
255 Klausner Street
Tel-Aviv 61392
ISRAEL

Dear Dr. Rosenbloom:

The Board of Directors for the Atlanta International School, Atlanta, Georgia, (United States) is personally inviting you to become a member of their board. Your name was suggested at the summer meeting of the Foundation of International Schools in Geneva, Switzerland.

Your credentials contain most of what our personnel are seeking. We are impressed with your work as a Professor of Psychology in Tel-Aviv and notice that you have done extensive work with youth groups. Dr. Rosenbloom, we have a great need for someone with your talent and experience. We feel you could make an outstanding contribution as a member of the Board of Directors here in Atlanta.

Please respond as quickly as possible. You may telephone me at 404-555-1454 or send an e-mail to me at Aistalk@aol.com.

Yours truly,

Dr. Lien Vandermark, President
Atlanta International School

[initials]

REPORT 15

Resume

Key the resume that is illustrated on page 206 using the same format. Follow these steps:

1. Use default margins.
2. Center and key the name in 14-point bold.
3. Center and key each line in the heading; then press ENTER 2 times.
4. Key the side heading *OBJECTIVE* in all caps and bold; then press ENTER 2 times.
5. Align the remaining text at the left margin. Leave a blank line between sections.
6. Leave a blank line before and after the bold side headings.

REPORT 16

Resume

Prepare a resume for yourself using the guidelines in this lesson. Include all sections that are applicable to your background. Do not include a section if you have no entries to place in that section.

PORTFOLIO Activity

Update Your Resume Add the resume you created in Report 16 to your portfolio. It is important to continue to "fine-tune" the resume as you continue taking courses or gaining additional work experiences.

You should also prepare a list of people you want to use as references, and ask those people for permission to list their names. Your list should include the references' names, titles, addresses, and telephone numbers. Update the list periodically so that when you are looking for a job you have the most complete and recent information. Follow your teacher's instructions for saving and printing your work.

SKILLBUILDING

C. Preview Practice

Key each line 2 times as a preview to the timed writings that follow.

Accuracy quickly compete realizing technology innovative information
Speed swift human entry same with time life five jobs who few new

D. 5-Minute Timed Writings

Take two 5-minute timed writings on the paragraphs. Note your speed and errors.

Goal: 36/5'/5e

Many factors changed in the workplace as we moved 11
into the new century. A stronger force in the economy at 23
this time is the rapid growth in the information industry. 34
The picture for employment is quickly being changed by 46
advances in technology. Just a few years ago, high school 58
graduates who were trained in most business skills could be 70
hired in entry jobs and grow in these same fields with 82
little or no training. 84

This is no longer true. Most office jobs now demand 94
workers with creative and innovative talents as well as 105
good human relations and computer skills. Many technical 117
school and college students are now realizing that most of 129
the skills they have learned may be outdated in five or six 141
years because of these swift changes. The world of work is 152
being changed so fast that workers must be willing and able 164
to adapt. Workers who compete are going to be those who are 176
learners for life. 180

SI 1.35

| 1 | 2 | 3 | 4 | 5 | 6 | 7 | 8 | 9 | 10 | 11 | 12

LESSON 59 APPLICATION LETTERS

OBJECTIVES:

- Improve keyboarding skills.
- Format application letters.

A. WARMUP

Key each line 2 times.

Speed	1	Janet works after school four hours a day at the town bank.
Accuracy	2	Buzz quickly designed five new projects for the wax museum.
Language Link	3	We changed the recipe by adding pecans, dates, and raisins.
Numbers/Symbols	4	Interest charged on the $7,000 loan is 15% (down from 17%).

| 1 | 2 | 3 | 4 | 5 | 6 | 7 | 8 | 9 | 10 | 11 | 12

ETHICS CONNECTION

Workplace Ethics An employee may believe that leaving work 10 minutes early each day is not significant. Imagine you are an employer of 60 employees who are making $15 an hour. If all 60 employees leave work 10 minutes early one day, the accumulated time lost is 10 hours. This costs you $150. Calculate how much your company would lose if this behavior went on for the five-day work week, the month (20 days), and the year (250 days). Key a paragraph describing your results and their significance for employers.

SKILLBUILDING

B. 12-SECOND SPRINTS

Take three 12-second timed writings on each line. Try to increase your speed each time.

5 The time had come for Bev to study for college final exams.
6 Be sure to relax, rest, and have a good meal before a test.
7 Sean scored better on this test than on the test last week.
8 Jo wants a drill that will be easy to read and fast to key.

| | | | |5| | | |10| | | |15| | | |20| | | |25| | | |30| | | |35| | | |40| | | |45| | | |50| | | |55| | | |60

LESSON 98 Letters With International Addresses

OBJECTIVES:

- Eliminate redundant wording.
- Key 36/5'/5e.
- Format and key letters with international addresses.

A. Warmup

Key each line 2 times.

Speed	1	You can opt to leave things as they are and make no change.
Accuracy	2	Jacqueline was vexed by the folks who got the money prizes.
Language Link	3	The vice president said, "Let's use dates we can maintain."
Numbers/Symbols	4	Take a 3-, 4-, and 5-minute timing on 186-C, pages 279-280.

| 1 | 2 | 3 | 4 | 5 | 6 | 7 | 8 | 9 | 10 | 11 | 12

Language Link

B. Composing at the Keyboard

Redundancy is using several words that mean the same thing. For example, instead of using the phrase, "the same identical items," use either "the same items" or "the identical items."

Key the following paragraph and eliminate the redundant wording.

When driving to school, I take the same identical route each day. I have a car that is small in size. Two friends ride along with me. Each and every day we get to class at about the same time. One day we tried another different route and got lost. We rode around in circles before we found our way. We repeatedly asked many times for directions. The only other alternative we had was to not repeat again the exact same route. We decided we would continue using our original old route.

C. PRETEST

Take a 1-minute timed writing on the paragraph. Note your speed and errors.

```
9       Most people work hard to improve their writing skills.  11
10  They make the nucleus of what they desire to say clearer    23
11  by poring over their rough drafts. They bring home their    34
12  point by rewriting, if necessary, and replacing some words. 46
    | 1 | 2 | 3 | 4 | 5 | 6 | 7 | 8 | 9 | 10 | 11 | 12
```

D. PRACTICE

SPEED: ***If you made 2 or fewer errors on the Pretest, key lines 13–20 two times each.***

ACCURACY: ***If you made more than 2 errors on the Pretest, key lines 13–16 as a group two times. Then key lines 17–20 as a group two times.***

Adjacent Reaches

```
13  tr trip trade trait strain trolls truck strive tromp trials
14  po polka potter pomp point pot pork power poster poker pore
15  re renter remember resting rewrite reptiles referees recite
16  sa sample sank salmon sap sack saws sags sable savor sabers
```

Jump Reaches

```
17  mo money motor motley most mock mower mop mobile monkey moo
18  br break brake brain bracket brick brook broke brat bramble
19  nu nut number nurture numb null nurse nuclear knuckle nutty
20  ce recede center cellular celery cement certain censor celt
```

E. POSTTEST

Repeat the Pretest. Compare your Posttest results with your Pretest results.

LANGUAGE ARTS CONNECTION

Describe Yourself Key the following paragraph, then key another paragraph below it that answers the following question: *How would you best describe yourself?* Follow your teacher's instructions for saving and printing your work.

The purpose of an application letter is to get an interview. When you go for an interview, dress neatly and appropriately. Be prepared to answer questions such as: Why do you think we should hire you for this job? How would you best describe yourself? What experience do you have? In addition, listen carefully to the interviewer, look at the interviewer when you speak, avoid nervous gestures, speak clearly, and answer questions honestly.

TABLE 40
Boxed Table

Create a 3-column, 9-row boxed table in portrait orientation. Merge cells 1 and 2 in row 9. Add 20 percent shading to row 2. Add a double line below row 2 and above row 9. Use the SUM formula to calculate the total salaries. Format the total with a comma and no decimals.

BRANCH MANAGER SALARIES **January 1, {year}**		
Office	**Manager**	**Salary**
Atlanta	Harrison Wilson	69,750
Boston	Audrey Pritchett	63,900
Chicago	Martin Sellers	62,800
Dallas	Leigh Martinez	68,500
Salt Lake City	William Beauchamp	64,350
Tulsa	Isabella Montgomery	68,890
TOTAL SALARIES		

TABLE 41
Boxed Table

Open Table 39 and make the following changes:

1. Insert row 8 at the bottom of the table.
2. Select row 8. Use the Custom option in the Borders tab to remove the inside borders in row 8; then key *TOTAL PURCHASES* at the left.
3. Use the SUM formula to calculate the total of column 3. Format the total with a dollar sign and two decimal places.
4. Add 15 percent shading to row 8.
5. Add a double line above row 8.

SOCIAL STUDIES CONNECTION

Create a Cultures and Color Chart In China, basic colors have specific associations. Create a new table with 2 columns and 7 rows. In the first row, key the title *COLOR ASSOCIATIONS IN CHINA*. Key the text below in column 1. Shade the cells in column 2 with the appropriate colors. Follow your teacher's instructions for saving and printing your work.

White is the color of mourning. / Black is associated with funerals. / Yellow represents prosperity. / Blue is the color of workers' uniforms. / Red is associated with good fortune and happiness. / Green, the color of jade, is considered lucky.

F. Application Letters

An application letter is written to apply for a position. Your resume should be enclosed with the letter. Since this may be the first impression an employer has of you, be sure that your letter and resume are each a single page, neat, accurate, and contain all the essential information.

An application letter should contain the following paragraphs:

Paragraph 1: The purpose of the letter, the job for which you are applying, and how you learned of the opening.
Paragraph 2: The qualifications that make you especially suited for the position. Mention experience you have that can help the employer and the company. Refer to the resume you are enclosing.
Paragraph 3: Special skills that will set you apart from other applicants. For example, do you work well with other people? Are you very well organized? Are you proficient at using various machines?
Paragraph 4: A request for an interview. Restate your interest in the job and indicate when you will be available. Include a telephone number where an employer can easily reach you.

*inter*NET CONNECTION

Compose an Application Letter Find out about the qualifications that you might need for different types of jobs. Go to the Online Learning Center at **KeyComps.glencoe.com>Internet Connection>Unit 3>Lesson 59**. Find a job description that you find interesting. Then compose an application letter for the position.

In the letter, describe your qualifications and why you are interested in the job. Mention that you are enclosing a resume. Format your letter correctly, and be sure to proofread it carefully and correct all errors. Ask your teacher or a classmate to review your letter to make sure it covers the content mentioned in Section F above. With your teacher's permission, print a copy of the letter for your portfolio.

C. PRACTICE

In the chart below, find the number of errors you made on the Pretest. Then key each of the designated drill lines 2 times.

Pretest Errors	0–1	2	3	4+
Drill Lines	12–16	11–15	10–14	9–13

Accuracy

```
 9 useful column divide multiply formulas required spreadsheet
10 work using useful effort subtract numbers software required
11 numbs numeric division formulate subtraction multiplication
12 actions addition columnar requisite effortless requisitions
```

Speed

```
13 column meets with will used know kind for one use and of by
14 tool soft save hour form ware sheet one can use add row how
15 working rowing tools knows your full cane can you use if to
16 subs work add use the add are you how add it an if is on or
```

D. POSTTEST

Repeat the Pretest. Compare your Posttest results with your Pretest results.

WORD PROCESSING APPLICATIONS

TABLE 39
Boxed Table

Create a 5-column, 7-row boxed table in landscape orientation. Center the table vertically and horizontally. Add 20 percent shading to row 2. Add a double line below row 2. Adjust the column widths so that all entries fit on a single line.

DATA WORKS, INC. **Monthly Hardware Purchases** **April {year}**				
Customer Name	**Account No.**	**Price**	**Telephone No.**	**Item Description**
Crockett, Rhonda	F901-76-3488	269.10	505-555-8900	17″ .42 mm flat panel monitor
Hembree, Eric	K854-00-3550	299.99	505-555-3409	48-bit color scanner
Luhn, Mario	L258-04-3891	529.99	505-555-7833	Color laser printer
Recendis, Rhet	P789-00-3548	149.95	505-555-6673	48X CD-RW and 16X CD-ROM drive
Upchurch, Joey	T901-75-3487	211.65	505-555-7834	15″ .28 mm flat panel monitor

LETTER 23

Personal-Business Letter in Block Style

Format the following application letter in block style. Review the format of a personal-business letter in Lesson 48.

June 12, {year}

Mrs. Carlotta Nguyen
Richardson Insurance Agency
One Washington Boulevard
Fort Worth, TX 76126

Dear Mrs. Nguyen:

One of the participants in a career fair at my high school, Mr. Curtiss Hall, mentioned that you have an opening for an office assistant in your downtown office. I would like to be considered as an applicant for that position.

My extensive training and experience in the use of various software programs will enable me to serve Richardson Insurance Agency as a competent employee. As you will see on my enclosed resume, my computer skills helped me win two awards in competitions at the regional and state levels. Also, I have excellent grades in all of my high school business courses.

I have taken an active leadership role in school. I was president of our chapter of Future Business Leaders of America, and I served as secretary of my class during my junior and senior years. These activities have provided me with valuable leadership and teamwork skills. They also gave me an opportunity to put my office skills to practical use.

I am very interested in working for Richardson Insurance Agency. I will telephone your office by the end of this week to arrange for an interview with you at your convenience. If you would like to speak with me before that time, please telephone me at my home number, 901-555-3245, after 4 p.m.

Sincerely,

Patrice McCrea
2316 S. Cravens
Fort Worth, TX 76132

Enclosure

LESSON 97 REVIEW

OBJECTIVES:

- Improve keyboarding skills.
- Reinforce tables with sums.

A. WARMUP

Key each line 2 times.

Speed	1	You must work very hard at this job to improve your skills.
Accuracy	2	Brown jars would prevent the mixture from freezing quickly.
Language Link	3	The president said, "Let's give support to our leadership."
Numbers/Symbols	4	The L & C 10 3/4% bonds (due 2013) are at 175; bid 169 3/8.

| 1 | 2 | 3 | 4 | 5 | 6 | 7 | 8 | 9 | 10 | 11 | 12

LANGUAGE ARTS CONNECTION

Create Examples of Alliteration Alliteration is the repetition of sounds, most often at the beginnings of words and syllables, such as *red rock.* Poets often use alliteration to create a mood.

Key the *A* sentence below. Then compose and key sentences for the letters *B, C,* and *D,* using as many alliterative words as possible. Follow your teacher's instructions for saving and printing your work.

Alice always agrees with Andrew about attracting an audience.

SKILLBUILDING

B. PRETEST

Take a 1-minute timed writing on the paragraph. Note your speed and errors.

5 A spreadsheet is a useful software tool if you know 11
6 how to use one. You can save hours of effort if you are 22
7 required to work with rows and columns of numbers by using 34
8 formulas to add, subtract, multiply, and divide numbers. 45

| 1 | 2 | 3 | 4 | 5 | 6 | 7 | 8 | 9 | 10 | 11 | 12

LETTER 24

Personal-Business Letter in Block Style

Format the following handwritten application letter in block style. Remember to include the current date and an enclosure notation. Use your name and address for the writer's name and address.

Mr. Darnell Makulski
Human Resources Department
The Rogers Group
21771 Telegraph, Suite 3000
Columbus, OH 43231

Dear Mr. Makulski:

I would like to apply for the position of Administrative Assistant for your company. My high school English teacher, Ms. Lorie Gold, informed me of this position.

The experience I gained working summers as a volunteer office clerk for the American Heart Society qualifies me for the position with your company. My enclosed resume shows that most of my duties involved daily use of keyboarding, filing, and communications skills. This experience would be especially beneficial to your company.

My computer skills and my English skills are well above average, and I feel that I could perform any of the jobs I would be called upon to do with a high degree of competence.

It would be a pleasure to work for your company as an administrative assistant. Please allow me the opportunity to discuss my special qualifications with you in greater detail during an interview. You can reach me at my home number, 301-555-4774, any time after 3 p.m.

Sincerely,

TABLE 36
Boxed Table

Create a 3-column, 8-row boxed table. Align the column headings as shown. Center the table vertically and horizontally, and automatically adjust the columns. Use the SUM formula to calculate the totals of columns 2 and 3.

QUARTERLY SALES REPORT **First Quarter**		
Salesperson	**Quarterly Total ($)**	**Quarterly Average ($)**
Cochran, Richard	34,757	11,586
Duffy, Theodora	39,154	15,829
Frances, Parker	49,721	16,778
Hebert, Theresa	43,198	13,862
Minichiello, Pat	40,500	13,754
TOTAL		

TABLE 37
Boxed Table

Open Table 30 and make the following changes:

1. Change the page orientation to landscape.
2. Remove all of the shading from the table.
3. Insert row 15 at the bottom of the table.
4. Merge cells 1, 2, 3, and 4 in row 15, and key *TOTAL COST* at the left.
5. Use the SUM formula to calculate the total of column 5. Format the total with a dollar sign and two decimal places.
6. Add 15 percent shading to rows of resources that cost over $20.

TABLE 38
Boxed Table

Open Table 32 and make the following changes:

1. Insert row 13 at the bottom of the table.
2. Merge cells 1 and 2 in row 13, and key *TOTALS* at the left.
3. Use the SUM formula to calculate the totals of columns 3 and 4.
4. Format the total of column 3 with a dollar sign, a comma, and no decimal.
5. Format the total of column 4 with a comma and no decimal.
6. Add a double line above row 13.
7. Add 10 percent shading to row 13.

LESSON 60 REVIEW

OBJECTIVES:

- Apply rules for semicolons.
- Key 33/3'/5e.
- Compose and key an application letter.
- Review personal-business and business letters.

A. Warmup

Key each line 2 times.

Speed	1	The old man paid for the yard work before he left for town.
Accuracy	2	Ezra jokingly vowed to question tax payments for his cabin.
Language Link	3	The woman, however, was unable to provide proper childcare.
Numbers	4	Send them to 6738 East 29 Street, Chicago, 60610 by May 19.

| 1 | 2 | 3 | 4 | 5 | 6 | 7 | 8 | 9 | 10 | 11 | 12

LANGUAGE LINK

B. Semicolons

Study the rule and the example that follows. Then correct any errors in punctuation in lines 5–8.

Rule 8: Use a semicolon between two independent clauses when one or both clauses have commas in them.

We ordered peanuts, popcorn, and candy; but only peanuts and candy were sent.

5 We saw Jake, Pat, and Leo but Jim, Hal, and Ray were gone.
6 Lea needs a mouse, a disk, and a CD but she has a printer.
7 Jay took music, art, and math he needs speech and science.
8 She got cards, gifts, and a cake I took her out to dinner.

C. PRACTICE

In the chart below, find the number of errors you made on the Pretest. Then key each of the designated drill lines 2 times.

Pretest Errors	0–1	2	3	4+
Drill Lines	12–16	11–15	10–14	9–13

Accuracy

```
9  similar involves subjects effective expressions appropriate
10 styles effect affects writing similar sentences expressions
11 choice always involve subjective similarity appropriateness
12 style express involving difference expressive appropriately
```

Speed

```
13 writes always makes what ways your the and but may in be to
14 express subject effect affect word idea read you all the in
15 choices choice differ words word what that ways sent and is
16 press tense rents want what read sent ice sub sty off to be
```

D. POSTTEST

Repeat the Pretest. Compare your Posttest results with your Pretest results.

E. Diagnostic Practice: Alphabet

Turn to the Diagnostic Practice: Alphabet routine on page SB1. Key one of the Pretest/Posttest paragraphs and identify any errors made. Then key the corresponding drill lines 2 times for each letter on which you made 2 or more errors and 1 time for each letter on which you made only 1 error. Finally, repeat the Pretest and compare your performance.

FORMATTING

F. Totals in Tables

A formula may be inserted into a table cell to perform various calculations. To add a row or column of numbers, you can use the **SUM function**. The SUM function is a built-in formula that adds a range of cells.

G. Software Features

STUDENT MANUAL

Formulas

Study Lesson 96 in your Student Manual. Complete all the practice activities while at your computer. Then complete the tasks that follow.

SKILLBUILDING

C. Preview Practice

Key each line 2 times as a preview to the timings that follow.

Accuracy	9	civil Morse major years amazing quickly seventeen telegraph
Speed	10	known short stood prior five code sent help dots not out it

D. 3-Minute Timed Writings

Take two 3-minute timed writings on lines 11–19. Note your speed and errors.

Goal: 33/3'/5e

11	Samuel Morse was an artist. Today, however, he's known	11
12	not for his major works of art but instead for inventing the	23
13	telegraph and the code it uses. With the help of his friend,	34
14	Alfred Vail, Morse made up a code of dashes and dots that	45
15	stood for numbers and letters. Text could be sent with this	57
16	code by using long and short signals.	67
17	Seventeen years prior to the Civil War, Samuel Morse	78
18	tapped out his very first message in Morse code. It was	89
19	quickly received an amazing thirty-five miles away.	99

SI 1.37

| 1 | 2 | 3 | 4 | 5 | 6 | 7 | 8 | 9 | 10 | 11 | 12

SOCIAL STUDIES CONNECTION

Compare Workweeks Key the following paragraph. Below the paragraph, key a description of your ideal workweek and hours. Follow your teacher's instructions for saving and printing your work.

The length of the workday and days of the week people work are different in various countries. Many companies, especially those in warmer climates, close their business for two to four hours during the middle of the day. In some countries, Thursday and Friday are days off with one day reserved for worship. The Korean workweek is Monday through Saturday and sometimes Sunday.

TOTALS IN TABLES

OBJECTIVES:

- Improve keyboarding skills.
- Apply the sum formula feature in tables.
- Reinforce the use of borders in tables.

A. WARMUP

Key each line 2 times.

Speed	1	Divide a big job into small tasks and do them step by step.
Accuracy	2	Six big men quickly won over Jeff despite his greater size.
Language Link	3	Mom said, “Who wants cake?” to which Becky replied, “I do.”
Numbers/Symbols	4	Invoice #23654, dated March 19, for 73 A-18 was 2/10, n/30.

| 1 | 2 | 3 | 4 | 5 | 6 | 7 | 8 | 9 | 10 | 11 | 12

LANGUAGE ARTS CONNECTION

Create a Time Management Table Key the following 1-column open table. Add a final row, then compose and key your own time management tip. Follow your teacher's instructions for saving and printing your work.

TIPS FOR TIME MANAGEMENT
Identify what must be done each day.
Prioritize your activities.
Develop a schedule to do the important things.

SKILLBUILDING

B. PRETEST

Take a 1-minute timed writing on the paragraph. Note your speed and errors.

5 Effective writing always involves the choice of words 11
6 and expressions. Sentences may express similar ideas, but 23
7 style is what makes the words affect readers in different 35
8 ways. Your style should be appropriate to your subject. 46

| 1 | 2 | 3 | 4 | 5 | 6 | 7 | 8 | 9 | 10 | 11 | 12

LETTER 25

Personal-Business Letter in Block Style

Compose and key a letter of application for the position in the classified ad shown below. Review Lesson 59 before you begin composing. Review the format for personal-business letters and block-style letters in Lesson 48.

> **ADMINISTRATIVE ASSISTANT**
>
> Fast-paced, downtown office seeks full-time administrative assistant. Applicants must key 40 wpm, be proficient in word processing, have some desktop publishing knowledge, and be detail oriented. We offer competitive salary and benefits. Send resume to:
>
> Human Resources Office
> Suite 200
> 4700 Village Road
> Columbus, Ohio 43235

LETTER 26

Business Letter in Modified-Block Style

Key the following letter in modified-block style. Use the current date and remember to add an enclosure notation and your reference initials.

Ms. Marcia Chisholm / 15 Lynch Street / Mobile, AL 36604 / Dear Ms. Chisholm:
¶Our conference on November 3 and 4 was a great success. Your expertise helped to generate solid plans for the program, and I thank you for two positive days.
¶Enclosed are the summary of notes from our meeting, a new outline of your book, and a list of concerns about the outline. Please review these materials and let me know if you have any changes. As you recall, we did not have time to discuss everything on our agenda at the meeting.
¶As you review the outline, please check for the correct sequence and whether or not it is complete. Please provide your suggestions and concerns to me by December 4. I look forward to hearing from you.
Sincerely yours, / Diane Daniels / Editorial Advisor

TABLE 33

Boxed Table

Open Table 25 and make the following changes:

1. Delete the last three rows in the table.
2. Insert three new rows at the bottom of the table, and add the following information:
   Row 10: April 7 / Pebblebrook High School / Home
   Row 11: April 12 / North Cobb High School / Away
   Row 12: April 15 / Dorsett Shoals High School / Home

TABLE 34

Boxed Table

Open Table 27 and make the following changes:

1. Change the subtitle to 1969-2005.
2. Delete rows 3, 4, 5, and 6.
3. Add 20 percent shading to the rows of presidents who were Democrats.

TABLE 35

Boxed Table

Open Table 34 and make the following changes:

1. Change the page orientation to landscape.
2. Change the title to **U.S. PRESIDENTS, VICE PRESIDENTS, PARTY, AND YEARS IN OFFICE.**
3. Insert a new column after column 1 with the heading **Vice President**.
4. Add the following entries to column 2: Gerald R. Ford / Spiro T. Agnew / Walter F. Mondale / George H. W. Bush / J. Danforth Quayle / Albert A. Gore, Jr. / Richard B. Cheney

Research the White House The White House has a rich historical heritage as the home and office of the president of the United States. Go to the Online Learning Center at **KeyComps.glencoe.com>Social Studies Connection>Unit 5>Lesson 95** and read the information about the history of the White House. Then create an open table similar to the one below and fill in the missing facts. Follow your teacher's instructions for saving and printing your work.

FACTS ABOUT THE WHITE HOUSE	
Address of the White House	
First President to Live in the White House	
Name of the President's Office	
Number of Rooms	
Owner of the White House	

UNIT 4 WORD PROCESSING

Lessons 61–80

OBJECTIVES

- Demonstrate keyboarding speed and accuracy on straight copy with a goal of 35 words per minute for 3 minutes with 5 or fewer errors.
- Demonstrate correct use of word processing features.
- Demonstrate an understanding of proofreaders' symbols by editing copy marked for revision.
- Demonstrate basic formatting skills on a variety of tables, reports with special features, and multipage reports from a variety of copy—arranged, unarranged, rough draft, and handwritten.
- Compose sentences and short paragraphs at the keyboard.
- Apply the rules for subject/verb agreement.
- Apply the rules for using semicolons, commas, and capitalization.

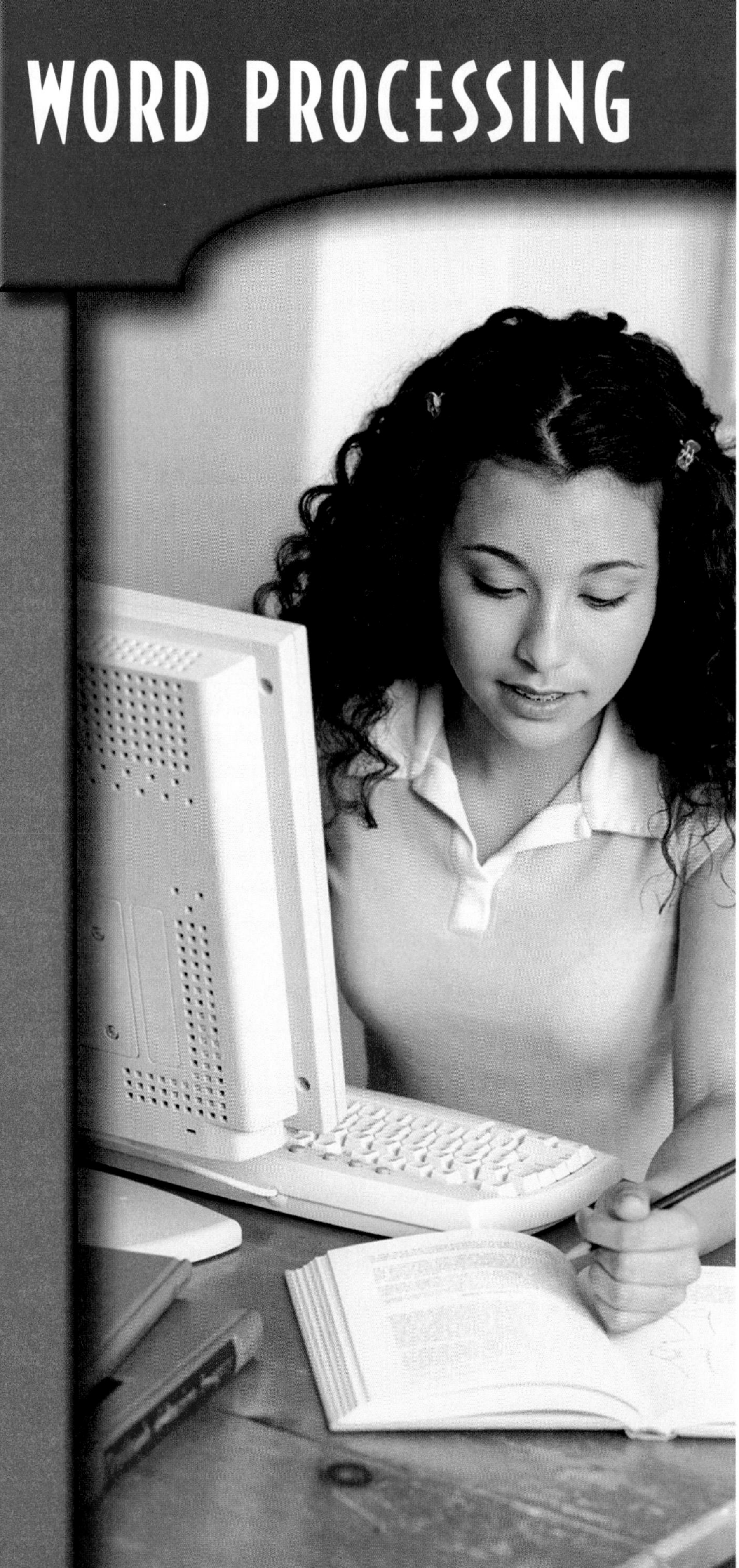

SKILLBUILDING

C. PRETEST

Take a 1-minute timed writing on the paragraph. Note your speed and errors.

```
9       If you think you might enjoy a vacation by the sea for   11
10  relaxing or catching some fish, a trip to your local travel  23
11  agent may provide you with all kinds of information to help  35
12  you. A little advance planning could improve your trip.      46
    | 1 | 2 | 3 | 4 | 5 | 6 | 7 | 8 | 9 | 10 | 11 | 12
```

D. PRACTICE

SPEED: ***If you made 2 or fewer errors on the Pretest, key lines 13–20 two times each.***

ACCURACY: ***If you made more than 2 errors on the Pretest, key lines 13–16 as a group two times. Then key lines 17–20 as a group two times.***

```
13  dark each felt fate harm idea abide barns clock depth earns
14  jobs kits lawn mark nail ours filed guest hotel judge lapse
15  pile rank self take used wage maple named often pairs range
16  with girl rake hand mail tops label moron felon flair throw

17  able bake camp film know lack about baked canal drink enjoy
18  nova only pack rank sink tank knack labor scout thank valid
19  vain acre have knew save wave acute blank candy habit known
20  lawn fact yolk lump cast limp hilly rests cages lumpy blame
```

E. POSTTEST

Repeat the Pretest. Compare your Posttest results with your Pretest results.

FORMATTING

F. SOFTWARE FEATURES

STUDENT MANUAL

Inserting Rows
Inserting Columns

Deleting Rows
and Columns

Study Lesson 95 in your Student Manual. Complete all the practice activities while at your computer. Then complete the tasks that follow.

WORDS TO LEARN

In the lessons, software, and Student Manual (SM), you will learn the following vocabulary terms for Unit 4.

cell (p. 235)
column headings (p. 242)
endnotes (p. 270)
footers (SM, Lesson 73)
footnotes (p. 270)
indents (SM, Lesson 72)
headers (SM, Lesson 73)
leaders (SM, Lesson 78)
merge cells (p. 251)
MLA style (p. 258)
parenthetical reference (p. 258)
postscript (p. 224)
table (p. 235; SM Lesson 65)

CAREER BYTE

AIR TRAFFIC CONTROLLER Air traffic controllers ensure the safe operation of commercial and private aircraft in and out of the airport. Relying on radar and visual observation, they closely monitor each plane. The Federal Aviation Administration (FAA) is currently developing and implementing a new automated air traffic control system. As a result, more powerful computers will help controllers deal with the demands of increased air traffic. Some traditional air traffic controller tasks—like determining how far apart planes should be kept—will be done by computer. Improved communication between computers on airplanes and those on the ground is making the controller's job a little easier.

LESSON 95

TABLES: ADD/DELETE COLUMNS AND ROWS

OBJECTIVES:

- Apply rules for quotation marks.
- Increase keyboarding speed and improve accuracy.
- Add and delete table columns and rows.

A. WARMUP

Key each line 2 times.

Speed	1	It takes two hands to make the dough for pizza flat enough.
Accuracy	2	Had Jeff's size helped him to win quickly over Gene Baxter?
Language Link	3	In the past two weeks, LaTasha has passed all of her tests.
Symbols	4	The word court can be a location. (I'll see them in court!)

| 1 | 2 | 3 | 4 | 5 | 6 | 7 | 8 | 9 | 10 | 11 | 12

LANGUAGE LINK

B. QUOTATION MARKS WITH DIRECT QUOTATIONS

Study the rule and examples below. Then edit lines 5–8 to correct any errors in the use of quotation marks.

Rule 20: Use quotation marks to enclose a **direct quotation,** that is, the exact words of a speaker or a writer. Notice that the punctuation is placed inside the final quotation mark.

Robert said, "That is the highest grade on this project."

5 Mrs. Woo said, Rea is being considered for the promotion.
6 Yes, Jill, you're still in the running, replied Ms. Paul.
7 Ben cried, Someone stole the library book I need tomorrow.
8 Diane asked me, When did they come to take your computer?

Letters With Copy and Delivery Notations

OBJECTIVES:

- Improve keyboarding skills.
- Format letters with copy and delivery notations.

A. Warmup

Key each line 2 times.

Speed	1	I feel sure he will be here in time to drive the boys home.
Accuracy	2	Six jumped from the quarry blaze, right into Lake Cragview.
Language Link	3	Li has red, blue, and pink; but she needs green and yellow.
Numbers/Symbols	4	Ryan saw Jack's dog's leash on Tim's brother's front porch.
		| 1 | 2 | 3 | 4 | 5 | 6 | 7 | 8 | 9 | 10 | 11 | 12

SKILLBUILDING

B. 30-Second Timed Writings

Take two 30-second timed writings on lines 5–6, then two 30-second timed writings on lines 7–8. Try to increase your speed each time.

5	Rush to finish the drill lines before time runs out.	11
6	Keep wrists and arms quiet as your fingers strike the keys.	23
7	When the batter heard that sound of breaking glass, he	11
8	knew without looking that the home run had truly gone home.	23
	| 1 | 2 | 3 | 4 | 5 | 6 | 7 | 8 | 9 | 10 | 11 | 12	

C. Diagnostic Practice: Alphabet

Turn to the Diagnostic Practice: Alphabet routine on page SB-1. Key one of the Pretest/Posttest paragraphs and note your errors. Then key the corresponding drill lines 2 times for each letter on which you made 2 or more errors and 1 time for each letter on which you made only 1 error. Finally, repeat the same Pretest and compare your performance.

TABLE 32
Boxed Table

Change the page orientation to landscape. Then create a 4-column, 12-row boxed table. Center the table vertically and horizontally. Press ENTER 1 time before keying the column headings in columns 1 and 2. Align number columns at the right. Add 10 percent shading to row 2. Add a double line above row 2. Add double lines between columns. Adjust the column widths so they are similar to the illustration.

PROJECTIONS FOR HIGHER-PAYING CAREERS **2002-2012**			
Rank	**Occupation**	**Average Yearly Earnings**	**Average Yearly Openings**
1	General and Operations Managers	$68,200	76,000
2	Computer Systems Analysts	$62,900	23,300
3	Management Analysts	$60,300	25,500
4	Postsecondary Teachers	$49,100	96,000
5	Registered Nurses	$48,100	110,000
6	Accountants and Auditors	$47,000	40,500
7	Secondary School Teachers	$44,000	45,800
8	Special Education Teachers	$43,500	23,300
9	Police/Sheriff Patrol Officers	$42,300	31,300
10	Administrative Assistants	$33,400	42,400

PORTFOLIO *Activity*

Evaluate Tables Look through all of the tables that you have completed. Choose the best boxed table that includes a border style and shading. Add that table and the best open table to your portfolio. If necessary, correct any errors you may have made. Follow your teacher's instructions for saving and printing your work.

D. Copy Notations

When you send a copy of a letter to someone in addition to the addressee, key a **copy notation** on the letter.

1. Key the copy notation on the line below the reference initials or below the enclosure or attachment notation.
2. At the left margin, key a lowercase *c* followed by a colon *(c:)*.
3. Press the SPACE BAR 1 time, and key the name of the person receiving the copy. If more than one person is to receive a copy, key the names on one line, separated by a comma and space between each name.
4. Use a title before the name only if the first name or initial is unknown.

When you do not want the addressee to know that someone else is to receive a copy, use the notation *bc:* (blind copy). To add a blind copy notation:

1. Print one copy of the letter.
2. Key the *bc* notation on the copy of a letter only, 2 lines below the last item in the letter. Print one copy of the letter to send to the addressee; then add the blind copy notation and print another copy.

Please let us know if we may visit your department and what time and date would be most convenient for you.

Sincerely,

Jason DiMartini
President

ws
c: Carole Ames, David Morales, Michael Vasajian

bc: Ben Gladstone

TABLE 31
Boxed Table

Change the page orientation to landscape. Then create a 5-column, 12-row boxed table. Center the table vertically and horizontally. Align text columns at the left and number columns at the right. Automatically adjust the column widths to fit the content. Add 20 percent shading to row 2 and double lines below it.

PROJECTIONS FOR FAST-GROWTH OCCUPATIONS
2002-2012

Rank	Occupation	Percent of Projected Growth	States with Highest Projected Growth	Projected Earnings
1	Medical Assistants	59	Idaho, Arizona, Arkansas	$27,000
2	Data Communications Analysts	57	Idaho, Nevada, Utah	$64,000
3	Physician Assistants	49	Arizona, Idaho, Utah	$65,000
4	Social and Human Service Assistants	49	Idaho, Nevada, Arizona	$27,000
5	Home Health Aides	48	Arizona, Utah, Idaho	$20,000
6	Medical and Health Records Technicians	47	Arizona, Nevada, Idaho	$30,000
7	Physical Therapist Aides	46	Idaho, Utah, Arizona	$25,000
8	Computer Applications Software Engineers	46	Wyoming, New Hampshire, Utah	$78,000
9	Computer Systems Software Engineers	45	New Mexico, Montana, Utah	$80,000
10	Physical Therapist Assistants	45	Arizona, Idaho, Arkansas	$39,000

E. Delivery Notations

When a letter is being sent by a special method (fax, registered, certified, etc.), key the appropriate notation on the line below the reference initials. For example, a letter that is being faxed would have the notation *By fax* below the reference initials.

jrt
By fax

jrt
By registered mail
c: Chris Brunet

jrt
Enclosure
By Federal Express

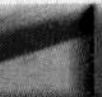

WORD PROCESSING APPLICATIONS

LETTER 27

Business Letter in Modified-Block Style

Format this letter in modified-block style. Address a No. 10 envelope to the addressee, and add it to the document.

(Current Date) / Mr. Theodis Chamberlin / 17934 Roscommon Lane / Detroit, MI 48227 / Dear Mr. Chamberlin: ¶Enclosed is the TSA loan form that you requested when we talked today. Please complete the form by filling out the highlighted areas, and return the form to me in the enclosed envelope.
¶If you elect to pay via checking account, please attach a voided check. If you elect to pay by savings account, fill out the information requested about your savings account.
¶I am pleased to tell you that I have been assigned as your financial advisor as of today. Call me if you have any questions about completing the form.
Yours truly, / Tamika Murphy / urs / Enclosures / c: Karl Mendoza

interNET CONNECTION

Online Banking Bank customers no longer need to write checks or wait on lines to deposit money. Today's technology-savvy customers can have paychecks sent electronically to their bank accounts, and they can also send checks directly from the bank's online resources. Find out more about using your computer to manage money by going to the Online Learning Center at **KeyComps.glencoe.com>Internet Connection>Unit 4>Lesson 61**.

(continued)

5 Sean (passed, past) the cycle driver (to, too, two) quickly to see who he was.
6 From (passed, past) experience, I have learned how (to, too, two) handle the job.
7 The (to, too, two) sisters were much (to, too, two) shy to go (to, too, two) the party alone.
8 Don said that he will go (to, too, two) the committee meeting tomorrow.

SKILLBUILDING

C. 30-Second OK Timed Writings

Take two 30-second OK (error-free) timed writings on lines 9–10. Then take two 30-second OK timed writings on lines 11–12. Goal: no errors.

9 We are expecting two quite sizable contracts in June 11
10 from Houston Federal Credit Union and Yonkers Savings Bank. 23

11 They were amazed that they were able to cut expenses 11
12 so quickly by reducing their television advertising budget. 23

| 1 | 2 | 3 | 4 | 5 | 6 | 7 | 8 | 9 | 10 | 11 | 12

FORMATTING

D. Tables: Page Orientation

The default page orientation for 8.5 × 11 inch paper is vertical, or **portrait.** A page may also be formatted in horizontal orientation, or **landscape.**

E. Software Features

STUDENT MANUAL

Changing Page Orientation

Study Lesson 94 in your Student Manual. Complete all the practice activities while at your computer. Then complete the tasks that follow.

LETTER 28

Business Letter in Block Style

Remember that a blind copy notation requires printing the letter a second time.

Format this letter in block style. Address a No. 10 envelope and add it to the document.

(Current Date) / Ms. Annette Birdsong / General Manager / Fabric Palace / 3799 Tower Place / Waterbury, CT 06704-0543 / Dear Ms. Birdsong:
¶I am happy to report that we do have washed silk in a variety of colors. It can be shipped to you the same day that your order is received.
¶Simply choose the colors you want from the attached sample card; then call 1-800-555-9877 to place your order. If you prefer, you can order securely online through our Web site. Hopefully, you will be able to take advantage of our "quantity discounts" that will allow you to pass along the savings to your customers.
¶We look forward to receiving your order soon. / Sincerely, / Stephen Leiberman / Sales Manager/ urs / Attachment/ c: James Hollingshead, Mary Lee / bc: Richard Holiday

LETTER 29

Business Letter in Modified-Block Style

Format this letter in modified-block style.

(Current Date) / Mr. Julio Sanchez / 233 Orchard Drive / Topeka, KS 66605 / Dear Mr. Sanchez:
¶Your financial planner, Craig Fulton, has shared with me your request to surrender your annuity policy with National Investors. Please consider the financial strength of our company before you make your final decision about this matter.
¶Before we process your request, we want to be sure you understand that a portion of the funds you withdraw may represent taxable income. You should contact your tax advisor to learn of the possible tax consequences of this withdrawal.
¶Please sign and return the enclosed Request for Surrender Information form indicating whether you wish to proceed with your request for surrender. If you have any questions, call our toll free number at 1-800-555-4885. / Yours truly, / Ali Faruk / Chief Executive Officer / urs / Enclosure / By fax / c: C. Fuller

LESSON 94 TABLES: PAGE ORIENTATION

OBJECTIVES:

- Identify confusing words.
- Improve keyboarding skills.
- Format and key tables in landscape orientation.

A. WARMUP

Key each line 2 times.

Speed	1	Each of us can learn to talk to others with poise and ease.
Accuracy	2	Mo brought back five or six dozen pieces of quaint jewelry.
Language Link	3	The trip to Grandma's house was farther than they expected.
Numbers/Symbols	4	She will visit our top offices (#1 & #2): DALLAS & EL PASO.

| 1 | 2 | 3 | 4 | 5 | 6 | 7 | 8 | 9 | 10 | 11 | 12

LANGUAGE LINK

B. CONFUSING WORDS

Study the confusing words and their meanings below. Then edit lines 5–8 on p. 341 by selecting the correct word.

passed (v.) past tense of *pass;* move beyond; transfer of ownership; to be approved; surpass; to happen

past (adj.) elapsed; former
(adv.) beyond
(n.) time before the present

to (prep.) toward
too (adv.) besides, also
two (adj.) one more than one

As we passed the house, we had fond memories of the past.

He too left to shop at the two stores.

(continued on next page)

LESSON 62 LETTERS WITH POSTSCRIPTS

OBJECTIVES:

- Compose sentences at the keyboard.
- Key 35/3'/5e.
- Format letters with postscripts.

A. WARMUP

Key each line 2 times.

```
Speed          1 It is easier to build good habits than to break bad habits.
Accuracy       2 Fritz quietly welcomed the five tax guides back from Japan.
Language Link  3 This food is in cans, bags, and boxes; now we must sort it.
Numbers        4 The 28 boys chose 29 books, 30 bags, 31 pens, and 32 disks.
                 | 1 | 2 | 3 | 4 | 5 | 6 | 7 | 8 | 9 | 10 | 11 | 12
```

LANGUAGE LINK

B. COMPOSING AT THE KEYBOARD

Go to the Online Learning Center to answer the questions that follow. Answer each question with a complete sentence.

Avoiding Viruses Businesses as well as individuals rely heavily on computers to process and store information. Unfortunately, computers can be damaged by harmful programs called viruses. Go to the Online Learning Center at **KeyComps.glencoe.com>Language Link>Unit 4>Lesson 62** to learn about computer viruses. Then key answers to the following questions using complete sentences:

```
5 What is a computer virus?
6 What kind of damage can a virus do?
7 What are two ways to help protect a computer from viruses?
```

TABLE 30

Boxed Table

Create a 5-column, 14-row boxed table. Center the table vertically and horizontally. Align the number column at the right. Automatically adjust the column widths. Add 10 percent shading to rows 2, 7, 11, and 14. Add double lines before and after row 2 and between all columns.

RESOURCES FOR ETHICS TRAINING

Topic	Title	Author/Editor	Medium	Cost
Confidentiality	Promise Not to Tell	Sara S. Teakworth	Book	23.75
Confidentiality	The Fax of the Matter	Stella Larue Parsons	Pamphlet	1.98
Copyright Laws	Interpreting the Law	Daniel V. Moeder	Pamphlet	1.25
Dishonesty	I Feel Sick Next Week	Rafael C. Lopez	Article	3.95
E-Mail Ethics	When Delete Doesn't	Connor T. Wue	DVD	39.99
Employee Theft	It Will Never Be Missed	Ralph M. Zbikowski	Book	24.95
Employee Theft	Petty Thieves	Twonette B. Greb	Book	17.95
Gossip	Have You Heard?	Rachel M. Stanley	Pamphlet	1.75
Gossip	The Invisible Enemy	Jake H. Hoffbrau	DVD	24.99
Integrity	Vendors Bearing Gifts	Carmen Golightly	Article	5.25
Software Pirating	E-Stealing	Cayla C. McCoy	Article	3.39
Software Pirating	May I Copy Your Disc?	Ron E. Shelton	DVD	15.99

SCIENCE CONNECTION

Fun Fjord Facts Did you know that fjords are deep, narrow valleys that stretch inland from the coasts of northern Europe, Scandinavia, and South America? Fjords were carved by huge glaciers that descended from mountains. Go to the Online Learning Center at **KeyComps.glencoe.com>Science Connection>Unit 5>Lesson 93** to learn more about fjords and complete the activity. Follow your teacher's instructions for saving and printing your work.

SKILLBUILDING

C. Preview Practice

Key each line 2 times as a preview to the timed writings that follow.

```
8 stack enough quickly produce reference examining Organizing
9 finished station better pencil permit spend small time such
```

D. 3-Minute Timed Writings

Take two 3-minute timed writings on the paragraph. Note your speed and errors.

Goal: 35/3'/5e

```
10      Organizing the work space where you spend most of your   11
11 time will permit you to work more quickly and also produce    23
12 more. Check to see that all work still to be done is in one   35
13 stack and all work just finished is in another. Do you have   47
14 enough pens and sharp pencils? Are small things, such as      58
15 paper clips, staples, and tape, kept in a handy place? Are    70
16 reference books easy to reach from the work station? Time     82
17 spent examining your work space now can save time later.      93
18 Getting organized can lead to better use of time and space.  105
                                                           SI 1.27
   | 1 | 2 | 3 | 4 | 5 | 6 | 7 | 8 | 9 | 10 | 11 | 12
```

LANGUAGE ARTS CONNECTION

Organization Evaluation Key at least four sentences describing yourself in terms of how organized you are. For example, do you keep your room neat? Then, rate yourself in terms of organization.

TABLE 28

Open Table

Create a 3-column, 14-row open table. Center the table vertically and horizontally. Center the column headings. Align all columns at the left. Automatically adjust the column widths. The table below is shown with faint gridlines as they will appear on the screen, but the gridlines will not print.

OLYMPIC FIGURE SKATING Women's Gold Medalists 1960-2002		
Name	**Country**	**Year**
Carol Heiss	United States	1960
Sjoukje Dijkstra	Netherlands	1964
Peggy Fleming	United States	1968
Beatrix Schuba	Austria	1972
Dorothy Hamill	United States	1976
Anett Poetzsch	East Germany	1980
Katarina Witt	East Germany	1984
Katarina Witt	East Germany	1988
Kristi Yamaguchi	United States	1992
Oksana Baiul	Ukraine	1994
Tara Lipinski	United States	1998
Sarah Hughes	United States	2002

TABLE 29

Boxed Table

Science Connection

Create a 4-column, 11-row boxed table. Center the table vertically and horizontally. Align number columns at the right. Press ENTER 2 times before keying the column heading in column 1. Adjust the column widths so that all columns are equal. Add 15 percent shading to rows 1 and 5. Add double lines above and below row 2.

THE SOLAR SYSTEM			
Planet	**Approximate Millions of Miles from the Sun**	**Approximate Days to Revolve around the Sun**	**Approximate Diameter in Miles**
Mercury	36	88	3,032
Venus	67	225	7,521
Earth	93	365	7,926
Mars	142	687	4,220
Jupiter	484	4,329	88,846
Saturn	887	10,753	74,898
Uranus	1,780	30,569	31,763
Neptune	2,800	59,758	34,504
Pluto	3,670	90,520	1,485

FORMATTING

E. Letters With Postscripts

A **postscript** (PS:) is an additional message in paragraph form at the end of a letter. To format a postscript:

1. Press ENTER 2 times after the last item in the letter.
2. For block paragraphs, key the postscript at the left margin. If paragraphs are indented, indent the postscript.
3. Key *PS:* followed by 1 space; then key the message.

Sincerely yours,

Bruce Bedarsky
Purchasing Department

urs

PS: Please let us know within a week whether or not it will be possible to have these items in stock for the holiday.

Sincerely yours,

Bruce Bedarsky
Purchasing Department

urs

PS: Please let us know within a week whether or not it will be possible to have these items in stock for the holiday.

WORD PROCESSING APPLICATIONS

LETTER 30

Business Letter in Modified-Block Style With Indented Paragraphs

Format the following letter in modified-block style with indented paragraphs. Remember to indent the first line of the postscript.

(Current Date) / Ms. Rachael Goldstein / 65 Sparks Avenue / Portland, ME 04102 / Dear Ms. Goldstein:
¶As you know, the National High School Student Council is having its annual meeting in Denver, Colorado, next summer. As president of your school student council, you were recommended to our National Board as being an energetic, enthusiastic, and knowledgeable leader.
¶We are looking for students who are willing to spend two to three weeks during June or July to help plan the annual National High School Student Council event. You would fly to Denver and stay with one of our host families. Each weekday we will be working at my high school, Lincoln High, for four to six hours. We will be making minor revisions to a general outline from last year's national meeting.
¶I look forward to hearing from you with your acceptance to be a part of this national high school event. Your participation will certainly be well received by any college you plan to attend. / Sincerely, / Nicholas Bono, President / urs / c: Jamie Bluto / PS: Please contact me as soon as possible by phone at 303-555-1800 or by e-mail at nbono@alhs.dpsd.k12.co.us.

SKILLBUILDING

C. Preview Practice

Key each line 2 times as a preview to the timed writings that follow.

Accuracy beyond express essential effective frequently communication
Speed skill point ideas need know work how way get for in up or a

D. 5-Minute Timed Writings

Take two 5-minute timed writings on the paragraphs. Note your speed and errors.

Goal: 37/5'/5e

In high school and beyond, the communication of ideas, 11
needs, wants, and feelings in the right way is a skill that 23
must be acquired. Parents and teachers may not be around 35
when you need them later. It is up to you to realize the 46
need for learning how to get your ideas and feelings across 58
to others clearly and to do so in a way that shows respect 70
both for yourself and for others. 77

Think of times when you wished you had the skill to 87
make your point. Perhaps you needed to know how to respond 99
in a job interview or how to bargain for work hours. These 111
situations call for good communication skills. Some people 123
find it easy to speak up for themselves, but many others 134
frequently receive negative reactions for their attempts. 146

It is up to you to examine your own needs and learn 156
how to express your ideas or feelings in an effective way. 168
This skill is essential in all dealings with other people. 180
Practice this skill often. 185

| 1 | 2 | 3 | 4 | 5 | 6 | 7 | 8 | 9 | 10 | 11 | 12 SI 1.39

LETTER 31

Business Letter in Block Style

Format the following letter in block style.

(Current Date) / Mr. Jon Nagata / Takata Motor Company / 5800 Alder Drive S. / Tempe, AZ 85283 / Dear Mr. Nagata:
¶Surprisingly, many of us do not want to say no—to customers, salespeople, or employees—especially if they smother us with kindness and cheer.
¶That is the ploy of many salespeople worldwide. In America, we know the push of the salesperson who takes us to lunch, finds us tickets to the ball game, finds us tickets to the theater, or tells us how much he or she thinks of our spouse or children. This is all done with the purpose of making us feel guilty when we are ready to negotiate on price or terms.
¶Do not be afraid to set limits. The more precise your limits, the greater respect you will receive. Most of us want to be liked, but we should not let human feelings get in the way of business judgment. Saying no and saying it firmly will make you feel better—and will help your organization.
¶I hope this "hint" about our culture will help you when you visit other companies in the United States next month, Mr. Nagata. / Sincerely yours, / Nick DelVichicco / Consultant / urs / By fax / PS: Our representative, Christine Chung, will meet you on the 20th and accompany you on your visits.

LETTER 32

Business Letter in Modified-Block Style

Format the following letter in modified-block style. Use the current date.

Ms. Heidi Flaharty / 2039 Northrup Street, Apt. 224 / Denver, CO 80205 / Dear Ms. Flaharty:
¶Thank you for agreeing to speak to the students in my Word Processing 2 class on the topic of the office of the future. I heard your interesting presentation on this topic at the Vocational Training Association Convention. I know your ideas are going to be interesting to my students. ¶The class meets on Mondays at 10:30 a.m. in the Buhl Building of our campus in Westchester. I am hopeful that your schedule will permit you to grant this request. ¶Please contact me at 303-555-3298 to let me know what date would be convenient for you to speak. After I speak with you, I will be able to finalize my syllabus. / Yours sincerely, / Sybil Belletarre / Instructor / urs / By next day express

LESSON 93 TABLES: REINFORCEMENT

OBJECTIVES:

- Compose a paragraph at the keyboard.
- Key 37/5'/5e.
- Reinforce table formats.

A. WARMUP

Key each line 2 times.

Speed	1	Some people seem to have more hours in the day than others.
Accuracy	2	Jeff quietly moved a dozen boxes last night by power truck.
Language Link	3	The committee will discuss building plans further tomorrow.
Numbers/Symbols	4	The invoice #740 for $189.32 is subject to a 6.5% discount.
		| 1 | 2 | 3 | 4 | 5 | 6 | 7 | 8 | 9 | 10 | 11 | 12

LANGUAGE LINK

B. COMPOSING AT THE KEYBOARD

Choose one of the scenarios below and complete it. Then continue composing until you have created a short paragraph of several sentences.

5 My friend and I were walking home after class when all of a sudden we saw...

6 I was driving home when I hit a patch of ice on the road. Next thing I knew...

7 Several of us were hiking up the steep mountain path when all of a sudden...

8 The building started to shake. As soon as I realized it was an earthquake, I...

LESSON 63 REINFORCEMENT: LETTERS

OBJECTIVES:

- Use semicolons with independent clauses.
- Improve keyboarding accuracy.
- Format letters in a variety of styles.

A. WARMUP

Key each line 2 times.

Speed	1	All of the fans were glad to hear news that their team won.
Accuracy	2	Jan very quickly froze both mixtures in the deep brown jar.
Language Link	3	I looked for fleas, ticks, and lice; but our dog was clean.
Numbers/Symbols	4	Our Orders #207 and #208 and #209 were paid by Check #1317.
		| 1 | 2 | 3 | 4 | 5 | 6 | 7 | 8 | 9 | 10 | 11 | 12

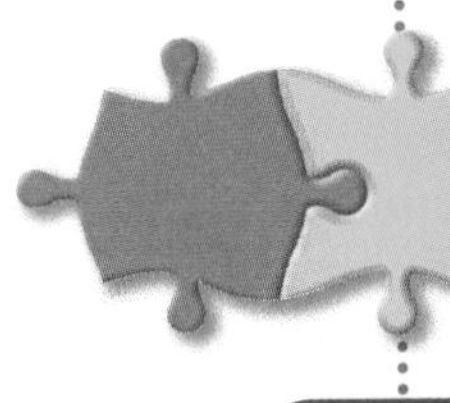

LANGUAGE LINK

B. SEMICOLONS WITH INDEPENDENT CLAUSES

Study the rule and the examples that follow. Then correct any errors in punctuation in lines 5–8.

Rule 9: Use a semicolon to join two closely related independent clauses that are not connected by a conjunction (such as *and, but, or,* or *nor*).

Melissa wanted to climb to the top of the mountain; Harry did not.

Harry was studying long hours; he was working days.

5 Last year I invested in stocks after that I had less cash.
6 They gave an excellent presentation mine was not terrific.
7 Rene was saving his money he looked forward to his cruise.
8 Buy bananas while you are out I will get the other fruits.

TABLE 26
Boxed Table

Create a 3-column, 14-row boxed table. Center the table vertically and horizontally. Align text columns at the left and number columns at the right. Adjust the column widths so that all columns are equal. Add double lines above row 2. Add 20 percent shading to row 2.

AVERAGE TEMPERATURES
Anchorage, Alaska

Month	High	Low
January	20	6
February	27	10
March	34	16
April	44	27
May	55	36
June	63	45
July	65	49
August	64	47
September	56	40
October	43	29
November	29	16
December	20	7

TABLE 27
Boxed Table

Social Studies Connection

Create a 3-column, 13-row boxed table. Center the table vertically and horizontally. Center the column headings. Adjust the column widths to look similar to the illustration. Add 20 percent shading to row 2. Add double lines above row 2 and between columns.

U.S. PRESIDENTS, PARTIES, AND YEARS IN OFFICE
1945-2005

President	Party	Term
Harry S Truman	Democrat	1945-1953
Dwight D. Eisenhower	Republican	1953-1961
John F. Kennedy	Democrat	1961-1963
Lyndon B. Johnson	Democrat	1963-1969
Richard M. Nixon	Republican	1969-1974
Gerald R. Ford	Republican	1974-1977
James E. Carter, Jr.	Democrat	1977-1981
Ronald W. Reagan	Republican	1981-1989
George H. W. Bush	Republican	1989-1993
William J. Clinton	Democrat	1993-2001
George W. Bush	Republican	2001-2009

SKILLBUILDING

C. 30-Second OK Timed Writings

Take two 30-second OK (error-free) timed writings on lines 9–10. Then take two 30-second OK timed writings on lines 11–12. Goal: no errors.

```
9       People make decisions each day; most are just routine,  11
10  but some require exact thinking and the ability to analyze.  23

11      Maxine had five jobs requiring zest and nearly perfect  11
12  work habits; I explained that a few jobs involve hazards.    23
    | 1 | 2 | 3 | 4 | 5 | 6 | 7 | 8 | 9 | 10 | 11 | 12
```

D. Diagnostic Practice: Numbers

Turn to the Diagnostic Practice: Numbers routine on page SB-4. Key one of the Pretest/Posttest paragraphs and identify any errors made. Then key the corresponding drill lines 2 times for each number on which you had 2 or more errors and 1 time for each number on which you made only 1 error. Finally, repeat the Pretest and compare your performance.

WORD PROCESSING APPLICATIONS

LETTER 33

Business Letter in Block Style

Format this letter in block style.

January 20, {year}/ Mrs. Blair Vance / 706 Middleton Avenue / Tunica, MS 39175 / Dear Mrs. Vance:

¶We at Dream Vacations are certainly able to assist you with your travel plans. We have years of experience helping our customers get the most for their travel dollar. One of our agents, Theresa Sullivan, will be happy to help you with ideas to make your trip to Alaska a memorable one.

¶I have enclosed several brochures giving descriptions both of cruises and airfare/hotel packages. Take some time now to look them over. Theresa will call you to work out the best time to meet as soon as you are ready.

¶If you have any questions or need additional information, please do not hesitate to call. It is a pleasure to be of service to you.

Cordially yours, / Carole Defazio / urs / Enclosures /c: Theresa Sullivan / bc: Carmella Rosito

C. Borders and Shading/Fill

GOLD MEDAL STANDINGS STATE TRACK MEETS	
School	**Gold Medals**
Spring Hills High School	35
Addison County High School	32
Montego Bay High School	27
Peachtree Heights Academy	17
Hopkins High School North	14

Table cells, rows, or columns can be highlighted by changing the border styles or by adding shading or fill. In the illustration at the left, row 2 has been highlighted by adding heavier lines above and below and 15 percent shading. Heavier lines have also been added between columns.

Shading or a fill pattern should not exceed 20 percent so that text in the shaded cell is easy to read.

D. Software Features

STUDENT MANUAL

Using Shading/Fill   Changing Borders

Study Lesson 92 in your Student Manual. Complete all the practice activities while at your computer. Then complete the tasks that follow.

WORD PROCESSING APPLICATIONS

TABLE 25

Boxed Table

Create a 3-column, 12-row boxed table. Center the table vertically and horizontally. Center the column headings. Automatically adjust the column widths to fit the content. Add double lines above and below row 2 and between the columns.

GIRLS' TRACK SCHEDULE Spring Hills High School		
Date	**School**	**Location**
March 3	Walton City High School	Home
March 10	Peachtree Heights Academy	Away
March 18	Bentwood Day Academy	Away
March 22	Trenton Valley High School	Home
March 26	J. C. Carlton High School	Away
March 31	Addison County High School	Home
April 2	Montego Bay High School	Home
April 8	Hopkins High School North	Away
April 16	Rockwall Senior High School	Home
April 22	South Pewitt High School	Home

LETTER 34

Personal-Business Letter in Modified-Block Style

Format this personal-business letter in modified-block style.

June 4, {year}/ Mr. Lyle Martin / Director, Customer Relations / Speedy Striders, Inc. / 8406 Hull Street / Henderson, NV 89015 / Dear Mr. Martin:

¶I purchased a pair of Speedy Striders, Model X7, from The Sports Store in the Dequindre Mall on April 15. Although I have always had good service from your shoes, this pair turned out to be defective.

¶I ran practice laps in the shoes during April and May with no problem. When I wore them in the Memorial Day Fun Run on May 30, I had a problem with my right shoe. The sole of the shoe ripped apart from the sides of the shoe; I was forced to drop out of the race. This was a serious problem for me because participation in the marathon was a requirement in my Health 155 class at Hillsdale College.

¶When I took the shoes back to the store, the manager refused to exchange the shoes or refund my money. This situation has been very frustrating for me. I would appreciate your help in getting a refund and clearing up this matter with the instructor of my physical education class. A copy of my sales slip is enclosed along with a photograph of the shoes.

Yours truly, / Kia Strobe / 45 East Windside Street / Thousand Oaks, CA 91360 / Enclosures / By registered mail

LANGUAGE ARTS CONNECTION

Write a Customer Letter Write a brief paragraph about an experience where you or someone you know had to contact a company about its product or service. The experience could be a negative one, like the one described in Letter 34, where the customer made a justified complaint. You might prefer to write about a good experience when you received extra special service or were particularly pleased with a product.

After you have written the details of the experience, use the information to write a letter to the business that was involved. Try to use specific examples, descriptions, and dates, like the writer does in Letter 34. If you think the company needs to resolve a problem, include your proposed solution in the letter.

LESSON 92 TABLES: BORDERS/SHADING

OBJECTIVES:

- Improve keyboarding skills.
- Apply word processing features.
- Format and key tables with borders and shading.

A. WARMUP

Key each line 2 times.

Speed	1	We can all speak well if we think about what we are saying.
Accuracy	2	Because he was very lazy, Jake paid for six games and quit.
Language Link	3	Ty drove farther than he should have; then he bought a map.
Numbers/Symbols	4	Hasn't our July Check #830 for $149.56 been mailed to them?

| 1 | 2 | 3 | 4 | 5 | 6 | 7 | 8 | 9 | 10 | 11 | 12

SKILLBUILDING

B. 12-SECOND SPRINTS

Take three 12-second timed writings on each line. Try to increase your speed each time.

5 The goal is to do the work we have to do as well as we can.
6 Key at a speed where you can have control over your errors.
7 She can save a lot of time and effort by planning the work.
8 She cannot count on luck as a means of getting ahead today.

||||5||||10||||15||||20||||25||||30||||35||||40||||45||||50||||55||||60

LANGUAGE ARTS CONNECTION

Define Homophones Create an open table similar to Table 22 on p. 331. Enter the following pairs of homophones: **affect/effect, bazaar/bizarre, chord/cord, peer/pier, rain/reign, ring/wring**. Enter a short definition for each word. If you need help defining the words, use a print or online dictionary. Follow your teacher's instructions for saving and printing your work.

LETTER 35

Business Letter in Modified-Block Style with Indented Paragraphs

Format the following letter in modified-block style with indented paragraphs.

June 15, {year}

Ms. Juvetta Dishman
7337 Westfalia Street
Charlotte, TN 37036
Dear Ms. Dishman:

Thank you for volunteering to participate in the PLSO study. Enclosed are two consent forms, a baseline questionnaire, a baseline locator form, and a postage-paid envelope in which to return these forms.

Please read the entire consent form carefully before signing it. Keep one copy of the consent form for your records. If you have any questions about the form, please call Lynn or Vanda at 555-8706. Answer each question to the best of your ability. If there are some questions you are not able to answer, indicate that on the form, and an interviewer will telephone you for more information.

Place the completed forms (unfolded) in the envelope provided and mail them back to us. We would appreciate it if you would take time right now to fill out the forms and return them. Thank you for your assistance in this important health study of older adults.
Sincerely,

Nolan Goydos, M.D.
Principal Investigator
Enclosures
c: M. Bryant, M.D., R. Welsh, M.D.

TABLE 23
Open Table

Create a 2-column, 8-row open table. Automatically adjust the column widths. Center the table vertically and horizontally. The table below is shown with faint gridlines as they will appear on the screen, but the gridlines will not print.

HONOR SOCIETY OFFICERS **Central High School**	
President	Marcus Wilson
Vice President	Kathy Chou
Secretary	LaTasha Bennett
Treasurer	Angel Florez
Reporter	Holly Koskoski
Historian	Kahlid Jordan
Parliamentarian	Benjamin Hertz

TABLE 24
Open Table

Create a 4-column, 10-row open table. Automatically adjust the column widths. Center the table vertically and horizontally. The table below is shown with faint gridlines as they will appear on the screen, but the gridlines will not print.

MAJOR LEAGUE BASEBALL TEAMS **[year]**			
American League Teams		**National League Teams**	
Anaheim Angels	Minnesota Twins	Arizona Diamondbacks	Milwaukee Brewers
Baltimore Orioles	New York Yankees	Atlanta Braves	New York Mets
Boston Red Sox	Oakland Athletics	Chicago Cubs	Philadelphia Phillies
Chicago White Sox	Seattle Mariners	Cincinnati Reds	Pittsburgh Pirates
Cleveland Indians	Tampa Bay Devil Rays	Colorado Rockies	San Diego Padres
Detroit Tigers	Texas Rangers	Florida Marlins	San Francisco Giants
Kansas City Royals	Toronto Blue Jays	Houston Astros	St. Louis Cardinals
		Los Angeles Dodgers	Washington Nationals

LETTER REVIEW

OBJECTIVES:

- Increase keyboarding speed and improve accuracy.
- Review various letter formats.

A. WARMUP

Key each line 2 times.

Speed	They do not feel it is their duty to fix the flat for free.
Accuracy	Did she realize big yellow quilts from Jack were expensive?
Language Link	Seven-digit codes were assigned; you should have yours now.
Numbers	2301 3402 4503 5604 6705 7806 8907 2301 3402 4503 5604 6705
	| 1 | 2 | 3 | 4 | 5 | 6 | 7 | 8 | 9 | 10 | 11 | 12

SKILLBUILDING

B. 12-SECOND SPRINTS

Take three 12-second timed writings on each line. Try to increase your speed on each timed writing.

When you go to get your pen, will you also please get mine.
He did the job well and was paid by the maid who was there.
Now that we have the time to sit back and read, it is cold.
The red leaves fell from the maple tree when the wind blew.
| 1 | 2 | 3 | 4 | 5 | 6 | 7 | 8 | 9 | 10 | 11 | 12

C. PRETEST

Take a 1-minute timed writing on the paragraph. Note your speed and errors.

The name high tech is given to a basic and useful type 12
of design that is changing our concept of modern living and 24
things we use daily. It has long enjoyed a quiet appeal in 36
places like restaurants and stores. 43
| 1 | 2 | 3 | 4 | 5 | 6 | 7 | 8 | 9 | 10 | 11 | 12

FORMATTING

E. Removing Borders

As you learned in Lesson 65, tables are created either with borders (boxed tables) or without borders (open tables). In this lesson, you will create open tables by removing the borders.

F. Software Features

STUDENT MANUAL

Table Borders

Study Lesson 91 in your Student Manual. Complete all the practice activities while at your computer. Then complete the tasks that follow.

WORD PROCESSING APPLICATIONS

TABLE 22

Open Table

Create a 2-column, 7-row open table. Automatically adjust the column widths. Center the table vertically and horizontally. Key each pair of homophones in one cell and press ENTER 1 time after the second word. The table below is shown with faint gridlines as they will appear on the screen, but the gridlines will not print.

FAMILIAR HOMOPHONES	
allowed aloud	permitted with a loud voice
foreword forward	an introduction send, move ahead
it's its	contraction for "it is" relating to itself
lead led	marking part of a pencil was the first to guide
patience patients	persistence, endurance people under medical care
stationary stationery	not moving; inactive paper for writing

D. PRACTICE

In the chart below, find the number of errors you made on the Pretest. Then, key each of the designated drill lines 2 times.

Pretest Errors	0–1	2	3	4+
Drill Lines	16–20	15–19	14–18	13–17

Accuracy

13 own basic quiet stores design concept expensive restaurants
14 built style pipes range bright rubber window appeal designs
15 use and are wild tech living modern useful quietly changing
16 now but used come water things colors coming places enjoyed

Speed

17 glass daily wide sign such tire come like home with has not
18 homes given high tech name type long used they last now are
19 appeal living useful given basic things daily long type use
20 colors bright stores water pipes style glass range wind are

E. POSTTEST

Repeat the Pretest. Compare your Posttest results with your Pretest results.

WORD PROCESSING APPLICATIONS

LETTER 36

Business Letter in Modified-Block Style with Indented Paragraphs

Current Date
Mr. Taylor Coates
President, News Guild
28 West Adams Street, Suite 1308
Alamonte Springs, FL 32714
Dear Mr. Coates:

Because of the extraordinarily high number of claims, we have found it necessary to increase our rates. This increase is required under Part 5, page 3-PR, of Policy Amendment 15. Accordingly, we are increasing the life insurance rate to .80/$1,000 for active members and .94/$1,000 for retirees.

In addition, the amount of dependent life insurance will be reduced from $10,000 to $5,000 along with extending the current policy for one year. If you think it would help, I am willing to come to your next membership meeting to answer questions.

Sincerely,
Patrick Tecumseh
Account Representative
PS: A summary of all changes we are recommending is enclosed for your review.

C. Preview Practice

Key each line 2 times as a preview to the timed writings that follow.

Accuracy	quite values linked identity satisfied examining individual
Speed	gives peace adult hold help role life way joy too who in to

D. 5-Minute Timed Writings

Take two 5-minute timed writings on the paragraphs. Note your speed and errors.

Goal: 37/5'/5e

Most decisions about your present lifestyle have been *11*
made for you by your parents. Your current way of life is *23*
quite often defined by your role as a member of a family *34*
and as a student. Your personal identity is closely related *46*
to how you live. In fact, your lifestyle and who you are as *58*
an individual are often linked. *64*

As an adult, you will make almost all of the choices *75*
that will determine your lifestyle. These decisions might *87*
help you define your personal identity. It is never too *98*
early to begin examining lifestyle features that you desire *110*
to have when you are older. When you can describe those *121*
traits, you can start setting goals and selecting options *133*
that will help you achieve the way of life you want to have *145*
as an adult. *147*

To live your life in a way that gives you peace and *158*
joy, your needs must be satisfied, most of your wants must *170*
be realized, and your style of living should be true to the *182*
values you hold. *185*

| 1 | 2 | 3 | 4 | 5 | 6 | 7 | 8 | 9 | 10 | 11 | 12 SI 1.37

COMMUNICATION FOCUS

Give Clear Directions It is important to communicate clearly when giving directions. Think about how you get from your house to your school. Create a new table. Key each step in the directions from your house to school in a separate row. Follow your teacher's instructions for saving and printing your work.

LETTER 37

Business Letter in Modified-Block Style

Format this letter in modified-block style. Make the corrections indicated.

June 18, {year}

Ms. Kia Strobe
45 E. Windside Street
Thousand Oaks, CA 93160

Dear Ms. Strobe:

You were justified [in] being angry. We are sorry for the problems you[#]had with your Speedy striders, model X7, which forced you to drop out of the Memorial Day Fun Run. I have telephoned your physical education instructor and sent her a letter explaining your reason for[#]not completing the class assignment. We are grateful to you for bringing this matter to our attention. The photo you sent was especially helpful.

¶ After we recieved your letter, we conducted an investigation of our equipment. We discovered that the equipment use[d] in sewing the Model 7X shoe is faulty. All of our dealers now have been informed of this situation, and the Model X7 Shoes have been removed from store shelves. Please take the damaged shoes to the Dequinder Mall store. The Store Manager, Mr. Kelly, has been contacted and instructed to refund your money in full.

Sincerely yours,

Lyle Martin
Director, Customer Relations

Enclosure
c: Paul Kelly

PS: We have enclose[d] a coupon entitling you to a free pair of shoes of your choice. We hope that this will restore your faith in speedy striders and that you [will] enjoy many more miles of successful marathon runs.

By Overnight Express

Tables: Remove Borders

OBJECTIVES:

- Reinforce keyboarding skills.
- Key 37/5'/5e.
- Apply software features.
- Format open tables.

A. Warmup

Key each line 2 times.

Speed	1	It will be very cold in a few hours when the sun goes down.
Accuracy	2	Jack keyed four dozen requisitions for hollow moving boxes.
Language Link	3	Then Coach said the prize went to whoever ran the farthest.
Numbers/Symbols	4	The citation for the case is 795 F.2D 1423 (9th Cir. 1996).

| 1 | 2 | 3 | 4 | 5 | 6 | 7 | 8 | 9 | 10 | 11 | 12

SKILLBUILDING

B. Technique Checkpoint

Key each line 2 times. Focus on the techniques at the left.

Lines 5–6: Space without pausing.

5 You can do much more work than you do each day of the week.
6 They will use the pay for the one day of work that she did.

Lines 7–8: Press and release the CAPS LOCK key without pausing.

7 Our SEVENTH ANNUAL MEETING will be held in MOBILE, ALABAMA.
8 The DAY COMPANY will sponsor our ADVISORY COUNCIL luncheon.

LETTER 38

Business Letter in Block Style

Format this letter in block style. Make the corrections indicated by the proofreaders' marks.

(Current Date)

Mrs. Christine Piantidosi
824 England avenue
Kansas City, KS 66801

Dear Mrs. Piantidosi:

After our telephone conversation thismorning concerning late delivery of three model 60 camcorders to your store, I found that the cam corders were shiped in error to Kansas City, MO. Our headquaters upgraded the system computer which required many hours of re-entering invoices. Obviously, the error in your order happened at that time. Our records are now correct. Because of the inconveneince this errors has caused you the shipping and handling charges have been removed from the your bill. Your orders is being sent today by express delivery, and you should receive it in 24 hours. We value your patronage and we look forward to serving you for many years to come.

Sincerely,

Marlon Chevron
Manger
By fax

c:Darryl Adams

MEMO 4
Template

Key the following memo. Use the first memo template in your word processing software.

TO: David J. Bacon / FROM: Wayne S. Goodin / DATE: Current / SUBJECT: Marketing Questionnaire
¶One of the questionnaires that was sent to your office at the beginning of the month should be completed by the 31st of this month. As a reminder, Section III must be completed for questions 8, 12, 18, 24, and 27. The results of the questionnaires are going to be used to compare our product sales with those of the other district offices in the eastern region. Thank you very much for your immediate response. / urs

COMMUNICATION FOCUS

Create a Fax Cover Sheet When you send a fax, you need to include a cover sheet so that the proper recipient will pick up the papers at a shared fax machine. Choose a fax cover-sheet template in your word processing software and key the information below into the appropriate areas. Complete the template, following the example below. Follow your teacher's instructions for saving and printing your work.

To: Mr. Alton Hathcoat Fax number: 512-555-8801	**A facsimile from** **The Quarry** 9027 Round Rock Road Austin, TX 78752 Phone: 512-555-3377 Fax: 512-555-3379
Date: [Current]	
Regarding: Confidential	
Comments: This transmittal has four pages, including this cover sheet.	

TABLES: CREATING

OBJECTIVES:

- Apply subject/verb agreement rules.
- Improve keyboarding skills.
- Create tables.

A. WARMUP

Key each line 2 times.

Speed	1	Heavy rain fell fast and hard on the game later in the day.
Accuracy	2	Jeff quickly took away five dozen more boxes of light pens.
Language Link	3	The express elevator broke; I had to walk up eight flights.
Numbers/Symbols	4	($95.15) ($59.26) ($60.37) ($71.48) ($82.59) ($90.60) ($$$)

| 1 | 2 | 3 | 4 | 5 | 6 | 7 | 8 | 9 | 10 | 11 | 12

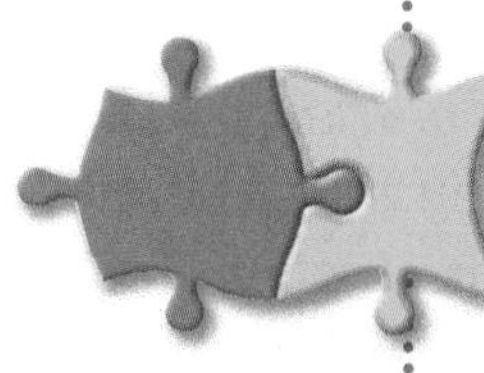

LANGUAGE LINK

B. SUBJECT/VERB AGREEMENT

Study the rule and examples that follow. Then edit lines 5–8 for subject/verb agreement.

Rule 10: Disregard any intervening words that come between the subject and verb when establishing agreement.

The lost box of books has been found.

The buses covered with green paint were moving very fast.

5 The books in the bookcase (was/were) rearranged by May last week.
6 The students working on this project (is/are) doing a great job.
7 One of the programmers (has/have) written and tested that program.
8 This contract, including all attachments, (is/are) due Wednesday.

LETTER 57

Business Letter in Modified-Block Style

Key the following letter in modified-block style.

(Current Date) / Alkens Industries / 750 South Filmore Street / Denver, CO 80209-5072 / Attention: Human Resources / Ladies and Gentlemen:
¶Mr. Warren Thomas was recently treated by me at Wilson Hospital. During his hospitalization, I placed him on a disability leave. I felt his condition was such that he could not return to work until his symptoms had resolved.
¶Mr. Thomas has continued in my care. He has shown good progress in recovery. On reevaluation, it is apparent that he would be able to return to work on the 15th of next month. This is sooner than I anticipated, but it reflects his positive progress.
¶If there are any other questions, please contact my office.
Sincerely, / John Blackburn, M.D. / urs / c: Mr. Warren Thomas

MEMO 3

Template

Key the following memo. Use the first memo template in your word processing software.

TO: Shelby Taylor / FROM: Kenneth Anderson / DATE: July 12, {year} / SUBJECT: Company Newsletter
¶Your first issue of the *Brownfield Quarterly* was fantastic, and I want to extend my heartfelt congratulations for a job well done. Even though this was your first edition of the newsletter using our new desktop publishing software, I think the finished product was great!
¶The Projects Update on page 2 was especially informative because you let us know the major projects our employees have been working on this quarter. We certainly need to know what is going on throughout the plant. I have heard many other employees make very favorable comments about the newsletter, especially this section.
¶Keep up the good work, Shelby. / urs

SCIENCE CONNECTION

Compose a Summary Memo Choose a memo template in your word processing software. If you had a friend who had missed a science class, how would you explain to your friend what he or she had missed? Use the template to compose a memo that gives your friend a brief summary of your last science class. Follow your teacher's instructions for saving and printing your work.

SKILLBUILDING

C. Technique Timed Writings

Take two 30-second timed writings on each line. Focus on the technique at the left.

Press the* SPACE BAR *with a quick down-and-in motion.

```
9  go to it go do so go be on us we do to on it at bet tip top
10 We want to go on and see that band at the park play for us.
11 Now it is my turn to tell them that we do not want it done.
12 How do you get it all done and stay in top form for us now?
   | 1 | 2 | 3 | 4 | 5 | 6 | 7 | 8 | 9 | 10 | 11 | 12
```

D. Paced Practice

Turn to the Paced Practice routine beginning on page SB-7. Take three 2-minute timed writings, starting at the point where you left off the last time.

FORMATTING

E. Parts of a Table

1. **Tables** are grids that arrange text or data in vertical columns and horizontal rows. The intersection of a column and row is called a **cell**. Information is keyed in the cells.
2. Tables may be formatted with lines (a boxed table) or without lines (an open table). A boxed table is shown in the illustration below.
3. When a table appears on a page by itself, it should be vertically and horizontally centered.
4. Align text columns at the left; align number columns at the right.

Accounting and Finance	Richards College of Business
Management and Business Systems	Richards College of Business
Mass Communications	College of Arts and Sciences
Physical Education and Recreation	College of Education

LETTER 56

Business Letter in Block Style

Key the following letter in block style.

(Current Date) / Ms. Ruthe Barichello, Department Chair / English Department / Central High School / 3474 Maple Avenue / Carrollton, GA 30118 / Dear Ms. Barichello:
Subject: Effective Leadership
¶As we discussed at our meeting last week, there are certainly several traits that we should consider when selecting the next members of the department. Effective leaders should:

1. Make others feel important and emphasize others' strengths and contributions, not their own. If leaders' goals are self-centered, followers will lose their enthusiasm quickly.
2. Promote a vision. Followers need a clear idea of where they are being led. A leader needs to provide that vision.
3. Follow the golden rule. A leader should treat followers the way he/she likes to be treated. That means admitting mistakes.
4. Criticize others only in private. Public praise encourages others to excel.

¶Our first interview is scheduled for next Monday in the board conference room at 9 a.m. I look forward to seeing you then. / Sincerely, / Casey Javonovich / Board Chairman / urs

COMMUNICATION FOCUS

Identify Leadership Qualities In the letter above, you keyed information about ways to lead effectively. Who comes to mind when you think of an outstanding leader? Compose a sentence explaining who that person is. Make a numbered list of five positive qualities that person possesses. Choose one of these qualities and describe what a person can do to strengthen that attribute. Follow your teacher's instructions for saving and printing your work.

F. Software Features

STUDENT MANUAL

Creating Tables

Study Lesson 65 in your Student Manual. Complete all the practice activities while at your computer. Then complete the following tasks.

WORD PROCESSING APPLICATIONS

TABLE 1

Boxed Table

Create a table with 2 columns and 4 rows. Use the TAB key to move from column to column as you key the information.

Accounting and Finance	Richards College of Business
Management and Business Systems	Richards College of Business
Mass Communications	College of Arts and Sciences
Physical Education and Recreation	College of Education

TABLE 2

Boxed Table

Create a table with 3 columns and 4 rows. Use the TAB key to move from column to column as you key the information.

Grand Canyon	United States	217 miles long
Great Barrier Reef	Australia	1,200 miles long
Mt. Everest	Nepal and Tibet	29,000 feet high (est.)
Nile River	Egypt and Sudan	4,160 miles long

ETHICS CONNECTION

Evaluate Ethics People do not become honest or trustworthy overnight. They develop those traits as a result of consistent, daily decisions. Read the following situations; then explain how an honest person might respond. Use complete sentences. Key your responses, and then follow your teacher's instructions for saving and printing your work.

1. Ryan found a man's gold watch in the parking lot of a discount store. No one was around when he picked it up.
2. On Monday morning Lora remembered that she had a book report due that day, but she had read only half the book. She knew that she could find information on the Internet to complete her report.

REVIEW

OBJECTIVES:

- Reinforce keyboarding techniques.
- Improve keyboarding skills.
- Reinforce letter and memo formats.

A. WARMUP

Key each line 2 times.

Speed	1	Mack wants to have a few of the boys come over for a visit.
Accuracy	2	Why would quick brown foxes want to jump over any lazy dog?
Language Link	3	Rather than go any farther, they stopped to get directions.
Numbers/Symbols	4	Only 4% of our current PCs are equipped with CD-ROM drives.

| 1 | 2 | 3 | 4 | 5 | 6 | 7 | 8 | 9 | 10 | 11 | 12

SKILLBUILDING

B. TECHNIQUE TIMED WRITINGS

Take two 30-second timed writings on lines 5–6. Then take two 30-second timed writings on lines 7–8. Focus on the technique at the left.

Keep your eyes on the copy.

5 Try to key every letter of the alphabet as quickly as 11
6 you can without having to stop to look where the keys are. 23

7 As you key, think about where the letters are located. 11
8 Then key with your eyes closed to test if you learned well. 23

| 1 | 2 | 3 | 4 | 5 | 6 | 7 | 8 | 9 | 10 | 11 | 12

C. PACED PRACTICE

Turn to the Paced Practice routine beginning on page SB7. Take three 2-minute timed writings, starting at the point where you left off the last time.

LESSON 66

TABLES: COLUMN SIZE AND POSITION

OBJECTIVES:

- Key 35/3'/5e.
- Adjust column widths.
- Center tables on a page.

A. WARMUP

Key each line 2 times.

```
Speed          1 He may find time to go today if Dan will help with the car.
Accuracy       2 James Boxell, the banquet speaker, analyzed a few carvings.
Language Link  3 All of the girls except Suzy have purchased their uniforms.
Symbols        4 Attention: Dear Mr. Westin: Subject: Gentlemen: Ladies: Re:
                 | 1 | 2 | 3 | 4 | 5 | 6 | 7 | 8 | 9 | 10 | 11 | 12
```

*inter*NET CONNECTION

Prevent Carpal Tunnel Syndrome Go to the Online Learning Center at **KeyComps.glencoe.com>Internet Connection> Unit 4>Lesson 66** to learn about carpal tunnel syndrome. Learn what causes it and how to treat it. Use the information to create a simple table with columns for symptoms, causes, and treatments. Follow your teacher's instructions for saving and printing your work.

SKILLBUILDING

B. PREVIEW PRACTICE

Key each line 2 times as a preview to the timed writings that follow.

```
Accuracy  5 experts adequate stressful everything difference management
Speed     6 check tips other will same time done item due use may is be
```

F. Software Features

STUDENT MANUAL

Using Templates

Study Lesson 89 in your Student Manual. Complete all the practice activities while at your computer. Then complete the tasks that follow.

WORD PROCESSING APPLICATIONS

MEMO 1

Template

Key the following memo using the first memo template listed in your word processing software.

MEMO TO: Darrell Stevens / **FROM:** Jim Goodwin / **DATE:** August 12, {year} / **SUBJECT:** Executive Meeting
¶Our next Executive Meeting will be held on August 22, and I'd like to present your report from the systems committee evaluation at the meeting. Since I have invited other department heads to attend, please bring a minimum of 20 copies of your report.
¶I appreciate all the hard work you've put into this project, and I look forward to presenting your report next week. / urs

MEMO 2

Template

Key the following memo using the first memo template listed in your word processing software.

MEMO TO: Janie Lane / **FROM:** Allen T. Wilson / **DATE:** September 21, {year} / **SUBJECT:** Industry Certification
¶I would like to congratulate you and the members of your department for receiving industry certification in April. All of you have worked very hard during the last two years preparing for this process, and I am extremely proud of this accomplishment for you and for our school.
¶Being industry-certified indicates that our Business Education Department has met the standards set by business and industry for meeting the needs of our students. I truly believe that they will be better employees and better citizens after taking our business courses. The industry certification distinction will definitely help to recruit students.
¶Congratulations for a job well done from the entire staff and student body! / urs

C. 3-Minute Timed Writings

Take two 3-minute timed writings on the paragraph. Note your speed and errors.

Goal: 35/3'/5e

```
     Time is a gift we all have. A day is the same length        11
for all of us. Some people always appear to have time for        22
everything and everyone. Other people just never seem to be      34
well organized to do all the things they want to do. This        46
difference may be due to people not having an adequate plan      58
to manage the time they have. Experts in time management         69
have decided on several tips for better use of time. Make        81
lists of things to do and check each item as it is done.         92
Your day will be less stressful if you manage your time         104
wisely.                                                         105
| 1 | 2 | 3 | 4 | 5 | 6 | 7 | 8 | 9 | 10 | 11 | 12       SI 1.28
```

FORMATTING

D. Column Widths and Table Position

When you create a table, the table is **horizontally centered**. That means that it is centered between the side margins. When you insert a new table, it automatically extends from the left margin to the right margin. All columns are the same width.

If a column contains long entries or short entries, you may want to change the width of the columns to make the table more readable or more attractive. Once you change the column widths, the table may no longer be horizontally centered. Therefore, you must reposition the table so that it is an equal distance from the right and left margins.

When a table appears on a page by itself, it should also be **centered vertically**, or an equal distance from the top and bottom margins.

SKILLBUILDING

C. 30-Second OK Timed Writings

Take two 30-second OK (error-free) timed writings on lines 9–10. Then take two 30-second OK timed writings on lines 11–12. Goal: no errors.

```
9       I did not realize that Kevin quietly joined the team      11
10  six months before he was graduated from Paul High School.     22

11      Analyze the quality of these extra blank cartons that     11
12  they gave us with the monthly shipment mailed this June.      22
    | 1 | 2 | 3 | 4 | 5 | 6 | 7 | 8 | 9 | 10 | 11 | 12
```

D. Technique Checkpoint

Key each line 2 times. Tab to begin each line. Focus on the technique at the left.

Keep other fingers in home position while reaching to the Tab.

```
13  Thomas Edison was born in Ohio.
14  His childhood home is now a museum.
15  He is best known for inventing the lightbulb.
16  He also invented a talking doll.
17  He was a close friend of Henry Ford.
```

FORMATTING

E. Memo Templates

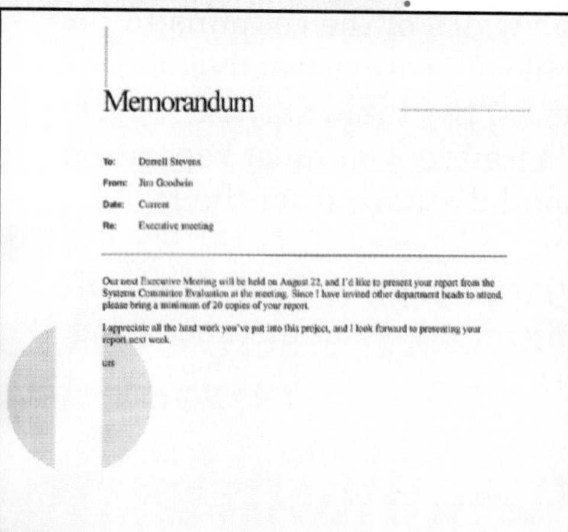

Memorandum

To: Darrell Stevens

From: Jim Goodwin

Date: Current

Re: Executive meeting

Our next Executive Meeting will be held on August 22, and I'd like to present your report from the Systems Committee Evaluation at the meeting. Since I have invited other department heads to attend, please bring a minimum of 20 copies of your report.

I appreciate all the hard work you've put into this project, and I look forward to presenting your report next week.

urs

Memos are written messages sent from one person to another in the same organization or business. Memos are less formal than letters and do not have salutations or closing lines.

Most word processing programs now include memo templates. **Templates** are forms that have been designed so that you can move quickly from one data entry area to the next to fill in necessary information. Memo templates usually include the following guide words:

TO:, *FROM:*, *DATE:*, and *SUBJECT:* or *RE:*.

STUDENT MANUAL

Selecting Columns and Rows

Table Position

Adjusting Column Widths

Study Lesson 66 in your Student Manual. Complete all the practice activities while at your computer. Then complete the following tasks.

WORD PROCESSING APPLICATIONS

TABLE 3

Boxed Table

Create a table with 3 columns and 4 rows. Enter the information in the cells. Use the TAB key to move from cell to cell. Automatically adjust the column widths. Center the table vertically and horizontally.

Your table should look like the following table when you have completed it.

Hill, James	Manager	Boston
Karen, Mark	Assistant Manager	Dallas
Renfro, Julia	Shipping Supervisor	Minneapolis
Street, Meridy	Personnel Director	San Francisco

TABLE 4

Boxed Table

Create a table with 3 columns and 5 rows. Automatically adjust the column widths. Center the table vertically and horizontally.

adapt	adopt	adept
lose	loose	loss
rein	rain	reign
site	sight	cite
too	to	two

TABLE 5

Boxed Table

Create a table with 3 columns and 5 rows. Automatically adjust the column widths. Center the table vertically and horizontally.

Coca Cola	KO	NYSE
Intel Corporation	INTC	NASDAQ
Microsoft	MSFT	NASDAQ
Nike	NKE	NYSE
Walt Disney Co.	DIS	NYSE

MEMO TEMPLATES

OBJECTIVES:

- Identify confusing words.
- Apply word processing features.
- Format and key memos using templates.

A. WARMUP

Key each line 2 times.

Speed	1 We will plan to cook on the grill when we meet at the lake.
Accuracy	2 All four mixtures in the deep brown jug froze very quickly.
Language Link	3 We usually vacation at a place that is south of the border.
Numbers/Symbols	4 Invoice #70-2 read: 653# "Extra" @ $4.89 per lb., less 10%.

| 1 | 2 | 3 | 4 | 5 | 6 | 7 | 8 | 9 | 10 | 11 | 12

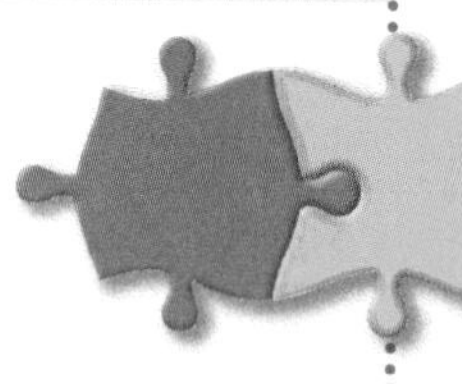

LANGUAGE LINK

B. CONFUSING WORDS

Study the confusing words and their meanings shown below. Then edit lines 5–8 by selecting the correct word.

than (conj. or prep.)	in comparison with
then (adv.)	at that time
farther (adv.)	to a greater measurable distance
further (adv.)	to a greater extent; additionally

5 Rather (then/than) stay at home, we saw a movie and (then/than) had pizza.
6 After studying the map (further/farther), we realized we were 50 miles (further/farther) (then/than) we should have been.
7 First we visited Niagara Falls, (then/than) we drove (further/farther) into Canada to visit Toronto.
8 The board members agreed to discuss the matter (further/farther).

TABLES: COLUMN HEADINGS

OBJECTIVES:

- Compose a paragraph at the keyboard.
- Increase keyboarding speed and improve accuracy.
- Format tables with column headings.

A. WARMUP

Key each line 2 times.

Speed	1	Take good care of this car, and it should last a long time.
Accuracy	2	Jeff's size had helped him to win quickly over Gene Baxter.
Language Link	3	Hundreds of acres of land are needed for the new reservoir.
Numbers/Symbols	4	Using the 8% increase, we bought 25# of #112 and #64 nails.
		| 1 | 2 | 3 | 4 | 5 | 6 | 7 | 8 | 9 | 10 | 11 | 12

LANGUAGE LINK

B. COMPOSING AT THE KEYBOARD

Answer one of the following questions with a short paragraph.

5 How is cheating on a test dishonest?
6 Why do you want friends who are honest?
7 Would your best friend say you are honest? Why?

SOCIAL STUDIES CONNECTION

Research Capital Cities Create a two-column table with three rows. Choose three countries, and key them in alphabetical order in the first column. In the second column, key the capital of each country. Use an encyclopedia or a search engine to find the capitals, if necessary. Follow your teacher's instructions for saving and printing your work.

LETTER 55
Business Letter in Block Style

Key this letter in block style.

(Current Date) / Mr. Sullivan D'Amico / D'Amico & McGrawth Legal Firm / 404 West Broadway / Suite 220 / Denver, CO 80501 / Dear Mr. D'Amico:

¶Thank you for your letter asking about my new book, *Listening Is an Art*. In the book, I stress that listening is not a spectator sport. It requires active participation.

¶As a listener, you need to encourage your speaker by visibly paying close attention. Body language on your part is often a great encouragement to the speaker. Listed below are several of the topics I cover in the book:

1. Paraphrase the content. In your own words, repeat what you are hearing. Encourage the speaker by letting him/her know that you are listening.
2. Be involved in the conversation. Go beyond paraphrasing to enforce understanding by adding comments to the person's discussion.
3. Feed back feelings. Reflect the feelings you hear by expressing your opinion about the topic being discussed. If you can, ask direct questions of the speaker.

¶I hope, Mr. D'Amico, that this gives you an idea of what I'm writing about. I've mailed you an autographed copy of my book for your enjoyment.

Yours truly, / Bonnie Ryan, Author / urs

LANGUAGE ARTS CONNECTION

The Interrobang The interrobang is a punctuation mark that combines the question mark and the exclamation point: ‽. It was intended to be used after an alarming question, such as "Is that a tornado‽" The interrobang was never widely accepted as an authentic punctuation mark, but the word itself has migrated into computer terminology.

You can insert an interrobang into text by changing to the Wingdings 2 font, holding down the Alt key, and entering one of these numbers on the numeric keypad: 61533, 61534, 61535, or 61536. When you release the Alt key, the interrobang will appear. Each number will produce an interrobang in a different font.

Practice inserting each of four interrobangs. Then compose and key four exclamatory questions and insert an interrobang after each one. Follow your teacher's instructions for saving and printing your work.

SKILLBUILDING

C. 12-Second Sprints

Take three 12-second timed writings on each line. Try to increase your speed on each timed writing.

8 It is always a good idea to take time to do your best work.
9 Take enough time to think about it and plan each step well.
10 If you rush into a job, you may just make many more errors.
11 Now is the time you should use these tips to do a good job.
|||| 5 |||| 10 |||| 15 |||| 20 |||| 25 |||| 30 |||| 35 |||| 40 |||| 45 |||| 50 |||| 55 |||| 60

D. PRETEST

Take a 1-minute timed writing on the paragraph. Note your speed and errors.

12 Cecil must know more about my past than he does about 11
13 his own. As we walked in the hazy sunshine with friends, he 23
14 spoke above the noise around us. I was pleased that he was 35
15 able to remember things we did when we were young. 45
| 1 | 2 | 3 | 4 | 5 | 6 | 7 | 8 | 9 | 10 | 11 | 12

E. PRACTICE

SPEED: ***If you made 2 or fewer errors on the Pretest, key lines 16–23 two times each.***

ACCURACY: ***If you made more than 2 errors on the Pretest, key lines 16–19 as a group two times. Then key lines 20–23 as a group two times.***

Up Reaches

16 ce cell once mice rice slice cease cedar fleece niece juice
17 me lime mime meal mere melon plume metal become slime smell
18 hi high hits hive nigh thigh chime whine chirps whips hires
19 lo lost love flow loam plods solos clots slower plops loans

Down Reaches

20 ca case cast pica carp carve cards cable capers laces cabin
21 im whim slim aims time limps crimp blimp chimes limes prime
22 rm harm worm arms army perms alarm charm squirm farms warms
23 ba bask bark barb paba bards bawls balms turban samba baits

F. POSTTEST

Repeat the Pretest. Compare your Posttest results with your Pretest results.

FORMATTING

F. Letters With Numbered Lists

A numbered list is often included in the body of a letter. Use the automatic numbering feature to create the list. Leave a blank line before and after each numbered item.

WORD PROCESSING APPLICATIONS

LETTER 54

Business Letter in Modified-Block Style

Key the following letter in modified-block style.

(Current Date) / Dr. Jaune Sakyesva / 2042 East Bellview Parkway / Suite 109 / Denver, CO 80202-1956 / Dear Dr. Sakyesva:

¶We are happy to respond to your letter requesting information about our next seminar on current ISSUES IN SOCIETY. This series of seminars has been successful because we have addressed some of the major issues our society faces today, and we have offered helpful suggestions on how to deal with them.

1. The seminar will be held August 21 from 9 a.m. until 3 p.m. at the Inn of the Rockies, 404 West Mountain Drive. A map is enclosed with this letter.
2. Lunch will be provided by Epicurean Delight. Call 699-555-1245 to specify your luncheon choice from those items listed in our brochure.
3. There will be three speakers and a chance for questions after each talk.
4. Tapes from other seminars will be available for purchase in the lobby during the luncheon break and at the conclusion of the seminar.

¶As soon as we have confirmations from the speakers, I'll send you literature regarding each speaker and his/her qualifications. Thank you for your interest in the seminar.

Sincerely, / Maya Harris / Public Relations Director / urs / Enclosure

FORMATTING

G. Tables: Column Headings

Column headings describe the data in each column of a table. To format column headings:

Salesperson	**Territory**	**No. of Units**
Dawson, Angelique	Midwest	1,245
Goodfellow, Robin	Southeast	1,137
Karampalas, Stephen	Northeast	1,089
Saad, Gamal	Western	1,764

1. Key the column headings in initial caps and bold.
2. Align column headings at the left over text columns, at the right over number columns, or centered over all columns if all columns contain text only.
3. If a column heading is much wider than the data in the column, you may want to let it wrap to the next line or break the heading into two lines by pressing ENTER at an appropriate point. (See Table 8, page 243.)

WORD PROCESSING APPLICATIONS

TABLE 6

Boxed Table

Language Arts Connection

Create a 3-column, 6-row table. Key the column headings in bold. Adjust the column widths; then center the table vertically and horizontally.

Present Tense	**Past Tense**	**Past Participle**
go	went	have/had gone
run	ran	have/had run
do	did	have/had done
see	saw	have/had seen
ring	rang	have/had rung

TABLE 7

Boxed Table

Create a 2-column, 7-row table. Adjust the column widths; then center the table vertically and horizontally.

Month	**Birthstone**
January	Garnet
February	Amethyst
March	Aquamarine
April	Diamond
May	Emerald
June	Pearl

SKILLBUILDING

C. PRETEST

Take a 1-minute timed writing on the paragraph. Note your speed and errors.

```
9       In the past decade, computers have affected almost       12
10  every job in the business office. Today, it is very common   22
11  to see computers being used that are smaller and six to ten  34
12  times quicker than they were only a few short years ago.     45
    | 1 | 2 | 3 | 4 | 5 | 6 | 7 | 8 | 9 | 10 | 11 | 12
```

D. PRACTICE

In the chart below, find the number of errors you made on the Pretest. Then key each of the designated drill lines 2 times.

Pretest Errors	0–1	2	3	4+
Drill Lines	16–20	15–19	14–18	13–17

Accuracy

```
13 just during decade faster smaller invaded business addition
14 past about coming become common powerful possible computers
15 now have would popular horizon machines business technology
16 six more find would quite become smaller possible computers
```

Speed

```
17 office being today every this task all now are the it in so
18 years their time more were used find this that not of is to
19 become makes will hard that they then much new and on be or
20 times today find such does much just work few ago use on of
```

E. POSTTEST

Repeat the Pretest. Compare your Posttest results with your Pretest results.

ETHICS CONNECTION

Photocopy Confidential Information Safely When photocopying confidential information, you need to be especially careful to keep the information safe. Key the following safeguards as a numbered list. Add an appropriate title. Follow your teacher's instructions for saving and printing your work.

1) Arrange to be alone while using the copier. 2) Keep all copies in your possession while copying. 3) Do not leave the copier unattended. 4) Do not make extra copies. 5) Remove any partially printed sheets inside the copier if the copier jams.
6) When you finish, take all originals, copies, and unwanted sheets with you.

TABLE 8

Boxed Table

Create a 3-column, 7-row table. Press ENTER to break the column headings as shown. Then adjust the column widths and center the table vertically and horizontally.

City of Origin	City of Destination	Date of Travel
Anchorage	Vancouver	January 1
Atlanta	Calgary	December 13
Chicago	Quebec	March 15
New York City	Montreal	May 27
Niagara Falls	Halifax	September 10
San Francisco	Toronto	October 7

SOCIAL STUDIES CONNECTION

Identify Spanish-Speaking Countries How many Spanish-speaking countries can you name? Enter "Spanish-speaking countries" in a search engine. Create a two-column table to list each country that you find and the geographic region of the country (for example, Central America, Europe, or Caribbean). Key an appropriate heading for each column. Follow your teacher's instructions for saving and printing your work.

PORTFOLIO Activity

Create a Table with Cities and States Revise Table 8 if you made any errors. Then create a 2-column, 7-row table. Title the first column City and the second column State.

Enter each city that is listed in the first column of Table 8 in the first column of the new table. Then key the state where it is located in the second column. If you are not sure of the correct state, use a print or online dictionary or almanac to find the information. Follow your teacher's instructions for saving and printing the file for your portfolio.

Letters With Numbered Lists

OBJECTIVES:

- Apply capitalization rules for compass points.
- Improve keyboarding skills.
- Format and key letters with numbered lists.

A. Warmup

Key each line 2 times.

Speed	1	Richard can ask what size tent he should take for the trip.
Accuracy	2	Jena quickly seized the wax buffer and removed a big patch.
Language Link	3	Thirty-seven people received ten 55-minute training videos.
Numbers/Symbols	4	The booklets are AB-GN, catalog item XH479/162CLW @ $13.50.

| 1 | 2 | 3 | 4 | 5 | 6 | 7 | 8 | 9 | 10 | 11 | 12

B. Capitalization

Study the rule and examples below. Then correct any errors in capitalization in lines 5–8.

Rule 19: Capitalize compass points (such as *north, south,* or *northeast*) only when they designate definite regions.

The forecaster said that the cold front was moving from the west and would blanket the Midwest with snow by Thursday.

5 If you are traveling to the north today, be careful of fog.
6 Paula lived in the north until she moved south to Florida.
7 Karen sold the most homes in the southern part of the city.
8 The flooding was severe in the southeast and midwest.

TABLES: NUMBER COLUMNS

OBJECTIVES:

- Key 35/3'/5e.
- Format tables with number columns.

A. WARMUP

Key each line 2 times.

Speed	*1*	We took a long trip and saw many fine sights while on tour.
Accuracy	*2*	Joe Pott quickly won over six men because of his good size.
Language Link	*3*	One of the students has been selected to go to the contest.
Numbers	*4*	5201 6202 7203 8204 9205 1206 2207 3208 4209 5210 6211 7212

| 1 | 2 | 3 | 4 | 5 | 6 | 7 | 8 | 9 | 10 | 11 | 12

*inter*NET CONNECTION

Relieve Stress Go to the Online Learning Center at **KeyComps.glencoe.com>Internet Connection>Unit 4> Lesson 68** to learn how to deal with stress. Create a one-column, seven-row table with the heading: **Ways to Relieve Stress**. Then list six healthy ways to relieve stress. Follow your teacher's instructions for saving and printing your work.

SKILLBUILDING

B. PREVIEW PRACTICE

Key each line 2 times as a preview to the timed writings that follow.

Accuracy	*5*	experts extended shoulders exercises stretching revitalized
Speed	*6*	stress breaks might gears ease desk step feel not may to of

LETTERS 51–53

Business Letter in Block Style

Create a data file with these field names:* Title, FirstName, LastName, Address, CityStateZIP, Physician, State. *After you have created the data file with these field names, create the following three records.

Record 1	**Record 2**	**Record 3**
Ms. Faye Hayes	Mr. Alvin Morgan	Mr. Lloyd Blairstone
450 Marshall Avenue	742 Huck Road	7500 Lada Lane
Hickory, NC 28611	Lexington, SC 29072	Thomaston, GA 30286
Dr. Millhouse	Dr. Stewart	Dr. Abernathy
North Carolina	South Carolina	Georgia

After you create the data records, key the following form letter in block style. Note that two of the data fields appear within the body of the letter. Then, merge the data records with the form letter to create Letters 51–53.

June 6, {year}

<<Title>> <<FirstName>> <<LastName>>
<<Address>>
<<CityStateZIP>>

Dear <<Title>> <<LastName>>:

¶Your physician, <<Physician>>, recommended you as a person who might benefit from participating in a research study on the problems of aging. This study is being conducted through the medical school at Wayne State University. The examinations included in the study will be at no cost to you.
¶Please read the brochure describing the study, complete the enclosed questionnaire, and return it to me by June 30. A postage-paid return envelope is also enclosed for your convenience.
¶Your participation in this study will help us reach our goal for the number of respondents we hope to include from <<State>>. If you have any questions, call me at 810-555-4575. I look forward to including you in this study.

Sincerely,

Donald L. Gaddis, M.D.
Project Director

urs
Enclosures

C. 3-Minute Timed Writings

Take two 3-minute timed writings on the paragraphs. Note your speed and errors.

Goal: 35/3'/5e

Workers may hesitate to take work breaks because they 11
feel they should not take the time. Extended sitting at a 23
computer can cause muscle pain. Experts say we should take 34
short breaks to refresh body and mind. Get out of your seat 46
and step around your desk. Walk to a different section of 58
the office. Do exercises that will relax your shoulders and 70
your neck. Just stretching at your desk might help to ease 82
stress. A quick change of pace can give your mind a chance 94
to shift gears. Then, you can return to work revitalized. 105

| 1 | 2 | 3 | 4 | 5 | 6 | 7 | 8 | 9 | 10 | 11 | 12 SI 1.29

FORMATTING

D. Tables: Number Columns

To format numbers in table columns:

1. Right-align the numbers in a column.
2. Right-align column headings over number columns. Entries such as telephone numbers, dates, and time periods are considered text, so column headings in these cases would be aligned left or centered.
3. If necessary, adjust the width of narrow number columns to balance them with the remaining columns in the table.

E. Software Features

STUDENT MANUAL

Aligning Text in Columns

Study Lesson 68 in your Student Manual. Complete all the practice activities while at your computer. Then complete the tasks that follow.

LETTER 50

Business Letter in Modified-Block Style

Key the following handwritten letter in modified-block style with indented paragraphs.

(Current Date)

Ms. Kateri Tahoma
Administrative Assistant
Diabo Construction Company
330 Cooper Avenue
Lincoln, NE 68506

Dear Ms. Tahoma:

You are invited to attend a seminar entitled "Listening Skills—Do You Hear When You Listen?" It will be held at the Cornhusker Hotel in Lincoln on June 17 from 9 a.m. until 3 p.m.

The registration fee of $50 includes the seminar and a luncheon from noon until 1:30. Your employer, Diabo Construction, will pay your registration fee.

This seminar will be well worth the time away from the office if you take the right approach. Here are a few suggestions that will help you turn this seminar into a valuable experience. Prepare yourself by reading the information provided by your company. List at least five specific questions you want answered. Use break time to network and talk to your peers. Bring business cards to exchange. When you receive one, make a note on the back about the person giving it to you. Collect handouts from all the speakers. Read your notes. Review and prepare a summary of what you experienced and learned. You also might listen for suggestions on how to be a better listener. The presenters will give the audience time to role-play and use specific techniques of listening.

If you follow these little hints, the seminar will be informative as well as enjoyable for you. We are looking forward to seeing you at the Cornhusker.

Sincerely,

Dana Olsen, Coordinator
Climbing the Ladder, Inc.

TABLE 9

Boxed Table

Create a 3-column, 6-row table. Align the column headings and the text columns at the left; align the column heading and the number column at the right. Automatically adjust the column widths. Center the table vertically and horizontally.

Teacher	Course	Room
Blackhawk, B.	Word Processing	109
Gorman, M.	Financial Planning	110
Maxey, S.	Applied Economics	2570
Sykes, B.	Beginning Japanese	315
Wicker, P.	Music Appreciation	2957

TABLE 10

Boxed Table

Create a 3-column, 8-row table. Break the column headings as shown. Align the number columns at the right. Automatically adjust the column widths. Center the table vertically and horizontally.

Snack Items	Total Caloric Count	Percent of Calories From Fat
Sell Well Chips	340	21
Mini Bits of Chips	290	10
Muncharoos	215	11
Cheddar Wafers	200	12
Snacker Crackers	190	8
Bagel Bits	150	8
Perfectly Crisp Pita Chips	120	0

TABLE 11

Boxed Table

Create a 3-column, 6-row table. Align the first column heading at the left. Align the second and third column headings at the right. Align the number columns at the right. Automatically adjust the column widths. Center the table vertically and horizontally.

Name	Gross Pay ($)	Tax ($)
Boldt, David	1,246	248
Johnson, Jay	942	188
Miller, Joan	846	168
Sipowitz, Rocky	1,050	210
Vandenburg, Harlan	976	194

C. 5-Minute Timed Writings

Take two 5-minute timed writings on the paragraphs. Note your speed and errors.

Goal: 36/5'/5e

Pollution of the earth refers to all of the ways in 11
which we spoil our natural surroundings. Mankind fouls the 22
air with smoke, ruins the soil with harsh pesticides and 34
fertilizers, and poisons the water with wastes. The earth 45
can be spoiled quickly in many ways. We unjustifiably ruin 57
the charm of the landscape when we toss ugly litter on the 69
ground and into the water. It seems we cause damage at one 81
time or another. 85

Pollution of the air, soil, and water is one of the 96
gravest issues that our world faces at this time. All of 107
these resources are basic to the survival of plants and 118
animals. Sickness and death can be caused by extreme air 130
pollution. Fish and other marine life are killed by water 141
that is badly polluted. Soil pollution reduces the number 153
of acres of land that can be used for food crops, and food 165
shortages can lead to famines. Polluted soil can also cause 177
deadly diseases. 180

SI 1.44

| 1 | 2 | 3 | 4 | 5 | 6 | 7 | 8 | 9 | 10 | 11 | 12

COMMUNICATION FOCUS

Identify Uses for Form Letters Form letters can be used for almost any kind of mass mailing. How would politicians and people running for office use form letters?

Key three ways that a politician would use form letters. Be sure to use complete sentences. Follow your teacher's instructions for saving and printing your work.

LESSON 69 TABLES: REINFORCEMENT

OBJECTIVES:

- Apply subject/verb agreement rules.
- Improve keyboarding skills.
- Apply table formats.

A. WARMUP

Key each line 2 times.

Speed	1	Rita will go to town and order two pairs of shoes for them.
Accuracy	2	Brown jars prevented the mixture from freezing too quickly.
Language Link	3	Most of the trees in this forest were saved from that fire.
Numbers/Symbols	4	You will get (1) more for the money and (2) better quality.

| 1 | 2 | 3 | 4 | 5 | 6 | 7 | 8 | 9 | 10 | 11 | 12

LANGUAGE LINK

B. SUBJECT/VERB AGREEMENT

Study the rule and the examples below. Then correct any errors in subject/verb agreement in lines 5–8.

Rule 11: Subjects joined by *and* take a plural verb unless the compound subject is preceded by *each, every,* or *many a (an).*

Many a computer and printer was purchased during the first quarter.

The physician and the anesthesiologist were in a patient conference.

Every student and instructor is hoping to obtain the test results soon.

5 Each girl and boy (has/have) received a ticket to the senior play.
6 Many a skier and skater (has/have) experienced very painful falls.
7 Both Louis and Ricki (is/are) taking a trip to Europe this fall.
8 Every dog and cat (has/have) to be vaccinated for rabies annually.

LESSON 87 REVIEW

OBJECTIVES:

- Key 36/5'/5e.
- Review business letter formats.
- Apply mail merge.

A. WARMUP

Key each line 2 times.

Speed	1	You can stay in shape with a brisk walk three times a week.
Accuracy	2	Dr. Baxter was quick to analyze the four major food groups.
Language Link	3	The philanthropist gave $24 million to Children's Hospital.
Numbers/Symbols	4	Donald and Darlene paid $5.08 for 4 pamphlets @ $1.27 each.
		| 1 | 2 | 3 | 4 | 5 | 6 | 7 | 8 | 9 | 10 | 11 | 12

SKILLBUILDING

B. PREVIEW PRACTICE

Key each line 2 times as a preview to the timed writings that follow.

Accuracy	5	pollution pesticides fertilizers surroundings unjustifiably
Speed	6	cause faces water world soil fish land into air be in of by

C. Diagnostic Practice: Alphabet

Turn to the Diagnostic Practice: Alphabet routine on page SB-1. Key one of the Pretest/Posttest paragraphs and identify any errors made. Then key the corresponding drill lines 2 times for each letter on which you made 2 or more errors and 1 time for each letter on which you made only 1 error. Finally, repeat the Pretest and compare your performance.

D. Alphabet Review

Key each line 2 times. Repeat if time permits.

```
 9 axle aide ache away bite brag brim bowl caps come crew chip
10 duet drag down dive east etch ends exit feud fame from flat
11 gale give glow grip hope have hill help ills into iced idea

12 joke jump jail jest knit kiln keep know line late lump lost
13 maze more mist melt norm nice nail numb odor over oath open
14 paid pour prod pest quad quip quiz quay ride reap rake room

15 sing stay sort shop team task thin tray ugly upon used unit
16 vote vast vine vest wage when wire worm axis oxen exit flax
17 yell yard year yolk yawl type zinc zeal zone zero zany buzz
```

ETHICS CONNECTION

Prevent Gossip A gossip is someone who spreads hurtful rumors about another person. Office or school gossip can cause serious problems by damaging relationships among people who must work together. The task of tracking and squelching gossip has been compared to catching smoke in the wind—it is impossible. There are, however, steps a person can take to prevent gossip.

Key the steps below. Under each numbered item, compose an acceptable response that you might make. An example is given after the first item. Follow your teacher's instructions for saving and printing your work.

1. Refuse to repeat gossip; keep confidences.
   "I really cannot talk about that."
2. Refuse to listen to gossip.
3. Speak up when you know that something is untrue.
4. Say positive, encouraging things to colleagues.

WORD PROCESSING APPLICATIONS

LETTERS 46–49

Business Letter in Block Style

Create a data file with the field names shown below, then create the four records. After the data records are complete, key the form letter in block style. Insert the fields where necessary. Merge the data file and form letter to create Letters 46–49.

Field Names: Title, FirstName, LastName, Address, City, State, ZIP

Record 1	Record 2	Record 3	Record 4
Mrs.	Dr.	Mr.	Mrs.
Jasmine	Lewis	Cameron	Nichole
Graham	Garcia	Wingert	McCullum
7457 E. 71st Street	3284 S. Yale Avenue	8130 W. Pine Street	948 S. Union Avenue
Tulsa	Tulsa	Tulsa	Tulsa
OK	OK	OK	OK
74136	74105	74136	74112

October 1, {year}

<<Title>> <<FirstName>> <<LastName>>
<<Address>>
<<City>>,<<State>> <<ZIP>>

Dear <<Title>> <<LastName>>:

We appreciate your recent purchase of an appliance from our Shalimar Mall store. A coupon book is enclosed that should be used to make your monthly payments.

Please be sure that our mailing address shows in the window part of the envelopes that are also enclosed. For your convenience, payments may also be made at the store. We look forward, <<Title>> <<LastName>>, to serving your appliance needs in the coming years.

Sincerely,

Wilbert Crawford
Accounts Manager

Enclosures

TABLE 12

Boxed Table

Create a 3-column, 7-row table. Center the column headings. Center the table vertically and horizontally.

Name of Show	Day/Date	Time
All Against Violence	Wed., October 16	3:30 p.m.–5:00 p.m.
Hooping It Up	Wed., November 15	10:30 a.m.–11:00 a.m.
Learning Rainbow	Monday-Friday	2:30 p.m.–3:00 p.m.
Magic Schoolroom	Sundays	10:30 a.m.–11:00 a.m.
Rock and Roll Times	Sunday-Thursday	8:00 p.m.–10:00 p.m.
The Science Guru	Monday-Friday	4:00 p.m.–4:30 p.m.

TABLE 13

Boxed Table

Create a 3-column, 8-row table, and align the column headings as follows: Left align the first column heading (press ENTER 1 time within the cell before you key it so that it aligns at the bottom with the multiline column headings). Align the second and third column headings at the right. Break the column headings into 2 lines as shown. Automatically adjust the column widths. Center the table vertically and horizontally.

Sandwich Items	Total Calorie Count	% of Calories From Fat
O'Brien's Lean Burger	320	10
Barbey's Lite Beef	294	10
Lucy's Grilled Chicken	290	6
BQ Broiler Chicken	280	10
Barbey's Chicken Lite	276	7
Lucy's Junior Burger	270	9
Andy's Turkey Lite	260	6

TABLE 14

Boxed Table

Open Table 8 and make the following changes:

1. Delete the hard returns in the column headings to place them on one line.
2. Change the third column heading to **Flight Number**.
3. Replace the dates in the third column with the following numbers: 1507, 557, 2330, 1991, 49, 275.
4. Align the first two column headings at the left. Align the last column heading at the right.
5. Right-align the numbers in the third column.
6. Re-center the table horizontally.

C. PRETEST

Take a 1-minute timed writng on the paragraph. Note your speed and errors.

Symbol Diagnostic

9 J&J Nursery numbered their plants. They sold 5 of #76, 11
10 69 of #42, and 25 of #38. I bought 20 bulbs* @ $2.49; now I 23
11 have to plant them. This is 20 + 40 = 60 that I have bought. 35
12 Red flowers @ $2.49 each show a profit of 8%. I'm thrilled! 47
| 1 | 2 | 3 | 4 | 5 | 6 | 7 | 8 | 9 | 10 | 11 | 12

D. PRACTICE

Key lines 13–21 twice. Then repeat any of the lines that stress the symbol errors you noted in the Pretest.

@ 13 Frank sold 15 @ 11, 20 @ 22, 25 @ 33, 30 @ 44, and 35 @ 55.
* 14 Earl selected *Rome, *Venice, *Paris, *Berlin, and *Madrid.
# 15 We see that #9 weighs 56#, #7 weighs 34#, and #8 weighs 2#.

$ 16 The seven girls saved $9, $10, $38, $47, $56, $72, and $89.
% 17 On those days the market rose 3%, 5%, 7%, 8%, 12%, and 18%.
& 18 The leaders are Kim & Dave, Robert & Mary, and Kay & Peter.

() 19 Li chose Marco (Florida), Daisy (Georgia), and Alta (Utah).
– 20 The cartons were labeled as 29-92, 38-56, 47-10, and 59-28.
+ = 21 Eb said that 28 + 65 = 93, 47 + 15 = 62, and 10 + 99 = 109.

E. POSTTEST

Repeat the Pretest. Compare your Posttest results with your Pretest results.

COMMUNICATION FOCUS

Conquer Glossophobia Do you have glossophobia? The majority of the people around you right now probably suffer from it to some degree. Glossophobia is the fear of speaking in public, and it ranks near the top on most lists of people's fears. Anyone can, however, take steps to overcome this phobia.

With a partner, discuss ways to conquer the fear of public speaking. Compose a numbered list of at least five ways to overcome glossophobia. Use complete sentences. Follow your teacher's instructions for saving and printing your work.

Tables: Titles, Subtitles, and Braced Column Headings

OBJECTIVES:

- Improve keyboarding skills.
- Format tables with titles, subtitles, and braced column headings.

A. Warmup

Key each line 2 times.

Speed	1	To reach your goal, you must learn to keep your mind on it.
Accuracy	2	Jars prevented the brown mixture from freezing too quickly.
Language Link	3	Each pattern and bow requires at least two yards of ribbon.
Numbers	4	Today's homework is to study Chapter 15, pages 136 and 137.

| 1 | 2 | 3 | 4 | 5 | 6 | 7 | 8 | 9 | 10 | 11 | 12

SKILLBUILDING

B. 30-Second Timed Writings

Take two 30-second timed writings on the first paragraph. Then take two 30-second timed writings on the second paragraph. Try to key with no more than 2 errors on each timed writing.

5 Very seldom will you be asked to work from exact copy 11
6 that has no errors. You will often have to make changes. 22

7 Most keying is done from rough-draft copy. On the job 11
8 you must be able to make a decision about correct format. 22

| 1 | 2 | 3 | 4 | 5 | 6 | 7 | 8 | 9 | 10 | 11 | 12

LESSON 86 MERGE: FORM LETTERS

OBJECTIVES:

- Improve keyboarding skills on symbol keys.
- Create a form letter and a data file.
- Merge a form letter with a data file.

A. WARMUP

Key each line 2 times.

Speed	1	The report cover is the first part of a report that we see.
Accuracy	2	Joey requested help to research weekly executive magazines.
Language Link	3	This science textbook is $63, but that math text is $44.17.
Numbers/Symbols	4	You may reach Don any weekday at (404) 555-7139, Ext. 3286.

| 1 | 2 | 3 | 4 | 5 | 6 | 7 | 8 | 9 | 10 | 11 | 12

SKILLBUILDING

B. 30-SECOND TIMED WRITINGS

Take two 30-second timed writings on lines 5–6. Then take two 30-second timed writings on lines 7–8. Try to increase your speed each time.

5 Making a speech is a frightening prospect for many of 11
6 us because we lack experience in making oral presentations. 23

7 Planning, preparing, and practicing are the best ways 11
8 to prepare for delivering an oral report to most audiences. 23

| 1 | 2 | 3 | 4 | 5 | 6 | 7 | 8 | 9 | 10 | 11 | 12

C. Number and Symbol Review

Key each line 2 times.

9 They found 10 @ 56, 56 @ 47, 47 @ 38, 38 @ 29, and 29 @ 10.
10 Our new scale shows #10 at 29#, #38 at 47#, and #29 at 56#.
11 Gray,* Moletti,* Young,* Hernandez,* and Jones* won prizes.

12 Our show tickets should cost us $10, $29, $38, $47, or $56.
13 Your sales increased 10%, 29%, 38%, 47%, and 56% last year.
14 Lea & Madera, Yung & Poe, and Day & Cole are all attorneys.

15 Label the square cartons as 47-10, 56-38, 38-47, and 10-29.
16 We know that 38 + 47 = 85, 29 + 10 = 39, and 56 + 70 = 126.
17 Lund (Utah), Leon (Iowa), and Troy (Ohio) were represented.

FORMATTING

D. Tables With Titles and Subtitles

Tables may have titles and subtitles in the first row, as shown in the example below. To format a table with a title and a subtitle:

1. **Merge**, or combine, the cells in the first row of the table.
2. Center and key the title in all caps, bold, and a 14-point font.
3. Press ENTER 1 time.
4. Center and key the subtitle in initial caps, bold, and a 12-point font.
5. Press ENTER 1 time to leave a blank line.

E. Braced Column Headings

Braced column headings are headings that apply to more than one column of a table. In this example, *First Quarter* and *Second Quarter* are braced headings. To create a braced heading:

1. Select the cells for the braced row and merge them.
2. Center the heading.
3. Key each braced column heading in bold and initial caps.

VISITATION REPORT **June 30, {year}**			
First Quarter		**Second Quarter**	
Month	City	Month	City
January	New York City	April	New Orleans
February	San Francisco	May	Kansas City
March	Philadelphia	June	Jacksonville

G. Software Features

STUDENT MANUAL

Mail Merge
Data Source
Return to the Main Document

Study Lesson 85 in your Student Manual. Complete all the practice activities while at your computer. Then complete the tasks that follow.

WORD PROCESSING APPLICATIONS

LETTERS 44–45

Business Letters in Block Style

Create a data file with the field names shown below; then create the two records. After the data records are complete, key the form letter in block style. Merge the data file and form letter to create Letters 44–45.

Field Names	**Record 1**	**Record 2**
Title	Ms.	Mr.
FirstName	Teresa	Tom
LastName	Belle	Carlisle
Address	7168 Olympia Avenue	16687 E. Latimer Place
City	Dalton	Westlake
State	GA	OH
ZIP	30720	44145

January 19, {Year}

<<Title>> <<FirstName>> <<LastName>>
<<Address>>
<<City>>,<<State>> <<ZIP>>

Dear <<FirstName>>:

¶Congratulations! You are a winner in the Bold Journey Contest sponsored by *Outdoor Magazine*. You have won an entire week at Outdoor Adventure Camp in Big Branch, Utah—all expenses paid. We hope, <<FirstName>>, that you are looking forward to joining the other 49 high school students across the country who are also winners.
¶Next week we will send you all the details concerning your travel arrangements, needed equipment, and the type of clothing you should bring.
¶We look forward to seeing you at Big Branch.
Sincerely, / Brandon T. Dillard / Editor in Chief / urs

STUDENT MANUAL

Merge Cells

Study Lesson 70 in your Student Manual. Complete the practice activities while at your computer. Then complete the tasks that follow.

WORD PROCESSING APPLICATIONS

TABLE 15

Boxed Table

Create a 2-column, 10-row table. Merge the cells in the first row. Center and key the title and subtitle. Insert a blank line after the subtitle. Center the column headings. Center the table vertically and horizontally.

NATURAL WONDERS OF THE WORLD **(Listed by World Travelers and Explorers)**	
Name	**Location**
Angel Falls	Venezuela
Giant Sequoia Trees	United States (California)
Grand Canyon	United States (Colorado River)
Great Barrier Reef	Australia
Mount Everest	Nepal
Mount Fuji	Japan
Paricutin (young volcano)	Mexico
Victoria Falls	Zimbabwe

TABLE 16

Boxed Table

Create a 4-column, 6-row table. Merge the cells in the first row. Center and key the title and subtitle. In the second row, merge the cells in columns 1 and 2; then merge the cells in columns 3 and 4. Center all of the column headings. Center the table vertically and horizontally.

SEMI-ANNUAL VISITATION REPORT **June 30, {year}**			
First Quarter		**Second Quarter**	
Month	**City**	**Month**	**City**
January	New York City	April	New Orleans
February	San Francisco	May	Kansas City
March	Philadelphia	June	Jacksonville

SKILLBUILDING

C. PRETEST

Take a 1-minute timed writing on the paragraph. Note your speed and errors.

```
9       To merge many addresses with one letter is truly quite   11
10 a job for certain people. However, this vexing task can be    23
11 completed very simply and in an amazingly little amount of    35
12 time with concentrated effort to learn the right technique.   47
   | 1 | 2 | 3 | 4 | 5 | 6 | 7 | 8 | 9 | 10 | 11 | 12
```

D. PRACTICE

SPEED: If you made 2 or fewer errors on the Pretest, key lines 13–20 two times each.

ACCURACY: If you made more than 2 errors on the Pretest, key lines 13–16 as a group two times. Then key lines 17–20 as a group two times.

Left Reaches

```
13 rer red were crow break dread cheer chore dream toast clerk
14 asa ask base lane flash saint hasty sauce spasm salty treat
15 rtr art dirt trim ports chart tract short trade sport train
16 tet jet team kite meter beets meets sweet liter miter white
```

Right Reaches

```
17 iui suit quit unit ruin build equip quiet quick guilt fruit
18 oio toil coil riot boil joins lions joist avoid doing onion
19 pop pods chop pose stop spoil sport adopt depot topic power
20 lol poll lots jolt told molds older holds soles folds holes
```

E. POSTTEST

Repeat the Pretest. Compare your Posttest results with your Pretest results.

FORMATTING

F. MERGE: DATA SOURCE/FORM LETTER

Often it is necessary to send the same letter to many different people. A **form letter** is a letter that is keyed only once but can be sent to many different people. To prepare a form letter:

1. Create a data file that contains the variable information within the letter (for example, the names and addresses of all the people to whom you want to send the letter).
2. Create a form letter with fields for the missing data.
3. Merge the form letter with the data.

LESSON 71 TABLES: REVIEW

OBJECTIVES:

- Apply subject/verb agreement rules.
- Increase keyboarding speed and improve accuracy.
- Apply knowlege of table formats.

A. WARMUP

Key each line 2 times.

Speed 1 The goal of the girl is to work to be the best she can be.
Accuracy 2 Dave froze the mixtures in the deep brown jug too quickly.
Language Link 3 Many a husband and wife has made a plan for spending money.
Numbers/Symbols 4 I purchased 13 dozen pens @ $11.05. (The sale ends today!)

| 1 | 2 | 3 | 4 | 5 | 6 | 7 | 8 | 9 | 10 | 11 | 12

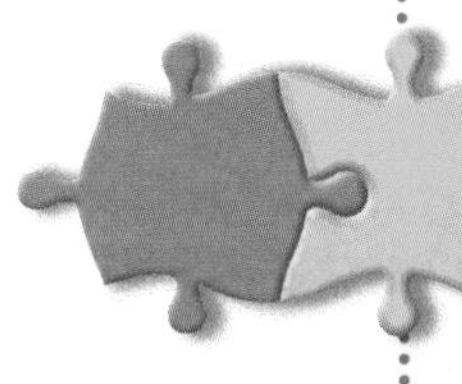

LANGUAGE LINK

B. SUBJECT/VERB AGREEMENT

Study the rule and the examples that follow. Then correct any errors in subject/verb agreement in lines 5–8.

Rule 12: If two subjects are joined by *or, either / or, neither / nor,* or *not only / but also,* the verb should agree with the subject nearer to the verb.

Either the lifeguard or the swimmers have reported a shark in the water.

Not only the page proofs but also the color template is ready to be returned.

5 Either the CEO or two board members (has/have) to sign the check.
6 Neither Bo nor the children (was/were) allowed to watch the show.
7 Not only the students but also the teacher (wants/want) to attend.
8 Either you or your classmates (is/are) to collect money for Wes.

MERGE: FORM LETTERS

OBJECTIVES:

- Compose paragraphs at the keyboard.
- Increase keyboarding speed and improve accuracy.
- Create form letters with a mail merge.

A. WARMUP

Key each line 2 times.

Speed	1	You can learn to key at a rapid speed if you will practice.
Accuracy	2	Olmec, Zapotec, Mixtec, and Aztec were early civilizations.
Language Link	3	Almost one-third of the class was unable to go on the trip.
Numbers/Symbols	4	Our company will buy 1/3 of their stock @ 22 7/8 per share.
		| 1 | 2 | 3 | 4 | 5 | 6 | 7 | 8 | 9 | 10 | 11 | 12

B. COMPOSING AT THE KEYBOARD

Choose one of the sentence fragments below, complete it, and continue composing until you have created a short paragraph with at least three sentences.

5 I was never a believer in UFOs until...
6 The road was dark and deserted. All of a sudden...
7 My phone never stopped ringing after I...
8 While sailing on a very windy day, we suddenly...

SOCIAL STUDIES CONNECTION

Create Composition Starters Think about what you have studied in your Social Studies class so far this year. Key three sentence fragments that relate to different areas that you have studied, such as "The legislative branch is...." Trade sentence fragments with a partner, and compose and key a paragraph with one of your partner's sentence fragments. Follow your teacher's instructions for saving and printing your work.

C. 30-Second OK Timed Writings

Take two 30-second OK (error-free) timed writings on lines 9–10. Then take two 30-second OK timed writings on lines 11–12. Goal: no errors.

9 I quickly explained that only a few big jobs involve 11
10 hazards, but the managers say we need more safety measures. 23

11 Peter reviewed the subject before giving Kay and Max a 11
12 quiz. Both of them like using the computer to take tests. 23

| 1 | 2 | 3 | 4 | 5 | 6 | 7 | 8 | 9 | 10 | 11 | 12

D. PRETEST

Take a 1-minute timed writing on the paragraph. Note your speed and errors.

13 Can you name the five steps in the cycle of processing 11
14 information? First is input. The next step is processing. 23
15 Output is the third step. The fourth step is distribution. 35
16 The last step is storage. 40

| 1 | 2 | 3 | 4 | 5 | 6 | 7 | 8 | 9 | 10 | 11 | 12

E. PRACTICE

In the chart below, find the number of errors you made on the Pretest. Then key each of the designated drill lines 2 times.

Pretest Errors	0–1	2	3	4+
Drill Lines	20–24	19–23	18–22	17–21

Accuracy

17 quire words future format mailed certain involves publicize
18 saves input phase public fourth output retrieval processing
19 modes backs third others lasted storage changed information
20 next steps named saving inform getting require distribution

Speed

21 files other words done this back last all the can use on be
22 store disks forms some them five mode and has job put up to
23 first cycle right name form have been rib you out for is in
24 names which third mail that four sets may mat his her of or

F. POSTTEST

Repeat the Pretest. Compare your Posttest results with your Pretest results.

LETTER 43

Business Letter in Modified-Block Style

Key the following handwritten letter in modified-block style. Use the current date and be sure to add your initials as reference initials.

DeskData Company
5339 Westhampton Court
Tempe, AZ 85284
Attention: Information Consultant

Ladies and Gentlemen:
Subject: New Desktop Publishing System

We have implemented the recommendations your company made to improve our communications at Swift Industrials. Our new desktop publishing software is providing us with printing capabilities that were not possible in the past.

We are experiencing tremendous savings in printing costs with the new system, and I know that our image has been improved because of the quality of our correspondence and reports.

Thank you for evaluating our old system and for recommending such a fine new one. We are already very pleased with the new system, and I know that as we all learn to use its full capabilities, we will find it even more valuable to our operations.

Sincerely,
Jake E. Ford
President

TABLE 17

Boxed Table

Create a 3-column, 8-row table. Right-align the number column. Automatically adjust the column widths. Center the table vertically and horizontally.

MAJOR U.S. RIVERS (From U.S. Geographic Textbook)		
River	**Length**	**Origin**
Arkansas	1,460	Colorado
Colorado	1,450	Colorado
Columbia	1,240	British Columbia
Mississippi	2,350	Minnesota
Missouri	2,320	Montana
Tennessee	900	North Carolina

TABLE 18

Boxed Table

Create a 4-column, 10-row table. Center the braced headings. Right-align the number columns. Automatically adjust the column widths. Center the table vertically and horizontally.

PARKS HIGH SCHOOL HONOR GRADUATES (GPA From 4.00 to 3.50)			
4.00 GPA to 3.75 GPA		**3.74 GPA to 3.50 GPA**	
Student	**GPA**	**Student**	**GPA**
Bryce Bynum	4.00	Aaron Christopher	3.73
Jennifer Click	4.00	Shelley Lyons	3.70
Samuel Dornbusch	3.98	Kelley Lavender	3.65
Rose Barstow	3.97	James Crawford	3.62
Isaac Heyman	3.90	Brandon Lee	3.57
Charlotte Mendosa	3.85	Karen Brackett	3.52
Charlotte Diaz	3.80	Neil Pacioni	3.50

COMMUNICATION FOCUS

Identify Workplace Skills Employers look for employees who can solve problems, make decisions, prioritize, work in teams, and listen well.

Create a table with two columns and six rows. Title the first column *Qualities*, and enter each of the qualities listed above in the rows. Title the second column *Examples* and key an example of each quality. Follow your teacher's instructions for saving and printing your work.

LETTER 42

Business Letter in Block Style

Key the following business letter in block style. Make the corrections indicated by the proofreaders' marks.

Current Date

Attention Purchasing Agent
Ladies and gentlemen

Solar supply co.
917 west madison street
Johnson City, tn 37601

We appreciate your check in payment of order no. 16543, however, I am returning the check to you by registered mail since the correct amount of $195.18 and your signature were omitted. Please fill in these items and return the check to us. Your order for the compact disc player model no. 34109 has been forwarded to our regional office in Dallas Texas. We should recieve it in this office by the 28th of this month. When it arrives, I will inspect it personally and send it to you immediately. Please let us know, if there is any other way we can be of service to you.

sincerely,

charles t. walker
sales manager

COMMUNICATION FOCUS

Compare Customer Service Consider the ways that businesses offer customer services: face-to-face, by telephone, and through Web sites that offer e-mail forms and Frequently Asked Questions (FAQs) information. Key three paragraphs explaining the advantages and disadvantages of each method, which you prefer and why. Follow your teacher's instructions for saving and printing your work.

TABLE 19

Boxed Table

Create a 6-column, 8-row table similar to the illustration below. Center all column headings. Automatically adjust the column widths. Center the table vertically and horizontally.

ANTARCTICA EXPLORATIONS (Expeditions to the South Pole)					
1773–1928			**1929–1989**		
Year	**Explorer**	**Mode of Travel**	**Year**	**Explorer**	**Mode of Travel**
1773	Cook	Ship	1929	Byrd	Airplane
1908	Shackleton	Pony sled	1935	Ellsworth	Airplane
1911	Amundsen	Dog sled	1946	Ronne	Airplane
1912	Scott	Dog sled	1958	Thiel	Tractor
1928	Wilkins	Airplane	1989	Murden & Metz	Skis

PORTFOLIO *Activity*

Identify the Parts of a Table Revise Table 19 if you made any errors. Change the vertical alignment from *Center* to *Top*.

Below Table 19, create a 2-column table and identify the parts of Table 19 as shown in the partial example below. Follow your teacher's instructions for saving and printing your work.

Title	Antarctica Explorations
Subtitle	
First braced column heading	
First column heading	

E. Subject Line

Ladies and Gentlemen:

Subject: New Desktop Publishing System

We have implemented the recommendations your company made to improve our communications at Swift Industrials. Our new desktop publishing software is providing us with printing capabilities that were not possible in the past.

We are experiencing tremendous savings in printing costs with the new system, and I know that our image has been improved because of the quality of our correspondence and reports.

Thank you for evaluating our old system and for recommending such a fine new one. We are already very pleased with the new system, and I know that as we all learn to use its full capabilities, we will find it even more valuable to our operations.

Sincerely,

Jake E. Ford
President

urs

A **subject line** briefly identifies the main topic of a letter. To format a subject line:

1. Key the salutation, then press ENTER 2 times.
2. Key the subject line in initial caps at the left margin.
3. Follow the word *Subject* with a colon and 1 space.
4. Press ENTER 2 times and begin the body of the letter.

WORD PROCESSING APPLICATIONS

LETTER 41

Business Letter in Modified-Block Style

Key the following letter in modified-block style.

(Current Date) / Allied Automotive Corporation / 3259 Bellevue Boulevard / Novato, CA 94949 / Attention: Customer Relations Department / Ladies and Gentlemen:

¶A few weeks ago I purchased a new SouthStar from AAA Motors in Carrollton, Georgia. Since I have worked as a sales representative for an automobile dealership in the past, I know it is not too often that you receive letters that say, "Thank you." That is the reason I want to take a few minutes to tell you how pleased I am with my new SouthStar and how much I appreciate the way I was treated by your two AAA sales representatives.

¶Everything about this vehicle has measured up to my expectations. The salespeople were most courteous and helpful—there was no high-pressure sales pitch. They gave me some valuable information about the use and upkeep of the vehicle, too.

¶Congratulations! You have a fine vehicle and a super dealership in Carrollton, Georgia! / Sincerely, / David Jackson / urs

Reports With Parenthetical References and Quotes

OBJECTIVES:

- Key 35/3'/5e.
- Format references and quotations.
- Format an academic report.

A. Warmup

Key each line 2 times.

Speed	1	The team has worked hard to solve the problem for the firm.
Accuracy	2	Six big jet planes quickly zoomed over the five old towers.
Language Link	3	Neither the colt nor the calves were afraid of the coyotes.
Numbers	4	Our 15 girls and 25 boys ate 8 pies, 8 cakes, and 9 pizzas.
		| 1 | 2 | 3 | 4 | 5 | 6 | 7 | 8 | 9 | 10 | 11 | 12

SKILLBUILDING

B. Preview Practice

Key each line 2 times as a preview to the 3-minute timed writings that follow.

Accuracy	5	relax beliefs improve realize physical positive differently
Speed	6	smile often well urge know good back each hug may how to be

C. Concentration

Key the following lines. As you key, change every masculine pronoun to a feminine pronoun (his to her), and change every feminine pronoun to a masculine pronoun (she to he).

```
9  She will complete the sales report as soon as she receives it.
10 He must give her the sales figures so that she can compile it.
11 Her final copy is past-due; her boss has already asked for it.
12 Her boss will then give it to his boss, the director of sales.
```

FORMATTING

D. Attention Line

When a letter is addressed directly to a company, an **attention line** may be used to route it to a particular person or department. If you use an attention line:

1. Key the inside address, then press ENTER two times.
2. Key the word *Attention*, followed by a colon and 1 space.
3. Key the name of the person or department to whom the letter is being directed.
4. Press ENTER 2 times and key the salutation. Use a salutation such as *Ladies and Gentlemen:*, *Gentlemen:*, or *Ladies:* with an attention line.

Current Date

DeskData Company
5339 Westhampton Court
Tempe, AZ 85283

Attention: Information Consultant

Ladies and Gentlemen:

C. 3-Minute Timed Writings

Take two 3-minute timed writings on the paragraphs. Note your speed and errors.

Goal: 35/3'/5e

When it comes to health, our minds matter more than we 11
know. Some studies say that a person may have feelings and 22
beliefs that can improve physical well being. People might 33
act differently when they realize that how they think might 47
affect how they feel. 51

Relax more. Be positive. Enjoy each day. Get back to 62
nature. Listen to the music you like. Practice the habit of 74
a hug a day from friends or family. Take breaks and quiet 86
time for yourself. Smile more often. Doctors urge us to 97
think good thoughts to live better lives. 105

| 1 | 2 | 3 | 4 | 5 | 6 | 7 | 8 | 9 | 10 | 11 | 12 SI 1.34

FORMATTING

D. Reports With Parenthetical References

When you write a report that uses facts, ideas, and information from other people, you must give credit to those people. One acceptable way to give credit, or cite your sources, is called MLA style, a format developed by the Modern Language Association.

MLA style uses **parenthetical references.** In this style, a quotation is followed by the author's or source's name in parentheses. Follow these guidelines to format parenthetical references:

1. In parenthesis, include the author's name and the page number(s) of the source; for example, (Adams 157–158).
2. If the author's or source's name is mentioned before the quote, include only the page number(s) in parentheses; for example, (157–158).
3. If there are two or three authors of the source, include all authors' names in parentheses; for example, (Jones, Cass, and Noel 199).

(continued on next page)

LESSON 84 LETTERS WITH ATTENTION AND SUBJECT LINES

OBJECTIVES:

- Improve keyboarding skills.
- Format and key letters with attention and subject lines.

A. WARMUP

Key each line 2 times.

Speed	1	A strong dollar makes it easier for interest to be lowered.
Accuracy	2	An aqueous liquid was used externally to prevent abscesses.
Language Link	3	We bought seven pies and seven dozen cookies for the party.
Numbers/Symbols	4	The S & P's 500 index (dividends + gains) was just over 9%.

| 1 | 2 | 3 | 4 | 5 | 6 | 7 | 8 | 9 | 10 | 11 | 12

MATH CONNECTION

Explain Credit Card Interest Rates When you pay for a product with a credit card, you get charged an annual percentage rate (APR) if the balance of the account is not paid each month. Go to the Online Learning Center at **KeyComps.glencoe.com>Math Connection>Unit 5>Lesson 84** to learn more about credit card interest rates. Complete the activity.

SKILLBUILDING

B. 12-SECOND SPRINTS

Take three 12-second timed writings on each line. Try to increase your speed each time.

5 Many good stocks showed slow gains even in the bull market.
6 Your credit card rate will go up if you pay late too often.
7 The people in this country save much less than they should.
8 A bank savings account is a safe way to save your earnings.

| | | | 5 | | | | 10 | | | | 15 | | | | 20 | | | | 25 | | | | 30 | | | | 35 | | | | 40 | | | | 45 | | | | 50 | | | | 55 | | | | 60

(continued)

4. If there are four or more authors, include the first author's name followed by *et al.;* for example, (Martin et al. 215–217).
5. If there is no author, include a shortened version of the title and the page number(s) in parentheses; for example, (Critical Essays 59).

E. Quotations In Reports

MLA style uses the following guidelines for quotations:

Short Quotations (less than 4 lines):

1. Enclose direct quotations in quotation marks. Do not use quotation marks with indirect quotes or paraphrased remarks.
2. Key the parenthetical reference 1 space after the closing quotation mark or the last word of an indirect quote.
3. Key the ending punctuation mark after the reference. **Example:** "...until we receive confirmation" (Barton 96).

Long Quotations (4 or more lines):

1. Do not use quotation marks.
2. Indent the quote 1 inch from the left margin.
3. Key the parenthetical reference 1 space after the ending punctuation mark. **Example:** ...by tomorrow at the latest. (Johnson 41)

F. Software Features

STUDENT MANUAL

Indents

Study Lesson 72 in your Student Manual. Complete all the practice activities while at your computer. Then complete the tasks that follow.

*inter*NET CONNECTION

Identify MLA Format The guidelines for formatting academic reports in this book are based on the MLA (Modern Language Association) style. To find out more about the MLA go to the Online Learning Center at **KeyComps.glencoe.com>Internet Connection>Unit 4> Lesson 72**. Complete the activity about the organization and its guidelines.

(continued)

¶Travel agencies will make hotel and rental car reservations. You can tell your travel agent exactly what you want in the way of a rental car, specify a certain hotel or motel, and ask for reservations on a specific airline. Usually, your agent will be able to fulfill the majority of your requests.

¶Before visiting a foreign country, get information about customs and cultures. Knowledge about cultural differences is vital. It will help you avoid offending someone in a foreign country. Don't be surprised if foreigners do not make eye contact. Some may make long eye contact, while others view eye contact as disrespectful. If you're confused about cultural differences, question someone who knows the culture. Most countries have days that commemorate special events. Information about social customs is very important.

¶Get to know a country's currency, and bring a translation dictionary with you so that you can refer to it for some of your basic communication needs.

¶GLOBAL TRAVEL can easily make airplane and hotel reservations for you. By making reservations in advance, you can save money and be certain you're getting the schedules you want.

¶Next week, we will be sending you a helpful booklet, *Traveling Abroad,* containing numerous helpful tips for traveling. Also included in the booklet are several detailed maps of the most popular travel destinations. These maps identify travel mileage between many cities and also highlight major scenic attractions that you may wish to visit during your trip.

¶We hope you will consider using GLOBAL TRAVEL for your travel needs. We look forward to helping you make your reservations for what we believe will be your most enjoyable travel adventure. / Sincerely, / Conrad McMurphy / Travel Agent / urs

REPORT 17

Academic Report

Key the following report in academic style. Double-space the report. If necessary, refer to formatting instructions on page 139 for academic reports.

(Your Name)
(Your Teacher's Name)
(Class Name)
(Current Date)

Employee Absenteeism

"Absence makes the heart grow fonder" (Bayly 1). This quote may apply to the absence of a loved one; however, it is not true in the case of employee absence.

Some feel that a paycheck is enough incentive to come to work. Others feel that what happens once employees arrive can increase absenteeism. Hawkens writes in his book, <u>Management by Communication</u>:

> It will help to work with employees rather than manage them and to keep open lines of communication. There is no greater obstacle to successful communications than the refusal of a manager to willingly communicate with those who are under his or her direct line of control and an unwillingness to practice this activity on a day-to-day basis. (22–23)

Employers have studied reports explaining why employees are absent. They have found that lack of good quality child care is one big factor. In response to this need, some employers have set up child care facilities at the work site (Stone and Burlingham 47).

The solution to the problem of employee absenteeism will take effort on the part of both workers and employers. Workers must understand how their job performance affects business success—and whether or not they will even have a job. Employers need to continue to try to help employees overcome factors that cause them to be absent.

(continued)

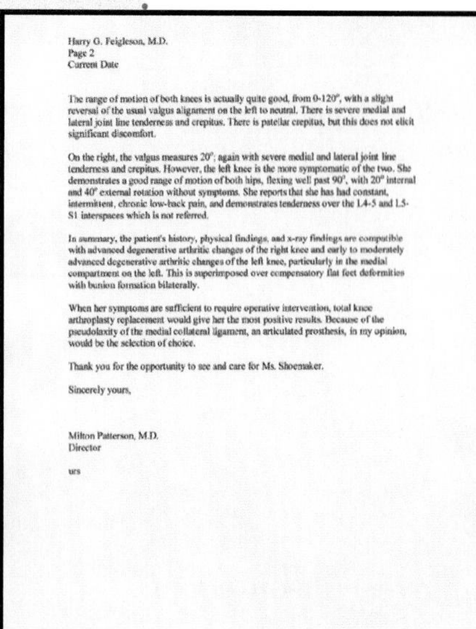

Harry G. Feigleson, M.D.
Page 2
Current Date

The range of motion of both knees is actually quite good, from 0-120°, with a slight reversal of the usual valgus alignment on the left to neutral. There is severe medial and lateral joint line tenderness and crepitus. There is patellar crepitus, but this does not elicit significant discomfort.

On the right, the valgus measures 20°; again with severe medial and lateral joint line tenderness and crepitus. However, the left knee is the more symptomatic of the two. She demonstrates a good range of motion of both hips, flexing well past 90°, with 20° internal and 40° external rotation without symptoms. She reports that she has had constant, intermittent, chronic low-back pain, and demonstrates tenderness over the L4-5 and L5-S1 interspaces which is not referred.

In summary, the patient's history, physical findings, and x-ray findings are compatible with advanced degenerative arthritic changes of the right knee and early to moderately advanced degenerative arthritic changes of the left knee, particularly in the medial compartment on the left. This is superimposed over compensatory flat feet deformities with bunion formation bilaterally.

When her symptoms are sufficient to require operative intervention, total knee arthroplasty replacement would give her the most positive results. Because of the pseudolaxity of the medial collateral ligament, an articulated prosthesis, in my opinion, would be the selection of choice.

Thank you for the opportunity to see and care for Ms. Shoemaker.

Sincerely yours,

Milton Patterson, M.D.
Director

urs

4. For all continuing pages, add a header that includes the addressee's name, the page number, and the date of the letter; align at the left margin. (See the illustration.) For a simplified continuation page, use a header to add only a right-aligned page number.
5. Use widow/orphan protection to avoid single lines of a paragraph at either the top or bottom of the page.

WORD PROCESSING APPLICATIONS

LETTER 40

Business Letter in Modified-Block Style

Key this letter in modified-block style. Create a header for the second page.

(Current Date) / Ms. Josephine Morello / 348 Douglas Boulevard / Atlanta, GA 30303 / Dear Ms. Morello:
¶Thank you for your request for travel information.
¶You have several options for travel arrangements. You can use a travel agency, your company's travel department, or your computer (for online reservation service), or you can make all the contacts yourself. Travelers are more and more frequently using the Internet to make their airline reservations.
¶If you choose a travel agency, you will receive assistance in making airline, rental car, or hotel/motel reservations. Travel agencies use computerized databases and can find the lowest fares and most convenient flight schedules. So that you can get the exact flight and fare you want, you will need to provide the travel agent with your preferred arrival and departure dates, and cities from which you will depart. Also provide your arrival time, times of travel, and travelers' names. You may also need to provide photographs or birth certificates if you are traveling to overseas destinations.

(continued on next page)

REPORTS WITH WORKS CITED PAGE

OBJECTIVES:

- Improve keyboarding technique.
- Compose paragraphs at the keyboard.
- Create headers and footers.
- Format a works cited page.

A. WARMUP

Key each line 2 times.

Speed	*1*	You will need to learn new ways to work and save more time.
Accuracy	*2*	The judge quickly gave back six of the prizes to the women.
Language Link	*3*	Not only they but also I am playing golf and swimming soon.
Numbers/Symbols	*4*	Report #R102 (prepared by Rothe & Roy) shows a 2% increase.

| 1 | 2 | 3 | 4 | 5 | 6 | 7 | 8 | 9 | 10 | 11 | 12

B. COMPOSING AT THE KEYBOARD

Answer one of the following questions with a short paragraph.

5 Who are three people you would most like to meet, and why would you like to meet them?

6 If you could travel with a historical or famous person, who would that be, and why did you choose that person?

7 If you could design your dream vacation spot, what would it be like?

C. 5-Minute Timed Writings

Take two 5-minute timed writings on the paragraphs. Note your speed and errors.

Goal: 36/5'/5e

```
     The term credit means buying now and paying later. It   11
is similar to borrowing cash. One reason people use credit   23
is because they do not have the money to pay for something   35
at the time they want to buy it.                             41
     Many people now use credit cards to purchase things.    52
Credit cards are easy to obtain and use, and people are      63
quick to use them as borrowed money for extra things they    75
cannot afford. They build up debts they cannot pay.          85
     Adults of all ages and all income levels can quickly    96
get into debt with credit cards. They do not realize that   108
using credit comes with a high price. Often, cardholders    119
pay finance charges or interest on unpaid bills.            129
     In spite of this, most people will need to establish a 140
good credit record. They will need a steady job with stable 152
income, and they must prove that they will repay any money  164
they borrow. Once people have their good credit ratings,    175
they must maintain them.                                    180
| 1 | 2 | 3 | 4 | 5 | 6 | 7 | 8 | 9 | 10 | 11 | 12   SI 1.39
```

FORMATTING

D. Two-Page Letters

HAYES MEDICAL CENTER
3231 Riverside Drive
Perrysburg, OH 43551-1001
Phone 419-555-7800 Fax 419-555-7890
Excellence in Medical Service for Over 50 Years

SURGERY UNIT

Current Date

Harry G. Feigleson, M.D.
356 South Main Street
Bowling Green, OH 43402-1011

Dear Dr. Feigleson:

Subject: Frances Shoemaker

Ms. Shoemaker was seen in consultation today concerning increasing problems she has been having with both lower extremities, but primarily her left knee. She is a 58-year-old woman who recognizes that she is overweight. She works as a secretary at Bowling Green State University, where she has been employed for 32 years.

She reports that, as best she can remember, her knee problems started with the right knee that she hit on a desk about 5 years ago, which resulted in an arthroscopic procedure to the right knee. It has improved, but it has shown some progressive evidence of deterioration with a lateral migration. Dr. Lewis treated the left knee with an arthroscopic procedure for torn cartilage 3 years ago. It has not consistently improved, and Ms. Shoemaker has had intermittent aching. These findings, associated with flat feet and bunion formation, have contributed to her present level of disability.

She has sleep interference 1 or 2 nights per week. The left knee bothers her the most; next are the feet and ankles; then her right knee. She avoids stairs when possible. She finds that any prolonged standing is limited, and that she has now had to give up walking for pleasure or exercise. She is at a point where she requires help with her foot hygiene.

On physical examination she is notably overweight at 251 lb. Her current height is 5' 5 ½". She is able to get in and out of a chair independently utilizing the armrests. She hesitates to initiate motion and ambulates with bilateral flat feet and valgus alignment of the right knee, measuring 9" between her medial malleoli with her knees touching, primarily because of the left knee and bilateral ankle valgus. The overall contour of the feet is not remarkable with the exception of bilateral hallux valgus with bunion formation. The pronated flat feet are believed to be compensatory, as maximum dorsiflexion with the foot in neutral is -10°, indicating short heel cords.

Long business letters are often continued on a second page. To format a multipage letter:

1. Key the first page of the letter on letterhead paper; key continuing pages on plain paper of the same quality as the letterhead used for the first page.
2. Use an approximate 2-inch top margin (press Enter 6 times) for the first page.
3. Use a 1-inch top margin for continuation pages. If a letterhead is used, start the first page on the third line below the letterhead.

(continued on next page)

SKILLBUILDING

C. Technique Timed Writings

Take two 30-second timed writings on each line. Focus on the technique at the left.

Space without pausing.

```
 8 Now that I have my own car, I can drive to all of my games.
 9 If I have to see him just now, he must come to this window.
10 My dad took a long trip and fished in the river for a week.
11 Our mom went to a spa to rest and relax while our dad read.
   | 1 | 2 | 3 | 4 | 5 | 6 | 7 | 8 | 9 | 10 | 11 | 12
```

FORMATTING

D. Works Cited Page

In MLA-style reports, the **works cited page** is an alphabetical list of all the sources you have cited. To format a list of works cited:

Acacio 5

Works Cited

Berenholc, Fatima. "Reading Body Language Cues." Management In Depth Feb. 2006: 138-153, 184.

LaCuesta, Cara. Grow a True International Corporation. Philadelphia: Business International Press, 2006.

N'Sonde, Corrinne J. "Developing Global Business Implications: Now Is the Time." Market Research Monthly 78 (2005): 236-281.

Stadnyk, Douglas S., and Theda Rao. "Lost in Translation: A Growing Issue." Daily Times Herald 24 Oct. 2005: 4A+.

"Truth-Telling: Conducting Business Efficiently in Today's Russia." New International Journal 28 Jan. 2006: 47.

"Twenty Ways to Grow Your International Partnership." UW-UG Business Department Online. 2005. University of Wisconsin-Union Grove. 14 Dec. 2005 <http://www.uwug.edu/business/international.html>.

1. Every page of an MLA-style report has a **header** at the top, with the author's name and page number aligned at the right margin; for example, Acacio 1. When creating the header, press ENTER one time after keying the page number.
2. Begin the works cited section on a new page, continuing the page numbers from the report.
3. Use the same side margins as in the report, and use double spacing.
4. Center and key the title *Works Cited* in initial caps approximately 1 inch from the top of the page.
5. Arrange the list alphabetically by authors' last names.
6. Begin each entry at the left margin, and indent carry-over lines 0.5 inch (use a hanging indent).

LESSON 83 TWO-PAGE LETTERS

OBJECTIVES:

- Key 36/5'/5e.
- Format and key a two-page business letter.

A. WARMUP

Key each line 2 times.

Speed	1 We must drive cautiously during the rush hours in the city.
Accuracy	2 Gazelles are Bovidae herbivores living from India to Egypt.
Language Link	3 We need to buy 16 bars of soap. We have seven bars on hand.
Numbers/Symbols	4 Martin & Wills sent a check for $2,195; the bill is $3,468.
	| 1 | 2 | 3 | 4 | 5 | 6 | 7 | 8 | 9 | 10 | 11 | 12

SKILLBUILDING

B. PREVIEW PRACTICE

Key each line 2 times as a preview to the timed writings on page 300.

Accuracy	5 maintain purchase something borrowing establish cardholders
Speed	6 prove repay spite good ages debt cash now pay all not do at

FACT FILE

Explain Credit Reports Anyone who makes a purchase and pays for it later has a record of information called a credit report. Go to the Online Learning Center at **KeyComps.glencoe.com>Fact File>Unit 5> Lesson 83** to find information about credit reports. Find out who uses these reports and how they are used. Then complete the online activity.

STUDENT MANUAL

Headers and Footers

Study Lesson 73 in your Student Manual. Complete all the practice activities while at your computer. Then complete the tasks that follow.

WORD PROCESSING APPLICATIONS

REPORT 18

Academic Report

Key the following report in academic style. Key the works cited page as the last page of the report. Use your name, your teacher's name, your course title, and the current date in the heading. Create a header that includes your last name and the page number.

Paying College Costs

¶It is assumed that students will continue their education beyond high school. Some graduates will attend community colleges or four-year colleges and universities immediately after high school graduation. Some graduates will work part-time and take classes over an extended period of years. Ravolett states that:

> Some will obtain vocational skills by attending career-specific schools and training programs. No matter what path is taken, all who seek training after high school face the problem of paying the ever-increasing costs of higher education. Next to your home, this may be the most expensive investment you make. (2)

¶Financial aid can be the answer. It is best to begin by examining the several types of financial aid available. There are scholarships, loans, and grants that do not have to be repaid. There are work-study programs and internships, which allow students to work and earn tuition. Some scholarships are granted by extracurricular organizations and may require a formal membership or a period of active participation. It is important to start your research early so that you have enough time to locate and meet application deadlines for a variety of awards (Kilgore 97).

¶The U.S. Department of Education offers six main student financial aid programs: Pell Grants, Federal Supplemental Education Opportunity Grants, Federal Work-Study, Federal Perkins Loans, Stafford Loans, and PLUS Loans (Blake 202). Published guidelines showing the requirements needed to qualify for each of these programs are available. Everyone, no matter what his or her income level, can benefit by completing the paperwork for governmental financial aid.

(continued on next page)

D. POSTTEST

Repeat the Pretest. Compare your Posttest results with your Pretest results.

E. Paced Practice

Turn to the Paced Practice routine beginning on page SB7. Take three 2-minute timed writings, starting where you left off the last time.

F. Technique Checkpoint

Key each line 2 times. Repeat if time permits. Focus on the technique at the left.

Press and release the* Shift *keys without hesitating.

```
19 Hal traveled to the Isle of Hope to visit Kelly and Jackie.
20 Nancy traveled to London, Paris, Madrid, and Oslo in March.
21 Frances passed West Dublin on the way to East Dublin today.
22 As in the past, the Wild West Rodeo will be in Thomasville.
```

G. PRETEST

Take a 1-minute timed writing on the paragraph. Note your speed and errors.

```
23      Recycling is the process of using goods more than one    11
24 time. Since many kinds of wastes can be reused, we must       22
25 learn just how important it is to start recycling. Glass,     34
26 cans, plastic, newspapers, and old tires can be used again.   46
   | 1 | 2 | 3 | 4 | 5 | 6 | 7 | 8 | 9 | 10 | 11 | 12
```

H. PRACTICE

In the chart below, find the number of errors you made on the Pretest. Then key each of the designated drill lines 2 times.

Pretest Errors	0–1	2	3	4+
Drill Lines	30–34	29–33	28–32	27–31

Accuracy

```
27 melted process ground turned products purposes requirements
28 paper bottles realize materials gasoline recycled newsprint
29 pulp reuse exact useful bottle highway substances important
30 such used make glass using tires clean should wastes melted
```

Speed

```
31 kinds more than time many cans into then made tires one how
32 paper ones just meet that very from must can be for new car
33 items tires then from are and for the how be if to as is it
34 goods clean down into down made time make news than old off
```

I. POSTTEST

Repeat the Pretest. Compare your Posttest results with your Pretest results.

(continued)

¶There are even financial aid programs earmarked for students with disabilities (Sandoval and Whittier 16). Each year millions of dollars are available as assistance for disabled students and their families. These programs are open to disabled applicants from high school through postdoctoral studies. Students with physical disabilities as well as learning disabilities (such as dyslexia) are eligible.

¶Probably the best place to begin the search for information on sources for college financial aid is in the counseling office of your school. Also, contact the financial aid office at the schools you are interested in attending as suggested by Derrick (112). The task of locating ways to fund college costs may seem overwhelming. It is made easier if you start early and are well-organized in your search.

Works Cited

Blake, Lauren. Free Cash for College. Minneapolis: Fact File Press, 2005.

Derrick, Edward. "Guidelines for Finding College Cash." Business Week 14 Sept. 2006: 112-113.

Kilgore, Donald M. Loans and Grants for Undergrads: Step-by-Step. New York: Indelible Ink Press, 2004.

Ravolett, Boyce D. Secrets to Finding College Financing, 11th ed. Chicago: Student Aid Publishing Division, 2006.

Sandoval, Julie Lynn, and Philip Gregory Whittier. Financial Opportunities for Students with Disabilities. Redwood City: Redwood Publishers, 2005.

*inter*NET CONNECTION

Search for Colleges Where do you want to go to continue your education after high school? Are you interested in going to a college or university, or would you prefer to learn a particular skill in a technical school?

Go to the Online Learning Center at **KeyComps.glencoe.com>Internet Connection>Unit 4>Lesson 73** to find information about post-secondary schools in the United States. Choose three schools that you find interesting, then create a table that lists the names, cities, states, and one reason you would want to attend each of these institutions. Follow your teacher's instructions for saving and printing your work.

LESSON 82 SKILLBUILDING

OBJECTIVES:

- Increase keyboarding speed and improve accuracy.
- Reinforce keyboarding techniques.

A. WARMUP

Key each line 2 times.

Speed	1	Four students from our school will run in the state finals.
Accuracy	2	The quadrant has been a survey device since medieval times.
Language Link	3	The accountant had 100 five-column pads in his desk drawer.
Numbers/Symbols	4	Invoice 836-259 for $1,274.50 is subject to a 12% discount.
		| 1 | 2 | 3 | 4 | 5 | 6 | 7 | 8 | 9 | 10 | 11 | 12

SKILLBUILDING

B. PRETEST

Take a 1-minute timed writing on the paragraph. Note your speed and errors.

5 The lady who lives at 160 North Street has 37 pairs 11
6 of shoes and 28 purses. She also has 4 sweaters, 5 skirts, 23
7 and 6 coats. She spends at least $98 each month on clothes 35
8 and $80 on pet food. She has 9 guppies, 1 bird, and 3 cats. 47
| 1 | 2 | 3 | 4 | 5 | 6 | 7 | 8 | 9 | 10 | 11 | 12

C. PRACTICE

Key each line 2 times.

1	9	We saw 11 computers, 11 boards, 11 monitors, and 11 drives.
2	10	By 2:22 p.m. on the 2d, they had 2.0 or 2.2 inches of rain.
3	11	The programs were found in seats 3, 30, 31, 32, 33, and 34.
4	12	Last night the scores were 40 to 4, 42 to 41, and 48 to 44.
5	13	The student scores on the 15th were 51, 53, 55, 57, and 59.
6	14	The spreadsheet cells listed 6, 16, 26, 36, 46, 56, and 66.
7	15	January 7, March 7, April 7, May 17, and July 17 were open.
8	16	Can Jerry add these: 1/8, 2/8, 3/8, 4/8, 5/8, 6/8, and 7/8?
9	17	They found $9.99, $9.19, $9.29, and $9.69 in the registers.
0	18	It isn't difficult to total 10, 20, 30, 40, 50, 60, and 70.

LESSON 74 REPORTS REVIEW

OBJECTIVES:

- Increase keyboarding speed and improve accuracy.
- Format an agenda and an academic report.

A. WARMUP

Key each line 2 times.

Speed	1	When you go to look for a job, dress well and arrive early.
Accuracy	2	Jackie quietly gave most of his prize boxers to dog owners.
Language Link	3	Not only those newspapers but also the magazine is missing.
Numbers	4	You can telephone Myron at 318-555-2647 or at 318-555-2648.

| 1 | 2 | 3 | 4 | 5 | 6 | 7 | 8 | 9 | 10 | 11 | 12

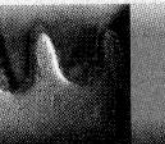

SKILLBUILDING

B. PACED PRACTICE

Turn to the Paced Practice routine beginning on page SB-7. Take three 2-minute timed writings, starting at the point where you left off the last time.

WORD PROCESSING APPLICATIONS

REPORT 19
Agenda

Key the following agenda in the correct format. Refer to directions for formatting Agendas on page 156.

ASIF TECHNOLOGY CONFERENCE / Meeting Agenda / August 12-15, {year}

1. Registration/Lobby
2. Demonstration: Wireless Networking/Mott Suite
3. Break/Curtise Suite
4. Computerized Accounting Software/Carriage B
5. Awards Luncheon/Chrysler A/B
6. Managing Files on a Computer/Carriage B
7. Break/Curtise Suite
8. Introduction: Interactive Communications/Mott Suite
9. Discussion and Evaluation/Chrysler B

(continued)

MN 21 M may mix mad make mind month N new nor now note next noise
OP 22 O own old oil oath ouch ought P peg par pay prod plea purge
QR 23 Q qua qui quo quip quit quest R rod rig rug raft ream right
ST 24 S ski six sod salt sent scale T tag tin toy tend toil toast
UV 25 U uke urn use undo unit using V vow van vie volt vile virus
WX 26 W why won wet wipe wrap waver X vex fox mix lynx text waxen
YZ 27 Y yam yes yaw yoke year yards Z zag zip zoo zinc zing zesty

E. POSTTEST

Repeat the Pretest. Compare your Posttest results with your Pretest results.

F. Technique Checkpoint

Key each line 2 times. Repeat if time permits. Focus on the technique at the left.

Space between words without pausing.

28 He is the one who will pay if we go to the ball game today.
29 When all of us have gone out, you need to stay in the room.
30 You need to save as much of your pay as you can to be safe.
31 There is no one but you who knows how to lead the band now.

G. Paced Practice

Turn to the Paced Practice routine beginning on page SB7. Take three 2-minute timed writings, starting at the point where you left off the last time.

PORTFOLIO Activity

Create an Alphabetic Timed Writing Some timed writings, such as the ones on p. 281, are alphabetic. They contain every letter of the alphabet, in order to test your keying ability thoroughly. Compose a short paragraph that contains every letter of the alphabet. The paragraph should be approximately four lines long and can be on any topic.

Save and print your work according to your teacher's instructions. Then trade your paragraph with another student and see if you can key the timed writing in less than one minute.

REPORT 20

Academic Report

Key the following report in academic style. Include the works cited page as the last page of the report. Use your name, your teacher's name, your course title, and the current date in the heading. Add a header with your last name and the page number.

Managing Your Money 101

¶It is not easy to manage money, but this is a very important part of becoming an independent adult. When you start your first job (which will probably be a part-time job), you will be expected to take on some of the financial responsibilities for your own care that were previously met by your parents or guardians. Perhaps you will have to buy your own clothes. You will certainly have to pay for your own lunches and for your transportation to and from work. "You will have to learn to live within your means, which means spending less than you earn and not buying things for which you cannot pay" (Molina and Satsukawa 154).

¶If you are to be successful in living within your means, you must have a plan for spending. People who do not plan often end up in trouble with credit accounts. College students are particularly at risk of overdoing it with credit if they use the many unsolicited credit cards that come to them in the mail almost as soon as they check into the dormitory. Jefferson tells parents to be sure that their college-age students leave for college with a sensible spending plan and lessons on how to use credit (29).

¶In order to have a realistic spending plan, you need to think about your plans—both long-range and short-range. If you want to purchase a house, for example, you will need to begin saving money for a down payment.

> One of the most important things you can do is to think of saving as you think of paying your bills—something that you do every month without fail. Think of savings as a bill you pay yourself. Add savings to your budget, and pay yourself first. Certainly, saving requires discipline (Yusko 114).

¶Single adults and families with young children should consider saving money for the future or providing for emergencies by investing in insurance (Toliver 145). Income-protection insurance will provide income for the single person or young family in case the breadwinner is unable to work. There is homeowner's insurance to cover unexpected losses of property. Car insurance is also a must. For many people, the purchase of insurance is a good way to save money for future expenses. There are many different kinds of insurance to be considered when putting together a spending plan.

(continued on next page)

(continued)

Rule 18: Spell out the words *million* and *billion* in even amounts. Do not use decimals with even amounts. Spell out fractions.

The multimillionaire gave almost $2 million to charity.

Each of them paid $50 for a ticket and $12.50 for parking.

About one-half of the graduating class participated in the graduation ceremony.

Jan got 2 dozen pastries and a pot of coffee.
The agenda listed twenty-five items to be covered today.
779 students were there.
The musician recorded 7 6-track demo tapes.
After taxes, he was worth $4,000,000.00.
Only 1/3 of the students had summer jobs.

SKILLBUILDING

C. PRETEST

Take a 1-minute timed writing on the paragraph. Note your speed and errors.

American President Andrew Jackson was a self-made man. 11
He fought for and was liked by the common man. His votes 23
came from farmers in the South, settlers in the West, and 34
workers in the East. 38

| 1 | 2 | 3 | 4 | 5 | 6 | 7 | 8 | 9 | 10 | 11 | 12

D. PRACTICE

Key each line 2 times.

AB A ale and ant aunt aide aisle B bid bay bud belt bulk balmy
CD C cut cat cod cove cube clerk D did dry dim dorm debt doubt
EF E ear elm end ease etch edges F fir few fly foil four front
GH G gun gag gap gaze goal grant H hit hot hue have half hitch
IJ I ice imp ire into idea infer J jam jar jet jury just joker
KL K key keg kid keen kind kayak L law lad let land lamb laugh

(continued on next page)

(continued)

¶There is help available for people who find themselves in need of help with money matters. General information can be obtained free of charge from government publications. Also, banks employ people who can provide you with information on savings and investments (Galyean et al. 194–201). It would be worth your while to invest your time and money in a class to learn how to manage your money. Remember, no matter how much you earn, how you manage your money will determine the type of lifestyle you will be able to achieve.

Works Cited

Galyean, Rachel, et al. Financial Guidelines That Work for Working Couples. New York: David Wynan Brothers, 2005.

Jefferson, Randi. "Teaching Little Ones to Spend Wisely." Quintessence May 2006: 29–30.

Molina, Kendra, and Hui Satsukawa. Stabilizing Your Finances. Bloomington: Golden Publishing, 2004.

Toliver, Daniel. "Financial Freedom." Money Managers Dec. 2005: 142–146.

Yusko, Victoria Tapp. Frugal Family Finances. San Diego: Plimsoll Publishers, 2006.

MATH CONNECTION

Describe Your Savings Plan Key a brief paragraph describing something that you want to save for and your plan for saving. Why is it important enough to make you want to save? How much could you save every week or month, and how long will it take to achieve your goal?

Create a two-column table. In the left column, list the dates for each week or month in which you plan to put money away for your purchase. In the right column, key the amount you intend to save during that period. Then total the right column. It should add up to the amount of your final goal. Follow your teacher's instructions for saving and printing your work.

LESSON 81 SKILLBUILDING

OBJECTIVES:

- Apply rules for number expression.
- Increase keyboarding speed and improve accuracy.
- Reinforce keyboarding techniques.

A. WARMUP

Key each line 2 times.

Speed	1	The little black puppy ran to the door to greet his master.
Accuracy	2	Jeff amazed the audience by quickly giving six new reports.
Language Link	3	Terry is taking English Literature 215 on Tuesday mornings.
Numbers/Symbols	4	Can't they find Check #953 for $840, which is dated May 16?

| 1 | 2 | 3 | 4 | 5 | 6 | 7 | 8 | 9 | 10 | 11 | 12

LANGUAGE LINK

B. NUMBER EXPRESSION

Study the rules and examples below. Then edit lines 5–10 on page 295 to correct any errors in number usage.

Rule 16: In general, spell out numbers one through ten. Use figures for numbers above ten.

Only three walls have been painted.

We purchased 15 pairs of socks, 11 jackets, and 23 scarves.

Rule 17: Spell out numbers used as the first word in a sentence. Also spell out the smaller of two adjacent numbers.

Nineteen applications were processed today.

Each participant will receive three 45-minute tapes to listen to.

(continued on next page)

Footnotes and Endnotes in Reports

OBJECTIVES:

- Apply rules for commas with introductory expressions.
- Key 36/3'/5e.
- Format a report with footnotes and endnotes.

A. Warmup

Key each line 2 times.

Speed	*1*	`We know that a good thing to do is to rest and read a book.`
Accuracy	*2*	`The lazy judge was very quick to pay tax money for the box.`
Language Link	*3*	`Either Kay and Hal or Rodger is going to deliver the meals.`
Numbers/Symbols	*4*	`Lee & Lou and Nate & Nat paid for 534# of #80 tape @ $1.28.`

| 1 | 2 | 3 | 4 | 5 | 6 | 7 | 8 | 9 | 10 | 11 | 12

B. Commas

Study the rule and the examples below. Then correct any errors in comma usage in lines 5–8.

Rule 13: Use a comma after an introductory expression (unless it is a short prepositional phrase).

In my opinion, the cars should be repaired immediately.

No, you may not take the ferry to the island.

After the flood, we sold our house and moved to a condominium.

In 1790 the first U.S. census was taken by marshals on horseback.

(continued on next page)

WORDS TO LEARN

In the lessons, software, and Student Manual (SM), you will learn the following vocabulary terms for Unit 5.

data source (SM Lesson 85)
form letter (p. 309)
formulas (p. 348)
landscape (p. 341)
mail merge (SM Lesson 85)
memo (p. 323)
page orientation (p. 341)
portrait (p. 341)
template (p. 323)

CAREER BYTE

COURT REPORTER Court reporters key verbatim reports of speeches, conversations, legal proceedings, meetings, or other events when written accounts of spoken words are necessary for correspondence, records, or legal proof. Court reporters use stenotype machines, which enable them to record combinations of letters representing sounds, words, or phrases. The symbols are recorded on computer disks, which are then loaded into a computer that translates and displays the symbols in English.

Stenotype machines that link directly to the computer are also used for real-time captioning. That is, as the symbols are keyed, the computer instantly transcribes them into words. This is used for closed captioning for the deaf or hearing-impaired on television, in courts, classrooms, or meetings.

(continued)

5 As we discussed Friday the will must be probated by May 1.
6 After you see those shoes you may decide not to keep them.
7 Yes this is the last day to turn in your loan application.
8 In 1777 the Continental Congress passed the first Flag Act.

SKILLBUILDING

C. Preview Practice

Key each line 2 times as a preview to the 3-minute timed writings below.

Accuracy 9 enjoy seven acquire analyze aptitudes throughout roadblocks
Speed 10 happy want next they over also any few six set for do be if

D. 3-Minute Timed Writings

Take two 3-minute timed writings on the paragraphs. Note your speed and errors.

Goal: 36/3'/5e

11 Students seldom think about their future careers in 11
12 the first six or seven years of school. They do not know 22
13 what they want to do or which skills they need to acquire 34
14 over the next few years of their lives. 42
15 It is important for students to think about and plan 52
16 for their careers. They must analyze their personal goals 64
17 and aptitudes when they choose a career. They must also set 76
18 goals throughout their lives. Any failures must not become 88
19 roadblocks in their pursuit of their goals. They should 99
20 enjoy their careers if they want to be happy. 108

SI 1.30

| 1 | 2 | 3 | 4 | 5 | 6 | 7 | 8 | 9 | 10 | 11 | 12

UNIT 5
LESSONS 81–100

WORD PROCESSING

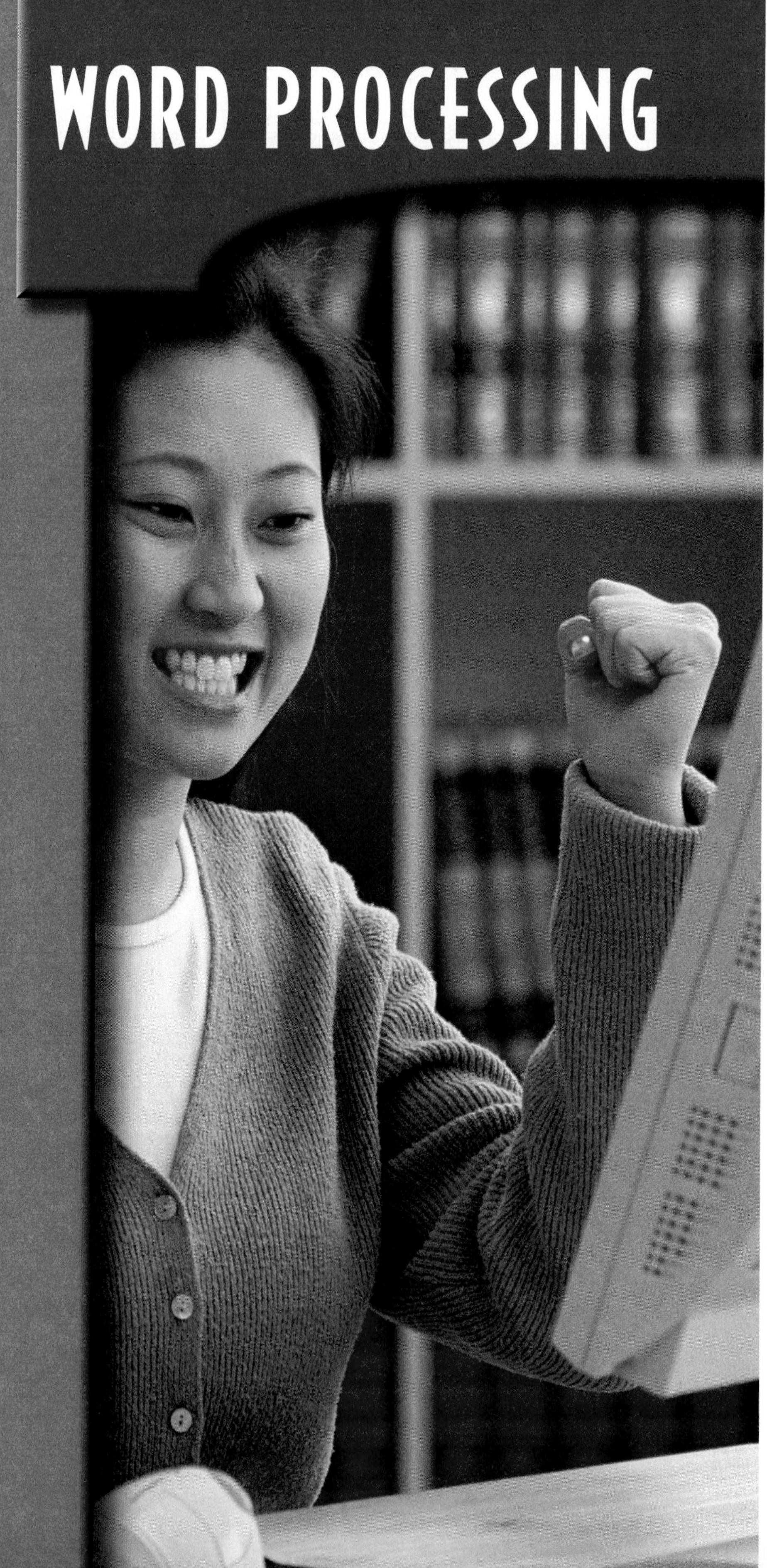

OBJECTIVES

- Demonstrate keyboarding speed and accuracy on straight copy with a goal of 36 words per minute for 5 minutes with 5 or fewer errors.
- Demonstrate correct use of word processing features.
- Demonstrate an understanding of proofreaders' symbols by editing copy marked for revision.
- Demonstrate advanced formatting skills on a variety of reports, letters, memos, and tables from a variety of copy—arranged, unarranged, rough draft, and handwritten.
- Compose paragraphs at the keyboard.
- Apply grammar and punctuation rules.
- Create form letters and data files; merge form letters with data files.

FORMATTING

E. Footnotes and Endnotes

In Lesson 72 you gave credit to sources of information in reports using parenthetical references. Two other acceptable methods for giving credit are footnotes and endnotes. Footnotes and endnotes should include the name of the author, the title of the book or article, the publisher, the place and year of publication, and the page numbers being referenced.

2. Be sure your message is clear, concise, and grammatically correct.[3]
3. If the information is extremely sensitive, try to deliver the message in person to avoid misunderstandings.
4. If you do not want anyone else to know what you are saying or writing, speak with the recipient directly. Neither voice mail nor e-mail is totally secure.

Used properly, voice mail and e-mail are a significant help to professionals. With courteous and thoughtful use, people can increase their own efficiency and become more responsive to others.[4]

---

[3] Blanca Velazquez, "How to Use E-Mail and Voice Mail," *The Business Educator*, Vol. 94, November 2006, p. 17.
[4] Ardith E. Neal, "Technology in Communications," *Business Now*, June 21, 2004, p. 11.

Footnotes

1. **Footnotes** give credit or additional information and appear at the bottom of the page on which the reference appears.
2. Footnotes are referenced in the body of a report with consecutive superscript numbers.

2. Be sure your message is clear, concise, and grammatically correct.[iii]
3. If the information is extremely sensitive, try to deliver the message in person to avoid misunderstandings.
4. If you do not want anyone else to know what you are saying or writing, speak with the recipient directly. Neither voice mail nor e-mail is totally secure.

Used properly, voice mail and e-mail are a significant help to professionals. With courteous and thoughtful use, people can increase their own efficiency and become more responsive to others.[iv]

---

[i] Brian V. Hofstra, *Business Practices and Procedures*, 7th ed., Boston Pioneer Publishers, Boston, Massachusetts, 2006.
[ii] Elizabeth M. Mulanax, *Increase Efficiency in Your Workplace*, Liberty Press, Sacramento, California, 2005.
[iii] Blanca Velazquez, "How to Use E-Mail and Voice Mail," *The Business Educator*, Vol. 94, November 2006, p. 17.
[iv] Ardith E. Neal, "Technology in Communications," *Business Now*, June 21, 2004, p. 11.

Endnotes

1. **Endnotes** give credit or additional information and appear at the end of a report, either on the last page or on a separate page.
2. Endnotes are referenced in the body of a report with consecutive superscript numbers. Lower-case Roman numerals is the default setting for creating endnote reference numbers.

LETTER 39

Business Letter in Modified-Block Style

Mrs. Emerson prefers letters formatted in modified-block style with blocked paragraphs. Her preferred complimentary closing is "Sincerely yours," followed by her name and title on separate lines.

Please send this letter today. Correct all errors in spelling, punctuation, and grammar.

Mr. Lesterr Romero / Romero Industries, Inc. / 272 Burdette Street / Akron, OH 44319 / Dear Mr. romero:

We are indebted to you for allowing community Way to use your facility as the ~~cite~~ site for this year's fund-raising dinner. Last Friday, 300 guests enjoyed fine dining, ~~dancing~~ listening to music, and dancing. Your lovely ~~spacious~~ ball room provided the perfect setting this for exciting event.

As you probably know, this event is one of our major fundraising activities. This year Project Upgrade, our major project is which will provide training for ~~countless~~ displaced workers in our Community. Thanks to ~~your~~ the support of caring individuals such as you, community way will be able to provided valuable services to some of our less fortune ate neighbors.

Again, thankyou for your kind support

TABLE 21

Boxed Table

Prepare the following table. Center the table vertically and horizontally, and automatically adjust the column widths. Align the numbers on the right.

AKRON CORPORATE CONTRIBUTORS January–May 2006		
Business	**Street Address**	**Amount ($)**
Akron Auto Body Professionals	224 Industrial Parkway	400
Akron Publishing Company	1599 Main Street	800
American Chemco	1990 Sawyer Avenue	650
Amparan Legal Group	45 Main Street	900
Boston Brick Manufacturer	500 Firestone Parkway	1,000
Cuyahoga Lumber and Millwork	303 State Road	1,100
Dawson Dairy Inc.	515 Waterloo Road	775
Donley Systems Corporation	400 Firestone Parkway	1,850
Esteban Incorporated	15 Union Road	750
First Bank of Akron	17 Cascade Plaza	500
Keller Furniture	225 Broadway Street	725
Safe Harbor Imports	7205 Barlowe Road	1,500
Scone Zone	1404 Drury Lane	450
Zesty Cola Bottling Company	900 Triplett Boulevard	2,500

F. Software Features

STUDENT MANUAL

Footnotes   Formatting Endnotes

Study Lesson 75 in your Student Manual. Complete all the practice activities while at your computer. Then complete the tasks that follow.

WORD PROCESSING APPLICATIONS

REPORT 21

Business Report

Key the following business report with single spacing. Format all references as footnotes. The text for the footnotes is at the end of the report.

MAKING VOICE MAIL AND E-MAIL WORK FOR YOU

¶Just a few short years ago, the way we most often communicated with others was by telephone or letter. Often, using the telephone meant playing what business workers referred to as "telephone tag."[1] This name resulted from a caller's having to leave a message for someone to call back, then not being available when the call was returned. If you communicated via letters, you could never be sure exactly when the letter would be delivered.

¶With advances in technology, we now have many more options available. Among these options are voice mail and e-mail. Voice mail enables you to leave a message for someone even if you know the person is not available. It enables the person being called to answer the telephone or wait until a more convenient time to get any messages. E-mail enables you to send "written" messages to anyone at any time and have those messages delivered instantly. This is particularly useful if you must communicate with someone in a different time zone. You can send your message at a convenient time for you, and the receiver can respond at a convenient time for him or her.

¶Each of these options also has negative aspects. Many people do not like voice mail because they do not like to be greeted by a recording; others refuse to leave messages. Companies that rely on voice mail to answer and route all incoming calls risk losing the business of people who want to speak with a "real" person.[2] Have you ever been frustrated by having to listen to a long recording or a list of options before your call could be completed?

(continued on next page)

REPORT 31
Business Report

Prepare this report in left-bound format. Be sure to proofread and correct any errors when you finish.

FITNESS FOR WORK

¶The company expects all employees to be physically and mentally able to perform their jobs and otherwise meet the demands of their jobs and conditions of employment, except as required by applicable law. The company provides medical and dental benefits, which are fully described in the benefit information material, and counseling services, which are part of our employee assistance program.

¶This section explains the responsibility of the manager and the employee when an employee cannot report to work because of a medical condition.

ILLNESSES AND INJURIES

¶**The Employee's Responsibilities.** An employee who is incapable of performing his/her job adequately because of a medical condition or whose presence at work might infect other employees should remain at home. In the case of a contagious disease, an employee should inform the manager of the extent to which he or she may have exposed co-workers.

¶**The Manager's Responsibilities.** When an employee is absent due to a medical condition for six or more consecutive working days, or due to a job-related injury for one or more days, the employee's manager must notify the human resources office by completing an absence notification form. When the employee returns to work, the manager must complete a return-to-work form and send it to the human resources office.

ABSENTEEISM AND TARDINESS

¶The company counts on its employees to be at work on time and on a regular basis to carry out the responsibilities of their jobs. The company expects employees to be conscientious about their attendance and punctuality. Although some absence or tardiness can be accepted, excessive absence or tardiness will not be tolerated and will be cause for discipline, up to and including termination of employment.

¶Employees are not "given" a number of sick days per year. The company plan protects employees when they need it, but the plan is not a "time-off" plan. If an employee's absence record becomes excessive, he/she may be subject to disciplinary action.

¶If employees must be delayed or absent, they must notify their manager as far in advance of their starting time as possible of the fact and reason for the delay or absence.

¶Employees who are absent for three or more consecutive working days without notifying their manager may have their employment terminated.

(continued)

¶E-mail has provided us with a way to send messages instantly. However, this ease of sending messages has dramatically increased the number of unimportant messages being sent. (In other instances, using e-mail has proved to be very costly. The informality of e-mail often causes people to respond without thinking and send messages that should never be sent.) In addition, e-mail is not totally secure. Information that you do not want others to know should not be sent via e-mail.

¶Here are four general guidelines for using voice mail and e-mail:

1. Keep your message professional and courteous.
2. Be sure your message is clear, concise, and grammatically correct.[3]
3. If the information is extremely sensitive, try to deliver the message in person to avoid misunderstandings.
4. If you do not want anyone else to know what you are saying or writing, speak with the recipient directly. Neither voice mail nor e-mail is totally secure.

¶Used properly, voice mail and e-mail are a significant help to professionals. With courteous and thoughtful use, people can increase their own efficiency and become more responsive to others.[4]

1. Brian V. Hofstra, *Business Practices and Procedures*, 7th ed., Boston Pioneer Publishers, Boston, Massachusetts, 2006.
2. Elizabeth M. Mulanax, *Increase Efficiency in Your Workplace*, Liberty Press, Sacramento, California, 2005.
3. Blanca Velazquez, "How to Use E-Mail and Voice Mail," *The Business Educator*, Vol. 94, November 2006, p. 17.
4. Ardith E. Neal, "Technology in Communications," *Business Now*, June 21, 2004, p. 11.

COMMUNICATION FOCUS

Voice Mail Etiquette Key the following paragraph. Then compose a final sentence to conclude the paragraph. Follow your teacher's instructions for saving and printing your work.

When you are leaving a message on voice mail, be sure to speak clearly, state the essential facts quickly, and give your name and telephone number slowly. It is also a good idea to repeat your telephone number again at the end of the message. If your message contains any unusual names, you may want to spell those names. Analyze your messages and think of ways in which you can improve them.

C. PRACTICE

In the chart below, find the number of errors you made on the Pretest. Then, key each of the designated drill lines 2 times.

Pretest Errors	0–1	2	3	4+
Drill Lines	12–16	11–15	10–14	9–13

Accuracy

```
9  thermometer indicate presence pleasing threats humans cause
10 winter becomes highest chilling pleasure pleasant temperate
11 beings please making thermal windiest chilliest threatening
12 by colder become pleasing indicated thermometer temperature
```

Speed

```
13 a to of it is by be the out are can low than when high wind
14 a this cold make come chill cause death please threat human
15 be to on dear come when wind cloth treat threat death there
16 mom hen his ten man see low his hill that meter press three
```

D. POSTTEST

Repeat the Pretest. Compare your Posttest results with your Pretest results.

WORD PROCESSING APPLICATIONS

E. Orientation

You will be working in the offices of the Community Way, City Center, Suite 100, 14 South Main, Akron, OH 44308. Community Way is a nonprofit community-service organization. Today is June 6. Mrs. Alice Emerson is the director. Her assistant is Hugh Michaelson. You will help him to prepare documents for Mrs. Emerson's approval. She depends on her assistant (and on you) to format the documents correctly and to catch any errors.

Prepare the following table. Center it vertically and horizontally, and automatically adjust the column widths.

TABLE 20

Boxed Table

ABSENCE AND TARDINESS GUIDELINES				
Rating	**Absence**		**Tardiness**	
	6 Months	**12 Months**	**6 Months**	**12 Months**
Commendable	0–1 days	0–2 days	0–1 times	0–2 times
Acceptable	2 days	3–5 days	2–3 times	3–5 times
Poor	3–4 days	6–8 days	4–5 times	6–9 times
Unacceptable	5+ days	9+ days	6+ times	10+ times

LESSON 76

REPORTS: MULTIPAGE, LEFT BOUND

OBJECTIVES:

- Increase keyboarding speed.
- Format and key multipage, bound reports.

A. WARMUP

Key each line 2 times.

Speed	1	When the cat rests, it wants to lie down in the same place.
Accuracy	2	Jack was too lazy for the farm job; he proved quite vexing.
Language Link	3	By the end of the week, it had rained more than last month.
Numbers/Symbols	4	We will earn 12% more on #31 & #46 if they are sold @ $200.
		| 1 | 2 | 3 | 4 | 5 | 6 | 7 | 8 | 9 | 10 | 11 | 12

SKILLBUILDING

B. 12-SECOND SPRINTS

Take three 12-second timed writings on each line. Try to increase your speed each time.

5 He may not play ball if he did not yet take that math test.
6 We might have a very nice profit if the order is a big one.
7 That job might very well take much longer than you thought.
8 Justin had time to do the job because it was planned early.
||||5||||10||||15||||20||||25||||30||||35||||40||||45||||50||||55||||60

LANGUAGE ARTS CONNECTION

Compare Footnotes and Endnotes In the last lesson, you learned about footnotes and endnotes, which you will be using in upcoming reports. In your own words, key a sentence about one similarity between footnotes and endnotes. Then key a sentence about one difference between footnotes and endnotes. Follow your teacher's instructions for saving and printing your work.

LESSON 80 SIMULATION

OBJECTIVES:

- Increase keyboarding speed and improve accuracy.
- Format and key a variety of office documents.

A. WARMUP

Key each line 2 times.

Speed	1	Dale saw a small cabin at the end of the winding dirt road.
Accuracy	2	Four lawyers quickly rejected a luxury prize given to them.
Language Link	3	Marge sent the project to the Advertising Department today.
Numbers/Symbols	4	Their tax was $35,489 (26% sales + 10% excise)--incredible!

| 1 | 2 | 3 | 4 | 5 | 6 | 7 | 8 | 9 | 10 | 11 | 12

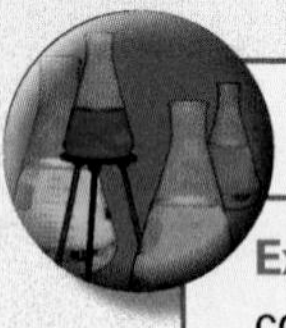

SCIENCE CONNECTION

Explain Wind Chill The Skillbuilding activities below discuss the concept of wind chill. Go to the Online Learning Center at **KeyComps.glencoe.com>Science Connection>Unit 4>Lesson 80** to find information about wind chill and complete an activity. Follow your teacher's instructions for saving and printing your work.

SKILLBUILDING

B. PRETEST

Take a 1-minute timed writing on the paragraph. Note your speed and errors.

Science Connection

5 The presence of wind makes it seem colder out than is 11
6 indicated by a thermometer. This can be pleasing when the 23
7 temperature is high. When temperatures are low, wind chill 34
8 becomes a threat to human beings and may cause death. 45

| 1 | 2 | 3 | 4 | 5 | 6 | 7 | 8 | 9 | 10 | 11 | 12

FORMATTING

C. Left-Bound Reports

In a left-bound report, the left margin must be wider to allow room for the binding. To format a left-bound report, change the left margin to 1.5 inches. Do not change the default right margin.

WORD PROCESSING APPLICATIONS

REPORT 22

Business Report

Key the following business report as a left-bound report. Format all the references as endnotes. Remember to add the page number to the second page of the report.

LISTENING

¶Everyone appreciates a good listener. Good listeners make good friends. People who are good listeners not only gain insight into other people, but they also learn about the world around them. If you want to be a good listener, you must make a conscious decision to listen. The following suggestions should help you become a better listener.

BE QUIET

¶Pause for several seconds before you start to talk after the one speaking to you stops. This pause allows the speaker to catch a breath and gather his or her thoughts. The speaker may want to continue. This pause also gives you time to form your response. Preparing your response while you are trying to listen often leads to missing the main point.

MAINTAIN EYE CONTACT

¶Look at the person who is speaking. It shows you are listening and keeps your mind from wandering. Looking directly at the speaker enables you to watch body language and behavior. Don't stare, but look into the speaker's eyes often.

DISPLAY OPENNESS

¶Your facial expressions and body positions convey openness. Sit or stand up straight. Do not cross your arms and legs. Do not have any physical barriers, such as a desk or a pile of books, between you and the other person.

(continued on next page)

(continued)

inches high. The backboard must be mounted 4 feet inside the end line.[3] [[3] Ron Salopek, "Basketball: The Sport of Champions," *On the Line*, September 2004, p. 7.]

¶Official games played in elementary school, high school, and college and by professionals use regulation basketballs, courts, baskets, and backboards. Following these standards makes the game fairer for both teams.

CLOSING

¶Basketball has grown in the past decade to become one of the most popular spectator sports. It is played in almost every country in the world, is popular with both young and old, and attracts both men and women players. It has been an Olympic sport for many years and will likely grow in popularity for years to come.

REPORT 28
Title Page

Prepare a title page for Report 27b. Use your keyboarding teacher's name, the keyboarding course in which you are enrolled, and the current date.

REPORT 29
Table of Contents

Prepare a table of contents from the information in Report 27b. Use the side headings and paragraph headings as your entries.

REPORT 30
Bibliography

Prepare a bibliography from the sources in Report 27b. Number the bibliography as the final page in the report.

PORTFOLIO Activity

Review of Reports For your portfolio you will create documents in order to review and practice some of the skills you have learned in this unit.

Open Report 22. Proofread it and correct any errors. Then create each of the following documents for Report 22:

1. A title page
2. A table of contents
3. A bibliography

Follow your teacher's instructions for saving and printing your work.

(continued)

LISTEN WITHOUT RESPONSE

¶Don't interrupt the speaker even if you feel that you cannot wait to express your opinions, suggestions, and comments. Caroline Frederick suggests, "Don't always have a bigger or better one of whatever the speaker is telling you about."[i] Watch your nonverbal expressions, such as shrugs and frowns. They may keep the other person from finishing the message.

SEND ACKNOWLEDGMENTS

¶Send acknowledgments. It is important to let the speaker know you are still listening throughout the conversation. A frequent "OK," "Yes," or nod of the head lets the speaker know that you are interested in what is being said. These signals do not imply that you agree with the speaker; they indicate only that you are hearing what is being said.[ii]

¶Being a good listener is hard work. Sometimes it takes more effort to be a good listener than it does to be a good speaker. If you put these suggestions into practice, they will pay you big dividends.

[i] Caroline Frederick and Douglas O. Frederick, "Listen to Learn," *Journal of Communications*, July 2006, p. 21.

[ii] Joseph Thomas O'Brien, *Communications for Everyday People*, Bravado Press, College Station, Texas, 2005, p. 65.

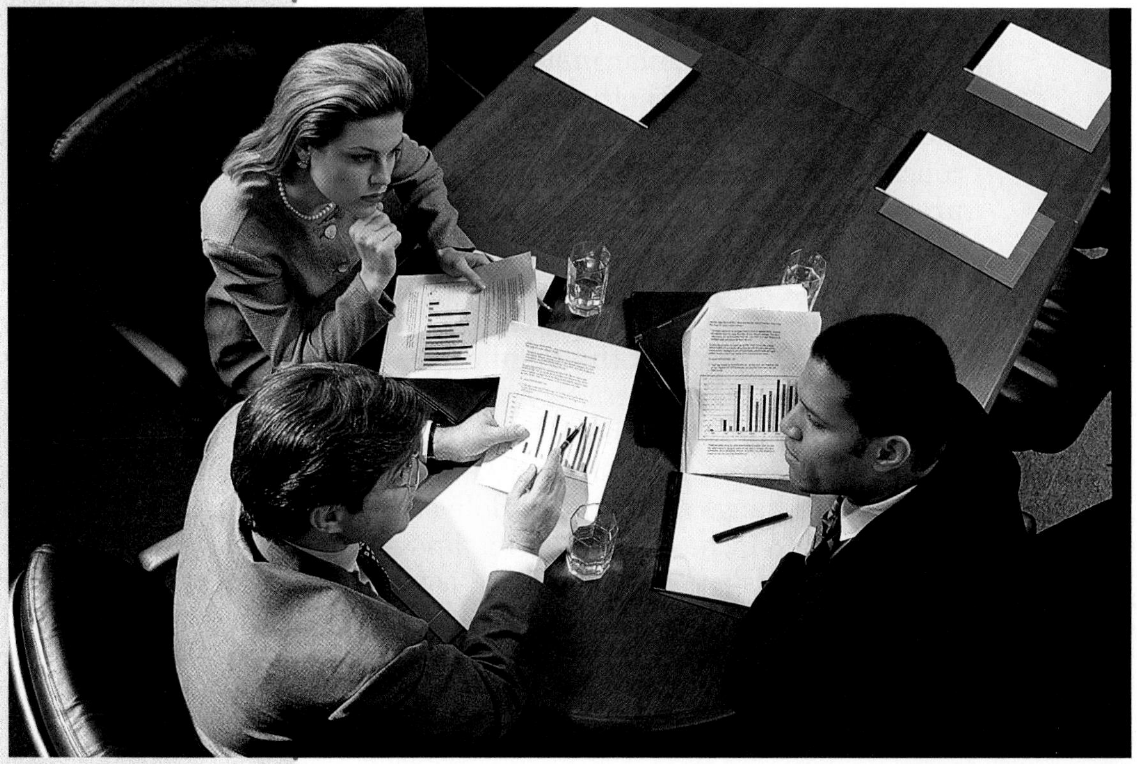

WORD PROCESSING APPLICATIONS

REPORT 27
Outline

REPORT 27b
Business Report

Key an outline for the business report below. Use the major headings and the paragraph headings as your entries for the outline. Then key the report as a left-bound report. Add a byline below the title (press ENTER 1 time) that contains the word "By" followed by your name. Format the references as footnotes. The text for each footnote follows the superscript number and is enclosed in brackets.

BASKETBALL SPECIFICS

INTRODUCTION

¶The game of basketball is one of the most widely played and watched sports in the world. The game is played by two teams consisting of five players each. Nearly all elementary schools, high schools, and colleges in the United States have organized basketball teams.[1] [[1] William Phelps, "Basketball," *Sports Encyclopedia*, 2005 ed., pp. 101–102.]

¶Basketball is truly America's game since it was invented in the United States in 1891. The popularity of the game has steadily increased over the years because it is exciting to play and to watch.

DIMENSIONS

¶Three very important features of the official game include the specific dimensions of the basketball, the court, and the basket and backboard.

¶**The Basketball.** The ball measures about 30 inches in circumference and weighs from 20 to 22 ounces. It can be made of leather, plastic, rubber, or similar material, and it is inflated with air.

¶**The Court.** The basketball court is a hard, level surface. Most indoor courts are made of wood. Outdoor courts are made of asphalt, concrete, or any other solid material. Most high school courts measure 84 feet long by 50 feet wide. College and professional courts measure 94 feet long by 50 feet wide. The court has two sidelines, a division line, which divides the court in halves, two free-throw lanes, and two free-throw lines. Two circles, the center circle and the restraining circle, mark the middle of the court.[2] [[2] Richard E. Lange and Nina Elliott, *Regulations for Standard Basketball*, Dawning Publications, Inc., Wilmington, North Carolina, 2006, pp. 121–122.]

¶**The Basket and Backboard.** A white-cord net basket attached to a backboard hangs above the middle of each end line. The net hangs down 15 to 18 inches from the ring and slows the ball as it passes through the basket. The backboard is made of glass, metal, wood, or any other hard material. It must be white or transparent and rectangular or fan-shaped. Rectangular backboards measure 72 inches wide by 48 inches high. Fan-shaped backboards are 54 inches wide by 35

(continued on next page)

LESSON 77 REPORTS: MULTIPAGE, LEFT BOUND

OBJECTIVES:

- Apply rules for capitalization.
- Increase keyboarding speed.
- Format and key multipage, bound reports.

A. WARMUP

Key each line 2 times.

Speed	1	You should always be honest with yourself about your goals.
Accuracy	2	David quickly put the frozen jars away in small gray boxes.
Language Link	3	Although Bill said it wasn't, Jason thought it was farther.
Numbers/Symbols	4	Two items (#20 & #21) were sold for $33 each--a great loss!
		| 1 | 2 | 3 | 4 | 5 | 6 | 7 | 8 | 9 | 10 | 11 | 12

LANGUAGE LINK

B. CAPITALIZATION

Study the following rules and examples. Then correct any errors in capitalization in lines 5–8.

Rule 14: Capitalize common organizational terms (such as *advertising department* and *finance committee*) when they are the actual names of the units in your own organization and when they are preceded by the word *the*.

> *The monthly update will be presented by the Marketing Department today.*
>
> *I applied for a position as an assistant in a marketing department.*

(continued on next page)

SKILLBUILDING

C. Preview Practice

Key each line 2 times as a preview to the timed writings that follow.

Accuracy	8	join apply realize inquire activities experience leadership
Speed	9	skills least first would great look soon help ask use of to

D. 3-Minute Timed Writings

Take two 3-minute timed writings on the paragraph. Note your speed and errors.

Goal: 36/3'/5e

10	You may soon be asked to write a resume to use when	11
11	you inquire about your first job. Employers realize that	22
12	you may not have a great deal of work experience, so they	34
13	tend to look more at school activities and interests. It	45
14	would be a good idea to get involved in the activities of	57
15	any clubs for business students. Your school is sure to	68
16	have at least one that you could join. If not, ask your	79
17	teacher to help you start one. You can apply what you have	91
18	learned in your classes, gain leadership skills, and make	102
19	friends with like interests.	108

| 1 | 2 | 3 | 4 | 5 | 6 | 7 | 8 | 9 | 10 | 11 | 12 SI 1.31

SOCIAL STUDIES CONNECTION

Adapt to Cultural Differences Different cultures have different social rules for interacting with people. Key the following table. With a partner, add one additional guideline in each row of column 2. Follow your teacher's instructions for saving and printing your work.

ADAPTING TO CULTURAL DIFFERENCES	
Be Observant	Notice how people greet each other, how close they stand to each other, and how they make eye contact. Then follow their lead.
Be Polite	Good manners are always correct. Smile, speak courteously, and treat others with kindness.
Be Respectful	Acknowledge customs and habits that are new to you without criticism.

(continued)

Rule 15: Capitalize names of specific course titles but not the names of subjects or areas of study.

She enrolled in Advanced Physics 201 and will also take a psychology course.

5 The editorial staff of the office technology unit worked very well together.

6 He took one class in word processing and another in database management.

7 The computer support unit works with us to keep our computers running smoothly.

8 I studied economics and took the course business communications 301.

SKILLBUILDING

C. 30-Second Timed Writings

Take two 30-second timed writings on lines 9–10. Then take two 30-second timed writings on lines 11–12. Try to increase your speed each time.

9 Driving in the country in the fall is a real treat if 11
10 you can stop and visit some local vendors along the way. 22

11 A visit to some small villages is like a trip back in 11
12 time because they work to keep things the way they were. 22

| 1 | 2 | 3 | 4 | 5 | 6 | 7 | 8 | 9 | 10 | 11 | 12

REVIEW

OBJECTIVES:

- Compose paragraphs at the keyboard.
- Key 36/3'/5e.
- Reinforce report formats.

A. WARMUP

Key each line 2 times.

Speed	1	The grass has grown tall, and it must be mowed by Thursday.
Accuracy	2	Paz visited the Zagros Mountains near the Strait of Hormuz.
Language Link	3	In the past, we have had our Billing Department sell candy.
Numbers/Symbols	4	If 33% (1/3 of total) attends #26 or #45, we will earn $90.

| 1 | 2 | 3 | 4 | 5 | 6 | 7 | 8 | 9 | 10 | 11 | 12

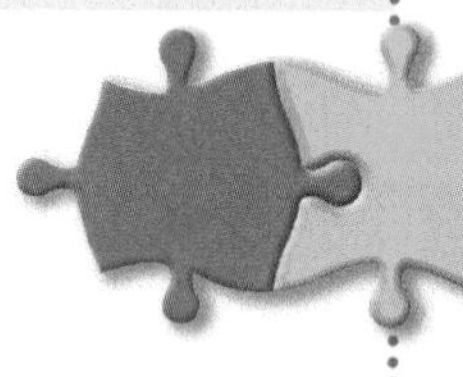

LANGUAGE LINK

B. COMPOSING AT THE KEYBOARD

Use a print dictionary to look up the definition of each of the words in bold below. Key the answer to each question as a short paragaph.

It is illegal and unethical to take someone else's literary, artistic, or scientific work and claim that it is your own original work.

5 What is **plagiarism**? How can a person avoid plagiarizing?

6 What is **copyright**?

7 What is **copyright infringement**?

LANGUAGE ARTS CONNECTION

Develop Report Titles The title of a report should be a short phrase that tells the reader the main topic of the report and gets the reader's attention. Reread the sentences that you keyed to answer question 5 above. Key three titles that you could use for a report on avoiding plagiarism. Follow your teacher's instructions for saving and printing your work.

REPORT 23

Business Report

Key the following report as a left-bound business report. Format all references as footnotes. The text for each footnote follows the superscript number and is enclosed in brackets.

VOICE RECOGNITION: THE FUTURE IS NOW

¶Many newspapers, magazines, and technology demonstrations are featuring voice recognition as the wave of the future. But, is voice recognition really new?

HISTORICAL PERSPECTIVES ON VOICE RECOGNITION

¶People have been able to recognize each other's voices since language first began. You need only to watch the face of a cat or dog when its owner speaks to know that the animal has heard and recognized the voice. Call centers and other kinds of businesses have been using a type of voice (speech) recognition for years.

¶Think for a moment, though, how exciting it would be to speak to your computer and have it understand what you said. Then, it would format what you said into what you need—a letter, a report, a table, a memo, or whatever, all with your voice telling your computer what to do. Is this really possible?

SPEECH RECOGNITION IN ITS INFANCY

¶While Bell Laboratories of Lucent Technologies created the first speech recognizer in 1952, the first speech recognition capability for PCs was finally developed in the 1980s. The world's first discrete speech dictation system was developed by Dragon Systems in 1990. Following that innovation was the world's first commercially available software-only dictation system.[1] [[1] "Dragon Systems Lead the Industry," *Dragon Product Specifications*, July 12, 2005, pp. 3–5.]

¶In 1997, Jim and Janet Baker excited the speech recognition arena with the first dictation software to handle continuous speech. The spotlight focused on *Naturally Speaking*, another Dragon Systems' product.[2] [[2] "There is Much to Say," *Technology Now*, August 14, 2004, p. 73.]

VOICE RECOGNITION MARCHES ON

¶The technology movement had begun in earnest. Several companies jumped into the race to capture the market and produce software capable of higher and higher feats of accuracy. Software and portable device manufacturers came out with new programs and devices. Companies such as Sony, Norcom, Olympus, Dragon Systems, Lernout & Hauspie, and IBM, to name a few, began to find this field exciting.[3] [[3] Marcia G. Flowers, "It Knows Your Voice," *The World of Business*, June 2006, p. 55.] Philips, Grover Industries, and others followed the thrill of voice recognition development with hardware and software utilities. For example, Grover Industries' Web-TalkIt is an easy-to-use voice command and control utility for your default Web browser. Just say the Web site you wish to visit, and Web-TalkIt will go to the URL address.

(continued on next page)

E. Bibliography

5

BIBLIOGRAPHY

Beauducel, Christie, *Create a Successful Interview*, Gaudium Press, New York, 2005.

Dolfeld, Kim B., and Lisa Simmons, *Interview to Get the Job*, Figureroa Books, Monrovia, California, 2006.

Gokaraju, Chris, "After the Interview," *Communications*, Vol. XXVII, No. 8, May 2005, pp. 15-22.

Lymanski, Quentin, et al., "Keys to Interviewing: Style and Organization," *HR Expert*, Vol. LXVII, No. 7, October 2005, pp. 50-58.

"Prepare for the Interview," *Marketing Today*, Vol. XXXV, No. 3, August 19, 2005, pp. 102-105.

Tafoya, Jake, "Get the Job! Top Ten Interview Tips for Grads," *College of Georgia Career Center Online*, June 2005, College of Georgia, July 6, 2005 <http://www.collegeofgeorgia.edu/students/careercenter.html>.

A **bibliography** is an alphabetical listing of sources used in a report. It is placed at the end of the report. To format a bibliography:

1. Use the same side margins as the report.
2. Center and key the title, *BIBLIOGRAPHY,* in all caps, bold, and a 14-point font approximately 2 inches from the top of the page (press ENTER 6 times). Press ENTER 2 times after the title.
3. Entries are single spaced with a hanging indent and a 12-point font. Leave a space between entries.
4. Alphabetize by authors' last names. If there is no author, alphabetize by the title of the article or book.
5. Arrange book entries as follows: author's name, title (in italics), publisher, place of publication, and year.
6. Arrange journal articles as follows: author's name, article title (in quotation marks), journal title (in italics), journal series, volume, issue numbers; date and page numbers.
7. Arrange online sources as follows: author's name, article or Web page title (in quotes), complete title of the Web site (in italics), date of online publication, name of the organization that owns the site, date you visited the site and the full URL of the page (in angle brackets).

F. Software Features

STUDENT MANUAL

Dot Leaders

Study Lesson 78 in your Student Manual. Complete all the practice activities while at your computer. Then complete the tasks that follow.

WORD PROCESSING APPLICATIONS

REPORT 24
Title Page

Prepare a title page for Report 23. Use your name, the name of your keyboarding teacher, and the current date.

REPORT 25
Table of Contents

Prepare a table of contents for Report 23. Use the side headings for the major entries.

REPORT 26
Bibliography

Prepare a bibliography for Report 23. Use the footnotes as the entries for the bibliography.

(continued)

USERS OF VOICE RECOGNITION

¶Large mail order and customer service companies as well as utilities, banks, airlines, stockbrokers, manufacturers, and couriers are some of the major users of voice recognition. Customers or clients can use these voice recognition systems to obtain information, service, or to order products without human contact in most instances. Adding natural language processing to speech recognition gives us an entirely new user interface, notes Jeremy T. Monroe of *Electronics Magazine*.[4] [[4] Jeremy T. Monroe, "Speed Equals Profits," *Electronics Magazine*, September 21, 2006, p. 13.]

¶Voice recognition programs are enabling many physically challenged persons to use their computers more efficiently and effectively. Molly Hanover does not have use of her hands, but she successfully holds a job in the Billing Department of Carson, Inc., using a voice-activated computer.[5] [[5] Pamela Nicole Denison, "Bridging the Gap," *Update Source*, October 24–25, 2006, pp. 15–16.]

¶Financial traders, lawyers, and physicians are using voice recognition software. Minneapolis lawyer Jim Anderson has been using a voice recognition system for the past three years. He has developed personalized dictation macros that insert blocks of text with one- or two-word commands. For example, when Mr. Anderson says "contract one," the software inserts the standard first paragraph for a contract. After he has added the personal information, Mr. Anderson continues with "contract two," and so on.[6] [[6] Preston McMinn, "No-Hands Computing: The Counselor Wins," *Networking Newsletter*, Fall, 2005, ALA Law Practice Management Section, 2005–06, American Law Association, pp. 6–7.]

¶Physicians are finding voice recognition ideal for dictating chart notes after patient sessions. They say they often get more accurate notes because they can say more than if they were writing charts by hand.

¶More and more applications will be developed and more people will avail themselves of voice recognition technology as it is perfected and as accuracy levels improve above the 95-98 percent level.

TAKING IT ONE STEP FURTHER INTO THE FUTURE

¶What does the future hold for voice recognition technology? Forecasters say the sky is the limit. Computers will probably arrive loaded with voice recognition software; you will be able to access the Internet quickly, and you will be able to go from link to link just by saying what topic you want to request. Innovative software and equipment will make the lives of the blind, the deaf, and others with different physical difficulties more efficient by enabling them to access their computers without using their hands.

¶Some new processors can zoom through the math used in speech recognition, making it possible to "train" the new computer to understand the user in less than five minutes. Software developers that harness the power of these new processors predict that speech recognition will be a standard PC

(continued on next page)

C. Title Page

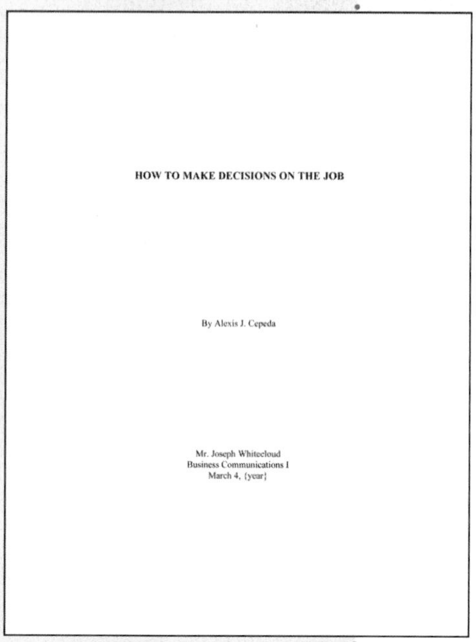

HOW TO MAKE DECISIONS ON THE JOB

By Alexis J. Cepeda

Mr. Joseph Whitecloud
Business Communications I
March 4, {year}

A **title page** is the first page of a report. It gives the title of a report, the name of the writer, the name of the person for whom the report was prepared, and the date. For academic reports, it also contains the name of the course. To format a title page:

1. Use single spacing, and center the page vertically.
2. Center all lines of text horizontally.
3. Key the report title in all caps, bold, and a 14-point font. If there is a subtitle, double-space and key the subtitle in initial caps.
4. Press ENTER 12 times and key *By* in a 12-point font followed by your name as the writer. If there is more than one writer, single-space the names of the writers.
5. Press ENTER 12 times. Then, using single spacing, key the name of the person for whom the report was written, the name of the course (if appropriate), and the current date.

D. Table of Contents

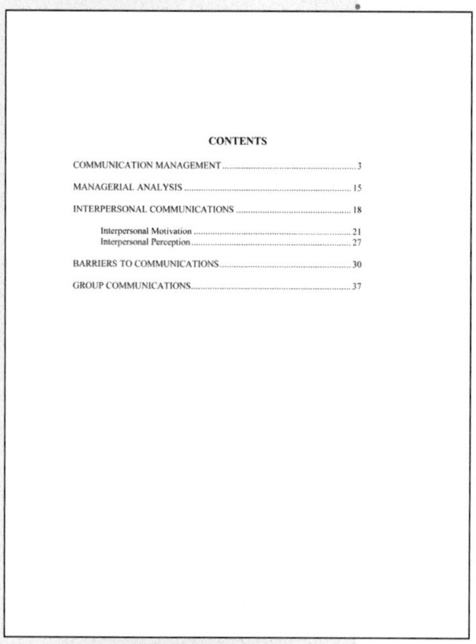

CONTENTS

COMMUNICATION MANAGEMENT 3

MANAGERIAL ANALYSIS 15

INTERPERSONAL COMMUNICATIONS 18

Interpersonal Motivation 21
Interpersonal Perception 27

BARRIERS TO COMMUNICATIONS 30

GROUP COMMUNICATIONS 37

A **table of contents** may follow the title page. It is an outline of the headings in a report and the pages on which they are found. To format a table of contents:

1. Use the same margins as those used in the report.
2. Center and key the word *CONTENTS* in a 14-point font approximately 2 inches from the top of the page (press ENTER 6 times) in all caps and bold, followed by a double space.
3. Key major headings in all caps and a 12-point font; leave a blank line before and after them.
4. Indent subheadings and key them with initial caps and single spacing.
5. Align page numbers at the right and precede them with **dot leaders**—a series of periods that help guide the reader's eye from the headings to the page numbers.

(continued)

feature by the end of the year.[7] [7 Andrew Dryden, "Computers That Hear," *The Cutting Edge*, July 14, 2006, p. 15.]

¶Is voice recognition in your future? Keep your ears sharp, watch for new developments, and you will probably be a voice recognition technology user soon!

COMMUNICATION FOCUS

Format a Resume as a Table A resume should stand out and make a great first impression. One way to do this is to format it as a table.

Study the example shown below. Create a similar table. Make the table as large as possible on the page, leaving a one-inch margin on all sides. If you already have a resume, you can copy and paste some of that information into the resume table. Join cells where appropriate. Follow your teacher's instructions for saving and printing your work.

Joshua T. Zondervan
7944 Ridgeway Road
Commerce, TX 75428
903-555-8330
jtzond@comp.net

OBJECTIVE	To obtain an office position that requires telephone, communications, keyboarding, and general computer application skills.
EDUCATION	Commerce High School Commerce, TX 75428 Graduated May 2005
	Kilgore College Kilgore, TX 75662 Office Technology Program Completed December 2006 GPA: 3.44
OFFICE SKILLS	Keyboarding (65 wpm) Proficiency using numeric keypad by touch Proficiency using word processing, spreadsheet, and data base
HONORS AND ACTIVITIES	Outstanding Office Technology Student, 2006 First place in business applications contest, area and state, 2005 Senior class treasurer, 2004-05 Co-captain, Commerce High School soccer team, 2004-05
EXPERIENCE	2005-2006 Office Assistant, Elysian Entertainment, Inc., 405 N. Judson Road Longview, TX 75604 903-555-3797
	2004-2005 Cashier, Warner Quick Stop, 1492 Oak Avenue Commerce, TX 75428 903-555-4004
REFERENCES	References will be provided upon request.

Reports: Title Page, Contents, Bibliography

OBJECTIVES:

- Improve keyboarding accuracy.
- Format and key title, contents, and bibliography pages.

A. Warmup

Key each line 2 times.

Speed	1	Edward saved his files on the hard drive and on a diskette.
Accuracy	2	Vic quickly mixed grape juice with the frozen strawberries.
Language Link	3	It is too soon for Will to know whether he passed spelling.
Numbers/Symbols	4	Hamilton & Jones expected a 12% increase in sales--$35,890.
		| 1 | 2 | 3 | 4 | 5 | 6 | 7 | 8 | 9 | 10 | 11 | 12

SKILLBUILDING

B. 30-Second OK Timed Writings

Take two 30-second OK (error-free) timed writings on lines 5–6. Then take two 30-second OK timed writings on lines 7–8. Goal: no errors.

5	Peg was amazed by the fact that time management skills	11
6	are magic tools for learning very quickly how to mix tasks.	23
7	Sixty men went to a quaint village in the back country	11
8	of western New Zealand and fished for pike, jack, and gar.	23
	| 1 | 2 | 3 | 4 | 5 | 6 | 7 | 8 | 9 | 10 | 11 | 12	